BEST 170
LAW SCHOOLS

The Princeton Review

PrincetonReview.com

BEST 170 LAW SCHOOLS

2008 EDITION

Eric Owens, Esq., John Owens, Esq., Julie Doherty, and The Staff of The Princeton Review

Random House, Inc.
New York

The Princeton Review, Inc.
2315 Broadway
New York, NY 10024
E-mail: bookeditor@review.com

© 2008 by The Princeton Review, Inc.

ISBN: 978-0-375-76628-2

Editorial Director: Robert Franek
Director, Production Editorial: Christine LaRubio
Director, Print Production: Scott Harris
Account Manager: David Soto
Editors: Adrinda Kelly, Adam Davis, and Laura Braswell

Printed in the United States of America.

9 8 7 6 5 4 3 2 1

2008 Edition

ACKNOWLEDGMENTS

Eric Owens would like to say, "Thank you, John Katzman, for pretty much everything."

Thanks also to Laura Braswell for the support and guidance on this book and many others and to Bob Spruill for his LSAT expertise.

In addition, many thanks should go to David Soto and Ben Zelevansky for spearheading the law school data collection efforts. Their survey, along with the support and assistance of Jen Adams, allowed for the completion of a totally cohesive stat-packed guide. Candace Pinson also deserves a standing ovation for her tireless work coordinating student surveys and profile reviews at 170 law schools.

A special thanks must go to our production team: Scott Harris and Christine LaRubio. Your commitment, flexibility, and attention to detail are always appreciated in both perfect and crunch times.

—Eric Owens

I'd like to send my thanks:

To Eric Owens, my quasi-cousin, who kept me in mind for this project.

To my editors at The Princeton Review, who trusted me (and the other Eric Owens) enough to give me the chance.

To my family and friends, who support me in the things I do.

To the law students who took the time to complete the law student survey.

—John Owens

I would like to thank my parents, Brucine and Francis Doherty, the staff of The Princeton Review, and Arturo Meade.

—Julie Doherty

CONTENTS

PREFACE

Welcome to *The Best 170 Law Schools*, The Princeton Review's truly indispensable guide for anyone thinking about entering the law school fray. This is not simply a reprint of the garden-variety fluff in each law school's admissions booklet. We have attempted to provide a significant amount of essential information from a vast array of sources to give you a complete, accurate, and easily digestible snapshot of the best law schools in the country. Here you'll find a wealth of practical advice on admissions, taking and acing the Law School Admissions Test (LSAT), choosing the right school, and doing well once you're there. You'll also find all the information you need on schools' bar exam pass rates, ethnic group and gender breakdown percentages, tuition, average starting salaries of graduates, and much more. For 170 ABA-approved law schools, you'll find descriptive profiles of the student experience based on the opinions of the only true law school experts: current law school students. Indeed, with this handy reference, you should be able to narrow your choices from the few hundred law schools in North America to a handful in no time at all.

Never trust any single source of information too much, though—not even us. Take advantage of all the resources available to you, including friends, family members, the Internet, and your local library. Obviously, the more you explore all the options available to you, the better decision you'll make. We hope you will be happy wherever you end up and that this guide will be helpful in your search to find the best law school for you.

Best of luck!

ALL ABOUT LAW SCHOOL

CHAPTER 1
SO YOU WANT TO GO TO LAW SCHOOL

Congrats! Law school is a tremendous intellectual challenge and an amazing experience. It can be confusing and occasionally traumatic—especially during the crucial first year—but the cryptic ritual of legal education will make you a significantly better thinker, a consummate reader, and a far more mature person over the course of three years.

The application process is rigorous, but it's not impossible. Here's our advice.

WHAT MAKES A COMPETITIVE APPLICANT?

It depends. One of the great things about law schools in the United States is that there are a lot of them, and standards for admission run the gamut from appallingly difficult to not very hard at all.

Let's just say, for example, you have your heart set on Yale Law School, arguably the finest law school in all the land. Let's also say you have stellar academic credentials: a 3.45 GPA and an LSAT score in the 99th percentile of everyone who takes it. With these heady numbers, you've got a whopping 2 percent chance of getting into Yale, at best. However, with the same 3.45 GPA and LSAT score in the 99th percentile, you are pretty much a lock at legal powerhouses like Duke University School of Law and Boston College Law School. With significantly lower numbers—say, a 3.02 GPA and an LSAT score in the 81st percentile—you stand a mediocre chance of getting into top-flight law schools like Case Western or Indiana. With a little bit of luck, these numbers might land you a spot at George Washington or UCLA.

> *Fascinating Acronyms*
>
> **LSAC:** Law School Admission Council, headquartered in beautiful Newtown, Pennsylvania
>
> **LSAT:** Law School Admissions Test
>
> **LSDAS:** Law School Data Assembly Service
>
> **ABA:** American Bar Association

This is good news. The even better news is that there are several totally respectable law schools out there that will let you in with a 2.5 GPA and an LSAT of 148 (which is about the 36th percentile). If you end up in the top 10 percent of your class at one of these schools and have even a shred of interviewing skill, you'll get a job that is just as prestigious and pays just as much money as the jobs garnered by Yale grads. Notice the important catch here, however: You *must* graduate in the top 10 percent of your class at so-called "lesser" schools, while almost every Yale Law grad who wants a high-paying job can land one.

Ultimately, there's a law school out there for you. If you want to get into a "top-flight" or "pretty good" school, you're in for some fairly stiff competition. Unfortunately, it doesn't help that the law school admissions process is somewhat formulaic; your LSAT score and your GPA are vastly more important to the process than anything else about you. If your application ends up in the "maybe" pile, your recommendations, your major, the reputation of your college alma mater, a well-written and nongeneric essay, and various other factors will play a larger role in determining your fate.

THE ADMISSIONS INDEX

The first thing most law schools will look at when evaluating your application is your "index." It's a number (which varies from school to school) made up of a weighted combination of your undergraduate GPA and LSAT score. In virtually every case, the LSAT is weighted more heavily than the GPA.

While the process differs from school to school, it is generally the case that your index will put you into one of three piles:

(Probably) Accepted. A select few applicants with high LSAT scores and stellar GPAs are admitted pretty much automatically. If your index is very, very strong compared with the school's median or target number, you're as good as in, unless you are a convicted felon or you wrote your personal statement in crayon.

(Probably) Rejected. If your index is very weak compared with the school's median or target number, you are probably going to be rejected without much ado. When Admissions Officers read weaker applications (yes, at almost every school every application is read) they will be looking for something so outstanding or unique that it makes them willing to take a chance. Factors that can help include ethnic background, where you are from, or very impressive work or life experience. That said, don't hold your breath because not many people in this category are going to make the cut.

Well . . . Maybe. The majority of applicants fall in the middle; their index number is right around the median or target index number. People in this category have decent enough LSAT scores and GPAs for the school, but not high enough for automatic admission. Why do most people fall into this category? For the most part, people apply to schools they think they have at least a shot of getting into based on their grades and LSAT scores; Yale doesn't see very many applicants who got a 140 on the LSAT. What will determine the fate of those whose applications hang in the balance? One thing law schools often look at is the competitiveness of your undergraduate program. On the one hand, someone with a 3.3 GPA in an easy major from a school where everybody graduates with a 3.3 or higher will face an uphill battle. On the other hand, someone with the same GPA in a difficult major from a school that has a reputation for being stingy with A's is in better shape. Admissions Officers will also pore over the rest of your application—personal statement, letters of recommendation, resume, etc.—for reasons to admit you, reject you, or put you on their waiting lists.

ARE YOU MORE THAN YOUR LSAT SCORE?

Aside from LSAT scores and GPAs, what do law schools consider when deciding who's in and who's out? It's the eternal question. On the one hand, we should relieve you hidebound cynics of the notion that they care about nothing else. On the other hand, if you harbor fantasies that a stunning application can overcome truly substandard scores and grades, you should realize that such hopes are unrealistic.

Nonquantitative factors are particularly important at law schools that receive applications from thousands of numerically qualified applicants. A "top 10" law school that receives 10 or 15 applications for every spot in its first-year class has no choice but to "look beyond the numbers," as admissions folks are fond of saying. Such a school will almost surely have to turn away hundreds of applicants with near-perfect LSAT scores and college grades, and those applicants who get past the initial cut will be subjected to real scrutiny.

Less competitive schools are just as concerned, in their own way, with "human criteria" as are the Harvards and Stanfords of the world. They are on the lookout for capable people who have relatively unimpressive GPAs and LSAT scores. The importance of the application is greatly magnified for these students, who must demonstrate their probable success in law school in other ways.

CAN PHYSICS MAJORS GO TO LAW SCHOOL?

"What about my major?" is one of the more popular questions we hear when it comes to law school admissions. The conventional answer to this question goes something like, "There is no prescribed, pre-law curriculum, but you should seek a broad and challenging liberal arts education, etc."

Translation: It really doesn't matter what you major in. Obviously, a major in aviation or hotel and restaurant management is not exactly ideal, but please—we beg you!—don't feel restricted to a few majors simply because you want to attend law school. This is especially true if those particular majors do not interest you. Comparative literature? Fine. American studies? Go to town. Physics? No problem whatsoever. You get the idea.

Think about it. Because most would-be law students end up majoring in the *same* few fields (e.g., political science and philosophy), their applications all look the *same* to the folks in law school Admissions Offices. You want to stand out, which is why it is a good idea to major in something *different*. Ultimately, you should major in whatever appeals to you. Of course, if you want to major in political science or philosophy (or you already have), well, that's fine too.

DOES GRAD SCHOOL COUNT?

Your grades in graduate school will not be included in the calculation of your GPA (only the UGPA, the undergraduate grade point average, is reported to the schools) but will be taken into account separately by an Admissions Committee if you make them available. Reporting grad school grades would be to your advantage, particularly if they are better than your college grades. Admissions Committees are likely to take this as a sign of maturation.

ADVICE FOR THE "NONTRADITIONAL" APPLICANT

The term "nontraditional" is, of course, used to describe applicants who are a few years or many years older than run-of-the-mill law school applicants.

In a nutshell, there's no time like the present to start law school. While it's true that most law students are in their early to mid-20s, if you aren't, don't think for a minute that your age will keep you from getting in and having a great experience. Applicants for full-time and part-time slots at U.S. law schools range in ages from 21 to 71 and include every age in between. Some of these older applicants always intended to go to law school and simply postponed it to work, travel, or start a family. Other older applicants never seriously considered law school until after they were immersed in other occupations.

Part-time attendance is especially worth checking into if you've been out of college for a few years. Also, dozens of law schools offer evening programs—particularly in urban centers.

Waiting Lists

If a law school puts you on its waiting list, it means you may be admitted depending on how many of the applicants they've already admitted decide to go to another school. Most schools rank students on their waiting list; they'll probably tell you where you stand if you give them a call. Also, note that schools routinely admit students from their waiting lists in late August. If you are on a school's waiting list and you really, really want to go there, keep your options at least partially open. You just might be admitted in the middle of first-year orientation.

MINORITY LAW SCHOOL APPLICANTS

Things are definitely looking up. According to figures published by the American Bar Association's Committee on Legal Education, in 1978 more than 90 percent of the law students in the ABA's 167 schools were White. In recent years, however, the number of non-Whites enrolled in law school has nearly doubled, from about 10 percent to more than 20 percent. Taking an even longer view, figures have tripled since 1972, when minority enrollment was only 6.6 percent. These days, the American Bar Association and the legal profession in general seem pretty committed to seeking and admitting applicants who are members of historically underrepresented minority groups.

WOMEN IN LAW SCHOOL

During the past decade, the number of female lawyers has escalated rapidly, and women undeniably have become more visible in the uppermost echelons of the field. According to statistics compiled by the American Bar Association (ABA), more than 16 percent of all law firm partners are women, and women make up more than 29 percent of all lawyers.

More and more women are going to law school as well. At a solid majority of the ABA-approved law schools in the United States, the percentage of women in the student population is 49 percent, and women make up more than half of the students at a handful of schools.

Gender discrimination certainly lingers here and there, though. You might want to check certain statistics on the law schools you are interested in, such as the percentage of women on Law Review and the percentage of female professors who are tenured or on track to be tenured. (Nationally, nearly 33 percent of all full law school professors are women, and 25 percent of tenured faculty are women.) Also, visit each law school and talk with female students and female professors about how women are treated at that particular school. Finally, see if the school has published any gender studies about itself. If it has, you obviously ought to check those out too.

Engineering and Math Majors Make Great Law Students

A disproportionate number of law students with backgrounds in the so-called "hard sciences" (math, physics, engineering, etc.) make very high grades in law school, probably because they are trained to think methodically and efficiently about isolated problems (which is what law students are supposed to do on exams).

CHAPTER 2
CHOOSING A LAW SCHOOL

There are some key things you should consider before randomly selecting schools from around the country or just submitting your application to somebody else's list of the Top 10 law schools.

LOCATION

It's a big deal. If you were born and raised in the state of New Mexico, care deeply about the "Land of Enchantment," wish to practice law there, and want to be the governor someday, then your best bet is to go to the University of New Mexico. A school's reputation is usually greater on its home turf than anywhere else (except for some of the larger-than-life schools, like Harvard and Yale). Also, most law schools tend to teach law that is specific to the statutes of the states in which they are located. Knowledge of the eccentricities of state law will help you immensely three years down the road when it comes time to pass the bar exam. Even further, the Career Services Office at your school will be strongly connected to the local legal industry. As a purely practical matter, it will be much easier to find a job and get to interviews in Boston, for example, if you live there. Still another reason to consider geographical location is the simple fact that you'll put down professional and social roots and get to know many really great people throughout your law school career. Leaving them won't be any fun. Finally, starting with geographic limitations is the easiest way to reduce your number of potential schools dramatically.

SPECIALIZATION

Word has it that specialization is the trend of the future. General practitioners in law are becoming less common, so it makes sense to let future lawyers begin to specialize in school. At certain schools, you may receive your JD with an official emphasis in, say, taxation. Specialization is a particularly big deal at smaller or newer schools whose graduates cannot simply get by on their school's reputation. Just between us, it's kind of hard to specialize in anything at most law schools because every graduate has to take this huge exam—the bar—that tests about a dozen topics. Most of your course selections will (and should) be geared toward passing the bar, which leaves precious few hours for specialization. You'll almost certainly specialize, but it's not something to worry about until you actually look for a job. All of that said, if you already know what kind of law you want to specialize in, you're in good shape. Many schools offer certain specialties because of their locations. If you are very interested in environmental law, you'd be better off going to Vermont Law School or Lewis and Clark's Northwestern School of Law than to Brooklyn Law School. Similarly, if you want to work with children as an attorney, check out Loyola University Chicago's Child Law Center. So look at what you want to do in addition to where you want to do it.

Dean's List

According to a letter signed by just about every dean of every ABA-approved law school in the country, the following are the factors you should consider when choosing a law school:

- *Breadth and support of alumni network*
- *Breadth of curriculum*
- *Clinical programs*
- *Collaborative research opportunities with faculty*
- *Commitment to innovative technology*
- *Cost*
- *Externship options*
- *Faculty accessibility*
- *Intensity of writing instruction*
- *Interdisciplinary programs*
- *International programming*
- *Law library strengths and services*
- *Loan repayment assistance for low-income lawyers*
- *Location*
- *Part-time enrollment options*
- *Public interest programs*
- *Quality of teaching*
- *Racial and gender diversity within the faculty and student body*
- *Religious affiliation*
- *Size of first-year classes*
- *Skills instruction*
- *Specialized areas of faculty expertise*

JOINT-DEGREE PROGRAMS

In addition to offering specialized areas of study, many law schools have instituted formal dual-degree programs. These schools, nearly all of which are directly affiliated with a parent institution, offer students the opportunity to pursue a JD while also working toward some other degree. Although the JD/MBA combination is the most popular joint-degree sought, many universities offer a JD program combined with degrees in everything from public policy to public administration to social work. In today's perpetually competitive legal market, dual degrees may make some students more marketable for certain positions. However, don't sign up for a dual-degree program on a whim—they require a serious amount of work and often a serious amount of tuition.

YOUR CHANCE OF ACCEPTANCE

Who knows how law schools end up with their reputations? Everything else being equal, you really do want to go a to a well-respected school. It will enhance your employment opportunities tremendously. Remember, whoever you are and whatever your background, your best bet is to select a couple of "reach" schools, a couple of schools at which you've got a good shot at being accepted, and a couple of "safety" schools where you are virtually assured acceptance. Remember also that being realistic about your chances will save you from unnecessary emotional letdowns. Getting in mostly boils down to numbers. Look at the acceptance rates and the average LSATs and GPAs of incoming classes at various schools to assess how you stack up.

The Dreaded Bar Exam

Once you graduate, most states require you to take a bar exam before you can practice law. Some state bar exams are really, really hard; New York's and California's are examples. If you don't want to take a bar exam, consider a law school in beautiful Wisconsin. Anyone who graduates from a state-certified Wisconsin law school does not need to take the state bar exam to practice law in the Badger State, as long as they are approved by the Board of Bar Examiners.

PERSONAL APPEAL

A student at a prominent law school in the Pacific Northwest once described his law school to us as "a combination wood-grain bomb shelter and Ewok village." Another student at a Northeastern law school told us her law school was fine except for its "ski-slope classrooms" and "East German Functionalist" architecture. While the curricula at various law schools are pretty much the same, the weather, the surrounding neighborhoods, the nightlife, and the character of the student populations are startlingly different. An important part of any graduate program is enjoying those moments in life when you're not studying. If you aren't comfortable in the environment you choose, it's likely to be reflected in the quality of work you do and your attitude. Before you make a $10,000 to $80,000 investment in any law school, you really ought to check it out in person. While you are there, talk to students and faculty. Walk around. Kick the tires. *Then* make a decision.

EMPLOYMENT PROSPECTS

Where do alumni work? How much money do they make? What percentage of graduates is employed within nine months of graduation? How many major law firms interview on campus? These are massively important questions, and you owe it to yourself to look into the answers before choosing a school.

YOUR VALUES

It is important that you be honest about defining your criteria for judging law schools. What do you want out of a law school? Clout? A high salary? A hopping social life? To live in a certain city? To avoid being in debt up to your eyeballs? A non-competitive atmosphere? Think about it.

MAKE A LIST

Using these criteria (and others you find relevant), develop a list of prospective schools. Ideally, you'll find this book useful in creating the list. Assign a level to each new school you add (something like *reach*, *good shot*, and *safety*).

Did You Know?

According to the people who take the LSAT, the average applicant applies to four or more law schools.

At your *reach* schools, the average LSAT scores and GPAs of incoming students should be higher than yours. These are law schools that will probably not accept you based on your numbers alone. In order to get in, you'll need to wow them with everything else (e.g., personal statement, stellar recommendations, work experience).

Your *good shot* schools should be the schools you like that accept students with about the same LSAT scores and GPA as yours. Combined with a strong and *cohesive* application, you've got a decent shot at getting into these schools.

At your *safety* schools, the average LSAT scores and GPAs of current students should be below yours. These schools should accept you pretty painlessly if there are no major blemishes on your application (e.g., a serious run-in with the law).

CHAPTER 3
APPLYING TO LAW SCHOOL

Our advice: Start early. The LSAT alone can easily consume 80 or more hours of prep time, and completing a single application form might take as much as 30 hours if you take great care with the essay questions. Don't sabotage your efforts through last-minute sloppiness or by allowing this already-annoying process to become a gigantic burden.

WHEN TO APPLY

Yale Law School's absolute final due date is February 1, but Loyola University—Chicago's School of Law will accept your application up to April 1. There is no regular pattern. However, the longer you wait to apply to a school, regardless of its deadline, the worse your chances of getting into that school may be. No efficient Admissions Staff is going to wait to receive all the applications before starting to make their selections.

If you're reading this in December and hope to get into a law school for next fall but haven't done anything about it, you're in big trouble. If you've got an LSAT score you are happy with, you're in less trouble. However, your applications will get to the law schools after the optimum time and, let's face it, they may appear a little rushed. The best time to think about applying is early in the year. Methodically take care of one thing at a time, and *finish by December*.

Early Admissions Options. A few schools have Early Admissions options (for instance, New York University's Early Admission deadline is on or about October 15), so you may know by December if you've been accepted. Early Admission is a good idea for a few reasons. It can give you an indication of what your chances are at other schools. It can relieve the stress of waiting until April to see where you'll be spending the next three years of your life. Also, it's better to get wait listed in December than in April (or whenever you would be notified for regular admission); if there is a "tie" among applicants on the waiting list, they'll probably admit whoever applied first. Of course, not every school's Early Admission option is the same (and many schools don't even have one), so do your research.

Rolling Admissions. Many law schools evaluate applications and notify applicants of admission decisions continuously over the course of several months (ordinarily from late fall to midsummer). Obviously, if you apply to one of these schools, it is vital that you apply as early as possible because there will be more spots available at the beginning of the process.

Applying Online. Almost all law schools allow applicants to submit applications online. The LSAC online service (LSAC.org) has a searchable database and applications to ABA-approved schools.

LAW SCHOOL ADMISSIONS COUNCIL: THE LAW SCHOOL APPLICATION MAFIA

In addition to single-handedly creating and administering the LSAT, an organization called the Law School Admissions Council (LSAC) maintains the communication between you and virtually every law school in the United States. It runs the Law School Data Assembly Service (LSDAS), which provides information (in a standard format) on applicants to the law schools. They—not you—send your grades, your LSAT score, and plenty of other information about you to the schools. You'll send only your actual applications directly to the law schools themselves. Oh, by the way, the fee for this service is $113 of your hard-earned money plus $12 (or more) every time you want LSDAS to send a report about you to an additional law school.

THE BIG HURDLES IN THE APPLICATION PROCESS: A BRIEF OVERVIEW

Take the LSAT. The Law School Admission Test is a roughly three-and-a-half-hour multiple-choice test used by law schools to help them select candidates. The LSAT is given in February, June, October (or, occasionally, late September), and December of each year. It's divided into five multiple-choice sections and one writing sample. All ABA-approved and most non-ABA-approved law schools in the United States and Canada require an LSAT score from each and every applicant.

Register for LSDAS. You can register for the Law School Data Assembly Service at the same time you register to take the LSAT; all necessary forms are contained in the *LSAT and LSDAS Registration Information Book* (hence the name). It can also be done, of course, online.

Get applications from six or seven schools. Why so many? Because it's better to be safe than sorry. As early as July, select a couple of *reach* schools, a couple of schools to which you've got a good shot at being accepted, and a couple of *safety* schools to which you are virtually assured of acceptance. Your safety school—if you were being realistic—will probably accept you pretty quickly. It may take a while to get a final decision from the other schools, but you won't be totally panicked because you'll know your safety school is there for you. If, for whatever reason, your grades or LSAT score is extremely low, you should apply to several safety schools. Most schools won't post online applications until mid-September at the earliest. Still, it is a good idea to familiarize yourself with the previous year's applications as soon as possible, as law schools tend not to radically alter components of their applications from one year to the next.

Write your personal statement. With any luck, you'll only have to write one personal statement. Many, many schools will simply ask you the same basic question: "Why do you want to obtain a law degree?" However, just in case you need to write several personal statements and essays, you need to select your schools fairly early.

Obtain two or three recommendations. Some schools will ask for two recommendations, both of which must be academic. Others want more than two recommendations and want at least one to be from someone who knows you outside traditional academic circles. As part of your LSDAS file, the LSAC will accept up to three letters of recommendation on your behalf, and they will send them to all the schools to which you apply. This is one of the few redeeming qualities of the LSAC. The last thing the writers of your recommendations are going to want to do is sign, package, and send copies of their letters all over the continent.

Update/create your resume. Most law school applicants ask that you submit a resume. Make sure yours is up to date and suitable for submission to an academic institution. Put your academic credentials and experience first—no matter what they are. This is just a supplement to the rest of the material; it's probably the simplest part of the application process.

Get your academic transcripts sent to LSDAS. When you subscribe to LSDAS, you must request that the Registrar at every undergraduate, graduate, and professional school you ever attended send an official transcript to Law Services. Don't even think about sending your own transcripts anywhere; these people don't trust you any farther than they can throw you. *Make these requests in August.* If you're applying Early Decision, start requesting transcripts as early as May. Law schools require complete files before making their decisions, and LSDAS won't send your information to the law schools without your transcripts. Undergraduate institutions can and will screw up and delay the transcript process—even when you go there personally and pay them to provide your records. Give yourself some time to fix problems should they arise.

Write any necessary addenda. An addendum is a brief explanatory letter written to explain or support a "deficient" portion of your application. If your personal and academic life has been fairly smooth, you won't need to include any addenda with your application. If, however, you were ever on academic probation, arrested, or if you have a low GPA, you may need to write one. Other legitimate addenda topics are a low/discrepant LSAT score, DUI/DWI suspensions, or any time gap in your academic or professional career.

An addendum is absolutely not the place to go off on a rant about the fundamental unfairness of the LSAT or how that evil campus security officer was only out to get you when you got arrested. If, for example, you have taken the LSAT two or three times and simply did not do very well, even after spending time and money preparing with a test prep company or a private tutor, simply tell the Admissions Committee that you worked diligently to achieve a high score. Say you explored all possibilities to help you achieve that goal. Whatever the case, lay out the facts, but let them draw their own conclusions. Be brief and balanced. Be fair. Do not go into unneccessary detail. Explain the problem and state what you did about it. This is no time to whine.

Send in your seat deposit. Once you are accepted at a particular school, that school will ask you to put at least some money down to hold your place in that year's class. A typical fee runs $200 or more. This amount will be credited to your first-term tuition once you actually register for classes.

Do any other stuff. You may find that there are other steps you must take during the law school application process. You may request a fee waiver, for example. Also make sure to get a copy of the LSAC's *LSAT/LSDAS Registration and Information Book*, which is unquestionably the most useful tool in applying to law school. It has the forms you'll need, a sample LSAT, admissions information, the current Law Forum schedule, and sample application schedules.

The Princeton Review	LAW SCHOOL APPLICATION CHECKLIST (suitable for framing)
January	• **Take a practice LSAT.** Do it at a library or wherever you won't be interrupted. Also, take it all at once.
February	• **Investigate LSAT prep courses.** If you don't take one with The Princeton Review, do *something*. Just as with any test, you'll get a higher score on this one if you prepare for it first.
March	• **Obtain an *LSAT/LSDAS Registration and Information Book*.** The books are generally published in March of each year. You can get one at any law school, by calling the LSAC at 215-968-1001, or by stopping by The Princeton Review office nearest you. You can also download one in PDF format at www.lsac.org.
April	• **Register for the June LSAT.** • **Begin an LSAT prep course.** At the very, very least, use some books or software.
May	• **Continue your LSAT prep.**
June	• **Take the LSAT.** If you take the test twice, many schools will average them. Your best bet is to take it once, do exceedingly well, and get it out of your hair forever.
July	• **Register for LSDAS.** • **Research law schools.**
August	• **Obtain law school applications.** You can call or write, but the easiest and cheapest way to get applications is via the Internet. This is, of course, only necessary if you plan to send in paper applications. Go to www.lsac.org to access and submit online applications. • **Get your undergraduate transcripts sent to LSDAS.** Make sure to contact the registrar at each undergraduate institution you attended.
September	• **Write your personal statements.** Proofread them. Edit them. Edit them again. Have someone else look them over for all the mistakes you missed. • **Update your resume,** or create a resume if you don't have one. • **Get your recommendations in order.** You want your professors to submit recommendations exactly when you send your applications (in October and November).
October	• **Complete and send early decision applications.**
November	• **Complete and send all regular applications.**
December	• **Chill.** • **Buy holiday gifts.** • **Make plans for New Year's.**

CHAPTER 4
THE LSAT

As you may know, we at The Princeton Review are pretty skeptical of most of the standardized tests out there. They make us a lot of money, of course, and we like that, but they are hideously poor indicators of anything besides how well you do on that particular standardized test. They are certainly not intelligence tests. The LSAT is no exception. It is designed to keep you out of law school, not facilitate your entrance into it. For no good reason we can think of, this 125-question test is *the single most important factor in all of law school admissions*, and, at least for the foreseeable future, we're all stuck with it.

Unfortunately, with the possible exception of the MCAT (for medical school), the LSAT is the toughest of all the standardized tests. Only 24 to 26 of the 125 questions have a "correct" answer (Logic Games), as opposed to Arguments and Reading Comprehension, for which you must choose the elusive "best" answer. As ridiculous as they are, the GMAT, GRE, SAT, MCAT, and ACT at least have large chunks of math or science on them. There are verifiably correct answers on these tests, and occasionally you even have to know something to get the right answers. *Only the LSAT requires almost no specific knowledge of anything whatsoever, which is precisely what makes it so difficult.* The only infallible way to study for the LSAT is to study the LSAT itself. The good news is that *anybody* can get significantly better at the LSAT by working diligently at it. In fact, your score will increase exponentially directly in proportion to the amount of time and work you put into preparing for it.

HOW IMPORTANT IS THE LSAT?

The LSAT figures very prominently in your law school application, especially if you've been out of school for a few years. Some law schools won't even look at your application unless you achieve a certain score on your LSAT. Most top law schools average multiple LSAT scores, so you should aim to take it only once. By the way, each score you receive is valid for five years after you take the test.

LSAT STRUCTURE

Section Type	Sections	Questions Per Section	Time Per Section
Logical Reasoning (Arguments)	2	24–26 2 sections, about 25 questions each	35 minute sections
Analytical Reasoning (Games)	1	24–26	35 minutes
Reading Comprehension	1	27–28	35 minutes
Experimental	1	24–26	35 minutes
Writing Sample	1	1	35 minutes

Each test has approximately 125 questions. Neither the Experimental section nor the Writing Sample counts toward your score. The multiple-choice sections may be given in any order, but the Writing Sample is always administered last. The Experimental section can be any of the three types of multiple-choice sections and is used by the test writers to test out new questions on your time and at your expense.

The Writing Sample is not scored, and unlikely to be read by anyone other than you. However, the law schools to which you apply will receive a copy of your writing sample, so you should definitely do it. A blank page would stand out like a sore thumb, and you wouldn't want the Admissions Office to think you were some kind of revolutionary.

WHAT'S ON THE LSAT, EXACTLY?

We asked the experts in the LSAT Course Division of The Princeton Review for the lowdown on the various sections of the LSAT. Here's what they had to say.

Registering for the LSAT

You can register for the LSAT by mail, over the phone, or online. To register by mail, you will need a copy of the Registration and Information Bulletin, which you may request from Law Services or pick up from your pre-law advisor. You may also register for the LSAT online at www.lsac.org. The LSAT fee is currently a whopping $123; if you're late, it's an extra $62. To avoid late fees, mail your registration form at least six weeks — six weeks — before the test. Also, by registering early, you are more likely to be assigned your first choice of test center. You can reach the Law School Admissions Council at

Phone: 215-968-1001

www.lsac.org

lsacinfo@lsac.org

Analytical Reasoning: If you've ever worked logic problems in puzzle books, then you're already somewhat familiar with the Analytical Reasoning section of the LSAT. The situations behind these problems—often called "games" or "logic games"—are common ones: deciding in what order to interview candidates, or assigning employees to teams, or arranging dinner guests around a table. The arrangement of "players" in these games is governed by a set of rules you must follow in answering the questions. Each Analytical Reasoning section is made up of four games, with five to seven questions each. Questions may ask you to find out what *must* be true under the rules or what *could* be true under the rules; they may add a new condition that applies to just that question; or they may ask you to count the number of possible arrangements under the stated conditions. These questions are difficult mostly because of the time constraints under which they must be worked; very few test-takers find themselves able to complete 24 questions on this section in the time allotted.

Logical Reasoning: Because there are two scored sections of them, Logical Reasoning questions on the LSAT are the most important to your score. Each Logical Reasoning—sometimes called "arguments"—question is made up of a short paragraph, often written to make a persuasive point. These small arguments are usually written to contain a flaw—some error of reasoning or unwarranted assumption that you must identify to answer the question successfully. Questions may ask you to draw conclusions from the stated information, to weaken or strengthen the argument, to identify its underlying assumptions, or to identify its logical structure or method. There are most often a total of 50 or 51 argument questions between the two sections—roughly half of the scored questions on the LSAT.

As of June 2007 a modification, called Comparative Reading, appears as one of the four sets in the LSAT Reading Comprehension section. In general, Comparative Reading questions are similar to traditional Reading Comprehension questions, except that Comparative Reading questions are based on two shorter passages that together are roughly the same length as one Reading Comprehension passage. A few of the questions that follow a Comparative Reading passage pair might concern only one of the two passages, but most questions will be about both passages and how they relate to each other. Also, beginning with the June 2007 LSAT, test-takers no longer are randomly assigned one of two different kinds of writing prompt—decision or argument—for the writing sample. All test-takers will be assigned a decision prompt. The Writing Sample will continue to be unscored.

We strongly recommend that you prep for this test. Although we provide the best prep for the LSAT, you certainly don't have to take The Princeton Review's course (or buy our book, *Cracking the LSAT*, or sign up for our awesome distance learning course), as much as we'd obviously like it. There are plenty of books, software products, courses, and tutors out there. The people who make the LSAT will gleefully sell you plenty of practice tests as well. The key is to find the best program for you. Your first step should be taking a free full-length practice LSAT given under realistic testing conditions (we offer them across the country), so you can gauge where you stand and how much you need to improve your LSAT score. Whatever your course of action, however, make sure you remain committed to it, so you can be as prepared as possible when you take the actual test.

WHEN SHOULD YOU TAKE THE LSAT?

Here is a quick summary of test dates along with some factors to consider for each.

JUNE

The June administration is the only time the test is given on a Monday afternoon. If you have trouble functioning at the ordinary 8:00 A.M. start time, June may be a good option. Furthermore, taking the LSAT in June frees up your summer and fall to research schools and complete applications. However, if you are still in college, you'll have to balance LSAT preparation with academic course work and, in some cases, final exams. Check your exam schedules before deciding on a June LSAT test date.

OCTOBER/SEPTEMBER

The October test date (which is sometimes in late September) will allow you to prepare for the LSAT during the summer. This is an attractive option if you are a college student with some free time on your hands. Once you've taken the LSAT, you can spend the remainder of the fall completing your applications.

DECEMBER

December is the last LSAT administration that most competitive law schools will accept. If disaster strikes and you get a flat tire on test day, you may end up waiting another year to begin law school. December test-takers also must balance their time between preparing for the LSAT and completing law school applications. Doing so can make for a hectic fall, especially if you're still in college. You should also remember that, while a law school may accept December LSAT scores, taking the test in December could affect your chances of admission. Many law schools use a rolling admissions system, which means that they begin making admissions decisions as early as mid-October and continue to do so until the application deadline. Applying late in this cycle could mean that fewer spots are available. Check with your potential law schools to find out their specific policies.

FEBRUARY

If you want to begin law school in the following fall, the February LSAT will be too late for most law schools. However, if you don't plan to begin law school until the *next* academic year, you can give yourself a head start on the entire admissions process by taking the LSAT in February, then spending your summer researching schools and your fall completing applications.

UPCOMING LSAT TEST DATES		
TEST DATE	**Registration Deadline**	**Late Registration Ends**
September 29, 2007*	August 28, 2007	August 29–September 4, 2007
December 1, 2007*	October 30, 2007	October 31–November 6, 2007
February 2, 2008*	January 2, 2008	January 3–January 8, 2008

* The test is available the following Monday for those who cannot take a Saturday exam for religious purposes.

HOW IS THE LSAT SCORED?

LSAT scores currently range from 120 to 180. Why that range? We have no idea. The table on page 16 indicates the percentile rating of the corresponding LSAT scores between 141 and 180. This varies slightly from test to test.

Your raw score (the number of questions you answer correctly) doesn't always produce the same scaled score as previous LSATs. What actually happens is that your raw score is compared with that of everyone else who took the test on the same date you did. The LSAC looks at the scales from every other LSAT given in the past three years and "normalizes" the current scale so that it doesn't deviate widely from those scaled scores in the past.

LSAT Score	Percent Below	LSAT Score	Percent Below
180	99.9	160	82.2
179	99.9	159	79.1
178	99.9	158	76.5
177	99.8	157	72.6
176	99.7	156	68.7
175	99.6	155	65.7
174	99.5	154	61.5
173	99.3	153	57.3
172	99.0	152	53.2
171	98.5	151	49.1
170	98.1	150	44.9
169	97.5	149	41.0
168	96.7	148	37.0
167	95.7	147	33.4
166	94.6	146	29.6
165	93.2	145	26.4
164	91.4	144	23.3
163	89.7	143	20.2
162	87.3	142	17.7
161	84.9	141	15.2

A GOOD LSAT SCORE

A good score on the LSAT is the score that gets you into the law school you want to attend. Remember that a large part of the admissions game is the formula of your UGPA (undergraduate grade point average) multiplied by your LSAT score. Chances are, you are at a point in life where your UGPA is pretty much fixed (if you're reading this early in your college career, start getting very good grades pronto), so the only piece of the formula you can have an impact on is your LSAT score. We cannot emphasize enough the notion that you must prepare for this test.

A LITTLE IMPROVEMENT GOES A LONG WAY

A student who scores a 154 is in the 62nd percentile of all LSAT-takers. If that student's score was 161, however, that same student would jump to the 85th percentile. Depending upon your score, a 7-point improvement can increase your ranking by more than 25 percentile points.

COMPETITIVE LSAT SCORES AROUND THE UNITED STATES

The range of LSAT scores from the 25th to 75th percentile of incoming full-time students at U.S. law schools is pretty broad. Here is a sampling.

Law School	Score 25 to 75 percentile
Widener University, School of Law, Harrisburg	151–155
Gonzaga University, School of Law	152–156
Rutgers University-Newark, School of Law	154–161
University of Pittsburgh, School of Law	157–161
Northeastern University, School of Law	159–163
Temple University, James E. Beasley School of Law	160–163
University of Florida, Levin College of Law	156–162
University of Tennessee, College of Law	155–161
Case Western Reserve University, School of Law	157–161
University of Alabama, School of Law	160–164
Southern Methodist University, School of Law	155–164
Loyola University Chicago, School of Law	159–163
Boston University, School of Law	163–166
Emory University, School of Law	161–165
University of Southern California, The Law School	164–167
George Washington University, Law School	163–166
Duke University, School of Law	165–169
University of Michigan, Law School	166–169
Stanford University, School of Law	167–172
University of Chicago, Law School	168–172
Yale University, Yale Law School	168–175

PREPARING FOR THE LSAT

No matter who you are—whether you graduated *magna cum laude* from Cornell University or you're on academic probation at Cornell College—the first thing you need to do is order a recent LSAT. One comes free with every *Official LSAT Registration Booklet*. Once you get the test, take it, but not casually over the course of two weeks. Bribe someone to be your proctor. Have them administer the test to you under strict time conditions. Follow the test booklet instructions exactly, and do it right. Your goal is to simulate an actual testing experience as much as possible. When you finish, score the test honestly. Don't give yourself a few extra points because "you'll do better on test day." The score on this practice test will provide a baseline for mapping your test preparation strategy.

If your practice LSAT score is already at a point where you've got a very high-percentage shot of getting accepted to the law school of your choice, chances are you don't need much preparation. Order a half dozen or so of the most recent LSATs from LSAC and work through them over the course of a few months, making sure you understand why you are making specific mistakes. If your college or university offers a free or very cheap prep course, consider taking it to get more tips on the test. Many of these courses are taught by pre-law advisors who will speak very intelligently about the test and are committed to helping you get the best score you can.

If, after you take a practice LSAT, your score is not what you want or need it to be, you are definitely not alone. Many academically strong candidates go into the LSAT cold because they assume that the LSAT is no more difficult than or about the same as their college courses. Frankly, many students are surprised at how poorly they do the first time they take a dry run. Think about it this way: It's better to be surprised sitting at home with a practice test than while taking the test for real.

If you've taken a practice LSAT under exam conditions and it's, say, 10 or 15 points below where you want it to be, you should probably consult an expert. Test preparation companies spend quite a bit of money and time poring over the tests and measuring their students' improvement. We sure do. Ask around. Assess your financial situation. Talk to other people who have improved their LSAT scores and duplicate their strategies.

Whatever you decide to do, make sure you are practicing with real LSAT questions and you take full-length practice tests under realistic testing conditions—again and again and again.

SOME ESSENTIAL, DOWN-AND-DIRTY LSAT TIPS

Slow down. Way down. The slower you go, the better you'll do. It's that simple. Any function you perform, from basic motor skills to complex intellectual problems, will be affected by the rate at which you perform that function. This goes for everything from cleaning fish to taking the LSAT. You can get 25 questions wrong and still get a scaled score of 160, which is a very good score (it's in the 84th percentile). You can get at least six questions wrong per section or, even better, you can ignore the two or three most convoluted questions per section, *still* get a few more questions wrong, and you'll get an excellent overall score. Your best strategy is to find the particular working speed at which you will get the most questions correct.

> **Princeton Review's Hyperlearning LSAT Course**
> We offer the very best in LSAT prep, combining personal attention with intensive class sessions. You'll take six full-length practice tests and be ready to ace the LSAT on test day—we guarantee it. Visit PrincetonReview.com for fantastic resources, free practice material, and information on The Princeton Review's classroom and online courses.

There is no penalty for guessing. If you don't have time to finish the exam, it's imperative that you leave yourself at least 30 seconds at the end of each section in which to grab free points by bubbling in some answer to every question before time is called. Pick a letter of the day—like B—don't bubble in randomly. If you guess totally randomly, you might get every single guess right. Of course, you may also get struck by lightning in the middle of the test. The odds are about the same. *You are far more likely to miss every question if you guess without a plan.* However, if you stick with the same letter each time you guess, you will definitely be right once in a while. It's a conservative approach, but it is also your best bet for guaranteed points, which is what you want. By guessing the same letter pretty much every time as time runs out, you can pick up anywhere from two to four raw points per section. Be careful about waiting until the very last second to start filling in randomly, though, because proctors occasionally cheat students out of the last few seconds of a section.

Use process of elimination all the time. This is absolutely huge. On 75 percent of the LSAT (all the Logical Reasoning and Reading Comprehension questions), you are *not* looking for the *right* answer, only the *best* answer. It says so right there in the instructions. Eliminating even one answer choice increases your chances of getting the question right by 20 to 25 percent. If you can cross off two or three answer choices, you are really in business. Also, very rarely will you find an answer choice that is flawless on the LSAT. Instead, you'll find four answer choices that are definitely wrong and one that is the least of five evils. You should constantly look for reasons to get rid of answer choices so you can eliminate them. This strategy will increase your odds of getting the question right, and you'll be a happier and more successful standardized test-taker. We swear.

> **Law School Trivia**
> The last president to argue a case before the United States Supreme Court was Richard Nixon (a Duke alumnus). He argued the case between his tenure as vice president and his presidency. The case was Time, Inc. v. Hill (1967), a rather complicated First Amendment case.

Attack! Attack! Attack! Read the test with an antagonistic, critical eye; look for holes and gaps in the reasoning of arguments and in the answer choices. Many LSAT questions revolve around what is wrong with a particular line of reasoning. The more adept you become at identifying what is wrong with a problem before going to the answer choices, the more successful you'll be.

Write all over your test booklet. Actively engage the exam, and put your thoughts on paper. Circle words. *Physically cross out wrong answer choices you have eliminated.* Draw complete and exact diagrams for the logic games. Use the diagrams you draw.

Do the questions in whatever order you wish. Just because a logic game question is first doesn't mean you should do it first. There is *no order of difficulty* on the LSAT—unlike some other standardized tests—so you should hunt down and destroy those questions at which you are personally best. If you are doing a Reading Comprehension question, for example, or tackling an argument, and you don't know what the hell is going on, then cross off whatever you can, guess, and move on. If you have no idea how to solve a particular logic game, don't focus your energy there. Find a game you can do and milk it for points. Your mission is to gain points wherever you can. By the way, if a particular section is really throwing you, it's probably because it is the dastardly Experimental section (which is often kind of sloppy and, thankfully, does not count toward your score).

CHAPTER 5
WRITING A GREAT PERSONAL STATEMENT

There is no way to avoid writing the dreaded personal statement. You'll probably need to write only one personal statement, and it will probably address the most commonly asked question: "Why do you want to obtain a law degree?" This question, in one form or another, appears on virtually every law school application and often represents your only opportunity to string more than two sentences together. Besides your grades and your LSAT score, it is the most important part of your law school application. Your answer should be about two pages long, and it should amount to something significantly more profound than "A six-figure salary really appeals to me," or "I watch *Law & Order* every night."

Unlike your application to undergraduate programs, the personal statement on a law school application is not the time to discuss what your trip to Europe meant to you, describe your wacky chemistry teacher, or try your hand at verse. It's a fine line. While you want to stand out, you definitely don't want to be *overly* creative here. You want to be unique, but you don't want to come across as a weirdo or a loose cannon. You want to present yourself as intelligent, professional, mature, persuasive, and concise because these are the qualities law schools seek in applicants.

THE BASICS
Here are the essentials of writing essays and personal statements.

Find your own unique angle. The admissions people read tons of really boring essays about "how great I am" and how "I think there should be justice for everyone." If you must explain why you want to obtain a law degree, strive to find an angle that is interesting and unique to you. If what you write *isn't* interesting to you, we promise that it won't be remotely interesting to an Admissions Officer. Also, in addition to being more effective, an interesting essay will be far more enjoyable to write.

In general, avoid generalities. Again, Admissions Officers have to read an unbelievable number of boring essays. You will find it harder to be boring if you write about particulars. It's the details that stick in a reader's mind.

Good writing is easily understood. You want to get your point across, not bury it in words. Don't talk in circles. Your prose should be clear and direct. If an Admissions Officer has to struggle to figure out what you are trying to say, you'll be in trouble. Also, legal writing courses make up a significant part of most law school curricula; if you can show that you have good writing skills, you have a serious edge.

Buy and read *The Elements of Style* by William Strunk Jr. and E. B. White. We can't recommend it enough. In fact, we're surprised you don't have it already. This little book is a required investment for any writer (and, believe us, you'll be doing plenty of writing as a law student and a practicing attorney). You will refer to it forever, and if you do what it says, your writing will definitely improve.

Have three or four people read your personal statement and critique it. If your personal statement contains misspellings and grammatical errors, Admissions Officers will conclude not only that you don't know how to write but also that you aren't shrewd enough to get help. What's worse, the more time you spend with a piece of your own writing, the less likely you are to spot any errors. You get tunnel vision. Ask friends, boyfriends, girlfriends, professors, brothers, sisters—somebody—to read your essay and comment on it. Use a computer with a spellchecker. *Be especially careful about punctuation!* Another tip: Read your personal statement aloud to yourself or someone else. You will catch mistakes and awkward phrases that would have gotten past you otherwise because they sounded correct in your head.

Don't repeat information from other parts of your application. It's a waste of time and space.

Stick to the length that is requested. It's only common courtesy.

Maintain the proper tone. Your essay should be memorable, without being outrageous and easy to read, without being too formal or sloppy. When in doubt, err on the formal side.

Being funny is much harder than you think. An applicant who can make an Admissions Officer laugh never gets lost in the shuffle. The clever part of the personal statement is passed around and read aloud. Everyone smiles and the Admissions Staff can't bear to toss your application into the "reject" pile. But beware! Most people think they're funny, but only a few are able to pull it off in this context. Obviously, stay away from one-liners, limericks, and anything remotely off-color.

WHY DO YOU WANT TO GO TO LAW SCHOOL?

Writing about yourself often proves to be surprisingly difficult. It's certainly no cakewalk explaining who you are and why you want to go to law school, and presenting your lifetime of experiences in a mere two pages. On the bright side, the personal statement is the only element of your application over which you have total control. It's a tremendous opportunity to make a great first impression as long as you avoid the urge to communicate your entire genetic blueprint. Your goal should be much more modest.

Websites about Getting into Law School

www.PrincetonReview.com

You can access tons of information about law school and the LSAT at our site.

www.lsac.org

This site is home to the people who bring you the LSAT and the LSDAS application processing service.

DON'T GET CARRIED AWAY

Although some law schools set no limit on the length of the personal statement, you shouldn't take their bait. You can be certain that your statement will be at least glanced at in its entirety, but Admissions Officers are human, and their massive workload at admissions time has an understandable impact on their attention spans. You should limit yourself to two or three typed, double-spaced pages. Does this make your job any easier? Not at all. In fact, practical constraints on the length of your essay demand a higher degree of efficiency and precision. A two-page limit allows for absolutely no fluff.

MAKE YOURSELF STAND OUT

We know you know this, but you will be competing against thousands of well-qualified applicants for admission to just about any law school. Consequently, your primary task in writing your application is to separate yourself from the crowd. Particularly if you are applying directly from college or if you have been out of school for a very short time, you must do your best to ensure that the Admissions Committee cannot categorize you too broadly. Admissions Committees will see innumerable applications from bright 22-year-olds with good grades. Your essay presents an opportunity to put those grades in context, to define and differentiate yourself.

WHAT MAKES A GOOD PERSONAL STATEMENT?

Like any good writing, your law school application should be clear, concise, and candid. The first two of these attributes, clarity and conciseness, are usually the result of a lot of reading, rereading, and rewriting. Without question, repeated critical revision by yourself and others is the surest way to trim and tune your prose. The third quality, candor, is the product of proper motivation. Honesty cannot be superimposed after the fact; your writing must be candid from the outset.

In writing your personal statement for law school applications, pay particularly close attention to the way your essay is structured and the fundamental message it communicates. Admissions Committees will read your essay two ways: as a product of your handiwork and as a product of your mind. Don't underestimate the importance of either perspective. A well-crafted essay will impress any Admissions Officer, but if it does not illuminate, you will not be remembered. You will not stand out. Conversely, a thoughtful essay that offers true insight will stand out unmistakably, but if it is not readable, it will not receive serious consideration.

THINGS TO AVOID IN YOUR PERSONAL STATEMENT

"MY LSAT SCORE ISN'T GREAT, BUT I'M JUST NOT A GOOD TEST-TAKER."

If you have a low LSAT score, avoid directly discussing it like the plague in your personal statement. Law school is a test-rich environment. In fact, grades in most law-school courses are determined by a single exam at the semester's end, and as a law student, you'll spend your Novembers and Aprils in a study carrel, completely removed from society. Saying that you are not good at tests will do little to convince an Admissions Committee that you've got the ability to succeed in law school once accepted.

Consider also that a low LSAT score speaks for itself—all too eloquently. It doesn't need you to speak for it too. The LSAT may be a flawed test, but don't go arguing the merits of the test to Admissions Officers, because ordinarily it is the primary factor they use to make admissions decisions. We feel for you, but you'd be barking up the wrong tree. The attitude of most law school Admissions Departments is that while the LSAT may be imperfect, it is equally imperfect for all applicants. Apart from extraordinary claims of serious illness on test day, few explanations for poor performance on the LSAT will mean much to the people who read your application.

About the only situation in which a discussion of your LSAT score is necessary is if you have two (or more) LSAT scores and one is significantly better than another. If you did much better in your second sitting than in your first, or vice versa, a brief explanation couldn't hurt. However, your explanation may mean little to the committee, which may have its own hard-and-fast rules for interpreting multiple LSAT scores. Even in this scenario, however, you should avoid bringing up the LSAT in the personal statement. *Save it for an addendum.*

The obvious and preferable alternative to an explicit discussion of a weak LSAT score would be to focus on what you *are* good at. If you really are bad at standardized tests, you must be better at something else, or you wouldn't have gotten as far as you have. If you think you are a marvelous researcher, say so. If you are a wonderful writer, show it. Let your essay implicitly draw attention away from your weak points by focusing on your strengths. There is no way to convince an Admissions Committee that they should overlook your LSAT score. You may, however, present compelling reasons for them to look beyond it.

"MY COLLEGE GRADES WEREN'T THAT HIGH, BUT . . ."

This issue is a bit more complicated than the low LSAT score. Law school Admissions Committees will be more willing to listen to your interpretation of your college performance but only within limits. Keep in mind that law schools require official transcripts for a reason. Members of the Admissions Committee will be aware of your academic credentials before ever getting to your essay. As with low LSAT scores, your safest course of action is to *explain low grades in addendum.*

If your grades are unimpressive, you should offer the Admissions Committee something else by which to judge your abilities. Again, the best argument for looking past your college grades is evidence of achievement in another area, whether in your LSAT score, your extracurricular activities, your overcoming economic hardship as an undergraduate, or your career accomplishments.

"I'VE ALWAYS WANTED TO BE A LAWYER."

Sure you have. Many applicants seem to feel the need to point out that they really, really want to become attorneys. You will do yourself a great service by avoiding such throwaway lines. They'll do nothing for your essay but water it down. Do not convince yourself in a moment of desperation that claiming to have known that the law was your calling since age six (when—let's be honest—you really wanted to be a firefighter) will somehow move your application to the top of the pile. The Admissions Committee is not interested in how much you want to practice law. They want to know *why.*

"I WANT TO BECOME A LAWYER TO FIGHT INJUSTICE."

No matter how deeply you feel about battling social inequity, between us, writing it down makes you sound like a superhero on a soapbox. Moreover, though some people really do want to fight injustice, way down in the cockles of their hearts, most applicants are motivated to attend law school by less altruistic desires. Among the nearly one million practicing lawyers in the United States, there are relatively few who actually earn a living defending the indigent or protecting civil rights. Tremendously dedicated attorneys who work for peanuts and take charity cases are few and far between. We're not saying you don't want to be one of them; we're merely saying that people in law school admissions won't *believe* you want to be one of them. They'll take your professed altruistic ambitions (and those of the hundreds of other personal statements identical to yours) with a (huge) grain of salt.

If you can, in good conscience, say that you are committed to a career in the public interest, show the committee something tangible on your application and in your essay that will allow them to see your statements as more than mere assertions. If however, you cannot show that you are already a veteran in the good fight, don't claim to be. Law school Admissions Committees certainly do not regard the legal profession as a saints versus sinners proposition, and neither should you. Do not be afraid of appearing morally moderate. If the truth is that you want the guarantee of the relatively good jobs a law degree practically ensures, be forthright. Nothing is as impressive to the reader of a personal statement as the ring of truth, and what's wrong with wanting a good job, anyway?

CHAPTER 6
RECOMMENDATIONS

The law schools to which you apply will require two or three letters of recommendation in support of your application. Some schools will allow you to submit as many letters as you like. Others make it clear that any more than the minimum number of letters of recommendation is unwelcome. If you've ever applied to a private school (or perhaps a small public school) then you know the drill.

Unlike the evaluation forms for some colleges and graduate programs, however, law school recommendation forms tend toward absolute minimalism. All but a few recommendation forms for law school applications ask a single, open-ended question. It usually goes something like, "What information about this applicant is relevant that is not to be found in other sources?" The generic quality of the forms from various law schools may be both a blessing and a curse. On the one hand, it makes it possible for those writing your recommendations to write a single letter that will suffice for all the applications you submit. This convenience will make everybody much happier. On the other hand, if a free-form recommendation is to make a positive impression on an Admissions Committee, it must convey real knowledge about you.

WHOM TO ASK

Your letters of recommendation should come from people who know you well enough to offer a truly informed assessment of your abilities. Think carefully before choosing them to do this favor for you, but, as a general rule, pick respectable people whom you've known for a long time. If the writers of your recommendations know you well and understand the broader experience that has brought you to your decision to attend law school, they will be able to write a letter that is specific enough to do you some good. You also want people who can and are willing to contribute to an integrated, cohesive application.

The application materials from most law schools suggest that your letters should come, whenever possible, from people in academic settings. Some schools want at least two recommendations, both of which must be academic. Others explicitly request that the letters come from someone who has known you in a professional setting, especially if you've been out of school for a while.

HELP YOUR RECOMMENDATION WRITERS HELP YOU

Here, in essence, is the simple secret to great recommendations: Make sure the writers of your recommendations know you, your academic and professional goals, and the overall message you are trying to convey in your application. The best recommendations will fit neatly with the picture you present of yourself in your own essay, even when they make no specific reference to the issues your essay addresses. An effective law school application will present to the Admissions Committee a cohesive picture, not a montage. A great way to point your recommendation writers in the right direction and maximize their abilities to contribute to your overall cause is to provide them with copies of your personal statement. Don't be bashful about amiably communicating a few "talking points" that don't appear in your personal statement, as well.

Helpful Websites

www.findlaw.com
This site is the mother lode of free information about law, law schools, and legal careers.

www.ilrg.com
Mother lode honorable mention.

www.hg.org/students.html
Another honorable mention.

www.canadalawschools.com
Pretty much everything you ever wanted to know about Canadian law schools.

www.jurist.law.pitt.edu
The University of Pittsburgh School of Law's splendid "Legal News and Research" website offers a wealth of useful information.

ACADEMIC REFERENCES

Most applicants will (and should) seek recommendations from current or former professors. The academic environment in law school is extremely rigorous. Admissions Committees will be looking for assurance that you will be able not just to survive but to excel. A strong recommendation from a college professor is a valuable corroboration of your ability to succeed in law school.

You want nothing less than stellar academic recommendations. While a perfunctory, lukewarm recommendation is unlikely to damage your overall application, it will obviously do nothing to bolster it. Your best bet is to choose at least one professor from your major field. An enthusiastic endorsement from such a professor will be taken as a sign that you are an excellent student. Second—and we hope that this goes without saying—you should choose professors who do not immediately associate your name with the letter C.

Specifics are of particular interest to Admissions Officers when they evaluate your recommendations. If a professor can make *specific* reference to a particular project you completed, or at least make substantive reference to your work in a particular course, the recommendation will be strengthened considerably. Make it your responsibility to enable your professors to provide specifics. Drop hints, or just lay it out for them. You might, for example, make available a paper you wrote for them of which you are particularly proud. Or you might just chat with the professor for a while to jog those dormant memories. You might feel uncomfortable tooting your own horn, but it's for the best. Unless your professors are well enough acquainted with you to be able to offer a very personal assessment of your potential, they will greatly appreciate a tangible reminder of your abilities on which to base their recommendation.

ESCAPING THE WOODWORK

If you managed to get through college without any professors noticing you, it's not the end of the world. Professors are quite talented at writing recommendations for students they barely know. Most consider it part of their job. Even seemingly unapproachable academic titans will usually be happy to dash off a quick letter for a mere student. However, these same obliging professors are masters of a sort of opaque prose style that screams to an Admissions Officer, "I really have no idea what to say about this kid who is, in fact, a near-total stranger to me!" Although an Admissions Committee will not outrightly dismiss such a recommendation, it's really not going to help you much.

REELING IN THE YEARS

Obviously, the longer it has been since you graduated, the tougher it is to obtain academic recommendations. However, if you've held on to your old papers, you may still be able to rekindle an old professor's memory of your genius by sending a decent paper or two along with your request for a recommendation (and, of course, a copy of your personal statement). You want to provide specifics in any way you can.

NON-ACADEMIC REFERENCES

Getting the mayor, a senator, or the CEO of your company to write a recommendation helps only if you have a personal and professional connection with that person. Remember, you want the writers of your recommendations to provide specifics about your actual accomplishments. If you're having trouble finding academic recommendations, choose people from your workplace, from the community, or from any other area of your life that is important to you. If at all possible, talk to your boss or a supervisor from a previous job who knows you well (and, of course, likes you).

SEND A THANK-YOU NOTE

Always a good idea. It should be short and handwritten. Use a blue pen so the recipient knows for sure that your note is no cheap copy. As with any good thank-you note and any good recommendation, mention a specific. (Send a thank-you note if you have an interview at a law school, too.)

CHAPTER 7
REAL-LIFE WORK EXPERIENCE
AND COMMUNITY SERVICE

WORK EXPERIENCE IN COLLEGE

Most law school applications will ask you to list any part-time jobs you held while you were in college and how many hours per week you worked. If you had to (or chose to) work your way through your undergraduate years, this should come as good news. A great number of law schools make it clear that they take your work commitments as a college student into consideration when evaluating your undergraduate GPA.

WORK EXPERIENCE IN REAL LIFE

All law school applications will ask you about your work experience beyond college. They will give you three or four lines on which to list such experience. Some schools will invite you to submit a resume. If you have a very good one, you should really milk this opportunity for all it's worth. Even if you don't have a marvelous resume, these few lines on the application and your resume are the only opportunities you'll have to discuss your post-college experience meaningfully—unless you choose to discuss professional experience in your personal statement as well.

The kind of job you've had is not as important as you might think. What interests the Admissions Committee is what you've made of that job and what it has made of you. Whatever your job was or is, you want to offer credible evidence of your competence. For example, mention in your personal statement your job advancement or any increase in your responsibility. Most important, though, remember your overriding goal of cohesive presentation—you want to show off your professional experience within the context of your decision to attend law school. This does not mean that you need to offer geometric proof of how your experience in the workplace has led you inexorably to a career in law. You need only explain truthfully how this experience influenced you and how it fits nicely into your thinking about law school.

COMMUNITY SERVICE

An overwhelming majority of law schools single out community involvement as one of several influential factors in their admissions decisions. Law schools would like to admit applicants who show a long-standing commitment to something other than their own advancement.

It is certainly understandable that law schools would wish to determine the level of such commitment before admitting an applicant, particularly since so few law students go on to practice public interest law. Be forewarned, however, that nothing—*nothing*—is so obviously bogus as an insincere statement of a commitment to public interest issues. It just reeks. Admissions Committees are well aware that very few people take the time out of their lives to become involved significantly in their communities. If you aren't one of them, trying to fake it can only hurt you.

CHAPTER 8

INTERVIEWS

The odds are very good that you will never have to sit through an interview in the law school admissions process. Admissions Offices just aren't very keen on them. They do happen occasionally, however, and if you are faced with one, here are a few tips.

Be prepared. Interviews do make impressions. Some students are admitted simply because they had great interviews; less often, students are rejected because they bombed. Being prepared is the smartest thing you can do.

Don't ask questions that are answered in the brochures you got in the mail. You have to read those brochures—at breakfast before the interview would be an ideal time.

If there is a popular conception of the school (e.g., Harvard is overly competitive), don't ask about it. Your interviewer will have been through the same song and dance too many times. While you don't want to seem off the wall by asking bizarre questions, you don't want to sound exactly like every other boring applicant before you.

Look good, feel good. Wear nice clothes. If you aren't sure what to wear, *ask the Admissions Staff*. Get a respectable haircut. Don't chew gum. Clean your fingernails. Brush your teeth. Wash behind your ears. You can go back to being a slob as soon as they admit you.

Don't worry about time. Students sometimes are told that the sign of a good interview is that it lasts longer than the time allowed for it. Forget about this. Don't worry if your interview lasts exactly as long as the assistant said it would. Don't try to stretch out the end of your interview by suddenly becoming long-winded or asking questions you don't care about.

CHAPTER 9
MONEY MATTERS

Law school is a cash cow for colleges and universities everywhere and, especially at a private school, you are going to be gouged for a pretty obscene wad of cash over the next three years. Take University of Southern California Gould School of Law, where tuition is more than $36,000 a year. If you are planning to eat, live somewhere, buy books, and (maybe) have health insurance, you are looking at about $53,000 per year. Multiply that by three years of law school and you get $159,000. Now faint. Correct for inflation (USC certainly will), add things like computers and other miscellany, and you can easily spend $165,000 to earn a degree. Assume that you have to borrow every penny of that $165,000. Multiply it by 8 percent through 10 years (a common assumption of law school applicants is that they will be able to pay all their debt back in 10 years or less). Your monthly payments will be about $2,002.

On the bright side, while law school is certainly an expensive proposition, the financial rewards of practicing can be immensely lucrative. You won't be forced into bankruptcy if you finance it properly. There are tried-and-true ways to reduce your initial costs, finance the costs on the horizon, and manage the debt with which you'll leave school—all without ever having to ask, "Have you been in a serious accident recently?" in a television commercial.

LAW SCHOOL ON THE CHEAP

Private schools aren't the only law schools, and you don't have to come out of law school saddled with tens of thousands of dollars of debt. Many state schools have reputations that equal or surpass some of the top private ones. It might be worth your while to spend a year establishing residency in a state with one or more good public law schools. Here's an idea: Pack up your belongings and move to a cool place like Minneapolis, Seattle, Berkeley, Austin, or Boulder. Spend a year living there. Wait tables, hang out, listen to music, walk the Earth, write the great American novel, and *then* study law.

COMPARISON SHOPPING

Here are the full-time tuition costs at law schools around the country. The two schools listed for each state are randomly paired schools in the same region (one public and one private) and are provided to help you get a feel of what law school costs are going to run you. Those schools that have the same tuition in both columns are private law schools.

Law School	In-State	Out-of-State
University of Florida, Levin College of Law	$9,861	$29,227
University of Miami, School of Law	$32,840	$32,840
Indiana University-Bloomington, School of Law	$14,980	$29,507
University of Notre Dame, Law School	$33,670	$33,670
The University of Tennessee, College of Law	$9,142	$24,198
Vanderbilt University, Law School	$36,000	$36,000
The University of Iowa, College of Law	$13,374	$28,818
Drake University, Law School	$25,800	$25,800
Louisiana State University, Law Center	$10,722	$19,818
Tulane University, Law School	$30,350	$30,350
University of California, Hastings College of Law	$22,190	$33,415
University of San Francisco, School of Law	$32,110	$32,110
The University of Texas at Austin, School of Law	$14,948	$27,238
Baylor University, School of Law	$30,156	$30,156
University of Illinois, College of Law	$18,102	$29,100
Northwestern University, School of Law	$40,410	$40,410
University of Pittsburgh, School of Law	$20,758	$29,056
University of Pennsylvania, Law School	$37,020	$37,020
University of Oregon, School of Law	$18,690	$23,262
Lewis & Clark College, Northwestern School of Law	$27,670	$27,670

LOAN REPAYMENT ASSISTANCE PROGRAMS

If you are burdened with loans, we've got more bad news. The National Association of Law Placement (NALP) shows that while salaries for law school graduates who land jobs at the big, glamorous firms have skyrocketed in the past few years, salaries of less than $85,000 are more common than salaries of $100,000 to $130,000 for the general run of law school grads. There are, however, a growing number of law schools and other sources willing to pay your loans for you through loan forgiveness programs in return for your commitment to work in public interest law.

While doing a tour of duty in public service law will put off dreams of working at a big firm or becoming the next Mark Geragos, the benefits of these programs are undeniable. Here's how just about all of them work. You commit to working for a qualified public service or public interest job. As long as your gross income does not exceed the prevailing public service salary, the programs will pay off a good percentage of your debt. Eligible loans are typically any educational debt financed through your law school, which really excludes only loan sharks and credit-card debts.

The Skinny on Loan Repayment Assistance Programs

For a comprehensive listing of assistance programs and for other loan-forgiveness information, call Equal Justice Works at 202-466-3686, or look them up on the Web at www.napil.org.

MAXIMIZE YOUR AID

A simple but oft-forgotten piece of wisdom: If you don't ask, you usually don't get. Be firm when trying to get merit money from your school. Some schools have reserves of cash that go unused. Try simply asking for more financial aid. The better your grades, of course, the more likely schools are to crack open their safe of financial goodies for you. Unfortunately, grants aren't as prevalent for law students as for undergrads. Scholarships are not nearly as widely available either. To get a general idea of availability of aid at a law school, contact the Financial Aid Office.

PARENTAL CONTRIBUTION?!

If you are operating under the assumption that, as a tax-paying grownup who has been out of school for a number of years, you will be recognized as the self-supporting adult you are, you could be in for a surprise. Veterans of financial aid battles will not be surprised to hear that even law school Financial Aid Offices have a difficult time recognizing when apron strings have legitimately been cut. Schools may try to take into account your parents' income in determining your eligibility for financial aid, regardless of your age or tax status. Policies vary widely. Be sure to ask the schools you are considering exactly what their policies are regarding financial independence for the purposes of financial aid.

BORROWING MONEY

It's an amusingly simple process, and several companies are in the business of lending large chunks of cash specifically to law students. Your law school Financial Aid Office can tell you how to reach them. You should explore more than one option and shop around for the lowest fees and rates.

WHO'S ELIGIBLE?

Anyone with reasonably good credit, regardless of financial need, can borrow enough money to finance law school. If you have financial need, you will probably be eligible for some types of financial aid if you meet the following basic qualifications:

- You are a United States citizen or a permanent U.S. resident.

- You are registered for Selective Service if you are a male, or you have the documentation to prove that you are exempt.

- You are not in default on student loans already.

- You don't have a horrendous credit history.

- You haven't been busted for certain drug-related crimes, including possession.

> **Let the Law School Pick Up the Tab for Phone Calls Whenever Possible**
>
> Many schools have free telephone numbers that they don't like to publish in books like this one. If the number we have listed for a particular law school is not an 800 number, it doesn't necessarily mean that you have to pay every time you call the school. Check out the school's website, or ask for the 800 number when you call the first time.

WHAT TYPES OF LOANS ARE AVAILABLE?

There are three basic types of loans: federal, private, and institutional.

Federal

The federal government funds federal loan programs. Federal loans, particularly the Stafford Loan, are usually the first resort for borrowers. Most federal loans are need-based, but some higher-interest loans are available regardless of financial circumstances.

TABLE OF LOANS			
NAME OF LOAN	**SOURCE**	**ELIGIBILITY**	**MAXIMUM ALLOCATION**
Federal Stafford (Subsidized) Student Loan http://studentaid.ed.gov/students/publications/student_guide/index.html	Federal, administered by participating lender	Demonstrated financial need	$8,500/year. The maximum aggregate total for subsidized loans is $65,500. The maximum aggregate total includes any Stafford loans received for undergraduate study.
Unsubsidized Stafford Student Loan http://studentaid.ed.gov/students/publications/student_guide/index.html	Federal, administered by participating lender	Not need-based	The total Stafford loan limit is $18,500, including Unsubsidized loans and Subsidized loans not to exceed $8,500. The maximum aggregate total of Stafford loans is $138,500, including Unsubsidized loans and Subsidized loans not to exceed $65,500.*
Health Professions Student Loan/Primary Care Loan (HPSL) Contact school for more information	Federal, administered by school	Exceptional financial need; commitment to primary care	For first- and second-year students, the maximum allocation is the cost of attendance (including tuition, educational expenses, and reasonable living expenses). Third- and fourth-year students may receive allocations beyond this amount.
Perkins Loan (formerly NDSL) Contact school for more information	Federal, administered by school	Demonstrated financial need	$6,000/year, with aggregate of $40,000. Aggregate amount includes undergraduate loans.
Alternative Loan Program (ALP) www.aamc.org/programs/medloans	AAMC, administered under MEDLOANS division of AAMC	Not need-based	Cost of attendance minus other aid received. Aggregate: $250,000 (total educational indebtedness from all sources).

*Students pursuing certain health professions and enrolled in programs accredited by the appropriate approved accreditation agency are eligible to receive increased amounts of Unsubsidized Stafford loans. If a student is granted the maximum additional allocation, the maximum aggregate total will be $189,500. This number includes all undergraduate and graduate Subsidized and Unsubsidized Stafford loans. See "Increased Eligibility for Health Professions Students" in the Federal Student Aid Handbook for details and updates.

Private

Private loans are funded by banks, foundations, corporations, and other associations. A number of private loans are targeted to aid particular segments of the population. You may have to do some investigating to identify private loans for which you might qualify. As always, contact your law school's Financial Aid Office to learn more.

Institutional

The amount of loan money available and the method by which it is disbursed vary greatly from one school to another. Private schools, especially those that are older and more established, tend to have larger endowments and can offer more assistance. To find out about the resources available at a particular school, refer to its catalog or contact—you guessed it—the Financial Aid Office.

TABLE OF LOANS (continued)			
REPAYMENT AND DEFERRAL OPTIONS	**INTEREST RATE**	**PROS**	**CONS**
10–30 years to repay. Begin repayment 6 months after graduation. Forbearance possible for up to 3 years of residency training.	Variable 4% loan disbursement fee. Capped at *8.25%.	Most common medical school loan. Interest is paid by the government during school. Once you get a loan, later loans are at the same rate.	None
10–30 years to repay. Interest begins to accrue from day loan is disbursed; you can pay the interest or have it capitalized (added to principal). Begin repayment 6 months after graduation. Forbearance possible for up to 3 years of residency training.	Variable 4% loan disbursement fee. Capped at *8.25%.	Not need-based.	Interest is not paid by the government while you're in school.
10 years to repay, beginning 1 year after graduation. Deferrable during residency and under special circumstances.	Fixed, 5%.	Fixed, relatively low interest rate.	Very limited availability.
10 years to repay. Begin repayment 9 months after graduation. Can be deferred for 2 years during residency.	Fixed, 5%.	Fixed, relatively low interest rate.	Low maximum allocation.
Standard: 20 years of interest and principal payments. Alternative: 3 years of interest only and 17 years of interest and principal. Repayment generally begins 3–4 years after graduation, depending on length of residency.	Prime rate plus 1.25%; variable, adjusted monthly. (While in school, prime rate plus 0%. Variable, adjusted monthly.)	High maximum allocation; not need-based.	"Loan of last resort." High interest rate.

*Check http://studentaid.ed.gov/students/publications/student_guide/index.html

CHAPTER 10
LAW SCHOOL 101

IS IT REALLY THAT BAD?

The first semester of law school has the well-deserved reputation of being among the greatest challenges to your intellect and stamina that you'll ever face. It requires tons and tons of work and, in many ways, it's an exercise in intellectual survival. Just as the gung-ho army recruit must survive boot camp, so, too, must the bright-eyed law student endure the humbling effects of the first year.

Though complex and difficult, the subject matter in first-year law school courses is probably no more inherently difficult than what is taught in other graduate or professional schools. The particular, private terror that is shared by roughly 40,000 1Ls every year stems more from law school's peculiar *style*. The method of instruction unapologetically punishes students who would prefer to learn passively.

THE FIRST-YEAR CURRICULUM
The first-year curriculum in the law school you attend will almost certainly be composed of a combination of the following courses:

TORTS
The word comes from the Middle French for *injury*. The Latin root of the word means *twisted*. Torts are wrongful acts, excluding breaches of contract, over which you can sue people. They include battery, assault, false imprisonment, and intentional infliction of emotional distress. Torts can range from the predictable to the bizarre, from "Dog Bites Man" to "Man Bites Dog" and everything in between. The study of torts mostly involves reading cases to discern the legal rationale behind decisions pertaining to the extent of, and limits on, the civil liability of one party for harm done to another.

CONTRACTS
They may seem fairly self-explanatory, but contractual relationships are varied and complicated, as two semesters of contracts will teach you. Again, through the study of past court cases, you will follow the largely unwritten law governing the system of conditions and obligations a contract represents, as well as the legal remedies available when contracts are breached.

CIVIL PROCEDURE
Civil procedure is the study of how you get things done in civil (as opposed to criminal) court. "Civ Pro" is the study of the often dizzyingly complex rules that govern not only who can sue whom, but also how, when, and where they can do it. This is not merely a study of legal protocol, for issues of process have a significant indirect effect on the substance of the law. Rules of civil procedure govern the conduct of both the courtroom trial and the steps that might precede it: obtaining information (discovery), making your case (pleading), pre-trial motions, and so on.

PROPERTY
You may never own a piece of land, but your life will inevitably and constantly be affected by property laws. Anyone interested in achieving an understanding of broader policy issues will appreciate the significance of this material. Many property courses will emphasize the transfer of property and, to varying degrees, economic analysis of property law.

CRIMINAL LAW
Even if you become a criminal prosecutor or defender, you will probably never run into most of the crimes to which you will be exposed in this course. Can someone who shoots the dead body of a person he believes to be alive be charged with attempted murder? What if they were both on drugs or had really rough childhoods? Also, you'll love the convoluted exam questions in which someone will invariably go on a nutty crime spree.

CONSTITUTIONAL LAW

"Con Law" is the closest thing to a normal class you will take in your first year. It emphasizes issues of government structure (e.g., federal power versus state power) and individual rights (e.g., personal liberties, freedom of expression, property protection). You'll spend a great deal of time studying the limits on the lawmaking power of Congress as well.

LEGAL METHODS

One of the few twentieth-century improvements on the traditional first-year curriculum that has taken hold nearly everywhere, this course travels under various aliases, such as Legal Research and Writing or Elements of the Law. In recent years, increased recognition of the importance of legal writing skills has led more than half of the U.S. law schools to require or offer a writing course after the first year. This class will be your smallest, and possibly your only, refuge from the Socratic Method. Methods courses are often taught by junior faculty and attorneys in need of extra cash and are designed to help you acquire fundamental skills in legal research, analysis, and writing. The methods course may be the least frightening you face, but it can easily consume an enormous amount of time. This is a common lament, particularly at schools where very few credits are awarded for it.

In addition to these course requirements, many law schools require 1Ls to participate in a moot-court exercise. As part of this exercise, students—sometimes working in pairs or even small groups—must prepare briefs and oral arguments for a mock trial (usually appellate). This requirement is often tied in with the methods course so that those briefs and oral arguments will be well researched—and graded.

Tips for Classroom Success

- *Be alert. Review material immediately before class so that it is fresh in your memory. Then review your notes from class later the same day and the week's worth of notes at the end of each week.*

- *Remember that there are few correct answers. The goal of a law school class is generally to analyze, understand, and attempt to resolve issues or problems.*

- *Learn to state and explain legal rules and principles with accuracy.*

- *Don't want to focus on minutiae from cases or class discussions; always try to figure out what the law is.*

- *Accept the ambiguity in legal analysis and class discussion; classes are intended to be thought provoking, perplexing, and difficult.*

- *No one class session will make or break you. Keep in mind how each class fits within the course overall.*

- *Write down the law. Don't write down what other students say. Concentrate your notes on the professor's hypotheticals and emphases in class.*

- *Review the table of contents in the casebook. This is a simple but effective way of keeping yourself in touch with where the class is at any given time.*

- *If you don't use a laptop, don't sit next to someone who does. The constant tapping on the keys will drive you crazy, and you may get a sense that they are writing down more than you (which is probably not true).*

- *Don't record classes. There are better uses of your time than to spend hours listening to the comments of students who were just as confused as you were when you first dealt with the material in class.*

THE CASE METHOD

In the majority of your law school courses, and probably in all of your first-year courses, your only texts will be things called casebooks. The case method eschews explanation and encourages exploration. In a course that relies entirely on the casebook, you will never come across a printed list of "laws." Instead, you will learn that in many areas of law there is no such thing as a static set of rules, but only a constantly evolving system of principles. You are expected to understand the principles of law—in all of its layers and ambiguities—through a critical examination of a series of cases that were decided according to such principles. You will often feel utterly lost, groping for answers to unarticulated questions. This is not only normal but also intended.

In practical terms, the case method works like this: For every class meeting, you will be assigned a number of cases to read from your casebook, which is a collection of (extremely edited) written judicial decisions in actual court cases. The names won't even have been changed to protect the innocent. The cases are the written judicial opinions rendered in court cases that were decided at the appeals or Supreme Court level. (Written opinions are not generally rendered in lower courts.)

Your casebook will contain no instructions and little to no explanation. Your assignments will be to simply read the cases and be in a position to answer questions based on them. There will be no written homework assignments, just cases, cases, and more cases.

You will write, for your own benefit, summaries—or briefs—of these cases. Briefs are your attempts to summarize the issues and laws around which a particular case revolves. *By briefing, you figure out what the law is.* The idea is that, over the course of a semester, you will try to integrate the content of your case briefs and your notes from in-class lectures, discussions, or dialogues into some kind of cohesive whole.

THE SOCRATIC METHOD

As unfamiliar as the case method will be to most 1Ls, the real source of anxiety is the way in which the professors present it. Socratic instruction entails directed questioning and limited lecturing. Generally, the Socratic professor invites a student to attempt a cogent summary of a case assigned for that day's class. Hopefully, it won't be you (but someday it will be). Regardless of the accuracy and thoroughness of your initial response, the professor then grills you on details overlooked or issues unresolved. Then, the professor will change the facts of the actual case at hand into a hypothetical case that may or may not have demanded a different decision by the court.

The overall goal of the Socratic method is to forcibly improve your critical reasoning skills. If you are reasonably well prepared, thinking about all these questions will force you beyond the immediately apparent issues in a given case to consider its broader implications. The dialogue between the effective Socratic instructor and the victim of the moment will also force nonparticipating students to question their underlying assumptions of the case under discussion.

WHAT IS CLINICAL LEGAL EDUCATION?

The latest so-called innovation in legal education is ironic in that it's a return to the old emphasis on practical experience. Hands-on training in the practical skills of lawyering now travels under the name "Clinical Legal Education."

HOW IT WORKS

Generally, a clinical course focuses on developing practical lawyering skills. "Clinic" means exactly what you would expect: a working law office where second- and third-year law students counsel clients and serve human beings. (A very limited number of law schools allow first-year students to participate in legal clinics.)

In states that grant upper-level law students a limited right to represent clients in court, students in a law school's clinic might actually follow cases through to their resolution. Some schools have a single on-site clinic that operates something like a general law practice, dealing with cases ranging from petty crime to landlord-tenant disputes. At schools that have dedicated the most resources to their clinical programs, numerous specialized clinics deal with narrowly defined areas of law, such as employment discrimination. The opportunities to participate in such live-action programs, however, are limited.

> *Watch* **The Paper Chase.** *Twice.*
>
> *This movie is the only one ever produced about law school that comes close to depicting the real thing. Watch it before you go to orientation. Watch it again on Thanksgiving break, and laugh when you can identify prototypes of your classmates.*

OTHER OPTIONS

Clinical legal education is much more expensive than traditional instruction, which means that few law schools can accommodate more than a small percentage of their students in clinical programs. If that's the case, check out external clinical placements and simulated clinical courses. In a clinical externship, you might work with a real firm or public agency several hours a week and meet with a faculty advisor only occasionally. Though students who participate in these programs are unpaid, they will ordinarily receive academic credit. Also, placements are chosen quite carefully to ensure that you don't become a gopher.

There are also simulated clinical courses. In one of these, you'll perform all of the duties that a student in a live-action clinic would, but your clients are imaginary.

CHAPTER 11
How to Excel at Any Law School

Preparation for law school is something you should take very seriously. Law school will be one of the most interesting and rewarding experiences of your life, but it's also an important and costly investment. Your academic performance in law school will influence your career for years to come. Consider the following facts when thinking about how important it is to prepare for law school:

- The average full-time law student spends more than $125,000 to attend law school.

- The average law student graduates with more than $80,000 of debt.

- The median income for law school graduates in both public and private practice is only about $60,000.

> **Contact Law Preview**
>
> *Law Preview*
>
> *10 Cordage Park Circle, Suite 115*
>
> *Plymouth, MA 02360*
>
> *Phone: 888-PREP-YOU*
>
> *E-mail: admin@lawpreview.com*
>
> *Website: www.lawpreview.com*

As you can see, most law students cannot afford to be mediocre. Money isn't everything, but when you're strapped with close to six figures of debt, money concerns will weigh heavily on your career choices. Even if money is not a concern for you, your academic performance in law school will profoundly affect your employment options after graduation and, ultimately, your legal career. Consider these additional facts

- Students who excel in law school may have opportunities to earn up to $135,000 plus bonuses right out of law school.

- Only law students who excel academically have opportunities to obtain prestigious judicial clerkships, teaching positions, and distinguished government jobs.

As you can see, law students who achieve academic success enjoy better career options and have a greater ability to escape the crushing debt of law school. The point is obvious: Your chances of achieving your goals—no matter what you want to do with your career—are far better if you succeed academically.

Now comes the hard part: How do you achieve academic success? You are going to get plenty of advice about how to excel in law school—much of it unsolicited. You certainly don't need any from us. We strongly advise, however, that you pay close attention to what Don Macaulay, the president of Law Preview, has to say about surviving and thriving as a law student. Macaulay, like all the founders of Law Preview, graduated at the top of his law school class and worked at a top law firm before he began developing and administering Law Preview's law school prep course in 1998.

> *All B-pluses put you in the top quarter at most schools and in the top fifth at many.*

While there are many resources that claim to provide a recipe for success in law school, Law Preview is the best of the lot. They have retained some of the most talented legal scholars in the country to lecture during their week-long sessions, and they deliver what they promise—a methodology for attacking and conquering the law school experience.

We asked Macaulay a few questions to which we thought prospective law students might like to know the answers:

It is often said that the first year of law school is the most important year. Is this true and, if so, why?

It is true. Academic success during the first year of law school can advance a successful legal career unlike success in any other year because many of the top legal employers start recruiting so early that your first-year grades are all they will see. Most prestigious law firms hire their permanent attorneys from among the ranks of the firm's "summer associates"—usually second-year law students who work for the firm during the summer between the second and third years of law school. Summer associates are generally hired during the fall semester of the second year, a time when only the first year grades are available. A student who does well during the first year, lands a desirable summer associate position, and then impresses his or her employer, is well on his or her way to a secure legal job regardless of his or her academic performance after the first year.

In addition, first-year grades often bear heavily upon a student's eligibility for law review and other prestigious scholastic activities, including other law journals and moot court. These credentials are considered the most significant signs of law school achievement, often even more than a high grade point average. Many of the top legal employers in the private and the public sectors seek out young lawyers with these credentials, and some employers will not even interview candidates who lack these honors, even after a few years of experience. As a result, a solid performance during the first year of law school can have a serious impact upon your professional opportunities available after graduation.

Websites About Doing Well in Law School

www.lawpreview.com

Law Preview is an intensive week-long seminar designed to help you conquer law school. Learn why hundreds of students have made Law Preview their first step to Law Review.

www.LawBooksForLess.com

LawBooksForLess.com is the best place to purchase casebooks and legal study aids, cheap!

How does law school differ from what students experienced as undergraduates?

Many students, especially those who enjoyed academic success in college, presume that law school will be a mere continuation of their undergraduate experience, and that, by implementing those skills that brought them success in college, they will enjoy similar success in law school. This couldn't be further from the truth. Once law school begins, students often find themselves thrown into deep water. They are handed an anchor in the form of a casebook (they are told it's a life preserver), and they are expected to sink or swim. While almost nobody sinks in law school anymore, most spend all of their first year just trying to keep their heads above water. In reality, virtually every student who is admitted into law school possesses the intelligence and work ethic needed to graduate. But in spite of having the tools needed to survive the experience, very few possess the know-how to truly excel and make Law Review at their schools.

What makes the law school experience unique is its method of instruction and its system of grading. Most professors rely on the case method as a means for illustrating legal rules and doctrines encountered in a particular area of the law. With the case method, students are asked to read a particular case or, in some instances, several cases, that the professor will use to lead a classroom discussion illustrating a particular rule of law. The assigned readings come from casebooks, which are compilations of cases for each area of law. The cases are usually edited to illustrate distinct legal rules, often with very little commentary or enlightenment by the casebook editor. The casebooks often lack anything more than a general structure, and law professors often contribute little to the limited structure. Students are asked to read and analyze hundreds of cases in a vacuum. Since each assigned case typically builds upon a legal rule illustrated in a previous case, it isn't until the end of the semester or, for some classes, the end of the year, that students begin to form an understanding of how these rules interrelate.

One of the objectives of Law Preview's law school prep course is to help students to understand the big picture before they begin their classes. We hire some of the most talented law professors from around the country to provide previews of the core first-year law school courses: Civil Procedure, Constitutional Law, Contracts, Criminal Law, Property, and Torts. During their lectures, our professors provide students with a roadmap for each subject by discussing the law's development, legal doctrines, and recurring themes and policies that students will encounter throughout the course. By providing entering law students with a conceptual framework for the material they will study, Law Preview eliminates the frustration that most of them will encounter when reading and analyzing case law in a vacuum.

What is the best way to prepare for law school, and when should you start?

When preparing for law school, students should focus on two interrelated tasks: 1) developing a strategy for academic success, and 2) preparing mentally for the awesome task ahead. The primary objective for most law students is to achieve the highest grades possible, and a well-defined strategy for success will help you direct your efforts most efficiently and effectively toward that goal. You must not begin law school equipped solely with some vague notion of hard work. Success requires a concrete plan that includes developing a reliable routine for classroom preparation, a proficient method of outlining, and a calculated strategy for test-taking. The further you progress in law school without such a plan, the more time and energy you will waste struggling through your immense work-load without moving discernibly closer to achieving academic success.

You must also become mentally prepared to handle the rigors of law school. Law school can be extremely discouraging because students receive very little feedback during the school year. Classes are usually graded solely based on final exam scores. Midterm exams and graded papers are uncommon, and classroom participation is often the only way for students to ascertain if they understand the material and are employing effective study methods. As a result, a winning attitude is critical to success in law school. Faith in yourself will help you continue to make the personal sacrifices during the first year that you need to make to succeed in law school, even when the rewards are not immediately apparent.

Incoming law students should begin preparing for law school during the summertime prior to first year, and preparation exercises should be aimed at gaining a general understanding of what law school is all about. A solid understanding of what you are expected to learn during the first year will give you the information you need to develop both your strategy for success and the confidence you need to succeed. There are several books on the market that can help in this regard, but those students who are best prepared often attend Law Preview's one-week intensive preparatory course specifically designed to teach beginning law students the strategies for academic success.

What factors contribute to academic success in law school?

Academic success means one thing in law school—exam success. The grades that you receive, particularly during the first year, will be determined almost exclusively by the scores you receive on your final exams. Occasionally, a professor may add a few points for class participation, but that is rare. In most classes, your final exam will consist of a three- or four-hour written examination at the end of the semester or—if the course is two semesters long—at the end of the year. The amount of material you must master for each final exam will simply dwarf that of any undergraduate exam you have ever taken. The hope that you can "cram" a semester's worth of information into a one-week reading period is pure fantasy and one that will surely lead to disappointing grades. The focus of your efforts from day one should be success on your final exams. Don't get bogged down in class preparation or in perfecting a course outline if it will not result in some discernible improvement in your exam performance. All of your efforts should be directed at improving your exam performance in some way. It's as simple as that.

What skills are typically tested on law school exams?

Law school exams usually test three different skills: 1) the ability to accurately identify legal issues, 2) the ability to recall the relevant law with speed, and 3) the ability to apply the law to the facts efficiently and skillfully. The proper approach for developing these skills differs, depending on the substantive area of law in question and whether your exam is open book or closed book.

Identifying legal issues is commonly known as issue spotting. On most of your exams, you will be given complex, hypothetical fact patterns. From the facts you are given, you must identify the particular legal issues that need to be addressed. This is a difficult skill to perfect and can only be developed through practice. The best way to develop issue-spotting skills is by taking practice exams. For each of your classes, during the first half of the semester, you should collect all of the available exams that were given by your professor in the past. Take all of these exams under simulated exam conditions—find an open classroom, get some blue books, time yourself, and take the exams with friends so that you can review them afterward. It is also helpful for you to practice any legal problems you were given during the semester. Issue spotting is an important skill for all lawyers to develop. Lawyers utilize this skill on a daily basis when they listen to their clients' stories and are asked to point out places where legal issues might arise.

The ability to recall the law with speed is also very important and frequently tested. On all of your exams, you will be given a series of legal problems, and for each problem you will usually be required to provide the relevant substantive law and apply it to the facts of the problem. Your ability to recall the law with speed is critical because, in most classes, you will be under time constraints to answer all of the problems. The faster you recall the law, the more problems you will complete and the more time you will have to spend on demonstrating your analytical skills. For courses with closed-book exams, this means straight memorization or the use of memory recall devices, such as mnemonics. Do not be passive about learning the law—repeatedly reviewing your outline is not enough. You must actively learn the law by studying definitions and using memory-assistance devices like flash cards. When you have become exceedingly familiar with your flash cards, rewrite them so as to test your memory in different words. This is particularly critical for courses such as torts and criminal law where you must learn a series of definitions with multiple elements. For courses with open-book exams, this means developing an index for your outline that will enable you to locate the relevant law quickly. Create a cover page for your outline that lists the page number for each substantive subtopic. This will help you get there without any undue delay.

Books About Doing Well in Law School:

Getting to Maybe: How to Excel on Law School Exams, Professors Jeremy Paul and Michael Fischl

This book is excellent! While many books and professors may preach "IRAC"—Issue, Rule, Application, Conclusion—as a way of structuring exam answers, Getting to Maybe rightly points out that such advice does not help students correctly identify legal issues or master the intricacies of legal analysis.

Law School Confidential: A Complete Guide to the Law School Experience (Second Edition), Robert H. Miller, Esq.

Robert H. Miller, a former federal judicial clerk, Law Review editor, and graduate of University of Pennsylvania Law School, covers every aspect of the law school experience in thoughtful detail. Whether you are a college student just starting to think about law school, a student in the midst of law school applications, or someone who has already been admitted, Law School Confidential is a book you should not be without. An extensive new chapter is devoted to an exclusive one-on-one interview with Dean of Admissions Richard Geiger of the Cornell Law School, wherein closely guarded secrets of the increasingly competitive admissions process are discussed openly for the first time anywhere. In another chapter, Miller goes one-on-one with the hiring partners of two prestigious U.S. law firms about how to succeed in the hiring process, and what it takes to make it to partnership.

The final skill you need to develop is the ability to apply the law to the facts efficiently and skillfully. On your exams, once you have correctly identified the relevant issue and stated the relevant law, you must engage in a discussion of how the law applies to the facts that have been given. The ability to engage in such a discussion is best developed by taking practice exams. When you are practicing this skill, you should focus on efficiency. Try to focus on the essential facts, and do not engage in irrelevant discussions that will waste your energy and your professor's time.

Any final comments for our audience of aspiring law students?

The study of law is a wonderful and noble pursuit, one that I thoroughly enjoyed. Law school is not easy, however, and proper preparation can give you a firm foundation for success. I invite you to visit our website (LawPreview.com) and contact us with any questions (888-PREP-YOU).

CHAPTER 12
CAREER MATTERS

Okay, it's a long time away, but you really ought to be thinking about your professional career beyond law school from day one, especially if your goal is to practice with a major law firm. What stands between you and a job as an associate, the entry-level position at one of these firms, is a three-stage evaluation: first, a review of your resume, including your grades and work experience; second, an on-campus interview; and last, one or more call-back interviews at the firm's offices. It's a fairly intimidating ordeal, but there are a few ways to reduce the anxiety and enhance your chances of landing a great job.

YOUR RESUME

The first thing recruiters tend to notice after your name is the name of the law school you attend. Tacky, but true. Perhaps the greatest misconception among law students, however, is that hiring decisions are based largely upon your school's prestige. All those rankings perpetuate this myth. To be sure, there are a handful of schools with reputations above all others, and students who excel at these schools are in great demand. But you are equally well situated, if not better off, applying from the top of your class at a strong, less prestigious law school class than from the bottom half of a Top Ten law school class.

FIRST-YEAR GRADES ARE THE WHOLE ENCHILADA

Fair or not, the first year of law school will unduly influence your legal future. It's vital that you hit the ground running because law school grades are *the* critical factor in recruitment. An even harsher reality is that *first-year grades are by far the most critical in the hiring process.* Decisions about who gets which plum summer jobs are generally handed down before students take a single second-year exam. Consequently, you're left with exactly *no* time to adjust to law school life and little chance to improve your transcript if you don't come out on top as a first-year student.

WORK EXPERIENCE

If you're applying to law school right out of college, chances are your most significant work experience has been a summer job. Recruiters don't expect you to have spent these months writing Supreme Court decisions. They are generally satisfied if you show that you have worked diligently and seriously at each opportunity. Students who took a year or more off after college obviously have more opportunities to impress but also more of a burden to demonstrate diligence and seriousness.

Work experience in the legal industry—clerkships and paralegal jobs for instance—can be excellent sources of professional development. They are fairly common positions among job applicants, though, so don't feel you have to pursue one of these routes just to show your commitment to the law. You'll make a better impression by working in an industry in which you'd like to specialize (e.g., a prospective securities lawyer summering with an investment bank).

Making Law Review

Every law school has an academic periodical called Law Review, produced and edited by law students. It contains articles about various aspects of law—mostly written by professors. While some schools sponsor more than one Law Review, there is generally one that is more prestigious than all the others. In order to "make" Law Review, you will have to finish the all-important first year at (or very, very near) the top of your class or write an article that will be judged by the existing members of the Law Review. You might have to do both. Making Law Review is probably the easiest way to guarantee yourself a job at a blue-chip firm, working for a judge, or in academia. In all honesty, it is a credential you will proudly carry for the rest of your life.

A Couple Good Books

If you are thinking about law school, here are a few books you might find interesting:

The Princeton Review's Law School Essays That Made a Difference

Check out successful essays written for an assortment of selective schools.

Jeff Deaver, The Complete Law School Companion: How to Excel at America's Most Demanding Post-Graduate Curriculum

This straightforward law school survival guide gives excellent advice on how to brief cases, sample briefs, survive class, and plenty more.

THE INTERVIEWS

There are as many right approaches to an interview as there are interviewers. That observation provides little comfort, of course, especially if you're counting on a good interview to make up for whatever deficiencies there are on your resume. Think about the purpose of the initial 30-minute interview you are likely to have: it provides a rough sketch of not only your future office personality but also your demeanor under stress. The characteristics you demonstrate and the *impression* you give are more important than anything you say. Composure, confidence, maturity, articulation, and an ability to develop rapport are characteristics recruiters are looking for. Give them what they want.

CHAPTER 13
HOW TO USE THIS BOOK

It's pretty simple.

The first part of this book provides a wealth of indispensable information covering everything you need to know about selecting and getting into the law school of your choice. There is also a great deal about what to expect from law school and how to do well. You name it—taking the LSAT, choosing the best school for you, writing a great personal statement, interviewing, paying for it—it's all in the first part.

The second part is the real meat and potatoes of *The Best 170 Law Schools*. It contains portraits of 170 law schools across the United States and Canada. Each school has one of two possible types of entries. The first type of entry is a two-page descriptive profile. It contains data The Princeton Review has collected directly from law school administrators and textual descriptions of the school we have written based on our surveys of current law students. The second type of entry is a data listing, which includes all the same data that appears in the sidebars of the descriptive profiles but does not have the student survey-driven descriptive paragraphs. For an explanation of why all schools do not appear with descriptive profiles, turn to page 59. As is customary with school guidebooks, all data, with the exception of tuition (which should be for the current year if the school reported it by our deadline), reflects figures for the academic year prior to publication unless otherwise noted on the pages. Since law school demographics vary significantly from one institution to another and some schools report data more thoroughly than others, some entries will not include all the individual data described below.

The third part of the book hosts the "School Says . . ." profiles. The "School Says . . ." profiles give extended descriptions of admissions processes, curricula, internship opportunities, and much more. This is your chance to get even more in-depth information on programs that interest you. These schools have paid us a small fee for the chance to tell you more about themselves, and the editorial responsibility is solely that of the law school. We think you'll find these profiles add lots to your picture of a school.

WHAT'S IN THE PROFILES: DATA
The Heading: The first thing you will see for each profile is (obviously) the school's name. On the facing page, you'll find the school's snail mail address, telephone number, fax number, e-mail address, and website. You can find the name of the Admissions Office contact person in the heading, too.

INSTITUTIONAL INFORMATION
Public/Private: Indicates whether a school is state-supported or funded by private means.

Student/Faculty Ratio: The ratio of law students to full-time faculty.

Affiliation: If the school is affiliated with a particular religion, you'll find that information here.

% Faculty Part-time: The percentage of faculty who are part-time.

% Faculty Female: The percentage of faculty who are women.

% Faculty Minority : The percentage of people who teach at the law school who are also members of minority groups.

Total Faculty: The total number of faculty members at the law school.

> *Yet Another Good Book:*
> **One L: The Turbulent True Story of a First Year at Harvard Law School,** *Scott Turow*
> *This law school primer is equal parts illuminating and harrowing.*

SURVEY SAYS

The Survey Says list appears in the sidebar of each law school's two-page descriptive profile, and up to three Survey Says items will appear on each list. As the name suggests, these items communicate results of our law student surveys. There are 10 possible Survey Says items, each explained below. Of these 10, the 3 items that appear are those about which student respondents demonstrated the greatest degree of consensus. Survey Says items represent the agreement among students only at *that particular law school* and are not relative to how students at other law schools feel about that particular Survey Says item.

Liberal students: Students report that their fellow law students lean to the left politically.

Conservative students: Students report that their fellow law students lean to the right politically.

Students love Hometown, State: Students are pleased with the location of their law school.

Good social life: Students report a lively social life at the law school.

Students never sleep: Students report a low average number of hours of sleep each night. Little sleep in law school is often an indication of extra-long hours of study on a daily basis.

Heavy use of Socratic Method: Students report that their professors primarily employ the traditional Socratic Method in the classroom.

Beautiful campus: Students report that their law school campus is practical and beautiful.

Great research resources: Students report that the library, computer databases, and other research tools are good.

Great judicial externship/internship/clerkship opportunities: Students rate these opportunities as excellent.

Diverse opinions in classrooms: Students agree that differing points of view are tolerated in the classroom.

STUDENTS

Enrollment of Law School: The total number of students enrolled in the law school.

% Male/Female: The percentage of full-time students with an X and a Y chromosome and the percentage of students with two X chromosomes, respectively.

% Out-of-state: The percentage of full-time students who are out-of-state.

% Full-time: The percentage of students who attend the school on a full-time basis.

% Minority: The percentage of full-time students who represent minority groups.

% International: The percentage of students who hail from foreign soil.

# of Countries Represented: The number of different foreign countries from which the current student body hails.

Average Age of Entering Class: On the whole, how old the 1Ls are.

ACADEMICS

Academic Experience Rating: The quality of the learning environment, on a scale of 60 to 99. The rating incorporates the Admissions Selectivity Rating and the average responses of law students at the school to several questions on our law student survey. In addition to the Admissions Selectivity Rating, factors considered include how students rate the quality of teaching and the accessibility of their professors, the school's research resources, the range of available courses, the balance of legal theory and practical lawyering skills stressed in the curriculum, the tolerance for diverse opinions in the classroom, and how intellectually challenging the course work is. This individual rating places each law school on a continuum for purposes of comparing all law schools within this edition only. If a law school receives a "low" Academic Experience Rating, it doesn't mean that the

---

Law School Fun Fact

The least litigated amendment in the Bill of Rights is the Third Amendment, which prohibits the quartering of soldiers in private homes without consent of the owner.

---

school provides a bad academic experience for its students. It simply means that the school scored lower than other schools in our computations based on the criteria outlined above. Because this rating incorporates law student opinion data, only those law schools that appear in the section with the descriptive profiles based on student surveys receive an Academic Experience Rating.

Professors Interesting Rating: Based on law student opinion. We asked law students to rate the quality of teaching at their law schools on a scale from 60 to 99. Because this rating incorporates law student opinion data, only those law schools that appear in the section with the descriptive profiles receive a Professors Interesting Rating.

Professors Accessible Rating: Based on law student opinion. We asked law students to rate how accessible the law faculty members at their schools are on a scale from 60 to 99. Because this rating incorporates law student opinion data, only those law schools that appear in the section with the descriptive profiles receive a Professors Accessible Rating.

Hours of Study Per Day: From our student survey. The average number of hours students at the school report studying each day.

Academic Specialties: Different areas of law and academic programs on which the school prides itself.

Advanced Degrees Offered: Degrees available through the law school and the length of the program.

Combined Degrees Offered: Programs at this school involving the law school and some other college or degree program within the larger university, and how long it will take you to complete the joint program.

Grading System: Scoring system used by the law school. (Appears in the data listings section only.)

Academic Requirements: Most law schools require their students to complete some courses and/or programs that go beyond traditional legal theory, whether to broaden their understanding of and experience with the law or to develop important practical lawyering skills.

Clinical Program Required? Indicates whether clinical programs are required to complete the core curriculum.

Clinical Program Description: Programs designed to give students hands-on training and experience in the practice of some area of law. (Appears in the data listings section only.)

Legal Writing Course Requirement? Tells you whether there is a required course in legal writing.

Legal Writing Description: A description of any course work, required or optional, designed specifically to develop legal writing skills vital to the practice of law. (Appears in the data listings section only.)

Legal Methods Course Requirements? Indicates whether there is a mandatory curriculum component to cover legal methods.

Legal Methods Description: A description of any course work, required or optional, designed specifically to develop the skills vital to legal analysis. (Appears in the data listings section only.)

Legal Research Course Requirements? If a school requires course work specifically to develop legal research skills, this field will tell you.

Legal Research Description: A description of any course work, required or optional, designed specifically to develop legal research skills vital to the practice of law. (Appears in the data listings section only.)

Moot Court Requirement? Indicates whether participation in a moot court program is mandatory.

Moot Court Description: This will describe any moot court program, mandatory or optional, designed to develop skills in legal research, writing, and oral argument. (Appears in the data listings section only.)

Public Interest Law Requirement? If a school requires participation on a public interest law project, we'll let you know here.

Public Interest Law Description: Programs designed to expose students to the public interest law field through clinical work, volunteer opportunities, or specialized course work. (Appears in the data listings section only.)

Academic Journals: This field will list any academic journals offered at the school. (Appears in the data listings section only.)

ADMISSIONS INFORMATION

Admissions Selectivity Rating: How competitive admission is at the law school, on a scale of 60 to 99. Several factors determine this rating, including LSAT scores and the average undergraduate GPA of entering 1L students, the percentage of applicants accepted, and the percentage of accepted applicants who enrolled in the law school. We collect this information through a survey that law school administrators completed for the Fall 2008 entering class. This individual rating places each law school on a continuum for purposes of comparing all law schools within this edition only. All law schools that appear in this edition of the guide, whether in the section with the descriptive profiles based on student surveys or in the section with school-reported statistics only, receive an Admissions Selectivity Rating. If a law school has a relatively low Admissions Selectivity Rating, it doesn't necessarily mean that it's easy to gain admission to the law school. (It's not easy to get into any ABA-approved law schools, really.) It simply means that the school scored lower relative to other schools in our computations based on the criteria outlined in the previous page.

# of Applications Received: The number of people who applied to the law school's full-time JD program.

# of Applicants Accepted: The number of people who were admitted to the school's full-time class.

# of Acceptees Attending: The number of those admitted who chose to attend the school full-time.

Average LSAT/LSAT Range: Indicates the average LSAT score of incoming 1Ls, as reported by the school. The range is the 25th to 75th percentiles of 1Ls.

Average Undergrad GPA: It's usually on a 4.0 scale.

Application Fee: How much it costs to apply to the school.

> **Law School Trivia**
>
> The guarantee that each state must have an equal number of votes in the United States Senate is the only provision in the Constitution of 1787 that cannot be amended.

Regular Application Deadline and "Rolling": Many law schools evaluate applications and notify applicants of admission decisions on a continuous, rolling basis over the course of several months (ordinarily from late fall to midsummer). Obviously, if you apply to one of these schools, you want to apply early because there will be more places available at the beginning of the process.

Regular Notification? The official date by or on which a law school will release a decision for an applicant who applied using the regular admission route.

Early Application Program? Whether the law school has an early application program. If you are accepted to an Early Decision program, you are obligated to attend that law school. If you are accepted under an Early Action program, you have no obligation to attend. You just get to know earlier whether you got in.

Early Application Deadline: The official date by which the law school must receive your application if you want to be considered for its early application program.

Early Application Notification: The official date on which a law school will release a decision for an applicant who applied using the early application route.

Transfer Students Accepted? Whether transfer students from other schools are considered for admission.

Evening Division Offered? Whether the school offers an evening program in addition to its full-time regular program. Evening division programs are almost always part-time and require four years of study (instead of three) to complete.

Part-time Accepted? Whether part-time students may enroll in the JD program on a basis other than the standard full-time.

LSDAS Accepted? "Yes" indicates that the school utilizes the Law School Data Assembly Service.

Applicants Also Look At: The law schools to which applicants to this school also apply. It's important. It's a reliable indicator of the overall academic quality of the applicant pool.

RESEARCH FACILITIES (APPEARS IN THE DATA LISTINGS SECTION ONLY)

Research Resources Available: Online retrieval resources, subscription services, libraries, and databases available for legal research.

% of JD Classrooms Wired: The percentage of dedicated law school classrooms wired for laptops and Internet access.

Computer Labs: The number of rooms full of computers that you can use free.

School-Supported Research Centers: Indicates whether the school has on-campus, internally supported research centers.

INTERNATIONAL STUDENTS

TOEFL Required/Recommended of International Students? Indicates whether or not international students must take the TOEFL, or Test of English as a Foreign Language, to be admitted to the school.

Minimum TOEFL: Minimum score (paper and computer) an international student must earn on the TOEFL to be admitted.

FINANCIAL FACTS

Annual Tuition (Residents/Nonresidents): What it costs to go to school for an academic year. For state schools, both in-state and out-of-state tuition is listed.

Books and Supplies: Indicates how much students can expect to shell out for textbooks and other assorted supplies during the academic year.

Fees Per Credit (Residents/Nonresidents): That mysterious extra money you are required to pay the law school in addition to tuition and everything else, on a per-credit basis. If in-state and out-of-state students are charged differently, both amounts are listed.

Tuition Per Credit (Residents/Nonresidents): Dollar amount charged per credit hour. For state schools, both in-state and out-of-state amounts are listed when they differ.

Room and Board (On-/Off-campus): This is the school's estimate of what it costs to buy meals and to pay for decent living quarters for the academic year. Where available, on- and off-campus rates are listed.

Financial Aid Application Deadline: The last day on which students can turn in their applications for monetary assistance.

% First-Year Students Receiving Some Sort of Aid: The percentage of new JD students who receive monetary assistance.

% Receiving Some Sort of Aid: The percentage of all the students at the school presently accumulating a staggering debt.

% of Aid That Is Merit-Based: The percentage of aid not based on financial need.

% Receiving Scholarships: The percentage of students at the school who received some sort of "free money" award. This figure can include grants as well.

Average Grant: Average financial aid amount awarded to students that does not have to be paid back. This figure can include scholarships as well.

Average Loan: Average amount of loan dollars accrued by students for the year.

Average Total Aid Package: How much aid each student at the school receives on average for the year.

Average Debt: The amount of debt—or, in legal lingo, arrears—you'll likely be saddled with by the time you graduate.

EMPLOYMENT INFORMATION

Career Rating: How well the law school prepares its students for a successful career in law, on a scale of 60 to 99. The rating incorporates school-reported data and the average responses of law students at the school to a few questions on our law student survey. We ask law schools for the average starting salaries of graduating students, the percentage of graduating students who find employment after graduation, and the percentage of students who pass the bar exam the first time they take it. We ask students about how much the law program encourages practical experience; the opportunities for externships, internships, and clerkships; and how prepared to practice law they will feel after graduating. If a school receives a "low" Career Rating, it doesn't necessarily mean that the career prospects for graduates are bad; it simply means that the school scored lower relative to how other schools scored based on the criteria outlined above. Because this rating incorporates law student opinion data, only those law schools that appear in the section with the descriptive profiles receive a Career Rating.

Rate of Placement (nine months out): Percent of graduates who secured employment within nine months of graduating from law school.

Average Starting Salary: The average amount of money graduates of this law school make the first year out of school.

State for Bar Exam: The state for which most students from the school will take the bar exam.

Pass Rate for First-Time Bar: After three years, the percentage of students who passed the bar exam the first time they took it. It's a crucial statistic. You *don't* want to fail your state's bar.

Employers Who Frequently Hire Grads: Firms where past grads have had success finding jobs.

Prominent Alumni: Those who made it . . . *big*.

Grads Employed by Field: The percentage of students in the most recent graduating class who have obtained jobs in a particular field.

Academia: The percentage of graduates who got jobs at law schools, universities, and think tanks.

Business/Industry: The percentage of graduates who got jobs working in business, corporations, consulting, and so on. These jobs are sometimes law-related and sometimes not.

Government: Uncle Sam needs lawyers like you wouldn't even believe.

Judicial Clerkships: The percentage of graduates who got jobs doing research for judges.

Military: The percentage of lawyers who work to represent the Armed Forces in all kinds of legal matters, like Tom Cruise in *A Few Good Men*.

Private Practice: The percentage of graduates who got jobs in traditional law firms of various sizes or "put out a shingle" for themselves as sole practitioners.

Public Interest: The percentage of (mostly) altruistic graduates who got jobs providing legal assistance to people who couldn't afford it otherwise.

NOTA BENE

If a 60* appears for any of a law school's ratings, it means that the school's administrators did not report by our deadline all of the statistics that rating incorporates.

Please note that we target each law school for resurveying at least every other year, which means we rewrite each law school's descriptive profile at least every other year, too. Student surveys captured via our online survey (http://survey.review.com) are considered current for the purposes of our own rating, rankings, and Survey Says items for two years.

WHAT'S IN THE PROFILES: DESCRIPTIVE TEXT

Academics, Life, and Getting In Sections: The text of the descriptive profiles is broken out into three sections: Academics, Life, and Getting In. The Academics and Life sections of each descriptive profile are driven by the student survey responses collected from current law students at the school, and the quotations sprinkled throughout each of these sections come directly from the written comments students provided us with on their surveys. In the Academics section, we often discuss professors and their teaching methods, the workload, special clinical programs, the efficiency of the administration, and the helpfulness of the library staff. In the Life section, we often discuss how academically competitive the student body is, how (and if) students separate into cliques, clubs, or organizations students often join, and the amenities of the town in which the school is located. We don't follow a cookie-cutter formula when writing these profiles. Instead we rely on students' responses to the open-ended questions on our student survey and analysis of their aggregate responses to our multiple choice questions to determine each profile's major "theme." The information in the Getting In section is based on the data we collect from law school administrators and our own additional research.

DECODING DEGREES

Many law schools offer joint- or combined-degree programs with other departments (or sometimes even with other schools) that you can earn along with your Juris Doctor. You'll find the abbreviations for these degrees in the individual school profiles, but we thought we'd give you a little help in figuring out exactly what they are.

AMBA	Accounting Master of Business		MEM	Master of Environmental Management
BCL	Bachelor of Civil Law		MFA	Master of Fine Arts
DJUR	Doctor of Jurisprudence		MHA	Master of Health Administration
DL	Doctor of Law		MHSA	Master of Health Services Administration
EdD	Doctor of Education		MIA	Master of International Affairs
HRIR	Human Resources and Industrial Relations		MIB	Master of International Business
IMBA	International Master of Business Administration		MIP	Master of Intellectual Property
JD	Juris Doctor		MIR	Master of Industrial Relations
JSD	Doctor of Juridical Science		MILR	Master of Industrial and Labor Relations
JSM	Master of the Science of Law		MJ	Master of Jurisprudence
LLB	Bachelor of Law		MJS	Master of Juridical Study (not a JD)
LLCM	Master of Comparative Law (for international students)		MLIR	Master of Labor and Industrial Relations
LLM	Master of Law		MLIS	Master of Library and Information Sciences
MA	Master of Arts		MLS	Master of Library Science
MAcc	Master of Accounting		MMA	Master of Marine Affairs
MALD	Master of Arts in Law and Diplomacy		MOB	Master of Organizational Behavior
MAM	Master of Arts Management		MPA	Master of Public Administration
MM	Master of Management		MPAFF	Master of Public Affairs
MANM	Master of Nonprofit Management		MPH	Master of Public Health
MAPA	Master of Public Administration		MPP	Master of Public Planning or Master of Public Policy
MAUA	Master of Arts in Urban Affairs		MPPA	Master of Public Policy
MBA	Master of Business Administration		MPPS	Master of Public Policy Sciences
MCJ	Master of Criminal Justice		MPS	Master of Professional Studies in Law
MCL	Master of Comparative Law		MRP	Master of Regional Planning
MCP	Master of Community Planning		MS	Master of Science
MCRP	Master of City and Regional Planning		MSEL	Master of Studies in Environmental Law
MDiv	Master of Divinity		MSES	Master of Science in Environmental Science
ME	Master of Engineering or Master of Education		MSF	Master of Science in Finance
MEd	Master of Education		MSFS	Master of Science in Foreign Service
MED	Master of Environmental Design		MSI	Master of Science in Information

MSIA	Master of Science in Industrial Administration
MSIE	Master of Science in International Economics
MSJ	Master of Science in Journalism
MSPH	Master of Science in Public Health
MSW	Master of Social Welfare or Master of Social Work
MT	Master of Taxation
MTS	Master of Theological Studies
MUP	Master of Urban Planning
MUPD	Master of Urban Planning and Development
MURP	Master of Urban and Regional Planning
PharmD	Doctor of Pharmacy
PhD	Doctor of Philosophy
REES	Russian and Eastern European Studies Certificate
SJD	Doctor of Juridical Science
DVM	Doctor of Veterinary Medicine
MALIR	Master of Arts in Labor and Industrial Relations

LAW SCHOOLS RANKED BY CATEGORY

ABOUT OUR LAW SCHOOL RANKINGS

On the following few pages, you will find 11 top 10 lists of ABA-approved law schools ranked according to various metrics. It must be noted, however, that none of these lists purports to rank the law schools by their overall quality. Nor should any combination of the categories we've chosen be construed as representing the raw ingredients for such a ranking. We have made no attempt to gauge the *prestige* of these schools, and we wonder whether we could accurately do so even if we tried. What we have done, however, is presented a number of lists using information from two very large databases—one of statistical information collected from law schools and another of subjective data gathered via our survey of more than 18,000 law students at 170 ABA-approved law schools. We target each law school's student body for resurveying at least every other year. This means that schools'student opinion data is considered current for the book's rankings and descriptive profiles for two years.

Ten of the ranking lists are based partly or wholly on opinions collected through our law student survey. The only schools that may appear in these lists are the 170 ABA-approved law schools from which we were able to collect a sufficient number of student surveys to accurately represent the student experience in our various ratings and descriptive profiles.

One of the rankings, Toughest to Get Into, incorporates *only* admissions statistics reported to us by the law schools. Therefore, any ABA-approved law school appearing in this edition of the guide, whether we collected student surveys from it or not, may appear on this list.

New to our rankings this year is out Best Classroom experience list, based on student assessment of professors' teaching abilities, balance of theory and practical skills in the curricula, tolerance for differing opinions in class discussion, and classroom facilities.

Under the title of each list is an explanation of the criteria on which the ranking is based. For explanations of many of the individual rankings components, go back to page 46–47.

It's worth repeating: There is no one best law school in America, but there is a best law school for you. By using these rankings in conjunction with the descriptive profiles and data listings of the schools in this book, we hope that you will begin to identify the attributes of a law school that are important to you, as well as the law schools that can best help you to achieve your personal and professional goals.

The schools in each category appear in descending order.

TOUGHEST TO GET INTO

Based on the Admissions Selectivity Rating (see page 47 for explanation)

1. Yale University
2. Harvard University
3. Stanford University
4. University of Pennsylvania
5. University of California, Berkeley
6. Columbia University
7. University of Chicago
8. Northwestern University
9. University of Michigan
10. Georgetown University

PROFESSORS ROCK (LEGALLY SPEAKING)

Based on the Professors Interesting and Professors Accessible Ratings (see page 47 for explanations)

1. Boston University
2. University of Chicago
3. Stanford University
4. Loyola Marymount University
5. Chapman University
6. Washington and Lee University
7. Ave Maria School of Law
8. Pepperdine University
9. Mercer University
10. Wake Forest University

MOST COMPETITIVE STUDENTS

Based on law student assessments of: the number of hours they spend studying outside of class each day, the number of hours they think their fellow law students spend studying outside of class each day, the degree of competitiveness among law students at their school, and the average number of hours they sleep each night

1. Brigham Young University
2. Baylor University
3. Whittier College
4. St. Thomas University
5. Roger Williams University
6. Thomas M. Cooley Law School
7. St. John's University (NY)
8. Albany Law School
9. Ohio Northern University
10. St. Mary's University (TX)

BEST CAREER PROSPECTS

Based on the Career Rating (see page 49 for explanation)

1. Northwestern University
2. University of Michigan
3. University of Chicago
4. Harvard University
5. Boston College
6. Boston University
7. Vanderbilt University
8. University of Pennsylvania
9. University of Virginia
10. University of Notre Dame

BEST CLASSROOM EXPERIENCE

Based on student assessment of professors' teaching abilities, balance of theory and practical skills in the curricula, tolerance for differing opinions in class discussion, and classroom facilities

1. Loyola Marymount University
2. Duke University
3. Stanford University
4. Vanderbilt University
5. Boston University
6. University of Chicago
7. Chapman University
8. University of Michigan
9. Georgetown University
10. Northwestern University

CANDIDATES FOR CENTER FOR AMERICAN PROGRESS FELLOWSHIPS? (OR, STUDENTS LEAN TO THE LEFT)

Based on student assessment of the political bent of the student body at large

1. University of the District of Columbia
2. Northeastern University
3. City University of New York—Queens College
4. Lewis & Clark College
5. American University
6. Vermont Law School
7. University of Oregon
8. University of California, Berkeley
9. New York University
10. University of Maine

CANDIDATES FOR HERITAGE FOUNDATION FELLOWSHIPS? (OR, STUDENTS LEAN TO THE RIGHT)

Based on student assessment of the political bent of the student body at large

1. Regent University
2. Ave Maria School of Law
3. Brigham Young University
4. George Mason University
5. University of Notre Dame
6. Louisiana State University
7. University of Alabama
8. Campbell University
9. Texas Tech University
10. The University of Mississippi

BEST ENVIRONMENT FOR MINORITY STUDENTS

Based on the percentage of the student body that is from underrepresented minorities and student assessment of whether all students receive equal treatment by fellow students and the faculty, regardless of ethnicity

1. Howard University
2. St. Thomas University
3. University of Hawaii at Manoa
4. Florida International University
5. University of Southern California
6. Northwestern University
7. American University
8. Santa Clara University
9. Southern University
10. University of the District of Columbia

MOST DIVERSE FACULTY

BASED ON THE PERCENTAGE OF THE LAW SCHOOL FACULTY THAT IS FROM A MINORITY GROUP AND STUDENT ASSESSMENT OF WHETHER THE FACULTY MAKES UP A BROADLY DIVERSE GROUP OF INDIVIDUALS

1. Howard University
2. Florida International University
3. Southern University
4. City University of New York—Queens College
5. University of Hawaii at Manoa
6. University of the District of Columbia
7. North Carolina Central University
8. Northern Illinois University
9. Loyola Marymount University
10. University of New Mexico

BEST QUALITY OF LIFE

BASED ON STUDENT ASSESSMENT OF: WHETHER THERE IS A STRONG SENSE OF COMMUNITY AT THE SCHOOL, HOW AESTHETICALLY PLEASING THE LAW SCHOOL IS, THE LOCATION OF THE LAW SCHOOL, THE QUALITY OF THE SOCIAL LIFE, CLASSROOM FACILITIES, AND THE LIBRARY STAFF

1. Chapman University
2. University of St Thomas
3. Stanford University
4. Vanderbilt University
5. University of Virginia
6. University of Colorado
7. Regent University
8. University of Oregon
9. Samford University
10. Northwestern University

MOST WELCOMING OF OLDER STUDENTS

BASED ON THE AVERAGE AGE OF ENTRY OF LAW SCHOOL STUDENTS AND STUDENT REPORTS OF HOW MANY YEARS THEY SPENT OUT OF COLLEGE BEFORE ENROLLING IN LAW SCHOOL

1. City University of New York—Queens College
2. Lewis & Clark College
3. University of the District of Columbia
4. Seattle University
5. William Mitchell College of Law
6. Willamette University
7. Georgia State University
8. Hamline University
9. University of New Mexico
10. University of Utah

LAW SCHOOL DESCRIPTIVE PROFILES

In this section you will find the two page descriptive profile of each of the 170 ABA-approved law schools. As there are currently a total of 193 ABA-approved law schools in the country, there are obviously many law schools not appearing in this section; those schools appear in the following section, Law School Data Listings.

In order for a law school to appear in this section, we had to collect the opinions of a sufficient number of current law students at that school to fairly and responsibly represent the general law student experience there. Our descriptive profiles are driven primarily by 1) comments law students provide in response to open-ended questions on our student survey, and 2) our own statistical analysis of student responses to the many multiple-choice questions on the survey. While many law students complete a survey unsolicited by us at http://survey.review.com, in the vast majority of cases we rely on law school administrators to get the word out about our survey to their students. In an ideal scenario, the law school administration e-mails a Princeton Review–authored e-mail to all law students with an embedded link to our survey website (again, http://survey.review.com). If for some reason there are restrictions that prevent the administration from contacting the entire law student body on behalf of an outside party, they often help us find other ways to notify students that we are seeking their opinions, like advertising in law student publications or posting on law student community websites or electronic mailing lists. In almost all cases, when the administration is cooperative, we are able to collect opinions from a sufficient number of students to produce an accurate descriptive profile and ratings of its law school.

There is a group of law school administrators, however, that doesn't agree with the notion that the opinions of current law students presented in descriptive profile and rankings formats are useful to prospective law school students trying to choose the right schools to apply to and attend. Administrators at the 23 ABA-approved law schools not appearing in this section are a part of this group. They either ignored our multiple attempts to contact them to request their assistance in notifying their students about our survey, or they simply refused to work with us at all. While we would like to be able to write a descriptive profile on each of these 23 schools anyway, we won't do so with minimal law student opinion. So if you are a prospective law school student and would like to read the opinions of current law students about your dream school(s), contact the missing school(s) and communicate this desire to them. (We include contact information in each of the data listings.) If you are a current law student at one of the 23 ABA-approved law schools not profiled in this section, please don't send us angry letters; instead, go to http://survey.review.com, complete a survey about your school, and tell all of your fellow students to do the same. If we collect enough current student opinion on your school in the coming year, we'll include a descriptive profile in the next edition of the guide.

SPECIAL NOTE ON THE TEXT OF EACH DESCRIPTIVE PROFILE

The Academics and Life sections of each descriptive profile are driven by the student opinions collected from current law students at the school, and the quotations sprinkled throughout each of these sections comes directly from the written comments with which students provided us on their surveys. The Getting In section is based on the data we collect from law school administrators and our own additional research. Every law school with a descriptive profile has its students resurveyed and its profile rewritten at least every other year.

SPECIAL NOTE ON THE SIDEBAR STATISTICS

Explanations of what each field of data signifies may be found in the How to Use This Book section, which begins on page 45.

ALBANY LAW SCHOOL

INSTITUTIONAL INFORMATION

Public/private	Private
Student-faculty ratio	14:1
% faculty part-time	49
% faculty female	37
% faculty minority	6
Total faculty	107

SURVEY SAYS...
Great library staff
Abundant externship/internship/
clerkship opportunities

STUDENTS

Enrollment of law school	731
% male/female	50/50
% out-of-state	22
% full-time	95
% minority	20
% international	2
# of countries represented	8
Average age of entering class	23

ACADEMICS

Academic Experience Rating	**74**
Profs interesting rating	71
Profs accessible rating	73
Hours of study per day	5.12

Academic Specialties
Business law, civil procedure, constitutional law, criminal law, environmental law, estate planning, family and elder law, government regulation and administration, health law, intellectual property law, international law, labor law, taxation.

Advanced Degrees Offered
LLM, MS (legal studies).

Combined Degrees Offered
JD 3 years, JD/MBA 3.5 to 4 years, JD/MPA 3.5 to 4 years, JD/MSW 3.5 to 4 years, JD/MRP 3.5 to 4 years, JD/MPP 3.5 to 4 years, JD/MS (bioethics) 4 years.

Clinical program required	No
Legal writing course requirement	Yes

Academics

Albany Law School "is the oldest independent law school in the nation" with "relatively small classes" and "great course offerings." The "very strong government law and administrative law program" is particularly noteworthy. "Hands down," though, Albany's best feature is its "field placement program." Again and again, students tell us that their school is "famed for its practical side." "The lack of nearby competing law schools," "Albany Law's geographic location," and a "deluge of internship opportunities" make it "all but a forgone conclusion that every student" will have "real-world experience." The school has a "monopoly" on "amazing juridical or state government internship opportunities." "I clerked at both the Attorney General's Office and the United States Attorney's Office," brags a 3L. "Needless to say, I learned more than I ever could in a classroom setting."

There are some "dud professors," but "By and large, the faculty here is excellent" and "excited about teaching." A few "legendary" professors are "heavyweights" who "have played instrumental roles in drafting and interpreting the laws." "We have some of the most respected practitioners in the state of New York," emphasizes one student. Though some "Socratic professors scare you into learning the material," all faculty members are "very accessible" and "really get to know their students."

"Discontent expressed about the administration has decreased in the past few years," one student notes. These days, the "extremely involved and helpful" administration "goes out of its way to ensure that every student is accommodated," and an "open-door policy" reigns supreme. You can't please everybody, though. Some students now complain that administrators "like to hold hands and coddle." Also, "Tuition has been raised at an incredible rate." The Financial Aid staff is highly unpopular as well. "No one is happy to be racking up this much debt," gripes a 3L. "To find an unfriendly face and an attitude greeting you at the door doesn't make handing over your first two years' salary . . . any easier."

The "helpful" Career Center works "tirelessly" and manages "time and again to deliver jobs to students." Some find that "if you are in the middle or bottom of the class, it is difficult to find a job," but this is clearly offset by Albany's reported graduate employment rate of 96 percent. That said, one student explains that "if you want a high paying, sexy job after you graduate, you have to do very well." Those who do excel find their hard work's reward "with some major law firms, especially in New York City."

The facilities, though "improving every day," are "serviceable but not amazing." The "beautiful Gothic building" offers "plenty of quiet spaces to study." "We have a decent library," says a 2L. It's "like a home away from home, except with less comfortable chairs." "The library staff is phenomenal," too. Students appreciate the "wireless" classrooms but find that some older classrooms "are freezing when they should be warm and warm when they should be cooler."

GAIL BENSEN, DIRECTOR OF ADMISSIONS
80 NEW SCOTLAND AVENUE, ALBANY, NY 12208
TEL: 518-445-2326 FAX: 518-445-2369
E-MAIL: ADMISSIONS@ALBANYLAW.EDU • INTERNET: WWW.ALBANYLAW.EDU

Life

The student population tends to be on the younger side but "The community embraces nontraditional students" as well. "The political atmosphere here is undoubtedly liberal," reports one student. "As with any other school," though, "you will find your (usually drunken) jocks, mouthy liberals, angry conservatives, slackers, overachievers, nice people, unfriendly people, over-competitive people, and those who just really don't care." One student notes that "when you have a school filled with people who want to argue for the rest of their lives, there is bound to be conflict. Every time a new issue arises at the law school, it's fought over the e-mail listserv, with every student feeling the need to weigh in on the issue."

Differences of opinions aside, "The community is tight-knit and people genuinely care about each other." "The student body is a great reason to come here, and often parties and socializes together," claims another. However, there are those who "concentrate themselves in small social cliques" exclusively. Extracurricular activities are plentiful with "many clubs and community events which most students get involved in. There are also a lot of receptions and free food and drinks." "There are always things to do on a Friday night." To the disappointment of students, the administration "no longer tolerates" on-campus "beer bashes."

The surrounding community of Albany is chock-full of "beautiful old buildings," and its "Gray winter months are great for studying indoors." "There is some nice off-campus housing if you look in the right places. The on-campus housing is okay, but it is much like a dorm," says one lodger. Most agree that "parking is a tremendous problem." This "might seem trite," admits one student, "but you try parking a mile away and walking through a 20-degree Albany winter at 7:30 A.M. to get to class."

Getting In

Students at the 25th percentile admitted into Albany Law School post an average LSAT score of 152 and GPAs of 2.86. Those students admitted at the 75th percentile have average LSAT scores of 158 and GPAs of 3.51.

EMPLOYMENT INFORMATION

Career Rating	76	Grads Employed by Field (%)	
Rate of placement (nine months out)	97	Academic	13
Average starting salary	$53,276	Business/Industry	17
State for bar exam	NY	Government	27
Pass rate for first-time bar	88	Judicial clerkships	6
Employers Who Frequently Hire Grads		Military	1
Private law firms; government agencies;		Private practice	52
business and industry; high tech industry		Public Interest	3
and corporations.			

Prominent Alumni
Thomas Vilsack, Governor of Iowa; Richard D. Parsons, chief executive officer, Time Warner; Andrew Cuomo, New York State Attorney General

Legal methods course requirement	Yes
Legal research course requirement	Yes
Moot court requirement	No
Public interest law requirement	No

ADMISSIONS
Selectivity Rating	74
# applications received	2,181
# applicants accepted	851
# acceptees attending	247
Average LSAT	155
LSAT Range	152–158
Average undergrad GPA	3.22
Application fee	$60
Regular application	3/1
Regular notification	Rolling
Rolling notification	Yes
Early application program	No
Transfer students accepted	Yes
Evening division offered	No
Part-time accepted	No
LSDAS accepted	Yes

Applicants Also Look At
American University, Brooklyn Law School, New York Law School, Pace University, St. John's University, State University of New York—University at Buffalo, Syracuse University, University of Miami.

International Students
TOEFL required of international students	Yes
Minimum paper TOEFL	600
Minimum computer TOEFL	250

FINANCIAL FACTS
Annual tuition	$34,949
Books and supplies	$1,000
Tuition per credit	$1,185
Room and board (off-campus)	$6,400
% first-year students receiving some sort of aid	98
% receiving some sort of aid	90
% of aid that is merit based	89
% receiving scholarships	35
Average grant	$15,337
Average loan	$31,163
Average total aid package	$36,650
Average debt	$80,000

AMERICAN UNIVERSITY
WASHINGTON COLLEGE OF LAW

INSTITUTIONAL INFORMATION

Public/private	Private
Student-faculty ratio	14:1
% faculty part-time	62
% faculty female	42
% faculty minority	15
Total faculty	221

SURVEY SAYS...
Abundant externship/internship/
clerkship opportunities
Liberal students

STUDENTS

Enrollment of law school	1,483
% male/female	44/56
% out-of-state	99
% full-time	82
% minority	34
% international	1
# of countries represented	37
Average age of entering class	24

ACADEMICS

Academic Experience Rating	**84**
Profs interesting rating	83
Profs accessible rating	81
Hours of study per day	4.5

Academic Specialties
Commercial law, corporation securities law, environmental law, government services, human rights law, intellectual property law, international law.

Advanced Degrees Offered
LLM (international legal studies) 12 to 18 months, LLM (law and government) 1 year, SJD 3 to 4 years.

Combined Degrees Offered
JD/MBA 3.5 to 4 years, JD/MA (international affairs) 3.5 to 4 years, JD/MS (justice) 3.5 to 4 years, LLM/MBA 2 to 3 years.

Clinical program required	No
Legal writing course requirement	No
Legal methods course requirement	Yes

Academics

American University's Washington College of Law is an "amazing place" for "public interest law." Students appreciate the "full-tuition scholarship" offered to "10 students every year with a dedicated commitment to social justice work." Adding to the school's civic focus, the issue of international human rights "seems to pervade nearly everything the school does." Also, "The range of courses relating to governmental ideas cannot be matched." "If you have any interest in government, come to this law school," says one student. Along with "an abundance" of "research opportunities," several "excellent study abroad opportunities," and "great clinical programs" are lauded with praise. "The opportunities for internships and externships" in the District of Columbia's courts, government agencies, and nonprofit sector "far exceed those offered by law schools in any other city."

Students note that "teachers really run the gamut" and "Some are very eccentric," but many reports echo the opinion of one student, who says, "Overall I have really liked most of my teachers and feel I have gotten a really good education." An "an amazing open-door policy" permeates WCL. There are many "captivating," "extraordinary teachers" who are "very good at relating their subject matter to social-justice issues." This faculty includes "attorneys on famous cases, a Supreme Court clerk, Ivy League grads, prominent scholars, and even a Jeopardy contestant." Professors here are also "astoundingly liberal." "My professors range between gay-rights-feminist activists and critical-race-theorist-anti-death-penalty activists," comments a 2L. "God help you if you say in Con Law that Roe v. Wade was a poorly reasoned decision," adds a 3L. "The liberal orthodoxy is downright oppressive (and I'm a liberal)."

Though "far from first-rate," WCL's facilities "are more than sufficient." A student explains, "We're starting to outgrow our building, so sometimes space is tight." The "cramped" library is "often crowded and loud." The e-mail program "could be more sophisticated" and "wireless Internet is intermittent, at best." However, "the library and some other offices have received makeovers lately," and the "clean and large" classrooms offer "plenty of space, as well as sufficient electrical outlets to accommodate the many laptops that students have."

All in all, "The school functions fairly smoothly." The administration is "very student-focused" though also "Byzantine" at times. The financial aid staff could stand "to improve communication." The Office of Career Development gets mixed reviews. "Perhaps the top third get interviews" at "midsize firms" in "the Mid-Atlantic region." "About the top 15 percent of students have a chance of being selected for on-campus interviews with the major international law firms," says a student. Another notes, "While George Washington is proclaimed to be so much better, every job I've had has been with GW students, so I have no idea what they are doing that we aren't."

Life

WCL is "pretty big." There is "a diverse student body" here "with differing nationalities, opinions, and goals." "There is really every kind of person at WCL, for better or worse," remarks a 2L. "I think generally for the better." Many students "have spent a year or two between law school (or more) doing really fascinating things with their lives." These "extremely intelligent" students "are still idealistic and strive to make the law a better profession and our society a better society." "A lot of students are very politically active." Several "used to work on the Hill." There is "a slight hippy streak," and "Everyone has a cause." Some lament that the "incredibly liberal" students are so "vocal about it" as "The aura of political correctness can be a bit suffocating at times."

Academically, though "somewhat of a competitive edge" is "lurking underneath," the atmosphere "isn't hyper-competitive." In fact, WCL is a "very friendly place" full of "genuinely nice people." There is "lots of sharing of notes and outlines." "There is an incredible sense of camaraderie," reports one student. Students are also "incredibly involved with the community." There is an "array" of guest lectures and symposia "every day" and "more academic activities than you could ever attend." "I have had many opportunities to meet students at American through clubs, activities, and community service projects," beams a 3L.

Students think that "it's great that [the school] is in DC" but say that "for being in DC," WCL "has a terrible location." Getting to and from campus can be "difficult" and "time consuming," meaning at times "It very much feels like a commuter school." In addition, students report that "no taxi cabs pass by the school when you're in a pinch." The closest subway station "is slightly over a mile away (though "There is a free shuttle that goes directly to the law school)." Parking remains "an ongoing struggle," especially for 1Ls. (For 2Ls and 3Ls, there is "a garage underneath the building"). On the bright side, "There are a lot of ways to cheat the system" if you drive. "Everyone has all the nooks and crannies figured out."

Getting In

Admitted students at the 25th percentile have LSAT scores of 158 and GPAs of about 3.15. Admitted students at the 75th percentile have LSAT scores of 163 and GPAs of 3.60. WCL says that it considers your highest score if you take the LSAT more than once.

Legal research course requirement	Yes
Moot court requirement	No
Public interest law requirement	No

ADMISSIONS

Selectivity Rating	**87**
# applications received	7,601
# applicants accepted	1,877
# acceptees attending	379
Average LSAT	162
LSAT Range	158–163
Average undergrad GPA	3.42
Application fee	$65
Regular application	3/1
Regular notification	Rolling
Rolling notification	Yes
Early application program	No
Transfer students accepted	Yes
Evening division offered	Yes
Part-time accepted	Yes
LSDAS accepted	Yes

Applicants Also Look At
Boston University, The Catholic University of America, Fordham University, George Mason University, The George Washington University, Georgetown University, University of Maryland.

International Students

TOEFL required of international students	No
TOEFL recommended of international students	No

FINANCIAL FACTS

Annual tuition	$34,400
Books and supplies	$950
Tuition per credit	$1,274
Room and board	$17,076
Financial aid application deadline	3/1
% first-year students receiving some sort of aid	84
% receiving some sort of aid	82
% of aid that is merit based	9
% receiving scholarships	38
Average grant	$12,410
Average loan	$38,196
Average total aid package	$39,905
Average debt	$106,758

EMPLOYMENT INFORMATION

		Grads Employed by Field (%)	
Career Rating	**85**		
Rate of placement (nine months out)	98	Academic	2
Average starting salary	$80,500	Business/Industry	17
State for bar exam	MD, NY, VA	Government	12
Pass rate for first-time bar	81	Judicial clerkships	11
Employers Who Frequently Hire Grads		Private practice	49
Akin, Gump, Strauss, Hauer, and Feld LLP;		Public Interest	9
Hogan and Hartson LLP; Jones Day;			
Arnold and Porter; Skadden Arps, U.S.			
Department of Justice.			
Prominent Alumni			
Benjamin R. Jacobs, managing partner,			
The JBG Companies; Honorable Robert C.			
Byrd, U.S. Senator.			

APPALACHIAN SCHOOL OF LAW

Academics

The Appalachian School of Law is a young, private institution, organized in 1994 and given full accreditation from the American Bar Association in 2006. The traditional-looking campus is very beautiful and the library is "new." Wireless Internet access is available and, in recent years, "The technology aspect of the Law School has shown a significant improvement."

Students report that "trial advocacy training," "moot court programs," and other "practical courses" are "first rate" at ASL. The mock trial team "has trounced big names" in national competitions. "The law school's emphasis on practical legal skills has thoroughly prepared me for everyday situations in the general practice of law," says a 3L. "I will graduate and know what to do in a courtroom besides espouse constitutional theory with opposing counsel at lunch." Appalachian also "distinguishes itself from the majority of other law schools by requiring 150 hours of community service." A summer externship is also "required of all first-year students." "The community-service requirement promotes student involvement in law school organizations, benefits the community, and strengthens the reputations of both ASL and the legal profession in general," explains one student. "The summer externship program provides all rising 2Ls with the opportunity to apply the knowledge they gained from first-year classes to real-life situations." There is also a "mandatory alternative dispute resolution requirement," though the school seems keener on this than the students.

The "knowledgeable" and "very approachable" professors here are "down-to-earth people who have a wide variety of legal experience" and "extensive practical and theoretical knowledge of the subjects they teach." Their dedication means that "they are exceptionally concerned with bar passage" and always "available outside of the classroom." "My experience at the Appalachian School of Law has been nothing short of exceptional," confides one student. "The teachers love interacting with the students and are our greatest cheerleaders, mentors, and leaders." "Faculty turnover" has been a problem, though. The "remote location" is "not the most appealing place" for academics to "hang their hats for the long term." However, "The town and area are progressing."

Students tell us that "the greatest strength" of their law school is its "concern and respect for students as individuals." "The administration, faculty, staff, and students have created a community where you can receive an excellent legal education in the midst of the natural beauty of the Appalachian Mountains," explains one student. However, there is a "communication gap between students and administration," meaning that "it often takes days to cut through whatever hidden red tape or underlying ineptness or unwillingness exists." "The administration is very unpredictable" as well. "I realize every new school needs to work out its quirks, but ASL especially needs to do so," gripes one student. Career Services could stand to be "more active," and there seems to be a revolving door regarding deans. "The school appears to promote diversity among our deans with the tenure running about a dean a year," observes a wry 2L.

Life

Grundy is a "small community" located near the convergence of Virginia, Kentucky, and West Virginia. "You can't go to the grocery store without seeing another law student." "The remote location of the school" helps to make "studying is [the] number-one priority." One student explains, "There's nothing to do but study in Grundy, so I went from a below-average college student to above average," adds a proud 3L. "I will

NANCY PRUITT, ADMISSIONS COUNSELORS
PO BOX 2825, GRUNDY, VA 24614
TEL: 276-935-4349 FAX: 276-935-8261
E-MAIL: ASLINFO@ASL.EDU • INTERNET: WWW.ASL.EDU

probably graduate with honors. I'm not so sure that's [because] of the law school itself . . . [or] the general area."

Town-gown relations are strained. "There is some resentment from locals toward law students and vice versa," most agree. "The rugged, desolate terrain" and "isolation" lead students to say that "Appalachian could benefit from more things to do in Grundy outside of law school activities." Students lament that "there isn't a bar or club in the town" where they could "relieve stress and get a drink." (In fact, there is "no liquor by the drink in the county.") "The three-screen movie theater is the most diversion many will get," says one student. That said, people here take a DIY approach to entertainment and "typically find or make [their] own fun to blow off the steam and stress of law school." "A culture of frugal bacchanalia persists in the form of student-hosted house parties." When cabin fever sets in, students take "sojourns" to the nearest bigger cities, "both of which are over the mountains and about 45 minutes away."

Not surprisingly, "You definitely develop a sense of family with the law school students and faculty." "The law students are a very tight-knit group," though beware as "gossip flourishes" and "Everyone's life is an open book." "With scant few exceptions, the student body is Caucasian." Most students would like to see "diversity promoted" at ALS, feeling that "out in town" "underlying discrimination" exists "based on race, sexual orientation, socioeconomic status, and even geographic origin."

Getting In

Appalachian Law School's admitted students at the 25th percentile have LSAT scores of 146 and GPAs of 2.60. Admitted students at the 75th percentile have LSAT scores of 152 and GPAs of 3.30.

ADMISSIONS

Selectivity Rating	**63**
# applications received	990
# applicants accepted	457
# acceptees attending	145
Average LSAT	148
LSAT Range	146–152
Average undergrad GPA	2.8
Application fee	$50
Regular application	4/1
Regular notification	Rolling
Rolling notification	Yes
Early application program	No
Transfer students accepted	Yes
Evening division offered	No
Part-time accepted	No
LSDAS accepted	Yes

International Students

TOEFL required of international students	No
TOEFL recommended of international students	No

FINANCIAL FACTS

Annual tuition	$19,900
Books and supplies	$2,500
Tuition per credit	$700
Room and board (off-campus)	$12,295
% receiving some sort of aid	64
Average grant	$6,468
Average loan	$21,372

EMPLOYMENT INFORMATION

Career Rating	**61**	**Grads Employed by Field (%)**	
Average starting salary	$45,000	Business/Industry	11
State for bar exam	VA, TN, KY, NC, WV	Judicial clerkships	19
Pass rate for first-time bar	52	Private practice	69

ARIZONA STATE UNIVERSITY
SANDRA DAY O'CONNOR COLLEGE OF LAW

Academics

Arizona State University's Sandra Day O'Connor College of Law "is a serious and challenging school" where "The tuition is cheap" and "There are a ton of pro-bono and clinical opportunities." "Students can gain practical experience in most any arena they plan on entering upon graduation." Over 150 students receive academic credit for partic- ipating in externships each year. "Our externship coordinator is great at finding positions for us in the legal community," commends a 2L. Pro-bono work isn't mandatory, "but almost all of the students participate" in order to "start getting practical experience out- side of the classroom." "The school offers a broad range of electives and particularly strong offerings" in intellectual property and technology law, and the nationally recog- nized Indian Legal Program helps train Native American lawyers and furthers an under- standing of the distinctions between the legal systems of Indian Nations and the United States. The cutting-edge Center for Law, Science, and Technology "offers a core of dedi- cated and professional professors" and sponsors speakers drawn from across the country.

The biggest beef among students here is the "terribly one-sided and unreachable" administration. "The administration at every school I've ever been familiar with is crap- py," says a well-traveled 2L. "ASU is no exception." On the other hand, ASU's "sup- portive," "truly motivated," and generally "world-class" professors give students "the opportunity to appreciate the nuances of the law." ASU's faculty has "a real talent and passion for teaching." Sandra Day O'Connor herself teaches courses here "and is a fre- quent visitor to the school." Outside the classroom, "it is obvious that nearly all of the professors genuinely care about the students' well-being." "Most professors maintain an open-door policy for questions, comments, laments, or coffee."

Students are seriously split regarding their employment prospects. Many students emphasize ASU's "quasi-monopoly" on "one of the hottest job markets" and say "A large number of employers recruit here." "If you plan to practice in Phoenix, ASU pro- vides a good connection to the local legal community," counsels a 3L. "However, there's very little opportunity to work outside of Arizona. Very few out-of-state firms recruit here and a degree from ASU does not travel well." "Phoenix is a small legal market," cau- tions another student, and "Opportunities for employment in the private sector, espe- cially larger private firms, are limited."

Many of the law school's facilities have "seen better days." There is an "overwhelming sense of Arizona off-pink décor," classrooms are "simply dated," and "The layout of some of the classrooms is flat-out strange." On the upside, "There is fancy-schmancy technology in nearly all the classrooms." Wireless access is great, and the law library is "state-of-the-art." Student say the library staff is "excellent and a very valuable resource." Also, "There is natural light coming through multiple large windows in the library, which makes it easier to stay awake and to concentrate on studying."

SHELLI SOTO, ASSOCIATE DEAN FOR ADMISSIONS AND FINANCIAL AID
PO BOX 877906, TEMPE, AZ 85287-7906
TEL: 480-965-1474 FAX: 480-727-7930
E-MAIL: LAW.ADMISSIONS@ASU.EDU • INTERNET: WWW.LAW.ASU.EDU

Life

Life here is "pretty laid-back." "The school is not very competitive" and even "somewhat lackadaisical." ASU is home to one of the largest groups of Native American law students in the nation and "There is a good blend of recent college grads and people who have been in the workforce, which brings a good range of opinions to class discussions." "There is also a good blend of out-of-state and in-state students," many of whom are married. "Students seem to genuinely like each other," though they can be "rather cliquish." "People are very social, and the size of the school is big enough that we aren't too into each other's business and small enough that it's easy to get to know a lot of people," explains a 1L.

ASU is "a bit of a commuter school, so it's important to live close by to avoid a lengthy commute and to be socially available." "Largely as a result of the commute, the student body is fairly apathetic when it comes to getting involved in organizations." Those who do decide to get involved enjoy "plenty of opportunity for leadership positions in some great activities." While Arizona State has a world-famous reputation as an undergraduate party school, some students tell us that the social scene for law students "is very lame." Others disagree. "The [law] students know how to have a good time," declares one happy soul. "There is a lot of involvement in intramurals, going out drinking after a particularly rough late-afternoon class, and partying on the weekends."

ASU's location—"minutes away from downtown Phoenix"—is "desirable," though "The beautiful weather can be a terrible distraction." "There's sunshine almost year-round," says one student. "If you have to spend all your time reading, you might as well be doing it by the pool."

Getting In

Admission to ASU's College of Law is competitive. Admitted students at the 25th percentile have LSAT scores of 155 and GPAs of 3.3. Admitted students at the 75th percentile have LSAT scores of 162 and GPAs of 3.8.

EMPLOYMENT INFORMATION			
Career Rating	82	**Grads Employed by Field (%)**	
Rate of placement (nine months out)	99	Academic	3
Average starting salary	$71,000	Business/Industry	6
State for bar exam	AZ	Government	15
Pass rate for first-time bar	79	Judicial clerkships	9
Employers Who Frequently Hire Grads		Private practice	61
Snell and Wilmer; Perkins Coie; Bryan		Public Interest	6
Cave; Gammage and Birnham; Lewis and			
Roca; Fennemore Craig; Jennings, Strouss			
and Salmon.			
Prominent Alumni			
Dan Burk, Oppenheimer, Wolff, and			
Donnelly professor, University of			
Minnesota Law School; Chief Justice Ruth			
McGregor, Arizona State Supreme Court.			

Legal research course requirement	Yes
Moot court requirement	Yes
Public interest law requirement	No

ADMISSIONS

Selectivity Rating	**85**
# applications received	2,944
# applicants accepted	617
# acceptees attending	165
Average LSAT	158
LSAT Range	155–162
Average undergrad GPA	3.54
Application fee	$50
Regular application	2/1
Regular notification	Rolling
Rolling notification	Yes
Early application program	Yes
Early application deadline	11/1
Early application notification	1/31
Transfer students accepted	Yes
Evening division offered	No
Part-time accepted	No
LSDAS accepted	Yes

Applicants Also Look At
University of Arizona, University of California—Hastings, University of California—Los Angeles, University of Denver, University of Nevada—Las Vegas, University of San Diego, University of Southern California.

International Students

TOEFL required of international students	Yes
Minimum paper TOEFL	550
Minimum computer TOEFL	213

FINANCIAL FACTS

Annual tuition (resident)	$13,180
Annual tuition (nonresident)	$23,766
Books and supplies	$1,280
Room and board (off-campus)	$7,400
Financial aid application deadline	3/1
% first-year students receiving some sort of aid	84
% receiving some sort of aid	84
% of aid that is merit based	40
% receiving scholarships	56
Average grant	$2,410
Average loan	$21,928
Average total aid package	$21,268
Average debt	$59,780

AVE MARIA SCHOOL OF LAW

Academics

If you are looking for "a challenging, rigorous education" in "a supportive, collegial environment," consider Ave Maria School of Law. This "unique" and "familial" bastion of legal education opened its doors in the Fall of 2000 thanks largely to the extraordinarily Catholic-oriented philanthropy of Tom Monaghan, the founder of Domino's Pizza. "Natural law theory, moral reasoning, [and Catholicism] pervade the school," as does a strong "commitment to training lawyers who will work for justice." One student explains, "The school does not dwell on policy and theory, but rather teaches the meat and potatoes, black-letter law that you should have a great grounding in to be successful upon graduation." In keeping with its religious foundation, "Every class is begun with prayer, usually the Lord's Prayer or Hail Mary."

Students tell us that Ave Maria is "intellectually rigorous [and] first-class in every aspect." Students also say the school's "Professors honestly love us and want us to do well." "They challenge students, but are respectful," says one student. "They are always available and extremely helpful inside and outside of the classroom." But their dedication doesn't end in the classroom: "They show up at student barbeques and picnics, care about our families, and are always 100 percent available," students boast. The "incredibly professional" administration is "prone to micromanaging" but otherwise "runs the school like clockwork [and] will bend over backward to help you." Ave is "really generous too." Full and nearly full scholarships absolutely abound.

Ave Maria's facilities are "spectacular." Students report that "you can always plug into an Internet port (they deliberately hard-wired everywhere for a better connection) and you also can always plug in your laptop to save precious batteries." One student swears, "It's the nicest law school facility I've seen." Everybody loves the "beautiful" library, where "the fusion of traditional resources and computer technology is wonderfully accomplished." Also (and this is a massive plus), "The library staff lets you eat, drink, and talk in the main reading room!" Students vigorously complain about the lack of parking though.

As a new law school, Ave Maria does have some disadvantages. Piquing the interest of law firms can be difficult. "It is difficult to attract employers when I must introduce, not only myself, but also my school," one student says. Ave Maria offers "widely available" externships and internships, but "There could be a stronger emphasis on the practical." Students feel "The school should increase its faculty so that further course offerings may be had." Overall, however, students are happy, and they are confident that the bells and whistles are just around the corner. In the meantime, Ave Maria boasts the highest bar passage rate in Michigan for "three of the last four years" and "an uncommon *esprit de corps*." One student asserts, "It is a place where students who have a passion for the law have the opportunity to let that passion flourish."

Life

The atmosphere at this little law school is "competitive without being too stressful." Camaraderie is strong, and "People genuinely try to help each other." One student expounds, "The students at Ave Maria are extremely competitive; however, they are highly cooperative. Perhaps this is oxymoronic to the rest of the legal profession, but it is nonetheless true."

RACHELE CONNER, ASSISTANT DIRECTOR OF ADMISSIONS
3475 PLYMOUTH ROAD, ANN ARBOR, MI 48105
TEL: 734-827-8063 FAX: 734-622-0123
E-MAIL: INFO@AVEMARIALAW.EDU • INTERNET: WWW.AVEMARIALAW.EDU

Ave Maria is home to "the kindest people on the planet." The "genuine" students at Ave Maria "place a strong interest on family priorities." One student says, "Ave is a great school for married students and parents. The school goes out of its way to support and involve families." Students feel that "the downside of our law school is the lack of diversity." Although they do say that "the school is actively working to recruit minorities and people with different life experiences," for the time being Ave Maria "basically [consists of] Catholic, conservative, White males."

Not surprisingly, "Many activities surround the Catholic faith" at Ave Maria. This strongly Catholic sentiment has advantages and drawbacks. On the plus side, "There is a pervasive sense that each student is important as a person," both in class and in social settings. Also, if following "the teachings of the Catholic Church" is important to you, you will have oodles of support. While Ave Maria is a bit too "right-wing" for some students' tastes, other students are not bothered. "It gets awkward once in a while, but on the whole I'm getting a high-quality legal education in a great setting among truly concerned people." "Nobody dislikes anybody here, even when they disagree fundamentally about things like abortion, gay rights, or Catholicism," asserts one student. As one student puts it, "It might well be [conservative], but reasonableness and intellectualism are what's demanded, not being conservative."

Getting In

For Fall 2006, admitted students at the 25th percentile had an LSAT score of 150 and a grade point average of 3.02. Admitted students at the 75th percentile have an LSAT score of 158 and a GPA of 3.61. Of those accepted, 25 percent scored in the top 13 percent on the LSAT.

ADMISSIONS

Selectivity Rating	**68**
# applications received	941
# applicants accepted	497
# acceptees attending	131
Average LSAT	153
LSAT Range	150–158
Average undergrad GPA	3.32
Application fee	$50
Regular application	6/10
Regular notification	Rolling
Rolling notification	Yes
Early application program	No
Transfer students accepted	Yes
Evening division offered	No
Part-time accepted	No
LSDAS accepted	Yes

Applicants Also Look At

Case Western Reserve University, George Mason University, Michigan State University—College of Law, Thomas M. Cooley Law School, University of Detroit Mercy, Valparaiso University, Wayne State University.

International Students

TOEFL required	
of international students	Yes
Minimum paper TOEFL	600
Minimum computer TOEFL	250

FINANCIAL FACTS

Annual tuition	$30,345
Books and supplies	$900
Room and board	
(off-campus)	$12,312
Financial aid	
application deadline	6/1
% first-year students	
receiving some sort of aid	84
% receiving some sort of aid	85
% of aid that is merit based	27
% receiving scholarships	55
Average grant	$16,437
Average loan	$28,489
Average total aid package	$48,476
Average debt	$76,482

EMPLOYMENT INFORMATION

Career Rating	**68**	**Grads Employed by Field (%)**	
Rate of placement (nine months out)	72	Academic	2
Average starting salary	$59,100	Business/Industry	24
State for bar exam	MI, IL, NY, NJ, FL	Government	8
Pass rate for first-time bar	75	Judicial clerkships	16
Employers Who Frequently Hire Grads		Military	6
Federal, state, and trial court judges;		Private practice	41
United States Military (JAG); federal government (DOJ); Butzel Long, PC.		Public Interest	3

BAYLOR UNIVERSITY
SCHOOL OF LAW

INSTITUTIONAL INFORMATION

Public/private	Private
Affiliation	Baptist
Student-faculty ratio	17:1
% faculty part-time	24
% faculty female	21
% faculty minority	6
Total faculty	33

SURVEY SAYS...

Heavy use of Socratic method
Great research resources
Beautiful campus

STUDENTS

Enrollment of law school	403
% male/female	57/43
% out-of-state	26
% full-time	100
% minority	12
% international	3
# of countries represented	2
Average age of entering class	23

ACADEMICS

Academic Experience Rating	**84**
Profs interesting rating	78
Profs accessible rating	83
Hours of study per day	5.68

Academic Specialties

Administrative practice, business litigation, business transaction, civil procedure, criminal law, estate planning.

Combined Degrees Offered

JD/MBA 3.5 to 4 years, JD/M (taxation) 3.5 to 4 years, JD/MPPA 3.5 to 4 years.

Clinical program required	Yes
Legal writing course requirement	Yes
Legal methods course requirement	Yes
Legal research course requirement	Yes
Moot court requirement	Yes
Public interest law requirement	No

Academics

While Baylor's Baptist ties show in its efforts to produce lawyers that are both "ethical and public-serving," it is predominantly a school that "teaches to the bar" and does it well. "It's a huge strength," says a 2L. "If you keep up with the work for class and put in the effort to prepare, you are almost guaranteed to pass the bar on your first try." In fact, Baylor's first-time bar-passage rate is an impressive 95 percent, according to the university. The school embraces a "practical approach" and is thorough in teaching students all the essentials of practicing law. "Other schools teach you about the law and leave it up to firms to make you a lawyer," a 3L reports. "But at Baylor you really become one before you have 'JD' at the end of your name." Skills are imparted via a "practice makes perfect" philosophy, which is exemplified by the school's Practice Court Program for 3Ls. "After going through Practice Court, I don't know how any new lawyer who hasn't gone through that process would ever know where to begin in the courtroom; I feel well prepared to be a trial lawyer," a program veteran notes. "Even if you don't become a litigator, it will help you communicate and be confident in your lawyering skills," another adds.

Students here describe their professors as "drill instructors" who "are not afraid to push students to realize their full potential." A 3L explains: "They aren't afraid of calling on you in Practice Court when you have a trial that afternoon, and then kicking you out because you aren't prepared and assigning you a memo due the next day." While tough, most students recognize that professors here "are some of the brightest in their fields" and are "interested in every student learning the material." "You can almost always find your professors in their offices, and they're always willing to help, even with problems outside of their particular classes," a 1L reports. Students also avow that Baylor "has the finest facilities in Texas—not just for a law school, but for any educational institution." "The classrooms and the library are fabulous and are equipped with the latest technology," a 2L brags. "I can get on LexisNexis or Westlaw right in class to get an exact quote from a case as the professor is quoting it."

"A harsh grading scale" where "a 3.24 is the top 15 percent" of the class tempers the mood at Baylor. Students believe this "makes it more difficult to compete with students from other law schools when looking for a job," particularly outside of Texas, where Baylor's name recognition is lower. However, as of the writing of this profile, "The grading scale is being changed . . . to help bring grades up to more reasonable standard." The school's quarter system—students start in either the spring, summer, or fall quarter—allows for smaller classes and uniformity in the academic experience, as every student takes a given course with the same instructor. Many here, however, warn that a "drawback of the quarter system is that there's never any letup on work; students are seemingly always preparing for exams." "Whereas most schools only have finals twice a year, we have them three times," a 1L gripes. Still, most here a buoyed by a belief that "few schools in the nation train their students better."

BECKY BECK CHOLLETT, DIRECTOR OF ADMISSIONS
ONE BEAR PLACE #97288, WACO, TX 76798
TEL: 254-710-1911 FAX: 254-710-2316
E-MAIL: BECKY_BECK@BAYLOR.EDU • INTERNET: LAW.BAYLOR.EDU

Life

"We have fun during the first month of the quarter, but after that we pretty much just hit the books," a 1L writes. While some say that Baylor's heavy workload fosters an "unparalleled sense of camaraderie between the students," others perceive "intense competition" over grades simmering just below the surface. "I work part-time in the library and I know firsthand that students at Baylor do hide books," a 2L reports. (Whether this undercurrent of tension dissipates with the new grading system is to be determined.) At least on the surface, however, students say their peers are "very friendly," and many at the school "compare it to the high school experience" as "The student body of about 400 is smaller than most people's graduating classes." Students report little diversity on campus but state that "no one should confuse the religiosity and famously conservative mindset of Baylor undergrad with Baylor Law School. As an attendee of both and a liberal, I can say that the liberal-to-conservative ratio at the law school is probably 40:60, compared to probably 25:75 at the undergrad [school]."

Students say hometown Waco offers "very few distractions." "There are really only three bars that students frequent," a 3L writes. "Scruffy's is the dive bar. Crickets is the college bar. Treff's is somewhere in between." Some find the positive in this, such as a 2L that admits "There isn't much to distract me from studying." Take heart, though, since "Even though Waco seems like it's in the middle of nowhere, the city lies in between the great cities of Dallas and Austin, so when law school stress starts to get to you, hop on the interstate and get away."

Getting In

Prospective students apply to the quarter in which they wish to enroll. The fall quarter is the most competitive, with a median GPA and LSAT of 3.75 and 162, respectively. Summer is the least competitive, with a median GPA and LSAT of 3.59 and 159, respectively. Students who apply to and are admitted to multiple quarters choose the one they most want to attend. Those rejected from the fall quarter are often encouraged to apply to another quarter.

EMPLOYMENT INFORMATION

Career Rating	87	Grads Employed by Field (%)	
Rate of placement (nine months out)	96	Academic	1
Average starting salary	$74,247	Business/Industry	6
State for bar exam	TX	Government	13
Pass rate for first-time bar	95	Judicial clerkships	9
Employers Who Frequently Hire Grads		Private practice	68
Akin Gump; Jenkins and Gilcrest;		Public Interest	1
Thompson and Knight; Strasburger and			
Price; Baker and Botts; Haynes and Boone;			
Bracewell and Patterson; Jackson Walker;			
Fulbright and Jaworski.			
Prominent Alumni			
Leon Jaworski, special prosecutor for the			
Watergate trials; William Sessions, former			
FBI director; Morris Havell, president of			
the ABA.			

ADMISSIONS

Selectivity Rating	86
# applications received	2,450
# applicants accepted	771
# acceptees attending	70
Average LSAT	162
LSAT Range	160–163
Average undergrad GPA	3.69
Application fee	$40
Regular application	3/1
Regular notification	Rolling
Rolling notification	Yes
Early application program	Yes
Early application deadline	11/1
Early application notification	3/1
Transfer students accepted	Yes
Evening division offered	No
Part-time accepted	No
LSDAS accepted	Yes

Applicants Also Look At

Southern Methodist University, Texas Tech University, University of Houston, The University of Texas at Austin.

International Students

TOEFL required of international students	No
TOEFL recommended of international students	Yes

FINANCIAL FACTS

Annual tuition	$30,156
Books and supplies	$1,785
Tuition per credit	$718
Room and board (on/off-campus)	$7,803/$9,645
% first-year students receiving some sort of aid	93
% receiving some sort of aid	92
% of aid that is merit based	25
% receiving scholarships	75
Average grant	$13,701
Average loan	$27,805
Average total aid package	$35,582
Average debt	$79,609

BOSTON COLLEGE
LAW SCHOOL

INSTITUTIONAL INFORMATION

Public/private	Private
Affiliation	Roman Catholic
Student-faculty ratio	14:1
% faculty part-time	56
% faculty female	39
% faculty minority	19
Total faculty	126

SURVEY SAYS...
Great research resources
Great library staff

STUDENTS

Enrollment of law school	781
% male/female	55/45
% out-of-state	65
% full-time	100
% minority	24
% international	2
# of countries represented	7
Average age of entering class	25

ACADEMICS

Academic Experience Rating	**92**
Profs interesting rating	90
Profs accessible rating	90
Hours of study per day	4.33

Academic Specialties
Business law, civil procedure, commercial law, constitutional law, corporation securities law, criminal law, environmental law, human rights law, intellectual property law, international law, labor law, legal history, legal philosophy, property, taxation.

Advanced Degrees Offered
JD 3 years, LLM 1 year.

Combined Degrees Offered
JD/MBA 4 years, JD/MSW 4 years, JD/MEd 3 years.

Clinical program required	No
Legal writing	
course requirement	Yes
Legal methods	
course requirement	Yes
Legal research	
course requirement	Yes

Academics

Boston College law students may "work really, really hard," but what the majority here find most remarkable about the school is how "interesting and enjoyable" it is. "So many people describe law school as being a bitter pill that one has to swallow in order to become an attorney," a 2L writes. "That's just not the case at Boston College." It's the people that make BC Law special, and professors are "truly extraordinary in their capacities as teachers, mentors, and friends." Faculty members here are at the "top of their field" and "challenge their students to think critically without subjecting [them] to cruel and unusual punishment." While some of the "Visiting professors are hard to follow," instructors "are always well-prepared for class and dedicated to their students." Reinforcing this dedication is the retreat held each year, lead by "approximately five faculty [members] and five students," . . . "that aims to help students discern their vocation in the law."

The "interesting, intellectual, and fun" students are another part of BC's appeal. Law schools are frequently places where egos run rampant, but BC students compliment their peers by calling them "highly normal" and "willing to help." While students would like to see more ethnic, geographic, and religious diversity on campus, there is "a high level of respect" among all in the BC community, and both faculty members and fellow students are "willing to use their personal contacts" to help advance a student's career. "Last year I was able to help two classmates get summer jobs," a 2L reports. Throw in "several events on campus with alumni and Boston attorneys," and students say you can "get a position at a top law firm with relative ease," though the employees in the Career Services Office often "seem limited in their knowledge of job markets to those in [the] major cities of the Northeast and Mid-Atlantic."

While the administration here is sometimes "disorganized" and has, in the past, created "difficult scheduling conflicts for students," others find it "approachable, flexible, and student oriented." By all accounts, the school is "incredibly accommodating to people with family commitments, children, and disabilities." "I have had friends that have had personal problems [and] illness, and the staff has been very helpful and understanding in allowing for help and guidance during difficult times and providing . . . things like make-up exams," a 1L writes. The school is less flexible, however, when it comes to what many students believe to be its "overly conservative" policies.

On the academic front, BC's legal writing program is "one of the best in the country" and "great for learning to write legal briefs." In addition, its "1L class introducing lawyering and ethics helps pull together the various stages of a trial which helped me through my various internships. The course allowed me to ask questions about the legal process in a safe environment instead of learning it through 'sink or swim later.'" Students do, however, call for "more concentrations outside of general corporate and public interest. Other big law schools are committing themselves to advancing IP studies or other 'hot' issues." While "Some of the older sections of the law school show their age," BC's "Classroom and research facilities are beautiful and brand new," and the "awe-inspiring" library particularly boasts "a legion" of "technologically savvy" "research librarians who are always more than willing to help with a particular problem. Many of them teach one-credit classes on legal research which students often take advantage of." A 1L sums up the BC experience: "Where else would your research librarian tell you to call her up over the summer if you have a research issue you need help with?"

Life

The Law Students Association (LSA) "sponsors monthly 'Bar Reviews' at Boston and Cambridge bars, as well as special events such as a fall Harbor Cruise, Halloween Party, and Spring Gala." The LSA has "also begun adding events for the incoming 1L class, such as a reception on Main Campus, a Duck Tour, and tailgating before home football games." As this just scratches the surface of student programming, it's not surprising that "people develop very strong friendships during their time here." Some go as far as to call BC "the Disneyland of law schools." When considering BC's social scene, however, its "massive workload" should not be overlooked.

The school is located "about a mile and a half down the road from BC's main campus, out in the suburb of Newton." While Newton is "a beautiful town," public transportation isn't easily accessible, which makes "the law school is somewhat isolated." Still, most BC law students choose to live in Boston, as there is no housing for law students on the Newton campus, and Newton itself is outside the budget of most students. Much to the chagrin of BC law students, however, there are "three freshman dorms" for undergraduate students on the Newton campus. While the law library "is off-limits for frosh, and the security people do a good job enforcing that," it "closes before midnight." A "cafeteria-type room [is] open all night," but "It is sometimes overridden with freshmen" who "are not particularly respectful of the peace and quiet needed to study late."

Getting In

Only about one in five applicants is admitted to BC Law, but the school offers prospective students some nice options. Through the school's early notification plan, you can submit your application by November 1 and receive a decision by December 15. You may also reactivate an application submitted in the previous year by submitting a new application form, personal statement, LSDAS report, and application fee.

Moot court requirement	No
Public interest law requirement	No

ADMISSIONS

Selectivity Rating	**92**
# applications received	6,322
# applicants accepted	1,224
# acceptees attending	257
Average LSAT	164
LSAT Range	162–166
Average undergrad GPA	3.58
Application fee	$75
Regular application	3/1
Regular notification	Rolling
Rolling notification	Yes
Early application program	Yes
Early application deadline	11/1
Early application notification	12/15
Transfer students accepted	Yes
Evening division offered	No
Part-time accepted	No
LSDAS accepted	Yes

Applicants Also Look At

American University, Boston University, Columbia University, Fordham University, The George Washington University, Georgetown University, New York University.

International Students

TOEFL required of international students	Yes
Minimum paper TOEFL	600
Minimum computer TOEFL	250

FINANCIAL FACTS

Annual tuition	$34,770
Books and supplies	$840
Room and board (off-campus)	$16,835
Financial aid application deadline	3/15
% first-year students receiving some sort of aid	92
% receiving some sort of aid	85
% of aid that is merit based	9
% receiving scholarships	51
Average grant	$15,019
Average loan	$29,389
Average total aid package	$42,541
Average debt	$76,189

EMPLOYMENT INFORMATION

Career Rating	**97**	Association.	
Rate of placement (nine months out)	98	**Grads Employed by Field (%)**	
Average starting salary	$100,000	Academic	1
State for bar exam	MA	Business/Industry	6
Pass rate for first-time bar	96	Government	8
Employers Who Frequently Hire Grads		Judicial clerkships	14
Bingham McCutchen; Brown Rudnick;		Military	1
Cadwalader; Choate Hall and Stewart; DLA		Private practice	65
Piper; Edwards, Angell, Palmer, and		Public Interest	5
Dodge.			
Prominent Alumni			
John Kerry, U.S. Senator/Democratic nominee for president; Debra Yang, former United States Attorney; Michael Greco, immediate past president, American Bar			

BOSTON UNIVERSITY
SCHOOL OF LAW

Academics

The Boston University School of Law boasts "an incredibly open and welcoming learning environment" along with "many dual-degree options." The writing program and mandatory first-year moot court program are "very strong." "BU sets it up so that 1Ls only have two 'real' (i.e., graded) classes first semester," explains one student. "This way, they give us a huge buffer zone. By the time second semester rolled around, we knew what to do, and only then did we take finals for the classes that went ungraded first semester. The system really helped me do well without becoming disheartened." "I don't think there is a law school in the country that could possibly be better than BU for the overall law school experience," adds a 2L.

BU's "incredibly personable" professors "love to teach." "They encourage debate and [a] thorough understanding of the material," explains one student. They "put 150 percent into every single class" and in return "expect a lot out of you which makes you work harder." Their "quirky teaching styles . . . make even tedious subjects interesting," leading one professor to "sing to us about restitution to the tune of 'SexyBack' by Justin Timberlake," says an impressed 1L. Not surprisingly, the faculty is "very approachable outside of the classroom," and students find it "very refreshing to have such a small-school feel at such a large university."

The "dedicated" and "very responsive" administration "constantly" solicits feedback and "doesn't pull any punches." Deans are "genuine" and "willing to speak with students about any issue." The Career Development Office is "well organized" and "friendly." Whatever career you want, "There is someone who can point you in the right direction." "The best firms from New York and Boston" interview here, and "A number of students" secure "big law" jobs. "Even students who don't finish in the top third" after the first year "have excellent chances of being recruited by the top firms in the Northeast." "There is a strong sense of commitment" to public interest law as well.

The "aging building" is BU's one big drawback, and most students agree that it "isn't exactly up to par with its very high academic excellence." The good news is that there have been "many improvements to the Law Tower." The "small" library is "old" yet "lacks the classic law-library feel." The "newly renovated" classrooms are "modern" but "nothing that'll blow you away." That said, there is "wireless Internet throughout" and "The chairs are very comfortable," not to mention the "fantastic" views of the city "from the tower." Despite the building's aesthetic issues, most students agree that "at the end of the day, would you rather have a nice library that you'll never use or would you rather have outstanding, engaging, entertaining professors who bring the law alive?"

Life

"Considering that everyone is brilliant and comes from great undergrads, the school has a surprisingly congenial atmosphere," observes a 1L. Students are mostly "willing to help each other" and "Everyone shares outlines." Nevertheless, there are some "hyper-competitive" types "trying to prove that their application was the one that Harvard inadvertently rejected."

Having "a great time out in the city" is easy. "There's never a lack of things to do to avoid doing work," says one student. "You would have to be a social pariah not to enjoy the social life." Those that "thought partying was done when law school started" are pleasantly surprised to find otherwise. "There's this little hole-in-the wall bar across the street called the Dugout" that "is absolutely infamous at BU," particularly when final exams end. The location "right along the Charles River" is tremendous. It's easy to "grab a meal at someplace local," and "There's lots to do right in the area." Fenway Park is "five-minute walk." On the other hand, "Housing is horrible for what you pay."

BU "attracts a group of people from different walks of life." "There are people who just graduated college, but there are also people who are quite a few years out." "Members of the student body can be a little odd," though "Politically, there is a good mix." There are "quite a few international students" as well. "There are a lot of gay students, and the faculty is very receptive" to their concerns. It's all shapes and sizes on campus with "plenty of Northeastern preppies," "snappy, funky dressers," "bikers and punk rockers," and other "loads of quirky characters." Some think BU "could do more to encourage racial diversity." Other students point out that BU is very integrated ethnically: "Everyone forms one big multicolored bundle of love." "I have never had so many multiracial friends in my life," proclaims a 2L. "Really, you should see us in a bar, it's like the beginning of a bad joke: 'So a Chinese guy, an Indian, a Jew, and an Italian exchange student are sitting in a bar . . . '"

Getting In

Academic credentials of incoming students are very high. BU's admitted students at the 25th percentile have LSAT scores of 163 and GPAs of 3.52. Admitted students at the 75th percentile have LSAT scores of 166 and GPAs of 3.83.

Clinical program required	No
Legal writing course requirement	Yes
Legal methods course requirement	No
Legal research course requirement	Yes
Moot court requirement	Yes
Public interest law requirement	No

ADMISSIONS

Selectivity Rating	**89**
# applications received	6,016
# applicants accepted	1,576
# acceptees attending	269
Average LSAT	165
LSAT Range	163–166
Average undergrad GPA	3.68
Application fee	$75
Regular application	3/1
Regular notification	Rolling
Rolling notification	Yes
Early application program	No
Transfer students accepted	Yes
Evening division offered	No
Part-time accepted	No
LSDAS accepted	Yes

Applicants Also Look At

Boston College, Columbia University, Fordham University, Georgetown University, New York University, The George Washington University, University of Pennsylvania.

International Students

TOEFL required of international students	Yes
Minimum paper TOEFL	600
Minimum computer TOEFL	250

FINANCIAL FACTS

Annual tuition	$34,674
Books and supplies	$1,206
Room and board (off-campus)	$11,008
Financial aid application deadline	3/1
% first-year students receiving some sort of aid	84
% receiving some sort of aid	83
% of aid that is merit based	7
% receiving scholarships	50
Average grant	$16,500
Average loan	$30,528
Average total aid package	$35,000
Average debt	$80,509

EMPLOYMENT INFORMATION

Career Rating	**97**	**Grads Employed by Field (%)**	
Rate of placement (nine months out)	99	Academic	5
Average starting salary	$135,000	Business/Industry	5
State for bar exam	MA, NY, CA, NJ, IL	Government	11
Pass rate for first-time bar	93	Judicial clerkships	10
Prominent Alumni		Private practice	65
Judd Gregg, U.S. Senator; William S.		Public Interest	4
Cohen, former Secretary of Defense; David			
Kelley, executive producer; Gary F. Locke,			
former Governor of Washington State;			
Honorable Sandra L. Lynch, U.S. Court of			
Appeals, First Circuit; Edward Brooke, for-			
mer U.S. Senator; Martha Coakley,			
Massachusetts Attorney General; Shari			
Redstone, president, National Amusements.			

BRIGHAM YOUNG UNIVERSITY
J. REUBEN CLARK LAW SCHOOL

Academics

Brigham Young University's J. Rueben Clark Law School prides itself on "an uplifting, enriching atmosphere" where "very high moral/ethical standards" "are taught as an integral part of law." "A fabulous clinical component" has "really blossomed over the past few years" as well, and international externship opportunities" abound. There are also "some good opportunities" if you are "interested in Federal Indian Law." Most importantly, though, at a three-year total of around $25,000, "you can't beat the price." "Tuition is ridiculously inexpensive" and, "at the same time," BYU Law provides "one of the greatest legal educations in the nation." Generous scholarships are just gravy.

BYU Law's vast resources are "well within the grasp of every student." "Everyone at the school wants you to succeed," and there is seemingly unlimited money to present papers, travel for trial and appellate advocacy competitions, and participate in anything that could benefit the school. BYU's "brilliant and inspiring" professors are "captivating teachers" who are "far too qualified to be teaching law school but eager to give back." In class, professors "keep it interesting" and "use the Socratic Method really well." Discussion is lively. Outside of class, they are "approachable" and "genuinely care." An "open-door policy reigns supreme." Administrators are "mostly very available" as well. The writing program is either "intense" or "could be a little more vigorous," depending on whom you ask. If they could change one thing, students say "some courses" need to be available more often.

The "amazing" Career Services Office "gets things done." Upon graduation, few students have any problems finding employment. "I am in the lower half of the class and I still expect to make $70,000 starting out," claims a 2L. BYU Law's "connections to alumni and supporters throughout the country and the world" are very useful in this regard. "Pick the city where you want to live," explains another 2L, "and there will be lawyers with BYU connections who are willing to get you an interview."

The law school building "was built in the 1970s" when "large concrete slabs" were all the rage. It's "not very pretty" and "does not have enough windows." Inside, though, "The facilities are fabulous." The library is "state-of-the-art" (despite some "really uncomfortable" chairs). "I am amazed at how many hours the library is open, and equally amazed at how large the library staff is," applauds a 2L. Also, "Each law student has an individual carrel in the law library" with "three drawers, two cabinets that lock, an Ethernet connection, and three electrical outlets." You even get a lamp. Technology, wireless Internet, and tech support are "top of the line" as well.

Life

BYU Law's affiliation with the Church of Jesus Christ of Latter-day Saints adds "an important spiritual component." "Many students read the Bible on a daily basis and openly talk about religion in the halls, classroom, and in their academic papers." BYU Law can seem "extremely homogeneous" but, "If you are comfortable in that environment, it's perfect." Students tell us that BYU is "doable for a non-Mormon," too, particularly "considering the price tag." "Take it from a non-member when I say that attending J. Reuben Clark Law School is well worth the sacrifice in giving up Friday night cocktail mixers in favor of Friday family barbeques," promises a 1L. "If nothing else, I guarantee a once-in-a-lifetime experience with enough bizarre situations to warrant a fabulous book in the future."

GaeLynn Kuchar, Director of Admissions
340 JRCB, Brigham Young University Law School, Provo, UT 84602
Tel: 801-422-4277 Fax: 801-422-0389
E-mail: kucharg@law.byu.edu • Internet: www.law.byu.edu

The thing to understand is that BYU is "very conservative." An honor code includes "dress and grooming standards" as well as a total ban on alcohol, drugs, and tobacco. No tea or coffee, either. "The strongest drink you will find at the BYU Law School is orange-flavored Metamucil." Single students "spend a lot of time together" but "If you're on the hunt for men and you're not Mormon, good luck." "Many students are married" with children. There are "all kinds of accommodations for families" including a trick-or-treat day through the study carrels. "Yeah," emphasizes one happy student, "it's that good."

BYU Law is "one of the most competitive schools in the country." It's "not an in-your-face type of competitiveness"; "No one would ever sabotage you, and notes are widely circulated." Instead, students here "will simply outwork you." "Everyone works ridiculously hard," says one student. "Everybody reads all their cases all the time." It's not uncommon to see "the library parking lot full on a Saturday morning at 8:00 A.M." "The students are machines." Despite the "exceptional" competitiveness, BYU is also very friendly. With a class size of roughly 150, "It is hard not to get to know your peers." "There is a real sense of community at the law school," relates a 1L. "The informal sense of friendship is profound and hard to explain, but I trust the other students to be looking out for me and they expect the same from me. It is a great atmosphere in which to study."

When, at last, students relax, BYU Law "has a ton of clubs" for "just about anything." "The clubs end up being social clubs with fun activities and dinners and other social events." Lectures and "fabulous intramural programs" are plentiful as well. Winters "get a little cold" but "You couldn't ask for a more beautiful setting." The campus is "within an hour" of world-class ski resorts and "outdoor adventures" galore. "Housing is crazy affordable" too. Basically, "If you don't mind driving 25 minutes to Salt Lake for the partying and clubbing that doesn't happen in Provo, then really there's nothing missing."

Getting In

Admitted students at the 25th percentile have LSAT scores of 161 and GPAs of about 3.5. Admitted students at the 75th percentile have LSAT scores of 166 and GPAs of better than 3.8. When you apply, you have to establish by way of a letter of recommendation that you will live in accordance with BYU's Honor Code. If you take the LSAT more than once, BYU Law will consider your highest score.

EMPLOYMENT INFORMATION

		Grads Employed by Field (%)	
Career Rating	89	Academic	1
Rate of placement (nine months out)	99	Business/Industry	13
Average starting salary	$81,782	Government	9
State for bar exam	UT, CA, NV, AZ, TX	Judicial clerkships	12
Pass rate for first-time bar	94	Military	1
Employers Who Frequently Hire Grads		Other	1
Allen Matkins; Alverson Taylor; Ascione		Private practice	52
Heideman; Baker and McKenzie; Ballard		Public Interest	1
Spahr; Bryan Cave; Carlsmith Ball;			
Christensen and Jensen.			
Prominent Alumni			
Steve Young, former quarterback, San			
Francisco 49ers; Honorable Dee V.			
Benson, senior judge, Federal District			
Court, Utah; Chris Cannon, Congressman.			

ADMISSIONS

Selectivity Rating	**95**
# applications received	917
# applicants accepted	260
# acceptees attending	145
Average LSAT	164
LSAT Range	161–166
Average undergrad GPA	3.63
Application fee	$50
Regular application	3/1
Regular notification	Rolling
Rolling notification	Yes
Early application program	No
Transfer students accepted	Yes
Evening division offered	No
Part-time accepted	No
LSDAS accepted	Yes

Applicants Also Look At
Georgetown University, Loyola Marymount University, University of Nevada, Las Vegas, University of Southern California, The University of Texas at Austin, University of Utah.

International Students

TOEFL required	
of international students	No
TOEFL recommended	
of international students	No
Minimum paper TOEFL	590
Minimum computer TOEFL	243

FINANCIAL FACTS

Annual tuition	$8,200
Books and supplies	$1,470
Room and board	$14,106
% first-year students	
receiving some sort of aid	86
% receiving some sort of aid	78
% of aid that is merit based	33
% receiving scholarships	50
Average grant	$2,300
Average loan	$13,400
Average debt	$41,000

BROOKLYN LAW SCHOOL

INSTITUTIONAL INFORMATION

Public/private	Private
Student-faculty ratio	20:1
% faculty part-time	63
% faculty female	33
Total faculty	189

SURVEY SAYS...

Abundant externship/internship/
clerkship opportunities
Students love Brooklyn, NY

STUDENTS

Enrollment of law school	1,494
% male/female	51/49
% out-of-state	45
% full-time	77
% faculty minority	26
% international	1
# of countries represented	34
Average age of entering class	24

ACADEMICS

Academic Experience Rating	**79**
Profs interesting rating	72
Profs accessible rating	71
Hours of study per day	4.01

Academic Specialties

Civil procedure, commercial law, constitutional law, corporate securities law, criminal law, environmental law, government services, health, human rights law, intellectual property law, international business law, international law, labor law, law and cognition, legal history, legal philosophy, property, science and public policy, taxation.

Advanced Degrees Offered

JD 3 to 4 years.

Combined Degrees Offered

JD/MA (political science) 4 to 6 years, JD/MS (city and regional planning) 4 to 6 years, JD/MBA 4 to 6 years, JD/MS (library/information science) 4 to 6 years, JD/M (urban planning) 4 to 6 years.

Clinical program required	No
Legal writing course requirement	Yes

Academics

Instructing prospective students that "there is no better place to begin your life as a lawyer," Brooklyn Law School in—where else?—Brooklyn, New York, is "the real deal." Boasting a diverse group of hardworking students, everyone at Brooklyn Law is "smart and ambitious, but also down to earth."

The level of instruction varies at Brooklyn Law, with most students expressing appreciation for their "accomplished and effective" professors, but many students have had their share of misses in the instructional department. "I personally feel I've lucked out with my professors; they're routinely engaging, witty, and all are universally brilliant. However, I know this isn't the case across the board. Some of my friends have professors that might as well be Charlie Brown's parents," a first-year student declares. Outside of the lecture halls, the clinical and moot court programs receive strong marks for bringing practical experience to Brooklyn Law students, and the school's rigorous legal writing program is described by one second-year student as a "major humbling experience."

The general consensus among students is that there is "nothing fantastic about the facilities." Spotty wireless access and classrooms that are nice, but "filled to capacity," forcing students to "sardine-can themselves in the back at separate desks." The school's location in Brooklyn—within spitting distance of the Brooklyn DA's Office, District Court, New York State Supreme Court, Criminal Court, and Bankruptcy Court—helps bring "great adjunct and visiting faculty" to the campus and provides much opportunity and excitement for students looking to see the law in action. As one student explains, "You can spend one hour seeing a mobster case in court, and then the next hour be sitting in the classroom." "You hear all too often that law school does not teach you what being a lawyer is really all about, but BLS seems to constantly turn to the question of how we can apply our skills in the real world," affirms another student. However, some students criticize the law school's credit limit on externships, "which is problematic if you already know what field you want to practice in since you can only get credit for an externship in a given field for two semesters."

The administration at Brooklyn Law receives almost universally negative reviews. Referred to as "completely absent, the source of many headaches, [and] not as responsive as it should be," many students share the sentiment of one wise second-year student who says: "If you have the patience and intelligence to deal with the school's administration, you're probably qualified to be a lawyer." The Career Center is also the source of much angst; many complain that if you're not in the top 10 percent of the class then "You're dead to them," and that much good could be done by "improving relations with mid-sized firms." "Opportunities to learn outside the classroom abound, with clinics, journals, moot court, and more internships then you can shake a stick at, but with no help from the Career Center, it's up to the student to go out and get them," says a 3L. Fortunately, many students are happy to take on the challenge. As one 2L explains, "I was not terribly involved in undergrad, but the richness of programs and other non-classroom events that go on are often just too interesting and varied to pass up."

Life

Though the atmosphere at Brooklyn Law "tends to be more liberal, the conservative students still speak up." However, some students say that the leftward slant "can create an annoying system of group thinking that sometimes stifles classroom discussion on more controversial issues." There is a palpable sense of competition amongst students at the law school (particularly the 1Ls), but everyone still seems to "really get along." Student housing is "terrific" thanks to the recent opening of the "aesthetically perfect" Feil Hall, the newly furnished residence building on campus (though "God help you if you bring a date back there, because everybody will know about it the next morning"). Indeed, the school can seem very cliquey, and one 3L warns that "you fall in with a niche, and there is minimal crossover." "When I'm in school I often feel like I'm in the 17th grade," agrees another. The school is mainly "dominated by Tristaters," and although this creates a sense of camaraderie among students, almost everyone is "involved in other communities, and law school socialization comes second." The Student Bar Association "tries hard to create a social community" by sponsoring events such as the Barrister's Ball and Open Mic Night. But when your campus is New York City, plenty of other social opportunities await you, and many of Brooklyn Law's students are "intelligent, fun people who enjoy hanging out with each other and drinking beers at the myriad bars that surround them."

Getting In

Students admitted at the 25th percentile had an average GPA of 3.2 and an average LSAT score of 162. Students admitted at the 75th percentile had an average GPA of 3.6 and an average LSAT score of 164. The school offers several interesting joint-degree programs, and admits that diversity plays a part in its selection process, from ethnicity and geographical background to prior life experiences.

Legal methods	
course requirement	Yes
Legal research	
course requirement	Yes
Moot court requirement	Yes
Public interest	
law requirement	No

ADMISSIONS

Selectivity Rating	88
# applications received	4,229
# applicants accepted	1,141
# acceptees attending	303
Average LSAT	163
LSAT Range	162–164
Average undergrad GPA	3.43
Application fee	$65
Regular application	Rolling
Regular notification	Rolling
Rolling notification	Yes
Early application program	Yes
Early application deadline	12/1
Early application notification	12/31
Transfer students accepted	Yes
Evening division offered	Yes
Part-time accepted	Yes
LSDAS accepted	Yes

Applicants Also Look At
American University, Fordham University, Yeshiva University.

International Students

TOEFL required	
of international students	No
TOEFL recommended	
of international students	Yes
Minimum paper TOEFL	600
Minimum computer TOEFL	250

FINANCIAL FACTS

Annual tuition	$37,174
Books and supplies	$1,000
Fees per credit	$326
Tuition per credit	$27,882
Room and board	
(off-campus)	$14,360
Financial aid application	
deadline	4/30
% first-year students	
receiving some sort of aid	65
% receiving some sort of aid	62
% of aid that is merit based	66
% receiving scholarships	46
Average grant	$14,020
Average loan	$34,120
Average total aid package	$36,500
Average debt	$89,125

EMPLOYMENT INFORMATION

Career Rating	84	Grads Employed by Field (%)	
Rate of placement (nine months out)	98	Business/Industry	20
Average starting salary	$87,405	Government	13
State for bar exam	NY, NJ, CA, MA	Judicial clerkships	5
Pass rate for first-time bar	85	Military	1

Employers Who Frequently Hire Grads

Other	1
Private practice	56
Public Interest	4

Cahill Gordon; Fried, Frank, Harris, Shriver and Jacobson; Pillsbury, Winthrop; Proskauer Rose; NYC Law Department.

Prominent Alumni

David Dinkins, former Mayor of New York City; Honorable Edward R. Korman, chief judge, U.S. District, EDNY; Russell Lewis, former president and CEO of New York Times Company.

CAMPBELL UNIVERSITY
NORMAN ADRIAN WIGGINS SCHOOL OF LAW

INSTITUTIONAL INFORMATION

Public/private	Private
Affiliation	Baptist
Student-faculty ratio	15:1
% faculty part-time	17
% faculty female	56
% faculty minority	12
Total faculty	189

SURVEY SAYS...

Heavy use of Socratic method
Diverse opinions accepted
in classrooms
Conservative students

STUDENTS

Enrollment of law school	346
% male/female	52/48
% full-time	100
% minority	8
Average age of entering class	26

ACADEMICS

Academic Experience Rating	**81**
Profs interesting rating	87
Profs accessible rating	88
Hours of study per day	5.46

Academic Specialties

Tracks in business/transactions and trial and appellate advocacy.

Advanced Degrees Offered

JD 3 years.

Combined Degrees Offered

JD/MBA.

Clinical program required	No
Legal writing course requirement	Yes
Legal methods course requirement	Yes
Legal research course requirement	Yes
Moot court requirement	Yes
Public interest law requirement	No

Academics

Be prepared for an intense first year at the Norman Adrian Wiggins School of Law, where classroom discussion is demanding and late-night study sessions are par for the course. A 3L tells us, "The Socratic Method is employed for at least your first three terms, and the core classes are beyond challenging at Campbell." Another student warns, "Campbell is not for the weak hearted. You must want to be a lawyer and be determined to persevere." However, with an excellent student/teacher ratio, a respectful Christian tradition, and a helpful teaching staff, Campbell is a kinder, gentler form of legal boot camp. "While professors are demanding of students in the classroom and rigorous in their implementation of the Socratic Method, outside of class they are approachable and eager to assist and love to engage students in dialogue," according to one student. Another goes on, "The faculty is outstanding. They are always available to talk to students about anything, even if it has nothing to do with law."

In addition to course difficulty, students tell us that Campbell upholds difficult marking standards, eschewing any form of grade inflation. "There seems to exist a friendly rivalry among the faculty as to who teaches the best [and] the hardest subject, who has the best jokes; however, the competition stops short of including which professor can give the most A's." Even so, students assure us that their hard work pays off in the long run. For one thing, "Campbell's bar-passage rate has been the highest in North Carolina in 10 of the last 13 years." On top of that, students say that Campbell has an excellent reputation among local firms, ensuring excellent career placement after graduation. "Campbell is a small private law school with a big reputation within North Carolina. After graduation, prepare to live up to the high standard that graduates before you have set for Campbell Law attorneys," admonishes a 2L. Students point to the support and guidance they receive from Campbell's top-notch Career Services as a big part of why the school has such a solid placement rate.

Speaking of career preparation, students say that Campbell leaves them well prepared for the practical aspects of practicing law through various programs, such as the Professionalism Lecture Series for first-year students. "Campbell's emphasis on professionalism is quite impressive," reports a 1L. "First-year students are required to go [to the lecture series] in order to . . . further develop the skill of thinking like a lawyer." As they progress, "Students get to participate in Law Review, moot court, trial teams, and any one of at least four pro bono projects," reports one student. "I believe this is why we have a reputation for being so well prepared to start our careers."

Affiliated with the Baptist Church, Campbell is committed to promoting the ethical practice of law. A student praises the school's Christian ethos: "Campbell not only provides a great legal education but [also] something that is less and less valued in the legal world today: a solid grounding in ethics and Christian principles." Another adds this warning: "Campbell Law is a wonderful place to learn, if you don't mind a Republican-conservative-professed-Christian atmosphere." However, non-Baptists need not avoid Campbell. As one student confides, "Even though the school has a religious affiliation, one which I am not a part of, I feel just as welcome as every student here."

ALAN D. WOODLIEF JR., ASSOCIATE DEAN FOR ADMISSIONS
PO BOX 158, 113 MAIN STREET, BUIES CREEK, NC 27506
TEL: 910-893-1754 FAX: 910-893-1780
E-MAIL: ADMISSIONS@LAW.CAMPBELL.EDU • INTERNET: WWW.LAW.CAMPBELL.EDU

Life

The small town of Buies Creek, North Carolina, doesn't offer much in the form of entertainment. Take it from the 2L who tells us, "The school is pretty much in the middle of nowhere, so you have to drive 45 minutes to get to a variety of social activities. There are a few restaurants and a movie theater close by, but that's about it." Another puts it even more bluntly: "Buies Creek itself is a great place to study law because there is not much else to do." As a result, Campbell students must rely on one another for fun and diversion. Luckily, the small school atmosphere engenders an intimate, friendly feeling within the student body. "Students at this small law school get to know each other, and in a sense you live together. There is a sense of family, because we all are going to represent why we went to Campbell one day," writes one student. Another adds, "Campbell encourages competitive attitudes, but not for the sake of self-aggrandizement or mere greed. People come first here; that is what matters."

Getting In

Accepted students to the class entering in Fall 2006 had a median GPA of 3.19 and a median LSAT score of 155. (Note that median and average LSAT scores can differ significantly.) In addition to common law school application requirements, Campbell does what few other law schools do: Prior to admission, students must also submit to a personal interview with the law school faculty. Invitations to interview are based on a student's application; most, but not all, applicants are invited to interview.

ADMISSIONS

Selectivity Rating	**83**
# applications received	1,032
# applicants accepted	272
# acceptees attending	122
Average LSAT	155
LSAT Range	152–157
Average undergrad GPA	3.19
Application fee	$50
Regular application	Rolling
Regular notification	Rolling
Rolling notification	Yes
Early application program	No
Transfer students accepted	Yes
Evening division offered	No
Part-time accepted	No
LSDAS accepted	Yes

Applicants Also Look At
Appalachian School of Law, North Carolina Central University, Regent University, Samford University, The University of North Carolina at Chapel Hill, University of South Carolina, Wake Forest University—MBA Program.

International Students

TOEFL required	
of international students	No
TOEFL recommended	
of international students	Yes

FINANCIAL FACTS

Annual tuition	$24,941
Books and supplies	$1,500
Room and board	
(on/off-campus)	$10,749/$13,063
Financial aid application	
deadline	3/15
% receiving some sort of aid	91
% receiving scholarships	51
Average grant	$5,825
Average loan	$32,770
Average debt	$85,015

EMPLOYMENT INFORMATION

Career Rating	69	Grads Employed by Field (%)	
Average starting salary	$55,000	Business/Industry	0
State for bar exam	NC, SC, VA, MD, UT	Government	8
Pass rate for first-time bar	87	Judicial clerkships	10
Employers Who Frequently Hire Grads		Private practice	76
Small to medium size private firms.		Public Interest	3
Prominent Alumni		Own firm	3
Elaine Marshall, North Carolina Secretary of State; Honorable John Tyson, North Carolina Court of Appeals; Richard Thigpen, general counsel, Carolina Panthers NFL Franchise; Honorable Ann Marie Calabria, North Carolina Court of Appeals; Honorable Laura Bridges, North Carolina District Court.			

CAPITAL UNIVERSITY
LAW SCHOOL

INSTITUTIONAL INFORMATION

Public/private	Private
Affiliation	Lutheran
Student-faculty ratio	23:1
% faculty part-time	36
% faculty female	21
% faculty minority	14
Total faculty	29

SURVEY SAYS...

Diverse opinions accepted
in classrooms
Great research resources
Abundant externship/internship/
clerkship opportunities
Students love Columbus, OH

STUDENTS

Enrollment of law school	683
% male/female	54/46
% out-of-state	27
% full-time	61
% minority	9
% international	1
# of countries represented	9
Average age of entering class	25

ACADEMICS

Academic Experience Rating	**70**
Profs interesting rating	70
Profs accessible rating	74
Hours of study per day	4.3

Academic Specialties

Children and family law, corporation securities law, dispute resolution, environmental law, government services, international law, labor law, taxation.

Advanced Degrees Offered

LLM (taxation) 1 to 6 years, LLM (business) 1 to 6 years, LLM (business and taxation) 1 to 6 years, MT 1 to 6 years.

Combined Degrees Offered

JD/MBA 3.5 to 6 years, JD/MSN 3.5 to 6 years, JD/MSA 3.5 to 4 years, JD/MTS 4 to 6 years.

Academics

Capital University Law School "in the heart of downtown" Columbus, Ohio "is a great place to study law," particularly if you seek a balance between "legal theory and actual practice." The "broad range of courses" here emphasizes "practical lawyering skills." "The legal writing program is awesome," says one student. A wealth of externships, internships, and clerkships offers "the best hands-on experience possible." The law school is "only a few short blocks from the Ohio Supreme Court" and is "nestled within two miles" of a bevy of other state and federal courthouses and agencies. Capital has "outstanding" part-time and evening programs and "All of the offices are open longer hours to accommodate this group of students." The "highly reputable" National Center for Adoption Law and Policy "offers a great way to gain expertise" and "get connected with family-law attorneys." Another plus is an Advanced Bar Studies course "designed to prepare 3Ls for taking the bar." It seems to be working. "We are ecstatic about our third-in-the-state passage rate this year," raves a 3L. Employment prospects are also good. Capital is "respected in the Columbus legal community" and has "a strong reputation with local government and private firms for producing students with strong research and writing skills and good practical knowledge." When "Many loyal alumni practice locally," it goes to say that students find plenty to keep them in Columbus and at Capital.

"With very few exceptions, the teaching faculty is top-notch as communicators and mentors." There is also "an excellent base of adjunct professors who are practitioners by day." Capital's "devoted, highly prepared, [and] usually pretty easygoing" professors "make an effort to stay easily accessible." "So far, minus one pompous and unhelpful professor, my experience with Capital's faculty has been amazing," comments a 1L. "Most professors emphasize the real-world aspects of the curriculum as well as what is required to perform well on the bar exam." Some professors "could make class more interesting," though. Also, be warned: "There is no grade inflation here." Something like "four to eight percent of students in first-year classes" receive an A. The "median grade" is more like a "B-minus." "When someone gets an A at Capital, it should be an unambiguous signal to an employer that the person is highly qualified in the subject matter," explains a student.

The "approachable" administration is "improving every year" and "open to criticisms and suggestions." The "Registrar, Career Services staff, and even the security guards are incredibly friendly and helpful." "Not a lot of people fall through the cracks." Organization can be "very lackluster sometimes," though. There are "small mix-ups (e.g., a classroom for the class not being large enough to accommodate all the students)," and the "terrible" scheduling process is "tiresome."

Capital's "aesthetically boring" facilities are "pretty much completely modern." So "don't be fooled by the gray, outdated exterior." Classrooms are "all equipped with state-of-the-art technology." "The wireless Internet throughout the school is wonderful," claims one student. The library "needs improvement" though and "The building is a maze." Also, some areas get "a little crowded with everyone's books and laptops."

Life

There is both "a strong sense of camaraderie" and "a somewhat competitive atmosphere" here. Capital is "small" and "very family-oriented." "Everyone is friendly and willing to help out," says one student. Competition for coveted A's can be stiff, though.

LINDA J. MIHELY, ASSISTANT DEAN OF ADMISSIONS AND FINANCIAL AID
303 EAST BROAD STREET, COLUMBUS, OH 43215-3200
TEL: 614-236-6310 FAX: 614-236-6972
E-MAIL: ADMISSIONS@LAW.CAPITAL.EDU • INTERNET: WWW.LAW.CAPITAL.EDU

"It is best not to mention grades except among close friends." "There seems to be a sort of divide among students at the law school." "Day and evening students don't interact much at all," and most agree that "the day program is much more competitive." "The evening program is much more relaxed in class" because "Most people have very busy lives outside of school." "Evening students are a different breed," explains one student. "I can honestly report that studying law with people whose resumes are already filled with diverse experience has been very rewarding."

"Students here are generally pretty vocal about issues that matter to them." Ethnically, "Students are mainly White," but "There is a great minority community." You'll find a very high number of "nontraditional law students" here and a "wide range in age" and "professions." "Some spend their days talking about drinking and parties, while other more serious students spend their days studying," observes a 2L. "It is quite obvious which students are fresh out of undergrad."

There are "lots of student organizations" and "ways to get involved." "Community-service projects are everywhere," and "The main law fraternities are very active." Capital sponsors "planned social hours" and "a lot of events and different opportunities for students to get to know each other." "It is very easy to find a group of people with similar interests both in and out of the legal field." Students give the city of Columbus reasonably high marks. "It's not San Francisco or Boston," but "There are usually student-group sponsored happy hours at various bars downtown" and "social nights in and around Columbus at other bars." "Often after classes are over on Friday or after a midterm, an impromptu group will just go out somewhere."

Getting In

Admitted students at the 25th percentile here have LSAT scores of about 150 and GPAs hovering just around 3.0. Admitted students at the 75th percentile have LSAT scores of 156 and GPAs of approximately 3.5.

Clinical program required	No
Legal writing course requirement	Yes
Legal methods course requirement	Yes
Legal research course requirement	Yes
Moot court requirement	No
Public interest law requirement	No

ADMISSIONS

Selectivity Rating	72
# applications received	1,575
# applicants accepted	624
# acceptees attending	255
Average LSAT	153
LSAT Range	151–156
Average undergrad GPA	3.21
Application fee	$40
Regular application	Rolling
Regular notification	Rolling
Rolling notification	Yes
Early application program	No
Transfer students accepted	Yes
Evening division offered	Yes
Part-time accepted	Yes
LSDAS accepted	Yes

Applicants Also Look At
Cleveland State University, Florida Coastal School of Law, Ohio Northern University, Thomas M. Cooley Law School, The University of Akron, University of Dayton, University of Toledo.

International Students
TOEFL required of international students	Yes

FINANCIAL FACTS

Annual tuition	$24,795
Books and supplies	$898
Fees per credit	$855
Tuition per credit	$855
Room and board (off-campus)	$10,580
Financial aid application deadline	4/1
% first-year students receiving some sort of aid	94
% receiving some sort of aid	93
% of aid that is merit based	40
% receiving scholarships	40
Average grant	$8,000
Average loan	$23,570
Average total aid package	$28,737
Average debt	$70,806

EMPLOYMENT INFORMATION

Career Rating	76	Grads Employed by Field (%)	
Rate of placement (nine months out)	95	Academic	4
Average starting salary	$59,849	Business/Industry	19
State for bar exam	OH	Government	21
Pass rate for first-time bar	87	Judicial clerkships	3

Employers Who Frequently Hire Grads

Military	1
Private practice	46
Public Interest	6

Law firms, government agencies, business and corporate employers.

Prominent Alumni

David Tannenbaum, partner, Fulbright Jaworski—Patent Law; Deborah Pryce, U.S. Congresswoman; Paul McNulty, Deputy Attorney General, U.S. Department of Justice; Robert Schottenstein, chairman, CEO, and president, M/I Homes, Inc.

CASE WESTERN RESERVE UNIVERSITY
SCHOOL OF LAW

INSTITUTIONAL INFORMATION

Public/private	Private
Student-faculty ratio	14:1
% faculty female	31
% faculty minority	8
Total faculty	52

SURVEY SAYS...

Diverse opinions accepted
in classrooms
Great research resources
Great library staff
Abundant externship/internship/
clerkship opportunities

STUDENTS

Enrollment of law school	673
% male/female	59/41
% out-of-state	59
% full-time	99
% minority	17
% international	1
# of countries represented	18
Average age of entering class	25

ACADEMICS

Academic Experience Rating	**85**
Profs interesting rating	83
Profs accessible rating	82
Hours of study per day	4.55

Academic Specialties

Commercial law, constitutional law, corporation securities law, criminal law, government services, human rights law, intellectual property law, international law, taxation, litigation, health law; law, technology, and the arts; public law.

Advanced Degrees Offered

LLM (U.S. legal studies), 1 year for international lawyers.

Combined Degrees Offered

JD/MBA (management) 4 years, JD/MNO (nonprofit management) 4 years, JD/CNM (certificate in nonprofit management) 3 years, JD/MSSA (social work) 4 years, JD/MA (legal history) 4 years, JD/MA (bioethics) 4 years, JD/MD (medicine) 7 years; JD/MPH (public health) 4 years.

Academics

Case Western Reserve University School of Law is a dynamic institution emphasizing technology and "practical lawyering skills." Numerous cutting-edge academic centers on campus offer instruction in a wide range of unique legal niches, including regulatory law and law and medicine. According to many students, the crown jewel among these centers is the International Law Center. The international law program is "one of the best in the entire country." Students participate in "research for the government's cases against Guantanamo Bay inmates" and do research for the international courts for Rwanda, Cambodia, Sierra Leone, and the former Yugoslavia. Concentration programs include law and technology, litigation, and health law. Dual-degree programs include a JD/MD and a JD/Master's in social work. Also, "If you're interested in community-service and public interest work, you have more options than you'd ever have time to pursue."

"Professors are excellent" at Case Law. They are "intelligent, dedicated, and experienced" and "They all seem to love teaching and love the law." Courses are generally "lively and interesting." "Many members of the faculty are younger and they bring energy and enthusiasm to the classroom along with pedagogical methods that keep pace with modern technology." "They have an amazing knack for generating excitement out of mundane material," raves a 2L. "I will enroll in any course that these professors teach, simply because they are so passionate and challenging." The "interesting" adjuncts are "almost always great" as well, "and often come from elite firms." "One adjunct professor, who teaches law of the music industry, won a Grammy." Outside of class, professors are "quite accessible and willing to grab a drink with you." The administration is "amazingly accessible" as well.

On the career front, students are mostly satisfied with the Career Services Office. The school's location in one of the nation's top 10 legal markets certainly doesn't hurt. "Case has a strong reputation," and "Students who do exceptionally well academically do not have much of a problem" getting "an incredibly high-paying job" in any number of major cities across the country. Case Law's reputation "does not extend greatly to the coasts," though. "Finding employment outside of the Midwest region has been a problem for some students," and "It can be very difficult" for less-than-stellar students to find work, particularly outside the surrounding area.

The "aesthetically pleasing" law school facility is situated between an art museum, a botanical garden, and "the beautiful $25 million dollar Geary-designed business school." "The area is beautiful and a pleasure to relax in after the stresses of law school." "The library staff is excellent and always more than happy to help." Recent renovations "have made the library a great place to study," and there are plenty of "private cubicles with comfortable desks and chairs." The main university library is nearby as well and "open 24 hours," which is "a very important plus." "The classrooms are pretty standard," but they are generously outfitted with wireless access and ample power sources for laptops. However, "The wireless Internet often quits working in class, although that is sometimes for the best," admits a 3L. Also, "The building is always freezing cold regardless of the season, but no one seems to know why."

Life

"There is a fair amount of race, gender, and social diversity" at Case Law. The majority of students in each class hail from "states other than Ohio," and many "don't plan to

ALYSON ALBER, INTERIM ASSISTANT DEAN FOR ADMISSIONS
11075 EAST BOULEVARD, CLEVELAND, OH 44106
TEL: 800-756-0036 FAX: 216-368-1042
E-MAIL: LAWADMISSIONS@CASE.EDU • INTERNET: WWW.LAW.CASE.EDU

stay" after graduation. Some students are competitive, but there are "very few overly competitive students." "Everyone is extremely helpful and people in the same class pass around outlines." "Although students at Case are competitive, there is a real sense of community here. Students help each other and don't try to undermine their classmates to get ahead." "There is a feeling of community where we all want to be successful and are proud of being Case Law students, and in that sense we compete together against the rest of the legal world."

Socially, "There is a decent sense of community." "You can make your life as social as you want." Students call the "extremely active" Student Bar Association "the best SBA anywhere." Receptions, speakers, and happy hours are frequent. "Every Thursday, you can go to the bars and see people at school on a social level and it's very laid-back," explains a 1L.

Of their environs, students say "The campus is beautiful," located in walking distance from a beautiful orchestra hall, art museum, botanical garden, and planetarium, and only 15 minutes from the bars, restaurants, and theaters of downtown Cleveland. Much of the rest of the Queen City is "less attractive" but, as one student notes, this feature makes it "a great place to study." "Coming to Case, I was most concerned about living in Cleveland—the 'mistake on the lake'—where even the river caught fire," confides a 3L. "But really, it's not a bad place to spend three years."

Getting In

Admitted students at the 25th percentile have LSAT scores of approximately 157 and GPAs around 3.0. Admitted students at the 75th percentile have LSAT scores of 161 and GPAs in the 3.5 range.

Clinical program required	No
Legal writing course requirement	Yes
Legal methods course requirement	Yes
Legal research course requirement	Yes
Moot court requirement	No
Public interest law requirement	No

ADMISSIONS

Selectivity Rating	**83**
# applications received	2,653
# applicants accepted	756
# acceptees attending	228
Average LSAT	159
LSAT Range	157–161
Average undergrad GPA	3.36
Application fee	$40
Regular application	4/1
Regular notification	Rolling
Rolling notification	Yes
Early application program	Yes
Early application deadline	11/15
Early application notification	12/20
Transfer students accepted	Yes
Evening division offered	No
Part-time accepted	Yes
LSDAS accepted	Yes

International Students

TOEFL required of international students	No
TOEFL recommended of international students	No
Minimum paper TOEFL	
Minimum computer TOEFL	

FINANCIAL FACTS

Annual tuition	$33,300
Books and supplies	$1,900
Tuition per credit	$1,288
Room and board (on/off-campus)	$12,700/$13,100
Financial aid application deadline	5/1
% first-year students receiving some sort of aid	89
% receiving some sort of aid	87
% of aid that is merit based	100
% receiving scholarships	47
Average grant	$10,000
Average loan	$35,200
Average total aid package	$49,000
Average debt	$74,004

EMPLOYMENT INFORMATION

		Grads Employed by Field (%)	
Career Rating	**86**		
Rate of placement (nine months out)	98	Academic	2
Average starting salary	$75,000	Business/Industry	20
State for bar exam	OH, NY, CA, IL, PA	Government	11
Employers Who Frequently Hire Grads		Judicial clerkships	6
Firms of all sizes throughout the country;		Military	1
corporate legal departments; government;		Private practice	51
judiciary; public interest.		Public Interest	9
Prominent Alumni			
Barry M. Meyer, chairman and CEO,			
Warner Bros. Entertainment; Katherine			
Hatton, vice president, general counsel,			
secretary, Robert Wood Johnson			
Foundation.			

THE CATHOLIC UNIVERSITY OF AMERICA
COLUMBUS SCHOOL OF LAW

Academics

"I feel that I'm leaving very prepared for a legal career in just about any field of law," observes a happy 3L at the Catholic University of America's Columbus School of Law. We can see why. Offerings in international law are strong, and moot court is "particularly good." Notable clinical programs, including the Advocacy for the Elderly and the Criminal Prosecution Clinic, allow students to work with real clients. CUA is also home to an array of institutes, including the Institute for Communications Law Studies, which offers more courses in communications law than any other U.S. law school. It also offers an assortment of externships with prestigious law firms, government agencies, and media organizations. The six-week International Business and Trade Summer Law Program allows students to put their studies to work in Cracow, Poland. "For evening students who work full-time, CUA offers an excellent program." Beyond the academic strengths of the program, CUA places "strong emphasis on ethical practices" and Catholic traditions of service, both of which are "imbued in all classes." Nonetheless, a few students even feel that the school "should focus more on showcasing its Catholic heritage." Even still, justice, mercy, morality, faith, and reason—are all here, along with a Center for Law, Philosophy, and Culture and an Interdisciplinary Program in Law and Religion.

Students tell us that the professors at CUA run the gamut. "There are a few professors who are just great. There are also some bad teachers who need to be weeded out." Faculty accessibility also receives mixed reviews. "I definitely think the professors should be more active in the daily life of the students beyond classes," asserts a 3L. "There are a few professors who bend over backward to help students, and others who should be doing more." The best thing about the professors, according to students, is probably their absolute wealth of practical experience. There are "lots of judges on faculty." "With few exceptions, my professors have had extensive practical experience in their fields," notes a 2L. "For students wishing to learn from practitioners, this is paradise."

In terms of its facilities, CUA is "great." The beautiful, state-of-the-art law building is relatively new (it was completed in the mid-1990s), and it is grandly spacious. After spending three years at the tree-lined campus, CUA grads face solid career prospects. More than 90 percent of all newly minted graduates are able to find a full-time lawyer gig within one year of graduation. The average yearly salary for students fresh out of CUA exceeds $70,000—not too shabby, and it's even higher for those who choose to enter private practice. The immense "opportunities for internships" available to students tend to help students network and market themselves within the profession. Given the school's location—just minutes away from the United States Congress, the Supreme Court, numerous federal courts and agencies, and a host of big firms and nonprofits—students really have no excuse not to graduate with some kind of interesting job or internship on their resumes.

SARAH E. REWERTS, DIRECTOR OF ADMISSIONS
CARDINAL STATION, WASHINGTON, DC 20064
TEL: 202-319-5151 FAX: 202-319-6285
E-MAIL: ADMISSIONS@LAW.EDU • INTERNET: WWW.LAW.EDU

Life

"If you want a practical, solid legal education among supportive classmates, come to CUA," advises a 3L. "Supportive" definitely seems to be the watchword at CUA, and the atmosphere among the impressively diverse student population is highly collegial. Entering classes ordinarily have about 300 students. Students report that there is "very little backstabbing [or] competitiveness." One student explains: "We compete hard with each other but in a fair and friendly way." Even among evening students, the relationships are "very tight-knit," with "lots of camaraderie."

When students put their books away, they do not lack choices. CUA boasts a very respectable number of student organizations. Outside the campus's realm, the District of Columbia offers virtually endless social options. The nearby Metro stop makes frequenting any number of venues a quick and easy prospect. Washington is a great restaurant city, with ethnic food of virtually every variety available. The shopping of Union Station is just a few stops away. The Capitol and scores of museums, galleries, theaters, and parks are also nearby. The nightlife of Dupont Circle, Adams Morgan, Chinatown, and Capitol Hill are all easily accessible as well. If you get really bored, you can always take in an oral argument at the Supreme Court.

Getting In

Enrolled students at the 25th percentile at Catholic have an LSAT score of 156 and a GPA of roughly 3.11. Enrolled students at the 75th percentile have an LSAT score of 160 and a GPA of 3.55. Students in the evening division have slightly lower grades and LSAT scores on average, yet all possess relevant professional experience.

Public interest law requirement	No

ADMISSIONS

Selectivity Rating	82
# applications received	2,679
# applicants accepted	876
# acceptees attending	169
Average LSAT	158
LSAT Range	156–160
Average undergrad GPA	3.3
Application fee	$65
Regular application	3/1
Regular notification	Rolling
Rolling notification	Yes
Early application program	Yes
Early application deadline	11/1
Early application notification	12/15
Transfer students accepted	Yes
Evening division offered	Yes
Part-time accepted	Yes
LSDAS accepted	Yes

International Students

TOEFL required of international students	Yes

FINANCIAL FACTS

Annual tuition	$33,230
Books and supplies	$1,500
Tuition per credit	$1,215
Room and board (off-campus)	$14,600
Financial aid application deadline	7/15
% first-year students receiving some sort of aid	87
% receiving some sort of aid	90
% of aid that is merit based	34
% receiving scholarships	31
Average grant	$11,397
Average loan	$39,080
Average total aid package	$43,375
Average debt	$92,000

EMPLOYMENT INFORMATION

Career Rating	71	Grads Employed by Field (%)	
Rate of placement (nine months out)	91	Business/Industry	24
Average starting salary	$64,000	Government	27
State for bar exam	MD, VA, PA, NY, NJ	Judicial clerkships	11
Employers Who Frequently Hire Grads		Other	1
Akin, Gump, Strauss, Hauer, and Feld;		Private practice	34
Clifford Chance; Jones Day; U.S.		Public Interest	3
Department of Justice.			

CHAPMAN UNIVERSITY
SCHOOL OF LAW

INSTITUTIONAL INFORMATION

Public/private	Private
Affiliation	Disciples of Christ
Student-faculty ratio	17:1
% faculty part-time	40
% faculty female	41
% faculty minority	12
Total faculty	64

SURVEY SAYS...

Diverse opinions accepted
in classrooms
Beautiful campus
Students love Orange, CA

STUDENTS

Enrollment of law school	540
% male/female	58/42
% out-of-state	16
% full-time	78
% minority	31
% international	1
# of countries represented	3
Average age of entering class	24

ACADEMICS

Academic Experience Rating	**90**
Profs interesting rating	95
Profs accessible rating	98
Hours of study per day	4.49

Academic Specialties

Advocacy and resolution, domestic
violence, elder law, entertainment
law, environmental law, international
law, property, prosecutional science,
taxation.

Advanced Degrees Offered

JD 3 years, LLM (tax), LLM (prosecutional science).

Combined Degrees Offered

JD/MBA 4 years.

Clinical program required	No
Legal writing	
course requirement	Yes
Legal methods	
course requirement	Yes
Legal research	
course requirement	Yes

Academics

Though Chapman University School of Law "does not yet carry the 'prestige' of the names of some other law schools," "There is a certain youthful exuberance about the place" that instills "a great sense of pride" in its students. Administrators here are "constantly working" "to raise the reputation of the school" and to "help [students] get jobs and have successful careers." They're also "incredibly receptive to student ideas. When we ask for things, they happen," a 1L reports. One example is Chapman's brand-new entertainment law certificate program, which incorporates "courses from [its] prestigious School of Film." Students are even more upbeat regarding Chapman's professors, who boast tremendous real-world experience: "I took civil procedure from a professor that was one of the attorneys in the Exxon Valdez litigation; my constitutional law professor clerked for Justice Thomas and is on a first-name basis with Justice Scalia; my criminal law professor's prior career was defending death-row candidates; and my evidence professor was an Assistant U.S. Attorney for a number of years," a 2L brags. While "Being taught by prestigious and experienced professors would be great on its own," professors here don't rest on their laurels, staying "in touch with their students, encourag[ing] feedback, and [remaining] very accessible for class-related discussions as well as life advice." All "keep open office hours, and even the busiest are keen to make appointments with interested students. It is great to know that some of the most knowledgeable people in the country in various areas of the law are merely a flight of stairs away," a 2L writes. It also doesn't hurt that they "give career advice and provide contacts."

If Chapman students can't get enough of their professors, clinics provide them the opportunity to get hands-on experience in a specific area of the law under the supervision of a faculty member. Many students flock to the tax law clinic; Chapman is "the only school in the area" to offer such a program. Regarding his constitutional jurisprudence clinic, a 2L tells us he is learning "the legal and constitutional implications of current situations (the NSA surveillance program was one of our topics). I also helped to prepare congressional testimony, amicus briefs, and other legal memoranda under the guidance of one of the country's more recognized constitutional scholars. While I don't doubt that there are institutions throughout the country with professors as knowledgeable and experienced . . . I highly doubt that any other school offers students the chance to interact and participate with those top scholars in the actual representation of clients in cases of particular constitutional import. I certainly don't know of many 2L students whose work is cited by the Senate Judiciary Committee!" In the area of academic support, a 1L writes: "All of my professors have been willing to meet with students to review exams and assignments, some even scheduling weeks of extended office hours to accommodate everyone and even holding meetings to conduct review problem sessions." In addition, many "successful upperclassmen run small study groups."

"Everyone takes pride" in the "immaculate" law building, which features a "polished marble" lobby and classrooms designed "with acoustics in mind." In addition, "Each classroom is equipped with a computer for the instructor, a projector, [a] document camera, [a] microphone, and a number of other gadgets. . . . There are power outlets everywhere and wireless Internet access is ubiquitous," though "ubiquitous" may mean "doesn't work in a few key rooms and certain places in the library." Students' biggest complaint remains that "people outside of Orange County have never heard of us, and that can make getting a job difficult." While some here suggest "more marketing" to boost the school's profile, a sanguine 2L asserts that as students here "graduate and disseminate into the legal community, Chapman's name grows," adding, "It is already very

TRACY SIMMONS, ASSISTANT DEAN OF ADMISSIONS AND FINANCIAL AID
ONE UNIVERSITY DRIVE, ORANGE, CA 92866
TEL: 714-628-2500 FAX: 714-628-2501
E-MAIL: LAWADM@CHAPMAN.EDU • INTERNET: WWW.CHAPMAN.EDU/LAW

well-respected within Orange County and is quickly gaining prominence in Los Angeles and San Diego. I feel that it is only a matter of time before Chapman's reputation matches the education it provides."

Life

Chapman students argue that the school's location in Orange—right in the middle of Orange County, California—"can't be beat." "It's 80 degrees in February, and you're only 20 minutes from the beach," a 1L writes. In the midst of the Southern California sun, students report, "Even though we are all enduring law school, everyone is quite pleasant and fun to be around." Students are "concerned about class rankings and job opportunities," but are still "very willing to assist each other with the material." A 2L explains, "Everyone wants to do well, but not at the expense of others. People are willing to share notes, books, space at a table in the library—[it's] a very cooperative environment that allows students to focus on their studies." Though some complain that "after the first year, [students] really still only socialize within their 1L track," most here don't seem to mind. "The environment is a bit high school–ish, but in a fun way," a 2L reports. "Everyone enjoys the daily gossip." "We all hang out on the weekends and after school," a 1L adds. It should be noted that "diversity is well accepted" at Chapman, though a "more diverse student body" is called for.

Getting In

Beginning with the Fall 2008 entering class, Chapman requires that all applicants apply online via the Law School Admission Council's website. As admissions decisions here are not driven by a mathematical index, care should be given to "soft factors," such as letters of recommendation and the personal statement. For the accepted class of 2006, students reported a median undergraduate GPA of 3.19 and a median LSAT of 158.

Moot court requirement	No
Public interest law requirement	No

ADMISSIONS

Selectivity Rating	**80**
# applications received	2,385
# applicants accepted	783
# acceptees attending	210
Average LSAT	158
LSAT Range	156–159
Average undergrad GPA	3.19
Application fee	$65
Regular application	4/15
Regular notification	Rolling
Rolling notification	Yes
Early application program	No
Transfer students accepted	Yes
Evening division offered	No
Part-time accepted	No
LSDAS accepted	Yes

Applicants Also Look At
California Western, Loyola Marymount University, Pepperdine University, Southwestern University School of Law, University of the Pacific, University of San Diego, University of San Francisco.

International Students

TOEFL required of international students	Yes
Minimum paper TOEFL	600
Minimum computer TOEFL	250

FINANCIAL FACTS

Annual tuition	$34,250
Books and supplies	$1,500
Room and board	$13,752
Financial aid application deadline	3/2
% first-year students receiving some sort of aid	94
% receiving some sort of aid	97
% of aid that is merit based	19
% receiving scholarships	43
Average grant	$8,454
Average loan	$35,118
Average total aid package	$39,284
Average debt	$80,665

EMPLOYMENT INFORMATION

		Grads Employed by Field (%)	
Career Rating	**80**	Academic	9.1
Rate of placement (nine months out)	96.5	Business/Industry	21.2
Average starting salary	$72,146	Government	7.3
State for bar exam	CA	Judicial clerkships	1.8
Pass rate for first-time bar	67	Other	4.3
Employers Who Frequently Hire Grads		Private practice	53.9
O'Melveny and Myers; Orange County		Public Interest	2.4
District Attorney; Orange County Public			
Defender; Rutan and Tucker			

Prominent Alumni

Allison LeMoine-Bui, associate, Rutan and Tucker; Bryan Gadol, associate, Greenberg Traurig; Melanie Triebel, associate, Sidley Austin; Steve Ruden, Knobbe Martens; Jason Rednour, Paul Hastings; Michelle Hribar, Rutan and Tucker; Susan Johnson, Allen Matkins; Shadi Hosseinioun, Gordon Rees; Richard Whitlow, Jones Day.

City University of New York

School of Law at Queens College

INSTITUTIONAL INFORMATION

Public/private	Public
Student-faculty ratio	12:1
% faculty part-time	37
% faculty female	59
% faculty minority	42
Total faculty	43

SURVEY SAYS...

Diverse opinions accepted
in classrooms
Great library staff
Liberal students

STUDENTS

Enrollment of law school	427
% male/female	34/66
% out-of-state	24
% full-time	99
% minority	31
% international	4
# of countries represented	57
Average age of entering class	27

ACADEMICS

Academic Experience Rating	**71**
Profs interesting rating	70
Profs accessible rating	84
Hours of study per day	4.51

Academic Specialties

Criminal law, human rights law,
international law, labor law.

Advanced Degrees Offered

JD 3 years.

Clinical program required	Yes
Legal writing course requirement	Yes
Legal methods course requirement	Yes
Legal research course requirement	Yes
Moot court requirement	No
Public interest law requirement	Yes

Academics

City University of New York School of Law is a unique urban law school with a distinctive mission, which is expressed in its motto, "Law in the Service of Human Needs." While CUNY will provide a quality education in all the foundational legal topics, the school's expressed mission is "to teach students to be lawyers who will use their skills to serve the public interest," a goal that permeates every aspect of the classroom, culture, and population at CUNY. A 1L explains, "The entire focus of the school is public interest law and community service. All of the courses are taught with this in mind, and clinical programs serving low-income people in the community are required." All law students are required to participate in free legal clinics that benefit needy New Yorkers; this program not only serves the community but also provides CUNY students with essential real-world experience. "The amount and variety of real situations and people in the legal system I have observed and dealt with helped to shape the theoretical perspective that will guide my practice upon graduation." One student reports, "I've written several briefs, memoranda of law, and complaints in my classes; and I even got the chance to represent clients in administrative hearings as a 2L."

The school's diversity in terms of "both its students and faculty, is beyond exceptional." A 1L writes: "The faculty mirrors [the students'] diversity of ethnicity and experience." Students describe their professors as "brilliant, committed, and on the cutting edge of liberal law." On top of that, "Students, professors, and administrators get to know each other on a first-name basis and have real, one-on-one interaction." United by a common vision, the CUNY community is "a unique environment in which the dedication to students' academic and professional growth is always the priority of faculty and students alike."

"If you are set on making a lot of money and practicing big law with a firm, CUNY is not for you. If you want to become a public interest lawyer because of, and not in spite of, your legal education, this is [the] best law school you could find." While most CUNY students feel right at home on this activist campus, a handful have difficulty living in a "political environment [that] makes John Kerry look like Pat Buchanan." One 3L gripes: "If you're anything but an ultra-progressive liberal, you will not be happy. If you want a job that pays above the poverty line, you will not be popular." In fact, a few feel that the school's mission impedes critical thinking, claiming that "it is hard to have a challenging discussion when everyone thinks alike." For better or for worse, the school's progressive reputation has an influence on the jobs that alumni are likely—and encouraged—to find. Career Services generally places students in low-paying public interest jobs and makes little effort to contact firms.

Students complain that "there are far too many required courses" and that this "makes it virtually impossible to plan a creative or interesting schedule." While CUNY students appreciate the fact that they "are paying a third of the average tuition for a fantastic legal education," they also note that, "due to the low cost of attendance, CUNY doesn't have the same resources as some private institutions." The school's location "in an old junior high across from a cemetery in a place aptly named Flushing could stand to be improved." Students say the campus is hard to reach via public transit systems, there is no campus cafeteria, and there have been sightings of cockroaches and mice. But many take the undesirable facilities in stride, telling us that "CUNY doesn't need frills and thrills to prove itself as a notable law school; it has heart and soul."

Yvonne Cherena-Pacheco, Assistant Dean for Enrollment Management
and Director of Admissions • 65–21 Main Street, Flushing, NY 11367-1358
Tel: 718-340-4210 Fax: 718-340-4435
E-mail: admissions@mail.law.cuny.edu • Internet: www.law.cuny.edu

Life

While united by a common vision of public service, CUNY students are otherwise extremely diverse. "CUNY Law School isn't beautiful, and it isn't housed in prestigious, ivy-covered buildings. It is a school full of very real people, many of whom had very real lives before they came to law school." At CUNY, "Almost two out of three students are female, there is a very large GLBT community, and almost a majority are people of color." One student says, "Most of our students come from nothing, and they fight for those with nothing. We fight with our soul and hearts, and that is what makes us the best lawyers." Students "bond intensely by sharing in an endless flow of deprecating comments about the environment. In this way, [they] show [their] love for one another and [their] zeal for martyrdom in the public interest." This zeal manifests itself in the CUNY experience: "During any given week, there are likely to be several student-sponsored panel discussions, film screenings, special guest speakers providing education, and discussions about important events affecting international human rights or politics."

Most students regard the academic environment as respectful and report that "students, even when they disagree politically (and no matter how hard the debate), still struggle to afford each other respect and consideration." However, occasionally "The passion [students] harbor for some of their ideological issues causes them to lash out against other students with vicious and crude attacks." For the most part, though, the "we're-all-in-this-together" vibe is strong. "Students are all committed to helping one another out. We share ideas, class notes, outlines, and support, rather than [compete] for the best grades." That said, CUNY "is predominantly a commuter school" and, as a result, "lacks a campus life."

Getting In

CUNY evaluates prospective students based on their demonstrated abilities and intellectual capacity to complete a rigorous legal program, using test scores, previous academic records, and, where applicable, post-college work experience. In addition to these factors, CUNY seeks students who can bring diversity of background and experience to the campus and who express a specific interest in and affinity for the values of the program. Finally, CUNY favors New York residents or students with a particular interest in serving the New York community.

EMPLOYMENT INFORMATION

		Grads Employed by Field (%)	
Career Rating	74		
Rate of placement (nine months out)	93	Academic	5
Average starting salary	$51,735	Business/Industry	13
State for bar exam	NY	Government	14
Pass rate for first-time bar	77	Judicial clerkships	16
Employers Who Frequently Hire Grads		Other	1
NYC District Attorney Offices; NYC Legal		Private practice	16
Aid Society; legal services offices; Nassau		Public Interest	25
County Attorney's Office; NJS Superior			
Court; NYC Law Department.			
Prominent Alumni			
Honorable Diccia Pineda-Kirwan, Civil			
Court, Queens County; Robert Bank, COO,			
Gay Men's Health Crisis; Daniel O'Donnell,			
New York State Assemblyman.			

ADMISSIONS

Selectivity Rating	75
# applications received	2,457
# applicants accepted	561
# acceptees attending	144
Average LSAT	153
LSAT Range	150–156
Average undergrad GPA	3.23
Application fee	$50
Regular application	3/15
Regular notification	6/15
Rolling notification	No
Early application program	No
Transfer students accepted	Yes
Evening division offered	No
Part-time accepted	No
LSDAS accepted	Yes

Applicants Also Look At
Brooklyn Law School, Hofstra University, New York Law School, Pace University, St. John's University, Touro University—-California.

International Students

TOEFL required of international students	No
TOEFL recommended of international students	Yes

FINANCIAL FACTS

Annual tuition (resident)	$8,900
Annual tuition (nonresident)	$14,800
Books and supplies	$1,400
Financial aid application deadline	5/1
% first-year students receiving some sort of aid	93
% receiving some sort of aid	88
% of aid that is merit based	41
% receiving scholarships	41
Average grant	$4,305
Average loan	$30,379
Average total aid package	$26,210
Average debt	$61,148

CLEVELAND STATE UNIVERSITY
CLEVELAND-MARSHALL COLLEGE OF LAW

Academics

Students agree that the universally well-regarded law school at Cleveland State University "is the sort of school that lets students know they matter." The "responsive" administration "works very hard to ensure that students make it through school and find jobs afterwards" and does so at roughly half the price of other institutions, offering "great bang for the buck." Though many would like to see Cleveland Marshall's reputation expand outside northeast Ohio, a second-year student testifies, "While I was interviewing for summer positions many interviewers told me that they liked Cleveland-Marshall students because we write well and work hard to prove ourselves."

At Cleveland Marshall, the "very approachable" professors are "understanding of the first-year experience" and "treat you like a colleague rather than an interruption." Students say "one particular professor will go to the lounge after class and allow students to ask in-depth questions they may have, as well as engage in a longer dialogue about legal issues of note." As one 3L claims, "These individuals are the school's most valuable asset." Cleveland-Marshall's "very experienced" faculty has extremely strong ties to the local community, and students claim that their involvement "helps the overall reputation of the school in the local area," adding to the school's cachet during the job hunt (the "huge alumni network" doesn't hurt, either). "If you want to stay in Cleveland after graduation, this is the best choice for a legal education."

Though there's great praise for the new law library and its "wall of windows where you can read and look outside to remember what it was like to have a life before law school," the law building as a whole receives lukewarm reviews, with students describing some of the older classrooms as "unchanged since the 1970s" and "resembling prison cells." "Even in some of the tech classrooms, there aren't enough plugs for everyone's computers," says one student. While most students agree that the library's staff is "particularly helpful with research assignments," there are some gripes about the support staff, which students describe as "overworked, underpaid, and uninterested in helping students."

Complaints about the workload of a first-year law student are nothing new, but the unique setup of the first year curriculum at Cleveland-Marshall seems to lend itself to a particularly "brutal second semester." One student claims that the schedule "essentially 'forces' you to become a night student, or at least take a few classes at night." Some claim that it "takes forever to get through the requirements and bar courses," leaving little time for outside academic interests. Also, "The bar-passage rate, though it went up this year, could be higher." However, the school's Moot Court Program is "exceptional," and its "great writing program" and "emphasis on practical (as opposed to theoretical) approaches to studying the law" are major advantages. One first-year student sums up a common sentiment: "I often feel like I am getting a better education than my friends who are paying twice as much money to study at a neighboring private law school."

CHRISTOPHER LUCAK, ASSISTANT DEAN FOR ADMISSIONS AND FINANCIAL AID
2121 EUCLID AVENUE, LB 138, CLEVELAND, OH 44115-2214
TEL: 866-687-2304 FAX: 216-687-6881
E-MAIL: ADMISSIONS@LAW.CSUOHIO.EDU • INTERNET: WWW.LAW.CSUOHIO.EDU

Life

Cleveland-Marshall's "racially diverse, culturally diverse, and socioeconomically diverse" group of people is "vibrant" and "friendly." Since the school is located in downtown Cleveland, "Parking is a nightmare," and though the law school building isn't winning any architecture awards, construction is underway to make it "more open and attractive," as well as to add a "great new student lounge." Though "local Bar Associations provide excellent resources and young adult socials," students complain that the school empties out on weekends. Cleveland-Marshall's large percentage of non-traditional students—many who come from Cleveland and its surrounding areas—help contribute to the ghost town effect.

Other students feel that "the part-time . . . and full-time students have a separate community" on campus. One student could not agree more: "Part-timers are not treated the same as full-time day students. I switched to day this year, and the difference is obvious. Faculty, administration, and Career Services absolutely cater to the younger full-timers." Differences aside, many students are pleased to find a lack of the competitiveness inherent among so many law schools; "Most students know one another" and "support each other." As one first-year student puts it, "Sometimes things are like high school, but ultimately that is not a bad thing, unless you make it such. We have lockers, you wait for girls to go to the bathroom before lunch, and there can be rumors, but take it all in stride, know your goals, and you should be fine."

Getting In

Getting into Cleveland-Marshall, while far from being a given, is slightly easier than average. While there are no cutoff numbers, last year's admitted students at the 25th percentile had an LSAT score of 151 and an average GPA of 3.0, while admitted students at the 75th percentile had an LSAT score of 157 and a GPA of 3.6. The school also stresses the importance of personal statements in the admissions process.

Moot court requirement	No
Public interest law requirement	No

ADMISSIONS

Selectivity Rating	**76**
# applications received	1,755
# applicants accepted	541
# acceptees attending	236
Average LSAT	154
LSAT Range	151–157
Average undergrad GPA	3.29
Application fee	$40
Regular application	5/7
Regular notification	5/7
Rolling notification	Yes
Early application program	No
Transfer students accepted	Yes
Evening division offered	Yes
Part-time accepted	Yes
LSDAS accepted	Yes

Applicants Also Look At
Capital University, Case Western Reserve University, Ohio Northern University, The Ohio State University, The University of Akron, University of Dayton, University of Toledo.

International Students
TOEFL required of international students	Yes

FINANCIAL FACTS

Annual tuition (resident)	$16,477
Annual tuition (nonresident)	$19,208
Books and supplies	$1,300
Fees per credit (resident)	$25
Fees per credit (nonresident)	$25
Tuition per credit (resident)	$538
Tuition per credit (nonresident)	$739
Room and board	$10,630
Financial aid application deadline	5/6
% first-year students receiving some sort of aid	90
% receiving some sort of aid	95
% of aid that is merit based	90
% receiving scholarships	37
Average grant	$6,457
Average loan	$24,070
Average total aid package	$24,906
Average debt	$59,458

EMPLOYMENT INFORMATION

Career Rating	**72**	**Grads Employed by Field (%)**	
Rate of placement (nine months out)	92	Academic	3
Average starting salary	$67,584	Business/Industry	21
State for bar exam	OH, NY, MD, MA, FL	Government	16
Employers Who Frequently Hire Grads		Judicial clerkships	2
Jones Day; Thompson, Hine; Squire,		Military	1
Sanders, and Dempsey; Calfee, Halter, and		Private practice	53
Griswold; Arter and Hadden; Ernst &		Public Interest	4
Young.			

Prominent Alumni
Tim Russert, senior vice president, NBC News; Honorable Louis Stokes, U.S. House of Representatives, retired; Justice Maureen O'Connor, Supreme Court of Ohio.

THE COLLEGE OF WILLIAM & MARY
MARSHALL-WYTHE LAW SCHOOL

INSTITUTIONAL INFORMATION

Public/private	Public
Student-faculty ratio	16:1
% faculty part-time	68
% faculty female	29
% faculty minority	6
Total faculty	102

SURVEY SAYS...

Diverse opinions accepted
in classrooms
Great library staff
Abundant externship/internship/
clerkship opportunities

STUDENTS

Enrollment of law school	611
% male/female	53/47
% out-of-state	54
% full-time	100
% minority	18
% international	1
# of countries represented	9
Average age of entering class	24

ACADEMICS

Academic Experience Rating	**90**
Profs interesting rating	90
Profs accessible rating	89
Hours of study per day	4.4

Academic Specialties

Civil procedure, commercial law, constitutional law, corporation securities law, criminal law, environmental law, human rights law, intellectual property law, international law, labor law, legal history, property, taxation.

Advanced Degrees Offered

JD 3 years, LLM (American legal system) 1 year.

Combined Degrees Offered

JD/Master (public policy) 4 years, JD/MBA 4 years, JD/MA (American studies) 4 years.

Clinical program required	No
Legal writing course requirement	Yes
Legal methods course requirement	Yes

Academics

Professors at the The College of William & Mary's Marshall-Wythe School of Law are "breathtakingly prepared, experienced, and—most importantly—focused on teaching." They want students "to learn the material and how to effectively express ideas, without having to feel stupid." "Class discussions range from the slightly dull to the side-splittingly funny," and the faculty "does an excellent job of emphasizing both ethics and the greater role that lawyers play in society." "The school's greatest strength is its dedication to graduating not merely lawyers, but citizen-lawyers," relates a 3L, "Attorneys who are not only competent but also of the highest ethical and moral character." "Most professors know every single student by first name," and "They are always willing to meet with students, offer letters of recommendation, or give advice." W&M's administration is "very helpful and organized" as well. Deans are "approachable" and "extremely accessible." "First-year students have a social with the dean before classes even begin," explains a 1L. "Everyone learns your name and greets you in the halls. I've never experienced anything else quite like it."

The "outstanding" Office of Career Services "has helped many students to get summer jobs [that] often lead to permanent employment." "W&M is the type of school that'll allow you to find the job you want, where you want, if you're willing to work for it." Washington, DC and New York City "are the most popular markets," but the staff "works really hard to help you to find jobs wherever you want to go." "Upon graduating from William & Mary, I'll be working in my dream job in Texas, an opportunity I would not have had at a more regional school," enthuses one satisfied customer.

There is "a lot of practical training in written and oral advocacy" here. The unique and time-consuming legal skills program combines legal research, writing, and ethics into a "valuable" two-year program. Groups of about 25 students are organized into mock law firms, which take mock clients through all stages of a trial—from initial contact to appeals. Over 50 percent of the students here receive (often substantial) scholarships or fellowships. About the only complaint we hear concerns the limited clinical program, which "needs to expand and improve."

"William & Mary has recently witnessed a facilities renaissance, with renovated classrooms, an expanded new library, and a more attractive lobby, main hallway, and front entranceway." Nevertheless, "The law school building is certainly not elaborate or first-class." There is "hardly any parking," and "There isn't a whole lot within a short distance, so if you're used to being 15 minutes from a city, it might not be the place for you." Despite these shortcomings, students here are overwhelmingly satisfied. "I believe that William & Mary is truly the most unique of law schools," attests a 1L. "Any school can profess to have a collegial student body, to have accessible professors, and to provide the most enriching legal education. William & Mary has delivered on each and every one of its promises, and has exceeded my expectations for what the law school experience could offer."

Life

While the student body is predominantly White, "There is a large group of minority students" at William & Mary. The "extremely intelligent and hardworking" students here "really are friendly and don't take themselves too seriously." "Most every student who decides to attend William & Mary Law School raves about the friendly and supportive atmosphere." They also applaud the Honor Code. "We take an oath to not lie,

FAYE SHEALY, ASSOCIATE DEAN
OFFICE OF ADMISSION, PO BOX 8795, WILLIAMSBURG, VA 23187-8795
TEL: 757-221-3785 FAX: 757-221-3261
E-MAIL: LAWADM@WM.EDU • INTERNET: WWW.WM.EDU/LAW

cheat, or steal," explains a 3L, "and students really do abide by it. I can leave my laptop, books, purse—everything—in the lobby, the lounge, or the library, and go to lunch. I know, without doubt, that it will all be there when I return."

W&M is "fairly small," "so students get to know each other very well." "There are social cliques, for sure," says a 2L. "But every person gets a chance to make friends." "Like most law schools, William & Mary can be a bit like high school at times, with the gossip mill running full tilt." With few bars in town," social outlets are somewhat limited, catalyzing drama." "The social life is surprisingly booming," though. "Fun is there if you wish to have it."

"William & Mary is located in one of the most historical and beautiful areas of United States: Colonial Williamsburg." "If you love history, you couldn't get any better." "It's a great source of pride to be able to say George Wythe, Thomas Jefferson, and John Marshall taught, walked, or slept here," relates one student. Other students observe that "Williamsburg is a great town in which to go to graduate school "because there are "no distractions." This might be an exaggeration, as Busch Gardens is nearby, "as well as plenty of nice parks, recreation centers, and shopping." There are "a lot of outdoorsy things to do" as well.

Getting In

Admitted students at the 25th percentile have LSAT scores of 162 and GPAs around 3.3. Admitted students at the 75th percentile have LSAT scores of 166 and GPAs just above 3.8. If you take the LSAT more than once, W&M "will evaluate the LSAT portion of the application by looking to the highest reported score."

Legal research course requirement	Yes
Moot court requirement	No
Public interest law requirement	No

ADMISSIONS

Selectivity Rating	89
# applications received	4,209
# applicants accepted	1,014
# acceptees attending	204
Average LSAT	163
LSAT Range	162–166
Average undergrad GPA	3.56
Application fee	$50
Regular application	3/1
Regular notification	3/30
Rolling notification	No
Early application program	No
Transfer students accepted	Yes
Evening division offered	No
Part-time accepted	No
LSDAS accepted	Yes

Applicants Also Look At
American University, George Mason University, Georgetown University, The George Washington University, University of Virginia, Washington and Lee University.

International Students

TOEFL required of international students	No
TOEFL recommended of international students	No
Minimum paper TOEFL	600
Minimum computer TOEFL	250

FINANCIAL FACTS

Annual tuition (resident)	$12,745
Annual tuition (nonresident)	$22,811
Books and supplies	$1,250
Room and board	$6,300
Financial aid application deadline	2/15
% first-year students receiving some sort of aid	91
% receiving some sort of aid	90
% of aid that is merit based	75
% receiving scholarships	23
Average grant	$4,772
Average loan	$24,101
Average total aid package	$26,990
Average debt	$67,338

EMPLOYMENT INFORMATION

Career Rating	88
Rate of placement (nine months out)	98
Average starting salary	$88,461
State for bar exam	VA, CA, NJ, NY, PA
Pass rate for first-time bar	92

Grads Employed by Field (%)

Academic	1
Business/Industry	11
Government	12
Judicial clerkships	16
Military	3
Private practice	53
Public Interest	4

COLUMBIA UNIVERSITY
SCHOOL OF LAW

INSTITUTIONAL INFORMATION

Public/private	Private
Student-faculty ratio	11:1
% faculty part-time	41
% faculty female	31
% faculty minority	11.6
Total faculty	198

SURVEY SAYS...

Diverse opinions accepted
in classrooms
Great research resources
Students love New York, NY

STUDENTS

Enrollment of law school	1,229
% male/female	55/45
% full-time	100
% minority	30
% international	7
# of countries represented	44
Average age of entering class	24

ACADEMICS

Academic Experience Rating	**90**
Profs interesting rating	83
Profs accessible rating	71
Hours of study per day	4.13

Academic Specialties

Civil procedure, commercial law, constitutional law, corporation securities law, criminal law, environmental law, government services, human rights law, intellectual property law, international law, labor law, legal history, legal philosophy, property, taxation.

Advanced Degrees Offered

LLM 1 year, JSD.

Combined Degrees Offered

JD/PhD 7 years, JD/MA 4 years, JD/MBA 3 to 4 years, JD/MFA (arts administration) 4 years; JD/MS (urban planning), JD/MS (social work) 4 years, JD/MS (journalism) 3.5 years, JD/MIA (international affairs) 4 years; JD/MPA (public administration) 4 years, JD/MPA (public affairs with Woodrow Wilson School at Princeton) 4 years, JD/MPH (public health) 4 years.

Academics

There is a "focus on international law," "a moot court requirement for 1Ls," and "a nice blend of theory and practice" at Columbia Law School, "although the school tilts [more] towards the theory." "The theoretical focus of the faculty is a good thing," explains one student. "We'll have plenty of time to learn practical job skills, but this is the only time many of us will have the leisure to study theoretical issues in the law." The recently revamped legal writing curriculum is "more than sufficient," and "No law school in America has access to more prestigious practitioners." "Leading lawyers teach practical courses, and clinics get access to all types of activities," applauds one 3L. "Couple that with a top-notch reputation, and you have the best law school in the world."

The "eclectic" faculty at Columbia is "an incredible array of superstars," and otherwise "really talented, motivated, interested, and interesting people." There are "a lot of young, dynamic, and engaging professors," and most "seem to consider their students their primary concern." "Even those who are fiercely Socratic and would grill students in class are quite friendly outside of it." Professors are "respectful of differing political views." There is a "willingness to openly discuss" gender and race issues in class "in a way that is non-prejudicial but still acknowledges and values differences."

The "ineffective" and "very bureaucratic" administration at CLS is "positively frustrating." "They treat you like a walking dollar sign and nothing more," charges one annoyed student. "Signing up for classes is too hard." "Student Services has cultivated an amazing air of indifference and sometimes disdain for students." "The only way I got the Housing Office to tell me I had an apartment the day before moving was to sic a law school dean on them," claims a student.

Career prospects are dreamy. "A Columbia degree opens countless doors." "The 'big law' opportunities couldn't be better." "If you come here, you will get a job," agrees a confident 1L, "no matter how well or poorly you do." "Law firms around the country are banging down my door and begging me to work at their firm for six-figure salaries," says another student. "It's unbelievable how mediocre you can be at Columbia and yet have any law firm job in the country." There is "a stellar Public Interest Office" as well, and "small pockets of students" are "extraordinarily dedicated to public interest and other alternative legal careers."

The "overly modern" law school facilities are "highly functional," but "ugly, especially in comparison to the undergrad campus." On the outside, the building is "a postmodern mistake." Inside, the "elegant, sleek" classrooms are "equipped with the latest technology." The "soulless and depressing" library is "not very comfortable." "The research librarians are gods," though, and students "have access to resources most people don't even know exist."

Life

"It turns out that (almost) everybody here gets a B or B-plus." "Even a B reflects a lot of hard work." "Everyone is competitive," but at the same time, "People are happy to share notes." "Although there is a small public interest community, it is dwarfed by the majority of students who want nothing more than high-paying big-firm jobs." "Most people are only passing through on their way to a six- or seven-figure salary."

Some of these "future corporate lawyers" are "spoiled rich brats" who "do nothing but party." Others are "awkward and dull" types who "only see the outside of the library when they close it for breaks." But, "for the number of inflated egos, advanced degrees, and native New Yorkers in the law school, it is a remarkably collegial place," observes a 1L. "There is a lot of camaraderie" but the location in New York City makes it "much harder to build a community of people." "Students who are involved, engaged, and active tend to be very involved, very engaged, and very active (and thus, very stressed out), while the majority of students mostly do class work and keep their eyes on their future employment." "It is also extremely easy to become socially isolated if you are from a working-class family and attended a public university for undergrad."

Hometown New York City "is a huge asset." "You have to like urban environments," advises a 2L, "but if you are a city person, the location can't be beat. It is a great combination of a traditional campus and a big-city school." There is "substantial subsidization of housing" (once you wade through the red tape of the Housing Office), for which students are grateful. "You cannot find cheaper space in all of Manhattan." The number of events, debates, speeches, receptions and other social opportunities is "mind-boggling." "Naturally everyone's out in the city a lot."

Getting In

Good luck. Admitted students at the 25th percentile have LSAT scores of 169 and GPAs of just over 3.5. Admitted students at the 75th percentile have LSAT scores of 174 and GPAs of around 3.8. If you take the LSAT more than once, Columbia will consider all of your scores.

Clinical program required	No
Legal writing course requirement	Yes
Legal methods course requirement	Yes
Legal research course requirement	Yes
Moot court requirement	Yes
Public interest law requirement	Yes

ADMISSIONS

Selectivity Rating	**98**
# applications received	8,020
# applicants accepted	1,169
# acceptees attending	378
Average LSAT	170
LSAT Range	168–173
Average undergrad GPA	3.64
Application fee	$70
Regular application	2/15
Regular notification	Rolling
Rolling notification	Yes
Early application program	Yes
Early application deadline	11/15
Early application notification	1/1
Transfer students accepted	Yes
Evening division offered	No
Part-time accepted	No
LSDAS accepted	Yes

Applicants Also Look At
Harvard University, New York University, Stanford University, Yale University.

International Students

TOEFL required of international students	No
TOEFL recommended of international students	No

FINANCIAL FACTS

Annual tuition	$38,120
Books and supplies	$950
Fees per credit	$1,906
Room and board (on-campus)	$16,951
Financial aid application deadline	3/1
% first-year students receiving some sort of aid	79
% receiving some sort of aid	84
% of aid that is merit based	35
% receiving scholarships	38
Average grant	$15,069
Average loan	$37,730
Average total aid package	$37,070
Average debt	$98,675

EMPLOYMENT INFORMATION

Career Rating	**93**	**Grads Employed by Field (%)**	
Rate of placement (nine months out)	99	Academic	1
Average starting salary	$145,000	Business/Industry	3
State for bar exam	NY, NJ, CA, FL	Government	2
Pass rate for first-time bar	90	Judicial clerkships	9
Employers Who Frequently Hire Grads		Private practice	80
Large international corporate law firms,		Public Interest	6

Employers Who Frequently Hire Grads
Large international corporate law firms, federal judges, federal government agencies, and public interest organizations.

Prominent Alumni
Justice Ruth Bader Ginsburg, U.S. Supreme Court; George Pataki, Governor of New York State; Franklin D. Roosevelt, former president; Paul Robeson, performing artist/civil rights activist.

CORNELL UNIVERSITY
LAW SCHOOL

Academics

Cornell University is a small school with a big name. Thanks to this favorable combination, Cornell students enjoy a world-class education in the context of a personal, student-oriented environment. Across the board, "The professors at Cornell are top scholars in their respective fields" whose "prodigious academic accomplishments" are a significant asset to the classroom experience. What's more, most professors "are witty and make the classes worth getting up early for." Despite their impressive names and backgrounds, Cornell professors invest a lot of time and energy into their roles as teachers and mentors. A 2L insists, "The faculty is focused on teaching, not only publishing, and are clearly the greatest asset at Cornell Law School."

While Cornell boasts the high level of scholarship one would expect to find at a top school, "The close relationship between faculty and students is what sets Cornell apart from its peers." There are few lecture halls at Cornell, and "Small class sizes allow professors to really get to know students." Outside of class, professors are available for academic assistance, mentorship, and advice. "It is an honor to have classes and discussions with my professors. I have never had anyone here meet my questions without enthusiasm or support," gushes one student. Don't mistake kindness for laxness. Cornell is tough, and students caution that "professors drive us hard." In fact, students are constantly scrambling to keep up with the demands of their educations. A 2L recalls that "Last year, I definitely spent more than nine hours a day studying outside of class."

It is unanimously agreed that "Cornell's strength is in its size," but there's a flip side to that coin, for students point out that Cornell's course offerings are narrower than they would likely be if the school were larger. In addition, since "The faculty is too small, we end up with way too many visiting professors." Still, for many students "small seminars with current topics make up for an otherwise small range of classes." In addition, Cornell provides a number of first-rate programs and opportunities within the law school and the greater university. In particular, many students mention the school's excellent international law program: "If you're interested in international law with a European focus, this is the place to be," advises one student. "The school is also adding to its international program by offering new classes in Asian law (e.g., Japanese law)." On top of that, Cornell students say they really benefit from their affiliation with the greater university. For example, "Cornell has a wide range of non–law school classes" for which law students are able to sign up. "A small community within a large university means that professors and students aren't stretched too thin, but we have ample opportunity for a broad curriculum if we try hard enough," is how one student puts it.

When it comes to the administration, students report that "Cornell is run like a well-oiled machine . . . everything is done quickly and efficiently." Another major benefit to a Cornell education is that the school enjoys "name recognition in NYC," and as a result, "Across the board, Cornell graduates seem to get the very best jobs." Students say that "Cornell's career office is amazing—knowledgeable, accessible, and well connected. I have absolutely no complaints. I just got my dream job for the summer—and most of my classmates will say the same thing." Some students would, however, like to see more connections in public interest firms, as well as outside of New York.

SARAH LEVY, ASSISTANT DIRECTOR OF ADMISSIONS
226 MYEARSON TAYLOR HALL, ITHACA, NY 14853-4901
TEL: 607-255-5141 FAX: 607-255-7193
E-MAIL: LAWADMIT@LAW.CORNELL.EDU • INTERNET: WWW.LAWSCHOOL.CORNELL.EDU

Life

Cornell attracts ambitious, interesting, and accomplished students who "come from all walks of life and experience." For at least one student, "My classmates are the most uniformly intelligent and ambitious group of which I've ever been a member." Despite their personal accomplishments and drive, "Students are cooperative. Everyone feels they are in this together and there is no point in trying to knock one another down."

The campus vibe is friendly and social, and "The very active student organizations provide numerous non-academic opportunities." That's good, since "Students here are uniformly amiable and like spending time together" even to the exclusion of other members of the Cornell community; "The majority of law students socialize only with other law students," reports one student.

Consider yourself warned: "People are warm; weather is cold" in Ithaca, NY. Indeed, if there is one resounding complaint among Cornell students, it is that "Ithaca is an isolated college town." Students joke that the best way to improve the atmosphere at Cornell would be to "put the whole school in a bio-dome and turn up the heat and sunshine." However, one student aptly adds, "Everyone knew that before they came here. [There is] not much night life to speak of, but that's not what I am here for." Students make the best of the situation, however, informing us that "Cornell is beautiful [and] it's a great place to study for the lack of distraction."

Getting In

Admissions to Cornell is highly competitive. The Admissions Committee weighs all aspects of an applicant's background, including extracurricular and community activities, graduate work, LSAT scores, letters of recommendation, and undergraduate transcripts. Applicants are also encouraged to submit a separate document that details how their ethnic, cultural, or linguistic background will contribute to the diversity of the school community.

Public interest law requirement	No

ADMISSIONS

Selectivity Rating	**93**
# applications received	4,177
# acceptees attending	193
Average LSAT	167
LSAT Range	165–168
Average undergrad GPA	3.7
Application fee	$70
Regular application	2/1
Regular notification	Rolling
Rolling notification	Yes
Early application program	No
Transfer students accepted	Yes
Evening division offered	No
Part-time accepted	No
LSDAS accepted	Yes

International Students

TOEFL required of international students	No
TOEFL recommended of international students	No

FINANCIAL FACTS

Annual tuition	$40,580
Books and supplies	$850
Room and board	$10,300
Financial aid application deadline	3/15
% receiving some sort of aid	80
% receiving scholarships	50

EMPLOYMENT INFORMATION

Career Rating	90	Grads Employed by Field (%)	
Rate of placement (nine months out)	99	Academic	4
Average starting salary	$125,000	Business/Industry	3
State for bar exam	NY	Government	2
Pass rate for first-time bar	94	Judicial clerkships	9
		Other	1
		Private practice	72
		Public Interest	2

CREIGHTON UNIVERSITY
SCHOOL OF LAW

Academics

Small Creighton University School of Law boasts a "solid reputation" "in the Midwest" and a "strong" alumni network. Students note that "the practical experience that you receive at Creighton is beyond comparison." "The practical aspects of the legal profession are stressed in every class" so that Creighton's graduates "can be effective in the legal world from the start." "A variety of trial practice courses" is available. Nebraska's Supreme Court "holds a session at the law school" each year for students to observe. Justice Clarence Thomas has co-taught a "truly remarkable" Supreme Court Seminar here. There is "a required moot court competition in the second year," and many students "participate in traveling moot court and trial teams." "Look at the results for any of the trial competitions in the nation, and you will find Creighton University near the top," guarantees a 3L. "Creighton is the place for you" if you are "interested in becoming a trial lawyer." Creighton also offers "a broad range of classes" (though it "could offer a broader selection of class times"). Some students confide that the legal writing program "isn't the greatest."

Expect "a great deal of hard work." "The teachers are hard; the reading is difficult," says one student. But take heart in the "wonderful and insightful" faculty. The vast majority of professors are "outstanding," "incredibly dedicated," and "capable teachers" who are "well-versed in all of their subjects." They "display a true passion for the subjects they teach, and that passion seems infectious." "Creighton professors really care that students learn the law and understand how to apply it." Here, the "very accessible" faculty "know you by name." "Professors are involved in the student organizations and often attend the student activities." "'Faculty row'" provides an all-access pass to law students. "The school's open-door policy really is an open-door policy," adds a student. "Your tuition dollars definitely buy you the right to extract knowledge from the professors."

The "very genuine and welcoming" administrators are "exceptionally devoted to catering to their students' needs." "They really care about the students as individuals" and "You're treated like a person, not just a number." Career Services is more of a mixed bag. Some students tell us that "opportunities for Creighton grads upon graduation seem excellent." "Everyone I know is employed," says one student. "Some have judicial clerkships; some are working for large corporations; and many are working for large firms." Other students complain that Career Services "is very unhelpful" and say that there is "almost no recognition outside of Omaha, especially out west."

Most students agree that the facilities "need to be updated." The building "was built in the 1970s and could use a makeover," says one student. "Some of the classrooms have been updated but the rest of them badly need renovating." The "somewhat drab" and "windowless" "main teaching halls" are "out of date." Also, "Some of the classrooms only have a few electrical outlets, which makes using a laptop difficult." On the plus side, "very reliable" wireless Internet "is available throughout the law school." Also, the "new and beautiful" library is "phenomenal."

ANDREA D. BASHARA, ASSISTANT DEAN
2500 CALIFORNIA PLAZA, OMAHA, NE 68178
TEL: 402-280-2872 FAX: 402-280-3161
E-MAIL: LAWADMIT@CREIGHTON.EDU • INTERNET: LAW.CREIGHTON.EDU

Life

Let's face it: Nebraska is "a very homogeneous state." Ethnic diversity is largely "non-existent" at Creighton. Students say the population is "mostly upper-middle-class White students." Geographically, many states are represented, though "Most students are from the Midwest—Nebraska and Iowa mostly." Students "range from ultra-competitive and pretentious all the way down to careless and unkempt." Politics aren't much of a big deal here. "The students are a lot less politically active than I anticipated," professes a 2L.

"Small class sizes help you have more individual contact with your teachers," explains one student. Thanks to this, "You get to really know all of your classmates" as well. Life at Creighton is "competitive," but "It's a very positive environment." "The students want to do well but not at the expense of others," says one student. Most happily report that "students are generally cooperative and easy to get along with." "Most people here are extremely friendly" as "that good old Midwestern hospitality" pervades, meaning that "everyone really gets along quite well." However, some note that social life can tend to have "many cliques," making it a bit "like going back to high school again."

Creighton students are a hardworking crowd, but "opportunities to be involved" socially are ample. "There is always something going on" and "almost everyone is always busy." "There are several student groups to get involved in" and "multiple out-of-school functions, which large portions of the student body attend." The Student Bar Association holds a solid number of "drink fests." Creighton's "gorgeous urban campus" in "downtown Omaha" provides "a pleasant metropolitan setting." "Creighton is not located in the best part of Omaha" and students note that "you have to be careful . . . off campus." However, students are confident that this will be a thing of the past as "the school and city are making great efforts to improve the area."

Getting In

Creighton's admitted students at the 25th percentile have LSAT scores of 153 and GPAs of 3.15. Admitted students at the 75th percentile have LSAT scores of 157 and GPAs of 3.67.

EMPLOYMENT INFORMATION

Career Rating	76	Grads Employed by Field (%)	
Rate of placement (nine months out)	97	Academic	2
Average starting salary	$57,125	Business/Industry	23
State for bar exam	NE, IA, MO, AZ, IL	Government	11
Pass rate for first-time bar	86	Judicial clerkships	7
Employers Who Frequently Hire Grads		Military	2
Kutak Rock; Stinson, Morrison, and		Private practice	52
Hecker; Blackwell, Sanders, Peper, Martin;		Public Interest	3
Shughart, Thompson, Kilroy; McGrath			
North; Fraser Stryker; Baird Holm; Koley			
Jessen.			
Prominent Alumni			
Michael O. Johanns, United States			
Secretary of Agriculture; Brig. Gen. David			
G. Ehrhart, Assistant Judge Advocate			
General for Military Law.			

Public interest	
law requirement	No

ADMISSIONS

Selectivity Rating	**74**
# applications received	1,277
# applicants accepted	513
# acceptees attending	155
Average LSAT	155
LSAT Range	153–157
Average undergrad GPA	3.4
Application fee	$45
Regular application	5/1
Regular notification	Rolling
Rolling notification	Yes
Early application program	No
Transfer students accepted	Yes
Evening division offered	No
Part-time accepted	Yes
LSDAS accepted	Yes

Applicants Also Look At
Drake University, University of
Denver, University of Nebraska—
Lincoln.

International Students

TOEFL required	
of international students	No
TOEFL recommended	
of international students	Yes

FINANCIAL FACTS

Annual tuition	$23,848
Books and supplies	$1,370
Fees per credit	$11
Tuition per credit	$795
Room and board	$13,500
Financial aid application	
deadline	7/1
% first-year students	
receiving some sort of aid	89
% receiving some sort of aid	92
% of aid that is merit based	13
% receiving scholarships	42
Average grant	$9,300
Average loan	$23,630
Average total aid package	$25,211
Average debt	$83,492

DePaul University
College of Law

INSTITUTIONAL INFORMATION

Public/private	Private
Affiliation	Roman Catholic
Student-faculty ratio	16:1
% faculty part-time	50
% faculty female	37
% faculty minority	7
Total faculty	111

SURVEY SAYS...
Diverse opinions accepted
in classrooms
Students love Chicago, IL

STUDENTS

Enrollment of law school	1,070
% male/female	51/49
% out-of-state	54
% full-time	68
% minority	17
# of countries represented	8
Average age of entering class	24

ACADEMICS

Academic Experience Rating	**87**
Profs interesting rating	87
Profs accessible rating	83
Hours of study per day	5.04

Academic Specialties
Commercial law, corporation securities law, criminal law, human rights law, intellectual property law, international law, labor law, taxation, family law, health law, information technology law, litigation and practice, public interest law.

Advanced Degrees Offered
LLM (health law) 1 to 3 years, LLM (taxation) 1 to 3 years, LLM (intellectual property law) 1 to 3 years.

Combined Degrees Offered
JD/MBA 3 to 4 years, JD/MS (public service management) 4 years, JD/MA (international studies) 4 years, JD/MA (computer science) 4 years, JD/MS (computer science) 4 years.

Academics

The School of Law at DePaul University is home to a slew of highly respected professors and satisfied students. "Every time I tell someone I go to DePaul they perk up," says one student. With six or more law schools located in the Chicago area, "There is a lot of concern among the students regarding summer employment positions and finding permanent positions upon completion of school" (though the same could be said of law school students in many big cities), and therefore many are thrilled with the "alumni connections" provided by the school. One student explains, "DePaul has a great reputation for being a law family. With all the time I spend at the law school, they really are!"

DePaul's "amazing" faculty "truly represent a global viewpoint," and many are "distinguished practitioners within the Chicago legal community." "Most of the professors love their job, and it shows," explains one student, and this is evidenced by their accessibility outside of the classroom. A large number of students speak highly of the vastly differing instruction methods used by DePaul teachers, and cite these "very different teaching styles and personalities" as a unique academic resource, though the rule of thumb that "you'll always have one you don't like" seems to ring true here. Even with such a diverse range of techniques, one thing is always clear: DePaul's "inspiring" professors are "dedicated to making sure the students grasp the relevant concepts and material." As one 1L puts it, "No one is out to embarrass us, though that doesn't mean we aren't challenged!"

The administration also receives widespread praise for being "extremely helpful and always available" and "taking the time out to make sure that students' concerns are answered," as well as keeping students up to date on "all academic support program activities at the school and at other local schools." Many students also mentioned the "very hands-on" Admissions Office, which even employs student help "to give a unique perspective to potential and incoming students." Student input is valued very highly in other areas of DePaul life; the "wonderful professor review" at the end of each semester is taken very seriously, and helps keep the faculty at the top of their game.

Since the facilities "are subject to the limitations of a high-rise in downtown Chicago," the law school building "can be a little bit cramped at times," and the "terrible" classrooms are "not spacious" and "can be depressing to be in." "It's a confusing building. After four months, I still can't find certain places," says one exasperated 1L. Many complaints are also directed at the Career Services Office and the "frustrating" legal writing program, which needs "more exact instruction" and offers "little-to-zero appropriate feedback" from which "students are able to learn from their mistakes." It's a tough legal environment, to be sure, but one 3L seems to sum up the sentiments of his peers when he says: "If I did it over again, I wouldn't change anything."

Life

Students speak fondly of each other and claim not to have noticed any undue competitive streak amongst their classmates. "You won't find anyone hiding books in the library so only they have access to it," says one. Though there is "a helpful, polite competitiveness" amongst the student body, it's "more of a fun competition between classmates." People "freely share outlines with one another," "post jokes, helpful study aids they have found, etc. on the section blackboard," and "It is noticeable that everyone cares about each other and has a genuine desire to support and encourage each other." Students find it easy to make friends; one first-year student "likes to think it is because . . . DePaul

MICHAEL S. BURNS, ASSOCIATE DEAN AND DIRECTOR OF ADMISSION
25 EAST JACKSON BOULEVARD, CHICAGO, IL 60604
TEL: 312-362-6831 FAX: 312-362-5280
E-MAIL: LAWINFO@DEPAUL.EDU • INTERNET: WWW.LAW.DEPAUL.EDU

attracts a certain type of student." "The school is committed to diversity and maintains its goal," making for a solid group of people committed to their studies and to helping each other do well.

"As an urban school, there's not a lot of hanging out after class, though most of us do end up at local bars at some point or other throughout the week," says a 1L. The school itself is located "close to both federal and county courthouses" as well as "a variety of social activities such as the art institute and millennium park." As one student declares, "Everything is here . . . [and there is] lots of opportunity to do stuff while going to school." The school's unbeatable location combined with students' contentment with the academics creates a "colloquial atmosphere," and "Everyone in a section becomes almost like a family." Luckily there are "only a few who think that they are god's gift to lawyering."

Getting In

Students admitted for the class of 2010 at the 25th percentile had an LSAT score of 157 and an average GPA of 3.0, while admitted students at the 75th percentile had an LSAT score of 161 and a GPA of 3.6. Like many schools, DePaul offers rolling admissions, but first-year students may only be admitted for the fall semester.

Clinical program required	No
Legal writing course requirement	Yes
Legal methods course requirement	No
Legal research course requirement	Yes
Moot court requirement	No
Public interest law requirement	No

ADMISSIONS

Selectivity Rating	**83**
# applications received	4,941
# applicants accepted	1,644
# acceptees attending	335
Average LSAT	160
LSAT Range	157–161
Average undergrad GPA	3.34
Application fee	$60
Regular application	3/1
Regular notification	Rolling
Rolling notification	Yes
Early application program	No
Transfer students accepted	Yes
Evening division offered	Yes
Part-time accepted	Yes
LSDAS accepted	Yes

Applicants Also Look At
Illinois Institute of Technology,
Loyola University—Chicago,
University of Illinois.

International Students

TOEFL required of international students	Yes
Minimum paper TOEFL	600
Minimum computer TOEFL	250

FINANCIAL FACTS

Annual tuition	$30,520
Books and supplies	$1,200
Fees per credit	$100
Tuition per credit	$1,000
Room and board	$19,984
Financial aid application deadline	4/1
% first-year students receiving some sort of aid	91
% receiving some sort of aid	90
% of aid that is merit based	15
% receiving scholarships	45
Average grant	$10,566
Average loan	$31,405
Average total aid package	$35,154
Average debt	$98,115

EMPLOYMENT INFORMATION

Career Rating	**78**	ComEd.	
Rate of placement (nine months out)	98	**Grads Employed by Field (%)**	
Average starting salary	$67,634	Academic	2
State for bar exam	IL, CA, NY, MI, WI	Business/Industry	18
Pass rate for first-time bar	89	Government	11
Employers Who Frequently Hire Grads		Judicial clerkships	2
Bell, Boyd, and Lloyd; Chapman and		Other	4
Cutler; Hinshaw and Culbertson; Kirkland		Private practice	55
and Ellis; Vedder Price; Winston and		Public Interest	8
Strawn; Cook County State's Attorney's			
Office.			

Prominent Alumni
Richard M. Daley, Mayor of Chicago; Mary Dempsey, commissioner, Chicago Public Library System; Frank Clark, president,

DRAKE UNIVERSITY
LAW SCHOOL

INSTITUTIONAL INFORMATION

Public/private	Private
Student-faculty ratio	15:1
% faculty part-time	36
% faculty female	33
% faculty minority	10
Total faculty	47

SURVEY SAYS...

Diverse opinions accepted
in classrooms
Great research resources
Great library staff
Abundant externship/internship/
clerkship opportunities

STUDENTS

Enrollment of law school	430
% male/female	51/49
% out-of-state	42
% full-time	98
% minority	11
% international	1
# of countries represented	3
Average age of entering class	24

ACADEMICS

Academic Experience Rating	**78**
Profs interesting rating	78
Profs accessible rating	82
Hours of study per day	3.99

Academic Specialties

Agricultural law, constitutional law, legislative practice, litigation and dispute resolution.

Advanced Degrees Offered

JD 3 years.

Combined Degrees Offered

JD/MBA 3 years, JD/MPA 3 years, JD/PharmD, JD/MA (political science) 3 years, JD/MS (agricultural economics) 3 years.

Clinical program required	No
Legal writing course requirement	Yes
Legal methods course requirement	Yes

Academics

Drake University's Law School "prides itself on educating practical lawyers," through an approach which contented students say offers "the perfect balance of academic tradition and excellence." Much of Drake's teaching methodology "is focused on effective lawyering" instead of law theory. A second-year student sums up Drake's unique approach eloquently: "Other schools graduate theoretically sound students of the law; Drake graduates lawyers."

Most of Drake's faculty members have worked within their respective fields, which is "readily apparent in their pragmatic approach to teaching." Students cite professors' practical experience and open-door policies as two of the school's greatest strengths. Students "spend a lot of time learning how to do research, how to write, and how to convey ideas in the best manner possible"—a simple enough course of study that often gets needlessly complicated at other law schools. "The professors are truly concerned that you not only know the material for an exam but that you comprehend the material for your career," says one 2L. They also take the time to "get to know students on a first-name basis as well as [learn about] our interests both in and out of the classroom." A first-year student even tells of a torts professor who "brought in all kinds of canned and boxed food for the kids who couldn't make it home for Thanksgiving. This was of course to prevent them from having a lonely Thanksgiving dinner of Beef-a-roni like he had to do as a 1L!"

Drake's "knowledgeable and experienced" administrators are "unbelievably accessible" and "always stop to say hello." However, some students claim that they can be "frequently rigid about course offerings and credits," and wish there was more flexibility allowed in the adding and dropping of courses. The first-year curriculum is known for its intensity and its "huge emphasis on writing," but many students cite visits from Supreme Court Justices and Drake's "one-of-a-kind" trial practicum program (which allows students to observe an actual trial at the school's legal clinic) as first-year high points. Drake also recently "totally reinvented" its Career Services Department, which now sets up on-campus interviews with recruiters from several top firms in the surrounding area. As a result, job opportunities are "much more available [now] than in the past," though some still think the school could stand to benefit from "greater exposure outside of the Midwest job market."

Though Drake's campus "surely ranks among one of the nation's least attractive," the school's "expansive" facilities received universal commendations for being "state of the art, fully electronic, with wireless network access campus wide," and for having a "good variance on classroom size that allows for small classes and survey courses." The library is "impressive in resources"—one student calls it the "highlight of the school"—and the school's location in the capital city of Des Moines "presents many opportunities for networking and clerkships."

Life

"Relations amongst students are what make Drake." The "collegial environment" provides a "helpful and healthy place to study and learn." "Cutthroat, competition-type behavior is virtually unheard of"—"There is always someone who will send notes if you miss a class." The school's "supportive" atmosphere is palpable from day one: "On our first day of orientation, instead of telling us to look to our right and our left and that at least one of us would be gone by graduation, the dean told us that these individuals would one day be our colleagues," says a first-year student.

With all of the classes located in one building (which is connected to the library) "It is very convenient to study between classes without losing a lot of time trekking around campus." The small size of the school "allows students to get to know one another well," and "It is not uncommon to be friendly with everyone in the law school." Fortunately, life at Drake isn't all work and no play. Aside from the "plethora of organizations to join," there is an official social event once a week where the majority of students "get together and enjoy each other's company outside of the law school," as well as "a popular law school fraternity that provides additional social opportunities for students." Concerned about the Des Moines winters? Take your cues from one third-year student who says, "If you haven't been to Iowa, you're missing out; where else can it be 50 degrees one day and negative 10 the next!"

Getting In

Though the admit rate at Drake is higher than at most law schools, the significant number of enrolled out-of-staters in a relatively sparsely populated state is a testament to Iowa's increasing popularity (and increasing selectivity). Last year's admitted students at the 25th percentile had an LSAT score of 154 and an average GPA of 3.1, while admitted students at the 75th percentile had an LSAT score of 157 and a GPA of 3.6. Though admission decisions are made on a rolling basis and scholarships are not awarded until after April 1, applicants are strongly encouraged to submit application materials early.

Legal research course requirement	Yes
Moot court requirement	Yes
Public interest law requirement	No

ADMISSIONS

Selectivity Rating	**73**
# applications received	1,109
# applicants accepted	508
# acceptees attending	140
Average LSAT	155
LSAT Range	154–157
Average undergrad GPA	3.4
Application fee	$40
Regular application	Rolling
Regular notification	Rolling
Rolling notification	Yes
Early application program	No
Transfer students accepted	Yes
Evening division offered	No
Part-time accepted	Yes
LSDAS accepted	Yes

Applicants Also Look At
Creighton University, Hamline University, University of Iowa, William Mitchell College of Law.

International Students

TOEFL required of international students	Yes
Minimum paper TOEFL	560
Minimum computer TOEFL	220

FINANCIAL FACTS

Annual tuition	$25,800
Books and supplies	$1,100
Tuition per credit	$900
Room and board (off-campus)	$11,000
Financial aid application deadline	3/1
% first-year students receiving some sort of aid	98
% receiving some sort of aid	98
% receiving scholarships	57
Average grant	$10,000
Average loan	$25,000
Average total aid package	$39,500
Average debt	$68,500

EMPLOYMENT INFORMATION

		Grads Employed by Field (%)	
Career Rating	**80**	Academic	1
Rate of placement (nine months out)	99	Business/Industry	16
Average starting salary	$51,572	Government	9
State for bar exam	IA, MN, MO, IL	Judicial clerkships	9
Pass rate for first-time bar	91	Military	2
Employers Who Frequently Hire Grads		Private practice	58
Davis, Brown; Nyemaster, Goode; Jag		Public Interest	5
Corps; Blackwell Sanders; Shughart			
Thompson; Bryan Cave.			

Prominent Alumni
Dwight D. Opperman, CEO, publishing company; former Chief Justice Louis Lavarato, Iowa Supreme Court; Robert Ray, former governor; Terry Branstad, former governor; Chief Justice Marsha Ternus, Iowa Supreme Court

DUKE UNIVERSITY
SCHOOL OF LAW

INSTITUTIONAL INFORMATION

Public/private	Private
Student-faculty ratio	12:1
% faculty part-time	33
% faculty female	41
% faculty minority	4
Total faculty	92

SURVEY SAYS...

Diverse opinions accepted
in classrooms
Great research resources
Abundant externship/internship/
clerkship opportunities

STUDENTS

Enrollment of law school	630
% male/female	57/43
% full-time	100
% minority	24
% international	1
Average age of entering class	25

ACADEMICS

Academic Experience Rating	94
Profs interesting rating	87
Profs accessible rating	91
Hours of study per day	3.86

Advanced Degrees Offered

JD 3 years, LLM 1 year, SJD
(international students only) 1 year.

Combined Degrees Offered

JD/MA 3.5 years, JD/MS (electrical
and computer engineering, mechanical engineering) 3.5 years, JD/MBA,
JD/MPP, JD/MEM, JD/MTS 4 years,
JD/MD 6 years, JD/PhD 7 years,
JD/LLM (international and comparative law) 3.5 years.

Clinical program required	No
Legal writing	
course requirement	Yes
Legal methods	
course requirement	Yes
Legal research	
course requirement	Yes
Moot court requirement	Yes
Public interest	
law requirement	No

Academics

The highly regarded School of Law at Duke University provides an "extremely unique academic environment" in which the students unquestionably "get [their] money's worth." The small size of the law school "allows for a great deal of interaction with faculty and a small community feel." Students also speak of the benefits of "not being pegged as a 'New York' school or a 'California' school." This allows them to "go anywhere for jobs." Under the instructional guidance of a "wide array of legal rock stars," Duke's graduates become a part of an "incredible network of successful individuals." With fewer than 200 students per class and no plans to expand, the school's small size also makes grads "a novelty in the legal market," though some students speak of a lack of assistance for those who want to pursue nontraditional legal careers or jobs at smaller firms.

"Accessible" seems to be the foremost trait of the knowledgeable faculty at Duke Law School. "I think most of my classmates, including myself, have been to at least one of our professors' homes for dinner," says one 2L. Though many students wish for "a more diverse faculty," students across the board rave about professors' open-door policies and "special interest in helping you succeed." Instructors "are proud to be a part of the Duke community," and it shows in their teaching. "My constitutional law professor from last year is now the advisor on my independent study, and he treats me like I'm a client—he always e-mails me back within a few hours, which is nuts since he always happens to be arguing in front of the Supreme Court!" Though the first year of classes follow the typical curriculum for beginning law students, 2Ls and 3Ls "have the opportunity to take a broad a range of classes." Duke also offers a wide variety of solid clinics, pro bono opportunities, and a lunchtime speaker series "full of notable speakers flying in to talk."

There is a great deal of warmth for those who run the school itself, and their devotion to the school's message of learning does not go unnoticed. "Our dean and her husband [also a professor at the law school] gave $100,000 of their own money to start a Loan Repayment Assistance Program endowment," offers a 3L as evidence. Student satisfaction "appears to be the highest priority of the administration," and administrators solicit student input "in everything from website design to selecting a new dean to shaping admissions policies." The administration's receptiveness "to student-initiated change" gives students "a real sense of ownership" in the school.

"If law school is the smart person's incubator, then I am happily incubated," says one 2L, happily describing the law school's facilities. The "beautiful" law building was just redone last year and includes state-of-the-art classrooms equipped with wireless Internet and personal power plug-ins, and this technology is "seamlessly integrated into the teaching and learning," making the building a "very comfortable place to spend time."

Life

Surprisingly for a law school of Duke's caliber, the level of competition among students is minimal: "I expected law school to be cutthroat and somewhat evil, to be honest. It's the exact opposite here," attests a second-year student. "We joke amongst ourselves regularly about how we must be the 'Kumbaya' law school." This "fosters a tremendous sense of community throughout the school," and "No one even thinks of being a psycho and hiding books." One student speculates on the reasoning behind this "collegial" and "supportive" environment: "We all know there are enough employers coming to hire us that we do not need to employ cutthroat tactics to steal jobs from our

WILLIAM J. HOYE, ASSOCIATE DEAN FOR ADMISSIONS AND FINANCIAL AID
PO BOX 90393, DURHAM, NC 27708-0393
TEL: 919-613-7020 FAX: 919-613-7257
E-MAIL: ADMISSIONS@LAW.DUKE.EDU • INTERNET: ADMISSIONS.LAW.DUKE.EDU

peers." However, the competitiveness inherent in students at a top-tier law school "is brought out on the softball field and in the bowling alley (we have the largest bowling league in North Carolina)."

Duke's location in Durham plays a key role in fostering the sense of community that its "down-to-earth" and "diversified" students applaud. "The lives of both students and faculty at Duke Law revolve around the law school—it is not like schools in major cities where people show up, come to class, and go home, never to see each other again," says a 2L. This "fun-loving" bunch "likes to go out, party, and have a good time," and the low cost of living means they can afford the "great restaurants, bars, arts, and nightlife" of the town, as well as those in nearby Raleigh. Taking all things into account, Duke is "a very pleasant place to go to school."

Getting In

Duke's 23 percent acceptance rate may be somewhat higher than expected for a top-tier law school that makes no bones about the fact that it wants only the best, most ambitious students. Students admitted for the class of 2010 at the 25th percentile had an LSAT score of 165 and an average GPA of 3.7, while admitted students at the 75th percentile had an LSAT score of 169 and a GPA of 3.9. Be sure to complete the optional essay, and know that applications received earlier in the admissions process are at a distinct advantage.

ADMISSIONS

Selectivity Rating	**96**
# applications received	4,341
# applicants accepted	1,011
# acceptees attending	205
Average LSAT	168
LSAT Range	165–169
Average undergrad GPA	3.78
Application fee	$70
Regular application	2/15
Regular notification	Rolling
Rolling notification	Yes
Early application program	No
Transfer students accepted	Yes
Evening division offered	No
Part-time accepted	No
LSDAS accepted	Yes

International Students

TOEFL required of international students	Yes
Minimum paper TOEFL	600

FINANCIAL FACTS

Annual tuition	$39,960
Books and supplies	$1,140
Room and board (off-campus)	$9,180
Financial aid application deadline	3/15

EMPLOYMENT INFORMATION

Career Rating	**91**	**Grads Employed by Field (%)**	
Average starting salary	$135,000	Business/Industry	6
State for bar exam	NY, NC, CA, MD, VA	Government	5
Pass rate for first-time bar	90	Judicial clerkships	19
		Other	0
		Private practice	66
		Public Interest	3

EMORY UNIVERSITY
SCHOOL OF LAW

INSTITUTIONAL INFORMATION

Public/private	Private
Affiliation	Methodist
Student-faculty ratio	13:1
% faculty part-time	39
% faculty female	32
% faculty minority	10
Total faculty	97

SURVEY SAYS...

Diverse opinions accepted
in classrooms
Great research resources
Abundant externship/internship/
clerkship opportunities
Students love Atlanta, GA

STUDENTS

Enrollment of law school	695
% male/female	54/46
% out-of-state	53
% full-time	100
% minority	6
% international	2
# of countries represented	23
Average age of entering class	24

ACADEMICS

Academic Experience Rating	**90**
Profs interesting rating	90
Profs accessible rating	85
Hours of study per day	4.54

Academic Specialties

Business law, comparative law, corporation securities law, environmental law, health law, human rights law, intellectual property law, international law, law and religion, legal theory, trial practice.

Advanced Degrees Offered

LLM 1 year, SJD.

Combined Degrees Offered

JD/MBA 4 years, JD/MTS 4 years, JD/MDIV 5 years, JD/MPH 3.5 years, JD/REES 3 years, JD/PhD (religion) 7 years, JD/MA (Judaic studies) 4 years.

Academics

Emory University School of Law offers "an extremely strong brand name" that "allows for amazing networking opportunities and instant recognition." "Emory has wonderful connections in the city of Atlanta" and "opportunities to practice law in field placements and other internships" are "diverse." Emory students are "routinely" placed "with the Georgia Supreme Court, the U.S. Attorney's Office, the Eleventh Circuit Court of Appeals," and "major Atlanta-based corporations." A 3L explains, "If you are interested in intellectual property, Emory has a program that works with Georgia Tech to give you real experience." "If you are into criminal justice, Emory works with the Georgia Innocence Projects." The Turner Environmental Clinic and the Barton Child Law and Policy Clinic are "active and renowned." The "joint-degree program with the theology school" is "a very unique and prolific source of scholarship on a range of issues at the nexus of law and religion." Emory's "Feminist and Legal Theory project" garners more raves.

Professors here are described as "world class." "Emory Law's faculty is one of the best kept secrets of any top 30 law school," asserts one student. "They have a great sense of humor and seem to genuinely enjoy teaching." "The professors go the extra mile in terms of helping students network for clerkships and jobs with top firms." This "brilliant," "engaging," and "very dynamic" faculty "includes a couple of the world's foremost human rights scholars (one of whom is the preeminent scholar in Islamic law)." Students are split on Emory's administration. One faction says that the "friendly, approachable, and straightforward" administration is "on the ball" and "willing to listen to student concerns." Others say that those in the administration "take themselves too seriously." "The administration at Emory Law is herding cats with a spatula," offers one student. "They are attempting an impossible task in the manner least likely to succeed."

Career prospects for Emory Law grads "abound" in Atlanta and "The Emory degree also carries significant weight outside of Atlanta, especially along the entire East Coast." "The Emory degree has legs," affirms a 2L. "It can take you places. I'm going to Washington, DC to work with a great firm. I had offers as far away as Houston, and I'm not near the top 10 percent." "I haven't known people to have significant trouble getting jobs in the Northeast or elsewhere," adds another 2L. Nevertheless, "many students complain" that Career Services is Emory's "biggest weakness."

"The library is beautiful, but the classroom building needs a facelift," says one student. Emory's "stale," "bland," facilities are "uninspiring." "The classrooms are in dire need of some sprucing up," speculates a 2L. "White walls and windowless classrooms give the school an institutional feel." "It seems every year they paint the building, but students are not fooled." "The technology sucks," too, though the "law library is amazingly nice." It's "bright and open with lots of tables and study carrels." An insider's tip: "The trek to the undergraduate library, surprisingly, is worth it if you want quiet study."

Life

Students say "Emory draws an interesting mix of folks from both North and South (though not as many from the West)." "Long Island kids" and "conservative Southerners" create a "strange dichotomy" and an "extremely dynamic student body." There are students fresh out of college and those who "took some time off and are coming in with families or significant others." Politically, there is a "liberal bent," but you will find "various" viewpoints. Emory's "ambitious" students are "impossibly smart" and "focused." Many

LYNELL A. CADRAY, ASSISTANT DEAN FOR ADMISSION
1301 CLIFTON ROAD, ATLANTA, GA 30322-2770
TEL: 404-727-6801 FAX: 404-727-2477
E-MAIL: LAWINFO@LAW.EMORY.EDU • INTERNET: WWW.LAW.EMORY.EDU

are "outgoing" and "sociable." Others "stay hidden behind the books the whole semester and you don't even know they are there until they win many of the high-paying jobs." As good as Emory is, "not everyone is thrilled" to be here. "Some think they should be elsewhere" and "have a chip on their shoulder." But as one student explains, "Overall, the quality of students here is very high, and the reputation of the school will only continue to improve."

"Classes are small, so there is a strong sense of community." Emory can be "moderately competitive," though. "Some students are just downright nasty to each other," claims a 3L. "During first year, it is a very stressful environment." That said, most of the students are "congenial, helpful, and fun to go out with."

Social life at Emory is just swell. There is "an amazing Barrister's Ball" and "The Harvest Moon Ball Halloween party is a howling good time year after year." "We have weekly 'Bar Reviews' around Atlanta," explains one student. "Each Thursday we have a keg in 'Bacardi Plaza' (our atrium)." Atlanta is "an exciting place" and "a great city for 20-somethings." It's "the economic hub of the South," but at the same time it's "very affordable for students." "Having moved here from New York City, I'm shocked at how much Atlanta has to offer and how easy it is to get off campus and get lost in a genuinely cool city," declares a happy 1L.

Getting In

Emory Law receives more than 3,800 applications for about 230 1L seats. The admitted students at the 25th percentile have LSAT scores of roughly 161 and GPAs of roughly 3.3. Admitted students at the 75th percentile have LSAT scores of about 165 and GPAs of about 3.6. Emory says that it will average scores if you take the LSAT more than once.

Clinical program required	No
Legal writing course requirement	Yes
Legal methods course requirement	Yes
Legal research course requirement	Yes
Moot court requirement	No
Public interest law requirement	No

ADMISSIONS

Selectivity Rating	**87**
# applications received	3,591
# applicants accepted	1,042
# acceptees attending	207
Average LSAT	164
LSAT Range	162–166
Average undergrad GPA	3.5
Application fee	$70
Regular application	3/1
Regular notification	Rolling
Rolling notification	Yes
Early application program	No
Transfer students accepted	Yes
Evening division offered	No
Part-time accepted	No
LSDAS accepted	Yes

Applicants Also Look At
Boston College, Boston University, Duke University, Fordham University, The George Washington University, Georgetown University, Vanderbilt University.

International Students

TOEFL required of international students	Yes
Minimum paper TOEFL	600
Minimum computer TOEFL	250

FINANCIAL FACTS

Annual tuition	$36,400
Books and supplies	$4,868
Room and board	$14,400
Financial aid application deadline	3/1
% first-year students receiving some sort of aid	95
% receiving some sort of aid	87
% of aid that is merit based	26
% receiving scholarships	39
Average grant	$17,360
Average loan	$37,189
Average total aid package	$41,748
Average debt	$92,030

EMPLOYMENT INFORMATION

Career Rating	**89**
Rate of placement (nine months out)	99
Average starting salary	$89,063
State for bar exam	GA
Pass rate for first-time bar	95

Employers Who Frequently Hire Grads
Alston and Bird; Arnall Golden Gregory; Cadwalader, Wickersham and Taft; Chadbourne and Parke; Dechert; Greenberg Traurig; Holland and Knight; Wyche Fowler, former U.S. Senator; Bobby Jones, golfer; Frank Hall and Anthony Alaimo, U.S. federal judges; Terri Plummer McClure, general counsel, UPS.

Prominent Alumni
Honorable Sanford Bishop, U.S. Congressman; Chief Justice Leah Sears, Georgia Supreme Court.

Grads Employed by Field (%)

Business/Industry	7
Government	5
Judicial clerkships	11
Private practice	70
Public Interest	7

FAULKNER UNIVERSITY*
THOMAS GOODE JONES SCHOOL OF LAW

INSTITUTIONAL INFORMATION

Public/private	Private
Affiliation	Church of Christ
Student-faculty ratio	11:1
% faculty female	40
% faculty minority	10
Total faculty	22

SURVEY SAYS...

Heavy use of Socratic method
Diverse opinions accepted
in classrooms

STUDENTS

Enrollment of law school	274
% male/female	60/40
% out-of-state	21
% full-time	66
% minority	10
Average age of entering class	26

ACADEMICS

Academic Experience Rating	**73**
Profs interesting rating	85
Profs accessible rating	88
Hours of study per day	4.48

Academic Specialties

Alternative dispute resolution, civil procedure, commercial law, constitutional law, corporation securities law, criminal law, environmental law, government services, human rights law, intellectual property law, international law, labor law, legal history, legal philosophy, property, taxation, alternative dispute resolution.

Clinical program required	No
Legal writing course requirement	Yes
Legal methods course requirement	No
Legal research course requirement	Yes
Moot court requirement	Yes
Public interest law requirement	No

Academics

Faulkner University's Jones School of Law in Montgomery, Alabama is "a Church of Christ–affiliated school" with "a non-intimidating environment." According to students here, it's "the best-kept secret in Alabama." The "bar-passage rate is very high;" in fact, students report that in 2006 Faulkner had "the highest bar-passage rate in the state of Alabama." "The trial advocacy program is top-notch." "The faculty and administration actually care about you as a person" and "make sure you have practical knowledge for the real world." Many appreciate that professors "treat them like a friend and not a subordinate." Some feel that Jones "could benefit from a broader curriculum." While the "small" campus can mean fewer opportunities, many students find that "the resources of the law school are growing everyday."

The many "very knowledgeable" and "distinguished" professors here "truly are a hidden gem." Their ranks include "some of the most experienced legal minds anywhere." They also "possess a great deal of real-world experience" and "give practical lessons about real-life lawyering." The faculty is pretty big on the "Socratic Method." A student explains that his torts professor "writes everyone's name on a playing card. Before class he draws three cards, and the three people have a roundtable discussion presenting the cases that were assigned. It is by far the most memorable first-year experience." "Small class sizes" "allow for greater participation" and "You are able to get to know your professors better." The intimacy "strongly encourages differing viewpoints and class discussion" as well. Professors here "truly care about your success and take an interest in your life outside of the classroom." "The amount of time each professor is willing to dedicate to each student never fails to impress me," agrees another student. "They genuinely want each student to succeed."

The "professional looking" facilities (featuring "marble and mahogany throughout") are "outstanding." There is also "Internet access throughout the school." "Every classroom is equipped with plenty of electrical outlets," notes one student. Nevertheless, an "increase in building size" would be good. Classrooms can "sometimes" get "very hot". "Regulate the temperature in the classrooms," urges a 1L. Most students would also like to see the library "open later hours."

The well-liked administration here is "always available and extremely helpful" It's worth noting that the Jones School of Law is currently provisionally approved by the American Bar Association. Provisional approval is an intermediate step between full approval and no approval. For students here, it basically means that they can take any bar exam in any state when they graduate just like graduates of all ABA-approved law schools."

* Provisionally approved by the ABA.

ANDREW R. MATTHEWS, ASSISTANT DEAN FOR STUDENT SERVICES
5345 ATLANTA HIGHWAY, MONTGOMERY, AL 36109
TEL: 334-386-7210 FAX: 334-386-7908
E-MAIL: LAW@FAULKNER.EDU • INTERNET: WWW.FAULKNER.EDU/LAW

Life

"There is a definite sense of community" since "Everyone knows everyone," but students insist that "that's a plus." At the same time, "There is a competitive environment, but that's what the real world is like." "We are all in this struggle together, and we help each other to survive," explains a 3L. "This includes saving someone who is drowning in class when briefing a case or forming study groups for exams." Faulkner University is definitively "Christian oriented," and overall, it's "a very conservative campus." The law school is "extremely conservative" as well, but people who aren't on the political right feel welcome here. "Even though I am very liberal and a bit outside the norm, the faculty and staff do not attempt to curtail my individuality," comments a 3L. "I do not hesitate to be vocal in my opinions and viewpoints (both in and out of class) and have never had any repercussions."

Ethnic diversity "leaves a lot to be desired." Geographic diversity is limited too. However, students do say that their peers "come from all strata of society and bring varying perspectives based upon their personal, professional and educational experiences." "There are people that are directly out of college as well as people that have been out of undergrad for 15 to 20 years," explains one student. Students tend to be a little bit older, though. The average age is just under 30.

Outside of class, there are "seminars, speakers," and "even school parties," but students feel "There should be a few more social opportunities, especially on the weekends." "There is nothing to do here, unless you are active in a church—any church—we have all varieties," promises one student. "I play basketball with friends," says an athletic 2L. "We also play flag football and get together for poker and other events to take our minds off school."

Getting In

Admitted students at the 25th percentile have LSAT scores of 147 and GPAs of 2.7. Admitted students at the 75th percentile have LSAT scores of 152 and GPAs of 3.35. If you take the LSAT more than once, Faulkner will use your highest score.

ADMISSIONS

Selectivity Rating	**64**
# applications received	316
# applicants accepted	184
# acceptees attending	106
Average LSAT	150
LSAT Range	147–152
Average undergrad GPA	3.02
Application fee	$25
Regular application	5/1
Rolling notification	Yes
Early application program	No
Transfer students accepted	Yes
Evening division offered	Yes
Part-time accepted	Yes
LSDAS accepted	Yes

International Students

TOEFL required of international students	No
TOEFL recommended of international students	No

FINANCIAL FACTS

Annual tuition	$22,000
Books and supplies	$2,000
Tuition per credit	$916
Room and board (off-campus)	$12,000
Financial aid application deadline	6/1
% receiving some sort of aid	29
% of aid that is merit based	90
% receiving scholarships	29

EMPLOYMENT INFORMATION

		Grads Employed by Field (%)	
Career Rating	**90**	**Grads Employed by Field (%)**	
Rate of placement (nine months out)	93	Business/Industry	6
State for bar exam	AL	Government	28
Pass rate for first-time bar	97	Judicial clerkships	10
Prominent Alumni		Private practice	54
Greg Allen, partner, Beasley, Allen, et al;		Public Interest	2
Associate Justice Patricia Smith, Alabama			
Supreme Court; Ernestine Sapp, partner,			
Gray, Langford, Sapp, et al; Bobby Bright,			
mayor of Montgomery; Tommy Bryan,			
judge, Court of Civil Appeals.			

FLORIDA INTERNATIONAL UNIVERSITY
COLLEGE OF LAW

Academics

At the brand-new Florida International University College of Law, "students and faculty all work together to improve the college," promoting a spirit of camaraderie, conscientiousness, and cooperation on campus. Having received full ABA accreditation in 2006, the school is quickly building its course offerings, teaching faculty, and regional reputation. Students love "the opportunity to be a part of the foundation of a rising law school" and applaud the strides the school has made in just five years of operation. As a 2L says, "I have been very impressed by the faculty and the administration because they developed a reasonably broad range of courses, including an evening program, while at the same time keeping the college on track for provisional accreditation at the earliest possible time. I give them all an A-plus."

At FIU, "The faculty is excited about teaching [at] a new school," a sentiment that translates into lively and engaging academic atmosphere. Having recently recruited and hired the entire teaching staff, you won't have any old, stodgy, tenured lecturers at FIU. "Our greatest strength is definitely in our faculty," says one student. "There is no dead weight here—only live wires!" Indeed, FIU students insist that "professors are top-notch across the board." On top of that, for a public school price tag, students point to many benefits of a tiny, private school. Despite the "cheap cost," the school maintains a small student body, keeping total enrollment below 300 students. FIU students report a strong sense of campus community; most classes are reasonably sized, and students have the opportunity to build strong relationships with the school's talented and diverse teaching staff. One content 3L says, "We have a small student body, creating a fantastic sense of collegiality."

While FIU's forward-thinking attitude is apparently unequivocally appreciated, there are a few drawbacks to studying at a newer institution. "The college needs to reduce its obsession with following the prescribed formalism of the ABA and develop its own personality," says a student, and others wish "the professors would lighten up a bit on the competition fixation." As far as the physical aspects of the school go, the recent move into brand-new facilities has eliminated any complaints about the former building.

FIU was founded in 2000 with the mission to serve the legal needs of Florida residents and residents of South Florida in particular. During their studies, FIU students have the opportunity to "make a substantial impact on the local community" through the school's clinical program and community-service program. In fact, students are required to participate in the community-service program, through which they participate in pro bono legal work in underserved Miami communities. After graduation, this real-world experience pays off—and FIU students have something of a corner on the Miami market. By all accounts, there are "many opportunities for local employment" in surrounding Miami, and FIU students are in the unique position to influence and direct Florida law.

ALMA O. MIRÓ, DIRECTOR OF ADMISSIONS AND FINANCIAL AID
FIU COLLEGE OF LAW, OFFICE OF ADMISSIONS AND FINANCIAL AID, RDB 1055, MIAMI, FL 33199
TEL: 305-348-8006 FAX: 305-348-2965
E-MAIL: LAWADMIT@FIU.EDU • INTERNET: LAW.FIU.EDU

Life

Even in such a short period of time, FIU has built a strong, friendly, diverse campus community. In fact, many students say that "the greatest strength of the law school is the non-competitive, tight-knit environment that exists" among classmates. Despite the rigors of course work, FIU maintains a largely cooperative environment. According to a 1L, "People seem to have their priorities in the right place and are not neurotic about competition, which is what I hear happens in other contexts." In fact, students "tend to depend on each other for help and understanding. Whenever times are stressful or confusing, you can always count on a fellow student for help or class notes. Maybe it's because we are a newly formed law school, or maybe it's the city of Miami. Either way, it's great!"

Outside the classroom, students say they get along well with their amiable and interesting classmates. A 3L says, "I know everyone in my class pretty well, and there's not a person among them I wouldn't cross the street to say hello to if I saw them outside of school." However, many of the evening students scoff at the idea of meeting their colleagues for dinner or drinks after class: "Most of us don't have a social life, neither in school nor outside it. There are just so many hours in a day."

Getting In

Florida International University College of Law "seeks to enroll a diverse group of students who have demonstrated academic and personal achievement." In addition to a student's undergraduate transcript and LSAT scores, the Admissions Committee evaluates a student's demonstrated leadership ability, ethics, commitment to public service, and understanding of global issues.

Moot court requirement	No
Public interest law requirement	Yes

ADMISSIONS

Selectivity Rating	**79**
# applications received	1,857
# applicants accepted	423
# acceptees attending	165
Average LSAT	154
LSAT Range	151–156
Average undergrad GPA	3.26
Application fee	$20
Regular application	5/1
Regular notification	Rolling
Rolling notification	Yes
Early application program	No
Transfer students accepted	Yes
Evening division offered	Yes
Part-time accepted	Yes
LSDAS accepted	Yes

Applicants Also Look At

Florida Coastal School of Law, Florida State University, Nova Southeastern University, St. Thomas University, Stetson University, University of Florida, University of Miami.

International Students

TOEFL required of international students	Yes
Minimum paper TOEFL	550
Minimum computer TOEFL	213

FINANCIAL FACTS

Annual tuition (resident)	$9,037
Annual tuition (nonresident)	$23,280
Books and supplies	$6,748
Fees per credit (resident)	$285
Fees per credit (nonresident)	$285
Tuition per credit (resident)	$292
Tuition per credit (nonresident)	$751
Room and board (on/off-campus)	$9,288/$10,008
Financial aid application deadline	3/1
% first-year students receiving some sort of aid	68
% receiving some sort of aid	71
% of aid that is merit based	20
% receiving scholarships	43
Average grant	$6,527
Average loan	$16,500
Average total aid package	$19,598

EMPLOYMENT INFORMATION

		Grads Employed by Field (%)	
Career Rating	**71**	**Grads Employed by Field (%)**	
Rate of placement (nine months out)	86	Business/Industry	7
Average starting salary	$59,115	Government	17
State for bar exam	FL	Judicial clerkships	2
Pass rate for first-time bar	79	Private practice	34
Employers Who Frequently Hire Grads		Public Interest	4
Dade County State Attorney's office; Astigarraga Davis; Holland and Knight; Greenberg Traurig; Squire, Sanders, and Dempsey.			
Prominent Alumni			
Doug Giuliano, associate attorney, Astigarraga Davis; Mauricio Rivero, associate attorney, Holland and Knight; Kimberly Donovan, associate attorney.			

FLORIDA STATE UNIVERSITY
COLLEGE OF LAW

Academics

The law school at Florida State University, a relatively small program "hidden within the confines of a major public university," is considered by many happy students to be "the best-kept secret in Florida legal education opportunities." Not only is their satisfaction level high, but the price is right, too. "If all goes well, I will be working after graduation at a firm with lawyers from the top 14 schools, but the difference in my student loan payments will allow me to buy that new BMW instead of pay back Harvard! " exclaims one second-year student.

In contrast to many of the horror stories spouted by shell-shocked students at other law schools, FSU's 1L survivors have nothing but praise for their trial-by-fire year. "All of the first-year teachers are memorable and qualified, and seem genuinely interested in making sure that students adjust," says one 2L. "One first-year contracts teacher went as far as starting a fantasy NASCAR league amongst students." Another says, "I loved the first-year required curriculum. Now that I can pick and choose my classes/extern-ships, I feel pleasantly overwhelmed with all the choices." Maybe it's the result of starting off on the right foot, but students remain pleased as punch with the faculty right up through graduation. Speaking of "approachable" teachers who "are readily available to lend their expertise to a student's scholarship in a particular field" and who "even roam the halls looking for pick-up interaction with students," students say selflessness is evident in all aspects of instruction. "Classroom teaching seems just as important—if not more so—than producing scholarly articles," says a 2L.

Students also sing the praises of FSU's "extremely eager" staff, who they see as being "fully committed to making students' three years of law school a memorable experience." "There is not a single person in the leadership of this school who I could not approach at any time," avers one. Career Services is lauded for encouraging employers to "interview more than the top 10 percent of the class," and the job situation is helped by "fantastic" alumni who believe in the "kinship that is felt by being a Florida State Seminole."

No one can argue that FSU's location—"in the capital, across the street from the First District Court of Appeal and a block away from the State Supreme Court"—is ideal for a student of the law looking for practical experience on "a law clerk's playground." "By being so close to the capitol I was able to have two former state senators on my list of references," says one graduating student. However, such hotspots have their downsides; as one student puts it, "It doesn't take a math major to discover that 750 vehicles can't park in 50 spaces." Facilities get average reviews, and some students would like to see "more classrooms" and a "nicer lounge." The school has funded renovations in recent years, demonstrating "a true sense of investment in the student body and in the success of the law school, and planning money has been appropriated for the law school to annex the 50,000-square-foot courthouse across the street."

SHARON J. BOOKER, DIRECTOR OF ADMISSIONS AND RECORDS
425 WEST JEFFERSON STREET, TALLAHASSEE, FL 32306-1601
TEL: 850-644-3787 FAX: 850-644-7284
E-MAIL: ADMISSIONS@LAW.FSU.EDU • INTERNET: WWW.LAW.FSU.EDU

Life

"Balanced" is a word that comes up a lot when FSU students describe various aspects of their lives. The small size of the law school helps foster a "tight-knit" "sense of community that is pronounced," but avoids "being so small that you are singled out." Political persuasions seem to run middle of the road, or, as one second-year student puts it, "If you're from one of the more liberal areas of the country, FSU students will seem very conservative. Native Floridians tell me that the school is considered 'liberal.'" While most students cop to some level of contest among their peers, they say almost all are "willing to share outlines and their previous experiences with the exams of various professors." Students waver on whether or not the academics are as challenging as those at some other schools, but the general consensus seems to be that the age-old adage "work hard and play hard" is in top form here.

Special events such as lectures and networking opportunities are available for students to participate in on a regular basis thanks to an "extremely active group of student organizations." Socials "are usually once a week and have pretty high attendance." The beautiful Floridian weather means there's much fun to be had outdoors, including involvement in the "law school golf association" and the "club for University of Florida students/fans called the LitiGators!" FSU is "generally a fun place to work and study every day. Well, as much as law school can be 'fun,'" sums up one student.

Getting In

The actual admissions rate runs about average here, but the freshman profile runs a bit higher than one would expect for a state school. Students admitted for the class of 2009 at the 25th percentile had an LSAT score of 158 and an average GPA of 3.3. The school does not offer a part-time or evening program, but does accept a few highly qualified transfer students from other ABA-accredited law schools, and those lucky few must be in the top third of their class.

Legal methods course requirement	Yes
Legal research course requirement	Yes
Moot court requirement	No
Public interest law requirement	Yes

ADMISSIONS

Selectivity Rating	85
# applications received	3,313
# applicants accepted	806
# acceptees attending	196
Average LSAT	159
LSAT Range	158–161
Average undergrad GPA	3.44
Application fee	$30
Regular application	3/15
Regular notification	Rolling
Rolling notification	Yes
Early application program	No
Transfer students accepted	Yes
Evening division offered	No
Part-time accepted	No
LSDAS accepted	Yes

Applicants Also Look At

American University, Duke University, Emory University, Stetson University, Tulane University, University of Florida, University of Georgia.

International Students

TOEFL required of international students	Yes
Minimum paper TOEFL	600

FINANCIAL FACTS

Annual tuition (resident)	$9,810
Annual tuition (nonresident)	$29,820
Books and supplies	$3,000
Room and board	$10,000
Financial aid application deadline	3/15
% first-year students receiving some sort of aid	85
% receiving some sort of aid	89
% of aid that is merit based	45
% receiving scholarships	45
Average grant	$1,500
Average loan	$19,415
Average debt	$46,486

EMPLOYMENT INFORMATION

		Grads Employed by Field (%)	
Career Rating	79	Academic	1
Rate of placement (nine months out)	99	Business/Industry	7
Average starting salary	$56,200	Government	32
State for bar exam	FL, GA, NC, NY, CA	Judicial clerkships	7
Pass rate for first-time bar	87	Military	3

Employers Who Frequently Hire Grads
Akerman Senterfitt; Alston and Bird LLP; Arnstein and Lehr LLP; Broad and Cassel; Carlton Fields, PA.

Private practice	45
Public Interest	5

Prominent Alumni
Mel R. Martinez, U.S. Senator; Jeffrey A. Stoops, SBA Communications Corporation; Sheila Marie McDevitt, senior vice president and general counsel, TECO Energy, Inc.

FORDHAM UNIVERSITY
SCHOOL OF LAW

Academics

Known as "the friendly law school" of New York City, Fordham University is an amiable oasis within the hustle and bustle of its hometown. While the curriculum is indisputably difficult, Fordham students are guided through the countless challenges they face with the encouragement and support of the school's accomplished faculty, who "are available, encouraging, incredibly knowledgeable of their subject matter, interesting, and personable. They take time and view students as people and individuals with whom they are working." Inside the classroom, Fordham professors are "genuinely enthusiastic about teaching" and "truly want their students to go beyond basic understanding of the law." The overall effect is an "extremely challenging intellectual environment" that is somehow "less mind-boggling" than its reputable name might suggest.

Many professors join the Fordham faculty with impressive professional experience. "I've been taught by judges, senior partners, authors, and participants on federal rule boards. One professor is actually the Chief Judge Emeritus of the United States Court of International Trade. Can't beat their backgrounds," is how one 3L puts it. Students also point out that "in addition to the already strong faculty, the school has added young, smart, and energetic people during the last few years." The teaching staff is, therefore, "a good mix of practicing lawyers and theoretical academics," creating excellent equilibrium between real-world and academic skills in the curriculum.

There is an "incredible range of courses and activities" at Fordham, and "The clinical and externship opportunities are unsurpassed and a great way to network and get valuable practical experience." Of the many special programs and courses offered at Fordham, the "Crowley Program in International Human Rights is unmatched in any other school because it gives students the opportunity to do actual hands-on human rights fieldwork in a Third-World country and publish a report about it." In the extracurricular arena, Fordham students get plenty of career experience in New York City and brag that "there is no more convenient location for externships, part-time work, or conducting your job search." But while "The location of the school is spectacular," students warn that "Fordham's building is not its forte" and that classroom facilities are "slightly outdated and not comparable [with] other schools in the same range of cost and prestige."

Upon graduation, prospects are good for Fordham grads. Located in "the center of the legal world" and "well known in the regional marketplace," the school affords direct access to a multitude of excellent career opportunities. Students maintain that "the Career Planning Center is great" and will go to great lengths to help students land a plum position. "Even if you don't get a summer job, they will help you," reports one student. "I didn't, and as a 3L, I still got into 'big law' with their help." Students who are interested in working in public interest law claim that the Career Planning Center places "too much emphasis on large law firms." However, "The Public Interest Resource Center is terrific and staffed with amazing people" who can help civic-minded students find ways to put their training to public use. Students can also turn to instructors, as "Many professors will go to extraordinary lengths to help students get the best jobs." In addition to these resources, "Fordham law alumni really look out for the law students, and the network is extremely strong." As a result of all these conduits into legal careers, you will find "Fordham law students at all of the best firms in the country."

JOHN CHALMERS, ASSISTANT DEAN OF ADMISSIONS
33 WEST SIXTIETH STREET, 9TH FLOOR, NEW YORK, NY 10023
TEL: 212-636-6810 FAX: 212-636-7984
E-MAIL: LAWADMISSIONS@LAW.FORDHAM.EDU • INTERNET: LAW.FORDHAM.EDU

Life

With a prime location on the west side of Manhattan, you might think the Fordham campus would get swallowed up in the noise of the city, leaving little by way of campus culture. Not so. At Fordham, "It's like you're not even in NYC when you walk through the doors, but a small town, where you're friends with everyone." On campus, students are encouraged to socialize, and "The school offers tons of pizza, ice cream, and cupcake nights, passes out free movie tickets, and has different speakers each week on pertinent topics to keep you in touch with the real world." True to its moniker, "the friendly law school," students describe Fordham as an "incredibly welcoming environment." How welcoming? "The cafeteria woman, Gloria, regularly inquires how we are doing and encourages us . . . we give and get hugs from 'Mom.' It's just too good for words," gushes a 3L.

The diverse student body at Fordham Law School reflects its urban environs. Fordham also "tends to attract older students who have worked in a variety of professional fields." By all accounts, diversity is an asset to the educational experience, and "Having these diverse perspectives in the classroom have been tremendously beneficial." While differing opinions are common, contention and competition are rare. A 2L explains, "The school is very respectful of the students' diverse backgrounds, including ethnic, religious, and sexual orientations," and there is a "sense of camaraderie among students and alumni." The diversity and social opportunities on campus are further enhanced by the school's propitious location in the urban environment of New York City. A 3L attests that "the location of the school is probably one of the best in the whole country, being situated in the middle of NYC. Cultural, political, and recreational activities are all practically within walking distance."

Getting In

Fordham receives about 7,500 applications for 480 first-year seats. That means it has to be quite selective, admitting only those students with a strong academic background and a high level of achievement in their undergraduate curriculum. The middle 50 percent of applicants submitted LSAT scores between 164 and 167 and had undergraduate GPAs between 3.4 and 3.8.

EMPLOYMENT INFORMATION

Career Rating	**90**	
Rate of placement (nine months out)	98	
Average starting salary	$103,311	
State for bar exam	NY, CA, FL, DC, PA	
Pass rate for first-time bar	87	

Employers Who Frequently Hire Grads
Cahill, Gordon, and Reindel; U.S. Department of Justice; Simpson, Thacher, and Bartlett; NY Legal Aid.

Prominent Alumni
James Gill, chairman, Battery Park City Authority; Geraldine A. Ferraro, first female vice presidential candidate; John D. Feerick, chair, Board of Directors of the American Arbitration.

Grads Employed by Field (%)

Academic	1
Business/Industry	3
Government	6
Judicial clerkships	5
Private practice	77
Public Interest	1

Clinical program required	No
Legal writing course requirement	Yes
Legal methods course requirement	Yes
Legal research course requirement	Yes
Moot court requirement	No
Public interest law requirement	No

ADMISSIONS

Selectivity Rating	**93**
# applications received	6,751
# applicants accepted	1,635
# acceptees attending	460
Average LSAT	165
LSAT Range	163–167
Average undergrad GPA	3.62
Application fee	$65
Regular application	3/1
Regular notification	Rolling
Rolling notification	Yes
Early application program	No
Transfer students accepted	Yes
Evening division offered	Yes
Part-time accepted	Yes
LSDAS accepted	Yes

Applicants Also Look At
Boston College, Brooklyn Law School, Columbia University, The George Washington University, Georgetown University, New York University, Yeshiva University.

International Students

TOEFL required of international students	No
TOEFL recommended of international students	No

FINANCIAL FACTS

Annual tuition	$36,670
Books and supplies	$925
Fees per credit	$275
Tuition per credit	$1,528
Room and board	$15,675
Financial aid application deadline	4/1
% first-year students receiving some sort of aid	75
% receiving some sort of aid	77
% of aid that is merit based	3
% receiving scholarships	31
Average grant	$9,846
Average loan	$35,836
Average total aid package	$38,867
Average debt	$90,082

GEORGE MASON UNIVERSITY
SCHOOL OF LAW

INSTITUTIONAL INFORMATION

Public/private	Public
Student-faculty ratio	16:1
% faculty part-time	73
% faculty female	25
% faculty minority	7
Total faculty	168

SURVEY SAYS...
Conservative students
Students love Arlington, VA

STUDENTS

Enrollment of law school	751
% male/female	62/38
% full-time	62
% minority	14
% international	2
Average age of entering class	25

ACADEMICS

Academic Experience Rating	**83**
Profs interesting rating	72
Profs accessible rating	69
Hours of study per day	4.31

Academic Specialties
Civil procedure, corporation securities law, criminal law, government services, intellectual property law, international law, law and economics, legal philosophy, regulatory law, taxation, technology law.

Advanced Degrees Offered
LLM, specializing in intellectual property or law and economics.

Combined Degrees Offered
JD/MA or PhD (economics), JD/MPP.

Clinical program required	No
Legal writing	
course requirement	Yes
Legal methods	
course requirement	No
Legal research	
course requirement	Yes
Moot court requirement	Yes
Public interest	
law requirement	No

Academics

George Mason University School of Law has "a very strong reputation in the surrounding area," and "It's got to be one of the best bangs for your buck in the country." A "robust legal clinic program" provides "clinics for almost everything you can imagine." GMU's location "on the outskirts of Washington, DC" means that "there is a plethora" of judicial internships and work opportunities within the federal government. A host of specialization programs includes intellectual property, technology law, and international business law. Probably the most unique feature here is the ubiquitous emphasis on the nexus between law and economics. "The law and economics approach pervades the curriculum" and "teaches you as much about how the world operates as it does about the law." "It's like getting two degrees for the price of one," says a satisfied 3L. However, "the extent of the econ bent" is the bane of some students. "If you want to focus on something else, you have to pick your classes very carefully," notes a critic. The "arduous," four-semester legal writing program requires an enormous investment of time and is "by far the biggest complaint" among students. Students also tell us that "there's a mandatory attendance requirements" (as per ABA regulations), and they warn that "the curve at Mason is tough."

GMU's "supportive" and "incredibly dedicated faculty" is full of "intelligent, witty," and approachable professors. "They are always happy to discuss career plans and even send your resume to their friends," beams a 2L. "Some professors are so brilliant that they can't teach," but most "engage the students" and "keep class lively." "Older teachers are more likely to adhere to the Socratic Method, whereas classes with younger teachers are more relaxed and laid-back." "Lots of classes are taught by adjuncts" (including a "large number of judges") who are able to offer "practical, job-related advice." GMU has a reputation as a "right-of-center" law school. For many students, "the collection of so many conservative and libertarian geniuses among the faculty is wondrous and nearly incomparable." "A strong argument from any perspective is always welcome," though. "I am a liberal in a school whose administration and faculty lean toward the conservative or libertarian side," counsels a 3L. "While I sometimes find myself at odds with their beliefs, I love the academic challenge they provide and have always felt accepted in the community."

Career Services on campus "will go to great lengths to try and assist you in finding a job." "Each year, more and more prestigious law firms and government agencies recruit" at Mason. Also, "Alumni are extremely interested in helping current students meet their career goals." "My class has graduates heading to top 10 firms in the most competitive legal markets," boasts a 3L.

"Technology resources are top of the line," but the facilities at GMU aren't great. The "dumpy" building is "new and shiny on the outside," but "generally unattractive" once you walk through the door. "It is seriously the ugliest law school I have ever seen," fulminates a 3L, while others chime in that buildings are "cold, stark, and lack windows." Luckily, the school has undertaken an interior renovation project that will hopefully spruce things up a bit. The elevators and the lack of parking are another source of vexation. Classrooms have poor acoustics "so it's often hard to hear," and they "are too small."

Life

Many students come to Mason "for the school's conservative reputation." Others "come for the cheap tuition." The student population is especially diverse "in terms of work and practical experience." Also, "All kinds of perspectives and political backgrounds are apparent." "The student body is hardly monolithic," explains a 3L. "Students are older" on the whole. "There is a noticeable chasm in social interaction between the straight-out-of-college group and the students who have worked for a few years." Competition for grades is minimal among these "unusually motivated and down-to-earth students." (The evening section is "less competitive than the day sections.") "There are only about 5 or 10 people who are hyper-competitive gunner types." "Except for the total spazzes and the slackers, the majority of us just want to get through it," confesses a 3L.

Some students complain that "there is absolutely no sense of community at Mason, mainly because everyone works at least 20 hours per week and only comes to campus for class." Some say their classmates "seem too busy to enjoy themselves." "Students may try to tell themselves that the social void thing is normal, but it's simply not," says a 2L. Other students perceive that "there's a wealth of school-sponsored social activities" and that GMU's location "in the heart of" suburban Virginia "provides unparalleled social and cultural opportunities." "We have an abundance of student groups with something for everyone—from the GMU Sports Club, to the Jewish Law Student Association, to ACLU, to the Mason Republicans," declares a 1L. "There are hermits and partiers," adds another student, "so you can always find a quiet evening out with friends, or a drunken evening stumbling through the bar-laden streets." "There is a large faction, myself included, who enthusiastically immerse ourselves in the culture and nightlife of DC and Northern Virginia," says a fun-loving 2L. "Thursday nights you'll find some of us having dollar beers and tacos at the Mexican restaurant up the road, and you might run into another group of Masonites at two-dollar mug night at Whitlow's in Clarendon."

Getting In

At George Mason, admitted students at the 25th percentile have LSAT scores in the range of 160 and GPAs in the range of 3.1 or so. Admitted students at the 75th percentile have LSAT scores of about 166 and GPAs of roughly 3.78.

ADMISSIONS

Selectivity Rating	92
# applications received	5,024
# applicants accepted	1,004
# acceptees attending	178
Average LSAT	164
LSAT Range	160–166
Average undergrad GPA	3.6
Application fee	$35
Regular application	4/1
Regular notification	4/15
Rolling notification	Yes
Early application program	Yes
Early application deadline	12/15
Early application notification	1/15
Transfer students accepted	Yes
Evening division offered	Yes
Part-time accepted	Yes
LSDAS accepted	Yes

Applicants Also Look At
American University, The Catholic University of America, The College of William & Mary, The George Washington University, Georgetown University, University of Maryland.

International Students

TOEFL required	
of international students	Yes
Minimum paper TOEFL	600
Minimum computer TOEFL	250

FINANCIAL FACTS

Annual tuition (resident)	$15,274
Annual tuition (nonresident)	$26,502
Books and supplies	$1,000
Tuition per credit (resident)	$546
Tuition per credit (nonresident)	$947
Room and board (off-campus)	$20,228
Financial aid application deadline	3/1
% first-year students receiving some sort of aid	90
% receiving some sort of aid	90
% of aid that is merit based	3
% receiving scholarships	9
Average grant	$8,270
Average loan	$28,424
Average total aid package	$29,084
Average debt	$35,041

EMPLOYMENT INFORMATION

		Grads Employed by Field (%)	
Career Rating	85		
Rate of placement (nine months out)	99	Academic	3
Average starting salary	$83,871	Business/Industry	14
State for bar exam	VA, MD, DC, CA, NY	Government	22
Employers Who Frequently Hire Grads		Judicial clerkships	12
Hunton and Williams; Finnegan		Military	3
Henderson; Pillsbury, Winthrop, Shaw,		Private practice	41
Pittman; Venable; McGuire Woods.		Public Interest	5
Prominent Alumni			
Honorable Richard Young, judge, U.S.			
District Court; Kathleen Casey, commis-			
sioner, Securities and Exchange			
Commission; Paul Misener, vice president			
of global policy, Amazon.com.			

THE GEORGE WASHINGTON UNIVERSITY
LAW SCHOOL

INSTITUTIONAL INFORMATION

Public/private	Private
Student-faculty ratio	15:1
% faculty part-time	67
% faculty female	29
% faculty minority	9
Total faculty	327

SURVEY SAYS...
Diverse opinions accepted in classrooms
Students love Washington, DC

STUDENTS

Enrollment of law school	1,693
% male/female	55/45
% out-of-state	96
% full-time	84
% minority	26
% international	1
# of countries represented	19
Average age of entering class	24

ACADEMICS

Academic Experience Rating	**90**
Profs interesting rating	91
Profs accessible rating	83
Hours of study per day	4.05

Academic Specialties
Civil procedure, commercial law, constitutional law, corporation securities law, criminal law, environmental law, government contracts, government services, human rights law, intellectual property law, international law, labor law, legal history, legal philosophy, property, taxation.

Advanced Degrees Offered
JD 3 to 4 years, Master of Laws 1 to 2 years, Doctor of Juridical Science 3 years.

Combined Degrees Offered
JD/MBA 4 years, JD/MPA 4 years, JD/MA (international affairs) 4 years, JD/MA (history) 4 years, JD/MA (women's studies) 4 years, JD/MPH 4 years.

Clinical program required	No

Academics

With more than 1,500 full- and part-time students, The George Washington University Law School is one of the largest legal training grounds in the country. Its fairly mind-boggling array of resources include "an interesting range of classes" and a host of dual-degree programs. Although, "the best thing about GW is its location in one of the best legal markets in the United States." Going along with the territory is "a strong emphasis on clinical and real-world legal work" and "the only international human rights law clinic in the country." Students say "Amazing opportunities abound for internships, clerkships, externships, and full-time jobs at law firms, government agencies, and non-profit organizations"—which is great, as "Many students are interested in public interest law, not just 'big firm' work." Without question, "if you want immediate access to high levels of government, GW is a great choice." If intellectual property is your bag, the "high-quality" IP law program is "taught by federal circuit judges" and boasts a four-week program in Munich, Europe's "Intellectual Property Capital." Also noteworthy is "an excellent trial advocacy program" and an evening program that "treats evening students quite well."

The "very accessible, down-to-earth" professors at GW are "nationally (even internationally) renowned, funny, and brilliant," many students tell us. "They are challenging and thought provoking, and it is a pleasure to go to class," explains one student. "While some schools teach policy and then just expect you to know the law for the exam, the faculty here makes sure students leave their classroom knowing how to apply the law and why." The faculty is also "diverse in interests, strengths, opinions, and styles [and represents a] wide political spectrum."

"My experience at GW has been far and above what I expected," says one student. "Our Financial Aid Office is the smoothest-run machine in all of the District of Columbia," and "The administration really wants to come through for us as students." Aesthetically, the law school and its facilities have recently undergone a "very modern" transformation. The law school "interior is filled with rich wood, glass, leather, and gold ornamentation" to the delight of students. "The entire school looks gorgeous. They have wireless Internet access throughout the entire school, state-of-the-art classrooms, nice lounge areas, and an incredible moot courtroom." One student says, "I love having wireless Internet in class and taking exams on laptops." Now, students hope for more lounges in which to study and a bigger, better library that doesn't feel "crowded." The renovations are "really nice, but there are not enough tables to do research."

Life

George Washington is home to "easygoing law school students from all different backgrounds." These "genuinely friendly and fun" future attorneys are "smart and driven but not to the point of insanity." "You can find every type of person here, from conservative to cutthroat liberal to punk-rock chick to kids from Germany. Everyone is very involved in school clubs, which is a great way to meet people." One student relates, "My conservative friends assure me that the student body is liberal, but I have never met so many Republicans in my life." It is apparent that "students are often cliquey with their section mates," but overall, "There is a lot of camaraderie." In fact, "If you miss class, at least three people will send you the notes before you even ask." Also, "Nobody is focused on success at the expense of others. This is a very supportive environment." Some students may be self-described "nerds, but we can still talk baseball, politics,

ANNE M. RICHARD, ASSOCIATE DEAN FOR ADMISSIONS AND FINANCIAL AID
700 TWENTIETH STREET, NORTHWEST, WASHINGTON, DC 20052
TEL: 202-994-7230 FAX: 202-994-3597
E-MAIL: JDADMIT@LAW.GWU.EDU • INTERNET: WWW.LAW.GWU.EDU

college football, travel, the law, and where we are going to be drinking this weekend." Overall, students at GW tell us, "We are much happier than the people I've met who attend other DC schools."

In addition, the nation's capital is a great place to attend law school. The cost of living "isn't exorbitant like New York City" (although "a lack of affordable housing" is a "big detractor"). GW "has the best location of the DC law schools" too. The "IMF is across the street, and the World Bank is two blocks away." The White House is also nearby. "Supreme Court Justices are sometimes spotted in the law school," and political bigwigs "including the president and the Secretary of State" often speak on campus. One student marvels, "Activities just today ranged from a roundtable discussion with a federal judge to a reception and discussion on sports and entertainment law." Social life is swell, even if some feel it "revolves around beer." The Student Bar Association definitely has its act together. "You can count on a keg on the back patio for Thirsty Thursday and a bunch of rowdy GW students at a local bar for Bar Review after that." Moreover, "If you don't like lawyers, you can stroll over to an undergrad party, talk to med students, or go to Dupont Circle or Adams Morgan and mingle with DC residents." At GW, "We have bake sales, lockers, and live auctions with tons of beer. It's like a twisted version of middle school, and I wouldn't choose to go to law school anywhere else."

Getting In

Admission to George Washington is highly competitive. It's not quite as hard to get in as it is at its crosstown rival, Georgetown, but it's close. You should have an LSAT score at or above the 90th percentile and an A-minus average to be seriously considered.

Legal writing course requirement	Yes
Legal methods course requirement	Yes
Legal research course requirement	Yes
Moot court requirement	No
Public interest law requirement	No

ADMISSIONS

Selectivity Rating	**92**
# applications received	9,829
# applicants accepted	2,325
# acceptees attending	550
Average LSAT	165
LSAT Range	162–166
Average undergrad GPA	3.59
Application fee	$80
Regular application	3/1
Regular notification	Rolling
Rolling notification	Yes
Early application program	Yes
Early application deadline	12/31
Early application notification	1/15
Transfer students accepted	Yes
Evening division offered	Yes
Part-time accepted	Yes
LSDAS accepted	Yes

Applicants Also Look At

Columbia University, Georgetown University, New York University, University of California—Berkeley, University of Michigan, University of Pennsylvania, University of Washington.

International Students

TOEFL required of international students	No
TOEFL recommended of international students	No

FINANCIAL FACTS

Annual tuition	$36,310
Books and supplies	$890
Tuition per credit	$1,277
Room and board	$12,150
% first-year students receiving some sort of aid	84
% receiving some sort of aid	85
% of aid that is merit based	48
% receiving scholarships	44
Average grant	$13,000
Average loan	$33,950
Average total aid package	$35,000
Average debt	$96,770

EMPLOYMENT INFORMATION

Career Rating	90	Grads Employed by Field (%)	
Rate of placement (nine months out)	96	Academic	1
Average starting salary	$93,759	Business/Industry	10
State for bar exam	NY	Government	16
Pass rate for first-time bar	88	Judicial clerkships	10
Employers Who Frequently Hire Grads		Military	1
Department of Justice; Howrey Simon;		Other	5
Finnegan, Henderson et al.; Akin, Gump, et		Private practice	54
al; Shearman and Sterling; Arnold and		Public Interest	3
Porter; Wiley, Rein, and Fielding; Arent			
Fox; Dickstein, Shapiro, Morin, and			
Oshinsky; various government agencies.			

GEORGETOWN UNIVERSITY
LAW CENTER

Academics

The Law Center at Georgetown University is "the perfect blend of old-school intellectualism, [and] modern pragmatism." The school's location in the heart of Capitol Hill means that "connections to political and judicial institutions abound." Frequent visitors to the law school include high-ranking government officials, legal scholars, and interest group leaders who pop on over after work to chat due to the school's location "right smack in the hub of Washington activity." In addition, "About 70 percent of the cases that go before the Supreme Court have had one of the arguing attorneys go through a practice run at Georgetown Law." Students can sign up to watch before observing the actual trial, providing "an unparalleled source of training for any legal student." "It's like going to a concert in undergrad, but now we go to watch the justices do their thing," says a first-year student.

Many professors are considered to be "masters of their fields," which "can at first be intimidating," but then "They will insist that you call them by their first name" and "You will find yourself wanting to hang out during their office hours." First-year classes tend to be big, but even in the larger lecture courses, the instructors are "are able to facilitate great conversation and debate." In the smaller classes, the "genius of conversational teaching is fully developed," and an ongoing orientation program offers first-year students lessons on how to take notes, study for exams, and develop other study skills. The Law Center's unique alternative First-Year Curriculum B concentrates on making law school applicable to the legal world, and focuses heavily on jurisprudence and historical context, combining Torts and Contracts into one year-long class. Though many claim that the curve makes things unduly difficult and "Expectations and academic rigor are high," students' stress levels remain low, in large part due to the "warm and approachable" faculty, some of whom "even offer to meet with students they don't have in class." The Law Center is also heralded for its teachings in international law, its wide variety of course offerings "in just about any theoretical or practical area you can imagine," and for having one of the best clinical programs in the country, with fourteen clinics providing enough variety to satisfy even the most obscure of interests. "There simply isn't that permeating fear of failure here because our attention, as students, is constantly pushed toward a focus on all of the incredible things that we can do with our knowledge and skills," explains a first-year student.

Students at the Law Center universally agree that its "Bureaucracy is navigable," and "The administration is always open to hearing student ideas on how to improve" one observes. "Doors are open and e-mails are returned really quickly." Students say Washington, DC is "the perfect place to get any type of internship." As one 1L puts it, "There's nothing better than studying law where it is made." The Career Center is "unbelievable"; each student is assigned a counselor who "basically acts as your life coach and gives you all the tools and advice you need." The law building is within walking distance of the Supreme Court, Congress, embassies, NGOs, the Smithsonian museums, administrative agencies, and dozens of public interest organizations. It boasts a "brand-new gym" and "two beautiful law libraries" with lots of group study rooms.

ANDREW P. CORNBLATT, DEAN OF ADMISSIONS
600 NEW JERSEY AVENUE, NORTHWEST, ROOM 589, WASHINGTON, DC 20001
TEL: 202-662-9010 FAX: 202-662-9439
E-MAIL: ADMIS@LAW.GEORGETOWN.EDU • INTERNET: WWW.LAW.GEORGETOWN.EDU

Life

"It is great that we have our own campus, apart from the undergrad and other graduate institutions, because a complete sense of community is fostered," claims one happy student. Despite the school's large size, the division of first-year students into smaller 100–120 person sections helps create a more intimate atmosphere from which students benefit. Students socialize frequently within their own sections, though "The intra-section drama gets tired pretty quickly." There are tons of social, political, ethnic, and religious groups on campus, and myriad extracurricular activities are available. "Bar reviews" are held at different bars throughout the city and "keg on the quad" on some Wednesday nights provides students with free beer and food. "The amount of school-sponsored boozing that goes on is mind boggling," attests a graduating student. Without a doubt, the group at GULC is a social bunch who "love to spend time together both in and outside class." The level of competition at the school is low, and students are "respectful of each other" and "extremely friendly across the board." "Everyone wants to do well, but we act cooperatively to reach that goal." Plus, it's Washington, DC, and "You can't go wrong living here."

Getting In

One of the most highly regarded law schools in the nation, the Law Center receives the most applications out of any law school, and the numbers for those that they do admit certainly are impressive: Recently admitted students at the 25th percentile had an LSAT score of 167 and an average GPA of 3.4, while admitted students at the 75th percentile had an LSAT score of 171 and a GPA of 3.8. Georgetown also offers early action/early decision programs.

Clinical program required	No
Legal writing course requirement	Yes
Legal methods course requirement	Yes
Legal research course requirement	Yes
Moot court requirement	No
Public interest law requirement	No

ADMISSIONS

Selectivity Rating	97
# applications received	11,237
# applicants accepted	2,400
# acceptees attending	587
Average LSAT	169
LSAT Range	167–171
Average undergrad GPA	3.71
Application fee	$75
Regular application	2/1
Regular notification	Rolling
Rolling notification	Yes
Early application program	Yes
Early application deadline	11/01 and 12/01
Early application notification	12/15
Transfer students accepted	Yes
Evening division offered	Yes
Part-time accepted	Yes
LSDAS accepted	Yes

International Students

TOEFL required of international students	No
TOEFL recommended of international students	No

FINANCIAL FACTS

Annual tuition	$39,390
Books and supplies	$875
Tuition per credit	$1,445
Room and board	$18,185
Financial aid application deadline	3/1
% first-year students receiving some sort of aid	89
% receiving some sort of aid	88
% receiving scholarships	33
Average grant	$14,325
Average loan	$35,615
Average total aid package	$40,630
Average debt	$100,800

EMPLOYMENT INFORMATION

Career Rating	93	Grads Employed by Field (%)	
Rate of placement (nine months out)		Academic	1
Average starting salary	$105,058	Business/Industry	4
State for bar exam	NY, MD	Government	8
Pass rate for first-time bar	91	Judicial clerkships	10
Prominent Alumni		Other	2
Honorable George J. Mitchell, chairman of		Private practice	71
the global board, DLA Piper; Michael		Public Interest	4
Powell, chairman, MK Powell Group; Joan			
Claybrook, president, Public Citizen;			
Patrick Leahy, U.S. Senator; Brendan V.			
Sullivan Jr., partner, Williams and			
Connolly.			

GEORGIA STATE UNIVERSITY
COLLEGE OF LAW

INSTITUTIONAL INFORMATION

Public/private	Public
Student-faculty ratio	16:1
% faculty part-time	26
% faculty female	38
% faculty minority	18
Total faculty	72

SURVEY SAYS...

Diverse opinions accepted
in classrooms
Great library staff
Abundant externship/internship/
clerkship opportunities
Students love Atlanta, GA

STUDENTS

Enrollment of law school	663
% male/female	50/50
% out-of-state	13
% full-time	68
% minority	19
% international	3
# of countries represented	8
Average age of entering class	28

ACADEMICS

Academic Experience Rating	**80**
Profs interesting rating	79
Profs accessible rating	68
Hours of study per day	3.8

Academic Specialties

Civil procedure, commercial law,
corporation securities law, criminal
law, environmental law, human
rights law, intellectual property law,
international law, taxation.

Combined Degrees Offered

JD/MBA 4 years, JD/MPA 4 years,
JD/MA (philosophy) 4 years,
JD/MCRP 4 years, JD/MHA 4 years,
JD/MSHA 4 years.

Clinical program required	No
Legal writing course requirement	Yes
Legal methods course requirement	No
Legal research course requirement	Yes

Academics

The College of Law at Georgia State University receives solid reviews from students who appreciate the "quality, affordable legal education" they're receiving in the state's capital. Indeed, praise of the school's bargain tuition is sung from the rooftops; one practical 3L says, "It made no sense to go to a law school with a $35,000 a year tuition when I could get an equally good education for $6,000 a year!" That six grand a year gets Georgia State students a "great caliber" of teachers, many of whom "have recently come from practicing or are still practicing, and thus are able to give . . . great insight into what it's 'really like' out there in the legal profession." This practical experience is a perfect complement to the grounded atmosphere of GSU, where students are more trained to become attorneys than to theorize about the law.

Multiple kudos go out to Georgia State's part-time program, which "allows not only for nontraditional students to obtain a law degree while potentially working full-time and/or caring for a family, but makes these night classes available for anyone who wishes to take them, allowing full- and part-time students to mingle." The school's significant nontraditional student body appreciates this flexibility, as many of them come from the working world and would not be able to attend law school otherwise. There are a few gripes from day students that the scheduling of professors and classes can seem "heavily weighted towards evening classes." Others with more adaptable schedules believe it "gives us the opportunity to learn from adjuncts who practice during the day and teach at night." "The faculty is nothing less than outstanding," proclaims one student.

Although the Urban Life Building in which the College of Law is located "is sometimes more 'urban' than 'life'" with some "security/theft issues," the school's "surprisingly pleasant" downtown Atlanta location provides a plentiful and "amazingly diverse selection of externship opportunities." Though "Everyone agrees that we need a new building" (there are plans for it down the road) and many speak of the depressing aspects of having almost all of their 1L classes in the same two auditoriums, the "high level of technology" in the current classrooms help diminish some of the building's downsides.

One major point of contention amongst GSUers is that the College of Law "has no set curve for non-required classes, meaning the curve in one corporations class could be a 90 while another corporations class could be an 81. This necessitates either willful indifference or the careful selection of classes so as to manipulate your GPA—a difficult choice even for the most ideal among us." This also puts GSU students "at a significant disadvantage in the competition for employment," and it doesn't help that the "Career Services Office is considerably below par." Luckily, "the Federal Reserve, the Eleventh Circuit, the State Capitol, and most large law firms in the South" are all located very close to GSU (some within walking distance).

Dr. Cheryl Jester-George, Director of Admissions
PO Box 4049, Atlanta, GA 30302-4049
Tel: 404-651-2048 Fax: 404-651-1244
E-mail: ADMISSIONS@GSULAW.GSU.EDU • Internet: LAW.GSU.EDU

Life

The "mature, unpretentious, hardworking, and real-world savvy" students at the College of Law often bring "more than a couple years of impressive life experience with them into the classroom," making class discussions "interesting and relevant." "We have students who used to be doctors, researchers, police officers, engineers, business owners, stay-at-home moms (and dads), teachers, etc.," explains one 3L. "There do not seem to be too many people who came to school because they had nothing else to do." Even though there is a large part-time student population and diverse ages represented on campus, students still claim to "spend a considerable amount of social time together." In fact, students agree that a sense of camaraderie pervades the campus. As one states, "I have never . . . felt the razor's edge of cutthroat competitiveness."

Concerning hometown Atlanta, a graduating student suggests that incoming first-years "get used to the idea of a homeless person snoozing in the library cubicle next to you! What can I say—it's not Emory. But you're not paying the Emory price tag either, so something has to give." The fact that "most people commute" and the impression that the law building "seems a little shunted off to a random corner" does "deter the school from ever really attaining a campus-like feel." Fortunately there is a way to combat any unwelcome feelings of isolation: "Joining student activities are a great way to meet people at GSU."

Getting In

Georgia State cops to the fact that both the LSAT and GPA are significant factors in its admissions decision, though personal statements and letters of recommendation do play a role. Recently admitted students at the 25th percentile had an LSAT score of 157 and an average GPA of 3.1, while admitted students at the 75th percentile had an LSAT score of 160 and a GPA of 3.6. For prospective students who have taken the LSAT more than once, all scores will be reviewed.

Moot court requirement	No
Public interest law requirement	No

ADMISSIONS

Selectivity Rating	**86**
# applications received	2,888
# applicants accepted	613
# acceptees attending	213
Average LSAT	159
LSAT Range	157–160
Average undergrad GPA	3.33
Application fee	$50
Regular application	3/15
Regular notification	Rolling
Rolling notification	Yes
Early application program	No
Transfer students accepted	Yes
Evening division offered	Yes
Part-time accepted	Yes
LSDAS accepted	Yes

Applicants Also Look At

Emory University, Mercer University, University of Florida, University of Georgia.

International Students

TOEFL required of international students	No
TOEFL recommended of international students	Yes
Minimum paper TOEFL	680

FINANCIAL FACTS

Annual tuition (resident)	$7,366
Annual tuition (nonresident)	$23,284
Books and supplies	$750
Fees per credit (resident)	$520
Fees per credit (nonresident)	$520
Tuition per credit (resident)	$264
Tuition per credit (nonresident)	$927
Room and board	$10,986
Financial aid application deadline	4/1
% first-year students receiving some sort of aid	65
% receiving some sort of aid	70
% of aid that is merit based	7
% receiving scholarships	10
Average grant	$3,542
Average loan	$14,951
Average total aid package	$15,341
Average debt	$45,326

EMPLOYMENT INFORMATION

Career Rating	**88**	**Grads Employed by Field (%)**	
Rate of placement (nine months out)	95	Business/Industry	11
Average starting salary	$67,049	Government	13
State for bar exam	GA	Judicial clerkships	7
Pass rate for first-time bar	93	Other	1
Employers Who Frequently Hire Grads		Private practice	62
Alston and Bird; Arnall, Golden, and		Public Interest	6
Gregory; Drew Eckl; Jones Day; Kilpatrick			
and Stockton.			
Prominent Alumni			
Dr. Claudia Adkinson, Executive Associate			
Dean, Emory University School of			
Medicine; Evelyn Ann Ashley,			
partner/founder, Red Hot Law Group of			
Ashley LLCA.			

GONZAGA UNIVERSITY
SCHOOL OF LAW

Academics

Relatively small Gonzaga University School of Law has quite a lot to offer. The Jesuit influence is notable in Gonzaga's "great tradition of public service," and the school offers great respect and support to those pursuing a career in public interest (all students must perform 30 documented public service hours to get a diploma). Another perk is the "fabulous legal research and writing program," which "provides an excellent understanding of how to effectively and efficiently explain complex legal issues." "A strong externship program" "provides real-world experience," and the "on-site" University Legal Assistance Clinic gives students "real-life experience while under the supervision of attorneys."

Academically, "It really seems that the professors and administration want you to succeed." The "very driven and dedicated" administration is "open and accessible." "The administration has been very helpful and friendly to even my most idiotic of questions," confides a 1L. The "collegial, approachable, [and] enthusiastic" professors maintain "an open-door policy" and "will find time to meet with you if their office hours don't work." "It is nice to be at a school where the faculty knows you by name and truly cares about your academic success," says a 2L. In class, a few professors are "absolutely horrible," but most are "absolutely incredible." Professors tend to have "unique backgrounds" and "relevant, real-world experience." "While the majority of the faculty is relatively young in comparison to other institutions," Gonzaga's professors "all have very strong backgrounds in their respective subject areas," which gives students "an opportunity to learn what the real practice of law is like."

Gonzaga has "many ties to the local community." "The lawyers in town are practically all from GU and participate in the events here often," notes a 2L. One contingent of students says that "Career Services works very hard to help you find work" and "aggressively" offers assistance with resumes, networking, and job opportunities. "Several times a year, Career Services will bring in attorneys from various fields and give students free pizza while the practitioners talk about their particular area of expertise and how to get into it." The pro-Career Services faction also says that "opportunities to practice in big cities are increasing" for Gonzaga students. "I know plenty of students who are getting into big firms," declares a 2L. However, another group of students says that "Career Services needs a lot of help" because "Too many students are worried about finding jobs in desirable locations." "If you want to practice in eastern Washington, Gonzaga is a great school," acknowledges one student. "If you want to practice in civilization, going to Gonzaga puts you at a great disadvantage."

Gonzaga's "brand-new" facility "sits right next to the Spokane River," affording "beautiful views." The building itself "has limited space for students to gather or study" but it's "almost in the very center of the city," so "commuting every morning is a breeze." "Modern technology" is everywhere and "very reliable" wireless Internet access is available "throughout." The "excellent" library boasts a "helpful staff" and "a large selection of resources." "Only a few" of the classrooms "are less than ideal, and this is only the case when larger classes are held in those particular rooms."

Life

There isn't "very much" ethnic diversity here. "See the handful of minority students in admissions brochures and [the] DVD?" asks a 2L. "They're the only ones." "The Catholic and Mormon students create a fairly conservative atmosphere" but there is more than enough political diversity to go around, with both liberals and conservative abounding.

SUSAN LEE, DIRECTOR OF ADMISSIONS
PO BOX 3528, SPOKANE, WA 99220
TEL: 800-793-1710 FAX: 509-323-3697
E-MAIL: ADMISSIONS@LAWSCHOOL.GONZAGA.EDU • INTERNET: LAW.GONZAGA.EDU

"The mandatory curve creates a very competitive environment, particularly among first-year students." "Students get especially competitive around finals." "For the most part," though, "fellow students are more than willing to lend a helping hand when you are lost." "It's not nearly as competitive as I expected it to be," emphasizes a 1L. The Student Bar Association routinely "provides review sessions for each first-year class and for each professor." During these sessions, "Students can ask questions in an environment that is less intimidating than the classroom."

"There are tons of opportunities to get involved" in extracurricular activities. Student organizations cover "almost every issue," and "Their participation in the law school community is prominent." "Like any smaller school, Gonzaga has its cliques," but overall "The sense of community is amazing." "We go to Gonzaga basketball games, run along the Spokane River, or just get together to watch football," says a 2L. "Spokane's small-town nature, the relatively small student body, and the fact that almost all the students are from elsewhere means that there is a tendency for the students to become very close," explains another student. Far and away, the "boring," "blue-collar" town of Spokane is the most griped-about aspect of life here. The cost of living is low, but students end most compliments there. "Spokane is one step above purgatory," reflects one student, "but it is not a very big step." On the bright side, "Glacier National Park, Banff, Seattle, Northern Idaho, and lower British Columbia are all within a few hours' drive." "There are awesome outdoor activities nearby" as well. "There's rock climbing and mountain biking" as well as "plenty of smooth asphalt for road cyclists." "Tons of great ski areas and golf courses" are nearby and "dirt cheap."

Getting In

Gonzaga's admitted students at the 25th percentile have LSAT scores in the range of 153 and GPAs hovering around 3.0. Admitted students at the 75th percentile have LSAT scores of about 157 and GPAs of about 3.6.

ADMISSIONS

Selectivity Rating	75
# applications received	1,599
# applicants accepted	606
# acceptees attending	206
Average LSAT	155
LSAT Range	153–157
Average undergrad GPA	3.3
Application fee	$50
Regular application	4/15
Regular notification	Rolling
Rolling notification	Yes
Early application program	No
Transfer students accepted	Yes
Evening division offered	No
Part-time accepted	Yes
LSDAS accepted	Yes

Applicants Also Look At
Lewis & Clark College, Seattle University, University of Denver, University of Idaho, University of Oregon, University of the Pacific, Willamette University.

International Students
TOEFL required of international students	Yes
Minimum paper TOEFL	600
Minimum computer TOEFL	250

FINANCIAL FACTS
Annual tuition	$27,840
Books and supplies	$5,740
Tuition per credit	$928
Room and board (off-campus)	$3,375
Financial aid application deadline	2/1
% first-year students receiving some sort of aid	100
% receiving some sort of aid	100
% of aid that is merit based	19
% receiving scholarships	67
Average grant	$9,000
Average loan	$35,345
Average total aid package	$42,345
Average debt	$84,000

EMPLOYMENT INFORMATION

		Grads Employed by Field (%)	
Career Rating	73		
Rate of placement (nine months out)	94	Academic	1
Average starting salary	$54,803	Business/Industry	13
State for bar exam	WA	Government	17
Pass rate for first-time bar	71	Judicial clerkships	12
Employers Who Frequently Hire Grads		Military	3
Various law firms in Spokane and throughout Washington; various local and state government entities including military.		Private practice	48
		Public Interest	6

Prominent Alumni
Christine Gregoire, Governor of Washington State; Justice Barbara Madsen, Washington State Supreme Court; Justice Mary Fairhurst, Washington State Supreme Court; Paul Luvera, plantiffs attorney, lead in tobacco litigation.

HAMLINE UNIVERSITY
SCHOOL OF LAW

INSTITUTIONAL INFORMATION

Public/private	Private
Affiliation	Methodist
Student-faculty ratio	16.5:1
% faculty female	44
% faculty minority	10
Total faculty	42

SURVEY SAYS...

Diverse opinions accepted
in classrooms
Great research resources
Abundant externship/internship/
clerkship opportunities

STUDENTS

Enrollment of law school	716
% male/female	48/52
% out-of-state	45
% full-time	70
% minority	11
% international	1
# of countries represented	8
Average age of entering class	27

ACADEMICS

Academic Experience Rating	**72**
Profs interesting rating	72
Profs accessible rating	85
Hours of study per day	4.71

Academic Specialties

Commercial law, criminal law, government services, health law intellectual property law, international law, labor law, property, corporations, social justice, alternative dispute resolution.

Advanced Degrees Offered

JD 3 years, LLM (international lawyers) 1 year.

Combined Degrees Offered

JD/MAPA (Masters of Public Administration) 4 years, JD/MANM (Masters Nonprofit Management) 4 years, JD/MAM (Masters in Management) 4 years, JD/MLIS (Masters Library and Information Science) 4 years, JD/MAOL (Masters Arts in Organizational Leadership) 4 years.

Academics

Hamline University's School of Law is a relatively new program that focuses on giving its legal education curriculum a family feel. Those studying within Hamline's confines speak warmly of their teachers, a "combination of full-time faculty and adjuncts" who "provide a good balance of theory and practice." This "accessible" group is "committed to student learning" and even goes as far "as giving out their home phone numbers and encouraging students to call" in order to make sure that students properly grasp the material. The majority of Hamline's "liberal" professors "don't use the Socratic Method after first year," which students say is a nice reprieve. As an added bonus, "Many of Hamline's professors have worked prior to teaching," which "brings great real-world experience to the classroom."

Located in St. Paul, Minnesota, school officials run the school with a heartland touch. The administration is "always open to hear concerns," creating a "supportive environment" that encourages "connections with the broader community." A third-year student offers an example of the administration's focus on community: "When I deployed to Afghanistan midway through the second semester of my first year, the administration bent over backwards to ensure that my slot remained open and my scholarship was put into a holding status. The faculty and students maintained contact with me during the next 24 months, sending me care packages and e-mails." This sense of devotion to the student body is complimented by Hamline's "strong" Career Services Office, which "is helpful in all different types of legal career paths (and quite a few grads go public interest or nonpracticing)." The school's concentration on real-world experience also plays a key role in both developing grads who entered law school fresh out of college, as well as helping educate the nontraditional students who are coming from outside careers. Hamline's diverse clinical programs offer students the chance to clerk for a judge, do public interest law, corporate law, or work for the DA, all of which is done for credit for during the semester.

Though it's not winning any prizes, the law building is described by students as "not bad," though some think it could benefit from more quiet locations for studying, and the law library is "more than adequate." Hamline's new Health Law Institute wins raves merely for "(preparing) its students for an area that will require attorney assistance long into the future," and the Alternative Dispute Resolution Program offers a unique specialization not found at many other schools. The unusual (and popular) weekend program is especially tailored to nontraditional working students, which "allows students juggling families and/or jobs [to have] some flexibility." However, for regular students, "Registration is tough when there is only one section of every class, even popular ones like Evidence or Corporations (that is, unless as a weekday student you want to go to a weekend class on Sunday morning)." Still, second- and third-year law students are given the opportunity to self-schedule finals, and the "quality of the legal education is competitive with the other area schools." One third-year student proclaims, "If you want a rigorous environment, but don't want to have to watch your back for three years, Hamline is for you."

Life

Students at the School of Law mention the word "community", and they mention it often. This group "is quite diverse in terms of race, geographic background, politics, sexual orientation, age, and careers before law school," and this diversity "adds a nice dynamic to classroom discussions." "Hamline certainly operates like a family, but it's really two families: the weekend students and the day students," says one student, to a chorus of agreement. "Weekend program students are a different breed," says one 2L. "We already have careers for the most part." Some claim that this difference in background and priorities adds flavor to the student body's eclectic mix, but others mention the divide between the two different sets as the source of a palpable tension. Though Bar Review on Thursday nights is a good social opportunity to mingle with classmates at local bars, the weekenders are "more likely to socialize while we are studying, or to meet for a nice, more formal dinner—or meet at McDonald's with [their] kids." Still, "everyone gets along and cares about one another" which makes Hamline "a far cry from the dog-eat-dog world of law school." "There are many different student organizations that are perfect for networking, support, or simply to build friendships," says a second-year student. Apropos of nothing, "As far as mid-life crises go, law school is cheaper than fast cars and fast women," says a 3L.

Getting In

With an admit rate of nearly 50 percent, no one would ever accuse Hamline of closing its doors to qualified students. The school's rolling admissions policy allows students to submit an application up until the July prior to the fall in which they would enter (though the preferred deadline is April 1). The average LSAT for last year's admitted students was 154.

Clinical program required	No
Legal writing course requirement	Yes
Legal methods course requirement	Yes
Legal research course requirement	Yes
Moot court requirement	No
Public interest law requirement	No

ADMISSIONS

Selectivity Rating	**71**
# applications received	1,500
# applicants accepted	716
# acceptees attending	250
Average LSAT	154
LSAT Range	150–158
Average undergrad GPA	3.36
Application fee	$50
Regular application	Rolling
Regular notification	Rolling
Rolling notification	Yes
Early application program	No
Transfer students accepted	Yes
Evening division offered	Yes
Part-time accepted	Yes
LSDAS accepted	Yes

Applicants Also Look At
Drake University, Marquette University, University of Denver, University of Minnesota, University of St. Thomas, University of Wisconsin, William Mitchell College of Law.

International Students

TOEFL required of international students	Yes
Minimum paper TOEFL	600
Minimum computer TOEFL	250

FINANCIAL FACTS

Annual tuition	$28,390
Books and supplies	$800
Tuition per credit	$1,015
Room and board (on/off-campus)	$10,453/$14,043
Financial aid application deadline	4/1
% first-year students receiving some sort of aid	95
% receiving some sort of aid	88
% of aid that is merit based	98
% receiving scholarships	48
Average grant	$18,934
Average loan	$26,960
Average debt	$85,199

EMPLOYMENT INFORMATION

Career Rating	**78**	**Grads Employed by Field (%)**	
Rate of placement (nine months out)	97	Academic	2
Average starting salary	$53,079	Business/Industry	30
State for bar exam	MN, WI, IL, NY, WA	Government	9
Pass rate for first-time bar	88	Judicial clerkships	9
		Private practice	44
		Public Interest	6

HARVARD UNIVERSITY
HARVARD LAW SCHOOL

INSTITUTIONAL INFORMATION

Public/private	Private
Student-faculty ratio	10.5:1
% faculty part-time	21
% faculty female	48
% faculty minority	11
Total faculty	260

SURVEY SAYS...
Great research resources
Great library staff
Abundant externship/internship/
clerkship opportunities

STUDENTS

Enrollment of law school	1,719
% male/female	55/45
% out-of-state	86
% full-time	100
% minority	31
% international	4
# of countries represented	73
Average age of entering class	24

ACADEMICS

Academic Experience Rating	**91**
Profs interesting rating	82
Profs accessible rating	63
Hours of study per day	3.74

Academic Specialties
Civil procedure, commercial law, constitutional law, corporation securities law, criminal law, environmental law, government services, human rights law, intellectual property law, international law, labor law, legal history, legal philosophy, property, taxation.

Advanced Degrees Offered
LLM 1 year, SJD.

Combined Degrees Offered
JD/LLM, JD/MBA, JD/MPP, JD/MPP/ID, JD/PhD, JD/MA, JD/MALD, JD/EdM, JD/MDiv, JD/MPH, JD/MUP.

Clinical program required	No
Legal writing course requirement	Yes

Academics

Welcome to Harvard Law School, where "the resources—financial and material—are ridiculous." "Everything you need is right at your fingertips," says one student. "It's like having a remote control for your legal education." There is a "tremendous variety of courses" along with an "amazing" alumni network ("Chief Justice Roberts, Senator Barack Obama, and Elle Woods . . . "). The perennial complaint here is the lack of "practical emphasis." "We need a stronger legal writing curriculum," gripes a 3L. Many worry that the first year of classes have "little or no bearing on actual law practice," and Harvard is currently at the forefront of law schools looking to overhaul their first-year curriculum to include a wider range of classes. Other students disagree, though, citing the "incredible" clinical programs. "Nothing could prepare me better for a career in litigation than the real experience I am getting in litigation," explains a 2L.

The "fabulous" professors "range from amazing scholars and teachers to true nuts who probably couldn't find employment outside of academia." "I'm being taught contracts by one of the most prominent contracts theorists in the world and a former Solicitor General," brags a 1L. "You can't really beat that." "The breadth of knowledge of the professors, along with their professional experience, continually amazes me," adds another 1L. "There is a lot to be said for simply having the ability to interact with a large number of the country's greatest legal minds." However, some find certain professors "arrogant" and "aloof." This means that the faculty can be "somewhat inaccessible." "There's an intimidation factor in approaching some profs," and others "are just too busy to pin down."

The "very responsive" administration is "concerned about student issues." Dean Kagan "rocks." "If we need it, we get it," claims a 3L. "The administration spoils us ridiculously, all in the name of making students happy." At times, though, "This school is too big" and "feels like a factory, albeit one that pumps out very smart and well-qualified products."

"The career counseling services are pretty good," says one student. Not that they really need to be since "The Harvard name will take you anywhere in the world." "As one professor told us last year, '80 percent of what Harvard will do for you it did on the day you were accepted.'" "If you have a pulse and you graduate from HLS, you can get an excellent job," promises one student, adding that "it will probably be at the highest possible level in whatever city you work." One truly spectacular feature of Harvard Law is the "generous financial support for students working in the public interest during and after law school." There is an "excellent loan repayment program" if you want to do "public interest, government, or low-income work."

The facilities here "are almost all recently renovated." "The only buildings that are truly ugly are the dorms," which are "supposed to be magnificent examples of Bauhaus architecture." Most classrooms "are beautiful and intimate" and have plenty of "high-tech additions." Wireless access is good, but there are "too few outlets for laptops." Students love that the "library has every book ever imagined." This comes as no surprise as it's the biggest law library in the world.

Life

Students find that "everyone is extraordinarily talented" at Harvard. "Accomplished, hardworking, [and] unnervingly bright" are just a few ways to describe these future lawyers. "Sitting in class, you can look around and realize these are the brightest people

TOBY STOCK, ASSISTANT DEAN FOR ADMISSIONS
1515 MASSACHUSETTS AVENUE, CAMBRIDGE, MA 02138
TEL: 617-495-3109 FAX: 617-496-9179
E-MAIL: JDADMISS@LAW.HARVARD.EDU • INTERNET: WWW.LAW.HARVARD.EDU

of our generation," says a 2L, "and 75 percent of the learning here is from engaging your classmates and friends." "The kids here tend to be serious and a bit socially awkward," though. Despite "stereotypes" claiming "They're not the nicest group of people," many note "how friendly, cooperative, and even fun the vast majority of Harvard's students are."

Harvard can be "competitive." Some students are "obsessed with prestige." However, "The Harvard Law depicted in *The Paper Chase* is dead, and in its place is a much more collegial, respectful place." "Approximately the top 10 or 20 percent of students are intensely competitive," one student explains. "Everyone else is content getting a top-firm job . . . and is hardly competitive at all."

"The school is a bit large," and "There is a thriving social atmosphere." "Dean Kagan's metaphor of HLS as the New York City of law schools is remarkably accurate," says one student. "Having so many students here provides for a tremendous wealth of student organizations, activities, clubs, and events." "Funding for all sorts of student projects" makes it "very easy to put together amazing extracurricular experiences that are fantastic skill and resume builders." "From BLSA to the Federalist Society, the California Club to the Shooting Club," "There is a lot going on, always." "We have free coffee morning and night, a law school ice rink in the winter, and sand volleyball courts in the fall and spring," says a 2L. "The gym is brand new and insanely good." There are even "free professional massages during finals." Ultimately, "It all makes for a highly caffeinated, active, and involved community."

Getting In

When students arrive at law school to hear the dean say—"The competition is over. You've won."—it's safe to say that getting in wasn't what most would call slightly difficult. Admitted students at the 25th percentile have LSAT scores of 169 and GPAs of about 3.72. Admitted students at the 75th percentile have LSAT scores of 175 and GPAs of about 3.95. (Note that Harvard tends to average multiple LSAT scores.)

Legal methods course requirement	Yes
Legal research course requirement	Yes
Moot court requirement	Yes
Public interest law requirement	Yes

ADMISSIONS

Selectivity Rating	**99**
# applications received	6,810
# applicants accepted	834
# acceptees attending	558
LSAT Range	169–175
Application fee	$75
Regular application	2/1
Regular notification	Rolling
Rolling notification	Yes
Early application program	No
Transfer students accepted	Yes
Evening division offered	No
Part-time accepted	No
LSDAS accepted	Yes

Applicants Also Look At
Columbia University, New York University, Stanford University, Yale University.

International Students

TOEFL required of international students	No
TOEFL recommended of international students	No

FINANCIAL FACTS

Annual tuition	$37,100
Books and supplies	$1,050
Room and board	$16,966
% first-year students receiving some sort of aid	73
% receiving some sort of aid	82
% receiving scholarships	42
Average grant	$17,131
Average loan	$36,391
Average total aid package	$45,213
Average debt	$99,367

EMPLOYMENT INFORMATION

Career Rating	98	Grads Employed by Field (%)	
Rate of placement (nine months out)	99	Business/Industry	4
Average starting salary	$110,000	Government	2
State for bar exam	NY, MA	Judicial clerkships	23
Pass rate for first-time bar	97	Private practice	65
Employers Who Frequently Hire Grads		Public Interest	5
Major national law firms; federal and state governments; investment banks; consulting firms; law schools.		Academia	1

HOWARD UNIVERSITY
SCHOOL OF LAW

INSTITUTIONAL INFORMATION

Public/private	Private
Student-faculty ratio	13:1
% faculty part-time	45
% faculty female	40
% faculty minority	78
Total faculty	67

SURVEY SAYS...
Diverse opinions accepted
in classrooms
Students love Washington, DC

STUDENTS

Enrollment of law school	402
% male/female	40/60
% full-time	100
% minority	94
Average age of entering class	25

ACADEMICS

Academic Experience Rating	**80**
Profs interesting rating	88
Profs accessible rating	81
Hours of study per day	4.65

Academic Specialties
Commercial law, constitutional law, corporation securities law, criminal law, environmental law, human rights law, intellectual property law, international law, labor law, property, taxation.

Advanced Degrees Offered
LLM (foreign lawyers only) 1 to 2 years.

Combined Degrees Offered
JD/MBA 4 years.

Clinical program required	No
Legal writing course requirement	Yes
Legal methods course requirement	Yes
Legal research course requirement	No
Moot court requirement	No
Public interest law requirement	No

Academics

In the tradition of the famous civil rights lawyer Charles Hamilton Houston, Howard University promotes its "legacy for cultivating social engineers." Because Howard is historically a Black institution, its students take their responsibility of serving as the next generation of minority attorneys very seriously. A 3L reports: "Many of our professors encourage us to think beyond the rules of the law and apply it to the real world and also to analyze the implications of the law, particularly as they apply to poor and minority communities." This classroom emphasis on "strong policy and social justice responses to the law" further provides students with the experience they need to succeed in their careers postgraduation.

Howard's Washington, DC, location "makes it easy to connect with professionals in a variety of fields, especially if you are going into public interest." Students find internships and jobs with the government, nonprofits, and lobby organizations. However, not everyone wants to engineer society from the trenches: "Corporate law is alive and well at Howard." A 2L reports, "Students focus on getting a job more than anything, especially those highly coveted six-figure law firm positions." The Career Placement Office staff members win approval from the students for their "tireless efforts to encourage firms to recruit and hire from Howard." Students feel as if they're in "the center of the recruiting universe," with plenty of "unique opportunities because of our institution's history."

Some students even feel that Howard has become too workforce-oriented and places too intense a focus on "teaching students how to be employees instead of leaders and innovators." Most, however, appreciate the "emphasis on practical experience," including clinics in criminal justice, immigration law, small business law, and alternative dispute resolution. In the classroom, students enjoy "a nontraditional dialogue approach," which allows them to get to know their professors, whom they consider "intense, dedicated, . . . absolutely brilliant, and true scholars in their respective fields." Beyond their achievements, the faculty is personally invested in the success of students. Professors "push hard" and "expect a lot," but also maintain the fine line between testing students' limits and keeping them afloat. Dean Kurt Schmoke, the former Mayor of Baltimore, also racks up popularity points for his "pleasant attitude and accessibility." His reputation mitigates some gripes with the rest of the administration, whose "Bureaucracy can be a little frustrating." Howard also offers "merit-based awards to the top 50 percent of the class" as a way of encouraging students to succeed.

One of the highlights of a Howard Law education is the Legal Research, Reasoning, and Writing Program, which trains students in the elusive arts of navigating a law library, formulating analogical reasoning, and writing readable legalese. "Legal and scholarly writing is very important, and recruiters are constantly commenting on the quality of the writing from this law school," notes a 3L. Students looking for courses beyond the scope of the Howard curriculum may take part in a summer program in Cape Town, where they have the chance to study international trade law and visit the South Africa Parliament. Additionally, the school runs an exchange program with Brigham Young University School of Law and the University of Vermont for students interested in environmental law.

REGINALD MCGAHEE, JD, ASSISTANT DEAN OF ADMISSION/DIRECTOR OF ADMISSIONS
2900 VAN NESS STREET, NORTHWEST, SUITE 219, WASHINGTON, DC 20008
TEL: 202-806-8008 FAX: 202-806-8162
E-MAIL: ADMISSIONS@LAW.HOWARD.EDU • INTERNET: WWW.LAW.HOWARD.EDU

On the Howard campus, you won't spot a law student without the required laptop, although some experience difficulty when they try to find a place to plug in and log on. "It's currently difficult to rely on Howard Law e-mail for communication from employers," writes a 3L. Students complain about classrooms with shabby furnishing and arctic temperatures in the winter. The brand-new library, however, earns praise for offering "lots of study space in a quiet and state-of-the-art building."

Life

A number of students describe the Howard student community as a "big extended family." Howard's "reputation attracts thousands of applicants of all races and ethnicities. Its familial atmosphere keeps them there." Another guiding philosophy at Howard, "Lifting As We Climb," means that "students who are [at] the top of the class are more than willing to take time to help other students who may be struggling." First-year students "don't even have to ask for help. Upperclassmen volunteer it out of love." There's no "ripping pages out of books in the library" here; everyone shares cases and invites each other to parties, "making it very easy to meet others" and creating a "community feeling I have never seen at any other educational institution."

Politically, students tend to "fall on the liberal side, for the most part," and make their opinions known both in and out of the classroom. Student organizations run the gamut, from *The Scroll*, a social justice Law Review (whose "reputation is on the rise"), to the Christian Legal Society and La Alianza, a Latino student group. The dean's lecture series addresses topics such as racial profiling, the implications of national elections, and the modern applications of historic legal decisions.

Getting In

The rolling admissions window runs from October to March for fall semester start only. Out of 2,550 applicants, roughly 421 are accepted and 155 subsequently enroll.

ADMISSIONS

Selectivity Rating	79
# applications received	2,550
# applicants accepted	421
# acceptees attending	155
Average LSAT	153
LSAT Range	148–158
Average undergrad GPA	3.3
Application fee	$60
Regular application	3/31
Regular notification	Rolling
Rolling notification	Yes
Early application program	No
Transfer students accepted	Yes
Evening division offered	No
Part-time accepted	No
LSDAS accepted	Yes

Applicants Also Look At
American University, The Catholic University of America, The George Washington University, Georgetown University, New York University, Texas Southern University, University of Maryland.

International Students

TOEFL required of international students	Yes
Minimum paper TOEFL	550

FINANCIAL FACTS

Annual tuition	$15,990
Books and supplies	$1,103
Fees per credit	$655
Tuition per credit	$724
Room and board	$10,169
Financial aid application deadline	3/1
% first-year students receiving some sort of aid	90
% receiving some sort of aid	95
% of aid that is merit based	58
Average grant	$13,000
Average loan	$18,500
Average total aid package	$29,000
Average debt	$60,000

EMPLOYMENT INFORMATION

Career Rating	84	**Grads Employed by Field (%)**	
Rate of placement (nine months out)	96	Academic	3
Average starting salary	$72,465	Business/Industry	13
Employers Who Frequently Hire Grads		Government	18
Law firms; judicial clerkships; government.		Judicial clerkships	15
		Military	1
		Private practice	43
		Public Interest	7

ILLINOIS INSTITUTE OF TECHNOLOGY
CHICAGO-KENT COLLEGE OF LAW

INSTITUTIONAL INFORMATION

Public/private	Private
Student-faculty ratio	7:1
% faculty part-time	61
% faculty female	30
% faculty minority	7
Total faculty	155

SURVEY SAYS...

Great research resources
Students love Chicago, IL

STUDENTS

Enrollment of law school	1,041
% male/female	53/47
% out-of-state	40
% full-time	78
% minority	20
% international	1
# of countries represented	14
Average age of entering class	24

ACADEMICS

Academic Experience Rating	**88**
Profs interesting rating	86
Profs accessible rating	77
Hours of study per day	3.77

Academic Specialties

Environmental law, intellectual property law, international law, labor law, litigation and alternative dispute resolution, public interest law.

Advanced Degrees Offered

JD 3 to 4 years, LLM 1 to 4 years.

Combined Degrees Offered

JD/MBA 3.5 to 5 years, JD/LLM 4 to 5 years, JD/MS (financial markets) 4 to 5 years, JD/MPA 3.5 to 5 years, JD/MS (environmental management) 3.5 to 5 years, JD/MPH 3.5 years.

Clinical program required	No
Legal writing course requirement	Yes
Legal methods course requirement	No
Legal research course requirement	Yes

Academics

If you're looking to "feel both challenged and encouraged to learn" rather than "beaten down by the stereotypical combination of sadistic professors and hyper-competitive classmates," then you might want to try the Chicago-Kent College of Law which works to create a scholarly community under the auspices of a science and engineering heavyweight. Placed "just high enough in the rankings to attract talented students who aren't arrogant, but not too high so that the professors are attracted for research rather than teaching," the school makes it clear up front that the experience "will be competitive," while also stressing "how important it is to not dwell on grades and rank even though they're important."

Known for its "intense" and "well-recognized" legal writing program (one of the few three-year programs in the country), students at Chicago-Kent must endure "several hellish weeks each semester" so that they can say, "The memo [I] did in the first three weeks of school is the equivalent of another school's 1L final project." "Every attorney I've worked with in the past three years has commented on the strength of my legal writing skills," boasts one third-year student. Other tough aspects of the school's curriculum include its grading curve, which gives transfer students an unfair advantage "because their GPA is not deflated by the first-year curve" and results in the school awarding more scholarships than students can retain "due to the academic standards that must be maintained." Many also cite the Intellectual Property Program and the variety of in-house clinics (in which students work with actual clients for credit) as strengths.

As one would expect judging from its parent institution, Chicago-Kent's "top-notch" classrooms are "enabled with the best educational technology," including myriad outlets, and the entire campus is blanketed with wireless Internet (some even claim the technology "outranks" the institute itself). The comprehensive library provides plenty of study space, and is run by a "knowledgeable" staff that is "willing to assist you with any issues." Chicago-Kent's location in the West Loop "is crucial to practical experience" and "maximizes chances for great externships," though summer jobs "aren't all that easy to come by with the competition of Northwestern, University of Chicago, U of I, and Michigan so close by."

Despite a large contingent of part-time faculty in the upper-level courses, professors at Chicago-Kent are "passionately engaged in the subject matter" and "totally committed to the students as well as to their research." They "work hard to encourage you and support you outside of the classroom," and are particularly good at "treating the students as adults and expecting them to perform at a higher level," according to a first-year student. Though they're not without complaints, most here say that the administration is "very accommodating [of] students' needs," and "are always quick to reply to questions." The general opinion of the Career Services Office is one of mild discontent, and a large number of students wish the school could "expand its ability to place students in the legal workplace nationwide" having noticed that most of the "prestigious" law firms only hire the top 10 percent of Chicago-Kent students. "For some reason, I say we are associated with IIT and people outside of the legal community think I am going to truck driving school," complains a 3L. After three years at Chicago-Kent, one student can safely say that "students are happy, teachers want to teach, and learning is fun, yet also difficult."

NICOLE VILCHES, ASSISTANT DEAN FOR ADMISSIONS
565 WEST ADAMS STREET, CHICAGO, IL 60661
TEL: 312-906-5020 FAX: 312-906-5274
E-MAIL: ADMIT@KENTLAW.EDU • INTERNET: WWW.KENTLAW.EDU

Life

Numerous clubs and organizations "for everything you can imagine" mean that "there is a constant flow of speakers and programs for students to attend that cover all areas of the law." After a hard day of classes and legal writing boot camp, students look forward to the Student Bar Association's monthly "Kent Nights," for which the SBA rents out a different downtown bar for a "really great way to get noses out of books and make the student body relax with each other to have a good time." The student body at Chicago-Kent is a friendly bunch, and while there is a "subtle" competitive streak throughout the years, most agree that "there is definitely a friendly, helpful attitude that prevails among students here," especially between the different sections of 1Ls. "I love being surrounded by individuals who allow me to have intelligent and insightful discussions about current issues or about what we are discussing in classes," says one student. However, a definite divide exists between day and evening students, with evening students complaining that most of the extracurricular activities are "pretty much unavailable to the evening students due to the timing of special events." While it's true that students live scattered all throughout the Chicago area, preventing some from attending certain events, others see it as a plus: "Most students will spend the better part of their day interacting with each other, instead of simply coming to class and then going home," explains a third-year student.

Getting In

Though admissions are on a rolling basis, Chicago-Kent's binding Early Decision Program is somewhat unique in the field of law school admissions. Recently enrolled students at the 25th percentile had an LSAT score of 158 and an average GPA of 3.3, while admitted students at the 75th percentile had an LSAT score of 164 and a GPA of 3.8.

Moot court requirement	Yes
Public interest law requirement	No

ADMISSIONS

Selectivity Rating	**86**
# applications received	3,034
# applicants accepted	887
# acceptees attending	215
Average LSAT	161
LSAT Range	158–164
Average undergrad GPA	3.5
Application fee	$60
Regular application	3/1
Regular notification	Rolling
Rolling notification	Yes
Early application program	Yes
Early application deadline	11/1
Early application notification	12/15
Transfer students accepted	Yes
Evening division offered	Yes
Part-time accepted	Yes
LSDAS accepted	Yes

Applicants Also Look At
American University, DePaul University, The George Washington University, The John Marshall Law School, Loyola University—Chicago, Northwestern University, University of Illinois.

International Students

TOEFL required of international students	No
TOEFL recommended of international students	No

FINANCIAL FACTS

Annual tuition	$31,150
Books and supplies	$610
Tuition per credit	$1,035
Room and board (on/off-campus)	$10,750/$13,860
% first-year students receiving some sort of aid	96
% receiving some sort of aid	91
% of aid that is merit based	22
% receiving scholarships	52
Average grant	$14,974
Average loan	$29,059
Average total aid package	$36,715
Average debt	$81,707

EMPLOYMENT INFORMATION

Career Rating	**87**	**Grads Employed by Field (%)**	
Rate of placement (nine months out)	96	Academic	1
Average starting salary	$77,608	Business/Industry	19
State for bar exam	IL	Government	13
Pass rate for first-time bar	90	Judicial clerkships	5
Employers Who Frequently Hire Grads		Military	2
Small firms; midsize to large firms; government; public interest; judicial clerkship.		Private practice	57
		Public Interest	3

Prominent Alumni
Honorable Ilana Diamond Rovner, U.S. Court of Appeals for the 7th Circuit; Honorable Anne Burke, Illinois Supreme Court; Thomas Demetrio, partner, Corboy and Demetrio; Barry Maram, director, Illinois Department of Public Aid.

INDIANA UNIVERSITY—BLOOMINGTON
SCHOOL OF LAW

INSTITUTIONAL INFORMATION

Public/private	Public
Student-faculty ratio	12:1
% faculty part-time	17
% faculty female	34
% faculty minority	12
Total faculty	56

SURVEY SAYS...
Great research resources
Great library staff

STUDENTS

Enrollment of law school	648
% male/female	59/41
% out-of-state	57
% full-time	100
% minority	17
% international	1
# of countries represented	21
Average age of entering class	24

ACADEMICS

Academic Experience Rating	87
Profs interesting rating	86
Profs accessible rating	82
Hours of study per day	4.65

Academic Specialties
Civil procedure, commercial law, constitutional law, corporation securities law, criminal law, environmental law, government services, human rights law, intellectual property law, international law, labor law, legal history, legal philosophy, property, taxation, telecommunications, trial and appellate advocacy.

Advanced Degrees Offered
SJD 1 year, LLM with thesis, LLM practicum, MCL.

Combined Degrees Offered
JD 3 years, JD/MBA 3 to 4 years, JD/MBAA 4 years, JD/MPA 4 years, JD/MSES 4 years, JD/MPA 4 years, JD/MA 4 years, MS 4 years, JD/MS 4 years, JD/PHD 5 years.

Clinical program required	No
Legal writing	
course requirement	Yes

Academics

Students at the Indiana University School of Law—Bloomington enjoy "first-rate resources and education" at "an excellent value." The law school boasts no fewer than 17 clinical programs and projects including a community legal clinic, an entrepreneurship law clinic, and an inmate legal assistance project. Externship programs include the Washington Public Interest Program, which allows 3Ls to earn credit for public interest internships with government agencies and nonprofits in Washington, DC. Students can study abroad in Florence, Barcelona, Beijing, Auckland, and a host of other international cities. Several interesting dual-degree programs and a bevy of specialization programs in taxation, international and comparative law, and intellectual property round out IU's "excellent" academic options.

The "extremely knowledgeable and accessible" faculty at IU "is really impressive." "When you go to class, you get the sense that your professors want to be in the classroom, and that makes engaging yourself in the material much easier," says a 2L. "There's a nice balance between professors who try to scare the pants off of you and the ones who really encourage you to take risks and push yourself, even if you turn out to be wrong." Even "boring" professors "really have a lot of important things to say." Outside the classroom, professors "participate in the law school social events" and "will go to great lengths to help students publish, research, and get placed" in jobs.

IU's administration "is genuinely concerned about students as individuals," and its "helpful and nice" Financial Aid Office "is the best in the country." Many students tell us that Career Services "does all it can to assist students in obtaining jobs." "I think they're great," declares a 1L. "They're not going to get a job for you, but they'll do pretty much everything else." "If you are near the top of the class," "You'll have the Indy firms drooling all over you" and you won't have a problem working at "any of the best firms in Chicago" "or even Washington, DC." Other students are more critical. "We have a good alumni base, but those in charge of the Career Services Office are ineffective at helping us take advantage of it," they say. "Career Services, while improving, has a long way to go," contends one student. "It is way too difficult for IU students to find a good job considering that it is a first tier school."

Everyone here agrees that the campus surrounding the law school is "beautiful," but the law school building itself is "worn and needs redecorating," though this should be partially alleviated by a new renovation completed in August 2007. "In general, the classrooms are uncomfortable" but "The entire building has wireless Internet" and "there are electrical outlets at each seat." The gem of IU is the law library, which students claim is "without equal in the world, in part because of its staff." "With large windows that look out on the forest in the middle of campus, it's easy to forget that you're in the middle of a Big Ten school."

Life

IU's Midwestern location helps encourage a collegial attitude that frowns on aggressive competition." Students "simply do not let the abstract, competitive nature of the grading system affect their outward nature or the way they see their classmates." "If there is a more laid-back group of students at any law school in the country, I'd like to see it," challenges a 2L. "Students find their groups and comfort zones relatively quickly." Smaller class sizes "contribute to some minor drama at times," but students "get to know each other better and have a closer relationship with the faculty." "You can learn as much law as well here as at Harvard or Yale," promises a 3L. "But you will pay less, will see people being nicer to each other, and don't have to live in a grungy New England city."

The law school is "settled into a big university" "far away from the real world" in "one of the greatest college towns in America." "The school is great for young undergraduates who appreciate a small-town environment." "Moving from a city to the boonies is still taking some getting used to," says one urbanite, "but the school offers some phenomenal cultural opportunities." There are "at least 30 ethnically diverse restaurants within a three-minute walk from the law school." Students here "work hard," but "There is great balance between the social life and the academic life." "The fitness and recreation facilities are superb" and "There are law school teams for intramurals." The Law and Drama Society "puts on a play in the school's moot court room." "The annual Women's Law Caucus Auction" is a big hit, as is an annual basketball game in IU's beloved Assembly Hall which pits students against professors. Mostly, though, "The social environment is aimed at those who like to go out and party." "We're very social, very involved, and very fun," boasts a 2L. "The school is the focal point around which life spins, but there's always something to do, somewhere to go, someone to talk to." "There are after-hours activities sponsored by the school or a student group almost each week, and if there's nothing going on students will always congregate somewhere to have fun."

Getting In

Admitted students at the 25th percentile have LSAT scores of about 158 and GPAs hovering around 3.24. Admitted students at the 75th percentile have LSAT scores of approximately 164 and GPAs of approximately 3.8.

Legal methods course requirement	No
Legal research course requirement	Yes
Moot court requirement	No
Public interest law requirement	No

ADMISSIONS

Selectivity Rating	85
# applications received	2,718
# applicants accepted	1,057
# acceptees attending	211
Average LSAT	163
LSAT Range	157–164
Average undergrad GPA	3.57
Application fee	$35
Regular application	Rolling
Regular notification	Rolling
Rolling notification	Yes
Early application program	Yes
Early application deadline	11/15
Early application notification	12/15
Transfer students accepted	Yes
Evening division offered	No
Part-time accepted	No
LSDAS accepted	Yes

Applicants Also Look At
University of Illinois, University of Iowa, University of Michigan, University of Notre Dame, University of Virginia, University of Wisconsin, Washington University.

International Students

TOEFL required of international students	Yes
Minimum paper TOEFL	600
Minimum computer TOEFL	250

FINANCIAL FACTS

Annual tuition (resident)	$14,980
Annual tuition (nonresident)	$29,507
Books and supplies	$1,558
Room and board	$12,600
Financial aid application deadline	4/1
% first-year students receiving some sort of aid	96
% receiving some sort of aid	96
% of aid that is merit based	70
% receiving scholarships	71
Average grant	$7,982
Average loan	$30,683
Average total aid package	$35,126
Average debt	$71,700

EMPLOYMENT INFORMATION

Career Rating	86	Grads Employed by Field (%)	
Rate of placement (nine months out)	99	Academic	3
Average starting salary	$75,300	Business/Industry	19
State for bar exam	IN, IL, NY, CA, OH	Government	11
Pass rate for first-time bar	92	Judicial clerkships	9
Employers Who Frequently Hire Grads		Military	1
Arnold and Porter; Baker and Daniels;		Private practice	52
Winston and Strawn; Ice Miller; Jones		Public Interest	5
Day; Kirkland and Ellis; Mayer Brown; U.S.			
Department of Justice.			
Prominent Alumni			
Chief Justice Shirley Abrahamson,			
Wisconsin Supreme Court; Lee Hamilton,			
former Congressman; Raphael Prevot,			
Labor Relations Counsel for the NFL.			

INDIANA UNIVERSITY—INDIANAPOLIS
SCHOOL OF LAW

INSTITUTIONAL INFORMATION

Public/private	Public
Student-faculty ratio	14:1
% faculty part-time	41
% faculty female	38
% faculty minority	6
Total faculty	81

SURVEY SAYS...

Great research resources
Beautiful campus
Students love Indianapolis, IN

STUDENTS

Enrollment of law school	913
% male/female	50/50
% out-of-state	32
% full-time	70
% minority	20
% international	4
# of countries represented	5
Average age of entering class	26

ACADEMICS

Academic Experience Rating	**76**
Profs interesting rating	70
Profs accessible rating	67
Hours of study per day	4.28

Academic Specialties

Constitutional law, criminal law, government services, health law, human rights law, intellectual property law, international law, taxation.

Advanced Degrees Offered

SJD.

Combined Degrees Offered

JD/MPA 4 years, JD/MBA 4 years, JD/MHA 4 years, JD/MPH 4 years, JD/MA (philosophy), 4 years, JD/MLS 4 years.

Clinical program required	No
Legal writing	
course requirement	Yes
Legal methods	
course requirement	Yes
Legal research	
course requirement	Yes
Moot court requirement	No

Academics

Despite being the lesser known of the two IU law schools (the other one is in Bloomington), the School of Law at Indiana University—Indianapolis still manages to carve out a well-regarded nook in the legal education world. Professors get solid reviews for their overall accessibility and for doing "a good job of engaging students in class discussions." "Besides ensuring academic success, faculty members take the initiative to help students find their niche in the legal community. There have been examples of professors reaching out to their contacts to obtain experiences for students," attests a 3L. IU-Indy's semester rotation system alternates the classes in IU's day and evening curriculum so that evening students learn from the same professors as do the day students, offering a good example of how the staff at IU—Indy "understands what [you're] taking on as [an] evening student." Students point out that the range of course selection and the legal writing program could use some work; many report of a muddled and unnecessarily lengthy legal writing program, which one student says "may as well be an upper-level foreign language [course] for me."

The "extremely student-friendly" administration is appreciated by most students, although there are detractors who claim that they are made to feel like "a tuition cow" and that "constant poor planning and communication cause a lot of unnecessary heartache for the students." However, for the most part, students are satisfied. "It is never a problem to schedule a meeting to sit down with the dean," says one. "Between the administration and the student groups, it seems that there's always some sort of activity being planned for us," backs up another. Career Services does its part for students as well; some would like to see more "firms from out of town" recruiting on campus, but others say that the office "has been helpful in reminding students that there are plenty of other wonderful jobs in small- to medium-sized firms, government jobs, as well as a myriad of other opportunities (all the while reminding us that those positions pay well too)."

With easy access to computer labs, advanced technology in all of the classrooms, wireless Internet, and many academic offerings available online (including online meetings with professors and remote speakers), the law school "promotes an environment that utilizes today's technology." The "spacious" and "bright" law building "is small enough to find someone easily but large enough to get away from the chit-chat and find a quiet place to study alone." "There is never a day that I dread being in the building, and that is a big deal considering how much time I spend in it!" chirps a first-year student. As an added benefit, the law school's location in Indianapolis ("for all intents and purposes, the center of the legal universe in Indiana") provides students access to many state and local resources for gaining practical experience, and IU-Indy "holds favorable rapport with all the largest firms in town." As the sole law school located in the state capital, networking opportunities are plentiful, and IU-Indy students "have a monopoly on available internships with government agencies and large corporations." "A student can take an internship in state government and walk there from class," says one.

ANGELA ESPADA, ASSOCIATE DEAN FOR STUDENT SERVICES AND ADMISSIONS
530 WEST NEW YORK STREET, INDIANAPOLIS, IN 46202-3225
TEL: 317-274-2459 FAX: 317-278-4780
E-MAIL: KHMILLER@IUPUI.EDU • INTERNET: WWW.INDYLAW.INDIANA.EDU

Life

Students at IU—Indy are a pleasant enough group, and "It's very easy to make new friends thanks to the various social activities, networking events, and classes" on campus. Though the social circuit seems to be less thriving for evening students, it's often due to outside responsibilities; as one night student puts it, "Anyone who complains about lack of social scene simply isn't trying to make friends or get out, because there is plenty to do if you're open to it." A large number of students speak of a need for more diversity within the student body, an issue the school has been trying to combat in recent years. Unfortunately, "Indiana still has a 'good ole boy' mentality present in many places," says a third-year. There is a certain amount of competitiveness "in the sense of not revealing grades or performance," but overall, students help foster an encouraging environment.

Without campus housing and with a large part-time, evening student contingent, IU—Indy is considered a commuter school, and people tend to scatter after classes end. Social life is "based strictly on friendship and/or social club membership." A 2L warns: "It is not the kind of school where all 100 people in your section will go grab a beer after class. It is a place where you can develop 10–20 really strong friendships." Once you do find these friendships, they are "great opportunities for leisure activities" both inside and outside of the school, as "Indianapolis is a cheap city." Be forewarned, however: "Parking is horrendous."

Getting In

When evaluating applicants for admission, Indy first looks at undergraduate GPA and LSAT scores, but also takes into account letters of recommendation. For applicants taking the LSAT more than once, the school will look at the best score. Applicants who are not admitted during the regular admissions cycle are considered for Indy's special summer program, meant for 30–40 students who the school feels can benefit from a rigorous, individualized summer course.

Public interest law requirement	No

ADMISSIONS

Selectivity Rating	**81**
# applications received	1,938
# applicants accepted	598
# acceptees attending	277
Average LSAT	155
LSAT Range	152–158
Average undergrad GPA	3.51
Application fee	$50
Regular application	3/1
Regular notification	Rolling
Rolling notification	Yes
Early application program	Yes
Early application deadline	11/30
Early application notification	12/31
Transfer students accepted	Yes
Evening division offered	Yes
Part-time accepted	Yes
LSDAS accepted	Yes

International Students

TOEFL required of international students	Yes
Minimum paper TOEFL	550
Minimum computer TOEFL	213

FINANCIAL FACTS

Annual tuition (resident)	$12,758
Annual tuition (nonresident)	$26,852
Books and supplies	$1,600
Fees per credit (resident)	$863
Fees per credit (nonresident)	$863
Tuition per credit (resident)	$376
Tuition per credit (nonresident)	$830
Room and board	$14,718
% first-year students receiving some sort of aid	59
% receiving some sort of aid	76
% of aid that is merit based	84
% receiving scholarships	35
Average grant	$5,000
Average loan	$17,965
Average total aid package	$20,000
Average debt	$51,676

EMPLOYMENT INFORMATION

		Grads Employed by Field (%)	
Career Rating	**74**	**Grads Employed by Field (%)**	
Rate of placement (nine months out)	94	Academic	4
Average starting salary	$65,000	Business/Industry	16
State for bar exam	IN	Government	11
Pass rate for first-time bar	78	Judicial clerkships	4
Employers Who Frequently Hire Grads		Other	12
Baker and Daniels; Barnes and Thornburg; Ice Miller.		Private practice	50
		Public Interest	3

Prominent Alumni

John Pistole, Deputy Director, FBI; Ellen Engleman, chairman, National Transportation Safety Board; Mark Roesler, president and CEO, CMG Worldwide, Inc.; Alan Cohen, chairman, president and CEO, The Finish Line Inc.

THE JOHN MARSHALL LAW SCHOOL*

INSTITUTIONAL INFORMATION

Public/private	Private
Student-faculty ratio	13:1
% faculty part-time	81
% faculty female	17
% faculty minority	4
Total faculty	290

SURVEY SAYS...

Diverse opinions accepted
in classrooms
Great library staff
Students love Chicago, IL

STUDENTS

Enrollment of law school	1,392
% male/female	55/45
% out-of-state	25
% full-time	72
% minority	18
% international	1
# of countries represented	13
Average age of entering class	24

ACADEMICS

Academic Experience Rating	**63**
Profs interesting rating	64
Profs accessible rating	63
Hours of study per day	4.34

Academic Specialties

Intellectual property law, international law, property, taxation.

Advanced Degrees Offered

LLM (taxation, intellectual property, real estate, information technology, comparative legal studies, international business and trade law, employee benefits) 1 year; MS (information technology).

Combined Degrees Offered

JD/MBA, JD/MPA, JD/MA, JD/LLM.

Clinical program required	Yes
Legal writing course requirement	Yes
Legal methods course requirement	Yes
Legal research course requirement	Yes

Academics

Smack-dab in the middle of Chicago's South Loop, the John Marshall Law School offers students a stimulating academic environment enhanced by the school's propitious location and extensive contacts in the Chicago legal community. Academically, "A few professors teach by the fear-of-God method (or the Socratic Method). Yet despite their toughness in the classroom, they are very accessible and open to discussion about course materials, legal trends, or the latest Cubs woes," writes a 3L. In particular, many students praise the adjunct staff, which "includes federal circuit judges and prosecutors" who "bring real-world experience right into the classroom, which is a breath of fresh air." It also "enables the students to gain a real-world perspective of the law." For those wishing to specialize, students point out the strength of the "Global Legal Studies Program, the Intellectual Property Law Program, and the amazing LLM programs," of which John Marshall offers seven: comparative legal studies, employee benefits, information technology, intellectual property, international business and trade, real estate, and tax.

John Marshall places a great deal of emphasis on fostering professional skills in future lawyers through training in appellate advocacy, alternative dispute resolution, client counseling, and negotiations. In addition, there is "great attention to legal writing," and "extracurricular activities—such as moot court, law journal, and the many symposiums held at the school—are a great benefit" to traditional studies. As a result, John Marshall graduates feel well prepared for their future careers and ready to "hit the ground running" once they receive their JD. A 2L advises, "If you are looking for legal theory, look elsewhere. At John Marshall, it is expected that you will practice upon graduation."

While they are introduced to legal skills in the classroom, the school's excellent location gives students direct access to a wide array of legal resources. Many say that "the school's location can't be beat," poised "right next door to the Chicago Bar Association and across the street from federal buildings." With so many important resources in the immediate vicinity, it's a piece of cake for students to interact directly with the Chicago legal community. "On my days off, I would take study breaks watching the Seventh Circuit oral arguments. Likewise, my internship was across the street—just walking distance from campus," recalls one 3L. At the hub of the city government, John Marshall maintains "great contacts" with the right people and institutions, just in case "You want to work for a judge or get involved in politics." On top of that, "Alumni relations seem to be particularly strong at JMLS."

While favorably located, students say the John Marshall campus could use a little face lift. "The facilities are somewhat mixed," explains a 2L. "It's two fairly large buildings slammed together to make one law school [making up] half a city block. There's a modern side, which is remodeled and has technical resources, and there's the antiquated side, [made up] of lecture halls fashioned from rooms that were distinctly not suited for lecturing." On the older side of campus there is a general grumble that it's "difficult to find a plug for your laptop," and several students mention that "it would be nice to have more student areas, a gym or workout center, and a day-care [center], especially for night students." However, the school has kept up with much of the latest classroom technology, and "wireless Internet is available throughout the school." Most important, John Marshall maintains world-class legal research facilities. Of particular note, "The library stores the reference material for the Chicago Bar Association, making it extremely resourceful compared [with] other institutions."

* Provisionally approved by the ABA.

WILLIAM B. POWERS, ASSOCIATE DEAN FOR ADMISSION AND STUDENT AFFAIRS
315 SOUTH PLYMOUTH COURT, CHICAGO, IL 60604
TEL: 800-537-4280 FAX: 312-427-5136
E-MAIL: ADMISSION@JMLS.EDU • INTERNET: WWW.JMLS.EDU

Life

Whether at work or play, there is a strong sense of camaraderie and friendship among students at the John Marshall Law School. Competition is mild, and no matter how tough things get, "Everyone wants their friends to do well" in class. With a total enrollment of more than 800 students, the school nonetheless maintains a low-key, intimate environment. In fact, students say "It feels like a small town community" where "Everyone knows everyone." In fact, a 2L notes, "If I bump into another student outside school, there is always a smile or an exchange of recognition, which is very comforting." Students in the part-time program report a similar sense of solidarity: "There is a great camaraderie among the evening students. We all have diverse careers and these add to the discussions in class," reports one 2L.

When they aren't hitting the books, John Marshall students are generally sociable and eager to unwind with their classmates. "When it's time to study, everyone is serious and focused, but when we can get a break, the drinks start flowing and the music starts cranking," explains a 2L. By all accounts, Chicago is an excellent backdrop for professional and personal pursuits; however, many point out that "John Marshall is located in a business area, and there is not really a lot to choose from in terms of social bars/restaurants to hang around in." In fact, students complain that it can be hard to find a decent gathering spot in and around John Marshall, as the surrounding area is not conducive, and "Student lounges need to be upgraded from old rat-infested couches and lawn chair–style seating on the fourth and fifth floors."

Getting In

John Marshall enrolls classes twice a year, admitting students for August and January. To apply to John Marshall, you must submit an undergraduate transcript, LSAT scores, a personal statement, and letters of recommendation. About one in three applicants is accepted.

Moot court requirement	No
Public interest law requirement	No

ADMISSIONS

Selectivity Rating	74
# applications received	3,172
# applicants accepted	1,127
# acceptees attending	329
Average LSAT	155
LSAT Range	153–156
Average undergrad GPA	3.12
Application fee	$60
Regular application	3/1
Regular notification	Rolling
Rolling notification	Yes
Early application program	No
Transfer students accepted	Yes
Evening division offered	Yes
Part-time accepted	Yes
LSDAS accepted	Yes

Applicants Also Look At
DePaul University, Illinois Institute of Technology, Loyola University—Chicago.

International Students

TOEFL required of international students	Yes
Minimum paper TOEFL	600

FINANCIAL FACTS

Annual tuition	$28,560
Books and supplies	$900
Tuition per credit	$952
Room and board (off-campus)	$17,620
% first-year students receiving some sort of aid	90
% receiving some sort of aid	90
% of aid that is merit based	10
% receiving scholarships	18
Average grant	$8,400
Average loan	$9,999
Average total aid package	$18,500
Average debt	$83,053

EMPLOYMENT INFORMATION

		Grads Employed by Field (%)	
Career Rating	62	Business/Industry	21
Average starting salary	$64,495	Government	12
State for bar exam	IL	Judicial clerkships	4
Pass rate for first-time bar	75	Private practice	56
Employers Who Frequently Hire Grads		Public Interest	1
Hinshaw and Culbertson; Cook County State's Attorney; Clausen Miller; City of Chicago Law Department; Sidley, Austin, Brown, and Wood.			

LEWIS & CLARK COLLEGE
LEWIS & CLARK LAW SCHOOL

INSTITUTIONAL INFORMATION

Public/private	Private
Student-faculty ratio	14:1
% faculty part-time	52
% faculty female	42
% faculty minority	5
Total faculty	143

SURVEY SAYS...
Great research resources
Liberal students
Beautiful campus

STUDENTS

Enrollment of law school	719
% male/female	53/47
% full-time	75
% minority	18
% international	1
# of countries represented	6
Average age of entering class	28

ACADEMICS

Academic Experience Rating	81
Profs interesting rating	83
Profs accessible rating	83
Hours of study per day	4.15

Academic Specialties
Commercial law, corporation securities law, criminal law, environmental law, government services, intellectual property law, labor law, property, taxation.

Advanced Degrees Offered
LLM (environmental and natural resources) 1 to 1.5 years.

Clinical program required	No
Legal writing course requirement	Yes
Legal methods course requirement	Yes
Legal research course requirement	Yes
Moot court requirement	Yes
Public interest law requirement	No

Academics

Students who take the legal plunge at Lewis & Clark Law School in beautiful Portland, Oregon, enjoy professors who are "uniformly excellent and approachable for discussion about class topics and other issues striking your fancy." The small size of the law school allows for an extremely personalized educational experience, and students benefit from this cozy setup on multiple levels, "from an academic perspective as well as from a functional perspective." "I have been lucky enough to develop solid mentor relationships with specific professors that were particularly inspirational," says a second-year student. Practically everyone involved in running the school, from the dean to the cafeteria staff, "seems to truly like each other," and the well-regarded faculty is given an "unusual amount of influence in the way that the school is run, and [in the] the school's policies."

Lewis & Clark Law School has a relatively small course load of required classes and offers a night program, bringing a large contingent of older and more experienced students to the classrooms which "adds a valuable, practical dimension to the learning experience." As one would expect from such an environmentally conscious institution, programs such as environmental and natural resources law and animal law are "unparalleled." On the other hand, some students say that if you're not looking to specialize in environmental or criminal law, "This school has very few courses to offer," especially for night students (this is hopefully tempered by the ability to pursue a certificate in numerous other areas). No matter what their specialization, the faculty is considered to be "inspirational and knowledgeable enough to stimulate thinking beyond what's required by the curriculum," and the school's size "allows for an ideal student/teacher ratio that goes further to foster a highly effective teaching environment."

Lewis & Clark's National Crime Victim Law Institute (NCVLI) is another source of pride for the school, "leading the way in an emerging field of law."

Administrators are friendly, accessible, "always willing to help out a student," and they keep the law school "running very smoothly." The research librarians are cited for being "very knowledgeable," and the Career Services Department also does its part to make sure students' needs are met, though some would like to see more non-metro area firms on campus. For students who are interested in staying in the area after graduation, there is "heavy support and involvement from the Portland legal community," and for others, "alumni are distributed all around the world."

Since the school and its student body are known for being nature-friendly, it follows that the buildings on campus are all "green" and "tucked into a forested state park." This is nice, students say, because "When you are facing the gut-wrenching pain of law school, a 'walk in the park' goes a long way." Students are quite pleased with the library and the newer building, Woodhall, but many are clamoring for an update of the other facilities. Portland is universally beloved as "a great place to live," though students say the parking situation could stand some improvements. A graduating student sums up life at the law school this way: "The professors are passionate about what they teach, and the students actually want to help each other get ahead in school. And where else do you get to study while in an overly large tree-house?"

SHANNON DAVIS, ASSISTANT DEAN FOR ADMISSIONS
LEWIS AND CLARK LAW SCHOOL, 10015 SOUTHWEST TERWILLIGER BOULEVARD, PORTLAND, OR 97219
TEL: 503-768-6613 FAX: 503-768-6793
E-MAIL: LAWADMSS@LCLARK.EDU • INTERNET: LAW.LCLARK.EDU

Life

No one would argue that "the school could definitely use a little diversity"; "liberal" describes the majority of those enrolled at Lewis & Clark, and as one 3L warns, "If you are conservative, religious, or a meat-eating capitalist, be prepared." Fortunately, the laid-back nature of the majority of the student body means that there is "a complete void of competition"; absolutely "No one participates in the awful game of one-upmanship or cutthroat competition," and "The students are genuinely interested in helping and supporting each other." The day and night students don't often interact outside of class, but this doesn't seem to be a source of much tension. There are plenty of clubs in which they can relate if they so choose, and students here "are spoiled with the number of lunchtime events," including speakers and panels. "Everyone is accepted for who they are," coos a 2L. A second-year student puts it in another way: "Good people go here."

Getting In

Gaining admission to Lewis & Clark isn't very difficult; the typical student has been in the work force for several years, which plays into the amount of weight placed on various admissions factors. GPA will factor in more heavily for recent grads, and applicants should make sure their letters of recommendation come from the appropriate sources (professors or employers). Recently admitted students at the 25th percentile had an LSAT score of 158 and an average GPA of 3.0, while admitted students at the 75th percentile had an LSAT score of 164 and a GPA of 3.6.

ADMISSIONS

Selectivity Rating	80
# applications received	2,067
# applicants accepted	882
# acceptees attending	186
Average LSAT	160
LSAT Range	158–164
Average undergrad GPA	3.3
Application fee	$50
Regular application	3/1
Regular notification	Rolling
Rolling notification	Yes
Early application program	No
Transfer students accepted	Yes
Evening division offered	Yes
Part-time accepted	Yes
LSDAS accepted	Yes

Applicants Also Look At

Santa Clara University, Seattle University, University of California—Hastings, University of Denver, University of Oregon, University of Washington, Willamette University.

International Students

TOEFL required of international students	No
TOEFL recommended of international students	Yes
Minimum paper TOEFL	600
Minimum computer TOEFL	250

FINANCIAL FACTS

Annual tuition	$27,670
Books and supplies	$4,690
Tuition per credit	$20,752
Room and board (off-campus)	$9,900
Financial aid application deadline	3/1
% first-year students receiving some sort of aid	93
% receiving some sort of aid	93
% of aid that is merit based	100
% receiving scholarships	42
Average grant	$9,076
Average total aid package	$42,260
Average debt	$72,296

EMPLOYMENT INFORMATION

Career Rating	75	**Grads Employed by Field (%)**	
Rate of placement (nine months out)	93	Academic	2
Average starting salary	$57,603	Business/Industry	15
State for bar exam	OR, CA, WA	Government	13
Pass rate for first-time bar	84	Judicial clerkships	10
Employers Who Frequently Hire Grads		Private practice	48
Numerous small and medium-sized firms;		Public Interest	12
state government (Oregon, Washington,			
Idaho, Alaska); Multnomah, Washington,			
and Clackamas Counties.			
Prominent Alumni			
Earl Blumenauer, U.S. Representative;			
Heidi Heitkamp, former Attorney General			
(ND) and 2000 Governor nominee.			

LOUISIANA STATE UNIVERSITY
PAUL M. HEBERT LAW CENTER

Academics

Often referred to as "LSU Junior High Law," due to its "rigorously enforced attendance policy," the Paul M. Hebert Law Center at Louisiana State University is "undeniably one-of-a-kind in America," according to the students in attendance. Much is made of the grueling 97-hour course load that students must endure in order to graduate (more than at most other law schools), and students definitely feel the burden of the extra work, because it forces them to place an "extremely strong focus on studying." The administration is "very strong" but is in a state of flux while a new chancellor is being chosen for the law school. Since most of the school's administration, including the chancellor, teach classes at the law center, they are "well known by the students and are extremely accessible," in recognition of the fact that "the student-teacher relationship extends beyond the classroom."

The thing that stands out most about the LSU Law Center is its curriculum. Students complete classes "in both common law and civil law studies," which means all graduating students are granted a Bachelor of Civil Law as well as the traditional Juris Doctorate, making them "marketable worldwide," a distinction that LSU students hold dear. "Knowledge of the civil law is an invaluable resource as the world continues to become a global market. We have some of the preeminent civil law scholars from around the world on the faculty of LSU Law," says one enthused 2L. Or, as a third-year student simply puts it, "We get two degrees! That makes us twice as good as everyone else." However, for many students not looking to practice international law or become law professors, there is a strong desire for a wider breadth of courses and specializations. This contingent believes that there's "way too much emphasis on a few fields of law and next to nothing in many other fields" and that "almost nothing practical is offered." "If you do not intend to practice in Louisiana, do not attend this school," warns a graduating student.

Luckily, there are all-around raves to be heard about the facilities and the "superior" technology found within its walls, including an "excellent" library as well as "well-maintained" classrooms. With the main LSU campus right next door, one can "look out the window of a classroom across to the parade ground." Faculty come from all corners of the United States, which "provides students with a wealth of diverse experiences and knowledge." "It's nice to be taught by the godfather of all Louisiana tort law, who is forever bringing his infinite theoretical knowledge to practical application, thereby showing us 'where our Porsche is parked,'" says a suitably impressed 1L. With some top names in legal education taking the podium, it's nice to see "The faculty truly engage their students" and heartening to know that professors "actually want their students to learn and enjoy doing it."

Career Services is not without its detractors, with more than a few gripes concerning the lack of encouragement or education about clerkships. "There is a lack of organized career counseling to guide the disillusioned and the misguided," claims a 2L in crisis. But a second-year student assures us: "After two years at LSU Law, I can truly say that I am impressed with the administration and faculty, assured about the quality of my legal education, and prepared to practice in the legal profession."

Life

"While the overall student body may be slightly conservative, there is certainly an equally present liberal segment," states a student. "Both views are equally accepted on campus and in the classroom." Others may disagree on the use of the qualifier "slightly," but overall, students on campus seem to get along. Most point out that there's a tension amongst competing students, especially among those at the top of the class, but no one would ever call it cutthroat. "They're still law students after all, but with a more normal human-being swagger," reasons a first-year student.

As for social outlets, "There is something for everyone, whether it be political organizations, SBA, practice area interest organizations, the LSU Law Football Club, intramurals, or occasional Law School Socials," with a healthy amount of drinking thrown in. Even more importantly, "If there isn't something out there the school is receptive and encourages you to create an organization to satisfy that need." Many are of the opinion that the sense of community is not as strong for "outsiders"—students who are not from Baton Rouge and/or did not attend LSU as an undergraduate—but agree that for the most part, "The social atmosphere is great at LSU. Lifelong friends are made and kept."

Getting In

Naturally GPA and LSAT scores play a huge role in LSU's admissions decisions, but the Admissions Office encourages applicants to submit other information that would help them evaluate the applicant's aptitude for the study of law, including evidence of personal leadership, professional and/or military service, and resumes. The committee also asks that all applicants be of "good moral character."

Public interest law requirement	No

ADMISSIONS

Selectivity Rating	**80**
# applications received	1,353
# applicants accepted	475
# acceptees attending	204
Average LSAT	156
LSAT Range	154–159
Average undergrad GPA	3.5
Application fee	$25
Regular application	2/6
Regular notification	2/6
Rolling notification	Yes
Early application program	No
Transfer students accepted	Yes
Evening division offered	No
Part-time accepted	No
LSDAS accepted	Yes

Applicants Also Look At

Loyola University—New Orleans, Tulane University, University of Mississippi.

International Students

TOEFL required of international students	Yes
TOEFL recommended of international students	Yes
Minimum paper TOEFL	600
Minimum computer TOEFL	250

FINANCIAL FACTS

Annual tuition (resident)	$10,722
Annual tuition (nonresident)	$19,818
Books and supplies	$1,500
Room and board (on/off-campus)	$13,142/$15,206
Financial aid application deadline	4/20
% first-year students receiving some sort of aid	79
% receiving some sort of aid	86
% of aid that is merit based	7
% receiving scholarships	13
Average grant	$8,166
Average loan	$18,779
Average total aid package	$17,203
Average debt	$59,590

EMPLOYMENT INFORMATION

Career Rating	64	Grads Employed by Field (%)	
Average starting salary	$58,701	Academic	1
State for bar exam	LA	Business/Industry	7
Pass rate for first-time bar	92	Government	14
Employers Who Frequently Hire Grads		Judicial clerkships	12
Adams and Reese; Baker and Hostetler;		Military	2
Breazeale, Sachse, and Wilson; Phelps		Other	2
Dunbar; McGinchey Stafford; Taylor,		Private practice	60
Porter, Brooks, and Phillips; Stone		Public Interest	2
Pigman; Vinson and Elkins; Chaffe, McCall,			
Phillips, Toler, and Sarpy; Cook, Yancey,			
King, and Galloway; Correro, Fishman,			
Haygood, Phelps, Weiss; Courtenay,			
Forstall, Hunter, and Fontana; Cox and			
Smith; Crawford and Lewis; Deutsch,			
Kerrigan, and Stiles.			

LOYOLA MARYMOUNT UNIVERSITY
LOYOLA LAW SCHOOL

INSTITUTIONAL INFORMATION

Public/private	Private
Student-faculty ratio	16:1
% faculty part-time	51
% faculty female	37
% faculty minority	28
Total faculty	116

SURVEY SAYS...
Diverse opinions accepted in classrooms
Great research resources

STUDENTS

Enrollment of law school	1,297
% male/female	52/48
% full-time	77
Average age of entering class	24

ACADEMICS

Academic Experience Rating	**95**
Profs interesting rating	97
Profs accessible rating	95
Hours of study per day	4.32

Academic Specialties
Cancer rights law, civil procedure, commercial law, constitutional law, corporation securities law, criminal law, election law, entertainment law, environmental law, government services, human rights law, intellectual property law, international law, labor law, legal history, legal philosophy, mediation, property, taxation.

Advanced Degrees Offered
LLM (taxation) 1 to 3 years, LLM (American law and international legal practice) 1 to 3 years.

Combined Degrees Offered
JD/MBA 4 years.

Clinical program required	No
Legal writing course requirement	Yes
Legal methods course requirement	Yes
Legal research course requirement	Yes
Moot court requirement	No

Academics

Whether dropping the names of celebrity alumni or discussing the high quality of their academic program, Loyola Marymount students sing the praises of their Southern Californian school. While you will get a rigorous legal education at Loyola, don't expect to attend an endless series of boring lectures. The school's "brilliant [and] accessible" teaching staff draws praises for being able to "communicate the complex clearly. They're also a damn funny lot, which goes a long way when you're slogging through a 14-week course on civil procedure." On top of that, the teaching staff is generally described as "wonderful and supportive," always willing to lend academic or personal support. A 1L recounts, "All of the professors really care about their students; I even had a criminal law professor that would bring cookies and brownies in for the class."

Loyola has built a reputation for producing renowned litigators. "The school places a strong emphasis on practical application, skills classes, and real-world experience. Loyola is known throughout the Los Angeles region for producing top-notch litigators (among them Mark Geragos, Robert Shapiro, and Gloria Allred), and the school maintains a "great reputation among employers in the Southern California area," as well as "a large alumni network of successful and respected lawyers in California." As a result, "The bulk of Loyola lawyers end up working somewhere in LA," A few note that because Loyola's national reputation does not mirror its strong regional reputation, it is sometimes more difficult to find a job in another state. At Loyola, "Students have abundant opportunities to acquire practical researching, writing, and courtroom skills through extensive connections to the judicial system, a well-respected Law Review, and excellent trial and appellate advocacy programs, as well as numerous practical skills courses. The trial advocacy program, particularly the Hobbs Program, enables students at Loyola to complete a trial advocacy course and then do an externship at the district attorney's office for school credit. This program enables the student to get courtroom experience by handling preliminary hearing and misdemeanor jury trials." A 3L tells us that for students set on working on Law Review, "Law Review is a write-on, and if you complete your paper for the competition, your chances of getting on are very, very good. With three Law Reviews, there are a lot of positions for staffers." Loyola also offers unique opportunities for study abroad. A 2L boasts, "I've been to Costa Rica and China through Loyola . . . I not only met people from other countries, but have made lasting friendships (and connections) all over the country."

While enjoying the sunny California weather, lucky Loyola students attend classes in a building designed by the famous architect Frank O. Gehry, a facility that one student describes as "almost like an Escher painting." An added benefit to the building is its location: It is set apart from the main undergraduate campus. This location fosters "a good sense of togetherness with an enclosed campus. Loyola's intimate campus means that you can have lunch with your professors any day you want, get your Con Law taught by the dean who clerked in the Supreme Court, all while being in the heart of one of the biggest legal cities in the country." While intimate and beautiful, Loyola has some drawbacks: "The classrooms are aesthetically different (à la industrial/loft chic), but have terrible acoustics. The professors complain about it incessantly." On top of that, students gripe that the wireless Internet network is often down. Improvements are in the making, though: The school recently constructed a new facility "designed specifically for trial advocacy and has several 'courtrooms' set up with video, Internet, and computer capability, all state of the art."

Life

"The students are an incredibly diverse population" at Loyola. Even though "Loyola is a Jesuit institution," students report that "there is no forced emphasis with regard to

JANNELL LUNDY ROBERTS, ASSISTANT DEAN OF ADMISSIONS
919 ALBANY STREET, LOS ANGELES, CA 90015
TEL: 213-736-1074 FAX: 213-736-6523
E-MAIL: ADMISSIONS@LLS.EDU • INTERNET: WWW.LLS.EDU

religion." A 2L writes, "My class consists of students of every nationality, religion, and political affiliation." Students boast about the "true sense of community the students have with one another," noting that "no one hides books in the library; everyone is willing to share outlines; and diverse opinions are tolerated." As a result of its diversity, "Loyola has an organization for almost every interest, from Bioethics to East Asian Law Society to OutLaw: Gay/Straight Alliance and everything in between." On this active campus, "There is something for everyone—and if not, the Student Bar Association is supportive and encouraging of starting a new organization. From inviting distinguished speakers to debate on controversial issues to providing hot chocolate with marshmallows during finals week, the student organizations always have ways for students to become more involved in the school and the community."

While it may be surprising to hear that a bunch of future litigators are actually friendly folks, Loyola students insist that their classmates are outgoing, supportive, and social. "You always have someone to catch happy hour with. Professors, librarians, your fellow students, and even alumni come back to hang out." That said, because Loyola is located in the business district of downtown LA, it tends to be a "commuter school" with an on-campus vibe that is more academic than social. A 3L explains, "In the first year, there are many social activities as the different sections start to bond. As the years progress, the large-scale social activities shift into smaller-scale social activities." Many students say they take advantage of the school's excellent location "in the heart of downtown Los Angeles, so close to all sorts of employment opportunities, cultural places of interest, and an extremely diverse community." Loyola students, a "well-rounded and socially comfortable" bunch, often end up going out to "some of the top nightclubs in LA." Finally, because Loyola "is not a suburban environment," but rather "in the middle of the hubbub," students warn that the neighborhood is "not the safest place."

Getting In

To be considered for admission to Loyola Law School, students must submit undergraduate transcripts, LSAT scores, and a personal statement. Students also must submit at least one and up to three letters of recommendation, of which at least one should be from an academic source.

Public interest law requirement	Yes

ADMISSIONS

Selectivity Rating	**85**
# applications received	4,013
# applicants accepted	1,248
# acceptees attending	352
Average LSAT	161
LSAT Range	159–163
Average undergrad GPA	3.36
Application fee	$65
Regular application	Rolling
Regular notification	Rolling
Rolling notification	Yes
Early application program	No
Transfer students accepted	Yes
Evening division offered	Yes
Part-time accepted	Yes
LSDAS accepted	Yes

International Students

TOEFL required of international students	No
Minimum paper TOEFL	N/A
Minimum computer TOEFL	N/A

FINANCIAL FACTS

Annual tuition	$33,515
Books and supplies	$1,000
Fees per credit	$258
Tuition per credit	$22,418
Room and board (off-campus)	$13,500
Financial aid application deadline	3/16
Average debt	$97,092

EMPLOYMENT INFORMATION

		Grads Employed by Field (%)	
Career Rating	**83**	Academic	2
Rate of placement (nine months out)	97	Business/Industry	20
Average starting salary	$86,451	Government	8
State for bar exam	CA	Judicial clerkships	2
Pass rate for first-time bar	75	Other	1
Employers Who Frequently Hire Grads		Private practice	59
O'Melveny and Myers; Los Angeles District		Public Interest	8

Employers Who Frequently Hire Grads
O'Melveny and Myers; Los Angeles District Attorney; Skadden, Arps, Slate, Meagher, and Flom; Paul Hastings; Jones, Day, Reavis and Pogue.

Prominent Alumni
Gloria Allred, trial attorney; Johnnie Cochran, trial attorney; Larry Feldman, trial attorney; Mark Geragos, trial attorney; Robert Shapiro, trial attorney.

LOYOLA UNIVERSITY—CHICAGO
SCHOOL OF LAW

INSTITUTIONAL INFORMATION

Public/private	Private
Affiliation	Roman Catholic
Student-faculty ratio	15:1
% faculty part-time	65
% faculty female	55
% faculty minority	7
Total faculty	83

SURVEY SAYS...

Diverse opinions accepted
in classrooms
Great library staff
Students love Chicago, IL

STUDENTS

Enrollment of law school	843
% male/female	46/54
% out-of-state	45
% full-time	71
% minority	21
% international	2
# of countries represented	15
Average age of entering class	25

ACADEMICS

Academic Experience Rating	**81**
Profs interesting rating	80
Profs accessible rating	74
Hours of study per day	3.56

Academic Specialties

Child and family law, corporation securities law, health law, intellectual property law, international law, labor law, taxation.

Advanced Degrees Offered

MJ (health law), MJ (child law), MJ (business law), LLM (health law), LLM (child law), LLM (tax law), SJD (health law), Dlaw (health law) 2 years.

Combined Degrees Offered

JD/MBA, JD/MSW, JD/MA (political science) 4 years.

Clinical program required	No
Legal writing course requirement	Yes
Legal methods course requirement	No

Academics

"A phenomenal health law program" and an "incredibly strong" tax program are academic standouts at this Jesuit-affiliated law school in downtown Chicago. This is also "one of the few schools that has specific elder law classes and an elder law clinic where students can gain experience practicing in the . . . field while in school." This makes sense, as one of the hallmarks of a Jesuit education is an "emphasis on public service." In addition, the school has a highly touted "trial advocacy program that allows a select number of students" to train with "the best trial lawyers in Chicago." A sizable evening program "draws unusually diverse and gifted students" who are mostly "working professionals" from the City of Chicago and its environs.

The "first rate" professors not only "have excellent resumes (Harvard, Yale, Chicago . . . DC clerkships, former assistant attorney generals, current judges, etc.)" but "Unlike many professors with sexy resumes they can actually teach!" They also are "easily accessible and always willing to answer any question." "They seem to put students above all else," explains one student. If that's not enough, they are also personable outside of the school setting: "One even invited an entire 1L section to his house for Thanksgiving dinner!" The few complaints there are about faculty center on "older or tenured professors" whose "level of interest or enthusiasm seems nonexistent."

Students have mixed feelings about the administration. Some believe it is "disorganized," pointing out that the school "didn't even have a full-time career resources person this year" and that the "Computer technology is a decade behind the times." Others counter that Dean Yellen, who began his tenure in 2005, "is really turning Loyola around." These students argue that the "quality of new educators has drastically improved, the administration is much more helpful and friendly, and the facilities have come out of the dark ages, specifically with adding wireless Internet to the law building and giving some students the option of taking their exams online." One thing students agree the administration should put at the top of its to-do list is climate control: "The heating/cooling systems are often unbearable." A Star Wars fan agrees, "It's hotter than the ninth circle of Hades in many of the rooms, and some are colder than Hoth."

"Overall Loyola is a solid school with a good reputation in the Midwest," says one student. Graduates find themselves in good company as the State's Attorney General and the Chief Justice of the Illinois Supreme Court are alumni of Loyola. Many students claim that, thanks to the "loyal, prestigious, and well-organized alumni," it is possible to find Loyola grads "in the best law firms in the country."

Life

Students agree that "Loyola is located in the heart of the best part of Chicago." There are "so many different activities one could do around campus" and "as it's near downtown," there's "wonderful nightlife [and] shopping." The school itself offers "many opportunities for students to socialize out of class" while also promoting good causes. For example, "The Student Bar Association hosts weekly bar nights and other special events like the Barrister's Ball and the No Talent Show" with the proceeds of the latter going to help support "abandoned children."

Temperamentally, "The Loyola law student community is extremely cooperative, with students sharing notes and outlines constantly." "Students are generally friendly," and

OFFICE OF ADMISSION AND FINANCIAL ASSISTANCE
25 EAST PEARSON, SUITE 1440, CHICAGO, IL 60611
TEL: 312-915-7170 FAX: 312-915-7906
E-MAIL: LAW-ADMISSIONS@LUC.EDU • INTERNET: WWW.LUC.EDU/SCHOOLS/LAW

"None of the horror stories you hear about law school are true at Loyola." Though some feel like they are "in high school," most students report "a great atmosphere" full of people who embrace Loyola's "spirit of service." Politically, "The school tends to attract a lot of Midwesterners with a slight liberal bent" and "no die-hard Bill O'Reilly fans."

There seems to be a bit of a split between the way full-time and evening division students view each other, which is typical at most law schools that offer part-time study options. Full-time day students are younger and allegedly more "cutthroat" than evening students, who "all are a little older, have families, kids, jobs, etc. and . . . are just trying to make it through law school." But let's just say that these views reside in the eye of the beholder.

Minuses in terms of student life include the fact that "parking is terrible and validations can still be pricey." However there is always Chicago's famed L-train service; though some students feel "Public transit is undesirable."

Getting In

About one in four applicants is accepted to Loyola Chicago. Typical students who are accepted and enroll here have an A-minus/B-plus undergraduate GPA and an LSAT score in the 80th to 90th percentile. Loyola is somewhat unique in that it at least says that applicants' personal statements and letters of recommendation are more important selection criteria than LSAT scores. Applicants to the evening division will face a slightly less rigorous bar to admission.

Legal research	
course requirement	Yes
Moot court requirement	Yes
Public interest	
law requirement	No

ADMISSIONS

Selectivity Rating	88
# applications received	3,894
# applicants accepted	771
# acceptees attending	193
Average LSAT	162
LSAT Range	160–164
Average undergrad GPA	3.49
Application fee	$50
Regular application	4/1
Regular notification	Rolling
Rolling notification	Yes
Early application program	No
Transfer students accepted	Yes
Evening division offered	Yes
Part-time accepted	Yes
LSDAS accepted	Yes

Applicants Also Look At
American University, Boston University, DePaul University, The George Washington University, Illinois Institute of Technology, Northwestern University, University of Illinois.

International Students

TOEFL required	
of international students	Yes
Minimum paper TOEFL	650
Minimum computer TOEFL	280

FINANCIAL FACTS

Annual tuition	$31,800
Books and supplies	$1,000
Fees per credit	$230
Tuition per credit	$1,060
Room and board	
(off-campus)	$12,900
Financial aid application	
deadline	3/1
% first-year students	
receiving some sort of aid	96
% receiving some sort of aid	96
% of aid that is merit based	41
% receiving scholarships	52
Average grant	$9,000
Average loan	$21,500
Average total aid package	$34,500
Average debt	$72,000

EMPLOYMENT INFORMATION

Career Rating	81	Grads Employed by Field (%)	
Rate of placement (nine months out)	87	Academic	1
Average starting salary	$82,673	Business/Industry	22
State for bar exam	IL	Government	15
Pass rate for first-time bar	92	Judicial clerkships	6
Prominent Alumni		Military	1
Lisa Madigan, Attorney General, IL; Henry		Private practice	54
Hyde, U.S. Senator; Philip Corboy, personal injury attorney; Jeff Jacobs, former president, Harpo Entertainment; Chief Justice Mary Ann McMorrow, Illinois Supreme Court.		Public Interest	1

LOYOLA UNIVERSITY—NEW ORLEANS
SCHOOL OF LAW

INSTITUTIONAL INFORMATION

Public/private	Private
Affiliation	Roman Catholic
Student-faculty ratio	18:1
% faculty part-time	27
% faculty female	30
% faculty minority	19
Total faculty	63

SURVEY SAYS...

Diverse opinions accepted
in classrooms
Students love New Orleans, LA

STUDENTS

Enrollment of law school	796
% male/female	45/55
% out-of-state	42
% full-time	82
% minority	25
% international	1
# of countries represented	9
Average age of entering class	25

ACADEMICS

Academic Experience Rating	**71**
Profs interesting rating	70
Profs accessible rating	72
Hours of study per day	4.35

Academic Specialties

Environmental law, international
law, public interest law.

Combined Degrees Offered

JD/MBA 4 years, JD/MA (religious
studies) 4 years, JD/MA (communications) 4 years, JD/MA (public administration) 4 years, JD/MA (urban and
regional planning) 4 years.

Clinical program required	No
Legal writing	
course requirement	Yes
Legal methods	
course requirement	Yes
Legal research	
course requirement	Yes
Moot court requirement	Yes
Public interest	
law requirement	Yes

Academics

At Loyola University—New Orleans, School of Law, students are divided on their opinions of nearly everything. "The professors are wonderful resources and teachers of the material we're required to know for the Louisiana and any other common law bar," states one, speaking for a large segment of the population. "They balance stuffy case law with real-world experience, providing the best of both worlds and preparing us for our careers." Another voice representing the (not as widely held) counterpoint says: "I would not take a future class from most of the professors whose classes I took." Perhaps this middle-of-the-road 2L has it right when she observes, "It definitely matters what professors you take at Loyola because while some are great, others seem to know very little about what they are teaching." More than a few students speculate about racial preferences at Loyola, citing administrators who give "extra help to minorities in instruc-tion [private and prior to law school orientation], scholarship, and rate of acceptance," though the administration claims this is untrue. "Merit takes the back seat at Loyola when making admittance and scholarship decisions," opines a student.

The school itself is undergoing a lot of construction (now in its final stages) due to Hurricane Katrina, and though complaints about the noise abound, students know that the new wing will "help the law school in its mission to serve the New Orleans area." Indeed, though New Orleans was hit hard by Katrina, every single student agrees that the administration exhibited nothing but grace under pressure. A second-year student tells of officials' devotion to the school: "The dean evacuated to Houston and without access to any files, Loyola e-mail, or the Loyola server, arranged for us to have a full cur-riculum at University of Houston's Law School. Professors and faculty who had lost their homes came and taught us—many commuting each week from Baton Rouge or from wherever their families had evacuated." Now back up and running and open for busi-ness, Loyola University—New Orleans is able to help the needy with "free legal advice through clinics which [also] allow students hands-on experience" and helps them fulfill their pro bono requirement, one register of the school's commitment to public interest.

In terms of Loyola's academic offerings, students especially commend the moot court, certificate, and legal research and writing programs for being "very practical," though many wish for more diversity in the classes that are offered. "Regular availability of courses on specific areas of law, such as education, health, and employment law would broaden the course offerings for upperclassmen," says one student. Financial aid servic-es receive a universal thumbs-down, as does the parking situation on campus, though the school hired an additional person to help in the Financial Aid Department, which is expected to dramatically increase the response time in the office. The vast majority of stu-dents at Loyola are thrilled with the school's Career Services Office ("amazing in helping to revise resumes and in finding job placement") and the ensuing employment opportu-nities available to them in New Orleans

K. Michele Allison-Davis, Dean of Admissions
7214 Saint Charles Avenue, Box 904, New Orleans, LA 70118
Tel: 504-861-5575 Fax: 504-861-5772
E-mail: ladmit@loyno.edu • Internet: law.loyno.edu

Life

"Come on now, it's New Orleans. . . ." As one can imagine, the social life here in the home of Mardi Gras is "booming." "A lot of the diverse student population are frequent visitors to local bars, mostly in the French Quarter," says one booster, and "There is always something to do or someone to hang out with," including a fair number of school-sponsored events. "At times the students seem judgmental," but "Once you get to know your classmates you find that they are, for the most part, enjoyable to be around." "Loyola is a small school so there is definitely a lot of gossiping," and as in high school, the student body can be "very cliquey in the sense that a huge number of people are locals who have known each other awhile, thus out-of-staters may feel out of place at first." There also exists a social rift "between common law and civil law students." As is their custom, students are also divided about the level of competitiveness running throughout the school. Opinions range from "cutthroat" to "We help each other as much as possible with things like informing each other of assignments and getting notes to people who were not able to make it to class." One thing is for certain, though: "New Orleans attracts a wide variety of people and takes a special kind of person to live here and enjoy it."

Getting In

At a nearly 60 percent acceptance rate, admission to Loyola University—New Orleans isn't all that difficult, though this rate is a direct result of the decrease in applications received since Hurricane Katrina, and is expected to fall as the school returns to its pre-storm state. The school prefers applicants to apply using the online application, with a priority application deadline of February 1. Though letters of recommendation are not required, they are encouraged, and the school also recommends that all applicants have an LSAT score no lower than 154 and a minimum GPA of 3.3.

ADMISSIONS

Selectivity Rating	74
# applications received	1,267
# applicants accepted	768
# acceptees attending	223
Average LSAT	153
LSAT Range	150–155
Average undergrad GPA	3.31
Application fee	$40
Regular application	Rolling
Regular notification	Rolling
Rolling notification	Yes
Early application program	No
Transfer students accepted	Yes
Evening division offered	Yes
Part-time accepted	Yes
LSDAS accepted	Yes

Applicants Also Look At

Florida Coastal School of Law, Louisiana State University, Mississippi College, Southern University, St. Thomas University, Tulane University, University of Miami.

International Students

TOEFL required of international students	No
TOEFL recommended of international students	Yes
Minimum paper TOEFL	580
Minimum computer TOEFL	237

FINANCIAL FACTS

Annual tuition	$29,109
Books and supplies	$1,500
Fees per credit	$836
Tuition per credit	$939
Room and board	$14,366
% first-year students receiving some sort of aid	69
% receiving some sort of aid	68
% of aid that is merit based	33
% receiving scholarships	41
Average grant	$11,009
Average loan	$23,788
Average total aid package	$47,245
Average debt	$88,324

EMPLOYMENT INFORMATION

		Grads Employed by Field (%)	
Career Rating	82	Academic	1
Rate of placement (nine months out)	91	Business/Industry	12
State for bar exam	LA, TX, FL, GA, MS	Government	15
Pass rate for first-time bar	76	Judicial clerkships	8
Employers Who Frequently Hire Grads		Private practice	61
Private firms, the judiciary, government agencies.		Public Interest	3

Prominent Alumni

Chief Justice Pascal Calogero, Louisiana Supreme Court; Moon Landrieu, secretary of HUD, Mayor of New Orleans, etc.; Carl Stewart, U.S. Court of Appeals, 5th Circuit; Theodore M. Frois, general counsel, Exxon Mobil International; Robert L. Wilkie, special assistant to the president, NSA.

MARQUETTE UNIVERSITY
LAW SCHOOL

INSTITUTIONAL INFORMATION

Public/private	Private
Affiliation	Roman Catholic
Student-faculty ratio	16:1
% faculty part-time	28
% faculty female	46
% faculty minority	8
Total faculty	41

SURVEY SAYS...
Diverse opinions accepted
in classrooms
Great library staff
Abundant externship/internship/
clerkship opportunities
Students never sleep

STUDENTS

Enrollment of law school	689
% male/female	60/40
% full-time	72
% minority	9
# of countries represented	6
Average age of entering class	25

ACADEMICS

Academic Experience Rating	**75**
Profs interesting rating	74
Profs accessible rating	84
Hours of study per day	4.21

Academic Specialties
Civil procedure, commercial law, constitutional law, corporation securities law, criminal law, dispute resolution, environmental law, intellectual property law, international law, labor law, legal history, property, sports law, taxation.

Combined Degrees Offered
JD/MBA 4 years, JD/MBA (sports business) 4 years, JD/MA (political science) 4 years, JD/MA (international relations) 4 years, JD/MA (philosophy) 4 years, JD/MA (history of philosophy) 4 years, JD/MA (bioethics) 4 years, JD/Certificate (dispute resolution) 3 years.

Academics

What would you say to a guarantee that you will be admitted to the bar if you graduate? Not many law schools can make such promises, but Marquette can. As one of only two Wisconsin law schools approved by the American Bar Association (University of Wisconsin is the other), Marquette enjoys a certain "diploma privilege. You do not have to pass a bar exam to be authorized to practice." In Wisconsin, that is. If you plan on practicing somewhere other than the Badger State, no such guarantee applies.

There is no dearth of professorial prestige at Marquette, either. "Our faculty includes a former State Supreme Courts Justice, a former U.S. Supreme Court Law Clerk, a U.S. Attorney, authors of several textbooks and practice guides, and advisors to federal and state lawmakers." Despite what you might assume given their credentials, "Administrators and professors are caring professionals who take the time to get to know students as individuals and future colleague," and friends. One student goes so far as to declare, "Personally, I expect several faculty members to attend my wedding next year." The school is Jesuit-run, and as a result, there is an "emphasis on social conscience/social justice. Every professor I've had seems committed to discussing this aspect of the law and public policy." As far as legal academic concentrations go, "Marquette has a great sports law program administered by professors who seem more at home on ESPN than in a classroom."

The law school's location in downtown Milwaukee affects the student experience in two major ways. First, it makes a part-time program very practicable for working professionals. Marquette's night program is reportedly "perfect for Milwaukee-area residents who want to attend law school but cannot afford to take time off from their regular day jobs. Students can graduate by taking entirely night classes." Because more than 20 percent of students here attend part-time, they don't get short shrift, as part-timers at other law schools sometimes do. "The regular-day professors rotate through the night classes, giving the [night] students the same access to quality teaching that day students have."

Second, "Marquette has the Milwaukee market covered when it comes to internships. Marquette has an internship in essentially every courtroom in the Milwaukee area (state trial courts, federal trial courts, state appellate courts, and even the Seventh Circuit)." Increasing the radius of opportunity, Madison is just a short drive from school; "Many students intern there with the Wisconsin Department of Justice or the Supreme Court." In these positions, students pick up "real lawyering experience as a 3L in the largest DA or public defender offices in the state. If you work for the DA, most every 3L will graduate having done at least one full jury trial. Some even do felony trials."

Students' complaints center on the physical plant of the law school. "The facilities are a bit old, some of the classrooms are extremely cramped," and classroom "Chairs are uncomfortable and of a style where they are all joined together, meaning that when one person in the row moves, everyone does. You can get seasick sitting in class." Technologically, the school is also a little behind, as "Only about half of the classrooms include outlets for laptop users." Finally, "The library is dark and dingy and not a fun place to be, despite the inordinate amount of time that students spend there."

SEAN REILLY, ASSISTANT DEAN FOR ADMISSIONS
SENSENBRENNER HALL, ROOM 116, PO BOX 1881, MILWAUKEE, WI 53201-1881
TEL: 414-288-6767 FAX: 414-288-0676
E-MAIL: LAW.ADMISSION@MARQUETTE.EDU • INTERNET: LAW.MARQUETTE.EDU

Life

"As far as the stories of competition in law school [are concerned], Marquette doesn't quite live up to that reputation." Most students believe that "Marquette is not as cut-throat and competitive as other schools," and that "students are generally cooperative and helpful to one another." But that doesn't mean everyone always acts like a grown-up. As is the case at many law schools, "Socially, Marquette is like high school. There are cliques, locker gossip, and an annual formal we lovingly refer to as 'prom.'" There is "not a lot of racial/ethnic diversity," and many students would like to see that change. With regard to the school's political bent, "There are equal numbers who are liberal and conservative. [It would not be] accurate to say that the average student is middle-of-the-road, because that implies a passivity. The students are political, just evenly divided among moderately conservative and moderately liberal."

On campus, the recreational options are thin and uninviting. "There is no natural light in the school building, even though the university finally took the covers off the windows. The student lounge is in the basement of the building, and it can feel like a dungeon. We finally got cable TV, though, so we at least know what is going on in the world." For some extracurricular balance, the school's "great location" in "downtown Milwaukee offers a lot of diverse social environments and activities."

Getting In

Admission is significantly less competitive than at UW. (Marquette admits at almost twice the rate of UW.) The law school employs a modified rolling admissions process, with the Admissions Committee typically beginning its evaluations in December. As is the case in all rolling admissions systems, there are more spaces available sooner rather than later—especially if you think you may be a borderline candidate quantitatively. An undergraduate GPA of B-plus and an LSAT score in the high 150s would make you solidly competitive for admission at Marquette.

Clinical program required	No
Legal writing course requirement	Yes
Legal methods course requirement	No
Legal research course requirement	Yes
Moot court requirement	No
Public interest law requirement	No

ADMISSIONS

Selectivity Rating	**77**
# applications received	1,712
# applicants accepted	705
# acceptees attending	177
Average LSAT	157
LSAT Range	155–159
Average undergrad GPA	3.47
Application fee	$50
Regular application	4/1
Regular notification	Rolling
Rolling notification	Yes
Early application program	No
Transfer students accepted	Yes
Evening division offered	Yes
Part-time accepted	Yes
LSDAS accepted	Yes

Applicants Also Look At
DePaul University, Illinois Institute of Technology, John Marshall Law School, Loyola University—Chicago, University of Wisconsin.

International Students

TOEFL required of international students	Yes
Minimum paper TOEFL	600
Minimum computer TOEFL	250

FINANCIAL FACTS

Annual tuition	$28,410
Books and supplies	$1,120
Tuition per credit	$1,175
Room and board (off-campus)	$11,550
Financial aid application deadline	3/1
% receiving some sort of aid	83
% receiving scholarships	44
Average grant	$6,000
Average debt	$84,532

EMPLOYMENT INFORMATION

Career Rating	**78**
Rate of placement (nine months out)	94
Average starting salary	$60,235
State for bar exam	MO, IL, MN, AZ, WI
Pass rate for first-time bar	97

Employers Who Frequently Hire Grads
Quarles and Brady; Godfrey and Kahn; Foley and Lardner; Whyte, Hirschboeck, Dudek; von Briesen and Roper; Reinhart, Boerner Van Dueren; Davis and Kuelthau.

Prominent Alumni
Honorable Diane Sykes, U.S. Court of Appeals; Honorable Terence Evans, U.S. Court of Appeals.

Grads Employed by Field (%)	
Academic	2
Business/Industry	11
Government	9
Judicial clerkships	5
Military	1
Other	1
Private practice	63
Public Interest	4

MERCER UNIVERSITY
WALTER F. GEORGE SCHOOL OF LAW

INSTITUTIONAL INFORMATION

Public/private	Private
Affiliation	Baptist
Student-faculty ratio	12:1
% faculty part-time	49
% faculty female	32
% faculty minority	7
Total faculty	69

SURVEY SAYS...
Diverse opinions accepted in classrooms
Great research resources
Great library staff

STUDENTS

Enrollment of law school	444
% male/female	58/42
% out-of-state	29
% full-time	100
% minority	17
% international	1
# of countries represented	3
Average age of entering class	23

ACADEMICS

Academic Experience Rating	**89**
Profs interesting rating	92
Profs accessible rating	99
Hours of study per day	5.12

Academic Specialties
Civil procedure, commercial law, constitutional law, corporation securities law, criminal law, environmental law, government services, intellectual property law, international law, Internet law, labor law, legal history, legal writing certificate program, professionalism/ethics, property, taxation, trial advocacy.

Advanced Degrees Offered
JD 3 years.

Combined Degrees Offered
JD/MBA 3.5 to 4 years.

Clinical program required	No
Legal writing course requirement	Yes

Academics

In Mercer, students find an institution that "rejects the 'survival of the fittest' mentality of most law schools," adopting instead a "no man left behind" approach. "Every single person—librarians, professors, classmates, and even the sweet lady in the bookstore—is there to help you if you need it," a 1L reports. "I remember once I had to give a presentation in class, and I didn't know how to work the projection equipment—a member of the janitorial crew stopped by and showed me how," a 2L adds. This "encouraging environment" reportedly "takes a huge burden . . . off the shoulders of incoming law students" and allows them to focus on actually learning the law. Mercer starts 1Ls off with its "Intro to Law class, a one-week sample course designed to introduce new students to the foreign world of case opinions and IRAC," which, according to one 1L, "made a world of difference on the first day of 'real' classes, as I knew what to expect." Throughout students' time here, they receive "great practical skills instruction," which includes an "unbeatable" legal writing program; "Mercer students and graduates have notably superior writing skills, and employers know this," a 3L asserts. With "a bar-passage rate of 90.6 percent," one might assume that its all practical skills all the time at Mercer, but the school also places an "emphasis on legal theory." In fact, a sanguine 1L boasts that Mercer offers "the best blend of theory [and] practice of law in the country."

The school is committed to producing lawyers who demonstrate "compassion for the client," and this goal is reinforced by professors who are accessible and "seem to really care about the student." Students agree that "at any given time, you can pop in on a professor"—one "literally unhinged the door to his office"—or "call [him or her] at home." "Not once have I ever been turned down," a 2L writes. Most Mercer professors are also engaging instructors, who "keep classroom discussions lively" and even—gasp—"make the law fun." "In evidence class, we get to run through mock trials, employing all of the objections," explains a 2L. Things are so chummy here that a 1L writes, "Sometimes I fear that the personal nature of the legal education at Mercer may not adequately prepare students for the harshness of the legal profession."

The physical plant is "one of the oldest buildings in Macon" (according to one student, it was "around during the Civil War") and features an "awe-inspiring" façade; the "awful" interior draws some boos. Aesthetics and ergonomics aside, Mercer "has done an excellent job" of "installing adequate access to electronic resources not only in the library and computer labs, but also in the individual classrooms." "Nearly every classroom seat is hard-wired for power and Internet for our school-issued laptops, and we're completing a new wireless Internet system," reports a 1L.

Students' biggest wish is the expansion of Mercer's "recruiting and reputation" beyond "Georgia and its neighboring states." However, student opinion is split on whether change is indeed on its way. For some, "The administration is extremely responsive to student needs" and displays "a positive attitude toward helping students thrive in the academic setting." Others find the deans "willing to listen to student input about things, but rarely take the initiative to improve the marketability of the students." "They want the students to propose why another journal is needed when we only have one, and employers basically require one to be on a journal." A 1L hypothesizes that "the location is what hinders [Mercer] from breaking into the top 50 law schools. If we moved it to Atlanta, it would provide those internships [and] externships that we lack."

MARILYN E. SUTTON, ASSISTANT DEAN OF ADMISSIONS AND FINANCIAL AID
1021 GEORGIA AVENUE, MACON, GA 31207
TEL: 478-301-2605 FAX: 478-301-2989
E-MAIL: MARTIN_SV@MERCER.EDU • INTERNET: WWW.LAW.MERCER.EDU

Life

"Walking in the first day of your 1L year can be very intimidating, but any apprehensions I had about starting law school were eased when I met the people that would go through the 'torture' with me," a student recalls. By all accounts, "Students feel not like competitors but colleagues." "Exam time is weird when you realize the same people you've been with all semester are the ones you're competing with for grades," a 1L writes. "Despite a slightly more conservative bent" on campus—many are "married" or "engaged"—"all races, genders, and lifestyles are accepted without any hesitation." Not surprisingly, "the single kids" here are more socially active "than the ones who are spoken for." Students generally find that although "Macon has a lot of history, beautiful architecture, and solid infrastructure," "The population is rapidly moving elsewhere," leaving a lack of things to do off campus. Some note that due to the town's small amount of "growth and development" the level of "crime (although not generally violent)" has started to rise. "There isn't a whole lot to do in Macon," a 1L reports. "But it's okay because when you're studying on a Friday night (which happens) you [won't] feel like you're missing out on much."

Getting In

Accepted applicants have average undergrad GPAs of 3.45 and LSAT scores of 156. Applicants to Mercer are automatically considered for a variety scholarships. Additionally, they may apply for Mercer's George W. Woodruff Scholarship and Walter F. George Foundation Public Service Scholarship—both full-tuition grants—by submitting all admissions materials by February 1.

Legal methods course requirement	Yes
Legal research course requirement	Yes
Moot court requirement	Yes
Public interest law requirement	No

ADMISSIONS

Selectivity Rating	79
# applications received	1,290
# applicants accepted	457
# acceptees attending	176
Average LSAT	156
LSAT Range	153–158
Average undergrad GPA	3.45
Application fee	$50
Regular application	3/15
Regular notification	Rolling
Rolling notification	Yes
Early application program	No
Transfer students accepted	Yes
Evening division offered	No
Part-time accepted	No
LSDAS accepted	Yes

Applicants Also Look At

Florida Coastal School of Law, Florida State University, Georgia State University, Samford University, Stetson University, University of Georgia, University of South Carolina.

International Students

TOEFL required of international students	No
TOEFL recommended of international students	Yes
Minimum paper TOEFL	600

FINANCIAL FACTS

Annual tuition	$30,146
Books and supplies	$1,000
Tuition per credit	$1,256
Room and board	$13,200
Financial aid application deadline	4/1
% first-year students receiving some sort of aid	90
% receiving some sort of aid	85
% of aid that is merit based	20
% receiving scholarships	30
Average grant	$20,000
Average loan	$28,000
Average total aid package	$37,000
Average debt	$79,178

EMPLOYMENT INFORMATION

Career Rating	78	Grads Employed by Field (%)	
Rate of placement (nine months out)	93	Academic	3
Average starting salary	$63,167	Business/Industry	4
State for bar exam	GA, FL, NC, SC, TN	Government	11
Pass rate for first-time bar	91	Judicial clerkships	5
Employers Who Frequently Hire Grads		Military	3
King and Spalding; McKenna, Long, and		Private practice	70
Aldridge; Moore, Ingram, Johnson, and		Public Interest	4
Steele; Martin Snow, LLP; Alston and Bird;			
James, Bates, Pope, and Spivey.			

Prominent Alumni

Griffin Bell, former U.S. Attorney General; Cathy Cox, former GA Secretary of State; John Oxendine, GA Insurance Commissioner; Justice Hugh Thompson, GA Supreme Court.

MICHIGAN STATE UNIVERSITY
COLLEGE OF LAW

INSTITUTIONAL INFORMATION

Public/private	Private
Student-faculty ratio	20:1
% faculty part-time	68
% faculty female	58
% faculty minority	16
Total faculty	100

SURVEY SAYS...

Great research resources
Great library staff
Beautiful campus
Students love East Lansing, MI

STUDENTS

Enrollment of law school	960
% male/female	56/44
% out-of-state	36
% full-time	76
% minority	16
% international	6
# of countries represented	14
Average age of entering class	24

ACADEMICS

Academic Experience Rating	**76**
Profs interesting rating	74
Profs accessible rating	76
Hours of study per day	4.82

Academic Specialties

Alternative dispute resolution, corporation securities law, criminal law, environmental law, family law, government services, health law, intellectual property law, international law, taxation.

Advanced Degrees Offered

LLM1 year, MJ 1 year.

Combined Degrees Offered

JD/MBA 4 years, JD/MS 4 years, JD/MA 4 years.

Clinical program required	No
Legal writing course requirement	Yes
Legal methods course requirement	No
Legal research course requirement	Yes

Academics

Known for a century as the Detroit College of Law, Michigan State University College of Law has been reborn with a new name, a mutually beneficial affiliation with Michigan State, and a "positive, up-and-coming attitude." A 2L writes, "Instead of seeming chaotic, the school and the students have embraced these changes and used them as a springboard for advancing new ideas, fostering ownership of the curriculum, and creating an infectious enthusiasm for the school." Two things haven't changed, though: the private school price tag and the third-tier ranking. In an ongoing effort to lure top students and continue the school's transformation, the administration is doling out merit-based scholarships and flashy laptops. Some students call the recruitment efforts "bait-and-switch tactics," warning that as few as one in ten scholarship recipients see their funding renewed for the second year. Most students, however, focus on the numerous improvements they see and consider MSU Law to be "a top-tier school that doesn't know it's a top-tier school."

This "best-kept secret" status may not last long, as everyone loves to talk about the school's state-of-the-art moot court, considered to be "easily one of the best in the nation." The "technologically sophisticated" renovations mean that the school now features plenty of flat screens, microphones, presentation equipment, and other "computer gadgets possessed by only a few of the most progressive courts." In the words of a 2L, "I can plug my computer in anywhere I sit." All administrative offices and classrooms are housed in a single impressive building, complete with relatively reliable wireless Internet access. "The building is conducive to learning and gives us a sense of pride. It's what a graduate school should look like." Recently, the deans transformed the hallways into a political art show, and this "makes walking to class entertaining and interesting." The library also facilitates scholarship, with "amazingly helpful and knowledgeable Lexis and Westlaw representatives on staff."

Professors are divided into those who "follow the Socratic Method strictly" and a newer group of instructors described by students as "extremely laid-back." One from this latter group shows a *South Park* episode on the first day of contracts to explain "that every time we take action as a lawyer, we risk bringing Janet Reno in a fuzzy bunny suit to our clients' homes. I've been fully impressed with the weight of my duty ever since." Professor Jack Apol, who ran for the Michigan legislature, "managed to make criminal law fun and interesting without disrespecting the subject matter or the victims of the many crimes that we studied." Nearly all instructors are "willing to involve themselves as mentors to various student organizations, providing useful legal insight as well as friendly career advice." They draw on impressive backgrounds as "the heads of corporate law departments for large successful law firms, as well as former federal judges and prosecutors." Politically, "The faculty range from the radical liberal to merely liberal." Rare issues arise around "brilliant and well-published" professors who were educated at "first-tier schools" and sometimes "show contempt for MSU students." Overall, students praise their professors for "promoting individual thought and challenging our answers"; they just wish for a few more of them to reduce the student/faculty ratio.

MSU Law is geared toward "entrepreneurial go-getters who want to get into a courtroom, practice the law, and make a real difference" rather than "high-brow ivory-towered theoreticians." Students appreciate "opportunities for dual-degree programs and advanced specialization for all law students" through connections with other MSU departments. The well-known Fieger Trial Practice Institute gives select students the

CORY BURKE, ASSISTANT DIRECTOR OF ADMISSIONS AND FINANCIAL AID
230 LAW COLLEGE BUILDING, EAST LANSING, MI 48824-1300
TEL: 517-432-0222 FAX: 517-432-0098
E-MAIL: ADMISS@LAW.MSU.EDU • INTERNET: WWW.LAW.MSU.EDU

benefit of "unique instruction in trial practice." Everyone loves their clinic classes, which get students arguing cases early in their law school careers: "You can be in trial by the end of your first week." Many students intend to work on behalf of local people, like the 2L who is "interested in helping the American worker earn an honest living in a steady, safe, and satisfying job." Others opt to work for the government or in private practice. While the school's East Lansing location provides some opportunities for government work in the capital, many students want to see more done to "market the school's name to law firms not just in Michigan, but also in other states."

Life

Typically, students at MSU Law are "committed to making a difference in our society." Most graduates plan to stay in the state after graduation, furthering the collegial alumnae network. Recently formed interest groups—including the Native American Law Students Association, the Society for Mental Health Law, Older Wiser Law Students (OWLS), the Family Law Society, the Triangle Bar Association, and the Student Animal Legal Defense Fund—promote professional bonding and fuel the school's progressive reputation. Students express "excitement about the changes that have occurred and the school's association with a Big Ten university."

Students report a "virtual lack of pretension and mean-spirited competition" and note that most opt to "get through the hell together." Many live in the graduate dorm right across from the law school and work to cultivate the kind of atmosphere in which study groups "drink a glass of wine over a civil procedure sample exam question." Most "recognize the importance of social life in law school" and "make strong efforts to include everyone in activities and events."

Getting In

Although the application deadline is officially March 1, the Admissions Committee recommends submitting materials earlier (as the school has rolling admissions). Letters of recommendation may not be required, but it's a good idea to submit them anyway. All applicants are automatically considered for merit-based and trustee scholarships, so there's no need to do anything extra to apply for these.

Moot court requirement	No
Public interest law requirement	No

ADMISSIONS

Selectivity Rating	**76**
# applications received	2,492
# applicants accepted	1,001
# acceptees attending	189
Average LSAT	157
LSAT Range	155–160
Average undergrad GPA	3.4
Application fee	$60
Regular application	3/1
Regular notification	Rolling
Rolling notification	Yes
Early application program	No
Transfer students accepted	Yes
Evening division offered	Yes
Part-time accepted	Yes
LSDAS accepted	Yes

Applicants Also Look At

Cleveland State University, Illinois Institute of Technology, Penn State University, Wayne State University.

International Students

TOEFL required of international students	Yes
Minimum paper TOEFL	600
Minimum computer TOEFL	250

FINANCIAL FACTS

Annual tuition	$27,956
Books and supplies	$1,260
Tuition per credit	$964
Room and board	$8,298
Financial aid application deadline	4/1
% first-year students receiving some sort of aid	88
% receiving some sort of aid	88
% of aid that is merit based	20
% receiving scholarships	34
Average grant	$20,304
Average loan	$21,427
Average total aid package	$39,811
Average debt	$73,201

EMPLOYMENT INFORMATION

		Grads Employed by Field (%)	
Career Rating	**76**		
Rate of placement (nine months out)	91	Academic	3
Average starting salary	$65,000	Business/Industry	16
State for bar exam	MI	Government	14
Pass rate for first-time bar	97	Judicial clerkships	8
Employers Who Frequently Hire Grads		Military	1
Dykema Gossett; Jaffe, Raitt, Heuer, and		Other	5
Weiss; Clark Hill; Michigan Court of		Private practice	48
Appeals; Honigman, Miller, Schwartz, and		Public Interest	5
Cohn; Miller, Canfield, Paddock, and Stone.			
Prominent Alumni			
Dennis Archer, Leadership; Geoffrey Fieger,			
trial lawyer; Marrianne Battani, U.S.			
District Attorney; Clif Haley, corporate law;			
Bernard Friedman, U.S. District Attorney.			

MISSISSIPPI COLLEGE
SCHOOL OF LAW

INSTITUTIONAL INFORMATION

Public/private	Private
Affiliation	Southern Baptist
Student-faculty ratio	22:1
% faculty part-time	58
% faculty female	37
% faculty minority	8
Total faculty	56

SURVEY SAYS...

Diverse opinions accepted
in classrooms
Great research resources
Great library staff
Abundant externship/internship/
clerkship opportunities

STUDENTS

Enrollment of law school	529
% male/female	60/40
% out-of-state	54
% full-time	100
% minority	10
# of countries represented	1
Average age of entering class	24

ACADEMICS

Academic Experience Rating	**75**
Profs interesting rating	85
Profs accessible rating	90
Hours of study per day	3.76

Academic Specialties

Certificate program in civil law
studies.

Advanced Degrees Offered

JD 3 years.

Combined Degrees Offered

JD/MBA 4 years.

Clinical program required	No
Legal writing	
course requirement	Yes
Legal methods	
course requirement	Yes
Legal research	
course requirement	Yes
Moot court requirement	Yes
Public interest	
law requirement	No

Academics

Mississippi College School of Law "really places an emphasis on practical lawyering" "in addition to the theory of the law." Students offer high praise for MC Law's moot court teams, which are "annually competitive on a national level." Practice rounds for national competition teams "are often coached or judged by sitting Federal Court Judges and State Supreme Court Justices." The "most distinctive feature" is "the visibility and availability of the administration." The dean is "highly committed," reportedly going so far as to occasionally mow the campus lawn. Administrators, professors, staff, security, and "even the custodians" are "very personable and friendly." "Every day you can find the deans and the professors sitting and chatting with the students in the common areas of the school or dropping by the classrooms." "Having come to MCSOL from another institution, I was amazed by the accessibility of professors and genuine interest in the progress of their students," elaborates a 3L. "It is not uncommon for professors to remain 30 to 45 minutes after class answering individual students' questions. This was virtually unheard of at the other institution I attended." "Their doors are always open to us," adds a 1L. "If an office door is closed, there is usually a student already in there." The "knowledgeable, caring, [and] highly motivated" professors are "very effective as instructors." "Their methods of teaching vary from the harsh Socratic Method to a friendlier, more accommodating style." "I like the diversity," observes a 1L. "Some are extremely serious while some make the class more fun."

The "very nice" facilities are "equipped with state-of-the-art technology," including "technology-friendly" classrooms. The three-story law library "is a scene from the 1970s," but it "contains most likely all the legal research materials a student could want or need" and "many private study rooms." If only the school would "invest in chairs that support the lumbar region."

Student opinion regarding the writing program is more mixed. Some say it is "strong"; others call it "pathetic." The bar-passage rate—while quite high—is typically lower than the state average, which irks some students. Also, students tell us they'd like to see "more specialization options." (There is a Louisiana Civil Law Certificate program for students who want to practice in Louisiana, but that's about it.)

Mississippi College is one of only two law schools in the Magnolia State and the "only law school in Mississippi located in a major metro area (where jobs can easily be found)." The campus is located "in the heart of Mississippi's capital city, two blocks from the state capitol and Supreme Court buildings and three blocks from the federal court house." Students have access to "very choice and prestigious" externships. Clerking is easy because the neighborhood is crawling with "judges, legislators, and the top state and regional law firms." A tremendous point of pride here is that MC Law is in the top 15 percent nationally in job placement. Career Services works "tirelessly" to give students networking opportunities, "so that even the students who are fighting to improve their grades have one foot in the door somewhere." "This regional school is trying to develop the first-rate regional reputation it deserves," explains one student. "I can think of no improvements besides the fact that our school gets no national recognition."

Life

Ethnically, Mississippi College is home to a pretty "a homogenous environment." Many students are graduates of Mississippi State or Ole Miss. "When I arrived from out of state," says a 2L, "I felt as if everyone already knew each other because the majority of my class attended one of those schools." Politically, it's more diverse. "The student body is about 50 percent liberal and 50 percent conservative." Students can be "competitive when it comes to grades" and "There are a few students who have the cutthroat mentality." Mostly, though, "MCSOL is a very strong community." Students are "very sociable" and "easy to talk to." The 2Ls and 3Ls "are helpful with guidance and assistance" and "make you feel like a junior colleague, not a rookie."

Social life can be "a bit cliquish" but a "family-type environment" tends to triumph on campus. "The students seem to generally have a good time." "The prevailing social scene at MCSOL is a continuation of most SEC undergrad scenes, just a little more grown up." "There are clubs and organizations for every interest and many school-wide activities in which to participate." "Golf tournaments, bowling tournaments, tennis tournaments, charity auctions, Halloween parties, and barrister's balls are all annual events."

The "conservative and slow" surrounding city of Jackson "is an extremely affordable place to live." "Rent is low, groceries are inexpensive, and social events are easy to afford." It's "a great town for married couples." As a bonus, "contrary to popular belief, neither Mississippi nor its capital city is a haven for . . . narrow-minded people." However, "The social scene in Jackson is terrible." "There's very little to do, and the city itself is unattractive at best," says one student. "The downtown area has not been preserved at all, so now it's one big blight."

Getting In

At Mississippi College, admitted students at the 25th percentile have LSAT scores in the range of 149 and GPAs hovering around 3.0. Admitted students at the 75th percentile have LSAT scores of about 153 and GPAs of about 3.5.

ADMISSIONS

Selectivity Rating	**66**
# applications received	1,122
# applicants accepted	507
# acceptees attending	195
Average LSAT	150
LSAT Range	147–152
Average undergrad GPA	3.32
Application fee	$50
Regular application	6/1
Regular notification	Rolling
Rolling notification	Yes
Early application program	No
Transfer students accepted	Yes
Evening division offered	No
Part-time accepted	No
LSDAS accepted	Yes

Applicants Also Look At
Louisiana State University, Samford University, University of Alabama—Tuscaloosa, University of Mississippi, University of Tennessee.

International Students

TOEFL required of international students	No
TOEFL recommended of international students	No

FINANCIAL FACTS

Annual tuition	$20,700
Books and supplies	$900
Tuition per credit	$690
Room and board (off-campus)	$9,000
Financial aid application deadline	5/1
% first-year students receiving some sort of aid	85
% receiving some sort of aid	80
% of aid that is merit based	22
% receiving scholarships	29
Average grant	$12,000
Average loan	$24,000
Average total aid package	$29,000
Average debt	$70,000

EMPLOYMENT INFORMATION

Career Rating	75	Grads Employed by Field (%)	
Rate of placement (nine months out)	85	Academic	1
Average starting salary	$65,424	Business/Industry	11
State for bar exam	MS, AL, TN, GA, LA	Government	10
Pass rate for first-time bar	93	Judicial clerkships	7
Employers Who Frequently Hire Grads		Private practice	52
International law firms; multi-state law firms; Mississippi law firms; state government; federal government; business.		Public Interest	4
Prominent Alumni			
Felicia Smith, senior vice president and corporate counsel, Prudential; Chief Justice James Smith, Mississippi Supreme Court; Amy Tuck, lieutenant govenor, Mississippi.			

NEW ENGLAND SCHOOL OF LAW

Academics

Students agree that "NESL is the true Boston gem." Many also note that it's only a matter of time until "NESL is formally considered a top-tier law school in this nation" and in turn "recognized for the quality institution it is." Everyone, including "students, faculty, and Boston's legal community already know this," but many find it "too bad many outside Massachusetts do not." Such comments reflect the scrappy, going-it-together attitude shared by faculty, students and administration alike. "The professors," for example, "recognize that NESL is not a first-tier school and thus focus very much on preparing students for the legal profession and passing the bar," which students do on their first try at an impressive rate. Another bonus is the lack of "academic snobbery, and minimal competition between students."

Many students claims NESL's "greatest strength" is "the practical experience that a student gains from interaction with the adjunct faculty." Students say that the "clinical program is amazing." The school's location provides for easy "access to Boston professionals" and allows for students "to get some real-world practice in before graduation."

The faculty "contains the entire spectrum of the legal community, from NESL grads to Harvard grads." Overall, they "are accessible, qualified, and have excellent practical and conceptual grasp of the subject material," and they spread the love; full-time day students aren't the only ones who get professors' attention. Students are "amazed at how willing the professors are to stay a couple hours after evening classes end, and even to come in on Saturdays to conduct a review session."

Students are also pleased to report that "The school's administration is very organized," "very accessible," and "responds to student concerns in a timely manner." Folks are "really helpful if you have a problem, especially Financial Aid and the Registrar." The administration makes a point of being proactive. Its recent renovation of the library, for example, has been well received by students, who describe the new look as "modern and elegant." In addition, over the past few years "The school has completely revamped NESL's technology. Not only is NESL technologically up-to-date with their Wi-Fi and online services, but their facilities are modern, clean, and laptop friendly." But not all things administrative are peachy for students. Many complain that Career Services "is terrible." "They are not willing to help anyone who is not in the top 10 percent of the class," claims one student. That said, some students appreciate that "the administration seems to hang in the background until needed."

Life

"NESL is not as well known as the other law schools in the area, and the professors and students know that," explains one student. Therefore, "Students here are some [of] the hardest-working students in Boston, and rightly so—they face pretty tough competition for law jobs compared to other schools in the area." Contrary to what might be expected in such circumstances, "There is not the highly competitive, cutthroat attitude among the students here" normally associated with law schools that have lots of students vying for few select jobs. New students are often surprised by the "camaraderie" and "helpfulness" "exhibited by the students." That said, socially the school can be "cliquish" and reminds more than a few students of "high school." They note that "rumors fly quickly and everyone wants to know everyone else's business." "Everyone knows everyone" here, but they remain a "generally friendly lot." Politically, "students are extremely

MICHELLE L'ETOILE, DIRECTOR OF ADMISSIONS
154 STUART STREET, BOSTON, MA 02116
TEL: 617-422-7210 FAX: 617-422-7201
E-MAIL: ADMIT@ADMIN.NESL.EDU • INTERNET: WWW.NESL.EDU

liberal. Everyone here wants to eventually take down big business, big oil, Wal-Mart, and the Bush administration."

Being located right in "the heart of Boston," students find themselves "minutes away from everything," and note that the campus is "very accessible from all areas by the T system." Drivers will be happy to note that it is also "conveniently located near parking facilities," though these are in one of the "lesser" (though safe in the daytime) neighborhoods in Boston. One student mentions that "it is a good idea to walk with a friend to the garage—especially at night."

"There are constantly social events at nearby places to give students a break from law." "One bar across the street is practically all NESL students" and the "food court across the street is loaded with students studying and socializing." In addition to this, the school plans "several social events at the beginning of the year [so they can] meet everyone." The school also offers "many panels of lawyers" who "come in to speak about various legal professions to help students better assess which field of law they might want to pursue."

Getting In

Getting in to NESL may be easier than getting into than some other Boston-area law schools, but this by no means makes admission a cakewalk. Successful applicants have a B/B-plus undergraduate academic record and LSAT scores in the low 150s. As is the case at most law schools offering both day and night courses, acceptance to the part-time evening division is slightly easier to achieve than acceptance to the full-time day division.

ADMISSIONS

Selectivity Rating	66
# applications received	2,762
# applicants accepted	1,356
# acceptees attending	270
Average LSAT	152
LSAT Range	150–154
Average undergrad GPA	3.27
Application fee	$65
Regular application	3/15
Regular notification	Rolling
Rolling notification	Yes
Early application program	No
Transfer students accepted	Yes
Evening division offered	Yes
Part-time accepted	Yes
LSDAS accepted	Yes

Applicants Also Look At
Hofstra University, New York Law School, Northeastern University, Quinnipiac University, Roger Williams University, Suffolk University, Western New England College.

International Students
TOEFL required	
of international students	Yes
Minimum paper TOEFL	600
Minimum computer TOEFL	250

FINANCIAL FACTS
Annual tuition	$25,800
Books and supplies	$1,150
Tuition per credit	$1,075
Room and board (off-campus)	$15,405
Financial aid application deadline	4/20
% first-year students receiving some sort of aid	87
% receiving some sort of aid	87
% of aid that is merit based	68
% receiving scholarships	38
Average grant	$7,141
Average loan	$30,030
Average total aid package	$32,159
Average debt	$81,679

EMPLOYMENT INFORMATION

Career Rating	70	Grads Employed by Field (%)	
Rate of placement (nine months out)	78.4	Academic	2
Average starting salary	$55,588	Business/Industry	12
State for bar exam	MA, NY, CT, PA, NJ	Government	18
Pass rate for first-time bar	81	Judicial clerkships	6

Employers Who Frequently Hire Grads
A partial list of employers who have hired New England School of Law graduates can be found on our website www.nesl.edu/cso/success.cfm.

Military	1
Other	13
Private practice	47
Public Interest	1

Prominent Alumni
Leonard P. Zakim, NE Anti-Defamation League; Honorable Susan J. Crawford, Convening Authority for Military Commissions.

NEW YORK LAW SCHOOL

INSTITUTIONAL INFORMATION

Public/private	Private
Student-faculty ratio	20:1
% faculty part-time	22
% faculty female	40
% faculty minority	9
Total faculty	163

SURVEY SAYS...

Diverse opinions accepted in classrooms
Liberal students
Students love New York, NY

STUDENTS

Enrollment of law school	1,511
% male/female	46/54
% full-time	76
% minority	21
% international	1
# of countries represented	22
Average age of entering class	25

ACADEMICS

Academic Experience Rating	**69**
Profs interesting rating	76
Profs accessible rating	71
Hours of study per day	3.98

Academic Specialties

Civil procedure, commercial law, constitutional law, corporation securities law, criminal law, environmental law, government services, human rights law, information law, intellectual property law, international law, labor law, legal history, legal philosophy, legal profession/ethics, property, real estate law, taxation.

Advanced Degrees Offered

JD 3 to 4 years, LLM (tax) 1 to 2 years.

Combined Degrees Offered

JD/MBA 4 years.

Clinical program required	No
Legal writing course requirement	Yes

Academics

If you are interested in learning the "practicalities of becoming a lawyer and the real issues that one will encounter in practice," then consider New York Law School. "The school's motto says it all: Learn Law. Take Action." According to students, the school is "focused only on teaching students to be lawyers with the skills they [will] need to be strong advocates for their clients."

A "great location" in the subtly chic neighborhood of Tribeca—it's "right near all the courts" of the biggest legal center in the world—is one thing NYLS certainly has going for it. Being situated where it is definitely "makes it easier [for students] to get worthy internship/externship experience all year-round."

The "top-notch" professors and a "competent, helpful, and always available" administration are other big draws for students. Professors have "superior career backgrounds [and] most of them have published books which have been given great reviews by the *New York Times, Time* magazine, etc. Nearly all of them attended Ivy League law schools, clerked for judges, and worked at large, prestigious law firms." The faculty is also a testament to how "incredibly open to diversity, even for New York City" NYLS is. "Many members of the faculty are minorities and/or lesbian/gay/bi." It somehow seems to follow that "this school is great for those interested in civil rights and employment law. We really do have some of the best people in the field (including the president of the ACLU)." Students agree that, on the whole, the faculty is "disgustingly liberal," which "makes constitutional law, well, a unique experience for right-leaning students."

On the administrative side, "The dean of the school is very accessible. He takes students' calls and e-mails directly, which is impressive with such a large student body. In addition, he holds informal monthly meetings in the student center to update us all on what is going on at the school and to listen to our comments, complaints, and ideas."

"Though the career services and recruitment programs are good, our school is ranked quite low, especially in comparison [with] every other law school in the immediate area, so we are definitely at a disadvantage, particularly if you are not on Law Review." That's not to say that NYLS students do not have options. Many students "would guess that the top 5 to 10 percent of students get offers for summer jobs with the large, prestigious firms in New York." If you happen to fall outside of that top 90 percent, don't fret: "NYLS alumni are always ready to help students in finding jobs."

To make the school even better, students would like to see two "time-wasting, required" skills classes, Lawyering and Applied Analysis, disappear: "Lawyering and Applied Analysis are experimental and generally useless." In addition, they tell us that the facilities need some updating. "This school is old." There seems to be "only one electrical outlet for every 20 students in the lecture halls" and, frankly, "The elevators are scary." The good news is that "the law school is in the process of major renovations to the library and facilities." Once completed, the school should be quite impressive.

Life

There are two basic schools of thought on the social scene at NYLS. First, there are those who believe that "it is very difficult for a school in New York City to have a strong social environment. People are independent." On the other side, plenty of students are "pleasantly surprised at the sense of community and camaraderie at our school." The opposing views could be tied into the local/not local divide. One student who grew up in the area notes that having "a slew of friends in the New York area precluded me from attempting to build a social network at the law school [while] students who came from far away to study in New York were able to bond together." Regardless of from where they hail, those who spend a good deal of time around one another outside of class seem to form friendships faster. "Students who live in the law school building have a stronger sense of community" than those living in the far-flung reaches of Gotham. Across the board, students seem to agree that "the location is perfect because when one needs to escape the law school atmosphere and company of law students, there are millions of other people to spend time with and tons of places to go where nothing will remind one of law school."

Whether students feel particularly close to their peers or not, gunners are not in abundance. "Everyone gets their work done, [but] notes and outlines are shared with no reservations."

For those hoping to meet a mate in law school, it is worth noting that more than a few students responding to our survey cited "the attractiveness of the student body" as one of this law school's strengths.

Getting In

Despite the fact that it's easier to get into NYLS than a few of the other law schools in New York City, it's harder to get into than others; it's by no means a cakewalk. Students should aim for an LSAT score in the mid-150s and a B average in their undergraduate grades. It should be mentioned that New York Law School was started in the late nineteenth century specifically for nontraditional students, and it continues that tradition today. Older students are treated very well in the school's admissions process.

Legal methods	
course requirement	Yes
Legal research	
course requirement	Yes
Moot court requirement	No
Public interest	
law requirement	No

ADMISSIONS

Selectivity Rating	**72**
# applications received	5,557
# applicants accepted	2,421
# acceptees attending	549
Average LSAT	155
LSAT Range	152–157
Average undergrad GPA	3.33
Application fee	$60
Regular application	4/1
Regular notification	Rolling
Rolling notification	Yes
Early application program	No
Transfer students accepted	Yes
Evening division offered	Yes
Part-time accepted	Yes
LSDAS accepted	Yes

Applicants Also Look At
Brooklyn Law School, Hofstra University, New York University, Pace University, Seton Hall University, State University of New York at Albany, Yeshiva University.

International Students

TOEFL required	
of international students	No
TOEFL recommended	
of international students	Yes
Minimum paper TOEFL	600
Minimum computer TOEFL	250

FINANCIAL FACTS

Annual tuition	$39,460
Books and supplies	$850
Fees per credit	$734
Tuition per credit	$30,426
Room and board	$19,050
Financial aid application	
deadline	4/1
% first-year students	
receiving some sort of aid	88
% receiving some sort of aid	86
% of aid that is merit based	10
% receiving scholarships	24
Average grant	$8,750
Average loan	$36,485
Average total aid package	$38,645
Average debt	$86,250

EMPLOYMENT INFORMATION

Career Rating	**80**	**Grads Employed by Field (%)**	
Rate of placement (nine months out)	92	Academic	1
Average starting salary	$78,500	Business/Industry	17
State for bar exam	NY, NJ, CT	Government	9
Pass rate for first-time bar	83	Judicial clerkships	7
Employers Who Frequently Hire Grads		Other	12
Government; judicial clerkships; private		Private practice	51
practice; business/industry.		Public Interest	3
Prominent Alumni			
Justice John Marshall Harlan, U.S.			
Supreme Court; Wallace Stevens, Pulitzer			
Prize–winning poet; David Kelley, U.S.			
Attorney for the Southern District of New			
York; Robert F. Wagner, U.S. Senator.			

New York University
School of Law

Academics

A fixture in the city and a mirror to its culture, New York University is a large, famous, diverse, and cosmopolitan law school, boasting a distinguished faculty and strong scholarly community. With many well-known names on the faculty, you may be surprised to learn that "most professors are incredibly accessible and wonderful teachers." In the words of a 3L, "The faculty here has, on the whole, been outstanding. That applies not only to my classroom experience, but also the atmosphere of accessibility that is an essential part of the school."

There are a wide variety of course offerings at NYU, and "Picking classes for upcoming semesters is pretty fun because there are usually some well-known names, sometimes judges." Of particular note, NYU offers a wide range of "international course offerings" as well as a staggering array of colloquia, seminars, institutes, centers, and special programs, such as the lauded Global Public Service Law Project.

Although many NYU alumni end up at top private law firms across the country, "NYU students are generally very down to earth and extremely dedicated to public service." A 3L attests that "the public interest reputation is well deserved, and I think it has a lot to do with the atmosphere and civic culture of NYU Law." The school's progressive vision is promoted through course work, extracurriculars, and special programs. For example, the Public Interest Law Center "guarantees $4,000 worth of funding if you elect to partake in a public interest internship over the 1L summer and $5,000 for a 2L summer," a program that "shows just how dedicated NYU is to placing students in public interest jobs." "Even though I've ultimately chosen to take a private job," one 3L shares, "I appreciate the promotion of the idea that everyone in the profession still has obligations to the public interest."

While the educational experience is undeniably first rate, NYU occasionally falls short in meeting the needs of every one of its 1,300-plus students. At this large school, classes are assigned by lottery, and "almost every class, even basic classes, such as evidence and criminal procedure, have waiting lists, sometimes with 70 people waiting to get in." Students also say that the presence of big-name faculty can also be a double-edged sword, as some professors can make students feel "like teaching is not important to them" and can occasionally "brush off" students in favor of professional or academic projects. Still, for one of the most prestigious law schools in the country, "It is amazing how much NYU gives back to the students in terms of career counseling, placement, access to professors, and the overall classroom experience."

The academic program at NYU places a great deal of emphasis on legal theory. Outside of the classroom, however, "NYU provides you with opportunities to do every kind of practical work imaginable," and, on top of that, "All the journals are great." The school's host of "incredibly interesting" extracurricular activities include public service-oriented organizations such as "PREP: Prisoners Rights and Education Project, which takes students into area women's correctional facilities to serve as teachers for a law clerk class." This program and others help students apply legal theory to the real-world situations they will encounter as practicing attorneys. "You can come out of school feeling like a third-year associate if you are diligent," reports one 2L. On that note, NYU students have little trouble securing the most coveted jobs after graduation. As one 2L succinctly puts it, "Career Services are great here. We all get awesome jobs pretty much no matter what."

DIRECTOR OF ADMISSIONS
161 AVENUE OF THE AMERICAS, ROOM 501, NEW YORK, NY 10013
TEL: 212-998-6060 FAX: 212-995-4527
E-MAIL: LAW.MOREINFO@NYU.EDU • INTERNET: WWW.LAW.NYU.EDU

Life

When it comes to life at New York University, the first two words of the name say it all. In terms of location for work, culture, or socializing, "It really doesn't get much better than the Village in NYC." As one 2L puts it, "The neighborhood is awesome, especially if you choose to live in the dorms (most people do, and they're not bad)." With so many students choosing to reside in campus housing, "There is a big sense of community." While law students certainly enjoy their favorable location for off-campus social pursuits, they always take the time to socialize on campus. In fact, there is a "social event every week with free alcohol and two huge parties a year."

Overall, NYU students describe their classmates as highly intelligent, diligent, and accomplished. "I was amazed when I first got here at how bright and motivated my colleagues were," notes a 2L. When it comes to the competitive atmosphere on campus, however, NYU students send mixed messages. On the one hand, some say, "Competition is almost nonexistent. People share outlines and notes. They are courteous in the library and at workstations." On the other hand, some students describe their classmates as "greedy, self-interested, competitive jerks," who are "just as cutthroat and competitive as anywhere else."

Getting In

You want to go to NYU? So do a lot of other smart people. NYU bases admissions decisions on the intellectual potential, academic achievement, character, community involvement, and work experience of each applicant, but with an average LSAT score of a near-perfect 170 for each incoming class, we would suggest that if you want to attend NYU School of Law, you prepare for the test—a lot. There is an extensive scholarship program for highly qualified applicants.

Moot court requirement	No
Public interest law requirement	No

ADMISSIONS

Selectivity Rating	**96**
# applications received	7,571
# applicants accepted	1,597
# acceptees attending	448
LSAT Range	168–172
Application fee	$85
Regular application	2/1
Regular notification	4/30
Rolling notification	No
Early application program	Yes
Early application deadline	11/15
Early application notification	12/31
Transfer students accepted	Yes
Evening division offered	No
Part-time accepted	No
LSDAS accepted	Yes

International Students

TOEFL required of international students	No
TOEFL recommended of international students	No

FINANCIAL FACTS

Annual tuition	$38,980
Books and supplies	$950
Room and board	$18,955
Financial aid application deadline	4/15

EMPLOYMENT INFORMATION			
Career Rating	**94**	**Grads Employed by Field (%)**	
Rate of placement (nine months out)	99	Business/Industry	1
Average starting salary	$125,000	Government	4
State for bar exam	NY	Judicial clerkships	12
Pass rate for first-time bar	93.4	Private practice	76
Employers Who Frequently Hire Grads		Public Interest	7
Private law firms; public interest organizations; government agencies; corporations; public accounting firms.			

NORTH CAROLINA CENTRAL UNIVERSITY
SCHOOL OF LAW

INSTITUTIONAL INFORMATION

Public/private	Public
Student-faculty ratio	22:1
% faculty part-time	33
% faculty female	59
% faculty minority	55
Total faculty	49

SURVEY SAYS...

Diverse opinions accepted
in classrooms
Great research resources
Great library staff
Abundant externship/internship/
clerkship opportunities

STUDENTS

Enrollment of law school	537
% male/female	39/61
% out-of-state	31
% full-time	79
% minority	64
Average age of entering class	27

ACADEMICS

Academic Experience Rating	61
Profs interesting rating	71
Profs accessible rating	64
Hours of study per day	2.52

Academic Specialties
Intellectual property law, taxation.

Advanced Degrees Offered
JD 3 to 4 years.

Combined Degrees Offered
JD/MBA 4 years, JD/MLS 4 years.

Clinical program required	No
Legal writing course requirement	Yes
Legal methods course requirement	Yes
Legal research course requirement	Yes
Moot court requirement	No
Public interest law requirement	No

Academics

With both women and minority students making up sizable majorities of the student body, and with nearly as many female professors as male, one can make a strong case for agreeing with students in calling North Carolina Central University the "best law school for minorities and women."

A "very strong curriculum and high expectations" await students who enroll at NCCU. Those high expectations are exemplified by the grade expectation curve, which for many students seems "atrocious." Fortunately, some help in beating that curve is not far away: "The professors are superb, and they are always available. They place a great emphasis on establishing relationships with the students [and] earnestly want them to learn." Because the school "is small in size, it's easy to get to know other students in the school. Smaller class size also allows professors to be more accessible." However, "communication between the new administration and the general student body" needs some work.

NCCU has a reputation as a "strong public interest school and for preparing highly competent trial lawyers." The latter is a product of the "the practical training we receive that is applied within the courtroom." There are many "trial preparation opportunities" through "the clinic, trial practice, trial team, etc.," of which many students take advantage. In addition to this training, "The law school has recently renovated the facility, and resources include new classrooms, study rooms, technology that assists with teaching (e.g., projector screens), and wireless [Internet] throughout the building." Students appreciate all the new bells and whistles but still believe they "need more access to computers, printers and copiers," specifically in the computer labs.

Though the school "could stand to improve in the opportunities available to students [through] the Career Services Department," students know that NCCU "produces attorneys that are on par with those of any other institution." Even "Governor Mike Easley went here." Students are keenly aware that "despite its size, more North Carolina judges attended NCCU Law than another other school." However, some students don't think they "get a good shot at midsize and large firms given that we are in constant competition with UNC, Duke, Wake Forest. We have a terrific program, but not as good a reputation."

The cost-conscious law student should not overlook NCCU. Even for out-of-staters (but especially for in-state students) "NCCU law school is an educational steal. Tuition is a fraction of the average undergraduate tuition."

Life

There's a "strong sense of community" at NCCU, and students tell us "The school is very family-oriented. Students help one another and work together because when one succeeds, everyone succeeds." The administration, which "cares very much about the law school environment and the students' success," contributes to this overall feeling. In all, NCCU "is a positive environment and one in which" most students feel "very fortunate to be a part of." Although "There is competition"—what with the grade expectation curve and all—it's "the healthy kind, and there's a lot of sharing among students." It's the kind of school where "Everybody tries to help you in your studies."

SANDRA BROWN BECHTOLD, ADMISSIONS COORDINATOR/INTERIM DIRECTOR
OF ENROLLMENT MANAGEMENT • 1512 SOUTH ALSTON AVENUE, DURHAM, NC 27707
TEL: 919-530-5243 FAX: 919-530-7981
E-MAIL: SBROWNB@NCCU.EDU • INTERNET: WWW.NCCU.EDU/LAW

Even though NCCU is a Historically Black University, that doesn't stop students from calling for more diversity. Things can seem especially challenging sometimes for the "minority" students at this minority school. As one White female student explains, many "of the scholarships available/positions available seem to focus on minorities, which is great for African American/Latino/Native American students. However . . . I feel like most opportunities presented do not apply to me/other students in need."

Students point out that "the school is located in a rough area" within Durham, which itself has always had the reputation as the grittiest of the three cities of the North Carolina Research Triangle (the other two cities being Raleigh and Chapel Hill). If you can handle that, remember that Raleigh and Chapel Hill are within an easy drive, and the Research Triangle itself was named the "Best Place to Live in the South" by *Money* magazine in 2000. Such a distinction is hardly surprising. The climate is temperate, housing prices are reasonable, jobs are aplenty, and the scenery is pretty spectacular.

Getting In

Though the academic profile of the most recent incoming class might suggest admission to NCCU is not as tough as it is at other schools, a good LSAT score is by no means a sure ticket in. The Admissions Office can be selective because an impressive number of students who are accepted ultimately choose to enroll. The Admissions Office starts accepting completed applications on October 1 and it employs a rolling admissions scheme. There are more spots available early in the process, so the earlier you apply, the better.

ADMISSIONS

Selectivity Rating	66
# applications received	1,752
# applicants accepted	437
# acceptees attending	190
Average LSAT	146
LSAT Range	143–151
Average undergrad GPA	3.2
Application fee	$40
Regular application	4/15
Regular notification	Rolling
Rolling notification	Yes
Early application program	No
Transfer students accepted	Yes
Evening division offered	Yes
Part-time accepted	Yes
LSDAS accepted	Yes

Applicants Also Look At
The University of North Carolina at Chapel Hill.

International Students

TOEFL required of international students	Yes

FINANCIAL FACTS

Annual tuition (resident)	$2,670
Annual tuition (nonresident)	$14,530
Books and supplies	$1,500
Room and board (on/off-campus)	$6,950/$10,450
Financial aid application deadline	4/15
% first-year students receiving some sort of aid	97
% receiving some sort of aid	98
% of aid that is merit based	22
% receiving scholarships	45
Average grant	$3,400
Average loan	$18,500
Average total aid package	$22,500
Average debt	$55,500

EMPLOYMENT INFORMATION

Career Rating	75	Grads Employed by Field (%)	
Rate of placement (nine months out)	74	Academic	3
State for bar exam	NC, VA, SC, GA, DC	Business/Industry	4
Pass rate for first-time bar	86	Government	6
Employers Who Frequently Hire Grads		Judicial clerkships	3
Public defender and district attorney		Military	2
offices; NC Department of Justice; Legal		Other	3
Aid of NC.		Private practice	43
Prominent Alumni		Public Interest	10
Michael Easley, governor of North Carolina;			
G. K. Butterfield, U.S. House of			
Representatives; Willie Gary, private practice.			

NORTHEASTERN UNIVERSITY
SCHOOL OF LAW

Academics

A "commitment to progressive lawyering and the co-op internship model" are the hallmarks of Northeastern University School of Law. Northeastern is "a truly unique school," firmly "grounded in experiential learning." Students here appreciate the "lack of formal grades (students are evaluated in 2–3 paragraph blurbs instead), and a refusal to rank students above each other." Thanks to this "lack of competition," students feel more comfortable to "reach out to each other to prepare for exams and research papers, offering support, sharing outlines and giving advice." On the contrary, while "The school has a great reputation in the Boston legal market," some students grumble that employment prospects in other cities seem dim because "No one wants to read a huge packet of written evaluations." Most don't find this to be too much of a problem though since "Northeastern's co-op program has direct connections with hundreds of employers all across the country," resulting in plenty of "legal internships" that often turn into "job offers."

Students say their "amazing" professors are "super-approachable" experts in their fields who "take the time to care about you and challenge you." Faculty members also "really take the time to write personalized evaluations for each student." Northeastern's administration either "welcomes student voices and opinions [or has] very little commitment to the overall health and well-being of law students," depending on whom you ask.

"In terms of the facilities, we're like the Red Sox," suggests one student. "We need a new building, but I'd sure miss the old one." We're not sure how much other students would miss it, though. Almost all agree that "the building is definitely lacking," describing it as "leaky and old (it's all cinder blocks) [with] notoriously uncomfortable [classrooms that] are alternately tropical or arctic." Without question, "The law school building needs an overhaul." But a student assures us that "a new facility is being built that should be completed in the next few years."

It is no doubt that Northeastern's crown jewel is its hands-on Cooperative Legal Education Program. After completing a mostly traditional 1L curriculum, 2Ls and 3Ls rotate every three months between working as full-time, paid legal interns and attending classes. Each student completes "four three-month internships during our three years of law school." This valuable program "is a fantastic opportunity to get twice as much hands-on experience as you would get at other schools," and "means each student has the opportunity to explore areas of interest and make contacts in those fields." One 2L declares, "After next summer I will have completed three internships, one with a judge, one with in-house counsel at a large computer company, and one with a large law firm." Another student adds, "If you want real-world legal experience and to be four internships ahead of all of the other graduating law students, Northeastern is ideal."

Life

"The unique grading system provides for [an] extremely cooperative atmosphere." One student notes, "There is not an overwhelming sense of competition that stifles your ability to concentrate on functioning and thinking like a lawyer." Another explains, "Northeastern isn't a place for people who think of the whole world as a set of adversarial relationships. Students here love to help each other, and there is an honest desire among students and faculty for everyone to do well."

MJ Knoll-Finn, Assistant Dean and Director of Admissions
400 Huntington Avenue, Boston, MA 02115
Tel: 617-373-2395 Fax: 617-373-8865
E-mail: lawadmissions@neu.edu • Internet: www.slaw.neu.edu

Many agree that Northeastern students are "good, solid, friendly people who are a pleasure to be around." "The level of diversity, activism, and intelligence at this school is simply amazing," says one student. However many find that "the school is diverse in every way except ethnically." Others note that while "there are some conservative and libertarian types, we are very liberal here." "The more progressive students essentially dominate the school," explains one student.

Socially, "The school seems to be pretty cliquish—it's actually frighteningly like being in high school." One student notes, "A majority of the students seem to have taken a year or more to work between undergrad and law school, and the student body is more mature, socially and politically aware, and motivated as a result." That said, the "older" student population can "hurt the dating life of the single students on the prowl" as "most are married." Northeastern can be "a bit of a commuter law school." Geographically speaking, "The community ultimately revolves around e-mail exchanges because half the school at any time is somewhere else in the country." On the plus side, "Boston is a fantastic place to live," and the campus "is within walking distance or a T ride away from" live music, all manner of sports, fabulous food, and "everything exciting in town."

Getting In

Thanks to the public-interest bent, Northeastern's student body is in some ways self selecting. For the class of 2008, admitted students at the 25th percentile had an LSAT score of 159 and a GPA of 3.1. Admitted students at the 75th percentile had an LSAT score of 163 and a GPA of 3.58. Keep in mind it's full-time or nothing at Northeastern. The nature of the co-op program makes it next to impossible to accommodate part-time or evening students.

Public interest	
law requirement	Yes

ADMISSIONS

Selectivity Rating	**85**
# applications received	3,355
# applicants accepted	988
# acceptees attending	218
Average LSAT	161
LSAT Range	156–163
Average undergrad GPA	3.4
Application fee	$75
Regular application	3/1
Regular notification	4/15
Rolling notification	Yes
Early application program	Yes
Early application deadline	11/15
Early application notification	1/15
Transfer students accepted	Yes
Evening division offered	No
Part-time accepted	No
LSDAS accepted	Yes

Applicants Also Look At

American University, Boston College, Boston University, Fordham University, The George Washington University, New England School of Law, Suffolk University.

International Students

TOEFL required	
of international students	Yes
Minimum paper TOEFL	600
Minimum computer TOEFL	250

FINANCIAL FACTS

Annual tuition	$34,620
Books and supplies	$2,890
Room and board	$14,510
Financial aid application	
deadline	2/15
% first-year students	
receiving some sort of aid	96
% receiving some sort of aid	95
% of aid that is merit based	53
% receiving scholarships	78
Average grant	$7,930
Average loan	$34,145
Average total aid package	$39,283
Average debt	$89,310

EMPLOYMENT INFORMATION

		Grads Employed by Field (%)	
Career Rating	**80**	Academic	1
Rate of placement (nine months out)	97	Business/Industry	15
Average starting salary	$61,000	Government	10
State for bar exam	MA	Judicial clerkships	13
Pass rate for first-time bar	94	Private practice	45
Employers Who Frequently Hire Grads		Public Interest	16

Employers Who Frequently Hire Grads
Committee for Public Counsel Services (public defender); Equal Justice Works Fellowships; Suffolk County District Attorney's offices; Mintz, Levin, Cohn, Ferris, Glovsky and Popeo; Greater Boston Legal Services; U. S. Department of Labor; Morgan, Brown and Joy; Massachusetts trial and appeals courts; Health Law Advocates; Bingham McCutchen, LLP.

NORTHERN ILLINOIS UNIVERSITY
COLLEGE OF LAW

INSTITUTIONAL INFORMATION

Public/private	Public
Student-faculty ratio	13:1
% faculty part-time	17
% faculty female	50
% faculty minority	33
Total faculty	24

SURVEY SAYS...

Diverse opinions accepted
in classrooms
Great research resources
Great library staff
Students never sleep

STUDENTS

Enrollment of law school	315
% male/female	49/51
% out-of-state	16
% full-time	94
% minority	22
% international	1
# of countries represented	1
Average age of entering class	27

ACADEMICS

Academic Experience Rating	**70**
Profs interesting rating	65
Profs accessible rating	76
Hours of study per day	3.65

Academic Specialties
Lawyering skills training.

Combined Degrees Offered
JD/MBA 4 to 5 years, JD/MPA 4 to 5 years. Dual degrees can be structured for students admitted to other graduate programs.

Clinical program required	No
Legal writing course requirement	Yes
Legal methods course requirement	No
Legal research course requirement	Yes
Moot court requirement	Yes
Public interest law requirement	No

Academics

As the only public school found within the environs of the greater Chicago area, NIUers are released into Illinois' sea of graduating law students equipped with a solid education at a fraction of the price. Known for its commitment to fostering a sense of community and responsibility and pointing its students in the direction of public service jobs, NIU places a high value on pro bono work and makes a number of "public interest stipends" available to its students each summer. The school "has placed a special emphasis on diversity, both amongst its faculty and its student body," and it shows in the number of "divergent viewpoints" that are represented both in and out of the classroom.

Professors are themselves one source of these divergent viewpoints, with many students claiming that "some of the professors are amazing while others clearly enjoy the benefits of tenure." While the vast majority of professors "are well above average" and "do a very good job," offering students a high level of approachability, many students claim to have had a few instructors who were below par. "Simply reciting material straight from the textbook is not teaching," observes a first-year student. For the most part, however, students are happy with the quality of teaching at NIU, and say that the school is very good at balancing theory with practice. "A number of the professors go out of their way to expand on topics illustrated in the text and to relate their real-world experiences to the matters at hand. The professors as a group make themselves accessible to students who have issues that need to be discussed," affirms a student. "The faculty and administration practically begs students to come in and talk to them." Other students would like to see a broader spectrum of courses offered; says a 1L, "This semester I was forced to take a number of classes that I didn't have any interest in, solely to keep myself on pace for graduation."

As for facilities, one student informs us that "the school has chosen to update a number of its classrooms with modern technology. Unfortunately, the main lecture hall where all of the most popular 2L and 3L classes are taught has been left behind." There's an all-around chorus of complaints for the law school building itself and the library, both of which "suffer from a chronic case of tiredness and 1970s décor," but students recognize that rehabilitation is on the way. One of the greatest resources offered to NIU students, many of whom are older, is the Career Opportunities Office, which "will definitively help you get started towards your career." Though some students speak of the disadvantages facing NIU grads—particularly the distance of the school from Chicago proper—who are not in the top three or four people in the class but who are looking to get into "big law," others are reassured by the Career Opportunities Office's strong networking prospects, which complement the school's well-established and reputable clinic and externship programs. "We have a lock on many state attorney and public defenders offices now, and an incredible number of alumni in the judiciary. If you want to be a government trial lawyer in Illinois, this is definitely the school to go to." As an exiting student avers, "The price was right, and if you are willing to do the work you can get a good education."

BERTRAND J. SIMPSON JR., ESQ., DIRECTOR OF ADMISSION AND FINANCIAL AID
SWEN PARSON HALL, COLLEGE OF LAW, ROOM 151, DE KALB, IL 60115
TEL: 815-753-8595 FAX: 815-753-5680
E-MAIL: LAWADM@NIU.EDU • INTERNET: LAW.NIU.EDU

Life

With a strong contingent of older, "second-career" individuals, "a high bar for maturity and professionalism within the student body" tends to be set on campus. Students are friendly enough, but hometown Dekalb can be a "pretty desolate place to kids accustomed to the party life of Champaign-Urbana, Bloomington-Normal, or other major college towns." Dekalb is "without much of the nightlife and amenities that students were accustomed to having from their undergrad experience." There are two fraternities on campus (one is "clearly the party frat, and the other is the academic frat"), and there are a number of student groups which students can join, though "a few struggle to survive" due to lack of participation. As for competition among students, a second-year student assures us that "the shark-eat-shark mentality of other law schools would not be tolerated here." "For one thing, the student body is too small, and we all know each other too well. For another, there's just more a sense of being practical and real-world here; we're 'type A' people, surely, but we've also mellowed with more life experience than your average law student straight out of undergrad."

Getting In

Northern Illinois encourages students to submit their application early, though they do accept applications after the suggested priority deadline of May 15. Recently admitted students at the 25th percentile had an LSAT score of 152 and an average GPA of 3.0, while students at the 75th percentile had an LSAT score of 158 and a GPA of 3.6.

ADMISSIONS

Selectivity Rating	78
# applications received	1,283
# applicants accepted	377
# acceptees attending	111
Average LSAT	155
LSAT Range	152–158
Average undergrad GPA	3.46
Application fee	$50
Regular application	Rolling
Regular notification	Rolling
Rolling notification	Yes
Early application program	No
Transfer students accepted	Yes
Evening division offered	No
Part-time accepted	Yes
LSDAS accepted	Yes

International Students

TOEFL required of international students	Yes
Minimum paper TOEFL	550
Minimum computer TOEFL	250

FINANCIAL FACTS

Annual tuition (resident)	$9,552
Annual tuition (nonresident)	$19,104
Books and supplies	$1,500
Fees per credit (resident)	$70
Fees per credit (nonresident)	$70
Tuition per credit (resident)	$398
Tuition per credit (nonresident)	$398
Room and board	$8,336
Financial aid application deadline	3/1
% first-year students receiving some sort of aid	92
% receiving some sort of aid	87
% receiving scholarships	21
Average grant	$9,552
Average loan	$18,500
Average total aid package	$24,200
Average debt	$38,616

EMPLOYMENT INFORMATION

Career Rating	75
Rate of placement (nine months out)	93
Average starting salary	$50,295
State for bar exam	IL
Pass rate for first-time bar	84

Employers Who Frequently Hire Grads

State's attorneys; public defenders; Illinois Appellate Defender; Illinois House of Representatives; private firms.

Prominent Alumni

Kathleen Zellner, won reversals of 7 murder convictions by DNA; Cheryl Niro, Top 10 Female IL Lawyers and former president of ISBA; Dr. Kenneth Chessick, firm specializes in medical negligence litigation.

Grads Employed by Field (%)

Business/Industry	14
Government	24
Judicial clerkships	1
Military	1
Private practice	51
Public Interest	9

NORTHERN KENTUCKY UNIVERSITY
SALMON P. CHASE COLLEGE OF LAW

INSTITUTIONAL INFORMATION

Public/private	Public
Student-faculty ratio	15:1
% faculty part-time	31
% faculty female	39
% faculty minority	10
Total faculty	48

SURVEY SAYS...

Heavy use of Socratic method
Diverse opinions accepted
in classrooms
Great research resources
Great library staff

STUDENTS

Enrollment of law school	524
% male/female	45/55
% out-of-state	33
% full-time	54
% minority	7
Average age of entering class	24

ACADEMICS

Academic Experience Rating	**82**
Profs interesting rating	82
Profs accessible rating	87
Hours of study per day	3.95

Academic Specialties
Labor law, taxation.

Combined Degrees Offered
JD/MBA 4 years.

Clinical program required	No
Legal writing course requirement	Yes
Legal methods course requirement	Yes
Legal research course requirement	Yes
Moot court requirement	No
Public interest law requirement	No

Academics

At Northern Kentucky University Salmon P. Chase College of Law, an unwavering commitment to quality teaching fosters a stimulating and engaging learning atmosphere. Recruiting and retaining superior teachers is a priority at Chase, and the school "has gone out of its way to get good professors, especially in the last few years." As a result, "Classes are rich and rewarding." The "student-oriented [professors] create an atmosphere that is comfortable but challenging." In the classroom, critical-thinking skills and student participation are emphasized, and professors make lectures engaging with their humor, enthusiasm, and intelligence. While material can be difficult and dry, Chase professors take a lighthearted approach to instruction. A 1L explains, "The majority of our professors use humor to keep us involved and challenge us to work through difficult theories instead of just giving us the answers or letting us off the hook." One professor even "came up with lyrics to a country song during property class to help us understand fees."

In addition to traditional course work in legal theory, students appreciate Chase's "good, structured curriculum geared toward preparing students for the bar." This excellent program has allowed Chase to claim the "highest first-time bar-passage rate in Kentucky" (with a 79 percent average). In addition, "Chase's emphasis on practical experience is found in such classes as interview and negotiation, trial ad, and externships. These classes/externships are offered on a regular basis [and] prepare the student for immediate success in the courtroom or the boardroom." "Chase's practical teaching methods and adherence to the principles of the ever-evolving legal world allow a student to learn how to practice law and not simply what the law is historically." This applied experience also plays out positively in career placement, as "Chase has a great local reputation for turning out lawyers who are capable of hitting the ground running."

Described by weary students as "exhausting and exhilarating," the Chase experience is extremely competitive. Students warn that "the work load is obscene," and they are further challenged by the school's Draconian grading policies. Traditonal first-year classes (contracts, torts, etc.) are graded on what is known as a C curve. On every exam the majority of the class will get a C. While this is at times harsh, it really helps to push students. "When you get an A, you know that it really means something. Also, this curve has helped to improve our bar-passage rating by making students work harder." Ultimately, "Chase is about helping people succeed"; to that end, "The faculty really go out of their way for students." One student reports, "My writing professor is not only a good lawyer and writer, but also a personable and kind individual. He seems genuinely concerned about my education and about me personally." According to another, "The faculty are always willing to have students to their offices to answer questions or help in finding jobs." On top of that, "There is a very personal relationship between the deans and the students," and the administration is active in establishing programs to help students adjust to and succeed in law school. In particular, "Chase truly works on transitioning students into their first classes." First-years can "enroll in a summer program designed to introduce them to the law school process. In addition, there is a required course, introduction to legal studies, for all first-years, which builds on the summer program. This made the first day of law school a lot less intimidating."

Chase's supportive atmosphere is particularly evident in the remarks of evening program participants. While part-time students at other law schools often feel overlooked or misunderstood, Chase is "accommodating for students who work full-time, have children, or have been out of the classroom for a long time." One night student reports, "As a part-time student with a more than full-time job, my professors value my experience. I find they incorporate our expertise in their questioning, which means they have taken the time to get to know us." Indeed, night students say that "there are a large number of older students with real-world work and life experience attending classes [along] with traditional students."

Life

There is a noticeable divide between the day and evening programs at Chase. While full-time students describe the campus as friendly and social, evening students tend to keep to themselves. A day student comments, "Most of our class has genuinely become friends with each other, and we hang out together whenever we get free time." Among full-timers, participation in clubs, campus events, and student parties is common. On the contrary, students in the evening program usually work full-time, so "relations among students outside the classroom are minimal (with exception of study groups)." While they may not socialize together, evening students maintain a generally noncompetitive and supportive atmosphere in the classroom. One shares, "Because the majority of my class is composed of nontraditional students, social relationships are nonexistent. Academic relationships, however, are much stronger than any I've seen."

On that note, all Chase students agree that the academic environment is collegial and supportive. "Although there is a definite competitive atmosphere due to the bell curve, students are not as cutthroat as they may be at other schools." Students write that the school's "strongest fault is the lack of diversity within our faculty and our students." A 2L laments, "The law school could improve on its diversity retention." The school does, however, maintain fairly active student communities, and "There are groups for every type of student: law fraternities, the Black Lawyers' Society, the Christian Legal Society, the Public Interest Group. You can find support almost everywhere you turn."

Getting In

In 2005, Chase matriculated 110 students with an average LSAT score of 155 and an average undergraduate GPA of 3.33. Chase principally considers LSAT scores, undergraduate GPAs, letters of recommendation, and personal statements in making admissions decisions. Chase looks for students with a broad liberal arts education and strong writing and verbal skills. While the school does not prefer any specific course of undergraduate study, political science, finance, and psychology were the most common undergraduate majors represented in the entering class.

ADMISSIONS

Selectivity Rating	**78**
# applications received	913
# applicants accepted	264
# acceptees attending	89
Average LSAT	155
LSAT Range	154–157
Average undergrad GPA	3.36
Application fee	$40
Regular application	3/1
Regular notification	Rolling
Rolling notification	Yes
Early application program	No
Transfer students accepted	Yes
Evening division offered	Yes
Part-time accepted	Yes
LSDAS accepted	Yes

Applicants Also Look At

University of Cincinnati, University of Dayton, University of Kentucky, University of Louisville.

International Students

TOEFL required of international students	Yes

FINANCIAL FACTS

Annual tuition (resident)	$11,112
Annual tuition (nonresident)	$24,240
Books and supplies	$3,060
Tuition per credit (resident)	$463
Tuition per credit (nonresident)	$1,010
Room and board (on/off-campus)	$5,548/$15,390
Financial aid application deadline	3/1
% receiving some sort of aid	74
% of aid that is merit based	7
% receiving scholarships	36
Average grant	$4,915
Average loan	$17,305
Average total aid package	$30,360
Average debt	$58,215

EMPLOYMENT INFORMATION

		Grads Employed by Field (%)	
Career Rating	**73**	**Grads Employed by Field (%)**	
Rate of placement (nine months out)	92	Academic	3
Average starting salary	$54,463	Business/Industry	21
State for bar exam	KY, OH	Government	10
Pass rate for first-time bar	74	Judicial clerkships	4
Employers Who Frequently Hire Grads		Private practice	53
Procter and Gamble; Dinsmore and Shohl;		Public Interest	9
U.S. Department of Labor; Kentucky			
Department of Public Advocacy; Taft,			
Stettinius, and Hollister; Freund, Freeze,			
and Arnold.			
Prominent Alumni			
Steve Chabot, United States Representative,			
1st District of Ohio; Patricia L. Herbold,			
United States Ambassador to Singapore.			

NORTHWESTERN UNIVERSITY
SCHOOL OF LAW

INSTITUTIONAL INFORMATION

Public/private	Private
Student-faculty ratio	11:1
% faculty part-time	38
% faculty female	38
% faculty minority	8
Total faculty	168

SURVEY SAYS...

Diverse opinions accepted in classrooms
Abundant externship/internship/clerkship opportunities
Students love Chicago, IL

STUDENTS

Enrollment of law school	768
% male/female	54/46
% out-of-state	80
% full-time	100
% minority	38
% international	4
# of countries represented	33
Average age of entering class	26

ACADEMICS

Academic Experience Rating	**97**
Profs interesting rating	88
Profs accessible rating	87
Hours of study per day	4.49

Academic Specialties

Business enterprise, civil litigation and dispute resolution, corporation securities law, human rights law, international law, law and social policy, taxation.

Advanced Degrees Offered

JD 3 years, LLM 1 year, SJD 5 years, LLM (taxation) 1 year, LLM (human rights) 1 year, JD (international lawyers) 2 years.

Combined Degrees Offered

JD/MBA 3 years, JD/PhD 6 years, JD/MA 4 years, MSJ/MSL 2 years, LLM (certificate in management) 1 year.

Clinical program required	No

Academics

Located "in the heart of Chicago," Northwestern University School of Law has a first-rate "national reputation" for "developing practical skills" and offering "world-class" clinics that give students "unbelievable" opportunities to work on "real cases." Many here agree that "it's hard to imagine getting a better mix of academic rigor and practical job training anywhere else." Other highlights at NU include study abroad programs all over the world, a highly touted JD/MBA program, and lots of "self-scheduled exams." One demerit is the "legal writing program" that students wish was "a pass/fail class" due to the "incredible amount of work" it requires.

Northwestern's "brilliant" and "very friendly" faculty is made up of "nationally and internationally renowned scholars" who have "a great sense of humor." Students have "an unparalleled opportunity to learn from the best, starting right at the beginning." "My classes and instruction have ranged from very good to simply outstanding," relates a 2L. "I'd go so far to say that my Constitutional Law class was one of the most intellectually stimulating courses I've encountered." Professors are "accessible" and "The professors seem to really enjoy talking to students outside of class." "It is not uncommon for them to stop me in the hallway and chat about a class topic, my journal comment, or even college football," explains a student. For the most part the administration is "receptive to student concerns" and "always approachable." "Everything goes pretty smoothly," and the atmosphere is "not very bureaucratic," though some note that "change is very slow to come" in regards to "accommodation for disabilities."

Students happily report that "if you do even moderately well in your 1L classes at Northwestern, you're going to have legal employers knocking down your door." "You'd be hard-pressed to find someone coming out of NU to a less-than-excellent job." "Most of us start out at big firms," adds a 1L. "The Chicago firms just love NU students." However, some students complain that "there should be a greater emphasis on public interest career choices" as "Not everybody wants to go to a big law firm upon graduation."

The architecture here is "nice, consisting of both old, more traditional buildings, and a newer building." "A quiet atmosphere prevails" and the "gorgeous" library overlooks Lake Michigan. Also, trust us: Lincoln Hall is exactly what a law school classroom should look like. While "good," the classrooms could use some "updating," and "There aren't enough areas to study." Also, "lighting conditions" in the library are "bad," and though "Wireless Internet continues to improve," it can still be "insufficient and annoying."

Life

"Northwestern places a huge emphasis on admitting students who have a couple years of work experience after undergrad, and it makes a huge difference," says one student. These future lawyers "come from a variety of backgrounds and offer amazing insights into a range of issues." They "are grounded and have balanced lives." "People have a better sense of the world around them and the realities of life beyond a classroom," observes a 2L. "This keeps the drama to a minimum and also assembles a group of people who've done some pretty interesting things—minor league ball, the military, symphonic bassoon, and so on." "There seems to be the misconception that the students at Northwestern are really old," clarifies another student. "For most students it is only about two years before we come to law school."

Don Rebstock, Associate Dean of Enrollment
357 East Chicago Avenue, Chicago, IL 60611
Tel: 312-503-8465 Fax: 312-503-0178
E-mail: admissions@law.northwestern.edu • Internet: www.law.northwestern.edu

"Class sizes are small" and "The school goes to great lengths to create and foster a sense of community among the students." In this "collegial" atmosphere, students are "intelligent, friendly, [and] laid-back." "There are not too many gunners," reports one student. "We're smart, personable people who mix well socially while doing topnotch legal work," says a 2L. However, some students project an "'I-don't-study-at-all' attitude in the middle of the semester, trying to throw others off base. Then, suddenly, the same person who 'never studies' has a 150-page annotated outline with hyperlinks to all of its sections and subsections."

Outside of class, Northwestern is "a very fun place to attend school." "The school sponsors many events for students every week" and there are "free lunches almost every day" along with "random social events put on by the many, many student organizations." "Lunchtime speakers, panels, and club meetings provide great opportunities to explore different facets of the law school experience and the legal profession without taking up too much time." In addition, "Chicago is a great city" with "a great mix of . . . hustle and bustle and Midwestern friendliness"—all of which starts right "next door" to campus with "Michigan Avenue's Magnificent Mile."

Getting In

Northwestern claims to be "the only law school in the country that strongly encourages all applicants to interview as a part of the admissions process." Understandably, knowing this, it behooves you to show up for an interview if you apply. With or without an interview, though, admission is unusually competitive. Admitted students at the 25th percentile have LSAT scores of 166 and GPAs of about 3.4. Admitted students at the 75th percentile have LSAT scores of 172 and GPAs of about 3.8.

Legal writing	
course requirement	Yes
Legal methods	
course requirement	No
Legal research	
course requirement	Yes
Moot court requirement	Yes
Public interest	
law requirement	No

ADMISSIONS

Selectivity Rating	**98**
# applications received	5,015
# applicants accepted	869
# acceptees attending	233
Average LSAT	170
LSAT Range	166–172
Average undergrad GPA	3.7
Application fee	$80
Regular application	2/15
Regular notification	Rolling
Rolling notification	Yes
Early application program	Yes
Early application deadline	12/1
Early application notification	12/31
Transfer students accepted	Yes
Evening division offered	No
Part-time accepted	No
LSDAS accepted	Yes

Applicants Also Look At
Columbia University, Georgetown University, Harvard University, New York University, University of California—Berkeley, The University of Chicago, University of Pennsylvania.

International Students
TOEFL required	
of international students	No
TOEFL recommended	
of international students	No

FINANCIAL FACTS

Annual tuition	$40,410
Books and supplies	$7,628
Tuition per credit	$2,020
Room and board	$12,078
Financial aid application	
deadline	2/15
% first-year students	
receiving some sort of aid	85
% receiving some sort of aid	85
% of aid that is merit based	50
% receiving scholarships	32
Average grant	$20,000
Average loan	$30,000
Average total aid package	$50,000
Average debt	$125,000

EMPLOYMENT INFORMATION

		Grads Employed by Field (%)	
Career Rating	**99**	**Grads Employed by Field (%)**	
Rate of placement (nine months out)	100	Business/Industry	8
Average starting salary	$135,000	Government	4
State for bar exam	IL	Judicial clerkships	14
Pass rate for first-time bar	95	Private practice	71
Employers Who Frequently Hire Grads		Public Interest	3

Employers Who Frequently Hire Grads
Skadden Arps; Cravath, Swain, and Moore; Sidley, Austin, Brown, and Wood; White and Case; Kirkland and Ellis; Latham and Watkins; Jones, Day, Reavis, and Pogue.

Prominent Alumni
Justice Justice John Paul Stevens, U.S. Supreme Court; Justice Arthur Goldberg, U.S. Supreme Court; Donald Washburn, chairman and president, Northwest Airlines.

NOVA SOUTHEASTERN UNIVERSITY
SHEPARD BROAD LAW CENTER

INSTITUTIONAL INFORMATION

Public/private	Private
Student-faculty ratio	14:1
% faculty part-time	45
% faculty female	45
% faculty minority	18
Total faculty	119

SURVEY SAYS...
Diverse opinions accepted
in classrooms
Good social life

STUDENTS

Enrollment of law school	927
% male/female	50/50
% full-time	80
% minority	24
% international	2
# of countries represented	8
Average age of entering class	24

ACADEMICS

Academic Experience Rating	**73**
Profs interesting rating	64
Profs accessible rating	66
Hours of study per day	3.55

Academic Specialties
Civil procedure, commercial law, constitutional law, corporation securities law, criminal law, environmental law, family law, government services, human rights law, intellectual property law, international law, labor law, legal history, property, taxation.

Combined Degrees Offered
JD/MBA, JD/MS (psychology), JD/MS (dispute resolution), JD/MS (computer), JD/MURP.

Clinical program required	No
Legal writing course requirement	Yes
Legal methods course requirement	No
Legal research course requirement	Yes
Moot court requirement	Yes

Academics

At Nova Southeastern University's Shepard Broad Law Center, students are given the unbeatable opportunity to receive a practical law experience while being surrounded by the beautiful beaches and perfect weather of southern Florida. NSU's unique dual-degree law programs with the University of Venice and the University of Barcelona are extremely popular, and offer students the opportunity to study both the common law system in the United States and the civil law systems of Italy or Spain. It's this sort of range of exposure that makes Nova "a great place for students with an aptitude for law who are unsure about the area of law in which they want to practice," though some students express a desire for specialized classes in fields such as constitutional law and trial advocacy. The school places a high importance on practical experience, to the point that all third-year law students are guaranteed a place in one of the clinics.

The professors at NSU get mostly positive but still mixed reviews: "Some professors are incredible, and some make you wonder how they ever got offered a job in the first place." Despite the occasional bad apple, students don't hesitate to give props to the number of "accessible" and "knowledgeable" teachers who are "very open to classroom participation." "While [the professors are] not the most esteemed in the world, they are very hardworking and usually willing to help you out in any way they can," says a graduating student.

Students' satisfaction levels with the administration are "lukewarm," and many criticize the administration's requirement that all students "take a Bar Review class that does not count for credit." However, some students point out that this could be due to the fact that the administration has been "working in reaction mode to the very low bar-passage rates at the school." A third-year student claims that this "'experimentation' with programs to help that problem has not been fun for the gerbils/students." Career Services fares a bit better in students' esteem; "The [school's] reputation among south Florida judges and attorneys is strong" and the networking prospects in Broward County are great. However, a good number of students speak of a need for "more national recognition for students who leave south Florida" to practice.

As for facilities and technology, "The buildings and campus are beautiful, and I couldn't imagine a better location," gushes a third-year student. Those who call the Nova law building home are nothing short of effusive about the excellent wireless coverage that is integrated into all classrooms and course work (including the ability to watch lectures online), a boon which one student claims "makes it very easy to do all of my work on campus between classes and in the library." This accessibility can have its negative aspects as well: "95 percent of students in class are surfing the Net or IM-ing the entire time. There is very little student participation in class discussions as a result," says a 3L.

Life

When "Campus is a picture-perfect tropical paradise" located near the beaches of Fort Lauderdale, one does not find many complaints about the quality of life. "What other school allows for beach cleanups, trips to the Everglades, and socials on South Beach and in downtown Ft. Lauderdale?" asks a first-year student. With such idyllic surroundings, it's no wonder that "student life at school is very social." Competition levels are minimal—in fact, a few students suspect that their classmates are merely "looking for a piece of paper that says JD"—but on the upside, this does mean that "there is no internal bickering and fighting to be number one." Student organizations abound, but these organizations are usually run by a dedicated handful of people with little help or participation from other members and students, who tend to be "apathetic when it comes to extracurricular activities." "There are a lot of active clubs on campus for every ideology, ethnic group, or however else you might classify yourself," says a 3L, including numerous American Law Associations (Caribbean Law Student Association, Italian-American Law Student Association, Celtic-American Law Society, etc.). The Goodwin Speaker series also brings several notable speakers to the campus every year.

Getting In

Though the admit rate may seem to run about average, this is more a result of self-selection than it is the result of a particularly tough admissions process, as gaining admission to Nova is not exceptionally difficult for qualified students. Recently admitted students at the 25th percentile had an LSAT score of 148 and an average GPA of 2.8, while admitted students at the 75th percentile had an LSAT score of 152 and a GPA of 3.3. For students who don't meet Nova's standards for admission, the school's AAMPLE summer conditional program provides students with low LSAT scores the opportunity to attend law school.

Public interest law requirement	No

ADMISSIONS

Selectivity Rating	**69**
# applications received	2,821
# applicants accepted	953
# acceptees attending	315
Average LSAT	150
LSAT Range	148–153
Average undergrad GPA	3.18
Application fee	$50
Regular application	3/1
Regular notification	3/1
Rolling notification	Yes
Early application program	No
Transfer students accepted	Yes
Evening division offered	Yes
Part-time accepted	Yes
LSDAS accepted	Yes

Applicants Also Look At
Florida Coastal School of Law, Florida International University, Florida State University, St. Thomas University, Stetson University, University of Florida, University of Miami.

International Students

TOEFL required of international students	Yes
Minimum paper TOEFL	600
Minimum computer TOEFL	250

FINANCIAL FACTS

Annual tuition	$27,050
Books and supplies	$17,400
Room and board (on/off-campus)	$6,100/$13,000
Financial aid application deadline	4/15
% first-year students receiving some sort of aid	82
% receiving some sort of aid	80
% of aid that is merit based	6
% receiving scholarships	9
Average grant	$18,487
Average loan	$31,162
Average total aid package	$35,404
Average debt	$94,698

EMPLOYMENT INFORMATION

		Grads Employed by Field (%)	
Career Rating	68		
Rate of placement (nine months out)	82	Academic	1
Average starting salary	$57,154	Business/Industry	15
State for bar exam	FL, NY, TX, NJ, WA	Government	23
Pass rate for first-time bar	74	Judicial clerkships	2
Employers Who Frequently Hire Grads		Private practice	57
Private law firms; local and state agencies;		Public Interest	2
state attorney's offices; public defender offices.			

Prominent Alumni
Honorable Melanie G. May, appeals court; Rob Brzezinski, vice president football operations, Minnesota Vikings; Ellyn Setnor Bogdanoff, Florida House of Representatives.

OHIO NORTHERN UNIVERSITY
CLAUDE W. PETTIT COLLEGE OF LAW

INSTITUTIONAL INFORMATION

Public/private	Private
Affiliation	Methodist
Student-faculty ratio	12:1
% faculty part-time	25
% faculty female	30
% faculty minority	3
Total faculty	30

SURVEY SAYS...
Great research resources
Great library staff

STUDENTS

Enrollment of law school	320
% male/female	51/49
% out-of-state	65
% full-time	100
% minority	15
% international	1
# of countries represented	8
Average age of entering class	25

ACADEMICS

Academic Experience Rating	**68**
Profs interesting rating	70
Profs accessible rating	80
Hours of study per day	5.5

Academic Specialties
Capital punishment, civil procedure, commercial law, constitutional law, corporation securities law, criminal law, environmental law, human rights law, intellectual property law, international law, labor law, legal history, legal philosophy, property, taxation.

Advanced Degrees Offered
JD 3 years.

Clinical program required	No
Legal writing course requirement	Yes
Legal methods course requirement	Yes
Legal research course requirement	Yes
Moot court requirement	No

Academics

At the small Claude W. Pettit College of Law, no one is a face in the crowd, so you can forget about sitting in the back row and remaining unnoticed. Thanks to small class sizes, "There is a high degree of accountability in the classroom," and students are expected to keep up with a hefty workload; a 2L warns, "You really have to be on your game for class every day." Students also feel the need to be on the ball outside the classroom. "I didn't realize when I came here that I would have to walk around with clever things to say in case a professor happened to be near when I was roaming the building. You never know when a professor will approach you in the hall or lounge to talk about anything from what you discussed in class to something they remembered about your application essay," reports one student. Indeed, at many other law schools, the top ten percent of the class eats up most of the attention of faculty and staff, but at ONU, "The dean knows not only who is number one in the class, but also who is fiftieth and who is last."

The intimate environment at ONU makes for a lively and competitive atmosphere. But "While there is competition, you get personal attention every step of the way." The school promotes an open-door policy for professors, and students tell us that "the faculty is always around and usually more than willing to help out, answer questions, or shoot the breeze." A 2L adds, "They are there to help you not only with legal concepts, but also how to go about starting your legal career." On that note, students say they get excellent career preparation through the clinical programs, for even though ONU is located in a tiny, rural town, "The clinic/externship program is one of the best," placing many students in jobs in the nearby city of Lima. So "If you want a placement somewhere, they can make it happen." On top of that, the school operates "tons of extracurriculars," such as moot court and Law Review, which are described as top-notch and highly competitive. However, ONU doesn't just cater to overachievers. "Our programs differ in ways that allow each student to maximize [his or her] potential," reports one 2L. For example, the school runs "extra help sessions taught by teaching assistants and the summer starter program, intended for those with lower LSAT scores."

The school has been receiving increasing prominence as of late, and the administration is eager to keep the ball rolling. A 2L explains, "As for the goals of the university, the school seems to be moving toward increasing the quality of the students and faculty and generally ensuring a better reputation for the future." Some feel that the higher-ups are now too focused on building status at the expense of building personal bonds with students, leading some students to report that "the relationship between the administration and students feels like it gets chillier every year."

Located in the tiny town of Ada, Pettit's pleasant campus is an excellent place to study, offering little distraction for the serious law student. Some campus buildings need to be renovated, according to students who also point out that classrooms are old and limited in outlets for laptops Others feel, however, that the school hits the mark in all the important areas: "The building could use some sprucing up," a 2L writes, "but what it lacks in looks it makes up for in having wireless everywhere and being a comfortable place to learn." On top of that, students praise the research facilities and staff: "The librarians are hands-on, holding workshops that complement the research assignments."

LINDA K. ENGLISH, ASSISTANT DEAN AND DIRECTOR OF LAW ADMISSIONS
OHIO NORTHERN UNIVERSITY, PETTIT COLLEGE, ADA, OH 45810-1599
TEL: 877-452-9668 FAX: 419-772-3042
E-MAIL: LAW-ADMISSIONS@ONU.EDU • INTERNET: WWW.LAW.ONU.EDU

Life

You might be surprised to learn that many students say ONU's location "in the middle of a cornfield" is among the school's greatest assets because for the overburdened law student, Ada is free of distractions and is "conducive to studying." In addition, "the actual location of the school is in a small town setting but only 10 minutes from the next city. You are right between Columbus, Dayton, and Toledo, so you can go wherever you wish to have fun" if you have a car, that is. The small-town environment "lacks the diversity of a big city," a condition that is mirrored by the campus population, but students insist that there is nonetheless some variety among the student population. "Despite our cultural diversity being rather low due to the area of the university," reports one 2L, "we have a great deal of different life experiences."

On campus the atmosphere is active, social, and friendly. "Our student body is very outgoing," writes one student. "This allows for many different organizations to be successful and for different events to be more enjoyable." Outside of class, it's easy to make friends among interesting and amiable classmates: "Throughout your time in law school you will make closer friends than you could possibly imagine, not only with people in your section, but [also] the whole school," reports a typical student. With such a small number of students, however, "The rumor mill is endless." As is the case at many law schools, "It's like high school, but you can drink now without hiding it from your parents."

Getting In

No surprises here. Undergraduate GPA and LSAT scores are the most heavily weighted factors for admission; however, the Admissions Committee will also consider factors such as graduate work, work experience that may have enhanced a student's communication and analytical skills, or a history of overcoming racial or ethnic barriers. Successful applicants usually submit an undergraduate GPA above 3.0 and LSAT scores above 150.

Public interest law requirement	No

ADMISSIONS

Selectivity Rating	**71**
# applications received	1,424
# applicants accepted	498
# acceptees attending	120
Average LSAT	152
LSAT Range	150–155
Average undergrad GPA	3.35
Application fee	$40
Regular application	Rolling
Regular notification	Rolling
Rolling notification	Yes
Early application program	No
Transfer students accepted	Yes
Evening division offered	No
Part-time accepted	No
LSDAS accepted	Yes

Applicants Also Look At
Capital University, University of Dayton, University of Toledo.

International Students

TOEFL required of international students	Yes
Minimum paper TOEFL	550

FINANCIAL FACTS

Annual tuition	$24,840
Books and supplies	$900
Room and board (on/off-campus)	$11,237/$12,137
Financial aid application deadline	4/6
% first-year students receiving some sort of aid	97
% receiving some sort of aid	97
% of aid that is merit based	23
% receiving scholarships	51
Average grant	$16,390
Average loan	$25,140
Average total aid package	$31,023
Average debt	$74,380

EMPLOYMENT INFORMATION

Career Rating	73	Grads Employed by Field (%)	
Rate of placement (nine months out)	95	Academic	3
Average starting salary	$50,000	Business/Industry	11
State for bar exam	OH, FL, PA, NC, MD	Government	13
Pass rate for first-time bar	78	Judicial clerkships	2
Prominent Alumni		Military	12
Michael DeWine, U.S. Senator; Honorable		Other	1
Gregory Frost, U.S. District Court; Benjamin		Private practice	54
Brafman, senior partner, Brafman and Ross;		Public Interest	4
Greg Miller, U.S. attorney.			

THE OHIO STATE UNIVERSITY
MICHAEL E. MORITZ COLLEGE OF LAW

INSTITUTIONAL INFORMATION

Public/private	Public
Student-faculty ratio	14:1
% faculty part-time	11
% faculty female	40
% faculty minority	21
Total faculty	52

SURVEY SAYS...
Diverse opinions accepted
in classrooms
Great research resources
Great library staff

STUDENTS

Enrollment of law school	688
% male/female	57/43
% out-of-state	36
% full-time	100
% minority	23
% international	2
# of countries represented	6
Average age of entering class	23

ACADEMICS

Academic Experience Rating	**83**
Profs interesting rating	84
Profs accessible rating	77
Hours of study per day	4.42

Academic Specialties
Alternative dispute resolution, civil procedure, constitutional law, criminal law, government services, intellectual property law, international law, labor law, property.

Advanced Degrees Offered
Masters of Law 1 year, LLM (international students) 1 year.

Combined Degrees Offered
JD/MBA 4 years, JD/MHA 4 years, JD/MPA 4 years.

Clinical program required	No
Legal writing course requirement	Yes
Legal methods course requirement	No
Legal research course requirement	Yes

Academics

Students graduate from the Ohio State University Michael E. Mortiz College of Law with a strong legal education and excellent career prospects but without the crushing debt typical to top-tier law schools. "The faculty is composed of some of the top legal scholars in the country," and students report that "many of [their] professors are prolific writers and widely known in the academic and legal communities." The value, then, of an Ohio State legal education is "exposure to top professors at a public school price." While the college's accomplished faculty brings prestige to the school and expertise to the classroom, students say that it is their "caring and student-focused" attitudes that really stand out. "Across the board," one 3L attests, "the faculty at Ohio State is approachable and dedicated to teaching students. Students always come before publishing and other personal endeavors." Adds another student, "The professors here are outstanding and care about the students 150 percent. They will put forth the effort for you not only in the classroom, but in your career preparation and job searching as well."

With about 145 courses offered annually, Ohio State students can choose from "an incredible number of classes in a number of interesting areas." While first-year course work is prescribed, as it is at most law schools, the final two years are largely elective, and students can design their own course of study within a legal specialty. Many first-year classes are limited in terms of enrollment, which students see as a benefit, and as "The law school is attached to a great university," there are "so many opportunities" academically and socially that students at unaffiliated law schools may not enjoy. Of particular strength is the college's "focus and reputation for alternative dispute resolution [ADR]," which attracts many lawyers with an interest in public service. In fact, Ohio State has a history as a fairly liberal and social justice–oriented school. A 2L explains, "Because of the lower cost, we are exposed to a less cynical side of lawyering. We can come out and actually help someone, rather than pay off debt."

The Ohio State academic experience focuses largely on legal scholarship; however, the school also offers a variety of opportunities for students to put their theory to work. From the first year on, "the school offers a fair number of practicum courses," including a variety of upper-level classes, many of which enroll no more than 20 students at a time. In addition, the school operates a number of legal clinics and student-published legal reviews. Not everyone, however, feels the school goes far enough in promoting practical lawyering skills and feel that the school needs "to balance all this ADR and constitutional and rights course work with material that lawyers actually practice."

Despite such complaints, most Ohio State students easily find jobs in the area since the college has "a great regional reputation as the best law school in Ohio." In addition, "The law school is always looking to improve," and, as a result, students say their national reputation is on an upward trajectory.

The administration maintains a very considerate, student-friendly attitude. In fact, the administration is so solicitous that some complain they "could use a little more backbone" and are "too nice and too concerned about student opinions." While they report general satisfaction with the higher-ups, some students are sorely disappointed in the fact that the "university recently backed away from supporting its GLBT students and allies in favor of avoiding a legal battle with the Christian Legal Society." A 3L advises, "If you want a school that doesn't use your tuition/public money to discriminate,

JIMMI NICHOLSON, ASSISTANT DIRECTOR
104 DRINKO HALL, 55 WEST TWELFTH AVENUE, COLUMBUS, OH 43210
TEL: 614-292-8810 FAX: 614-292-1492
E-MAIL: LAWADMIT@OSU.EDU • INTERNET: MORITZLAW.OSU.EDU

rethink applying to OSU. They refuse to take a stand on this and have allowed 'sincere religious beliefs' to trump their own nondiscrimination policy."

Life

By all accounts, "the student body and the faculty at Ohio State is quite diverse," both ethnically and culturally. A 3L details, "The male-female ratio is about even, there are large numbers of racial minorities, there are substantial numbers of gays and lesbians, and minorities excel in all areas at OSU." Despite the ethnic and cultural diversity, students say that there is a surprising uniformity in age and opinion. "A huge percentage of students come straight to Moritz directly out of Ohio State undergrad," notes one student. "This leads to 'group think' on a lot of issues. I'm not talking about racial or ethnic diversity—that seems pretty good. I'm talking diversity of ideas, which makes for a better learning environment." In fact, many say that the school's political environment leans largely to the left and that "a liberal viewpoint is always eagerly welcomed."

While some conservatives may moan about the school's liberal bias, most students agree that, for the most part, Ohio State is "a cohesive and welcoming community" and that competitiveness is kept to a minimum. In general, life at Ohio State is pleasant, laid-back, and casual, and students appreciate the slower pace of their Midwestern environs. In the words of one 3L, "Columbus is a great city to live in as a student because there's a low cost of living and the pace of life is not hectic." If you are looking for bright lights and big city, though, Columbus is not the place: "There's not a lot of variety to Columbus. Enough to keep you busy, but not a lot of variety," reports a 2L.

Getting In

Ohio State University admits students who have demonstrated ability to succeed in a rigorous legal program. In particular, the admissions committee carefully evaluates a student's undergraduate record, examining grades, grade trends, rigor of the course work and major curriculum, reputation of the undergraduate institution, and recommendations from academic faculty. About 42 percent of entering students in fall 2004 were residents of a state other than Ohio.

| Moot court requirement | Yes |
| Public interest law requirement | No |

ADMISSIONS

Selectivity Rating	**87**
# applications received	2,289
# applicants accepted	653
# acceptees attending	232
Average LSAT	161
LSAT Range	158–163
Average undergrad GPA	3.61
Application fee	$60
Regular application	3/15
Regular notification	Rolling
Rolling notification	Yes
Early application program	Yes
Early application deadline	11/14
Early application notification	12/20
Transfer students accepted	Yes
Evening division offered	No
Part-time accepted	No
LSDAS accepted	Yes

Applicants Also Look At
American University, Capital University, Case Western Reserve University, The George Washington University, Georgetown University, University of Cincinnati.

International Students
TOEFL required of international students	Yes
Minimum paper TOEFL	600

FINANCIAL FACTS
Annual tuition (resident)	$17,538
Annual tuition (nonresident)	$31,956
Books and supplies	$2,950
Room and board	$10,000
Financial aid application deadline	3/1
% receiving some sort of aid	82
% receiving scholarships	67
Average grant	$4,500
Average loan	$22,897
Average debt	$53,179

EMPLOYMENT INFORMATION

Career Rating	82	Grads Employed by Field (%)	
Rate of placement (nine months out)	98	Academic	4
Average starting salary	$76,761	Business/Industry	18
State for bar exam	OH, DC, NY, IL, CA	Government	15
Pass rate for first-time bar	86	Judicial clerkships	7
Prominent Alumni		Military	1
Jack Creighton, former CEO, Weyerhauser		Private practice	49
Corporation and United Airlines; John		Public Interest	6
Garland, president, Central State			
University; Erin Moriarity, *48 Hours*/CBS			
News journalist; Karen Sarjeant, vice presi-			
dent, Legal Services Corp.; George			
Voinovich, U.S. Senator.			

OKLAHOMA CITY UNIVERSITY
SCHOOL OF LAW

INSTITUTIONAL INFORMATION

Public/private	Private
Affiliation	Methodist
Student-faculty ratio	20:1
% faculty part-time	25
% faculty female	31
% faculty minority	11
Total faculty	35

SURVEY SAYS...

Heavy use of Socratic method
Diverse opinions accepted
in classrooms
Great library staff

STUDENTS

Enrollment of law school	684
% male/female	60/40
% out-of-state	55
% full-time	80
% minority	18
% international	1
# of countries represented	5
Average age of entering class	25

ACADEMICS

Academic Experience Rating	**67**
Profs interesting rating	77
Profs accessible rating	74
Hours of study per day	4.73

Academic Specialties

Certificates in business law and
public law.

Combined Degrees Offered

JD/MBA 4 years.

Clinical program required	No
Legal writing course requirement	Yes
Legal methods course requirement	Yes
Legal research course requirement	Yes
Moot court requirement	No
Public interest law requirement	No

Academics

A first-year at Oklahoma City University School of Law writes, "I was nervous about going to a school that did not have a better academic reputation on the national level, but quickly I realized that OCU Law is very competitive with respect to its curriculum and professors." In particular, "If you are going to practice in Oklahoma, OCU Law has a stellar reputation within the community and surrounding states." Students interested in dispute resolution and Native American law find top programs that are backed by "an unmatched Legal Research and Writing Department." Some students, particularly those in the part-time evening program, complain about sparse course options. Furthermore, a few gripe that "the first three semesters are largely mandatory courses." That said, "The school is working on obtaining adjunct professors to teach some of the more popular courses requested by the students," and students are optimistic about having a wider range of course options in the future.

The professors at OCU "range from the typical Ivy-League eggheads to those who worked their way through law school." Students value the "intellectual energy" and practical experiences of their instructors, most of whom can "make even the driest theoretical concept interesting." Take the property professor who "got on top of a desk and shouted, 'Never, never, never change a legal description of a property!'" Professors toss around "fun terms, like 'playground justice,'" and come up with "offbeat hypos that really stick in your memory." A 1L writes, "The classroom environment is open. Free discussions, dissenting opinions, and intellectual dialogues between students are welcomed." Above all, the faculty show they care. "We actually had a professor e-mail 1Ls on driving techniques in the snow because he knew that many of us had never been in those conditions." But don't mistake kind-hearted professors for pushovers. Small classes mean there's nowhere to hide when the Socratic grilling gets going, and "high grades must be truly earned."

When it comes to the administration, "The doors are open at every level." The school's "personal touch" means that faculty and administration members "remember your name even when you are not one of those students who is president of almost every organization." The monthly Dean's Forum "allows students to have lunch with the dean and discuss any matter freely and openly."

While the law library—described as "amazing on the outside, but run-down on the inside"—could use some updating, students write that "the beautiful, historic atmosphere of the building makes the somewhat outdated technology more bearable." Although they've seen some upgrades in recent years, less-generous respondents call the campus "Stone Age" and the elusive wireless signal "an absolute joke." Students sit in "broken, squeaky chairs" and take exams on paper. Some students find themselves "studying at Starbucks, OU Law School, or the public library, simply because [OCU] facilities aren't comfortable in many ways."

Job placement worries keep some OCU students up at night. The relatively low first-time Oklahoma bar-passage rate (60 percent), the area's depressed job market—which keeps "salary potential for OCU law students below national average"—and competition with University of Oklahoma grads make launching a career an all-too-difficult task for OCU grads. Come graduation time, a large percentage face that sinking feeling of having substantial debt and no job offer. Some like to fault the "unhelpful" career placement staff, which needs "to do a better job of promoting us to the judges." Students can keep their chins up, though, since there are many factors that mediate this bleak picture. Because the school is located just five minutes from the state capitol building, it remains "very connected to the government and local business." Students are able to build personal networks over their three years, thanks to the "high priority placed on community involvement through internships, externships, and volunteer opportunities." Students can also tap into the "very large and loyal alumni base in Oklahoma" once they've graduated.

Life

Law students at OCU refuse to give up their social lives just because they're pending professionals. "People here party more than the students at my undergraduate institution," admits one student, but this is sometimes to the chagrin of the studious types. The class size is "small enough to make it possible to be friends with your entire cohort"; there are a "plethora [of] clubs for everyone's tastes;" and the student body "organizes numerous activities for the whole school or just your class." "If you want to engage in any type of social activity, there is always something going on." As a result, "lots of people find great friends and relationships." The varied student body includes people of all ages, many of whom come from outside of Oklahoma; this diversity fosters "a welcoming and rich environment," according to a nontraditional student.

The convivial social environment carries over to the academic realm, in which students collaborate rather than compete with one another. "Even though we are pitted against each other in the curve, it is not cutthroat here," writes a 3L. The overriding "atmosphere of teamwork and togetherness" keeps morale high and study groups well attended. The campus may be "a beautiful oasis" in the middle of a "rough" neighborhood, but the cost of living is low, and the friendly campus security force "will always walk you to your vehicle without complaint, or even give you a ride to your off-campus apartment."

Getting In

OCU will accept applications until August 1, but nearly all applications are submitted by April 1. Requisite admissions criteria include LSAT scores, undergraduate GPA, personal statement, and letters of recommendation. If you are looking to study law in Oklahoma, then Oklahoma City University, like the University of Tulsa, is a good backup law school to the University of Oklahoma. It's also a good alternative to Texas schools like Southern Methodist University, Texas Tech University, and Texas Wesleyan University.

ADMISSIONS

Selectivity Rating	**65**
# applications received	1,351
# applicants accepted	639
# acceptees attending	202
Average LSAT	150
LSAT Range	148–152
Average undergrad GPA	3.18
Application fee	$50
Regular application	4/1
Regular notification	Rolling
Rolling notification	Yes
Early application program	No
Transfer students accepted	Yes
Evening division offered	Yes
Part-time accepted	Yes
LSDAS accepted	Yes

Applicants Also Look At

Florida Coastal School of Law, Texas A&M University System Health Science Center, Texas Southern University, Texas Wesleyan University, Thomas M. Cooley Law School, University of Oklahoma, The University of Tulsa.

International Students

TOEFL required of international students	Yes
Minimum paper TOEFL	560
Minimum computer TOEFL	220

FINANCIAL FACTS

Annual tuition	$26,100
Books and supplies	$1,500
Tuition per credit	$870
Room and board	$8,000
Financial aid application deadline	3/1
% first-year students receiving some sort of aid	87
% receiving some sort of aid	91
% of aid that is merit based	27
% receiving scholarships	31
Average grant	$13,244
Average loan	$32,628
Average total aid package	$35,681
Average debt	$92,225

EMPLOYMENT INFORMATION

Career Rating	**72**	**Grads Employed by Field (%)**	
Rate of placement (nine months out)	83	Academic	3
Average starting salary	$54,403	Business/Industry	19
State for bar exam	OK, TX, IL, CO, MO	Government	12
Pass rate for first-time bar	88	Military	2
Employers Who Frequently Hire Grads		Private practice	59
Small to medium size law firms, government agencies.		Public Interest	5
Prominent Alumni			
Honorable Reta Strubhar, first woman on Oklahoma Court of Criminal Appeals; Andrew Benton, president, Pepperdine University; Nona Lee, vice president and general counsel, Arizona Diamondbacks.			

PACE UNIVERSITY
SCHOOL OF LAW

Academics

While not small by law school standards, Pace has an intimate vibe: "I know the names of probably 75 percent of the students in my graduating class," a 2L reports. This feeling extends to interactions with faculty and staff members, who maintain "an open-door policy" and "are always willing and available to help." "The school's administration . . . [has] always made me feel as if I was a customer of great importance and not just 'another student,'" a 3L writes. The school is currently in the process of updating its facilities: "More consistent wireless Internet access" is one serious need being addressed and students report that much of the campus "is looking pretty darn good," though there are "some portions that are either lagging behind" or "still a little 'classic.'" In addition to being "extremely knowledgeable in the subject areas in which they teach," professors here "really care whether you understand the concept or not." Upperclassmen supply their expertise through the Dean's Scholars program, which "provides a weekly tutoring session taught by a 3L who had the same professor in the same course when he/she was a 1L."

"I've discussed classes and theories with friends at top 25 schools and they are consistently amazed at the depth of the subject matter we've covered," says a 2L. Thoroughness is made possible by the frequent "opportunities for clinical and practical experience," which many here feel is the school's "greatest strength." "Because we are a smaller school, it sometimes feels like we have greater opportunities because we are not likely to get 'closed out' of a class or clinic or an externship," a 2L reports. Environmental and international law are the stand-out programs at Pace, and the school "regularly receives visiting scholars and lecturers who are tops in these fields." Students in the environmental law program are fêted with "outstanding professors," "numerous" course offerings, and "a wide variety of useful resources," including a "tremendous environmental law collection" in the school library. Students in the international law program appreciate their "miraculous" professors who create "many opportunities" for them, "such as summer internships and moot courts." Pace also hosts "the CISG database on international contracts" and students here "started the first ever 'International Criminal Court Moot Competition.'" With all the activity surrounding these two programs, a 2L remarks that "sometimes those of us with different concentrations (mine is constitutional law) get left behind." Similar students note that they have found their choices "limited" since "The basics are offered, but the choices are very difficult to schedule around."

On the job front, Pace's location "only 30 minutes from NYC" is a mixed blessing. The city boasts a large number of law firms, but it's also home to several "'big NYC' [law] schools" with stronger reputations than that of Pace. While all here agree that the school's Center for Career Development "offers a great deal of information," opinions of it are mixed. Some say its staffers "are readily available to students and are more than willing to spend extra time and effort to assist students seeking help." Others believe that "when it comes down to working hard for the individual student to assist in postgraduation employment opportunities, it falls way short." Fortunately, "faculty and alumni" "all seem to sincerely want to see everyone succeed, and so they are accessible for advice and job-hunting" help.

CATHY M. ALEXANDER, DIRECTOR OF ADMISSIONS
78 NORTH BROADWAY, WHITE PLAINS, NY 10603
TEL: 914-422-4210 FAX: 914-989-8714
E-MAIL: ADMISSIONS@LAW.PACE.EDU • INTERNET: WWW.LAW.PACE.EDU

Life

As Pace "give[s] students with lower LSAT scores a chance," it "doesn't seem to attract a lot of cutthroat types." By and large, students here are "down to earth and not too image conscious." "Most students commute, so campus clears out in the evenings and on the weekends," a 1L writes. Even if students did stick around, many are the type who "tends to study, even on the weekends." When students take a break from the books, they head to "the local pub" which "receives plenty of its business from Pace Law students." Pace does boast "many student groups, including ethnic and religious ones, various legal interests such as animal law, the environment, and international law, and also the Student Bar Association," and these groups sponsor "many events on campus throughout the semester." Unfortunately, these events are not always well attended, which leads a 1L to suggest that "club events should be more widely communicated" to the student body.

"It is nice that there is a campus as opposed to one building like most law schools," a 1L reflects. Boosters of Pace Law's White Plains location point out that the school is within "walking distance [of] a growing city center that has every amenity imaginable (including shopping, bars, and restaurants)" and "a short train ride away from Manhattan, yet, because it's in Westchester, we also have a great outdoor life, green grass, and trees!" However, other less-satisfied students say White Plains is "overpriced" and lacks a sense of "culture" and "community" unless "you already reside there."

Getting In

For a quick look to see if you've got the right stuff for Pace Law, consider this: admitted students at the 25th percentile had an LSAT score of 152 and a GPA of 3.1, and admitted students at the 75th percentile had an LSAT score of 156 and a GPA of 3.5. Make sure to put a human face to your application as interviews are strongly encouraged.

EMPLOYMENT INFORMATION			
Career Rating	**81**	**Grads Employed by Field (%)**	
Rate of placement (nine months out)	93	Academic	1
Average starting salary	$71,362	Business/Industry	25
State for bar exam	NY	Government	16
Pass rate for first-time bar	83	Judicial clerkships	3
Employers Who Frequently Hire Grads		Private practice	51
Small and medium-sized law firms; corpo-		Public Interest	2
rations; government employers.			
Prominent Alumni			
John Cahill, NY Chief of Staff, former NY			
governor George Pataki; Robert F. Kennedy			
Jr., co-director, Pace Environmental			
Litigation Clinic; Gerry Comizio, partner,			
Thacher Proffitt and Wood; Judith			
Lockhart, managing partne.			

Legal methods	
course requirement	Yes
Legal research	
course requirement	No
Moot court requirement	Yes
Public interest	
law requirement	No

ADMISSIONS

Selectivity Rating	**73**
# applications received	2,467
# applicants accepted	909
# acceptees attending	196
Average LSAT	154
LSAT Range	152–156
Average undergrad GPA	3.33
Application fee	$65
Regular application	3/1
Regular notification	Rolling
Rolling notification	Yes
Early application program	Yes
Early application deadline	11/4
Early application notification	12/15
Transfer students accepted	Yes
Evening division offered	Yes
Part-time accepted	Yes
LSDAS accepted	Yes

Applicants Also Look At

Brooklyn Law School; Fordham University; Hofstra University; New York Law School; Rutgers, The State University of New Jersey, School of Law at Camden; St. John's University; Touro University—California.

International Students

TOEFL required	
of international students	Yes
Minimum paper TOEFL	600
Minimum computer TOEFL	250

FINANCIAL FACTS

Annual tuition	$35,500
Books and supplies	$1,120
Tuition per credit	$1,126
Room and board	
(on/off-campus)	$13,400/$16,372
Financial aid application	
deadline	2/1
% first-year students	
receiving some sort of aid	90
% receiving some sort of aid	88
% of aid that is merit based	67
% receiving scholarships	40
Average grant	$12,000
Average loan	$26,000
Average total aid package	$36,000
Average debt	$78,000

PEPPERDINE UNIVERSITY
SCHOOL OF LAW

INSTITUTIONAL INFORMATION

Public/private	Private
Affiliation	Church of Christ
Student-faculty ratio	20:1
% faculty part-time	52
% faculty female	33
% faculty minority	17
Total faculty	89

SURVEY SAYS...
Beautiful campus
Students love Malibu, CA

STUDENTS

Enrollment of law school	704
% male/female	48/52
% out-of-state	40
% full-time	100
% minority	19
% international	1
# of countries represented	2
Average age of entering class	24

ACADEMICS

Academic Experience Rating	**90**
Profs interesting rating	91
Profs accessible rating	99
Hours of study per day	4.6

Academic Specialties
Commercial law, corporation securities law, dispute resolution, entrepreneurship, intellectual property law, international law, taxation.

Advanced Degrees Offered
LLM (dispute resolution).

Combined Degrees Offered
JD/MBA 4 years, JD/MDR 3 to 4 years, JD/MPP 4 years, JD/MDiv 5 years.

Clinical program required	Yes
Legal writing course requirement	Yes
Legal methods course requirement	No
Legal research course requirement	Yes
Moot court requirement	Yes

Academics

Students looking to be surrounded by "incredible" faculty and staff on possibly "the most beautiful campus in the country," at a school that retains the services of Kenneth Starr—a man who obviously "has a lot of great connections"—as dean, and regularly features "impressive speakers, symposiums, and opportunities to learn outside of the classroom" would be wise to check out Pepperdine. Students agree that Dean Starr is one of "several luminaries in the fields of constitutional and human rights law" on the faculty at Pepperdine and appreciate "how accessible he is to students." "He routinely hosts events at his house for students and will start up a conversation with a student like he is an old friend," explains one student. "He takes so much time making people feel comfortable . . . . The same is true for each and every professor I have had [here]." But don't let the picturesque location "mere yards away from the beach" and the dedicated faculty mislead you—"At best, you may see the beach from a library window. You certainly will not . . . be out surfing. Pepperdine is very demanding and our professors expect a lot from us," says a 1L.

Pepperdine boasts several stand-out programs, including "the internationally renowned Straus Institute for Dispute Resolution," which students feel "is the best program for learning negotiation, mediation, and arbitration techniques in the country." Students report that "the school also has amazing constitutional law professors and appears to be acquiring great additions to the faculty in the area of property law." Furthermore, its Palmer Center for Entrepreneurship and the Law "is completely unique and opens up a lot of doors for students to understand how the law can be used in many other careers." Students say "classes focus not just on theoretical concepts, but on the actual practice of law." A 3L opines: "I am convinced [that Pepperdine] is the equal or better of many 'top' law schools, including the other LA schools. Pepperdine students routinely outperform 'top school' students in summer clerkships because Pepperdine prepares you 'how to be a lawyer' while many of the 'top schools' focus more on theory. Pepperdine students have an excellent bar-passage rate and are very well prepared for the actual practice of law."

Pepperdine Law is "located next to a great legal market." "The only drawback," a 3L reports, "is fewer job opportunities than the 'top schools,' which is highly related to [Pepperdine's] ranking." By and large, however, students here are satisfied that "the school is working harder than any school in California to move up in the rankings, through getting current Supreme Court Justices and Chief Justices to teach and recruiting the best, brightest, and hardest-working students and professors." "In my interviews at big firms, Pepperdine seemed to be the new buzz," a sanguine 2L reports. "I found it easy to get a job with a big firm!" Helping matters, Pepperdine's "Career Services Center has been recently revamped, and is (thankfully) gaining momentum regarding on-campus interviews and networking." Also receiving attention are "the interior aesthetics of the law school"—"Pepperdine is in the process of refurbishing everything," a 1L reports—which seems to be a good move as one 3L reports that "the library carpet has a path in it." All these improvements cost money, however, and students here gripe about "financial aid and cost" of the school, as the latter is among the highest for U.S. law schools.

Life

Pepperdine students may describe themselves as "California casual," but they're also hard workers. "We're across the street from the beach, but we hardly go," a 1L reports. Regarding the student body's "conservative, religious" reputation, a 1L urges: "Don't let

SHANNON PHILLIPS, DIRECTOR OF ADMISSIONS
24255 PACIFIC COAST HIGHWAY, MALIBU, CA 90263
TEL: 310-506-4631 FAX: 310-506-7668
E-MAIL: SOLADMIS@PEPPERDINE.EDU • INTERNET: LAW.PEPPERDINE.EDU

that deter you—no one forces [their opinions] down your throat," though she adds that students "have to be somewhat tolerant of other views than [their] own." While the school is "making an effort to take more students who aren't straight in from undergrad," some would like to see "more diversity in minority and religion."

When you have "a lot of smart people competing for a limited number of good grades," "Competition is a fact." Some find this competition is "not palpable in student relations," while others discern a "level of tension." Under these conditions, Pepperdine "does an excellent job of creating a community in its law school." It divides first-year sections into three groups, "so you take the same classes with the same people and bond with them." In addition, the school "provides a great deal of social programming" to foster interaction. "There are Bar Reviews every Thursday," usually "in Santa Monica, where most of the college-aged students hang out." Other events include a "Barrister's Ball," "the Law Dinner," "an annual dodgeball tournament," and, for the service-minded, "humanitarian projects like hurricane relief trips to New Orleans [and] student mentoring for 1Ls."

Pepperdine is "located in a hillside canyon with 180-degree views of the Pacific Ocean, Los Angeles, and Catalina Island . . . It is paradise compared to every other law school out there," a 1L reports. While Pepperdine law students receive on-campus housing, many here wish there was "more affordable housing available in Malibu."

Getting In

Admitted students at the 25th percentile have an LSAT score of 157 and a GPA of 3.3. Admitted students at the 75th percentile have an LSAT score of 161 and a GPA of 3.7. According to the school, other factors that can play heavily in your favor come admissions time include "work or service experience," "a history of overcoming disadvantage," "unusual life experiences," and "racial and ethnic origin."

Public interest	
law requirement	No

ADMISSIONS

Selectivity Rating	**85**
# applications received	3,472
# applicants accepted	839
# acceptees attending	243
Average LSAT	159
LSAT Range	157–161
Average undergrad GPA	3.5
Application fee	$50
Regular application	3/1
Regular notification	Rolling
Rolling notification	Yes
Early application program	No
Transfer students accepted	Yes
Evening division offered	No
Part-time accepted	No
LSDAS accepted	Yes

Applicants Also Look At
Loyola Marymount University,
University of San Diego.

International Students

TOEFL required	
of international students	No
TOEFL recommended	
of international students	No

FINANCIAL FACTS

Annual tuition	$33,530
Books and supplies	$800
Tuition per credit	$1,230
Room and board	$14,590
Financial aid application	
deadline	4/1
% first-year students	
receiving some sort of aid	87
% receiving some sort of aid	87
% of aid that is merit based	20
% receiving scholarships	73
Average grant	$9,950
Average loan	$33,155
Average total aid package	$43,105
Average debt	$101,130

EMPLOYMENT INFORMATION

Career Rating	**81**	**Grads Employed by Field (%)**	
Rate of placement (nine months out)	96	Academic	1
Average starting salary	$80,000	Business/Industry	18
State for bar exam	CA	Government	8
Pass rate for first-time bar	76	Judicial clerkships	7
Employers Who Frequently Hire Grads		Other	2
Akin, Gump, Strauss, Hauer, and Feld; DLA		Private practice	62
Piper, Rudnick, Gray, Cary, US LLP; Fisher		Public Interest	2
and Phillips Gibbs; Giden, Locher, and			
Turner; Jones Day.			
Prominent Alumni			
Pierre Prosper, Ambassador-at-Large for			
War Crime Issues; Rod Blagojevich,			
Governor of Illinois; Todd Platts,			
Congressman, Pennsylvania.			

QUINNIPIAC UNIVERSITY
SCHOOL OF LAW

INSTITUTIONAL INFORMATION

Public/private	Private
Student-faculty ratio	13:1
% faculty part-time	49
% faculty female	30
% faculty minority	6
Total faculty	67

SURVEY SAYS...

Great research resources
Beautiful campus

STUDENTS

Enrollment of law school	459
% male/female	48/52
% out-of-state	47
% full-time	68
% minority	11
% international	1
# of countries represented	2
Average age of entering class	25

ACADEMICS

Academic Experience Rating	**80**
Profs interesting rating	79
Profs accessible rating	80
Hours of study per day	4.2

Academic Specialties

Civil advocacy, criminal law, dispute resolution, family and juvenile law, health law, intellectual property law, taxation.

Advanced Degrees Offered

JD 3 to 4 years, LLM health law.

Combined Degrees Offered

JD/MBA 4 years, JD/MBA (health care management).

Clinical program required	No
Legal writing course requirement	Yes
Legal methods course requirement	Yes
Legal research course requirement	No
Moot court requirement	Yes
Public interest law requirement	No

Academics

"Before I decided to go to Quinnipiac Law, I had never heard of the school," writes a 1L, but many students actively seek out the QUSL health law program. "Given that my career goal is to work in the health policy field, Quinnipiac was a perfect fit," writes a 3L. Other popular concentrations include tax law, criminal law, family law, intellectual property, civil advocacy, and dispute resolution. The school runs a traditional full-time day program and also offers part-time night classes. Both groups of students would like to see more higher-level courses offered in various practice areas. Night students in particular would like "more offerings outside of required areas." Because of their role as part of a "small law program on a much larger undergraduate campus," Quinnipiac students can broaden their scope through joint-degree opportunities, including a joint JD-MBA program.

Quinnipiac tends to focus more on the practical rather than the theoretical facets of law. "If you want to learn to practice law, come to Quinnipiac." Most students embrace this attitude, but some agree with one student who suggests that the school could "offer more theory-based courses and move away from traditional law school teaching styles, including the one-exam-equals-your-grade-for-the-course method."

The question keeping many up at night is whether graduates will have a place to exercise their professional filing skills after their three years. Three main concerns fuel the job-market fear: grade deflation, significantly less than adequate career services, and the debt that accompanies a Quinnipiac diploma. "Get rid of the curve!" begs a 2L, who emerged from her first year expressing concern about the law school's rigor in grading, supported in part by the school's suggested median grade of C-plus or B-minus for required first-year courses, and suggested median grade of B-minus or B for upper-level core electives. Students also seem to feel that the Career Placement Office "caters only to the students ranked one through ten." Though it does arrange "a wide variety of externships with local corporations and government organizations," many students "resort to sending cold resumes to area law firms as graduation approaches." Pressure mounts in the face of the "slightly outrageous price" of tuition at Quinnipiac, which ranks among the more costly law schools in the nation. Some get uneasy if they spend "too much time thinking about the expense of the lavish end-of-semester parties with white tablecloths and snappily attired wait staff."

The high cost of tuition also has its benefits. Quinnipiac has "arguably the most beautiful campus in New England." Furthermore, "Computers are available *ad nauseam*. Students don't need to buy laptops or even printer paper." The library, complete with comfortable study areas and a helpful research staff, is deemed "a great place to work." Classrooms, on the contrary, are kept at meat-locker temperatures year-round, and the wireless service is patchy. If students ever want to escape their slice of New England paradise, the summer program at Trinity College in Dublin is said to be "a total blast."

Praised for their "mentorship, thoughtful conversation, and candidness," Quinnipiac professors know the names and career aspirations of their students and get involved in law school life. "Every year at our public interest auction, there is one professor who offers a home-cooked dinner for the winner and three guests." In the classroom, instructors "command respect" while maintaining a "peer relationship." A 1L writes, "Our contracts professor stays until all hours of the night to meet with students to go over outlines."

EDWIN WILKES, EXECUTIVE DEAN OF LAW SCHOOL ADMISSIONS
275 MOUNT CARMEL AVENUE, (LW-ADM), HAMDEN, CT 06518-1908
TEL: 203-582-3400 FAX: 203-582-3339
E-MAIL: LADM@QUINNIPIAC.EDU • INTERNET: LAW.QUINNIPIAC.EDU

Certain professors employ an "interactive and Socratic style"; others sound more like "talking textbooks"; and a handful actually "insult students in front of their peers." Administrators dispel initial law school intimidation with their professional, courteous, and "surprisingly approachable" ways. Dean Saxton, in particular, earns praise for improving the school's image and ranking.

Life

"The classroom environment tends to be more lighthearted at night," and evening classmates consider themselves a generally more supportive group. One of the day students writes of the "fierce competition" that she witnessed during her first year. A third-year student assures, however, that after the first year, "students will have found the classmates whom they feel they can trust and pretty much stick to that group." Given the small class size, everyone knows everyone else, a phenomenon that sometimes fosters a "high school atmosphere" with the requisite rumor mill.

Some students are reportedly "more interested in playing stupid drinking games and watching television" than in debating legal issues during off-hours. Quinnipiac students, hailing mostly from the East Coast, like to raise their glasses at weekly events as well as at neighborhood and New Haven bars. As an alternative, many students also like to recharge by spending some quality time in nature. Fortunately for them, there is a picturesque state park right across the street.

Getting In

Quinnipiac fills its 150 seats from a pool of roughly 2,500 applicants annually. Those who don't have a 3.0 GPA still have a shot at acceptance, but applicants with LSAT scores lower than 150 would only rarely be competitive for admission. Although the school operates on a rolling admissions system, the priority application deadline is March 1. Therefore, early application is strongly advised. Students may take day classes on a part-time basis by special arrangement and even switch their enrollment status between terms.

ADMISSIONS

Selectivity Rating	**82**
# applications received	2,475
# applicants accepted	648
# acceptees attending	61
Average LSAT	159
LSAT Range	157–160
Average undergrad GPA	3.3
Application fee	$40
Regular application	Rolling
Regular notification	Rolling
Rolling notification	Yes
Early application program	No
Transfer students accepted	Yes
Evening division offered	Yes
Part-time accepted	Yes
LSDAS accepted	Yes

International Students

TOEFL required of international students	No
TOEFL recommended of international students	Yes

FINANCIAL FACTS

Annual tuition	$33,200
Books and supplies	$1,200
Fees per credit	$30
Tuition per credit	$1,160
Room and board (off-campus)	$12,645
% first-year students receiving some sort of aid	98
% receiving some sort of aid	94
% of aid that is merit based	68
% receiving scholarships	68
Average grant	$13,286
Average loan	$30,243
Average total aid package	$34,814
Average debt	$71,768

EMPLOYMENT INFORMATION

Career Rating	**75**	
Rate of placement (nine months out)	95	
Average starting salary	$57,136	
State for bar exam	CT, NY, NJ, MA, RI	
Pass rate for first-time bar	82	

Employers Who Frequently Hire Grads
Law firms; corporations; public defender offices; prosecutor offices; various government and public interest organizations.

Grads Employed by Field (%)

Academic	10
Business/Industry	22
Government	14
Judicial clerkships	8
Other	6
Private practice	38
Public Interest	2

REGENT UNIVERSITY
SCHOOL OF LAW

INSTITUTIONAL INFORMATION

Public/private	Private
Affiliation	Nondenominational
Student-faculty ratio	20:1
% faculty part-time	3.2
% faculty female	54
% faculty minority	11.2
Total faculty	23

SURVEY SAYS...
Conservative students
Beautiful campus

STUDENTS

Enrollment of law school	491
% male/female	49/51
% out-of-state	72
% full-time	94
% minority	12
% international	1
# of countries represented	3
Average age of entering class	25

ACADEMICS

Academic Experience Rating	**82**
Profs interesting rating	93
Profs accessible rating	93
Hours of study per day	4.92

Combined Degrees Offered

JD/MBA 4 years, JD/MA (management) 4 years, JD/MA (communication) 4 years, JD/MA (journalism) 4 years JD/MA (counseling) 4 years, JD/MA (divinity) 4 years, JD/MDiv 4 to 5 years, JD/MA (government) 4 years, JD/MA (public policy), JD/MPA.

Clinical program required	No
Legal writing course requirement	Yes
Legal methods course requirement	Yes
Legal research course requirement	Yes
Moot court requirement	Yes
Public interest law requirement	No

Academics

Founded 30 years ago by Christian heavyweight Pat Robertson, Regent University School of Law boasts a campus-wide emphasis on cooperation and support, offering its students an education that is "stressful, engaging, and even entertaining—a great balance for studying law." Regent's "community atmosphere" sets it apart from the vast field of "cutthroat competition . . . at other law schools." However, students say Regent's "academic rigor and challenge is not compromised by the motivation that we all have to see each other succeed."

"Who could imagine a law school where the professors actually wanted to see their students succeed?" Many of Regent's attorneys-in-training, apparently. These students gush over the accessibility of their professors, noting that they "are not only highly qualified, but extremely supportive and available for help when we need them." Professors are easy to track down "during and in between office hours. Not only that, but they respond to e-mails promptly—even on the weekends!" Students also appreciate the wealth of practical experience that faculty members bring to the classroom: "Since most of them were lawyers and judges, they teach you the law in realistic ways that you will be able to use in your practice, not just for law school exams or the bar exam." Other students wish the professors would take a slightly more hands-off approach to mentoring. In the words of one such student, "The *en loco parentis* model of instructing gets old quickly."

Regent engages "law from a Christian perspective." A glowing first-year tells us that the law school's greatest asset is "that God is at the forefront of the classes." Among the opportunities available are the Christian Legal Society and the Institute for Christian Legal Studies. There's also a law library, which earns high marks for its staff and resources, though students grumble that the physical layout is "awkward" and "stuffy," and that it's "time for new carpet!" The good thing about the library is that it's right next door to Robertson Hall, the home turf of the law school. In Robertson Hall, students find classrooms that are "up to date with the latest technology, including adequate places to plug in computers and Internet." In addition, "We have access to multiple full-size court rooms with the latest technology to practice our skills."

Regent's students tell us that all this adds up to a law school on the move. "In 2006 we won the ABA National Moot Court Competition," reports a student, "and in 2007 we won the Negotiation Competition." These successes can be attributed, in part, to a student body that sees law as more than just a career. As the school's motto says, "Law is more than a profession. It's a calling."

Life

Though most students at Regent are very focused on getting their law degree, they're not blind to the fact that RU is just "minutes from the beach and many other cultural and social activities." The campus itself, located in the Hampton Roads area of coastal Virginia, "is beautiful, with plenty of trees, fabulous architecture, and a fountain." Beyond the classroom, students discover "so many opportunities to be involved that no one should go through here without finding something they want to be involved in." When it comes to socializing, "Lots of people meet outside of school for fun." Typical after-hours activities include "Bible studies or just going out to dinner together."

BONNIE CREEF, DIRECTOR OF ADMISSIONS AND FINANCIAL AID
1000 REGENT UNIVERSITY DRIVE, ROBERTSON HALL, VIRGINIA BEACH, VA 23464
TEL: 757-226-4584 FAX: 757-226-4139
E-MAIL: LAWSCHOOL@REGENT.EDU • INTERNET: WWW.REGENT.EDU/LAW

The law school's student body is made up of "an interesting mix of young, out-of-college students who are always ready to socialize and have fun on the weekends mixed with a sizable population of older students who often have families waiting for them at the end of the day." The one thing that most of these students have in common is "a Christian worldview." A few disgruntled students say this manifests itself in the form of "intolerance for non-conservative or nonreligious views." Students for whom religion is not a top priority may have trouble finding their place, as one dissatisfied student explains: "This school needs a little less Bible thumping; we pray in the beginning of every single class. Coming from a private, liberal arts college on the West Coast, I had no idea it would be so intense out here. God forbid if you're pro-choice, pro–gay marriage, or the worst—a liberal Democrat!" But most students agree that Regent is "a great place for those who want to get a legal education and also mature in their relationship with the Lord."

Getting In

In 2006, the average LSAT score earned by an incoming law student was 153, and the average undergrad GPA was 3.3, but numbers are only part of the story at Regent. As the law school's Admissions Office states, "Strong academic credentials are crucial, but Regent Law also places significant importance on the personal statement and letters of recommendation." Application materials should not only reflect a clear desire to practice law, but also a personal and professional dedication to Christian principles.

ADMISSIONS

Selectivity Rating	70
# applications received	537
# applicants accepted	297
# acceptees attending	156
Average LSAT	153
LSAT Range	151–156
Average undergrad GPA	3.3
Application fee	$50
Regular application	6/1
Regular notification	Rolling
Rolling notification	Yes
Early application program	No
Transfer students accepted	Yes
Evening division offered	No
Part-time accepted	Yes
LSDAS accepted	Yes

Applicants Also Look At
College of William and Mary, Liberty University, University of Richmond, University of Virginia.

International Students

TOEFL required	
of international students	Yes
Minimum paper TOEFL	600
Minimum computer TOEFL	250

FINANCIAL FACTS

Annual tuition	$25,420
Books and supplies	$1,534
Tuition per credit	$820
Room and board	$6,700
Financial aid application deadline	6/1
% receiving some sort of aid	94
% of aid that is merit based	20
% receiving scholarships	72
Average grant	$5,215
Average loan	$27,820
Average total aid package	$29,307
Average debt	$81,281

EMPLOYMENT INFORMATION

		Grads Employed by Field (%)	
Career Rating	69		
Rate of placement (nine months out)	81	Academic	6
Average starting salary	$52,359	Business/Industry	14
State for bar exam	VA, NC, MD, CA, NY	Government	18
Pass rate for first-time bar	67	Judicial clerkships	6
Employers Who Frequently Hire Grads		Military	4
American Center for Law and Justice; Just		Other	3
Law International; U.S. Air Force JAG		Private practice	43
Corps; U.S. Army JAG Corps; Alliance		Public Interest	6
Defense Fund; Williams Mulle.			
Prominent Alumni			
Robert F. McDonnell, Attorney General for			
Virginia; Honorable April Wood Berg,			
North Carolina District Court; Honorable			
Ron Pahl, Oregon Circuit Court.			

ROGER WILLIAMS UNIVERSITY
RALPH R. PAPITTO SCHOOL OF LAW

INSTITUTIONAL INFORMATION

Public/private	Private
Student-faculty ratio	20:1
% faculty part-time	27
% faculty female	41
% faculty minority	9
Total faculty	54

SURVEY SAYS...
Great research resources
Great library staff
Beautiful campus
Students love Bristol, RI

STUDENTS

Enrollment of law school	593
% male/female	51/49
% out-of-state	79
% full-time	90
% minority	12
% international	3
# of countries represented	7
Average age of entering class	25

ACADEMICS

Academic Experience Rating	**76**
Profs interesting rating	87
Profs accessible rating	80
Hours of study per day	5.8

Academic Specialties
Commercial law, constitutional law, corporation securities law, criminal law, environmental law, human rights law, intellectual property law, international law, labor law, maritime law, property, public interest law.

Advanced Degrees Offered
JD 3 years.

Combined Degrees Offered
JD/MMA (marine affairs) 3.5 years, JD/MS (labor relations and human resources) 4 years, JD/MSCJ 3.5 years.

Clinical program required	No
Legal writing course requirement	Yes
Legal methods course requirement	Yes

Academics

A decidedly optimistic spirit permeates the atmosphere of the Ralph R. Papitto School of Law. At this young law school, students applaud the cooperative spirit, school pride, and dedication to excellence demonstrated by the entire community, noting that "everyone at the school—staff and students—seem dedicated to making Roger Williams as good as it can possibly be." With a dedicated and responsive administrative staff "willing to listen to new ideas and . . . open to suggestions," students at Roger Williams feel they have the unique opportunity to help shape their school's future. As a result, Papitto is constantly improving: "Every year brings new challenges, better qualified students, and further experienced professors," explains a 2L.

Over its short history, Roger Williams has focused on building a superior academic program. A 2L reports, "The administrators of Roger Williams were extremely smart in their hiring; they knew that the only way to take a fledgling law school and move it quickly up through the ranks was to hire the best faculty." As a result of these efforts, "The diverse backgrounds that the professors bring, the different teaching skills, and the rigorous expectations this young law school demands of its student body will lead it to great dimensions."

Papitto students must be primed to give their all in the classroom. A 3L explains, "The faculty are among the best and they don't take 'pass' for an answer. Preparedness is expected, and we're being grilled and graded as if we were at Harvard." Students insist that they are amply rewarded for their efforts: "The law school is extremely challenging, and the professors coax more from me than I ever believed I could give," reports one 2L. In addition, students reassure us that professors are dedicated to promoting academic success. By most accounts, professors are readily available to meet with struggling students, and "The smaller size and availability of the faculty allows for great communication and interactions outside the classroom." In addition, the school has instituted a number of programs to help students succeed academically, like the "excellent orientation program and seminar series continuing into the school year to teach and reinforce skills vital to 1L success."

Roger Williams is the only law school in the state of Rhode Island, a happy privilege that pays off in many ways. For example, "The local judiciary [including the chief justice of the Rhode Island Supreme Court] and legal community are highly involved with the school and frequently attend functions here." In fact, "The moot court competition involves arguing before the RI Supreme Court." In addition, "Internship opportunities abound because RWU has an exclusive franchise in the state." "I was able to work for a federal judge over the summer between my 1L and 2L years," recalls one 2L. When it comes to extracurriculars and externships, many students point out that "Roger Williams has an excellent public service focus" that likewise exerts a strong influence in the Rhode Island community; one student reports that "the Feinstein Institute for Public Service is the best thing about this school! They are amazing and have a huge range of placements available." After graduation, career prospects are good for Roger Williams' alumni, especially if they plan to practice in Rhode Island. After a recent revamp, "The new Career Services Department is outstanding!" While things already look good for RWU grads, students are convinced that their prospects improve with every passing year. As one enthusiastic 2L explains, "As more and more employers see the excellent caliber of students RWU turns out year after year, the school will continue to garner respect in the legal community."

MICHAEL BOYLEN, ASSISTANT DEAN OF ADMISSION
10 METACOM AVENUE, BRISTOL, RI 02809-5171
TEL: 401-254-4555 FAX: 401-254-4516
E-MAIL: ADMISSIONS@LAW.RWU.EDU • INTERNET: LAW.RWU.EDU

Life

Situated in Bristol, "Roger Williams is located in one of the most scenic locations in the country, Rhode Island's East Bay." "From my classroom I can see the bay and the sailboats out on a sunny day," reports one student. On campus "There are many clubs and organizations that make it a priority to put together different activities; anything from study groups and sports to parties and balls." Students say a decidedly social atmosphere pervades the campus, and students appreciate it. A 1L reasons, "I'd much rather spend three intensive years with classmates who can kick back and drink a beer on a Thursday night than with a competitive group of straight-A stress cases."

Thanks to an "extremely proactive admissions staff," Papitto attracts a "really interesting, fun student body" from all across the nation. By most accounts, "The students are by and large quite friendly and outgoing." Don't expect much by way of ethnic diversity: "Where are the minorities? I feel like I'm the only one sometimes, and usually I am," writes one 2L.

Getting In

LSAT scores and undergraduate GPA are generally considered to be the two most important factors in an application to Papitto. However, the school also considers graduate work, work experience, extracurricular activities, undergraduate curriculum, community involvement, and life experiences. A B-minus undergraduate GPA and an LSAT score above the 50th percentile puts you in the running, although it certainly doesn't guarantee admission.

Legal research course requirement	Yes
Moot court requirement	No
Public interest law requirement	Yes

ADMISSIONS

Selectivity Rating	**68**
# applications received	1,677
# applicants accepted	860
# acceptees attending	204
Average LSAT	153
LSAT Range	151–156
Average undergrad GPA	3.21
Application fee	$60
Regular application	Rolling
Regular notification	Rolling
Rolling notification	Yes
Early application program	No
Transfer students accepted	Yes
Evening division offered	No
Part-time accepted	No
LSDAS accepted	Yes

Applicants Also Look At

New England School of Law, Northeastern University, Pace University, Quinnipiac University, Suffolk University, Vermont Law School, Western New England College.

International Students

TOEFL required of international students	Yes
Minimum paper TOEFL	600
Minimum computer TOEFL	250

FINANCIAL FACTS

Annual tuition	$29,700
Books and supplies	$1,400
Room and board (on/off-campus)	$8,075/$7,570
Financial aid application deadline	3/15
% first-year students receiving some sort of aid	93
% receiving some sort of aid	93
% of aid that is merit based	23
% receiving scholarships	41
Average grant	$13,849
Average loan	$36,091
Average total aid package	$46,300
Average debt	$89,409

EMPLOYMENT INFORMATION

		Grads Employed by Field (%)	
Career Rating	**73**	Academic	3
Rate of placement (nine months out)	86	Business/Industry	18
Average starting salary	$56,207	Government	8
State for bar exam	RI, CT, MA	Judicial clerkships	12
Pass rate for first-time bar	80	Military	2
Employers Who Frequently Hire Grads		Private practice	48
New England judges (state and local);		Public Interest	9
small New England firms.			
Prominent Alumni			
Kenneth McKay, partner, Brown Rudnick, LLP; Brent Canning, partner, Hinckley, Allen, and Snyder, LLP; Cindy DeMarco, Assistant General Counsel, FBI; John Sutherland, III, vice president finance/CFO, Women and Infants Hospital.			

RUTGERS, THE STATE UNIVERSITY OF NEW JERSEY—CAMDEN
SCHOOL OF LAW

INSTITUTIONAL INFORMATION

Public/private	Public
Student-faculty ratio	5:1
% faculty part-time	58
% faculty female	31
% faculty minority	9
Total faculty	116

SURVEY SAYS...

Diverse opinions accepted
in classrooms
Great library staff
Abundant externship/internship/
clerkship opportunities

STUDENTS

Enrollment of law school	769
% male/female	58/42
% out-of-state	23
% full-time	73
% minority	11
Average age of entering class	25

ACADEMICS

Academic Experience Rating	**88**
Profs interesting rating	88
Profs accessible rating	87
Hours of study per day	4.26

Academic Specialties

Commercial law, constitutional law, corporation securities law, criminal law, environmental law, international law, labor law, taxation, health law, family law/dv, litigation.

Advanced Degrees Offered

JD 3 to 4 years.

Combined Degrees Offered

JD/MBA 4 years, JD/MPA 4 years, JD/MSW 4 years, JD/MS 3.5 years, JD/MCRP 4 years, JD/MD and JD/DO (with U. of Medicine and Dentistry of N.J.), JD/MPA 4 years.

Clinical program required	No
Legal writing course requirement	Yes
Legal methods course requirement	Yes
Legal research course requirement	No
Moot court requirement	Yes

Academics

If going to law school gives you the jitters, your fears will quickly be assuaged at Rutgers, The State University of New Jersey—Camden School of Law. Sure, just like other prestigious JD programs, Rutgers will treat you to a dose of the "Socratic thunderstorm approach," and there is the typical "never-ending workload" throughout the first year. However, Rutgers maintains a remarkably friendly and supportive academic environment. Students insist that "first-year classes don't intimidate you, as there's no fear of speaking your mind in class, and diversity in thinking is highly encouraged." Outside the classroom, Rutgers professors are personable, to say the least: "Every Wednesday afternoon, there's a veritable party in our torts professor's office during his office hours. So many students go to discuss both academic and non-textbook-related topics that there aren't enough chairs and people sit on the floor," recalls one 2L. In fact, "It's common for professors to take students out to lunch, to conferences, and even to show up at student-sponsored pub crawls." The administration draws similar praise from students, who believe it "tries to be very open door and available for anything we could possibly need." A 1L jokes, "I came to Rutgers expecting to witness students getting 'burned' by professors every day in class. Instead the only burn I got was on the roof of my mouth while eating pizza with the dean."

Students are impressed with the caliber of the Rutgers faculty, describing them as "knowledgeable and passionate about their subjects" and able pedagogues to boot. In the lecture hall, "The faculty is as intelligent as they are witty. Anecdotes from the real-world experiences are common in the classroom and make some of the drudgery more interesting." Many also point out the strength of the adjunct staff, who "come from varied fields, providing a unique and practical perspective to current topics." Indeed, a practical approach is emphasized at Rutgers, and classes may even include "spontaneous field-trips to the federal court house across the street from the campus just so we can view real-world motions to dismiss, jury selection, and final arguments." The school's active alumni network is also called upon to contribute to the JD experience, and students tell us that "in many courses, alumni return to give lectures on the practical aspects of the subject, and they have been willing to assist any student [who] has a question."

Among the greatest perks of Rutgers—Camden is its low tuition, offering a "fantastic and highly respected education at a very reasonable price." As a result, students do not experience the financial anxiety common to law students today. "Due to a scholarship and a summer internship at a Philadelphia law firm," reports one 2L, "I will graduate with a top-rate legal education and virtually no debt. That combination is hard to beat, and I expect it will free up my career options considerably." The downside to a low-cost education is that "because of prior decreases in state funds, the law school's physical facilities are limited," and many complain that the classrooms lack ample outlets for laptops. Many are quick to point out, however, that "the school has just received funding to build a new building," which will be available to future classes in 2007.

The school takes advantage of the resources in the surrounding community to instruct students in the playing out of law in the real world. "The federal courthouse is literally around the corner, the county courthouse a couple of blocks," and Rutgers students "have tremendous access to the judges in the area and several teach as adjuncts." Students also praise the fact that "the law school is very involved in the community through its pro bono clinics."

Rutgers is "located close to Philly, Trenton, and New York, so there are plenty of job opportunities." On that note, "Career Services are always on the job helping students get placed for both summer and permanent positions. They also expose students to the different options available to attorneys by having guests come to the law school to provide experiences in different areas." Rutgers is somewhat unique among law schools in that almost half of the graduating class takes judicial clerkship positions, more students than those who take positions in private practice.

Life

Attracting students from all across the nation and the world, the Rutgers student body is "extremely diverse in all aspects, including gender, socioeconomics, age, and interests." On this multicultural campus "There is an organization for just about any interest a person may have, [and] the SBA and other clubs do a great job of providing numerous social functions nearly every week." A 2L explains that "the environment is positive and students are involved with the school. Whether it be moot court, law journals, or politics, students are engaged in society and provide for a very strong sense of community." Off-campus "People are always looking to get together to study or to just go out socially," though most prefer hanging out in Philly to hitting the bars in the surrounding town of Camden. While some describe Camden as "the pit of despair," others tell us that "the waterfront on both sides of the Delaware River is beautiful." In addition, many appreciate the fact that "Philadelphia is exactly a mile away and provides for plenty of social opportunities."

Students warn that there are "a handful of students who are hell bent on getting a certain GPA." Most, however, value kindness and cooperation over competition. A 3L explains, "My school is both cooperative and competitive. Students here care deeply about being successful, but everyone is quick to lend a hand to bring someone else along for the ride." Indeed, many students praise the fact that "you can always find a good conversation outside after class."

Getting In

Rutgers—Camden recently began an experimental recruitment program, soliciting prospective law students based on their performance on the GRE or GMAT, rather than the LSAT. Therefore, there are a number of current law students who were previously pursuing advanced degrees in other subject areas. For all other prospective students, the admissions process is standard fare: Rutgers admits students who have demonstrated a high level of academic achievement, as well as strong standardized test scores.

EMPLOYMENT INFORMATION

Career Rating	83	Grads Employed by Field (%)	
Rate of placement (nine months out)	94	Academic	1
Average starting salary	$76,000	Business/Industry	9
State for bar exam	NJ, NY, PA, CA, TX	Government	6
Pass rate for first-time bar	81	Judicial clerkships	40
Employers Who Frequently Hire Grads		Military	1
All major Philadelphia, New Jersey, and		Other	5
Delaware law firms hire from Rutgers—		Private practice	37
Camden, as do numerous prestigious		Public Interest	1
firms from New York City, Washington,			
DC, and California.			
Prominent Alumni			
Honorable James Florio, former governor/U.S. Congressman; Honorable Joseph Rodriguez, U.S. federal district judge.			

Public interest	
law requirement	No

ADMISSIONS

Selectivity Rating	**87**
# applications received	2,152
# applicants accepted	562
# acceptees attending	219
Average LSAT	161
LSAT Range	160–162
Average undergrad GPA	3.41
Application fee	$60
Regular application	Rolling
Regular notification	Rolling
Rolling notification	Yes
Early application program	No
Transfer students accepted	Yes
Evening division offered	Yes
Part-time accepted	Yes
LSDAS accepted	Yes

Applicants Also Look At
Fordham University; The George Washington University; Rutgers, The State University of New Jersey—Newark; Temple University; University of California—Los Angeles; University of Maryland; University of Pennsylvania.

International Students

TOEFL required	
of international students	Yes
Minimum paper TOEFL	600
Minimum computer TOEFL	250

FINANCIAL FACTS

Annual tuition (resident)	$17,835
Annual tuition	
(nonresident)	$26,188
Books and supplies	$1,000
Fees per credit (resident)	$1,088
Fees per credit	
(nonresident)	$1,088
Tuition per credit (resident)	$738
Tuition per credit	
(nonresident)	$1,091
Room and board	
(on/off-campus)	$6,716/$8,000
Financial aid application	
deadline	4/1
% first-year students	
receiving some sort of aid	92
% receiving some sort of aid	92
% of aid that is merit based	25
% receiving scholarships	40
Average grant	$5,000
Average loan	$37,750
Average total aid package	$37,750
Average debt	$113,250

RUTGERS, THE STATE UNIVERSITY OF NEW JERSEY—NEWARK
SCHOOL OF LAW

INSTITUTIONAL INFORMATION

Public/private	Public
Student-faculty ratio	18:1
% faculty part-time	34
% faculty female	34
% faculty minority	26
Total faculty	62

SURVEY SAYS...

Diverse opinions accepted
in classrooms
Great library staff
Liberal students

STUDENTS

Enrollment of law school	817
% male/female	56/44
% out-of-state	29
% full-time	69
% minority	39
% international	2
# of countries represented	26
Average age of entering class	26

ACADEMICS

Academic Experience Rating	**80**
Profs interesting rating	79
Profs accessible rating	72
Hours of study per day	3.63

Academic Specialties

Civil procedure, commercial law, constitutional law, corporation securities law, criminal law, environmental law, global affairs, government services, human rights law, intellectual property law, international business, international law, labor law, legal history, legal philosophy, property, taxation.

Combined Degrees Offered

JD/MBA 4 years, JD/MD 6 years, JD/PhD (jurisprudence) 5 years, JD/MA (criminal justice) 4 years, JD/MCRP (city, regional planning) 4 years, JD/MSW 4 years.

Clinical program required	No
Legal writing	
course requirement	Yes
Legal methods	
course requirement	Yes

Academics

A "gem located in a very unexpected place," Rutgers, The State University of New Jersey—Newark, School of Law attracts a "top-notch" faculty who is "generally very invested in students that are interested or seek them out." Students commend their professors for being "witty and engaging" while simultaneously preparing them for the real legal world. One point of view suggests that the faculty is comprised of an "intriguing mix of academics and practitioners," enabling "students to engage with the material in both an intellectual and practical way." Another speaks to a shared sentiment of a "hands-on feel to the experience." As aptly summed up by one student, "none of [the] professors simply lecture, they all teach by making you work."

Students seem largely in favor of the administration, noting that it "is accessible and quick to respond to student concerns." One 2L attributes rebounding from a "rough start" and "disappointing grades" during the first semester of the program to the "extremely supportive, encouraging and helpful" attitude of the faculty and administration. However, others state that the "administration's efficiency is somewhat lacking" with regard to the red-tape entrenched registration process as well as grade dissemination. While some believe the administration "does not do enough to answer problems posed by the student body," others vouch for its commitment "to student success." Despite varied opinion, a common perception regarding Rutgers—Newark Law is that "it is truly a professional, graduate program"—students "get from it what [they] put in."

Some students call for an increase in course variety "to provide more theory and more specialty courses." Evening students in particular express dissatisfaction with limited course offerings "after 6:00 P.M." On the other hand, "Since patent law is a rapidly growing area, Rutgers—Newark has been actively adding more and more classes in this field" that are "taught by adjuncts who are partners in large patent law firms" imparting upon students their "vast practical knowledge."

For Rutgers—Newark's graduates, its proximity to New York City is considered to be its greatest strength. According to one student, "The vastness of opportunities that the New York City metro area holds is an immeasurable benefit to both the school and the students." While some feel "The students who do well often get jobs at the very best New York firms," the law school's Career Service Center itself receives mixed reviews. Students praise the current "dedicated" and "helpful" staff, but in the same breath remark that "Career Services could use some serious injection of resources," and that "the general glossing over" of the highly competitive job hunt "does not serve students well."

Virtually unanimous in opinion, students rave about the merits of the law library. The "excellent" and "never overcrowded" library "contains an extensive tax alcove" and a "brilliant" staff that is "amazing" and "very willing to help confused students through every stage of the research process." In general "facilities are worth mentioning," especially the law school building described as "a work of art" and the "universal wireless access" is a draw despite being "occasionally plagued with connection issues." "The six year young building makes for a very good learning environment" and students gladly report that "every three seats you can find an outlet for a laptop."

ANITA WALTON, ASSISTANT DEAN FOR ADMISSIONS
CENTER FOR LAW AND JUSTICE, 123 WASHINGTON STREET, NEWARK, NJ 07102
TEL: 973-353-5554 FAX: 973-353-3459
E-MAIL: LAWINFO@ANDROMEDA.RUTGERS.EDU • INTERNET: LAW.NEWARK.RUTGERS.EDU

Life

"There is a real camaraderie among the students" at Rutgers—Newark. The "non-competitive atmosphere, congenial student body and caring professors" "makes it a wonderful place to be." It seems as if "Everyone is very willing to help each other out." One student exclaims, "I asked a stranger for a class outline three days before the final, and she e-mailed it to me in 15 minutes." Another observes, "Competition between students is not noticeable but it does exist once interviewing for second-year jobs begins."

"It's law school; clearly the students aren't going to go out every night and party, but the school provides a vast array of different activities (quite a few that include open bar)." Students agree that "Thursday-afternoon happy hours are something to look forward to every week." Thankfully, "McGovern's (the Irish pub located across the street from the school)" provides a location for "a tradition that allows students to "let loose" and form lasting friendships." According to some, "While weekends in Newark leave everything to be desired, a student can always meet up with a classmate for dinner and drinks in nearby Hoboken (where many students choose to live)." Otherwise you can stay close to campus, as one student diplomatically explains, "Newark takes getting used to, but it grows on you very quickly."

Getting In

A unitary admissions system in place at Rutgers—Newark allows applicants to choose to compete for admissions with primary importance placed either on numerical values of their application, such as the LSAT and undergraduate GPA, or on non-numerical values, such as life experiences and achievements. Admitted students at the 25th percentile have an LSAT score of 154 and a GPA of 3.1. Admitted students at the 75th percentile have an LSAT score of 162 and a GPA of 3.6.

Legal research	
course requirement	Yes
Moot court requirement	Yes
Public interest	
law requirement	No

ADMISSIONS

Selectivity Rating	**84**
# applications received	3,010
# applicants accepted	713
# acceptees attending	184
Average LSAT	159
LSAT Range	154–162
Average undergrad GPA	3.34
Application fee	$60
Regular application	3/15
Regular notification	Rolling
Rolling notification	Yes
Early application program	No
Transfer students accepted	Yes
Evening division offered	Yes
Part-time accepted	Yes
LSDAS accepted	Yes

Applicants Also Look At
Boston University; Brooklyn Law School; Fordham University; The George Washington University; Rutgers, The State University of New Jersey—Camden, Seton Hall University; Yeshiva University.

International Students
TOEFL required	
of international students	No
TOEFL recommended	
of international students	No

FINANCIAL FACTS

Annual tuition (resident)	$17,835
Annual tuition	
(nonresident)	$26,187
Books and supplies	$4,225
Fees per credit (resident)	$892
Fees per credit (nonresident)	$892
Tuition per credit (resident)	$738
Tuition per credit	
(nonresident)	$1,090
Room and board	
(on/off-campus)	$13,908/$18,108
Financial aid application	
deadline	3/1
% receiving some sort of aid	90
% of aid that is merit based	13
% receiving scholarships	53
Average grant	$3,449
Average loan	$19,213
Average total aid package	$21,001
Average debt	$45,286

EMPLOYMENT INFORMATION

		Grads Employed by Field (%)	
Career Rating	**62**		
Average starting salary	$64,067	Academic	1
State for bar exam	NJ, NY, PA	Business/Industry	15
Pass rate for first-time bar	72	Government	5
Employers Who Frequently Hire Grads		Judicial clerkships	31
Federal judges; New Jersey State Court		Military	1
judges; large NJ and NY law firms;		Other	2
medium NJ firms, NY and NJ corpora-		Private practice	43
tions; legal services.		Public Interest	2
Prominent Alumni			
Robert Menendez, U.S. Senator; Justice			
Jaynee LaVecchia, NJ State Supreme Court;			
Ronald Chen, NJ public advocate; Justice			
Virginia Long, NJ State Supreme Court.			

SAMFORD UNIVERSITY
CUMBERLAND SCHOOL OF LAW

INSTITUTIONAL INFORMATION

Public/private	Private
Affiliation	Southern Baptist
Student-faculty ratio	18:1
% faculty female	26
% faculty minority	11
Total faculty	27

SURVEY SAYS...
Great research resources
Great library staff
Beautiful campus

STUDENTS

Enrollment of law school	481
% male/female	57/43
% out-of-state	52
% full-time	100
% minority	12
Average age of entering class	24

ACADEMICS

Academic Experience Rating	**86**
Profs interesting rating	88
Profs accessible rating	96
Hours of study per day	4.23

Academic Specialties
Trial advocacy and practical lawyering skills, Cumberland Community Center for Mediation.

Advanced Degrees Offered
Master of Comparative Law.

Combined Degrees Offered
JD/Master (accountancy) 3.5 to 4 years, JD/MBA 3.5 to 4 years, JD/MDivinity 5 years, JD/MPA 3.5 to 4 years, JD/MPH 3.5 to 4 years, JD/MS (environmental management) 3.5 to 4 years, JD/MA (theological studies) 3.5 to 4 years.

Clinical program required	No
Legal writing course requirement	Yes
Legal methods course requirement	Yes
Legal research course requirement	Yes
Moot court requirement	No

Academics

Samford University's Cumberland School of Law is, as one student puts it, "in the business of producing top-notch litigators." The school accomplishes this through an "exceptional focus on practical skills such as trial advocacy, negotiation, ADR, mediation, and client counseling." In fact, students quickly note that Cumberland's "trial advocacy program is tops in the nation." These future lawyers also benefit from "the legal writing classes [that] all first-years take"—classes that provide a firm foundation in the sort of communication skills that are incredibly marketable in the workforce. Cumberland offers students the opportunity to develop their lawyering skills in a traditional law school curriculum or through joint-degree programs, such as a JD/Master of Accountancy or a JD/Master of Science in Environmental Management. As one satisfied student says, "I am participating in a joint JD/MBA degree program. [This is the] only joint-degree I found in the country where you can graduate with both degrees in three years."

The students are quick to point out that none of these programs would be worth their salt if it weren't for the school's stellar faculty. A first-year beams, "The professors are masters of their craft. Not only are the professors extremely well-versed in their particular legal specialty, [but] they are terrific instructors." Not to mention accessible. Aside from tracking them down during office hours, "You can stop them in the hallway, corner them in the classroom, and call them on their cell phone if need be." A Cumberland first-year tells us, "I have enjoyed speaking with each of them to share my concerns, discuss a topic in class, or to just shoot the breeze." Even the administration has an "open-door policy" that one student is "willing to bet is unmatched at other schools." As one student explains, "I am on first-name basis with the majority of Career Services, professors, secretaries, and the library staff."

As far as resources go, Cumberland students admit that "the classrooms are older," but they are equipped with "the latest technology to enhance the learning experience." "The library is a stunning building with four floors of comfortable, quality furniture for long nights of study." In addition, "the Career Services Office does a great job matching students with potential job or externship opportunities." As one student assures us, "You constantly hear from recent alumni about how they were able to jump right into their practice upon graduation."

Life

Sure, "There is a competitive nature among the students" at Cumberland, but "They are all friendly and will not try to hide books from you at the library or steal pages from books so that you will not have the answers in class." As one first-year student says: "When I came to law school, I expected the 'survival of the fittest and at any cost' mentality. Instead, I found a group of highly supportive, incredibly enthusiastic people." All in all, "Cumberland is a close-knit community," and newcomers are absorbed into this community as soon as they arrive on campus, when they're placed into subgroups. As a 1L explains, "Each section consists of roughly 55 students, and during your first year you stay with those students throughout both semesters. It is a really great opportunity to form some close friendships." Cumberland students are hard workers, but they do not lose their civility and respect towards others in the pursuit of their goals. "Law school is stressful enough—it's nice that we do not have to worry about fellow classmates trying to undercut one another at every turn." The entire student body gets to mingle at the Thursday-night "social functions that anyone at Cumberland can attend." If you're looking for something a little more lively, though, you may have to "escape the conservative

M. GISELLE GAUTHIER, DIRECTOR OF ADMISSIONS
800 LAKESHORE DRIVE, BIRMINGHAM, AL 35229
TEL: 205-726-2702 FAX: 205-726-2057
E-MAIL: LAW.ADMISSIONS@SAMFORD.EDU • INTERNET: WWW.CUMBERLAND.SAMFORD.EDU

Baptist bubble that surrounds the university."

Students rave about Cumberland's physical setting. Picture "a beautiful campus full of cherry blossom trees, beautiful green spaces, and pristinely blue fountains." Located in the foothills of the Appalachians, Cumberland offers "a wonderful view of statuesque mountainsides and views of the city sitting below in the valley." That city, of course, is Birmingham—an old Southern metropolis boasting "a wonderful combination of nightlife, culinary variations, and cultural inspirations," and let's not forget the weather. As one student raves, "I'm writing this in February, and the temperature is 68 degrees outside."

Getting In

While Cumberland accepts applications on a rolling basis from October 1 through May 1, the Admissions Committee encourages prospective students to submit their materials by the February 28 priority deadline (when spots and scholarships begin to dwindle). In 2006, incomers arrived with an average undergrad GPA of 3.28 and an average LSAT score of 156. The school's application includes an open-ended personal essay. Take advantage of this opportunity to describe leadership and "other maturing experiences" that will set you apart from the field of applicants.

Public interest law requirement	No

ADMISSIONS

Selectivity Rating	**77**
# applications received	1,267
# applicants accepted	458
# acceptees attending	167
Average LSAT	156
LSAT Range	154–159
Average undergrad GPA	3.28
Application fee	$50
Regular application	5/1
Regular notification	Rolling
Rolling notification	Yes
Early application program	No
Transfer students accepted	Yes
Evening division offered	No
Part-time accepted	No
LSDAS accepted	Yes

Applicants Also Look At

Mercer University, The University of Alabama—Tuscaloosa, University of Georgia, University of Memphis, University of Mississippi, University of South Carolina, The University of Tennessee.

International Students

TOEFL required of international students	Yes
Minimum paper TOEFL	550
Minimum computer TOEFL	213

FINANCIAL FACTS

Annual tuition	$26,190
Books and supplies	$1,500
Room and board (off-campus)	$13,000
Financial aid application deadline	3/1
% first-year students receiving some sort of aid	83
% receiving some sort of aid	88
% of aid that is merit based	99
% receiving scholarships	38
Average grant	$13,895
Average loan	$32,610
Average total aid package	$38,086
Average debt	$90,015

EMPLOYMENT INFORMATION

		Grads Employed by Field (%)	
Career Rating	**79**	Academic	6
Rate of placement (nine months out)	96	Business/Industry	6
Average starting salary	$60,052	Government	10
State for bar exam	AL, FL, TN, GA, SC	Judicial clerkships	5
Pass rate for first-time bar	95	Military	3
Employers Who Frequently Hire Grads		Private practice	66
		Public Interest	4

Employers Who Frequently Hire Grads

Bradley, Arant, Rose and White; Burr and Forman; Balch and Bingham; Adams Reese; Cabaniss, Johnston, Gardner, Dumas and O'Neal; Sirote and Permutt; Alabama Attorney General's Office.

Prominent Alumni

Cordell Hull, founder of United Nations; Charlie Crist Jr., Governor of Florida; Justice Howell E. Jackson, U.S. Supreme Court; Justice Horace H. Lurton, U.S. Supreme Court.

SANTA CLARA UNIVERSITY
SCHOOL OF LAW

INSTITUTIONAL INFORMATION

Public/private	Private
Affiliation	Roman Catholic
Student-faculty ratio	20:1
% faculty part-time	36
% faculty female	48
% faculty minority	16
Total faculty	98

SURVEY SAYS...

Diverse opinions accepted
in classrooms
Beautiful campus
Students love Santa Clara, CA

STUDENTS

Enrollment of law school	932
% male/female	48/52
% out-of-state	19
% full-time	80
% minority	41
% international	2
# of countries represented	14
Average age of entering class	26

ACADEMICS

Academic Experience Rating	**72**
Profs interesting rating	68
Profs accessible rating	75
Hours of study per day	4.42

Academic Specialties

Intellectual property law, international law, public interest law.

Advanced Degrees Offered

LLM (U.S. law for foreign lawyers) 1 year, LLM (international and comparative law) 1 year, LLM (intellectual property law) 1 to 3 years.

Combined Degrees Offered

JD/MBA 3.5 to 4 years.

Clinical program required	No
Legal writing	
course requirement	Yes
Legal methods	
course requirement	No
Legal research	
course requirement	Yes
Moot court requirement	Yes

Academics

Many students at Santa Clara University School of Law are attracted by its "excellent regional reputation for high-tech law." "Since SCU is based in Silicon Valley, the opportunities for technology-based academia are profound." Specific programs that draw heaping praise include the "great IP [intellectual property] program, social justice program," and the "amazing study abroad options." SCU also "has an excellent part-time program" that brings lots of nontraditional students to the campus. Whatever track a student takes, she'll find an emphasis on "practical excellence and community service. SCU has a more genuine commitment to diversity and social justice than other, 'higher ranked' schools." With this solid selection of quality academic offerings in front of them, the 240 students at SCU are able to enjoy a "small-school feeling" with "big-school opportunities."

Students across the board reserved the highest praise for their professors. At SCU, "The professors are the bright spot. Most are approachable and readily accessible. Most are teaching and practicing so their lectures are a good combination of theory and practical application." The professors are so dedicated that, as one student tells us, "At least one professor will sleep in his office during finals so that he is always available for students." SCU students don't have such nice things to say about the administration, however. While some students say the administration is "extremely helpful" and "genuinely wants students to succeed," many claim the it's "ineffective, unprofessional, [and] can only seem to get it together for the initial seduction of incoming students."

In addition to a "wide range of guest lectures and events for networking," SCU students also enjoy plenty of good old-fashioned career counseling. The school "has a professional Career Services staff that puts on weekly events with alumni. The events help students figure out what area of law they'd like to practice in, mixers help them meet SCU alums, and they're great with intern/externships because there are so many SCU alumni out there." Plus, "The law school is very well respected, especially in the Bay Area. The location is amazing for anyone interested in high tech—this is the heart of Silicon Valley!"

Students say "The campus itself is indeed the highlight of the Santa Clara experience—the grounds are impeccable with peaceful gardens and perfectly manicured lawns." However, students gripe about the "woefully inadequate" classrooms and the "dim and dreary" library that is so "outdated" that studying becomes "harder than it already is." Also, "A lot of students would be happy if the school got rid of the mandatory grade curve and the additional upper-division writing requirement."

Life

"One of the greatest strengths of SCU Law is the collaborative attitude held by the students, faculty, and staff." "There is absolutely none of the cutthroat back-biting that you hear of at other schools," a current student says. "Aside from the usual stress at exam time, students are genuinely happy to be here." "Lots of the students [at SCU] are local residents," and "few live near or on campus." They "come from a variety of life and work backgrounds," which students find "especially enriching." The school's "collaborative atmosphere" helps to ensure that everyone gets along, though students "tend to form cliches with their own section." "Because of the part-time program, the student population is one of the most diverse anywhere (lots of engineers studying to be patent lawyers)."

Jeanette J. Leach, Assistant Dean for Admissions and Financial Aid
500 El Camino Real, Santa Clara, CA 95053
Tel: 408-554-5048 Fax: 408-554-7897
E-mail: lawadmissions@scu.edu • Internet: scu.edu/law

Academic life at SCU is supplemented by "many extracurricular activities from law journals to basketball leagues," all with "tremendous law student participation." There are "monthly bar nights" and "one or two lunches" every week where students can enjoy "speakers and food." Also, "March is banquet month, and every student organization puts on a party." Students say the Student Bar Association "does its best to put on social events for the law school. Some of the events have been a real success. But to say that any law student really has a social life is a joke. For three years, law school is your life."

"The immediate area around the campus is not really a 'college town' atmosphere. There are not a lot of areas for graduate students to go to hang out other than one or two places." "Your social life is what you make of it"—even if it sometimes "takes a little creativity and exploration of the neighboring towns." On the upside, SCU's location offers "easy access to downtown San Jose" and the true socialites among the student body "drive to San Francisco for fun."

Getting In

SCU's entering students earn an average score of 159 on the LSAT and a 3.32 undergraduate GPA. But the Admissions Committee strives to avoid "a mechanical approach to admissions." In other words, smart undergraduate course selection, improved academic record, and impressive life or professional experience can give a candidate the edge.

Public interest law requirement	No

ADMISSIONS

Selectivity Rating	**78**
# applications received	3,313
# applicants accepted	1,392
# acceptees attending	243
Average LSAT	159
LSAT Range	156–161
Average undergrad GPA	3.32
Application fee	$75
Regular application	2/1
Regular notification	Rolling
Rolling notification	Yes
Early application program	Yes
Early application deadline	11/1
Early application notification	12/20
Transfer students accepted	Yes
Evening division offered	Yes
Part-time accepted	Yes
LSDAS accepted	Yes

Applicants Also Look At

Loyola Marymount University, University of California—Davis, University of California—Hastings, University of San Diego, University of San Francisco.

International Students

TOEFL required of international students	No
TOEFL recommended of international students	No

FINANCIAL FACTS

Annual tuition	$33,600
Tuition per credit	$1,120
Room and board	$12,042
Financial aid application deadline	3/1
% first-year students receiving some sort of aid	90
% receiving some sort of aid	86
% of aid that is merit based	58
% receiving scholarships	33
Average grant	$12,452
Average loan	$32,574
Average total aid package	$35,373
Average debt	$98,424

EMPLOYMENT INFORMATION

Career Rating	**88**	**Grads Employed by Field (%)**	
Rate of placement (nine months out)	87	Academic	1
Average starting salary	$96,956	Business/Industry	27
State for bar exam	CA, WA, OR, AZ, NY	Government	9
Pass rate for first-time bar	79	Judicial clerkships	2
Employers Who Frequently Hire Grads		Military	1
Bingham McCutchen LLP; Blakely,		Other	7
Sokoloff, Taylor, and Zafman LLP; Cooley		Private practice	50
Godward LLP; Dewey Ballantine LLP; DLA		Public Interest	3
Piper; Fenwick and West LLP..			
Prominent Alumni			
Leon Panetta, former Chief of Staff under			
President Bill Clinton; Zoe Lofgren,			
Congresswoman, U.S. House of			
Representatives.			

SEATTLE UNIVERSITY
SCHOOL OF LAW

INSTITUTIONAL INFORMATION

Public/private	Private
Affiliation	Roman Catholic
Student-faculty ratio	15:1
% faculty part-time	37
% faculty female	39
% faculty minority	20
Total faculty	107

SURVEY SAYS...

Great research resources
Great library staff
Beautiful campus

STUDENTS

Enrollment of law school	1,092
% male/female	44/56
% out-of-state	25
% full-time	79
% minority	25
% international	1
# of countries represented	5
Average age of entering class	27

ACADEMICS

Academic Experience Rating	77
Profs interesting rating	67
Profs accessible rating	66
Hours of study per day	4.48

Academic Specialties

Commercial law, constitutional law, corporation securities, criminal law, environmental law, estate planning, health law and real estate, human rights law, intellectual property law, international law, labor law, legal writing, property, poverty law, taxation.

Advanced Degrees Offered

JD 3 to 3.5 years.

Combined Degrees Offered

JD/MBA 4 years, JD/MA (international business) 4 years, JD/MS (finance) 4 years, JD/MA (professional accounting) 4 years, JD/MPA 4 years, JD/MA (sports leadership) 4 years.

Clinical program required	No
Legal writing course requirement	Yes

Academics

"A fairly large school," the Seattle University School of Law offers an "outstanding," "very flexible, evening, part-time program" in addition to full-time day enrollment. "Course options are diverse and offered consistently." No fewer than 14 specializations include criminal practice, environmental law, and international law. The "tough but very good" legal writing curriculum is far and away the biggest point of pride here. It's "the class that you will despise while you are in it, but will be utterly grateful for when you are through." "This school has the best legal writing program and advocacy programs in the country," brags one student. "It is the best and most useful course I've ever taken at a school," adds a 3L. "The legal writing program really does prepare you for the real world and to a level of detail and precision I did not expect." A throng of externships and clerkships gives students the opportunity to "develop practical skills" "in all different areas of law." Seattle U's location "less than a mile from downtown Seattle businesses and law firms" allows students to walk to many courthouses and downtown law firms. Seattle U Law is also a Jesuit institution, and many students note that many organizations "are devoted to social justice." Other students tell us that "any mention of the Jesuit influence is off base." "If asked [about] the Jesuit tradition," jokes a 2L, many students would ask, "'Is that a type of mocha latte at Starbucks?'" The biggest gripe among students concerns the need to "reduce the size of the incoming classes" ("330-plus is just too much," says a student of past years). Also, warns a 3L, "The grading curve here is very tough. It can get daunting."

Professors "emphasize the practical side" of law and are "generally extremely capable, intelligent, and knowledgeable." It's the "really hit-and-miss" visiting professors whom "you have to watch out for." Outside of class, some faculty members are "extremely helpful and available." However, other professors are "very hard to access." "I wish that the professors were a bit more accessible," complains a 2L. "They are supposed to have set office hours, but none of the professors are held to that." Thoughts about the administration are similarly mixed. Some students say that the SU administration "is a distant, bureaucratic entity" that manifests "a seeming sense of apathy towards the individual student." Others assert that the deans "work hard to eliminate obstacles so that all you have to worry about is learning."

The Center for Professional Development "makes extraordinary efforts to find job placements for students." Also, "The alumni network is broad and very helpful." "The top 10 percent do great and get into private firms with the snap of a finger." Some students complain that SU "should be doing more to market students to regional and national employers." "Seattle University is a regional school," explains a 2L. "It is hard for students to find jobs outside of the Pacific Northwest."

Depending on which students you talk to, the facilities here are either "bordering on beautiful" or "stark and bleak" because "Everything is grey, and there is a severe lack of windows." Whatever the case, the law school is in "a new building with wireless technology" throughout and "very high-tech" gadgetry everywhere. "Superhumanly helpful and friendly research librarians" staff the law library, though "the lack of study space is a serious concern."

Life

"You can always get notes when you need them" at Seattle U Law; "However, there is still a healthy amount of competitiveness among students," who comprise "an interesting mix." "The right-out-of-undergrad students are obviously more competitive, but

CAROL COCHRAN, ASSISTANT DEAN FOR ADMISSION
901 TWELFTH AVENUE, SULLIVAN HALL, PO BOX 222000, SEATTLE, WA 98122-1090
TEL: 206-398-4200 FAX: 206-398-4058
E-MAIL: LAWADMIS@SEATTLEU.EDU • INTERNET: WWW.LAW.SEATTLEU.EDU

much more social too." Older students are "considerably more laid-back and have a completely different attitude." Students (and faculty) tend to lean to the left politically, though "the Federalist Society has a strong presence on campus." Few are particularly religious. "About the most religious this school gets is the Christmas tree and menorah that get put up during the holidays."

"Anyone with minimal social skills can make lifelong friends here," claims one student. "Nobody here is pretentious." "People at the school are tight-knit and supportive of one another." A host of on-campus events "promotes community interaction." However, there isn't much communication between the evening and the day programs. "For the night students who work full-time there aren't many opportunities to socialize with other students. Any socializing is done within the evening section and rarely are any day students involved."

"The school building itself is located just outside of downtown Seattle" in a lively neighborhood called Capitol Hill. "The school is in paradise," brags a 2L. "Seattle really is the greatest city in the world," beams another student. The Emerald City "is a great place to live for a variety of reasons, most notably the climate and the plethora of places to engage in outdoor activities."

Getting In

Admitted students at the 25th percentile have LSAT scores of 155 and GPAs of 3.2. Admitted students at the 75th percentile have LSAT scores of 161 and GPAs of 3.6. If you take the LSAT more than once, Seattle U Law "gives greater weight" to your highest score but also advises you to contextualize the difference in your scores in an addendum.

Legal methods course requirement	No
Legal research course requirement	Yes
Moot court requirement	No
Public interest law requirement	No

ADMISSIONS

Selectivity Rating	**82**
# applications received	2,880
# applicants accepted	822
# acceptees attending	289
Average LSAT	157
LSAT Range	155–160
Average undergrad GPA	3.3
Application fee	$50
Regular application	3/1
Regular notification	Rolling
Rolling notification	Yes
Early application program	No
Transfer students accepted	Yes
Evening division offered	Yes
Part-time accepted	Yes
LSDAS accepted	Yes

Applicants Also Look At

Gonzaga University, Lewis and Clark College, Santa Clara University, University of Oregon, University of San Francisco, University of Washington.

International Students

TOEFL required of international students	Yes
TOEFL recommended of international students	Yes
Minimum computer TOEFL	250

FINANCIAL FACTS

Annual tuition	$29,980
Books and supplies	$903
Tuition per credit	$996
Room and board	$12,925
% first-year students receiving some sort of aid	97
% receiving some sort of aid	96
% of aid that is merit based	45
% receiving scholarships	49
Average grant	$6,906
Average loan	$30,759
Average total aid package	$34,794
Average debt	$85,212

EMPLOYMENT INFORMATION

		Grads Employed by Field (%)	
Career Rating	**77**	Academic	2
Rate of placement (nine months out)	99	Business/Industry	29
Average starting salary	$60,000	Government	16
State for bar exam	WA, CA, OR, TX, IL	Judicial clerkships	7
Pass rate for first-time bar	84	Military	1
Employers Who Frequently Hire Grads		Private practice	42
Perkins Coie; Lane, Powell, Spears,		Public Interest	3

Employers Who Frequently Hire Grads
Perkins Coie; Lane, Powell, Spears, Lubersky; King County Prosecuting Attorney; Washington State Attorney General; Williams, Kastner, and Gibbs.

Prominent Alumni
Honorable Ralph Beistline, Federal District Court; Honorable Charles Johnson, WA State Supreme Court; Linda Stout, Deputy Chief Executive Officer, Port of Seattle; Honorable Elaine Houghton, WA Court of Appeals.

SETON HALL UNIVERSITY
SCHOOL OF LAW

Academics

As part of its mission statement, Seton Hall aspires to treat all individuals with dignity, justice, and compassion. In line with that philosophy, students at this large, New Jersey law school receive a rigorous legal education in the context of a nurturing and student-centered environment. By almost all accounts, the accomplished faculty is the school's greatest strength, bringing expertise, passion, and enthusiasm to the classroom. At Seton Hall, you will be taught by "great legal minds and leading experts in the fields of criminal procedure, property, and evidence, among others." Faculty brings more than impressive credentials to the table, though: "Professors view teaching as their first priority, so even though they have other responsibilities around the community, they are teachers ahead of anything. I can't stress how much of a relief this is as a first-year who is just learning the ropes," one student notes. Another adds, "From standing on tables barefoot, to portraying unilateral contracts using an analogy to *The Wizard of Oz*, to wearing a cheese-head throughout a lecture, to 'Porno Wednesday' in criminal law, the professors have demonstrated their mastery of presenting legal theory in a highly entertaining manner."

The student-centered approach extends well beyond the lecture hall, and "Professors can relate to a broad spectrum of individuals and can comfortably talk about anything ranging from the First Amendment to last night's Yankees–Red Sox game." Students love the surprisingly individualized attention they receive from the faculty and are quick to share anecdotes about their outgoing professors: "I have had professors make phone calls and e-mails on my behalf several times regarding jobs and internships," reports a 1L. A 2L recounts that "one professor called me at home on Thanksgiving night to answer a question I had that did not relate to school."

The Seton Hall administration demonstrates a "sincere interest in the students." In particular, "Seton Hall Law takes student evaluations very seriously and employs rigorous screening procedures for hiring new faculty members and in promoting current ones." Outside the classroom "The deans go out of their way to counsel 1Ls in making the transition into law school less painful" and work hard to maintain a number of special, student-friendly programs. Attentive to detail, the deans provide "those little touches that set the school apart from others." For example, "On the first day of orientation, Seton Hall gives you a key chain with the dean's home and cell phone numbers, and if you are sick, they'll send a car to pick you up at school and drive you to the health center." Unfailingly friendly, students say they "feel very welcome approaching almost all administrators," and a 3L tells us, "Dean Patrick Hobbs runs a great school, and can often be seen chatting with students well into the night." There are, however, some general grumbles that the administration can be inefficient in responding to individual students' concerns. In particular, many students complain that "Financial Aid takes their time in processing and delivering the loan checks to the students," which can lead to some damaging financial issues for struggling students.

The Seton Hall campus and facilities are first rate. "The building is relatively new, so the classrooms are big and clean, with outlets for pretty much every seat. The library is great and the staff is really helpful," comments one 2L. Located in Newark, New Jersey, the campus isn't set in the Garden of Eden, but it is nonetheless a propitious place for the ambitious law student. A 3L explains, "While Newark is not pretty, the district and circuit courts, as well as the U.S. Attorney's Office and Federal Defender, are all within a 10- to 15-minute (entirely safe) walk from school. The school's contacts with those offices are excellent." While Seton Hall focuses more on the theoretical aspects of legal education,

Ms. Gisele Joachim, Assistant Dean of Admissions and Financial Aid
One Newark Center, Newark, NJ 07102
Tel: 888-415-7271 Fax: 973-642-8876
E-mail: admitme@shu.edu • Internet: law.shu.edu

the clinical and externship opportunities in the surrounding area are nothing to sneeze at. A case in point: "The clinical program offered at Seton Hall Law is excellent. I participated in the immigration clinic, and I found it to be the most rewarding experience of my academic career." On top of that, Seton Hall has a "good reputation in the tristate area" and "has really great ties in New Jersey." Additionally, many are pleased to report that "each year we have more New York firms coming to campus to recruit students, as well as more firms participating in the resume drop. I've talked to alums from a few years back and they're really impressed with the response that many of us have gotten from New York firms."

Life

Seton Hall is home to a lively academic and intellectual atmosphere. After class, "Seton Hall Law provides many interesting seminars or presentations where prominent guests are featured or professors present lectures on practical aspects of law." On top of that, "The student government does a good job in holding social events for the students, as well as public service activities to help the community." However, given the fact that most students commute, the feeling of a campus community is not particularly strong. A 3L elaborates, "The school certainly suffers from the fact that most students commute to it from New York City and elsewhere in New Jersey. Let's face it: No one wants to live in Newark."

While Seton Hall is a historically Catholic institution, students hail from all backgrounds, cultures, and walks of life. A 1L elaborates, "It is a Catholic school, but there isn't a huge religious vibe. I have friends here who are Mormon, Jewish, Sikh, and agnostic." In fact, a 2L reports that the "law school has a fully supported gay and lesbian student group that functions well and is a leadership group within the school."

Getting In

Admissions to Seton Hall are competitive. Every year, the school receives almost 3,000 applications for about 310 first-year seats. Admissions decisions are based primarily on the strength of a candidate's undergraduate record and test scores; however, the Admissions Committee may take other factors into consideration, such as graduate education or work experience.

Public interest law requirement	No

ADMISSIONS

Selectivity Rating	84
# applications received	2,400
# applicants accepted	714
# acceptees attending	192
Average LSAT	160
LSAT Range	158–163
Average undergrad GPA	3.4
Application fee	$65
Regular application	4/1
Regular notification	Rolling
Rolling notification	Yes
Early application program	No
Transfer students accepted	Yes
Evening division offered	Yes
Part-time accepted	Yes
LSDAS accepted	Yes

Applicants Also Look At
Brooklyn Law School; Hofstra University; New York Law School, Rutgers, The State University of New Jersey; St. John's University.

International Students

TOEFL required of international students	No
TOEFL recommended of international students	Yes

FINANCIAL FACTS

Annual tuition	$35,010
Books and supplies	$1,100
Tuition per credit	$1,167
Room and board (off-campus)	$12,150
Financial aid application deadline	4/1
% first-year students receiving some sort of aid	85
% receiving some sort of aid	85
% of aid that is merit based	16
% receiving scholarships	41
Average grant	$13,880
Average loan	$39,000
Average total aid package	$48,000
Average debt	$78,978

EMPLOYMENT INFORMATION

Career Rating	77	Grads Employed by Field (%)	
Rate of placement (nine months out)	97	Academic	1
Average starting salary	$62,000	Business/Industry	15
State for bar exam	NJ, NY	Government	7
Pass rate for first-time bar	89	Judicial clerkships	35

Employers Who Frequently Hire Grads
Graduates are frequently hired by the nation's most prestigious firms, all national and state government agencies, public interest organizations and state and federal judges nationwide.

Private practice	41
Public Interest	1

Prominent Alumni
Honorable Michael Chagares, U.S. Court of Appeals, 3rd Circuit; Christopher Christie, U.S. Attorney for the State of New Jersey.

SOUTH TEXAS COLLEGE OF LAW

INSTITUTIONAL INFORMATION

Public/private	Private
Student-faculty ratio	22:1
% faculty part-time	54
% faculty female	31
% faculty minority	13
Total faculty	127

SURVEY SAYS...

Diverse opinions accepted
in classrooms
Great research resources
Great library staff
Students love Houston, TX

STUDENTS

Enrollment of law school	1,237
% male/female	55/45
% out-of-state	9
% full-time	74
% minority	20
Average age of entering class	26

ACADEMICS

Academic Experience Rating	**76**
Profs interesting rating	78
Profs accessible rating	75
Hours of study per day	3.84

Academic Specialties

Advocacy, alternative dispute resolution, corporate compliance, transactional skills.

Combined Degrees Offered

JD/MBA (with Texas A&M University).

Clinical program required	No
Legal writing	
course requirement	Yes
Legal methods	
course requirement	Yes
Legal research	
course requirement	Yes
Moot court requirement	No
Public interest	
law requirement	No

Academics

Centrally located in the heart of downtown Houston, students at South Texas College of Law can take full advantage of the school's proximity to surrounding courtrooms and law firms not to mention a "very strong network of alumni in practice." Second to none with 95 National Titles, "the pièce de résistance of STCL is its trial advocacy program." Students tell us that STCL "is a great school for practical lawyering skills and is a great choice for those students who wish to practice law in Texas." In addition, South Texas requires four hours of legal research and writing over the first two semesters and students cannot say enough about the legal research and writing program. According to one 2L, "It is the reason we continually win 'Best Brief' in the moot court competitions, and it will leave you well prepared for your summer clerkships." Another student concludes, "If you want to learn how to practice law instead of just learning theory, South Texas is a great place to be."

"The excellent and accessible faculty makes it a great school, even for part-time students who mainly attend evenings and weekends," says one student. Approachable both in and out of the classroom, the faculty's "love" of teaching, "sense of humor," and support is clearly felt by students who claim that "it is not difficult to excel in class given the great learning environment." Students agree that practical teaching is an aspect of STCL that distinguishes it from other law schools. STCL's professors hail from a variety of backgrounds, and the vast majority of the adjunct faculty are sitting judges or practicing attorneys. According to students, "This gives us a great sense of what is 'really' happening in the legal field versus the theoretical or purely academic focus of other schools." A 3L adds that practical learning, "builds the best practicing lawyers of tomorrow," while another boldly attests, "Our school will teach you how to litigate the day after you pass the bar."

Students note that "the Admissions Office is very professional, knowledgeable, and helpful." However, many express frustration over the fact that "the offices of the Registrar, Financial Aid, and Business Office are in three locations and don't seem to communicate well." In one student's experience, "One question regarding a semester's bill can require the student to visit each of the three offices." Fortunately, students report that past headaches surrounding registration have diminished due to the implementation of a campus-wide integrated database, resulting in a "smoother" process overall. While students admit that the administration has "streamlined many things lately which goes to show that they listen to students," others argue that "they need to be more responsive to the feedback of their customers—the students."

With regard to facilities at South Texas, students unanimously agree that the "state-of-the-art library is beautiful [and] includes an extensive collection of sources." "It's superior in every respect, and there is never a wait in one of its many computer labs," adds one student. One of its most valued features is the "amazing terrace on the sixth floor," which "provides a relaxing setting in downtown Houston" and can also be utilized for "reading, eating, sunbathing—whatever your pleasure." The only complaint about the library is that it "closes too early!" However, the same enthusiasm doesn't extend to the subject of "deplorable" parking. Due to its downtown location, parking at STCL continues to be the most widely cited grievance.

ALICIA K. CRAMER, ASSISTANT DEAN OF ADMISSIONS
1303 SAN JACINTO STREET, HOUSTON, TX 77002-7000
TEL: 713-646-1810 FAX: 713-646-2906
E-MAIL: ADMISSIONS@STCL.EDU • INTERNET: WWW.STCL.EDU

ADMISSIONS

Selectivity Rating	**71**
# applications received	2,185
# applicants accepted	992
# acceptees attending	339
Average LSAT	154
LSAT Range	151–156
Average undergrad GPA	3.22
Application fee	$50
Regular application	2/15
Regular notification	5/25
Rolling notification	No
Early application program	No
Transfer students accepted	Yes
Evening division offered	Yes
Part-time accepted	Yes
LSDAS accepted	Yes

Applicants Also Look At

St. Mary's University, Texas Tech University, Texas Wesleyan University, University of Houston, The University of Texas at Austin.

International Students

TOEFL required of international students	No
TOEFL recommended of international students	No

FINANCIAL FACTS

Annual tuition	$21,840
Books and supplies	$1,500
Room and board (off-campus)	$8,500
Financial aid application deadline	5/1
% first-year students receiving some sort of aid	91
% receiving some sort of aid	94
% of aid that is merit based	4
% receiving scholarships	57
Average grant	$5,338
Average loan	$22,536
Average total aid package	$25,792
Average debt	$79,448

Life

"The students in the part-time program are a great mix of experienced and right-out-of-college students, so class discussions are rich and varied," says one student. Diversity is reflected through classes that "explore all sides in a professional manner" and foster "creative and stimulating after class conversations with people that you may never have spoken to without the class discussion."

According to students, "While there is an inevitable degree of competition, [this] is not a cutthroat environment." Most here agree that "students work together and rely on each other for assistance." While there is no shortage of studying at South Texas, "Students looking for a social atmosphere can definitely find it here." In fact, one student reports, "The students at my school like to party. I have no idea where everyone finds the time, but we do."

In addition, students declare they "have more student interest organizations than you can count—this provides an opportunity to learn about practice areas that aren't covered in the classroom . . . fantastic!" "Each month, at least one student organization throws a shindig on the terrace of the library," states one student. Usually well attended, this type of event "breeds camaraderie among the student body. As a result, the law school atmosphere remains upbeat as we all move along the continuum together." Echoing this sentiment, one 2L muses, "I get a big sense of 'we're all in this together.' I only wish this prevailed post-graduation."

Getting In

Although LSAT scores and cumulative undergraduate GPA determine admission for many students applying to STCL, a significant portion of each class is admitted based on other factors including, but not limited to, exceptional personal or academic accomplishment, recommendation letters, and leadership potential. Admitted students at the 25th percentile have an LSAT score of 151 and a GPA of 3.0. Admitted students at the 75th percentile have an LSAT score of 156 and a GPA of 3.5.

EMPLOYMENT INFORMATION

		Grads Employed by Field (%)	
Career Rating	**79**		
Rate of placement (nine months out)	80	Academic	1
Average starting salary	$78,000	Business/Industry	12
State for bar exam	TX	Government	11
Pass rate for first-time bar	78	Judicial clerkships	2
Employers Who Frequently Hire Grads		Military	1
Large to midsized law firms; corporations;		Other	4
state and federal government entities.		Private practice	68
		Public Interest	1

SOUTHERN ILLINOIS UNIVERSITY
SCHOOL OF LAW

INSTITUTIONAL INFORMATION

Public/private	Public
Student-faculty ratio	12:1
% faculty part-time	21
% faculty female	47
% faculty minority	10
Total faculty	31

SURVEY SAYS...

Diverse opinions accepted
in classrooms
Great research resources
Great library staff

STUDENTS

Enrollment of law school	355
% male/female	59/41
% out-of-state	33
% full-time	99
% minority	8.5
Average age of entering class	25

ACADEMICS

Academic Experience Rating	**74**
Profs interesting rating	78
Profs accessible rating	90
Hours of study per day	4.46

Advanced Degrees Offered
JD 3 years, MLS 2 years, LLM 2 years.

Combined Degrees Offered
JD/MD 6 years, JD/MBA 4 years,
JD/MPA 4 years, JD/MAcc 4 years,
JD/MSW, JD/MSEd, JD/ PhD.

Clinical program required	No
Legal writing course requirement	No
Legal methods course requirement	Yes
Legal research course requirement	No
Moot court requirement	No
Public interest law requirement	No

Academics

Southern Illinois University's School of Law serves up a legal education that's "excellent for the price." A 3L says, "Because SIU is very inexpensive and has many grants and scholarships, I have been able to study abroad, and my debt after law school will still be way under the average [for] law school grads. Freedom from debt allows me to pick my field of practice after law school instead of being forced into doing something I don't want to do because of student loans." Low cost doesn't equal inferior legal training; SIU places a "strong emphasis on becoming a lawyer with both academic and practical skills," granting its students a well-rounded apprenticeship in the profession. "I think one of the school's greatest strengths is that it offers a lot of real world experience," avers an attorney-to-be. "We have an excellent clinic program as well as an externship program. We also have a 'writing across the curriculum' requirement for each class, so students really have a lot of opportunities to practice their writing skills and get feedback."

Students across the board give their professors high marks. A 1L interested in labor laws explains, "The professors doors are always open. They are always willing to discuss legal theory or current events. Numerous professors have gone out of their way to give advice which has been particularly beneficial to shaping my career aspirations and goals." A similarly chuffed student continues, "Many of them aren't simply professors, they're teachers—some of the best I've ever had. Most of them have had real world experiences which they share in order to better prepare you for the bar and for practice." Even more, these dedicated professors are so accessible that they "often sit in the lunch area and discuss topics of interest to the students." A first-year promises, "You need only show a modicum of enthusiasm and aptitude in order to have lots of people willing to mentor you and foster your skills."

Due in part to its small size, the law school "has a familial feel." Students rave about the school's "warm and friendly atmosphere," which "encourages cooperation and friendship." However, there is a downside to studying law in such a quaint setting, including "limited classrooms" and "many classes that conflict with either required courses or courses that are strongly recommended for passing the bar exam." Additionally, there's "a general lack of support for students wishing to take a nontraditional approach to legal education. The model of three years of law school, graduate, pass the bar, and practice law is rigidly held onto by the administration."

By and large, the school's facilities receive high marks. "Each seat in the classrooms has its own outlet which is very helpful since 99 percent of students here use laptops." In addition, "The library provides ample private study areas and there are two student lounges." One resource that's lacking, however, is the Office of Career Services. "There are not enough summer clerkship opportunities for law students," perhaps due to the school's relative lack of reputation as compared to other law schools. "Many people don't even know we exist!" exclaims one student.

Life

Life at the SIU School of Law begins with "orientation and study group programs" that give students "an opportunity to socialize and meet new people." Typically, everyone gets along with ease. A 2L tells us, "I'd be lying if I said we weren't competitive with each other, but that often takes a back seat to helping each other survive law school." In general, "The student body is very young. Most students came right out of undergrad, or took one year off, two at most." This youthful presence, combined with the small size of the school, sometimes makes SIU feel "like a high school." A 2L warns, "If you go here, don't expect to have a private life. People will usually find out everything about you."

The school is located in Carbondale, a city of 26,000 that's tucked among the hills of Illinois's southern corridor. The "beautiful wooded campus" and "the campus lake" allow students to enjoy the restorative powers of nature "on a tough day" without exiting SIU's gates. "If you like small-town living, this is a great place to be," says a first-year. "If you want big-city living, what the heck are you doing in Carbondale?" Nonetheless, a student promises that "Carbondale offers a wide variety of social opportunities. Whether it is the nightlife, wineries, or outdoor recreation, there is always something to take your mind off the books." One such distraction is local watering hole where, "on any given Thursday through Saturday night, one can go and find many law students (including those who do not drink)." On university grounds, "There are a lot of student organizations" that "do some cool things like visit immigration detention centers, philanthropic projects, etc."

Getting In

In recent years, approximately one in every three applicants was accepted to the SIU School of Law. Admitted candidates have an average undergrad GPA of 3.4 and a median LSAT score of 154. While these numbers are important, SIU also pays close attention to the "Admissions Committee memorandum" (personal statement). This is an opportunity for candidates to distinguish themselves as multidimensional individuals. Edit well.

ADMISSIONS

Selectivity Rating	71
# applications received	709
# applicants accepted	330
# acceptees attending	123
Average LSAT	152
LSAT Range	149–156
Average undergrad GPA	3.4
Application fee	$50
Regular application	3/1
Regular notification	Rolling
Rolling notification	Yes
Early application program	No
Transfer students accepted	Yes
Evening division offered	No
Part-time accepted	No
LSDAS accepted	Yes

Applicants Also Look At
Northern Illinois University.

International Students

TOEFL required of international students	Yes
Minimum paper TOEFL	600

FINANCIAL FACTS

Annual tuition (resident)	$9,720
Annual tuition (nonresident)	$26,640
Books and supplies	$1,080
Room and board	$11,674
Financial aid application deadline	4/1
% first-year students receiving some sort of aid	100
% receiving some sort of aid	91
% receiving scholarships	60
Average grant	$4,000
Average loan	$17,361
Average total aid package	$19,170
Average debt	$52,084

EMPLOYMENT INFORMATION

Career Rating	61
Average starting salary	$43,958
State for bar exam	IL, MO
Pass rate for first-time bar	90

Employers Who Frequently Hire Grads
Various Illinois State's Attorney's offices, large and small law firms, various public interest organizations.

Prominent Alumni
Tim Eaton, partner, Ungaretti and Harris; William Birkett, Associate General Counsel, INS.; Lisa Joley, general counsel, Anheuser-Busch; Chief Judge Patrick Murphy, U.S. District Court.

Grads Employed by Field (%)

Academic	4
Business/Industry	7
Government	20
Private practice	64
Public Interest	1

SOUTHERN METHODIST UNIVERSITY
DEDMAN SCHOOL OF LAW

INSTITUTIONAL INFORMATION

Public/private	Private
Affiliation	Methodist
Student-faculty ratio	14:1
% faculty female	37
% faculty minority	17
Total faculty	46

SURVEY SAYS...

Beautiful campus
Students love Dallas, TX

STUDENTS

Enrollment of law school	881
% male/female	50/50
% full-time	65
% minority	24
# of countries represented	19
Average age of entering class	25

ACADEMICS

Academic Experience Rating	**74**
Profs interesting rating	77
Profs accessible rating	73
Hours of study per day	3.84

Advanced Degrees Offered

LLM (taxation) 1 year, LLM (general) 1 year, LLM (comparative and international law) 1 year, SJD.

Combined Degrees Offered

JD/MBA 4 years, JD/MA (economics), 4 years.

Clinical program required	No
Legal writing	
course requirement	Yes
Legal methods	
course requirement	No
Legal research	
course requirement	Yes
Moot court requirement	Yes
Public interest	
law requirement	Yes

Academics

Students say the Dedman School of Law at Southern Methodist University has "a great reputation in Texas" and gives out "an incredible amount of scholarship money." (Roughly 50 percent of each class receives scholarship assistance.) "Diverse course offerings" in "everything from the philosophical to the tediously practical" define the curriculum here, and "The legal clinics are absolutely amazing." Externships and scholarly journals are abundant. Students say there are plenty of opportunities to get involved: "We have consistently won national moot court and mock trial competitions over the past two years and the school has a great Trial Advocacy program co-taught by practitioners and judges." A unique JD/MA program allows students to study economics as well as law, and students have the opportunity to study abroad in Oxford each summer. Academic complaints often revolve around the legal writing program, which "needs a massive overhaul" and "while informational, [can] feel more like fifth grade English in the way [it is] approached."

The "very distinguished" yet "easily approachable" professors "are very receptive to students and concerned with [their] learning" and "make an effort to be available." They are "demanding of their students," but "interesting and entertaining in the classroom." "There are a few who are quite reminiscent of *The Paper Chase* and make you stand to answer questions in class even if it is for the entire class period." Professors "make the classroom experience fun," gushes one student. "My civil procedure exam was one of the funniest things I have ever read, with witty undercurrents and subtle political satire." Opinions of the administration vary considerably. Some students say the deans seem "distant at times, but whenever you need them, they're available and helpful." Others tell us that the administration "does not care about the students" and gripe about "bureaucratic inefficiencies."

Job prospects are very promising for SMU grads. Career Services is "actually concerned with helping you find a job." "Dallas is a wonderful market that pays salaries on par with New York, but the quality of life is so much better," according to students here. "If you want to stay and practice in Dallas, you could not go to a better school." SMU's "exceptionally strong relationship with the Dallas legal market" provides an "extensive network of attorneys" "in every field imaginable." "The alums are very supportive and willing to help out." "A lot of doors are opened by attending the SMU Dedman School of Law, regardless of your class rank." "I was able to secure a six-figure job without being on law review or moot court," says a 3L. "There is definitely a huge hurdle" for students to face who do not want to practice in Texas, though.

The "gorgeous" campus is full of "very pretty, collegiate-looking brick buildings" and "nestled in one of the nicest, most affluent neighborhoods in the Dallas area." "The law school itself is further cloistered away from the rest of the university and, once inside, it is easy to forget you are sitting in the middle of a bustling metropolis." "Large oak trees provide shady walkways and outdoor study places are ample." "I always joke that our tuition goes straight toward landscaping," says a witty 3L. The majority of classrooms are "very comfortable and accommodating," and the "nearly flawless" wireless signal is "strong in every corner of the law school." The library is "amazing," "both with regard to holdings and ease of use."

VIRGINIA KEEHAN, ASSISTANT DEAN AND DIRECTOR OF ADMISSIONS
PO BOX 750110, DALLAS, TX 75275-0110
TEL: 214-768-2550 FAX: 214-768-2549
E-MAIL: LAWADMIT@MAIL.SMU.EDU • INTERNET: WWW.LAW.SMU.EDU

Life

"Most of the students are Texas natives," and "Overall, the people are young, fun, attractive, and smart." Some students are "cooperative, collegial, and very supportive of one another." Others are "very competitive." "There are a lot of married students, though not necessarily a lot older." SMU has its fair share of "obnoxious frat boys and catty, cliquey sorority girls." "There are definitely a few trust fund kids, but a lot of us are living off student loans as well," says one student. "The parking garage does boast an unusual concentration of BMWs and Hummers," agrees a 2L. "But as a non-Texan who shares a beat-up Honda with my wife, I've never felt out of place." "Political views run the gamut, but the large majority of students are tolerant of opposing views." SMU is also "remarkably GLBT-friendly."

Regarding social events on campus, students say "There's a club for everyone, whether you're a gun-toting Second Amendment crusader or a die-hard liberal." "The students put together a lot of fun activities," ranging from happy hours to baseball games to tailgating events. "The highlight of everyone's week is Bar Review where the Student Bar Association gets drink specials at a different local bar every Friday." There's also "a picnic/sports spectacular every semester." SMU's ritzy location is "great" in terms of safety but "can make finding student housing right next to school virtually impossible." Beyond the neighborhood surrounding campus, "Big D" is one of the liveliest cities in the South and "a fun place to live." "You get a great all-around legal education and have the resources of the Dallas-Fort Worth Metroplex right at your doorstep."

Getting In

At SMU, admitted students at the 25th percentile have LSAT scores in the range of about 155 and GPAs in the range of 3.3. Admitted students at the 75th percentile have LSAT scores of about 163 and GPAs approaching 3.8.

ADMISSIONS

Selectivity Rating	60*
# applications received	2,066
# applicants accepted	455
# acceptees attending	180
LSAT Range	158–164
Application fee	$60
Regular application	2/15
Regular notification	4/30
Rolling notification	Yes
Early application program	Yes
Early application deadline	12/1
Early application notification	1/31
Transfer students accepted	Yes
Evening division offered	Yes
Part-time accepted	Yes
LSDAS accepted	Yes

Applicants Also Look At
Baylor University, University of Houston, The University of Texas at Austin.

International Students

TOEFL required of international students	No
TOEFL recommended of international students	No

FINANCIAL FACTS

Annual tuition	$31,096
Books and supplies	$1,800
Fees per credit	$135
Tuition per credit	$1,140
Room and board (on/off-campus)	$6,000/$8,500
Financial aid application deadline	6/1
% of aid that is merit based	100
Average grant	$15,000
Average loan	$22,550

EMPLOYMENT INFORMATION

		Grads Employed by Field (%)	
Career Rating	83		
Rate of placement (nine months out)	97	Academic	2
Average starting salary	$87,700	Business/Industry	16
State for bar exam	TX	Government	6
Pass rate for first-time bar	90	Judicial clerkships	5
Employers Who Frequently Hire Grads		Military	1
Akin, Gump, Strauss, Hauer, and Feld;		Private practice	69
Baker Botts; Fulbright and Jaworski;		Public Interest	1
Haynes and Boone; Jones, Day, Reavis, and Pogue.			

Prominent Alumni
Michael Boone, founding partner, Haynes and Boone; Bill Hutchison, president, Hutchison Oil and Gas; Harriet Miers, former White House Counsel; Edward B. Rust Jr., chairman and CEO, State Farm Insurance.

SOUTHERN UNIVERSITY
LAW CENTER

Academics

"Historically Black" Southern University Law Center is an excellent and very affordable bastion of legal education in Baton Rouge—Louisiana's capital city and one of the fastest-growing cities in the South. The faculty is notoriously approachable. "Most professors are available, by phone, e-mail, or conference, from 7:00 A.M. to 9:00 P.M.," claims one satisfied student. "They are willing to meet with study groups, on or off campus, after class, or on the weekends." "Our faculty and staff are always accessible and willing to help," agrees a 2L, "so much so that this attitude filters down to the students. I remember being so overwhelmed by the hospitality of the students my first year that I began to get paranoid. But I soon learned not to worry." Professors also "have a great deal of practical knowledge to share."

As far as complaints, the administration generally receives lukewarm reviews. Basically, the front office has "a communication problem." "I never feel fully informed as a student," gripes a 3L. Some students are "worried about getting a job and making money." "The law school in general could help to create more opportunities for students to have a job upon graduation," says a 3L. The percentage of students employed six months after graduation is approximately 83 percent (with another 5 percent pursuing LLM degrees). A network of very loyal alumni is often a big help to students looking for their first gigs as real lawyers.

While a few students also suggest that Southern "could improve the diversity of the curriculum," most students feel that the course offerings are reasonably broad. There are full-time, part-time, and evening programs. Internships and externships abound. There are six different clinics. "Our law school's clinical program is a great asset and one which cannot be found at all law schools," boasts one student. "The clinical program provides hands-on experience with the realities of practicing law. It teaches what no textbook or case can teach and is an exceptional learning tool." For students who want to pursue the JD and MPA, the school offers a joint-degree program in cooperation with the Nelson Mandela School of Public Policy and Urban Affairs. There's also a study-abroad program in London, in which students take courses in International Criminal Law and Conflict of Laws. SULC also publishes two legal journals: its traditional Law Review as well as The Public Defender. SULC's students also get to experience the pleasure (and pain) of learning two different systems of law: Louisiana is a civil law jurisdiction (in the tradition of France and Continental Europe), while law in every other state is based on the common law tradition (of England). SU students learn both.

The Law Center itself is a nice place to spend a few years. The library is solid. Classrooms "offer cutting-edge technology and spacious seating designed so that every student has access to the professor and class discussion." "The entire Law Center is wireless, including the patio area." "Wireless printing" is another swell perk. However, "There are not enough outlets in the classrooms to accommodate wireless laptops for every student."

VELMA E. WILKERSON, COORDINATOR OF ADMISSION
A.A. LENOIR HALL, PO BOX 9294, TWO ROOSEVELT STEPTOE STREET, BATON ROUGE, LA 70813
TEL: 225-771-4976 FAX: 225-771-2121
E-MAIL: ADMISSION@SULC.EDU • INTERNET: WWW.SULC.EDU

Life

"The student population is very close-knit" at Southern, which allows you "to draw on the strengths of other students in areas" in which you "may be weak." "You like some people," of course, and "You can't tolerate others." In this sense, SU is "just like a grown-up high school." Overall, though, "There is a great sense of unity, primarily among 1Ls," despite the small contingent of "super-competitors and neurotic memorizers" that you'll find at pretty much any law school.

Southern is a unique law school in that it provides "a valuable education for many nontraditional students who otherwise would not have been given a chance to succeed in law school." The student population is nicely diverse, certainly the most diverse in Louisiana. The minority population at SULC is about 70 percent. Over 60 percent of the students are African American. "I think I attend the only law school in the nation where there is such a mixture of culture," explains a 2L. "Black students like myself constitute the majority" and, of course, "The state of Louisiana itself seems to be in another country." "Racial tension" between students from different ethnic groups is not a problem, though occasionally "There is definitely 'something' there."

Beyond the "friendly" confines of the Law Center, Baton Rouge is a student's Shangri-la, especially if you like music and food. Baton Rouge is home to unique art and culture, tons of festivals, and mouthwatering cuisine of every kind. When students take a break from hitting the books, a good number of bars and clubs and a raging live music scene keep life interesting.

Getting In

Southern University Law Center is a relatively small law school. About one-third of all applicants gain admission. Admitted students at the 25th percentile have an LSAT score of 142 and undergraduate GPA of 2.5. Admitted students at the 75th percentile have an LSAT score of 148 and an undergraduate GPA of 3.0.

ADMISSIONS

Selectivity Rating	**66**
# applications received	994
# applicants accepted	312
# acceptees attending	180
Average LSAT	147
LSAT Range	144–151
Average undergrad GPA	2.84
Application fee	$25
Regular application	2/28
Regular notification	Rolling
Rolling notification	Yes
Early application program	Yes
Early application deadline	2/28 of junior year
Early application notification	6/1
Transfer students accepted	Yes
Evening division offered	Yes
Part-time accepted	Yes
LSDAS accepted	Yes

Applicants Also Look At
Louisiana State University, Loyola University—New Orleans, Texas Southern University, Thomas M. Cooley Law School.

International Students

TOEFL required of international students	No
TOEFL recommended of international students	Yes

FINANCIAL FACTS

Annual tuition (resident)	$6,676
Annual tuition (nonresident)	$11,276
Books and supplies	$5,581
Tuition per credit (resident)	$5,494
Tuition per credit (nonresident)	$10,094
Room and board	$8,727
Financial aid application deadline	4/15
% first-year students receiving some sort of aid	86
% of aid that is merit based	20
% receiving scholarships	20
Average grant	$7,000
Average total aid package	$18,500

EMPLOYMENT INFORMATION

Career Rating		60*	Grads Employed by Field (%)	
State for bar exam	LA, FL, GA, IL, TX		Academic	1
Pass rate for first-time bar		61	Business/Industry	5
			Government	15
			Judicial clerkships	6
			Other	29
			Private practice	37
			Public Interest	7

Southwestern University

School of Law

INSTITUTIONAL INFORMATION

Public/private	Private
Student-faculty ratio	16:1
% faculty part-time	35
% faculty female	31
% faculty minority	15
Total faculty	100

SURVEY SAYS...

Diverse opinions accepted
in classrooms
Great research resources
Great library staff
Beautiful campus

STUDENTS

Enrollment of law school	931
% male/female	47/53
% out-of-state	15
% full-time	71
% minority	34
% international	2
# of countries represented	10
Average age of entering class	26

ACADEMICS

Academic Experience Rating	**81**
Profs interesting rating	80
Profs accessible rating	82
Hours of study per day	3.88

Academic Specialties

Civil procedure, commercial law, constitutional law, corporation securities law, criminal law, entertainment and media law, environmental law, government services, human rights law, intellectual property law, international law, labor law, legal history, legal philosophy, property, taxation.

Advanced Degrees Offered

LLM (entertainment and media law) 1 to 2 years.

Clinical program required	No
Legal writing course requirement	Yes
Legal methods course requirement	Yes

Academics

A "hidden gem" located in Los Angeles within easy commuting distance to the downtown district, Hollywood, and the Valley, Southwestern Law School is known for its flexibility and progressiveness. In addition to the traditional day and evening programs, the school offers a unique SCALE program, which gives students the ability to obtain a JD within two years, and the PLEAS program, a part-time day program that helps nontraditional students juggle the demands of work, family, and school, making for "an awesome way to get a great education and have a life too." The school recently saw a rise in the average GPA of entering students, which reflects its increasingly competitive applicant pool. With the increased local recognition comes "a better chance at competing for jobs with other local law schools," which students here appreciate.

SW's "eclectic" professors "don't just give lip service to an open-door policy, they encourage it," and they "seem to genuinely enjoy interaction with students." With many professors still practicing law, there's an "emphasis on real-world experience" inside the classroom. As one student explains, "The feelings of most SW students go from being completely overwhelmed upon entry (that's probably the same for all 1Ls), to feeling slightly inferior to other law schools in the area, then to the realization that you will have all the tools necessary to be a successful attorney when you leave and that earning a JD at SW is actually a fun and rewarding experience." Professor accessibility is "fantastic," as one appreciative student can attest: "One professor has gone out of his way to get me three internships in an area of law that is tough to get into." Though the school's program in entertainment law receives rave reviews, many think it would be great "if a wider array of courses were taught—especially in the business area."

The newly acquired Bullocks Wilshire building is "particularly gorgeous," "enormous," and situated on a "very clean and comfortable campus." Students cite Southwestern's "beautiful" library as one of the school's greatest strengths, and the research librarians are "very helpful. After just two years in office, the well-received new dean "is leading the school in all the right directions." The "administration has really come alive and is totally committed to helping students to make the best of their experience at Southwestern." The externship program at Southwestern is lauded by students, even if they tend to feel that their hard work is "underappreciated in the job force"; many here often feel that they live in the shadow of other local area law schools. Students also bemoan a lack of "alumni support" and help from the Career Services Office. "After my first year, I had an internship with a bunch of students from USC and UCLA and I was able to rattle all kinds of law off the top of my head while they all had to look it up. But I'm sure they all got a job and I couldn't," complains one critic. On the whole, though, students are satisfied with what they take away from their Southwestern experience. "Southwestern may not be perfect now, but it's definitely moving in an upward direction," says a third-year student. "It's a great time to be at Southwestern."

ANNE WILSON, DIRECTOR OF ADMISSIONS
675 SOUTH WESTMORELAND AVENUE, LOS ANGELES, CA 90005
TEL: 213-738-6717 FAX: 213-383-1688
E-MAIL: ADMISSIONS@SWLAW.EDU • INTERNET: WWW.SWLAW.EDU

Life

Because SW is a stand-alone law school, it "definitely has a small-school feel and a good sense of community." Students say this is an admirable trait for a school located in such a large and spread-out city, and they appreciate "the way the main promenade is open to the local community," which "helps to integrate the school within the surrounding neighborhoods." The school itself offers a wide variety of organizations and events for students to take part in, and many of these activities garner enthusiastic participation from students; why wouldn't they, when "Everyone gets along with everyone else." One first-year student says, "The environment is light hearted when it calls for it, and serious when it calls for it." While there is a "competitive edge" to students, for the most part "Everyone is very friendly and supportive of each other." "To my surprise, I have made so many new friends. Being from LA, I wouldn't have thought that I'd be interested in making new friends, because I already have a social network, but the people [at Southwestern] are great," says a 1L.

Getting In

Recently admitted students at the 25th percentile had an average LSAT score of 153 and GPA of 3.1. Students admitted at the 75th percentile had an average LSAT score of 158 and GPA of 3.6. Though undergrad GPA and LSAT scores count, Southwestern pays more attention to undergraduate activities and work experience than a lot of other institutions. The school looks at the difficulty level of the student's undergraduate course of study, as well as extracurricular activities and leadership examples. Up to three letters of recommendation may be submitted by the student; we recommend utilizing all of these.

Legal research	
course requirement	Yes
Moot court requirement	Yes
Public interest	
law requirement	No

ADMISSIONS

Selectivity Rating	**81**
# applications received	3,332
# applicants accepted	857
# acceptees attending	248
Average LSAT	156
LSAT Range	153–158
Average undergrad GPA	3.4
Application fee	$50
Regular application	6/30
Regular notification	Rolling
Rolling notification	Yes
Early application program	No
Transfer students accepted	Yes
Evening division offered	Yes
Part-time accepted	Yes
LSDAS accepted	Yes

Applicants Also Look At

Loyola Marymount University, Pepperdine University, University of California—Hastings, University of California—Los Angeles, University of San Diego, University of Southern California.

International Students

TOEFL required	
of international students	No
TOEFL recommended	
of international students	No

FINANCIAL FACTS

Annual tuition	$29,850
Books and supplies	$1,200
Tuition per credit	$995
Room and board	
(off-campus)	$15,600
Financial aid application	
deadline	6/1

EMPLOYMENT INFORMATION

		Grads Employed by Field (%)	
Career Rating	**78**		
Rate of placement (nine months out)	87	Academic	1
Average starting salary	$82,500	Business/Industry	21
State for bar exam	CA, NY, NV, WA, AZ	Government	6
Pass rate for first-time bar	69	Judicial clerkships	1
Employers Who Frequently Hire Grads		Other	15
Gibson, Dunn and Crutcher; Lewis, Brisbois,		Private practice	51
Bisgaard, and Smith; O'Melveny and		Public Interest	4
Meyers; Sedgwick, Detert, Moran and			
Arnold.			

Prominent Alumni

Tom Bradley, LA Mayor; Honorable Stanley Mosk, longest-serving California Supreme Court justice; Honorable Vaino Spencer, 1st African American woman judge in California and 3rd in the U.S.

St. John's University
School of Law

INSTITUTIONAL INFORMATION

Public/private	Private
Affiliation	Roman Catholic
Student-faculty ratio	16:1

SURVEY SAYS...

Heavy use of Socratic method
Great research resources
Great library staff
Abundant externship/internship/
clerkship opportunities

STUDENTS

Enrollment of law school	307
% male/female	52/48
% full-time	70
% faculty minority	22
Average age of entering class	23

ACADEMICS

Academic Experience Rating	**65**
Profs interesting rating	62
Profs accessible rating	61
Hours of study per day	4.07

Advanced Degrees Offered

JD 3 to 4 years, LLM bankruptcy, 1 to 3 years.

Combined Degrees Offered

JD/MBA, JD/MA(MS), BA(BS)/JD.

Clinical program required	No
Legal writing course requirement	Yes
Legal methods course requirement	Yes
Legal research course requirement	Yes
Moot court requirement	Yes
Public interest law requirement	No

Academics

Located in Jamaica, Queens, St. John's University is a fine place to get a strong, traditional legal education while benefiting from the many practical and professional opportunities available in the New York metropolitan area. With an emphasis on legal theory and the fundamentals of law, students say that "St. John's is old-fashioned, but in good ways." For example, "Professors' continued reliance on the Socratic Method is challenging, to be sure, but also stimulating and a great incentive to always read carefully!" The faculty makes up some of the country's top legal scholars, many of whom have published extensively or still hold prestigious positions as practicing attorneys or judges. In addition to their backgrounds, there is a lot of diversity within the teaching staff and many are "still very much involved in their fields and are very well known." What's more, students feel they have ample opportunity to learn from these great minds, as the school does not experience the scheduling hassles and class wait lists common to other law schools. Case in point: A part-time student tells us, "I am an evening student and they take care of us by having all professors rotate to the evening. We don't get gypped by going at night." While students mainly applaud the school's academic program, some feel that St. John's could benefit from "more classes about research and writing, which is the most important skill a lawyer can have."

Even so, there is no lack of practical opportunities at St. John's. Its hometown is a goldmine for the motivated student, and the school operates a number of applied learning programs, such as the domestic violence litigation clinic, elder law clinic, and immigration rights clinic. In addition, St. John's operates criminal, judicial, and civil law externships.

On campus, "The law school facilities are excellent, . . . clean, convenient, and efficiently designed." The building is "immaculate" and "features wireless Internet throughout, a great library, and plenty of room for students to study and socialize. In that vein, students report that "the library is generally a nice, quiet place to study, and the research librarians are very helpful."

If you are planning to practice in New York City, St. John's is an excellent place to do it, as the school has a strong regional reputation and extensive contacts in the legal community. In particular, St. John's alumni are a fantastic resource to students, as they are "extremely loyal and enthusiastic about giving St. John's students and alums opportunities in a cross-section of legal specialties." "The alumni are by far the greatest strength," reports one student. "Many are professors, full-time and adjunct, and all are perpetually upbeat, helpful with any academic concerns and pursuits." Not only do they teach at the school, many alumni "go above and beyond the call in trying to match students up with challenging and exciting employment opportunities."

ROBERT M. HARRISON, ASSISTANT DEAN FOR ADMISSIONS
8000 UTOPIA PARKWAY, QUEENS, NY 11439
TEL: 718-990-6474 FAX: 718-990-2526
E-MAIL: LAWINFO@STJOHNS.EDU • INTERNET: WWW.LAW.STJOHNS.EDU

Life

Like its hometown, "The law school is diverse," both ethnically and culturally. While they hail from a variety of backgrounds, St. John's students are generally friendly. In fact, many report that "the greatest strength of the law school is by far the close sense of community." "St. John's students tend to see each other as teammates rather than adversaries," writes a 1L. "One good example of the kind of atmosphere here was the Tsunami Relief Poker Tournament. The students and faculty raised more than $4,000 in one night through this poker tournament, and all proceeds went to tsunami victims."

While St. John's is well-located for jobs and externships, many students disparage the neighborhood surrounding the campus. One student cracks, "Located in the heart of Jamaica, Queens, there is a chance that your car will not be where you parked it when you return from class." If you want to leave your ride at home, think again; students complain that getting to Jamaica is "a hassle if you commute by public transportation." On top of that, Jamaica isn't exactly law school–friendly: "There is only one bar worth going to after class and only on school-sponsored nights," gripes a 3L. It should come as no surprise, then, that few students attend St. John's for the campus life. In fact, "Almost everyone is a commuter student, so the building clears out after classes end."

Getting In

St. John's University receives more than 4,000 applications annually for about 300 first-year spots. In addition to LSAT scores and undergraduate GPA, which are heavily weighted, St. John's considers factors that could be beneficial to the study of law and to the school community, such as graduate work, extracurricular activities, community service, work experience, or personal obstacles students may have overcome before or during their undergraduate studies.

ADMISSIONS

Selectivity Rating	**83**
# applications received	3,642
# applicants accepted	1,274
# acceptees attending	307
Average LSAT	160
LSAT Range	157–162
Average undergrad GPA	3.53
Application fee	$60
Regular application	4/1
Regular notification	Rolling
Rolling notification	Yes
Early application program	No
Transfer students accepted	Yes
Evening division offered	Yes
Part-time accepted	Yes
LSDAS accepted	Yes

International Students

TOEFL required of international students	No
TOEFL recommended of international students	Yes
Minimum paper TOEFL	600
Minimum computer TOEFL	250

FINANCIAL FACTS

Annual tuition	$32,700
Books and supplies	$1,000
Tuition per credit	$1,100
Room and board	$8,750
Average grant	$16,443
Average loan	$30,916
Average total aid package	$37,787
Average debt	$85,958

EMPLOYMENT INFORMATION

Career Rating	**89**	**Grads Employed by Field (%)**	
Rate of placement (nine months out)	97	Academic	3
Average starting salary		Business/Industry	21
State for bar exam	NY	Government	19
Pass rate for first-time bar	91	Judicial clerkships	4
Employers Who Frequently Hire Grads		Private practice	51
Many private law firms; corporations; governmental agencies; etc.		Public Interest	2

ST. MARY'S UNIVERSITY
SCHOOL OF LAW

INSTITUTIONAL INFORMATION

Public/private	Private
Affiliation	Roman Catholic
Student-faculty ratio	22:1
% faculty part-time	49
% faculty female	34
% faculty minority	17
Total faculty	77

SURVEY SAYS...

Diverse opinions accepted
in classrooms
Great research resources
Great library staff

STUDENTS

Enrollment of law school	742
% male/female	57/43
% out-of-state	11
% full-time	100
% minority	30
% international	1
# of countries represented	1
Average age of entering class	24

ACADEMICS

Academic Experience Rating	**73**
Profs interesting rating	73
Profs accessible rating	86
Hours of study per day	5.1

Academic Specialties

Advocacy, constitutional law, criminal law, human rights law, international law.

Advanced Degrees Offered

LLM (international and comparative law for U.S.-educated graduates), LLM (American legal studies for foreign-educated graduates).

Combined Degrees Offered

JD/MAcc 3.5 to 4 years, JD/MA 3.5 to 4 years, JD/MPA 3.5 to 4 years, JD/MA 3.5 to 4 years, JD/MA 3.5 to 4 years, JD/MS 3.5 to 4 years, JD/MS 3.5 to 4 years, JD/MBA 3.5 to 4 years, JD/MA 3.5 to 4 years.

Clinical program required	No
Legal writing course requirement	Yes

Academics

"Unfortunately, heart is not a criterion by which law schools are judged. If it were, St. Mary's would be at the top of the list," writes a 3L. Although the bar-passage rate at St. Mary's (80 percent for first-time test-takers) is on par with that of other schools in the Southwest region, many students express concern over what they perceive to be a particularly "low bar-passage rate," worrying that "the negative emphasis on the school's low bar-passage rate will become a self-fulfilling prophecy." Many, however, feel confident that the current administration has "taken the necessary steps to get the passage rate back up to where it was very soon." They put their trust in Dean Bill Piatt, who frequents student lounges and "seems more like a friend than a superior." A 1L praises, "Expect to see great things from this school as long as he's around." A practical bent characterizes the legal education at St. Mary's, an institution "with a strong dedication to creating practicing attorneys." Students would rather not take "useless survey classes," preferring instead course work that focuses on bar preparation and other practical skills. Indeed, St. Mary's already offers students ways to gain real-world experience. An emphasis on "clinical programs," "clerkships, internships, and writing and research" produces graduates ready for the working world, although a 3L cautions that "few obtain summer clerkship positions after their second year." Students see the importance of the legal writing requirement; they just wish they weren't "rushed through the material." They also ask for "a wider range of elective courses for students who may not intend to practice law in the traditional sense." Second-year students spend significant time in mock trial and moot court; this program "helps first-years realize there is something to strive for besides two more years of boring repetition."

"The faculty are extremely dedicated to providing the best education possible for their students. However, because the school does not have the resources or the reputation to attract the most sought-after professors, the quality of education is not comparable [with] that of most other upper-tier Texas schools." Nonetheless, students characterize their professors as "very accessible, helpful, and absolutely excellent." Instructors also earn praise for their effective teaching techniques. A 2L comments dryly, "They understand that the Socratic Method was a great teaching tool . . . in 300 B.C." To jazz things up, one torts professor "handcuffed two students together to demonstrate false imprisonment," and others "play short movie clips and project photos to accompany cases." These antics succeed in "pulling students easily into debate over the subject matter." A few instructors come from "strictly academic backgrounds with little experience in the practice of law," but most are "outstanding lecturers, prolific legal writers, and incredible achievers in their fields," according to a 3L. No matter how engaging the class, it's the GPA that matters, and the only topic as contentious as bar passage at St. Mary's is grades: "The mandatory curve is the devil and needs to go!" At minimum, students would like to see the curve raised slightly—"so that grades more accurately reflect achievement"—or even abandoned after the first year. "Among 1Ls, we all know that because of the forced curve, 20 percent of us will not be here next year." Many students take advantage of "the awesome tutoring program in place to help 1Ls" survive the difficult first year.

In terms of facilities and technology, "St. Mary's is like being stuck in the original *Star Trek* when all the other schools have upgraded to the *Next Generation*." Students sometimes come crashing to the ground during lecture because of sub-par classroom seating. In contrast, "The library facilities are expansive and modern, and for the few of us who use them every day, the staff knows us by name." Students find "comfortable places to study, as well as small meeting rooms, so you can get together with friends to review tough cases." The functional wireless network allows students to "sit outside in the sun working on [their] computers and then send something to the printer from the courtyard." "St. Mary's is San Antonio's law school, and the local bar association may as well be a second alumni association." The active student bar association cultivates strong ties with alumni, "allowing students to network with potential employers throughout law school." These connections compensate for a less-than-effective Career Services Office: "Options and opportunities seem to be clandestine topics with our career advisors," writes a 3L. Students note that many local positions require bilingual proficiency, an advantage for the school's many Spanish-speaking students.

Life

The student population shows diversity, "not just ethnically, but also in age and previous occupation." Students are split into four sections upon arrival, and they tend to "become very close with those in [their] groups," sometimes not even learning "who else is in the class until the end of the first year." A 2L describes the school as having an "air of collegiality and a growing community that trades textbooks and gives notes to each other." The overall "lackadaisical, mañana-style attitude" keeps stress levels low on the law school scale. The only time that the "great camaraderie and support among classmates" cracks seems to be during intramural athletic competition. Students find easy "access to both the social events and student organizations." In increasing numbers, students are joining the law journal, which "ranked the fourth most-cited among federal and state cases this past year." Although St. Mary's is a Catholic institution, students report that they "never feel pressure to alter [their] religious beliefs." Indeed, the school's religious affiliation doesn't seem to have as great an impact on social life as does the workload. While some students manage to find time "to go out three nights a week," many—especially first-years—find that "social life is relative to the amount of free time a 1L has: none."

Getting In

Falling well below the mean LSAT score (154) or GPA (3.15) doesn't necessarily result in rejection at St. Mary's. The committee carefully considers intangibles, such as maturity derived from previous career experience, the ability to overcome challenges, and cultural competence. They are looking for rigorous undergraduate course work and an inclination toward public service. It is best to get applications in soon after the Admissions Office starts accepting them in November.

Legal methods course requirement	Yes
Legal research course requirement	Yes
Moot court requirement	Yes
Public interest law requirement	No

ADMISSIONS

Selectivity Rating	72
# applications received	1,902
# applicants accepted	764
# acceptees attending	257
Average LSAT	154
LSAT Range	149–163
Average undergrad GPA	3.11
Application fee	$55
Regular application	3/1
Regular notification	5/1
Rolling notification	Yes
Early application program	No
Transfer students accepted	Yes
Evening division offered	Yes
Part-time accepted	Yes
LSDAS accepted	Yes

Applicants Also Look At
Baylor University, Southern Methodist University, Texas A&M University System Health Science Center, Texas Tech University, Texas Wesleyan University, The University of Texas at Austin, University of Houston.

International Students

TOEFL required of international students	No
TOEFL recommended of international students	Yes

FINANCIAL FACTS

Annual tuition	$22,258
Books and supplies	$1,300
Tuition per credit	$718
Room and board (on/off-campus)	$7,420/$7,230
Financial aid application deadline	3/31
% first-year students receiving some sort of aid	85
% receiving some sort of aid	85
% of aid that is merit based	6
% receiving scholarships	28
Average grant	$4,270
Average loan	$29,303
Average total aid package	$32,047
Average debt	$91,841

EMPLOYMENT INFORMATION

Career Rating	**73**	
Rate of placement (nine months out)	90	
Average starting salary	$65,431	
State for bar exam	TX, FL, MO, OK, NM	
Pass rate for first-time bar	80	

Employers Who Frequently Hire Grads
Bexar County District Attorney's Office; Fourth Court of Appeals; Cox Smith Matthew LLP; Texas Office of the Attorney General.

Prominent Alumni
John Cornyn, U.S. Senator; Charles Gonzalez, U.S. Congressman; Chief Justice Alma L. Lopez, Texas Court of Appeals.

Grads Employed by Field (%)

Academic	2
Business/Industry	16
Government	12
Judicial clerkships	5
Military	2
Other	4
Private practice	57
Public Interest	2

ST. THOMAS UNIVERSITY
SCHOOL OF LAW

Academics

Relatively small, relatively new, and markedly Catholic, St. Thomas University School of Law offers "small class sizes" and a consistent emphasis on ethics. "The practical experience is really good here." "A wide range" of opportunities to gain lawyering skills includes "very good" clinical programs for criminal and immigration law. "There are plenty of externship opportunities in both Miami-Dade and Broward counties" as well. A 40-hour pro-bono work requirement "provides a wide array of opportunities" to work in a variety of nonprofit offices, government agencies, and law firms. The tax law program is well respected. Joint-degree programs are available in—among other things—sports administration and accounting. There's a "cool Summer in Spain program" too. Without question, the biggest academic complaint among students here involves the bar-passage rate, which annually hovers below the state average.

"At St. Thomas, the professors make you work hard, and most students coming out of the school have a good work ethic as a result," says one student. The "extremely dynamic" faculty includes "many judges and prominent lawyers" from the area. Professors are "easily accessible" and "willing to spend as many hours on a subject that the student is willing to invest." "Their willingness to help students pass the bar and become successful, ethical attorneys is at its maximum," beams a 2L. Professors are "very experienced and very involved in the local community." There are some bad apples, though, who "shouldn't teach at a high school." "I had some professors who I felt were the best I'd ever had and others who didn't teach me anything," relates a 3L.

Student reviews of their administrators are decidedly mixed. Some students call the administration "helpful and caring" and tell us that the top brass is "genuinely striving to improve the overall experience at the school." Others counter that the administration is "unresponsive to students' issues" and "the pinnacle of bureaucratic inefficiency." "I have yet to see a final-exam day where the campus isn't pure pandemonium," says one student. "It seems, in all fairness, that many of the problems are associated with the parent university," notes a 1L. Nevertheless, Financial Aid is generally regarded as a mess and "Registering for classes is a disaster."

The facilities at St. Thomas are "nice, especially compared to other law schools around the Miami area." "Study areas abound" on the "very nice and open" campus, though students caution that it's "not in the best neighborhood." "Classrooms are great because of the wireless Internet. However, the air conditioning works too well. The classrooms are like igloos." Research resources are "quite extensive for such a small school, and there is an abundance of access to online resources through the library website." The library itself isn't much, though. "We need a bigger library," says a 2L.

Life

The student population "reflects the multicultural canvas of contemporary American society." "The international distinction of Miami as a gateway to all of the Americas results in professors and students that embody true diversity." "People from every part of the country" and all manner of every religions and ethnicities are studying law here. Politically, students describe a very good mix of liberals, conservatives, and everyone in between. There is a huge population of Hispanic students, and "a lot" of foreign students as well. Students are mostly single. "Miami is a great area to go to law school if you're straight out of undergrad, but it is not the most fun if you're over 25, have kids, or are

FAREZA KHAN, DIRECTOR OF ADMISSIONS
16401 NORTHWEST 37TH AVENUE, MIAMI GARDENS, FL 33054
TEL: 305-623-2310 FAX: 305-623-2357
E-MAIL: ADMITME@STU.EDU • INTERNET: WWW.STU.EDU

married." Most students "are focused on making it through school, enjoying Miami while they're here, and then going back to wherever they're from to settle down."

"The breezeway of the law school is the social hub" at STU—"a year-round outdoor gathering place that engenders social interaction on the way to and from classes." From early morning until late at night, people can be found sitting at the tables surrounded by their books and laptops or with their study groups, or sometimes just chatting with whoever happens to walk by. The Student Bar Association "sponsors many happy hours and picnics that a majority of students attend." Of course, "Miami is Miami." There is "great weather for most of the year" and finding something to do instead of reading case law is way too easy. Many students take "full advantage of South Beach on a nightly basis yet, surprisingly, still [find] time to study."

The social atmosphere at St. Thomas is "highly supportive." "Students are very friendly and cooperative with each other." "There is little or no cutthroat competitiveness." "Students get to know each other really quickly and are there right away to help each other out." While "Everybody knows everyone else," "There are a lot of cliques," but "You are able to develop great friendships while you study." "You learn; you compete; but you make friends," sums up a 3L. "At the end of the road, having some kind of social life, being able to make friends, and being happy overall is even more important than a law degree."

Getting In

At St. Thomas, admitted students at the 25th percentile have LSAT scores in the range of 148 and GPAs of about 2.6. Admitted students at the 75th percentile have LSAT scores of about 152 and GPAs of about 3.3. If you take the LSAT more than once, St. Thomas will average your scores.

Legal methods course requirement	Yes
Legal research course requirement	Yes
Moot court requirement	Yes
Public interest law requirement	Yes

ADMISSIONS

Selectivity Rating	**64**
# applications received	2,861
# applicants accepted	1,166
# acceptees attending	235
Average LSAT	150
LSAT Range	147–152
Average undergrad GPA	3
Application fee	$45
Regular application	5/1
Regular notification	Rolling
Rolling notification	Yes
Early application program	No
Transfer students accepted	Yes
Evening division offered	No
Part-time accepted	No
LSDAS accepted	Yes

Applicants Also Look At
Barry University, Florida Coastal School of Law, Florida International University, Nova Southeastern University, University of Miami.

International Students

TOEFL required of international students	No
TOEFL recommended of international students	Yes
Minimum paper TOEFL	550

FINANCIAL FACTS

Annual tuition	$25,340
Books and supplies	$1,000
Room and board (on/off-campus)	$10,341/$10,575
Financial aid application deadline	5/1
% first-year students receiving some sort of aid	95
% receiving some sort of aid	98
% of aid that is merit based	15
% receiving scholarships	39
Average grant	$11,000
Average loan	$25,500
Average total aid package	$29,660
Average debt	$82,000

EMPLOYMENT INFORMATION

Career Rating	63	Grads Employed by Field (%)	
Rate of placement (nine months out)	74	Business/Industry	16
Average starting salary	$60,000	Government	11
State for bar exam	FL, NY, GA	Judicial clerkships	1
Pass rate for first-time bar	63	Private practice	39
Employers Who Frequently Hire Grads		Public Interest	5

Employers Who Frequently Hire Grads
Private law firms of all sizes; government agencies, including the U.S. Department of Justice, the Florida State Attorney's Office, prosecutors' and public defenders' offices.

Prominent Alumni
Brett Barfield, partner, Holland and Knight; Mark Romance, partner, Richman Greer; Representative J.C. Planas, Florida House of Representatives.

STANFORD UNIVERSITY
SCHOOL OF LAW

INSTITUTIONAL INFORMATION

Public/private	Private
Student-faculty ratio	8.6:1
% faculty female	27
% faculty minority	19
Total faculty	48

SURVEY SAYS...

Great research resources
Great library staff
Abundant externship/internship/
clerkship opportunities

STUDENTS

Enrollment of law school	534
% male/female	57/43
% full-time	100
% minority	32
Average age of entering class	24

ACADEMICS

Academic Experience Rating	99
Profs interesting rating	98
Profs accessible rating	97
Hours of study per day	4.22

Academic Specialties

Civil procedure, commercial law, constitutional law, corporation securities law, criminal law, environmental law, government services, human rights law, intellectual property law, international law, labor law, legal history, legal philosophy, property, taxation.

Advanced Degrees Offered

MLS 1 year, JSM 1 year, LLM 1 year, JSD 4 years.

Combined Degrees Offered

JD/MBA 4 years, JD/MA 4 years, JD/PhD 7 years.

Clinical program required	No
Legal writing course requirement	Yes
Legal methods course requirement	No
Legal research course requirement	Yes
Moot court requirement	No

Academics

Students are emphatic that Stanford Law School "delivers on its claim of being a law school in paradise." "The facilities are top-notch" (even if they do look a bit "like corrugated cardboard"). Classrooms are "posh." The "newly redone" library is "luxurious." "You could sit in the chairs all day and, in fact, some people do." "The academic experience at SLS is wonderful." For some students, it "could not possibly be better." "Resources are deep, especially because the class is so small." The small class size "leads to countless opportunities to participate" in and out of the classroom. "There is a lot of freedom to chart your own academic course after your first semester." ("It's like a liberal arts college, only it's a law school," submits one student.) SLS has poured tons of resources into its clinical and public interest programs in the past five years. "Stanford now offers many courses geared towards public interest–minded individuals and the Public Interest Center offers much help in job placement." The "fast-expanding" clinical program provides "very practical and very profound pro-bono experience" and allows students to "work closely" and "on a daily basis" with "top lawyers in the country." "Academically, classes are often exceptionally interesting." Students can "learn about securities from a former SEC chair, [or] learn about Supreme Court opinions from the people who argued them."

The "first-rate" faculty is "less intellectually diverse" than some students would like, but there's no doubt that professors are "at the top of their fields." The "highly attentive" and "incredibly accessible" professors at Stanford "truly care about teaching" and are "desperate for student collaboration." "Whether you take them up on it is another thing, but they are there and willing to help," says another 1L. "Some are kind of quirky, but I have yet to meet a professor who isn't completely available to students." Stanford's administration "really cares about each and every one of its students" and the deans seek student input "on virtually everything." The administration often "proceeds at a California pace," though. "Everything always gets done, but not always as quickly as you might like."

"Jobs are very easy to get" for Stanford graduates. "You come here; you get a great job." "Grades are more important in relation to clerkships and public interest fellowships." "You can work really hard and achieve great things" or "You can coast through and have a great time while still getting the job you want upon graduation." Pickings are so sweet that one student told us, "You can fall out of bed and land a job for $145,000 if you want one." Career Services is "very helpful and proactive." There's a focus on jobs in California and large cities on the East Coast (particularly New York City), but "That may simply be because 90 percent of students here want to work in one of those two places, so the Career Services people are just filling demand." While "People who graduate from Stanford don't generally make less than $100,000 dollars a year unless they choose to," "The staff in public interest law is amazingly accessible and helpful" for students who do choose to pursue public interest careers. "SLS also boasts one of the most generous loan repayment programs in the country."

Life

Students at Stanford Law are "remarkably and uniformly intelligent" and "very supportive of one another." They are "intensely hardworking and super-motivated, but they're by no means outwardly competitive." "The place is full of closet studiers, the kind who say, 'Oh, man, I haven't even looked at that,' even though you saw them in the

Lillie V. Wiley-Upshaw, Vice Dean for Admissions and Financial Aid
309 O'Brian Hall, Buffalo, NY 14260
Tel: 716-645-2907 Fax: 716-645-6676
E-mail: law-admissions@buffalo.edu • Internet: www.law.buffalo.edu

library until midnight the night before," reports a 3L. Politically, "All of the people in power at the school are exceptionally liberal," but "It's no problem to be a conservative."

"Stanford is tiny." Social life here "is designed for the 22-to-25 set" and resembles undergraduate social life in many ways. "We sometimes have a fraternity-like culture," observes one student. "It's easy to feel excluded from the social scene" "for someone who's older," or "already has a partner and a life outside of school." "There is some drama and gossip." "It can get a bit incestuous at times," but "People are generally very social and friendly." "Everyone knows everyone else" and the intimate atmosphere "allows everyone the opportunity to do something cool, like run an organization, edit a journal, conduct independent research, or start a club."

"The weather is most definitely a plus." "The campus is gorgeous" and "huge and full of life." There is "hiking, biking, running, golf, and pickup soccer" year-round. "From yoga to horseback riding to bike clubs and ski clubs, athletic activities for low or no cost abound." "Sunny Palo Alto" is "a cultural vacuum" and "a crowded suburban hell" for some students, but "The Bay Area is really amazing" and "There is plenty to do in the surrounding area and in San Francisco." "Gorgeous destinations within a few hours' drive" include Tahoe, Napa, and Half Moon Bay. "Plan on bringing a car or else spending a lot of time bumming rides or waiting for the bus," though, because "You can't walk anywhere."

Getting In

Fewer than 10 percent of all applicants to SLS are admitted. The 25th percentile of admitted students has LSAT scores of 166 and GPAs in the 3.7 range. Admitted students at the 75th percentile have LSAT scores of 171 and GPAs approaching 4.0.

Public interest law requirement	No

ADMISSIONS

Selectivity Rating	99
# applications received	4,567
# applicants accepted	398
# acceptees attending	171
Average LSAT	170
LSAT Range	167–172
Average undergrad GPA	3.83
Application fee	$70
Regular application	2/1
Regular notification	4/30
Rolling notification	Yes
Early application program	No
Transfer students accepted	Yes
Evening division offered	No
Part-time accepted	No
LSDAS accepted	Yes

International Students

TOEFL required of international students	No
TOEFL recommended of international students	No

FINANCIAL FACTS

Annual tuition	$37,440
Books and supplies	$1,590
Room and board (on/off-campus)	$15,550/$18,034
Financial aid application deadline	3/15
% first-year students receiving some sort of aid	80
% receiving some sort of aid	77
% receiving scholarships	41
Average grant	$18,823
Average loan	$35,000
Average debt	$98,840

EMPLOYMENT INFORMATION

Career Rating	60*	Grads Employed by Field (%)	
State for bar exam	CA, NY, MD, NJ	Academic	1
Pass rate for first-time bar	91	Business/Industry	4
Prominent Alumni		Government	1
Justice Sandra Day O'Connor, U.S.		Judicial clerkships	26
Supreme Court; Warren Christopher, for-		Private practice	64
mer Secretary of State; Josh Bolten, White		Public Interest	4
House Chief of Staff; Max Baucus, U.S.			
senator; Jeff Bingaman, U.S. Senator.			

STATE UNIVERSITY OF NEW YORK—UNIVERSITY AT BUFFALO
LAW SCHOOL

Academics

Described by its students as "one of the best educational values going," University at Buffalo Law School offers a high-quality academic program for a low, public-school price tag. More than its affordability, its laid-back, student-centered attitude is what separates Buffalo from other institutions. For example, while other law schools talk about being noncompetitive, SUNY lives up to its claim. In fact, "Students are not ranked, and there is no GPA, which promotes a healthy working environment where students help each other instead of try to beat one another." Unlike most legal programs, which require students to follow an extensive prescribed curriculum, "UB is great because they allow you to pick whatever class you want during your final two years, and you have a lot of opportunities for hands-on experience." In this and many other ways, UB treats law students like the able-minded adults they are, allowing students to take active roles in designing their own educations.

Despite the large measure of autonomy they are afforded, law students do receive a great deal of encouragement and support from the administration and teaching staff, who promote cooperation and participation both in and out of the classroom. "The Socratic Method is used in classes, but not in a threatening way," explains a 1L. "Professors try to make sure everyone is involved in every class discussion, and everyone has a chance to voice their opinion." Professors further distinguish themselves through their casual, down-to-earth attitude; "The professors are top-notch, but still aren't afraid to wear jeans."

While many students appreciate the liberal, relaxed atmosphere at UB, others feel the academic experience could use more structure. One student is "disturbed by the excessive amount of flexibility professors are given in determining the curriculum for first-year classes. In my Constitutional Law class, we spent half the semester on equal protection, while I learned nothing about the full faith and credit clause." Students also feel that UB could do more to promote practical skills and bar preparation. Even so, students who are willing to take the initiative have many opportunities for gaining practical experience through the school's many journals, clinics, mock trial programs, and the "bridge classes" offered over the semester break.

"The Career Services officers give me about two hours a week of their time to help me find the summer job of my dreams," writes one satisfied 1L. Just keep in mind that "the vast majority of UB law graduates work in Buffalo, Rochester, or Syracuse, New York" While the academic program at UB is strong, many feel that the school's national recruitment and reputation is still lagging behind where it should be. A student close to graduating insists that "the school needs to stop catering to the local area . . . and start looking at creating a national name and reputation." On the bright side, UB students aren't nearly as hard-pressed as those from other schools to make six figures at a "big law" job as soon as they graduate, since the average UB student's total law school debt load doesn't even approach the national average of $80,000. On the contrary, "The better students coming out of UB can compete with almost anyone in the country for jobs and clerkships. And we pay a third or a fourth of the tuition that some of our fellow law students are paying."

Life

The students at UB Law School are "a nice mix. Some are bright minds who want to excel, many just want to do well, and others are great drinking partners for the weekend—but practically none [is] the stereotypical page-ripping, social-phobic, arrogant malcontents that you just want to muzzle." For the party crew, law school at UB is surprisingly fulfilling and fun. However, many lament that UB's social activities tend to revolve around drinking, leaving "almost no options for students with young children or singles not into the bar scene." A 2L complains, "People can be very nice and are not competitive, but at the same time there are a fair number of immature people. There are probably more frat types than there are type A's here."

Although there are 18 percent students of color, many say the school community would still benefit from more diversity. "As a minority student, I've encountered barriers that White students wouldn't," writes one. There is however, a working courtroom on the first floor of O'Brian Hall. Set in the suburbs, "The law school would be better suited downtown, in proximity to the courts, government offices, and many law firms." On the plus side, "The suburb of Amherst supports a higher standard of living and is a comfortable place to live and study."

Getting In

UB enrolls about 250 new students each year, evaluating applicants based on both qualitative and quantitative factors. In particular, the Admissions Committee seeks students whose academic backgrounds suggest a high probability for scholastic achievement in law school, who have demonstrated excellence in work or community activities, or who display potential for substantial contribution to the law after graduation.

Legal methods course requirement	No
Legal research course requirement	Yes
Moot court requirement	No
Public interest law requirement	No

ADMISSIONS

Selectivity Rating	**77**
# applications received	1,544
# applicants accepted	560
# acceptees attending	247
Average LSAT	155
LSAT Range	152–158
Average undergrad GPA	3.44
Application fee	$50
Regular application	3/15
Regular notification	Rolling
Rolling notification	Yes
Early application program	No
Transfer students accepted	Yes
Evening division offered	No
Part-time accepted	No
LSDAS accepted	Yes

Applicants Also Look At

Brooklyn Law School, The Catholic University of America, Hofstra University, State University of New York at Albany, Syracuse University.

International Students

TOEFL required of international students	Yes
Minimum paper TOEFL	650
Minimum computer TOEFL	280

FINANCIAL FACTS

Annual tuition (resident)	$12,170
Annual tuition (nonresident)	$18,270
Books and supplies	$1,534
Fees per credit (resident)	$53
Fees per credit (nonresident)	$53
Tuition per credit (resident)	$507
Tuition per credit (nonresident)	$761
Room and board	$9,581
Financial aid application deadline	3/1
% first-year students receiving some sort of aid	94
% receiving some sort of aid	90
% of aid that is merit based	49
% receiving scholarships	64
Average grant	$2,950
Average loan	$18,500
Average total aid package	$18,500
Average debt	$53,287

EMPLOYMENT INFORMATION

		Grads Employed by Field (%)	
Career Rating	**76**	**Grads Employed by Field (%)**	
Rate of placement (nine months out)	98	Academic	1
Average starting salary	$58,135	Business/Industry	11
State for bar exam	NY, PA, NJ, IL, MD	Government	10
Pass rate for first-time bar	82	Judicial clerkships	7

Employers Who Frequently Hire Grads

Ropes and Gray; Hodgson Russ; Phillips, Lytle; NYS Court of Appeals; NYS App. Div. 4th Dept.; Dewey Ballantine.

Prominent Alumni

Honorable Julio Fuentes, U.S. Court of Appeal for the 3rd Circuit; Herald Price Fahringer, constitutional lawyer; Honorable Paul Friedman, U.S. District Court; Susan Horwitz, MacArthur Foundation.

Military	3
Private practice	64
Public Interest	4

SUFFOLK UNIVERSITY
LAW SCHOOL

INSTITUTIONAL INFORMATION

Public/private	Private
Student-faculty ratio	18:1
% faculty part-time	60
% faculty female	34
Total faculty	208

SURVEY SAYS...
Great research resources
Beautiful campus
Students love Boston, MA

STUDENTS

Enrollment of law school	1,644
% male/female	51/49
% out-of-state	41
% full-time	63
% minority	14
% international	1
# of countries represented	18
Average age of entering class	25

ACADEMICS

Academic Experience Rating	**80**
Profs interesting rating	81
Profs accessible rating	72
Hours of study per day	4.45

Academic Specialties
Business law and financial services, civil litigation, civil procedure, commercial law, constitutional law, corporation securities law, criminal law, environmental law, government services, health care and biotechnology, human rights law, intellectual property law, international law, labor law, legal history, legal philosophy, property, taxation.

Advanced Degrees Offered
JD 3 to 4 years, LLM (global technology) 1 to 3 years, LLM (U.S. law for international business lawyers—study in Budapest, Hungary) 3 years.

Combined Degrees Offered
JD/MBA 4 to 5 years, JD/MPA 4 to 5 years, JD/MS (international economics) 4 to 5 years, JD/MS (finance) 4 to 5 years, JD/MS (criminal justice) 4 to 5 years.

Academics

The Suffolk University Law School "provides a wonderful mix of strong academics and opportunities for the practical application of law." Academics are enhanced by the "new, beautiful law school," which some call "the envy of all others in the Boston area." The school touts the "state-of-the-art technology" in its new building, but some students claim that "this is over-hyped," especially the wireless Internet system which one student said "cuts out constantly." That said, other facets of the technologies upgrade are working quite well. "The library is also totally wired, and the print volumes are more than you will ever need."

Suffolk also affords its future lawyers access to professors that "are amazing. All of them are accessible and quirky, on top of being incredibly challenging." A second-year tells us, "Whether students want to be in public interest," take classes "in Suffolk's excellent IP program," study to "be tax attorneys," or work "in corporate law," Suffolk "has the professors and talent to guide students and prepare them for lives in the law." The faculty typically takes "a more practical approach rather than a theoretical focus in the classroom, which enables students to become more engaged in discussion and debate." This practical emphasis has given way to the nine clinical experience programs for which Suffolk students are eligible. "I am currently in the Juvenile Justice Clinic, and my law school experience would not have been the same without it," says a 2L. "I am in court as a student attorney at least once a week and handle all of my own cases and clients. My experiences in the clinic have also given me an advantage in the job market."

The fiercely proud students at Suffolk are adamant that the law school deserves a stronger national reputation, even declaring that "the academics are comparable to" cross-town rival Harvard, but "without the fierce competition." One of the reasons its name is not so widely known, they suggest, is that the "Career Development Office needs a kickstart—especially for those students seeking work "outside of the Boston area." It should be noted, though, that among the school's "greatest strengths" is its "alumni network." A first-year says, "Over 19,000 strong, Suffolk alums are always willing to give both personal and professional advice to students, frequently offering to put in a good word on the behalf of students or make introductions to important networking contacts." Students also benefit from on-campus "speakers such as George H. W. Bush and Justice Ginsberg (both this year!). There are plenty of school- and student-sponsored events to keep you in the know."

Students note that the school's evening program lends significant weight to SULS's regional acclaim. One participant tells us, "As evening students, we have more of the adjunct faculty. They are all practitioners in the field and have practical and up-to-date information. The student body in the evening school is very diverse and brings a great deal of variety in viewpoints and life experience." "Overall, the school provides a quality, cohesive learning environment within the heart of one of nation's greatest cities," says a law student. A classmate adds, "After you get over the initial shock of the price and the ridiculous underrating that the school seems to have, you realize that the faculty, administration, and student body cannot be beat."

Life

In a way, the tenor of life at Suffolk comes down to circumstance. A 1L explains, "Some first-year sections are very friendly and social outside of the classroom, and others are not." The same can be said inside the classroom. While "Most people seem to understand the concept of 'we're not just classmates, but future colleagues' and want the respect of their peers," the typical stories about "ultra-competitive" law school students sometimes do play out at Suffolk. As one SULS first-year relays: "Everybody is quite competitive, but not in a way that is destructive to the community."

At Suffolk, "The students tend to be quite active in a plethora of activities and clubs, as well as competitions and Law Reviews and journals." Also, the SBA—or Student Bar Association—"is very active and responsive to the large student body." But Suffolk's law students don't always think about studying the law. "People want to party a lot," nods a student. Others like to shop, exercise, or just wander around Beantown. Students across the board agree that the location is "a boon" because SULS "is close to everything. Suffolk is right across from beautiful Boston Common, mere hundreds of yards away from the State House, and near several bars for after-class unwinding." "Midday shopping, errands, and part-time jobs in the heart of the city are even made possible by the great location."

Getting In

Suffolk's Admissions Committee seeks candidates who are poised to contribute to the life of the campus community as well as to the future of the legal profession. Prospective students can demonstrate their potential in these areas by getting involved in community service, extracurricular undergraduate organizations, and pre-professional societies. The 2006 incoming class scored a median 157 on the LSAT and boasted a 3.3 median undergraduate GPA.

Clinical program required	No
Legal writing course requirement	Yes
Legal methods course requirement	Yes
Legal research course requirement	Yes
Moot court requirement	Yes
Public interest law requirement	No

ADMISSIONS

Selectivity Rating	**75**
# applications received	2,429
# applicants accepted	1,136
# acceptees attending	331
Average LSAT	157
LSAT Range	154–159
Average undergrad GPA	3.3
Application fee	$60
Regular application	3/1
Regular notification	Rolling
Rolling notification	Yes
Early application program	No
Transfer students accepted	Yes
Evening division offered	Yes
Part-time accepted	Yes
LSDAS accepted	Yes

Applicants Also Look At
American University, Boston College, Boston University, New England School of Law, Northeastern University, Quinnipiac University, University of Connecticut.

International Students

TOEFL required of international students	Yes
Minimum paper TOEFL	600
Minimum computer TOEFL	250

FINANCIAL FACTS

Annual tuition	$35,948
Books and supplies	$900
Tuition per credit	$1,195
Room and board (off-campus)	$16,517s
Financial aid application deadline	3/1
% first-year students receiving some sort of aid	88
% receiving some sort of aid	88
% of aid that is merit based	36
% receiving scholarships	40
Average grant	$6,613
Average loan	$30,076
Average total aid package	$33,875
Average debt	$95,779

EMPLOYMENT INFORMATION

Career Rating	**83**	
Rate of placement (nine months out)	92	
Average starting salary	$71,663	
State for bar exam	MA, NY, FL	
Pass rate for first-time bar	90	

Employers Who Frequently Hire Grads
Large, medium, and small law firms in Boston; public sector; all levels of government service; serve on the judiciary.

Prominent Alumni
John Joseph Moakley, U.S. Congressman; James Bamford, author; Kristen Kuliga, principal, K Sports and Entertainment; Oliver Mitchell, chairman, Ford Motor Company Dealer Policy Board.

Grads Employed by Field (%)	
Academic	2
Business/Industry	22
Government	12
Judicial clerkships	10
Military	1
Other	4
Private practice	47
Public Interest	2

SYRACUSE UNIVERSITY
COLLEGE OF LAW

INSTITUTIONAL INFORMATION

Public/private	Private
% faculty female	46
% faculty minority	16
Total faculty	56

SURVEY SAYS...

Diverse opinions accepted
in classrooms
Great library staff
Beautiful campus

STUDENTS

Enrollment of law school	689
% male/female	56/44
% out-of-state	70
% full-time	99
% minority	20
% international	2
# of countries represented	8
Average age of entering class	24

ACADEMICS

Academic Experience Rating	**61**
Profs interesting rating	63
Profs accessible rating	63
Hours of study per day	5.5

Academic Specialties

Constitutional law, corporation securities law, criminal law, disability law, environmental law, family law, global law, government services, human rights, intellectual property law, international law, labor law, legal history, national security and counter-terrorism, taxation.

Combined Degrees Offered

JD/MPA 3 to 3.5 years; JD/MS 3 to 3.5 years, JD/MBA 3 to 3.5 years, JD/MA 3 to 3.5 years, JD/MS 3 to 3.5 years, JD/MSW 3 to 3.5 years, JD/MS or JD/PhD 3 to 3.5 years, JD/MS 3 to 3.5 years, JD/MA 3 to 3.5 years, JD/MBA 4 years.

Clinical program required	No
Legal writing course requirement	Yes
Legal methods course requirement	Yes

Academics

At Syracuse University College of Law, students have the opportunity to pursue a highly specialized legal education in one of a wide range of areas. With a large student body and extensive teaching staff, "Course selection is truly excellent, and once you get into your second and third years, many opportunities for specialization and exploration open up." In addition, the "Affiliation with Syracuse University makes for some unique joint-degree and study opportunities," allowing JD students to pursue master's degrees concurrently in communications, international relations, disability studies, public administration, or accounting, among other disciplines. According to one 3L, "The public administration program, which is very highly regarded, is quite popular, as are JD/MBA and JD/IR programs. A relatively high percentage of students pursue this amazing opportunity because the law school will actually shave a semester's worth of credits off of a joint-degree law student's degree requirements."

Despite the varied academic paths, there is no easy route through law school at Syracuse. The curriculum is challenging and students warn that "five-credit classes will break you." However, most appreciate the rigorous training, telling us that "professors are tough, but in a good way." In fact, the school's "committed, talented instructors" are able teachers who "are not merely experts in their respective fields. Their commitment to clearly conveying complex information to students is obvious." In addition to their skill as lecturers, professors are "very accessible and willing to help" struggling students outside the classroom.

In addition to the standard legal curriculum, Syracuse offers several applied learning programs, like trial practice, moot court, and a number of clinics, including the Family Law and Social Policy Center and the Global Law and Practice Center. In addition, the school operates summer abroad programs in London and Zimbabwe and participates in international moot court competitions, in which Syracuse has done quite well in the past. A 2L raves, "We have a great trial advocacy program and excellent clinical legal education opportunities. I loved practicing law my second year!" Practical approaches to law are also emphasized in the curriculum, and there are "some great practitioners in upper classes," though some feel that additional adjuncts would be a benefit to the learning experience.

Located on the same grounds as the greater university, the Syracuse campus is attractive, safe, and modern. After recent remodeling, classroom facilities are "nice and shiny with some good technology" and have all the nice touches, like "the soft swivel chairs in the classrooms that make life a little more comfortable." While doling out compliments, students admit that "the one glaring deficiency of the school, which overall is quite nice, is the library, which feels cramped and lacks adequate study space for students"; also, "The materials are limited, as are the computer facilities right in the library."

Syracuse has been going through many changes in recent years as the school attempts to build up its national reputation. Students specifically applaud the Syracuse administration for making efforts to improve the school's career placement opportunities. Among other measures, "The school has been making attempts to improve its academic reputation by instituting an upper-class grading curve, stricter attendance policies, and mandating the use of laptops." Many feel the changes have been a step in the right direction. However, some feel "The school lacks direction and focus in achieving its overall mission [and that] the administration does not seem to care about its existing students;

rather, it is focused on the quality of students it can enroll in the future." A 2L reassures us, however, that despite occasional misunderstandings, "In the end everything seems to come together as it should."

Life

Generally speaking, Syracuse students are a fairly homogenous bunch. While the school's sizable student body ensures that there is a little something for everyone, the school is home to "a large population of preppies from the suburbs of major cities in khakis and polo shirts with their collars up." However, everyone is able to find a niche on this active campus, and there are a wide range of campus clubs and interest groups. When it comes to socializing, the class is likewise diverse, depending on your definition of "diverse"; students report that "as far as social life is concerned, there are people who party and there are people who don't."

While the new grading policies have created some additional stress for Syracuse students, they have not generated unwanted or nasty competition between classmates. By most accounts "Students are competitive, but not to a point where you can't handle it." What's more, the faculty and administration do as much as possible to keep backstabbing at bay. A 2L explains, "The competitive nature of most law schools is not as evident at Syracuse, and any instances of extreme competition (e.g., hiding books) have been immediately reprimanded and corrected by the school."

Getting In

In addition to the numbers that go into your admissions index, the Admissions Committee closely analyzes a student's undergraduate transcript, considering difficulty of the course of study, caliber of the school attended, and course selection. Syracuse may also consider other subjective information about you, like graduate study or work experience, as well as commitment to the study of law. A B-plus undergraduate average and a LSAT score in the mid-150s makes you competitive at Syracuse.

Legal research course requirement	Yes
Moot court requirement	No
Public interest law requirement	No

ADMISSIONS

Selectivity Rating	76
# applications received	2,801
# acceptees attending	266
Average LSAT	155
LSAT Range	153–157
Average undergrad GPA	3.35
Application fee	$70
Regular application	4/1
Regular notification	Rolling
Rolling notification	Yes
Early application program	No
Transfer students accepted	Yes
Evening division offered	No
Part-time accepted	Yes
LSDAS accepted	Yes

Applicants Also Look At

American University; Brooklyn Law School; New York Law School; Rutgers, The State University of New Jersey; State University of New York at Albany; State University of New York-University at Buffalo; Temple University.

International Students

TOEFL required of international students	Yes
TOEFL recommended of international students	Yes
Minimum paper TOEFL	600
Minimum computer TOEFL	250

FINANCIAL FACTS

Annual tuition	$35,120
Books and supplies	$1,160
Tuition per credit	$1,536
Room and board	$11,270
Financial aid application deadline	2/15
% receiving some sort of aid	93
% of aid that is merit based	70
Average grant	$9,900
Average loan	$36,185
Average total aid package	$41,570
Average debt	$86,860

EMPLOYMENT INFORMATION

Career Rating	72	Grads Employed by Field (%)	
Rate of placement (nine months out)	92	Academic	4
Average starting salary	$56,300	Business/Industry	19
State for bar exam	NY, NJ, CA, PA, CT	Government	14
Pass rate for first-time bar	81	Judicial clerkships	13
Employers Who Frequently Hire Grads		Military	2
Medium sized law firms, federal and state government.		Private practice	43
Prominent Alumni		Public Interest	5
Joseph R. Biden Jr., U.S. Senator; Honorable Theodore A. McKee, Federal Appeals Court; Donald T. MacNaughton, partner, White and Case; Melanie Gray, partner and lit co-chair, Weil, Gotshal and Manges LLP.			

TEMPLE UNIVERSITY
JAMES E. BEASLEY SCHOOL OF LAW

INSTITUTIONAL INFORMATION

Public/private	Public
Student-faculty ratio	13:1
% faculty female	38
% faculty minority	25
Total faculty	64

SURVEY SAYS...

Diverse opinions accepted
in classrooms
Great research resources
Great library staff
Liberal students

STUDENTS

Enrollment of law school	1,004
% male/female	53/47
% out-of-state	35
% full-time	77
% minority	25
% international	1
# of countries represented	9
Average age of entering class	25

ACADEMICS

Academic Experience Rating	**85**
Profs interesting rating	89
Profs accessible rating	85
Hours of study per day	4.38

Academic Specialties

Commercial law, constitutional law, corporation securities law, criminal law, environmental law, government services, human rights law, intellectual property law, international law, public interest, taxation, trial advocacy.

Advanced Degrees Offered

JD 3 to 4 years, LLM (trial advocacy) 1 year, LLM (taxation), 0.5 to 1 year, LLM (transnational law) 0.5 to 1 year, graduate teaching fellowships 2 years, LLM (graduates of foreign law schools) 1 year, SJD.

Combined Degrees Offered

JD/MBA 4 years, JD/LLM (taxation and transnational law) 3.5 years, JD/individually designed joint-degrees.

Academics

Students here tell us that Temple University's James E. Beasley School of Law offers "the best value in a legal education, hands down." "It really is such a deal," affirms a 3L. Temple's "very approachable" professors are "passionate about their fields" and "genuinely interested in the success of their students." "Professors are not brutal with their use of the Socratic Method," says one student. "Every professor I've had has been unbelievably supportive." The adjunct faculty is "quite uneven" though. Far and away the biggest complaint here is the stiff grading system. "Temple curves to a lower grade," gripes a 3L, "making our students look worse than UPenn, Villanova, Rutgers, and Widener students." Temple's administration "does what it needs to" and sometimes even provides "awesome support." "Temple Law is a big school and, like any big school, there is opportunity if you seek it out," explains a 3L.

"Temple really emphasizes the practical skills required for legal work" and has a "strong reputation for producing litigators." The focus here is manifestly on "real-world law." The "year-long" trial advocacy program is "beyond amazing." "If you want to learn how to try a case—and win—you'll fit right in at Temple," guarantees a 3L. "You'll learn from some of the top prosecutors and trial lawyers in the country." Students also think the legal writing program "is the best in the nation" and appreciate that it "stresses the fundamentals and really teaches you what you need for success as a junior associate."

One of the law-school buildings here "is a great example of fortress-like architecture that gripped inner-city universities during the 1960s and 1970s." That said, Temple's interiors are "completely renovated." Also, "The other building, Barrack Hall, is one of the original buildings of the university and is gorgeous." Classrooms here are "all equipped with top-of-the-line technology," including wireless Internet that "is accessible everywhere." The library has a "helpful and knowledgeable" staff and contains "many nooks and crannies to hide out and study." Its major flaw is that it is "open to other floors and professors' offices, which sounds good in theory but is loud in fact."

The Career Planning Office is "excellent and extremely helpful." "Temple is deeply entrenched in the Philadelphia legal community, and that is invaluable" for students seeking "internships, externships, and jobs after graduation." "If you want to practice law in Philadelphia, Temple is the best choice," advises a 3L. "It's Temple grads who dominate the Philadelphia legal community." "Career opportunities are great" throughout other "Mid-Atlantic" states as well. A few students say that Temple "needs to do a better job of getting firms to interview on campus from areas outside the Delaware Valley."

Life

"There are students of all ages, walks of life, races, ethnicities, religions, etc.," reports a student. There is also a great deal of "diversity of student experiences prior to law school." Another student explains, "The students at Temple come from all different economic, professional, and ethnic backgrounds, which makes for great conversation and debate in class." Ultimately, "Nothing contributes more to the quality of the education than the diverse points of view provided by classmates."

Many find that "most" students are "friendly and supportive" and the overall environment "is one of 'we-are-in-this-together.'" "There is a huge difference between the

JOHANNE L. JOHNSTON, ASSISTANT DEAN FOR ADMISSIONS AND FINANCIAL AID
1719 NORTH BROAD STREET, PHILADELPHIA, PA 19122
TEL: 800-560-1428 FAX: 215-204-9319
E-MAIL: LAWADMIS@TEMPLE.EDU • INTERNET: WWW.LAW.TEMPLE.EDU

day program and night program," adds one student. "Day students have more time for community and studying. Evening students rely more on real experience to inform their studying, making up (somewhat) for less time." "There is less competition and more civility" in the evening program as well. "There are many student organizations, and they are always holding meetings, social events," and "happy hours." "We study together, go to lunch together, and most of us have formed lasting friendships with people in our classes," relates a 2L. "Students and faculty are very involved in law school life," reports a student. Others take into account the fact that many "students live throughout Philadelphia" and it can be "hard for students to get together and socialize."

Temple's law school is located in "one of the seedier areas" of Philadelphia, though "The campus itself is pretty safe." "It really can't be denied that the school is bounded on three sides with grinding poverty," admits a 2L. Nevertheless, many students think the area "has gotten a bad rap." There are always "many security guards around." A 2L explains, "Yes, you have to keep your eyes open. Yes, you shouldn't leave jewelry lying on your front seat. But these are things that could be said of any urban area." Beyond this, "The quality and cost of life in Philadelphia is remarkable." And "center city Philly" is only "five minutes away" on the subway.

Getting In

The 25th percentile of admitted students has LSAT scores of 161 and GPAs of 3.25. Admitted students at the 75th percentile have LSAT scores of 165 and GPAs of 3.7. Temple says that it doesn't average multiple LSAT score, however "all scores from the LSAT will be considered."

Clinical program required	No
Legal writing course requirement	Yes
Legal methods course requirement	No
Legal research course requirement	Yes
Moot court requirement	No
Public interest law requirement	No

ADMISSIONS

Selectivity Rating	**82**
# applications received	4,648
# applicants accepted	1,719
# acceptees attending	300
Average LSAT	161
LSAT Range	158–163
Average undergrad GPA	3.38
Application fee	$60
Regular application	3/1
Regular notification	Rolling
Rolling notification	Yes
Early application program	No
Transfer students accepted	Yes
Evening division offered	Yes
Part-time accepted	Yes
LSDAS accepted	Yes

Applicants Also Look At
American University, Fordham University, Georgetown University, Villanova University.

International Students

TOEFL required of international students	No
TOEFL recommended of international students	Yes

FINANCIAL FACTS

Annual tuition (resident)	$14,372
Annual tuition (nonresident)	$25,022
Books and supplies	$1,500
Tuition per credit (resident)	$556
Tuition per credit (nonresident)	$1,023
Room and board	$11,162
Financial aid application deadline	3/1
% receiving some sort of aid	87
% of aid that is merit based	93
% receiving scholarships	38
Average grant	$6,000
Average loan	$23,524
Average total aid package	$29,524
Average debt	$70,584

EMPLOYMENT INFORMATION

Career Rating	85	Grads Employed by Field (%)	
Rate of placement (nine months out)	94	Academic	3
Average starting salary	$73,283	Business/Industry	19
State for bar exam	PA	Government	10
Pass rate for first-time bar	91	Judicial clerkships	12
Employers Who Frequently Hire Grads		Private practice	49
District attorney; public defender; national law firms; state and federal judges; non-profit legal organizations.		Public Interest	7

TEXAS TECH UNIVERSITY
SCHOOL OF LAW

INSTITUTIONAL INFORMATION

Public/private	Public
Student-faculty ratio	15:1
% faculty part-time	25
% faculty female	30
% faculty minority	19
Total faculty	63

SURVEY SAYS...

Diverse opinions accepted
in classrooms
Great research resources
Great library staff

STUDENTS

Enrollment of law school	702
% male/female	55/45
% out-of-state	16
% full-time	100
% minority	10
% international	1
# of countries represented	1
Average age of entering class	24

ACADEMICS

Academic Experience Rating	**79**
Profs interesting rating	75
Profs accessible rating	89
Hours of study per day	4.64

Academic Specialties

Civil procedure, commercial law, constitutional law, corporate securities law, criminal law, environmental law, health law, intellectual property law, international law, labor law, law and bioterrorism, law and science, oil and gas, property, taxation, water law.

Combined Degrees Offered

JD/MBA 3 years, JD/MPA 3.5 years, JD/MS (agricultural economics) 3 to 3.5 years, JD/MS (accounting—taxation) 3 to 3.5 years, JD/MS (environmental toxicology) 3 to 4 years, JD/FFP (personal financial planning) 3 to 3.5 years, JD/MS (biotechnology) 3 to 4 years, JD/MS (crop science/horticulture/soil science/entomology) 3 to 4 years.

Academics

Described by its students as a "litigator factory," Texas Tech University takes a decidedly practical approach to the study of law, teaching students the basics of theory while providing rigorous training in research, writing, and courtroom technique. Many students choose Texas Tech because of its "emphasis on the practical side of law." In the state of Texas, the school has a "great reputation for turning out law students who are ready to practice law from day one." Indeed, practical skills are emphasized throughout the curriculum; in the classroom, students are introduced to "skills in client counseling, negotiating, and courtroom argument." Outside of the classroom, the school offers top-notch "clinical programs, strong moot court teams, and a required year-long legal research and writing course" as well as "opportunities to study abroad." The school is currently building a new, state-of-the-art mock courtroom to further promote its clinical programs.

While Texas Tech students appreciate the strength of their legal education, they caution that law school is no picnic. TTU students compare first-year classes with "boot camp," and a 1L tells us, "Everyone I know spends at least five to six hours a day studying; and if a day is missed to go out, then they make it up on the weekend." While the material and workload are decidedly challenging, the enthusiasm of the "incredibly awesome" teaching staff inspires students to achieve. A 3L tells us, "We have a lot of young professors who have a passion for the law and for teaching." In the words of a 1L: "Their great attitude and great sense of humor help you forget you're studying ridiculously dull topics." On top of that, students report that "the professors are willing to work with anyone who is having difficulties," and there is a campus-wide open-door policy for faculty and administrators. A 3L attests, "I have great relationships with all of my professors. . . . We truly have a law school family."

Administrators are generally described as "extremely helpful to students." A 1L says, "Professors and administration alike bend over backward to make sure you are understanding the concepts and learning to think like a lawyer." Another adds, "The administration—from the deans down to the secretaries—love what they do, and it shows; they strive to help each and every one of us." Texas Tech also has "regular peer tutoring offered to help us 1Ls survive our first semester," as well as a Mentor Program for first- and second-year students. Indeed, "you are not just a number at Texas Tech." With about 230 students per class, the school can offer small class sizes. However, the school's size also leads to some limitations; for example, some students write that "the range of topics of study needs to be much broader." On top of that, students report that the high number of required courses leaves "no wiggle room to explore fields of law that aren't on the bar exam," leaving little room to specialize. That said, many report that the Texas Tech administration members have listened to these concerns and "have employed new professors and are adding courses to their curriculum."

Out in the real world, TTU students find that their education leaves them well prepared for their future practice; the school consistently "turns out young lawyers who are not overwhelmed by the large disconnect between classroom and workplace legal skills." Many see the benefits of their education as early as their first internship placement. A 3L says, "From the time you start your first summer clerkship, you are ready to go." When it comes to career placement, students report that Texas Tech has a pretty single-minded "focus on criminal practice and finding jobs in high-paying firms." While some would like to see an expansion of the practice fields open to graduates as well as a more solid national reputation and recruiting, most note that "Texas Tech enjoys prestige

DONNA WILLIAMS, ADMISSIONS COUNSELOR
TEXAS TECH UNIVERSITY SCHOOL OF LAW, 1802 HARTFORD AVENUE, LUBBOCK, TX 79409
TEL: 806-742-3990 FAX: 806-742-4617
E-MAIL: DONNA.WILLIAMS@TTU.EDU • INTERNET: WWW.LAW.TTU.EDU

within the state of Texas" and that consequently, post-graduation in-state career prospects are auspicious. A 3L confirms, "I have received offers from law firms located throughout the state of Texas and have even considered a position with the Federal Bureau of Investigation after being accepted as an honors intern last summer."

Life

Located in the West Texas town of Lubbock, TTU's student population provides a little slice of the Lone Star State. A Dallas native exclaims, "I have never seen so many cowboy boots in all my life!" By most accounts, there is a distinctly Texan flavor to the politics and culture on campus, which most describe as unequivocally conservative and fairly religious. A 2L warns: "If you have one liberal bone in your body, be prepared to be an outcast here." According to many, the student body is largely lacking in ethnic, economic, and philosophical diversity. One student confides, "Diversity is said to be a priority here, but I haven't seen it yet, and there doesn't seem to be much support for it in the administration."

In addition to their conservative politics, Texans are famous for their upbeat, cheerful, and welcoming natures. A content 1L says, "The whole law school, from the administration to the students, reflects the friendly, caring West Texas atmosphere." Moreover, "While competition is encouraged, so are relationships and understanding." Students find one another "very willing to lend a helping hand or even a shoulder to cry on when it's needed." On campus, students say that "Tech has a great balance of academic, social, and community service. There is always something to do." As far as off-campus life is concerned, "Lubbock actually has a pretty good nightlife." Although it "isn't a hub of cosmopolitan splendor," it nevertheless "is very favorable to the law student." "Before you know it, this place grows on you."

Getting In

Texas Tech evaluates students based on their previous academic performance, LSAT scores, letters of recommendation, and personal statements. While no specific pre-law curriculum is required, the Admissions Committee favors students who have a background in public speaking, reading and writing skills, an understanding of public institutions and government, and the ability to think creatively and critically.

Clinical program required	No
Legal writing course requirement	Yes
Legal methods course requirement	Yes
Legal research course requirement	Yes
Moot court requirement	No
Public interest law requirement	No

ADMISSIONS

Selectivity Rating	**77**
# applications received	1,790
# applicants accepted	585
# acceptees attending	226
Average LSAT	154
LSAT Range	151–157
Average undergrad GPA	3.56
Application fee	$50
Regular application	2/1
Regular notification	Rolling
Rolling notification	Yes
Early application program	Yes
Early application deadline	11/1
Early application notification	1/15
Transfer students accepted	Yes
Evening division offered	No
Part-time accepted	No
LSDAS accepted	Yes

Applicants Also Look At

Baylor University, Southern Methodist University, University of Houston, University of New Mexico, University of Oklahoma, The University of Texas at Austin.

International Students

TOEFL required of international students	Yes
Minimum paper TOEFL	550
Minimum computer TOEFL	213

FINANCIAL FACTS

Annual tuition (resident)	$10,200
Annual tuition (nonresident)	$17,550
Books and supplies	$1,000
Room and board	$11,282
% first-year students receiving some sort of aid	87
% receiving some sort of aid	87
% of aid that is merit based	17
% receiving scholarships	78
Average grant	$6,391
Average loan	$17,739
Average total aid package	$21,978
Average debt	$50,545

EMPLOYMENT INFORMATION

		Grads Employed by Field (%)	
Career Rating	**78**	Business/Industry	3
Rate of placement (nine months out)	97	Government	13
Average starting salary	$68,800	Judicial clerkships	6
State for bar exam	TX, NM, CO, AZ	Private practice	77
Pass rate for first-time bar	91	Public Interest	1

Employers Who Frequently Hire Grads

Jones, Day, Reavis, and Pogue; Thompson and Knight; Haynes and Boone; Thompson and Coe; Cousins and Irons; Strasburger and Price; Cooper and Aldous.

Prominent Alumni

Karen Tandy, administrator, Drug Enforcement Administration; Honorable Kem Thompson Frost, Houston Court of Appeals.

TEXAS WESLEYAN UNIVERSITY
SCHOOL OF LAW

INSTITUTIONAL INFORMATION

Public/private	Private
Affiliation	Methodist
Student-faculty ratio	26:1
% faculty part-time	35
% faculty female	46
% faculty minority	10
Total faculty	29

SURVEY SAYS...

Heavy use of Socratic method
Diverse opinions accepted
in classrooms
Great library staff

STUDENTS

Enrollment of law school	725
% male/female	52/48
% out-of-state	
% full-time	65
% minority	21
Average age of entering class	24

ACADEMICS

Academic Experience Rating	**74**
Profs interesting rating	80
Profs accessible rating	88
Hours of study per day	4.06

Academic Specialties

Business planning/estate planning
and probate, criminal law, family
law, intellectual property law, labor
law.

Advanced Degrees Offered

JD 3 to 4 years.

Clinical program required	No
Legal writing course requirement	Yes
Legal methods course requirement	Yes
Legal research course requirement	Yes
Moot court requirement	No
Public interest law requirement	Yes

Academics

Whether fresh out of college or starting on a new career path, students feel stimulated and supported at Texas Wesleyan University School of Law. At this friendly Fort Worth school, professors are described as "dynamic and engaging, immensely knowledgeable, and easily accessible." "They have even been known to show up at small study groups at the request of their students." One 3L reports, "Never in my educational experience have I had so many people go out of their way to help me succeed. The professors are always available outside of class, and the administration is surprisingly willing to take any step necessary to help students both personally and professionally." Another student writes, "I feel more comfortable approaching my law professors than I did any of my undergraduate professors." With a total enrollment of only 700 students, the campus community is close-knit, and the administrators receive praise for being "helpful with questions, even if they are only minor problems."

Through clinics and course work, Texas Wesleyan students report that they are well prepared for the bar exam. The school boasts a "competitive bar-passage rate" (82 percent for first-time test-takers), which is comparable with—if not better than—many top Texas schools. In addition, the course work at Texas Wesleyan aims to prepare students for professional practice. A student explains, "Professors are genuinely interested not only in our successful completion of the program, but also in our bar exam performance and—more important—our professional competence." For a small school, "The courses offered are fairly broad," and students receive a comprehensive education. Students warn, however, that "no one subject has an extensive array of topics available under it for study," and some "would like to see a wider variety of course offerings, such as courses dealing with sexual orientation, gender, and civil rights."

One feature that distinguishes Texas Wesleyan from other law schools is its excellent evening and part-time programs, which offer "flexibility for full-time professionals who want to earn a law degree." Evening students (who account for 34 percent of the school's enrollment) have access to the full range of course offerings, and "night and weekend classes are all taught by top-tier faculty." A satisfied student attests, "Working full-time while attending school at night is difficult, but the school's flexible scheduling enables me to choose the classes I want and grants me access to all the support personnel I need to take care of administrative and other needs that come up." Many nontraditional students "have day jobs, spouses, children, and an embedded social group outside of school." For the most part, they "feel included in most of the extracurricular activities offered by the school and find the faculty to be particularly sensitive" to students with jobs and families. Even still, some wish the school offered more "activities geared toward our lifestyles."

Many note that the downtown Fort Worth "location is one of the school's greatest strengths." Situated across the street from the Tarrant County Bar Association, Texas Wesleyan is just "a step away from the legal community." While students are also in close proximity to the multitude of resources in neighboring Dallas, Fort Worth receives kudos for offering "a casual and friendly environment that affords greater access to local judges and lawyers." Established in 1989, Texas Wesleyan is steadily building its reputation in the greater Fort Worth area. A student explains, "Since we're a very young law school, we lack the academic reputation and alumni establishment of most other schools in our region." Students write, however, that their excellent education is starting to make an impression on the local community, and "More people are getting big firm jobs every year." As the school grows in age and reputation, enrollment, too, is slightly increasing.

LYNDA L. CULVER, DIRECTOR OF ADMISSIONS
1515 COMMERCE STREET, FORT WORTH, TX 76102
TEL: 800-733-9529 FAX: 817-212-4141
E-MAIL: LAWADMISSIONS@LAW.TXWES.EDU • INTERNET: LAW.TXWES.EDU

Life

Students at Texas Wesleyan write that their legal education is profoundly enhanced by the diversity of the student body. With its excellent part-time program, it's no surprise that the school attracts "people from all walks of life." One student confirms, "The diversity of the student body is a plus. I have been in classes with actors, parents of seven, recent college grads, candle makers, and police officers, and they all bring unique perspectives that could potentially not be found at other institutions."

The diversity at Texas Wesleyan breeds classroom debate and doesn't result in competition or contention. In fact, Texas Wesleyan students generally describe their classmates as "mature and mostly respectful, friendly, [and] helpful." A first-year writes, "I can always count on 2Ls and 3Ls for the inside scoop. Everyone wants the 1Ls to succeed and is always more than willing to help out." Students report that social life on campus is slightly lacking, since there isn't much to do in downtown Fort Worth. In addition to some safety issues in the vicinity, students gripe that "there are very few places within walking distance to eat or socialize" and that the only food options come from "vending machines that operate on a part-time basis."

Getting In

Admission to the school becomes slightly more competitive every year. In 2005, Texas Wesleyan received 2,088 applications, of which the school accepted roughly a third to fill 253 seats. In addition to a completed application and LSAT scores, applicants are required to submit two letters of recommendation and a personal statement. Texas Wesleyan welcomes students of different ages and backgrounds, and the school looks beyond test scores and grades when making admissions decisions.

ADMISSIONS

Selectivity Rating	72
# applications received	2,027
# applicants accepted	815
# acceptees attending	242
Average LSAT	154
LSAT Range	151–156
Average undergrad GPA	3.15
Application fee	$55
Regular application	3/31
Regular notification	Rolling
Rolling notification	Yes
Early application program	No
Transfer students accepted	Yes
Evening division offered	Yes
Part-time accepted	Yes
LSDAS accepted	Yes

Applicants Also Look At
Baylor University, Southern Methodist University, Texas Tech University, The University of Texas at Austin.

International Students

TOEFL required of international students	No
TOEFL recommended of international students	No

FINANCIAL FACTS

Annual tuition	$21,060
Books and supplies	$1,500
Fees per credit	$600
Tuition per credit	$715
Average grant	$5,000
Average loan	$20,000
Average debt	$55,000

EMPLOYMENT INFORMATION

Career Rating	**74**	**Grads Employed by Field (%)**	
Rate of placement (nine months out)	91	Academic	1
Average starting salary	$57,497	Business/Industry	18
State for bar exam	TX	Government	22
Pass rate for first-time bar	88	Judicial clerkships	1
Employers Who Frequently Hire Grads		Private practice	45
Small to midsize private practice firms; district attorneys' offices; government agencies; various corporations and businesses.		Public Interest	3

Thomas M. Cooley Law School

Academics

Thomas M. Cooley Law School "is a great school for a nontraditional student with a lot of self-discipline." The "flexibility of scheduling options" at Cooley makes the study of law possible for "many students who would not be able to go to law school if it weren't for programs like this." As a matter of fact, it's these students—those who would attend law school less than full-time—who make up more than 80 percent of the student body. One tells us that Cooley excels in providing the "opportunity to choose a schedule option that best fits the student's needs. You can attend school year-round or take semesters off if you prefer. You are not bound by the traditional fall/spring schedule." But even though the school makes it possible for so many students to study law, it doesn't make it easy for them: "Thomas Cooley is one of the easiest schools to get into, yet one of the hardest to survive at. If you come to this school, you better be willing to fight for your seat every single term." Students are dismissed for failing to maintain adequate grades.

In terms of enrollment, Cooley is the largest law school in the nation. "Because of its size, it is able to offer a wide variety of classes in many different fields." Unfortunately, "By the time students are done taking all their required courses [totaling 63 credits], they are left with about four electives though the school reports that technically students have the ability to enroll in 10 to 13 elective courses since 90 credits are required for gradua-tion." Heading those classes, at least, are professors who are "articulate, funny at times, and excellent in their specialty areas of the law." They come "from a variety of legal pro-fessions and have insight into practical examples of how the law has [been shaped through] 'real-life' experiences." Some even "have argued before the United States Supreme Court in big cases." Suffice it to say, they win most students' praise.

Students are not as enthusiastic about the administration. Many simply dismiss it as "overly bureaucratic and not very responsive to student concerns." On the contrary, stu-dents are pleased with the facilities. The new courtrooms/classrooms in the administra-tion building are great. They are very nice to look at, have plugs at every desk for lap-tops and offer wireless Internet." In addition, "The library is beautiful," which is staffed with competent and friendly people: "They will not only tell a student where to find a book; they will help the student track it down on one of the four floors of the large Cooley library."

Career Placement is not the greatest, but students acknowledge that the shortcomings in this department have much "to do with reputation problems." Things will improve, however, as firms begin to realize that "if you graduate from here, you will have worked harder than at other law schools."

Life

A variety of academic tracks segments the student body into groups that do not all have the same levels of social interaction. "The school has many students that attend night or weekend classes, which lends itself to making the school feel unsocial." This is because while "the weekday students form groups, friendships, and are able to clerk or volunteer in the legal profession, the others have family, work, and other time-consuming life requirements."

STEPHANIE GREGG, ASSISTANT DEAN OF ADMISSIONS
PO BOX 13038, 300 SOUTH CAPITOL AVENUE, LANSING, MI 48901
TEL: 517-371-5140 FAX: 517-334-5718
E-MAIL: ADMISSIONS@COOLEY.EDU • INTERNET: WWW.COOLEY.EDU

Cooley's main campus is located in Lansing, the capital of Michigan (Cooley also has two other campuses: one in Grand Rapids, Michigan and one at Oakland University in Rochester, Michigan). According to students, Lansing is a "great place to study law because there's not much else to do." But that's not entirely true. The location is good "in terms of gaining practical experience. Cooley is two blocks from the Michigan State Capitol, a federal courthouse, and county courts. Plus, there are lots of full- and part-time jobs around." It's the social outlets that are in somewhat short supply. However, "There are some jumpin' clubs over at Michigan State [in East Lansing], and a few bars around Cooley that are okay." On campus, there are also "tons of student organizations and activities that students are encouraged to get involved with." They do. In fact, "Student activities are regular and well attended."

Even though "good grades are extremely difficult to attain at Cooley, the school environment is not cutthroat. Students will work together in studying and sharing outlines, etc." You won't find "pages ripped out of books, and no material goes missing."

"Diversity is very important at Cooley." The campus is filled with "students from across the United States, [and] also from all around the world." It doesn't stop at geographic diversity, either. Its sheer size aids in reflecting "the diversity of the United States in all ways—race, gender, religion, political beliefs, etc. There is no 'prevailing political bent,' as all points of view are represented in both the student body and the faculty." This diversity "makes for interesting conversation and keeps most students very involved with school activities and social events."

Getting In

Cooley has one of the most objective admissions standards of all U.S. law schools. No personal statement or letters of recommendations are used in the decision-making process. Rather, Cooley relies solely on objective data (LSAT and undergraduate GPA). It's staying in Cooley that is difficult. They are serious about students maintaining satisfactory academic progress, and if a student fails to do so, the school will not hesitate in dismissing him or her, no matter how far along in the program he or she is.

Clinical program required	Yes
Legal writing course requirement	Yes
Legal methods course requirement	Yes
Legal research course requirement	Yes
Moot court requirement	No
Public interest law requirement	No

ADMISSIONS

Selectivity Rating	**61**
# applications received	5,718
# applicants accepted	3,802
# acceptees attending	1,691
Average LSAT	146
LSAT Range	144–149
Average undergrad GPA	3.05
Regular application	Rolling
Regular notification	Rolling
Rolling notification	Yes
Early application program	No
Transfer students accepted	Yes
Evening division offered	Yes
Part-time accepted	Yes
LSDAS accepted	Yes

Applicants Also Look At
Florida Coastal School of Law, Michigan State University—College of Law, St. Thomas University, Texas Southern University, University of Detroit Mercy, Widener University (DE).

International Students

TOEFL required of international students	No
TOEFL recommended of international students	Yes

FINANCIAL FACTS

Annual tuition	$24,220
Books and supplies	$800
Tuition per credit	$865
Room and board (off-campus)	$6,860
Financial aid application deadline	9/6
% first-year students receiving some sort of aid	88
% receiving some sort of aid	87
% receiving scholarships	57
Average grant	$7,507
Average total aid package	$18,500
Average debt	$93,067

EMPLOYMENT INFORMATION

Career Rating	**61**	
Rate of placement (nine months out)	82	
Average starting salary	$47,500	
State for bar exam	MI, NY, NJ, FL, IN	
Pass rate for first-time bar	63	

Employers Who Frequently Hire Grads
Michigan Court of Appeals, prosecutors, legal services programs, Michigan law firms.

Prominent Alumni
John Engler, former Governor of Michigan; Bart R. Stupak, U.S. Representative; Honorable Jane Markey, Michigan Court of Appeals; Chris Chocola, U.S. Representative.

Grads Employed by Field (%)	
Academic	2
Business/Industry	20
Government	13
Judicial clerkships	7
Military	4
Other	2
Private practice	46
Public Interest	6

TOURO COLLEGE
JACOB D. FUCHSBERG LAW CENTER

INSTITUTIONAL INFORMATION

Public/private	Private
Affiliation	Jewish
Student-faculty ratio	15:1
% faculty part-time	26
% faculty female	37
% faculty minority	10
Total faculty	59

SURVEY SAYS...

Diverse opinions accepted
in classrooms
Great research resources
Beautiful campus

STUDENTS

Enrollment of law school	733
% male/female	57/43
% full-time	68
% minority	20
% international	2
Average age of entering class	26

ACADEMICS

Academic Experience Rating	**73**
Profs interesting rating	85
Profs accessible rating	86
Hours of study per day	4.9

Academic Specialties

Commercial law, criminal law,
human rights law, intellectual property law, international law, health
care law.

Advanced Degrees Offered

JD 2.5 to 4 years, LLM (foreign law
graduates) 1 to 1.5 years, LLM
(general studies) 1 to 1.5 years.

Combined Degrees Offered

Dual Degree Programs: JD/MBA,
JD/MPA, JD/MSW.

Clinical program required	No
Legal writing course requirement	Yes
Legal methods course requirement	Yes
Legal research course requirement	Yes
Moot court requirement	No

Academics

Located on suburban Long Island, Touro Law Center boasts "many clinics on site." Five in-house clinics give full-time and part-time students the opportunity to serve real clients in civil rights litigation, immigration litigation, elder law, family law, and non-profit corporate law. Off-campus clinics include technology law and criminal law. The school also offers a fairly intensive, 20-hour-a-week rotation program with the United States Attorney's office. Touro's "focus on internships and externships" and its unique location, "only a five-iron shot" from federal and state courthouses, draws many students to the school. "Being located next to district, family, supreme, and federal courthouses gives Touro students a unique real-life look at what attorneys do while in court," explains one student. "I've randomly visited the court in the morning, and observed attorneys conduct direct and cross-examinations in a $150 million tort case." "We have a court visitation program for the 1Ls which is the first of its kind in law school academia," describes a 1L. "This program allows us access to more than just viewing a proceeding. With the hard work of the school staff, we have been given extra privileges at the court house including visits to chambers, personal audiences with both prosecutors, defense counsel, and all levels of court officers." "The direct contact with judges and attorneys and their input helps to [provide] insight into different areas of law." Also, "Having a better perspective on the various areas of law helps with deciding which area of law one may want to practice."

The course work at Touro "emphasizes legal writing and analysis." "Class sizes are pretty small, so it's not so intimidating to speak in front of everyone." The "smart, friendly, and approachable" professors are "excited to educate" (though there are a few "pretty boring ones"). "Plenty of judges and practitioners also teach classes." Accessibility is not a problem. "There is a high level of morale and the daily interaction between student and professor is priceless." Faculty members are "always willing to meet with and talk to the students outside the classroom," "no matter how long—or how many times—they have to go over a given concept." "Professors can be seen dining with students in the school's cafeteria while casually discussing the law," adds a 1L.

Some students call the Career Services Office "exceptional." "They will do their absolute best to make sure you are prepared for interviews and aware of upcoming opportunities," says one happy customer. Other students gripe that Career Services is "not at all helpful." Students also complain about Touro's "low" grade curve. Also, though Touro offers very flexible full-time and part-time programs, course scheduling is a huge problem. "There is not a lot of flexibility with regard to course selection" and "There are too many required courses after the first year." The administration, though "very accessible," seems "out of touch with the student body," "and they never seem to know what is going on."

The facilities here are "brand new," and students love them. Touro has a "state-of-the-art building" in which "Everything is high tech and top of the line." The "layout of the classrooms is odd" and "There are some problems with acoustics," but the "roomy" library has ample study space. There is a ton of free parking as well. The Law Center "follows a Jewish calendar" and one student notes that Touro "could improve by staying open on Saturday."

SUSAN THOMPSON, DIRECTOR OF ENROLLMENT
225 EASTVIEW DRIVE, CENTRAL ISLIP, NY 11722
TEL: 631-761-7010 FAX: 631-761-7019
E-MAIL: ADMISSIONS@TOUROLAW.EDU • INTERNET: WWW.TOUROLAW.EDU

Life

"Generally people get along very well" at Touro. "There is a good mix of both young and older, more experienced students." "The greatest strength of my law school is the sense of community that begins from the moment you enter the school," waxes a 3L. "In the full-time program you spend a full year with your incoming section and then half your classes the second year," adds a 2L. "This enables you to form strong bonds for study groups and lifelong friendships. Also, even though everyone studies a lot during the week, students find time to be social on Thursday or Friday nights."

"The location of the school is perfect from an educational standpoint because of the proximity to the courthouse." There's "an on-campus lecture-luncheon series with state and federal judges." The downside to life here is the "almost nonexistent social atmosphere." "The majority of the students commute from great distances which doesn't facilitate social opportunities." "People try to get involved and sponsor extracurricular social activities" and there are "plenty of opportunities to party and have fun," but you have to seek them out. "We need more social activities that cater to more students and bring us together as a community," suggests a 2L. The inescapable fact that "Central Islip is not exactly the party capital of the world" doesn't help. Fortunately, the culture and nightlife of New York City is only about an hour away.

Getting In

At Touro Law Center, recently admitted students at the 25th percentile have LSAT scores of approximately 150 and GPAs of approximately 2.8. Admitted students at the 75th percentile have LSAT scores of 153 and GPAs of roughly 3.4.

Public interest law requirement	Yes

ADMISSIONS

Selectivity Rating	60*
# applications received	2,403
# applicants accepted	923
# acceptees attending	266
Application fee	$60
Regular application	Rolling
Regular notification	Rolling
Rolling notification	Yes
Early application program	No
Transfer students accepted	Yes
Evening division offered	Yes
Part-time accepted	Yes
LSDAS accepted	Yes

International Students

TOEFL required of international students	No
TOEFL recommended of international students	Yes
Minimum paper TOEFL	600
Minimum computer TOEFL	250

FINANCIAL FACTS

Annual tuition	$32,000
Books and supplies	$700
Tuition per credit	$1,000
Room and board (off-campus)	$16,600
Financial aid application deadline	5/1
% first-year students receiving some sort of aid	89
% receiving some sort of aid	89
% of aid that is merit based	66
% receiving scholarships	61
Average grant	$5,068
Average loan	$27,163
Average total aid package	$30,925
Average debt	$79,000

EMPLOYMENT INFORMATION

Career Rating	71	Grads Employed by Field (%)	
Rate of placement (nine months out)	78	Business/Industry	15
Average starting salary	$58,875	Government	16
State for bar exam	NY	Judicial clerkships	3
Pass rate for first-time bar	79	Other	1
Prominent Alumni		Private practice	60
Justice Lewis Lubell, NYS Supreme Court;		Public Interest	5
Kathleen Rice, Nassau County district			
attorney; Seymour Liebman, corporate			
counsel, Canon USA; Jothy Narendran,			
partner, Certilman, Balin, Adler, and			
Hyman; Kenneth LaValle, New York State			
Senator.			

TULANE UNIVERSITY
LAW SCHOOL

INSTITUTIONAL INFORMATION

Public/private	Private
Student-faculty ratio	18:1
% faculty female	24
% faculty minority	12
Total faculty	50

SURVEY SAYS...

Students love New Orleans, LA
Good social life

STUDENTS

Enrollment of law school	800
% male/female	51/49
% out-of-state	84
% full-time	100
% minority	21
% international	3
# of countries represented	39
Average age of entering class	24

ACADEMICS

Academic Experience Rating	**86**
Profs interesting rating	86
Profs accessible rating	80
Hours of study per day	4.21

Academic Specialties

Admiralty and maritime law, civil law, environmental law, intellectual property law, international law, public interest law, sports law.

Advanced Degrees Offered

SJD 2 to 3 years, LLM 1 year, LLM (admiralty) 1 to 2 years, LLM (energy and environment) 1 to 2 years, LLM (international and comparative law) 1 year, LLM (American business law) 1 year.

Combined Degrees Offered

JD/BA or JD/BS 6 years, JD/MBA 4 years, JD/MHA 4 years, JD/MSPH 4 years, LLM/MSPH 2 years, JD/MSW 4 to 4.5 years, JD/MA Latin American studies 3 to 4 years, JD/MACCT 3.5 to 4 years, JD/MS (international development) 3 to 3.5 years.

Clinical program required	No

Academics

The oldest law school in the south, the Law School at Tulane University is the only first-tier law school that offers a dual curriculum in which students can study both common and civil law, an exceptional opportunity for those looking to practice internationally. Known for its strong international, environmental, and maritime law programs, the school has bounced back from the effects of Hurricane Katrina and in a big way. "Harvard itself couldn't pull me away from this place," states a clearly satisfied student.

Students are of conflicting opinion regarding those that run the school. The administration's actions and leadership during Katrina showed many students "that our roles as lawyers extend well beyond the courtroom to the community in which we live." However, upon returning to school after the hurricane (many students took classes at other law schools in the interim), some students have found the deans' expectations to be "frustrating" and unrealistic [and] particularly the administration's "almost blind adherence to pre-Katrina procedure while fully expecting complete understanding from students regarding the numerous areas in which administrative performance has been hampered, such as resource procurement, faculty retention and recruitment." Luckily, most students understand that this rebuilding and reparation period is temporary, and some have realized unexpected benefits in the aftermath of the disaster. "Post-Katrina Tulane is like no other law school in the country. We get the opportunity to study firsthand new situations and problems in a major U.S. city," says a third-year student. "The school is always holding seminars and conferences where lawyers and law students from across the country come to listen to our experiences and get our take on what could be done."

As far as instruction is concerned, students speak of a good blend of "senior" and "young professors," as well a mix of "pure academics and people who have actually practiced." This "wacky, intelligent, and entertaining" bunch of teachers has "very unique but effective teaching styles," which make for enjoyable classes. As one student explains, "The Socratic Method is used but only in a fun way." A lot of teachers try to veer away from this style when teaching the upperclassmen and use "more creative methods—panels and so forth." There is the problem of professor "poaching" by higher-ranked law schools, especially in the wake of the hurricane, but for the ones who have stayed "A sort of kinship has evolved between students and professors that might be missing at other schools." "My criminal law professor even gave us her cell phone number to call her during the exam if we had a question!" says a student.

With a JD program as well-recognized as Tulane's, employment opportunities are "national in scope" "with wonderful ties to New York and many other big markets." Alumni are "quick to accept requests for advice, and often pick up the tab for lunch." The law and business schools are located next to one another in the center of campus, allowing JD and MBA students the chance to "intermingle with students outside of their programs." The campus is adjacent to Audubon Park providing plenty of opportunities for outdoor activities. The law school building itself is "beautiful," not to mention the historic St. Charles Avenue neighborhood in which it is located. "New Orleans is in a transition period, but the city is still gorgeous." "Going to school here is a constant reminder of why you went to law school in the first place, and helps keep you from losing that idealism that so many law students tend to forget over time."

ERIN CRIXELL, ADMISSION COORDINATOR
WEINMANN HALL, 6329 FRERET STREET, NEW ORLEANS, LA 70118
TEL: 504-865-5930 FAX: 504-865-6710
E-MAIL: ADMISSIONS@LAW.TULANE.EDU • INTERNET: WWW.LAW.TULANE.EDU

Life

The diversity of Tulane means that "there are people here for everyone." "Students at Tulane are friends with other students at Tulane—[they're] not just classmates and competitors." In fact, there's very little competition to be found at all. "People who are 'there to win' don't belong at Tulane," says one student. Reflecting the city's reputation for around-the-clock distractions, students "work hard and play hard here." "If you can't balance school and Bourbon Street, don't go to Tulane," warns a 2L in true New Orleans form. "It is a uniquely Tulanian feature that you admire the cleverness of the students in your class by day, and revel in their pure stupidity in the French Quarter by night," says a student. Since very few of the "gutsy pirates and pioneers" who attend Tulane Law School are actually from the area, there's always someone willing to explore the social and cultural opportunities afforded by the school's location. "The food is amazing—yet not healthy at all," admits a second-year student guiltily. Students who want to take advantage of on-campus enrichment opportunities appreciate that Tulane offers a wide variety of organizations, journals, moot court teams, and sports clubs, and highly encourages pro bono work. As one graduating student sums up: "If you decide to come to Tulane, don't expect to sleep much—there's just too much to do."

Getting In

With close to 3,000 applications for just 250 seats, Tulane admissions can be quite selective. Though other factors play a part in the selection process, most offers are made to candidates whose "objective" credentials—undergrad GPA and LSAT scores—place them in the top third of the applicant pool. Enrolled students at the 75th percentile had a GPA of 3.75 and an LSAT score of 163. The school strongly urges candidates to submit applications electronically.

Legal writing	
course requirement	Yes
Legal methods	
course requirement	No
Legal research	
course requirement	Yes
Moot court requirement	Yes
Public interest	
law requirement	Yes

ADMISSIONS

Selectivity Rating	**86**
# applications received	2,400
# applicants accepted	800
# acceptees attending	275
Average LSAT	161
LSAT Range	159–163
Average undergrad GPA	3.56
Application fee	$60
Regular application	Rolling
Regular notification	Rolling
Rolling notification	Yes
Early application program	No
Transfer students accepted	Yes
Evening division offered	No
Part-time accepted	No
LSDAS accepted	Yes

Applicants Also Look At

American University, Boston College, Emory University, The George Washington University, Georgetown University, University of Miami, The University of Texas at Austin.

International Students

TOEFL required	
of international students	No
TOEFL recommended	
of international students	No

FINANCIAL FACTS

Annual tuition	$30,350
Books and supplies	$1,400
Fees per credit	$231
Tuition per credit	$3,035
Room and board	$9,375
Financial aid application	
deadline	3/15
% first-year students	
receiving some sort of aid	87
% receiving some sort of aid	87
% of aid that is merit based	90
% receiving scholarships	65
Average grant	$11,000
Average loan	$27,337
Average total aid package	$29,500
Average debt	$87,000

EMPLOYMENT INFORMATION

Career Rating	**86**	**Grads Employed by Field (%)**	
Rate of placement (nine months out)	95	Academic	1
Average starting salary	$88,500	Business/Industry	10
State for bar exam	NY, LA, TX, FL, DC	Government	12
Pass rate for first-time bar	93	Judicial clerkships	10

Employers Who Frequently Hire Grads

Military 2

Fulbright and Jaworski; Skadden Arps; Arnold and Porter; White and Case; Mayer, Brown, and Platt; Cleary Gottlieb; Schulte Roth.

Private practice 57

Public Interest 4

Prominent Alumni

Robert Livingston, former U.S. Representative; David Vitter, U.S. Senator; John Minor Wisdom, judiciary; Honorable William Suter, Clerk, U.S. Supreme Court.

THE UNIVERSITY OF AKRON
SCHOOL OF LAW

INSTITUTIONAL INFORMATION

Public/private	Public
Student-faculty ratio	13:1
% faculty part-time	45
% faculty female	31
% faculty minority	7
Total faculty	55

SURVEY SAYS...
Diverse opinions accepted in classrooms
Great research resources
Abundant externship/internship/clerkship opportunities

STUDENTS

Enrollment of law school	524
% male/female	57/43
% out-of-state	25
% full-time	58
% minority	14
% international	1
# of countries represented	1
Average age of entering class	24

ACADEMICS

Academic Experience Rating	**75**
Profs interesting rating	70
Profs accessible rating	71
Hours of study per day	4.4

Academic Specialties
Criminal law, corporate, general, intellectual property law, international law, litigation, taxation.

Advanced Degrees Offered
LLM (intellectual property) 1 to 2 years.

Combined Degrees Offered
JD/MBA 3.5 years, JD/MS (management in human resources) 3.5 years, JD/MA (taxation) 3.5 years, JD/MPA 3.5 years, JD/MA (applied politics) 3.5 years.

Clinical program required	No
Legal writing course requirement	Yes
Legal methods course requirement	Yes

Academics

Far away from the world of academic pretension and staggering student loans, The University of Akron is a laid-back and engaging place to earn a JD at a very reasonable price. One of the most inexpensive programs in the United States, Akron students ask us, "Where else can you get a well-respected law degree for less than $15,000 a year?" While Akron doesn't provide the posh classrooms and high-tech facilities you might find at a pricier program, the school delivers on every point that really matters. As one student explains, "Akron cuts out some of the unnecessary frills of law school but keeps the essential quality of faculty and passes on the savings to the student." In fact, students describe the teaching staff as no less than a "fleet of hard-core Ivy League pedagogues" who "genuinely care about our academic and professional success." But there are a few who seem "more worried about sticking to the Socratic Method . . . than ensuring that their students comprehend class materials."

Akron attracts a high-energy and accomplished student body and staff. One student elaborates, "The administration excels at recruiting high-caliber young professors and attracting students who are intelligent, skilled, and capable. In these areas Akron is accomplished and improving." The evening program draws a particularly interesting mix of students, including "physicians, teachers, paralegals, social workers, mid-level managers for *Fortune* 1000 companies, engineers of all sorts, police officers, business owners, amongst the usual part-time types." However, the professional diversity isn't limited to moonlighters; "Second and third year students often take a night class or two, and the two sections become intermixed after that first year."

Discussion, interaction, and practical applications of legal theory take precedence at Akron. "Many of the classrooms are set up like courtrooms, which give students the opportunity to have a courtroom experience, or meeting rooms, which provides the students with an excellent opportunity to discuss and engage in academic debate with the professor and one another," says one student. The school also employs a team of adjunct faculty who "teach the skills that will actually be needed to practice law." In addition, Akron offers a large number of courses that prepare you for the bar (the school boasts a very high bar-passage rate), as well as placing "a strong emphasis on legal research and writing." On top of that, students praise the school's "opportunities for practical experience via internships, clinic placements, trial team, trial practice, and pleading practice classes." For example, students may gain experience through the New Business Legal Clinic that "gives students hands-on transactional business law experience with real clients in the area."

When it comes to job and internship placement, Akron is competitive, especially in the local community. A current student elaborates, "It seems like the students who want big-firm summer associate positions fight for them and get them, just like at any 'higher ranked' school. I have not suffered from any shortage of opportunities here." However, students also complain that the school's "hard" grading policies negatively affect their job opportunities and create unnecessary competition amongst the student body. Plus, lower academic performance can negatively effect or cancel a student's scholarship package, which "the majority of students lose after the first year" due to the steep grading curve.

Life

While course work keeps them busy, "students at Akron are generally social and participate in community activities and student organizations." The school's "very active

LAURI S. FILE, ASSISTANT DEAN OF ADMISSIONS, FINANCIAL AID, STUDENT SERVICES
THE UNIVERSITY OF AKRON SCHOOL OF LAW, 302 BUCHTEL COMMONS, AKRON, OH 44325-2901
TEL: 800-425-7668 FAX: 330-258-2343
E-MAIL: LAWADMISSIONS@UAKRON.EDU • INTERNET: WWW.UAKRON.EDU/LAW

SBA," coordinates events with the SBA's at neighboring law schools." Students also like the fact that "professors are also present at most school/organizational functions supporting their students in their free time." As is the case for students in most professional programs, the evening division at Akron is less involved in the campus community, since they are usually balancing full-time work with school, and sometimes family. "Among evening students there is not a real sense of community because most of them have full-time jobs and families, and they just don't have time to 'hang out' outside of class," explains a current moonlighter.

Day students warn us that you'll see your share of "drama and gossip" amongst some members of the student body, many of whom are recent college graduates. However, students reassure us that the vibe is generally "very friendly and helpful" amongst their fellow students. One explains, "We attempt to help one another learn, because in the end the future clients are what matters most, and we want all clients, whether they are our own or not, to be represented in the best way possible." Whether of not they study or party together, "All students—evening students included—bond during their first year" thanks to the demanding workload. Don't discount the fact that despite all this work, students here "know how to have fun."

Getting In

In 2006, The University of Akron enrolled 119 students in the full-time day program, and 67 in the evening program. Both programs had roughly a 30 percent acceptance rate. The median LSAT score was 158 and 152 for the day and evening programs, respectively. The median undergraduate GPA for all entering students was 3.32. Non-Ohio residents made up approximately 25 percent of the entering class and 24 different states were represented.

Legal research course requirement	Yes
Moot court requirement	No
Public interest law requirement	No

ADMISSIONS

Selectivity Rating	79
# applications received	1,858
# applicants accepted	512
# acceptees attending	119
Average LSAT	156
LSAT Range	154–159
Average undergrad GPA	3.3
Regular application	Rolling
Regular notification	Rolling
Rolling notification	Yes
Early application program	No
Transfer students accepted	Yes
Evening division offered	Yes
Part-time accepted	Yes
LSDAS accepted	Yes

Applicants Also Look At
Capital U., Case Western Reserve U., Cleveland State U., The Ohio State U., Thomas M. Cooley Law School, U. of Dayton, U. of Toledo.

International Students

TOEFL required of international students	Yes
Minimum paper TOEFL	600
Minimum computer TOEFL	250

FINANCIAL FACTS

Annual tuition (resident)	$14,292
Annual tuition (nonresident)	$23,884
Books and supplies	$900
Fees per credit (resident)	$74
Fees per credit (nonresident)	$74
Tuition per credit (resident)	$476
Tuition per credit (nonresident)	$796
Room and board	$14,196
Financial aid application deadline	3/1
% first-year students receiving some sort of aid	70
% receiving some sort of aid	85
% of aid that is merit based	98
% receiving scholarships	34
Average grant	$11,910
Average loan	$19,286
Average total aid package	$19,622
Average debt	$45,924

EMPLOYMENT INFORMATION

Career Rating	73	Grads Employed by Field (%)	
Rate of placement (nine months out)	93	Academic	2
Average starting salary	$67,517	Business/Industry	30
State for bar exam	OH	Government	15
Pass rate for first-time bar	78	Judicial clerkships	7
Employers Who Frequently Hire Grads		Military	1
Buckingham, Doolittle, and Burroughs;		Other	1
Brouse and McDowell; Roetzel and		Private practice	40
Andress; Jones, Day, Squire, Sanders, and		Public Interest	4
Dempsey; Sughrue Mion.			

Prominent Alumni
Honorable Deborah Cook, Honorable Alice Batchelder, U.S. Court of Appeals 6th Circuit; Anthony Alexander, president and CEO, First Energy; Rochelle Seide, partner, Arent Fox; John Vasuta, counsel, Bridgestone Firestone.

THE UNIVERSITY OF ALABAMA AT TUSCALOOSA
SCHOOL OF LAW

INSTITUTIONAL INFORMATION

Public/private	Public
Student-faculty ratio	12:1
% faculty part-time	49
% faculty female	19
% faculty minority	8
Total faculty	94

SURVEY SAYS...
Great research resources
Great library staff
Abundant externship/internship/
clerkship opportunities

STUDENTS

Enrollment of law school	491
% male/female	63/37
% out-of-state	22
% full-time	100
% minority	13
Average age of entering class	25

ACADEMICS

Academic Experience Rating	**89**
Profs interesting rating	86
Profs accessible rating	93
Hours of study per day	4.56

Advanced Degrees Offered
LLM (taxation) 2 years, LLM (international graduate program) 1 year.

Combined Degrees Offered
JD/MBA 3 to 4 years, dual enrollment with various university graduate programs.

Clinical program required	No
Legal writing course requirement	Yes
Legal methods course requirement	No
Legal research course requirement	Yes
Moot court requirement	Yes
Public interest law requirement	No

Academics

Students seeking a very good and very affordable legal education might want to check out The University of Alabama School of Law. "It is unlikely that you will receive a better legal education for the amount of tuition anywhere in the country," ventures a 3L. "The bang for the buck can't be beat." UA offers "small" class sections, a "broad range of courses," and "a wide variety of clinical opportunities" which allow students to get practical experience at the school in exchange for academic credit. "Great study abroad and exchange programs" send students to Switzerland and Australia. In a word, the "overall academic experience is excellent."

"The administration and faculty are friendly and seem to genuinely care about the students." "Alabama professors integrate theory with real-world practicality." "The faculty's mission is not to turn out legal academics, but rather to prepare capable attorneys for real-world situations." In terms of teaching, professors are either "excellent in the classroom" or "deplorable." "There aren't a whole lot of middle-of-the-road professors," explains one student. "I've had the best professors in my life at this school—and the worst." Outside of class, "Professors get to know their students" and "welcome the opportunity to help students in a variety of endeavors." The administration is "top-notch" and "extremely accessible to students." The deans are much beloved and "ready, able, and willing to help you out." In general, staff members "request, listen to, and act on feedback from students," though they "can lag in response time."

"Career Services is still a work in progress, but it is improving." "Because the school is so inexpensive," "Alabama is a no-brainer" for students who are interested in public interest careers. For students interested in private-sector work, UA's reputation is "still regional." Students are "confident" that their degrees "will open doors" throughout the Southeast, but they admit that Career Services tends to "focus on the big regional firms and because of that, most of the attention goes to the students at the very top of the class." "Attracting more out-of-state firms to on-campus recruiting" would be a big improvement.

The facilities here are mostly excellent. The library "screams 1970s," but "has more than sufficient resources." "The new building is terrific." UA "just completed a new wing that has two large, very high-tech seminar classrooms; several high-tech courtrooms; a new dining area and lounge area for students; a new bookstore; and new rooms and offices for all of the law clinics."

Life

The UA law student population is "not very diverse." "There is a small group of Black students and very few Hispanic and Asian students. There are just a couple of older students." "The average student is young and direct from college," and "usually" from Alabama "or from a neighboring state." Students describe themselves as "very smart" and "down-to-earth." Politically, it's a pretty conservative atmosphere, and "expressing a more liberal viewpoint can sometimes be intimidating.'"

Academically, some students are "very grade-oriented" ("bordering on obsession") but, overall, "The competition appears healthy." "Civility among students is paramount," and "The atmosphere at Alabama is extremely collegial." "People at the top are very competitive with each other. But there is also a sort of community with those people as well." "We don't have too many gunners or too many of the socially inept," says

Ms. Claude Reeves Arrington, Senior Assistant Dean
Box 870382, Tuscaloosa, AL 35487
Tel: 205-348-5440 Fax: 205-348-5439
E-mail: admissions@law.ua.edu • Internet: www.law.ua.edu

a 2L. "It's friendly competition, because we know we'll all be working together throughout our careers." "Students share course outlines freely."

Socially, UA is "really a great place to study the law." "Students are overwhelmingly friendly and very cooperative." "It has been very easy for me to make several good friends among very diverse individuals with differing interests," says a 2L. "While we study a great deal, we also find time to hit up the bars in large groups." "The Student Bar Association throws parties every other week, and the students all socialize together." Tuscaloosa offers "great weather" and it's "a great college town." If you're not "super-interested" in football, though, "That's sacrilegious down here." Alabama's social scene generally "revolves around sports," and "Football is a near-religious experience." Devotion to the Crimson Tide definitely extends to the law school. Students have their own cheering section, "right there with the fraternities." "We schedule our work so that we can attend Crimson Tide ball games," says a 1L. If you "don't like football, you'll probably have a harder time finding your niche." "However, it is possible to escape that and do your own thing." "Birmingham is an awesome city a mere 45 minutes away from Tuscaloosa and it offers everything an urbanite could need," including "fantastic shopping, excellent restaurants, lots of young singles, a sense of community, and even a little bit of the hipster scene (somewhat of a rarity in Alabama)."

Getting In

At the University of Alabama, admitted students at the 25th percentile have LSAT scores of 159 and GPAs of nearly 3.3. Admitted students at the 75th percentile have LSAT scores of 165 and GPAs just over 3.8.

ADMISSIONS

Selectivity Rating	89
# applications received	1,109
# applicants accepted	354
# acceptees attending	171
Average LSAT	163
LSAT Range	159–165
Average undergrad GPA	3.56
Application fee	$35
Regular application	3/1
Regular notification	Rolling
Rolling notification	Yes
Early application program	No
Transfer students accepted	Yes
Evening division offered	No
Part-time accepted	No
LSDAS accepted	Yes

International Students

TOEFL required of international students	Yes

FINANCIAL FACTS

Annual tuition (resident)	$9,736
Annual tuition (nonresident)	$19,902
Books and supplies	$1,168
Room and board (on/off-campus)	$7,098/$7,310

EMPLOYMENT INFORMATION

Career Rating	80	Grads Employed by Field (%)	
Rate of placement (nine months out)	99	Academic	1
Average starting salary	$68,353	Business/Industry	7
State for bar exam	AL, GA, FL, TN, NC	Government	8
Pass rate for first-time bar	98	Judicial clerkships	8
Employers Who Frequently Hire Grads		Military	1
Bradley, Arant, Rose, and White LLP;		Other	2
Maynard, Cooper, and Gale, PC; Balch and		Private practice	69
Bingham LLP; Burr and Forman LLP;		Public Interest	4
Lightfoot, Franklin, and White, LLC;			
Kilpatrick Stockton LLP; Alston and Bird			
LLP; Sirote and Permutt, PC; Baker,			
Donelson, Bearman, Caldwell, and			
Berkowitz, PC; Adams and Reese LLP.			

UNIVERSITY OF ARIZONA
JAMES E. ROGERS COLLEGE OF LAW

INSTITUTIONAL INFORMATION

Public/private	Public
Student-faculty ratio	12:1
% faculty part-time	42
% faculty female	40
% faculty minority	20
Total faculty	83

SURVEY SAYS...

Diverse opinions accepted
in classrooms
Abundant externship/internship/
clerkship opportunities
Students love Tucson, AZ

STUDENTS

Enrollment of law school	463
% male/female	51/49
% out-of-state	30
% full-time	100
% minority	28
% international	1
# of countries represented	3
Average age of entering class	26

ACADEMICS

Academic Experience Rating	88
Profs interesting rating	87
Profs accessible rating	91
Hours of study per day	4.2

Academic Specialties

Commercial law, constitutional law,
corporation securities law, criminal
law, environmental law, human rights
law, Indian law, intellectual property
law, international indigenous peoples'
rights and policy, international law,
international trade law, legal history,
legal philosophy, property, taxation.

Advanced Degrees Offered

JD 3 years, LLM (international
trade) 1 year, LLM (indigenous peoples' law and policy) 1 year, SJD 3
years.

Combined Degrees Offered

JD/PhD 6 years, JD/MBA 4 years,
JD/MPA 4 years, JD/MA 4 years,
JD/MA 4 years, JD/MA 4 years,
JD/MA 4 years, JD/MMF

Clinical program required	No

Academics

The University of Arizona James E. Rogers College of Law offers "small class sizes"; "a very friendly, welcoming environment"; and "a price tag that lets students pursue careers in public service and nonprofit organizations" without racking up a gargantuan debt. Opportunities to gain practical experience are plentiful. The "strong" judicial externship program "can accommodate students interested in everything from bankruptcy court to superior court to district court." Clinics offer "hands-on experience" in six areas including immigration, child advocacy, and indigenous peoples' law.

"This school is the most student-focused academic institution I have ever attended," says a happy 3L. The small size "limits the number of advanced classes" available but students tell us that the personal attention they receive more than compensates. Faculty members "truly care about their students" and "are available constantly." In the classroom, professors "make every effort to make the classes interesting and enjoyable" and "The small-section format during first year allows students to build a relationship with at least one professor." "They encourage discussion before and after class and are more than willing to provide letters of recommendation and reference." "They are approachable, friendly, and most even greet you by name as they pass you in the lobby or going to and from class." "Most are around campus all day and not just available during their office hours." "I e-mailed my property professor on a Sunday at roughly 10:30 P.M., with a pretty lengthy question," describes a 2L. "The question was answered at length by 10:45 P.M." "The administration is great too," enthuses a 1L. "Everyone is very helpful and interested in you getting a good education." "The dean is fantastic." "She's approachable" and "will bend over backwards for you." Ideological diversity among the "very left-wing" faculty and administration is limited, though. "The professors do not hide the fact that they are liberal; the student body is liberal; and if you are conservative, you are made to feel like a two-headed monkey monster."

Some students tell us that the "very helpful" Career and Professional Development Office at the U of A is "active in helping students connect with amazing internship and job opportunities in both the public sector and in law firms" in Arizona, California, and other Western states. Other students complain that the Career Office "is less than helpful" and "does not bring in that many employers compared to other law schools." "Their attitude seems to be that they don't care what job you get, as long as you get one somewhere and they can mark you on their statistic sheet," complains a 3L.

The classrooms here are "freezing" but "very nice and technologically advanced." Otherwise, the "pretty basic and unattractive" law school facilities "leave something to be desired," but students emphatically promise that "massive renovations" will make things much better very soon. "Construction on a new library begins in the summer of 2007" and "The physical space will be reconfigured and completely redesigned."

Life

There is a "relaxed Arizonan attitude" among the "amazingly friendly, smart" students at the U of A. "There is definitely competition here, as is unavoidable, but the school has a very laid-back atmosphere that allows you to keep things in perspective." "The second- and third-year students are very active in assisting the first-years adapt to law school through tutorials for all first-year classes," and teaching assistants "help with briefing and outlining." "Despite the curve, grades are not a big issue among students, and we tend to

TERRY SUE HOLPERT, ASSISTANT DEAN FOR ADMISSIONS
PO BOX 210176, COLLEGE OF LAW, UNIVERSITY OF ARIZONA, TUCSON, AZ 85721-0176
TEL: 520-621-3477 FAX: 520-626-1839
E-MAIL: ADMISSIONS@LAW.ARIZONA.EDU • INTERNET: WWW.LAW.ARIZONA.EDU

be excited for others' successes," declares a 1L. "This place is the opposite of cutthroat." Small sections for first-year students "are really conducive to forming lasting friendships." "I became very close with the other 26 students in my small section and continue to be good friends with several of them," says a 2L. "There is an overriding sense that everyone, from faculty to administration to students, really wants to be at the school and wants to see the school succeed."

The social atmosphere is "very vibrant." "I have had so much fun in law school," gushes a 1L. "There are dozens of student groups and lots of social events." "Almost every day, there are informative and thought-provoking guest speakers, panel discussions, or film screenings, especially during the lunch hour." Intramural sports are also popular. Social tends to be "polarized between younger people coming straight out of college and older students with families." "The crowd divides into three groups," elaborates a 3L, "the married/serious relationship/older crowd, the nerds who rarely go out, and those who are trying to extend their undergraduate experience by going to law school." Without question, if you are "interested in partying, you cannot beat the University of Arizona bar scene."

The U of A campus itself is "beautiful, complete with palm trees and a gigantic, ideal student union." "The weather is ideal." The low cost of living is "fabulous, especially from a student's perspective," but "Tucson itself does not offer much for a social life outside of the undergraduate Greek life scene." If you like outdoor activity, there are "myriad" activities within minutes of campus, including hiking, biking, swimming, and rock climbing.

Getting In

Admitted students at the 25th percentile have LSAT scores in the range of about 158 and GPAs in the range of 3.3 or so. Admitted students at the 75th percentile have LSAT scores of about 164 and GPAs approaching 3.8.

Legal writing	
course requirement	Yes
Legal methods	
course requirement	No
Legal research	
course requirement	Yes
Moot court requirement	No
Public interest	
law requirement	No

ADMISSIONS

Selectivity Rating	87
# applications received	2,484
# applicants accepted	660
# acceptees attending	154
Average LSAT	162
LSAT Range	158–164
Average undergrad GPA	3.52
Application fee	$50
Regular application	2/15
Regular notification	Rolling
Rolling notification	Yes
Early application program	Yes
Early application deadline	11/15
Early application notification	12/22
Transfer students accepted	Yes
Evening division offered	No
Part-time accepted	No
LSDAS accepted	Yes

Applicants Also Look At

Arizona State U., U. of California—Davis, U. of California—Hastings, U. of California—Los Angeles, U. of San Diego, U. of Southern California, The U. of Texas at Austin.

International Students

TOEFL required	
of international students	Yes

FINANCIAL FACTS

Annual tuition (resident)	$16,201
Annual tuition	
(nonresident)	$25,991
Books and supplies	$1,000
Room and board	
(on/off-campus)	$8,864/$12,688
Financial aid application	
deadline	3/1
% first-year students	
receiving some sort of aid	80
% receiving some sort of aid	82
% of aid that is merit based	50
% receiving scholarships	78
Average grant	$5,000
Average loan	$13,500
Average total aid package	$18,000
Average debt	$50,000

EMPLOYMENT INFORMATION

		Grads Employed by Field (%)	
Career Rating	78		
Rate of placement (nine months out)	93	Academic	8
Average starting salary	$65,657	Business/Industry	7
State for bar exam	AZ, CA, WA, NV, DC	Government	15
Pass rate for first-time bar	88	Judicial clerkships	22
Employers Who Frequently Hire Grads		Military	3
Snell and Wilmer; Perkins Coie; Lewis and		Private practice	42
Roca; Kirkland and Ellis; Heller Erhman;		Public Interest	3
Quarles and Brady; Bryan Cave; Greenberg			
Traurig; Squire Sanders; Gibson Dunn.			
Prominent Alumni			
Morris K. Udall, former U.S. Congressman;			
Stewart Udall, former U.S.Congressman			
and Secretary of Interior; Dennis			
DeConcini, former U.S. senator.			

UNIVERSITY OF ARKANSAS—FAYETTEVILLE
SCHOOL OF LAW

INSTITUTIONAL INFORMATION

Public/private	Public
Student-faculty ratio	14.23:1
% faculty part-time	28
% faculty female	33
% faculty minority	16
Total faculty	34

SURVEY SAYS...

Diverse opinions accepted
in classrooms
Great research resources
Students love Fayetteville, AR
Good social life

STUDENTS

Enrollment of law school	428
% male/female	56/44
% out-of-state	30
% full-time	100
% minority	26
% international	1
# of countries represented	2
Average age of entering class	25

ACADEMICS

Academic Experience Rating	**73**
Profs interesting rating	67
Profs accessible rating	72
Hours of study per day	3.77

Advanced Degrees Offered
LLM (agricultural law) 1 academic year.

Combined Degrees Offered
JD/MBA 4.5 years, JD/MPA 4 years, LLM/MS 2.5 years.

Clinical program required	No
Legal writing course requirement	Yes
Legal methods course requirement	No
Legal research course requirement	No
Moot court requirement	No
Public interest law requirement	No

Academics

The very affordable University of Arkansas School of Law in Fayetteville provides "some of the best opportunities in the nation to develop real-world skills in trial advocacy." "This campus is the primary source in the state for legal information and is a huge asset to students, as well as local and visiting practitioners and scholars." Clinical opportunities "are few," but skills-based courses are ample. There are "many competitions" which "let students put their skills to practice." "Several ongoing collaborative community projects" involve externships and pro bono work. The school offers a traditional JD/MBA program and a unique JD/MA in international law and politics. In addition, students can pursue summer study-abroad programs in Cambridge, England and St. Petersburg, Russia.

You'll find "a diverse range of professors" here, "from the weathered courtroom practitioner to the young vibrant scholar." "While the Socratic Method employed in the classroom is stressful by nature, all of my professors seem to truly care about whether students understand the material," relates a 1L. "They will challenge you, mentor you, and teach you how to be the best advocate possible." "All of my professors have relevant experience that allows them to relate the cases in the book to something they have done in the real world, making those concepts easier to remember in the long run," adds another 1L. Outside the classroom, "All the professors have open-door policies, so you can stop in at anytime to ask anything." Reviews of the administration are mixed. Some students "can't stand the administration." Others call the administration "warm, welcoming, and personable." "They know the majority of the students on a first-name basis" and the deans are "truly helpful in any pursuit you may have, such as disseminating student organization information, providing general and tailored advice about internship searching, and providing pragmatic feedback."

Employment prospects following graduation are fair. "The school seems to have very good clout within the state and pretty good clout around the region." Plenty of students find employment in Little Rock and in smaller communities across the state. Other students don't find jobs in Arkansas because, they say, "There are no jobs available in this state." Northwest Arkansas in particular "is saturated with lawyers and so the starting salaries are depressed."

Facilities at the school "consist of a really ugly old building merged with a really ugly new building." The new building is "high-tech, comfortable, [and] beautiful" on the inside. "The library is now large and very modern. The new classrooms are extremely nice and are very technologically advanced." "With several study rooms, a coffee shop, a brand-new computer lab, a beautiful new courtroom, and many other additions, the U of A Law School facilities rival any other in the nation." Naturally, the new building is now "overrun with undergraduate students who are drawn to the coffee shop and study space." "Ironically, I often go to the campus' main library to study," says a 2L.

Life

The "vibrant and interesting" student population here is seriously diverse. This is either really great or a source of tension, depending on whom you talk to. Some students say that "too much emphasis is placed on diversity," "There is no sense of community," and "There are lots of cliques." "Social circles divide on the basis of race and ethnicity," adds one student. "The student chapter of BLSA (Black Law Student Association), of which I am a member, is strong and active but not overly inclusive of non-Black students,"

JAMES K. MILLER, ASSOCIATE DEAN FOR STUDENTS
UNIVERSITY OF ARKANSAS SCHOOL OF LAW, FAYETTEVILLE, AR 72701
TEL: 479-575-3102 FAX: 479-575-3937
E-MAIL: JKMILLER@UARK.EDU • INTERNET: LAW.UARK.EDU

observes a 3L. "It's a great support [network] but also a segregating factor." Other students disagree entirely. "I am amazed at the diversity in the law school, both among students and faculty," beams a 1L. "I've never noticed a racial divide." "Social circles seem to be quite diverse." "The majority of the campus and classes aren't divided or walking on eggshells about this issue." "I am originally from Los Angeles and I had some concerns that such a divide would exist in a Southern law school," explains a 3L. "I was pleasantly surprised with the racial interaction and harmony among the law students."

With only about 150 students per class, "everyone knows everybody." "Competitiveness among the student body varies widely by groups. Some are very competitive, others not so much." Mostly, "Students are courteous and friendly" and "generally willing to help each other study." When students put away their casebooks, there are "many social events to attend coordinated by the law school." "The social life is quite good," and it's really good if you like "drinking at different locations." The surrounding college town of Fayetteville oozes with "hometown charm" and is "a great place to be." According to one student, "Northwest Arkansas is the most beautiful part of the country."

Getting In

Recently admitted students at the 25th percentile have LSAT scores of about 152 and GPAs in the 3.0 range. Admitted students at the 75th percentile have LSAT scores of about 159 and GPAs approaching 3.7.

ADMISSIONS

Selectivity Rating	81
# applications received	1,334
# applicants accepted	386
# acceptees attending	159
Average LSAT	155
LSAT Range	151–159
Average undergrad GPA	3.48
Regular application	Rolling
Regular notification	Rolling
Rolling notification	Yes
Early application program	No
Transfer students accepted	Yes
Evening division offered	No
Part-time accepted	No
LSDAS accepted	Yes

International Students

TOEFL required of international students	Yes
Minimum paper TOEFL	550
Minimum computer TOEFL	213
Internet TOEFL	80

FINANCIAL FACTS

Annual tuition (resident)	$9,713
Annual tuition (nonresident)	$19,486
Books and supplies	$1,000
Room and board	$14,492
Financial aid application deadline	4/1
% first-year students receiving some sort of aid	74
% receiving some sort of aid	74
% of aid that is merit based	65
% receiving scholarships	40
Average grant	$6,000
Average loan	$18,500
Average debt	$48,794

EMPLOYMENT INFORMATION

Career Rating	71
Rate of placement (nine months out)	91
Average starting salary	$51,780
State for bar exam	AR, TN, MO, OK, TX
Pass rate for first-time bar	80

Employers Who Frequently Hire Grads
The majority of our grads go into small firms.

Prominent Alumni
George W. Haley, former Ambassador to Gambia; Philip S. Anderson, former ABA president; Honorable Morris S. Arnold, U.S. Court of Appeals, 8th Circuit; Rodney Slater, former U.S. Secretary of Transportation.

Grads Employed by Field (%)

Business/Industry	14
Government	11
Judicial clerkships	7
Private practice	61
Public Interest	7

UNIVERSITY OF ARKANSAS—LITTLE ROCK
WILLIAM H. BOWEN SCHOOL OF LAW

Academics

For the prospective law student interested in practicing in the state of Arkansas or regionally, it's hard to beat the "location" and "quality of instruction for your dollar" that the William H. Bowen School of Law offers. Because the school "is in the capital of the state, there are many opportunities for practical experience" such as "externships . . . for justices in the Arkansas Supreme Court, Federal District Court, and the U.S. Court of Appeals for the Eighth Circuit." The location also likely has something to do with the sizable part-time JD program offered here. Many say that "it is great for part-time students" and that the "school does not push off adjunct professors on the part-time students; instead full-time faculty members are required to also teach in the part-time division." In terms of price, tuition and fees clock in at less than $10,000 a year for in-state students—what you might call a legal steal.

The school has reportedly "spent $1 million . . . in renovations" in recent years. Results include "wireless and plugs for laptops at every seat" and "high-tech teaching workstations with projectors and cameras to video capture the class for students that are not there. They also have high-tech sound systems with microphones throughout the room so everybody can be heard." The "incredible" library has "an abundance of private study areas and more than adequate [research] resources." Most students agree that the school should focus its next round of capital improvements on dining facilities. "The lunch room and general access to food is terrible. There is no place within walking distance to get a cup of coffee!" says one student. The solution? "Build a cafeteria."

Professors at Bowen "are not in any shape, form, or fashion second-rate: They all have some pretty impressive resumes and most of them have practical experience" to inform the theories they teach. "They all seem genuinely engaged in teaching law" and "really care about your health [and] your well-being" as a student. They are "knowledgeable," "not haughty," and "demand high effort from students." This faculty is complemented by a "very helpful and approachable" administration.

The school promotes a "friendly" and "supportive" environment that fosters "an atmosphere of cooperation" rather than "abound[ing]" competition. But expect a challenge. "Everyone wants you to do the best that you possibly can with the best resources and the most thorough understanding, and then they want to beat you," explains one student. However students would like to see the grading curve "raised" or see the school "get rid" of it since many find that though they enjoy "being challenged on the level of graduates from across the country," "Our grades make us look inferior" to students from law schools with more forgiving curves.

AARON N. TAYLOR, ASSISTANT DEAN FOR ADMISSIONS
1201 MCMATH AVENUE, LITTLE ROCK, AR 72202-5142
TEL: 501-324-9903 FAX: 501-324-9433
E-MAIL: LAWADM@UALR.EDU • INTERNET: WWW.LAW.UALR.EDU

Life

The relatively small Bowen School of Law has a very solid mix of full-time and part-time students and "there are a lot of opportunities for students to meet each other and mix." "If you want a social life, there is always someone who wants to go out with you," says one student. "The hard part is actually refusing temptation."

The part-timers, who represent the other third of the student population, apparently have an easier time resisting the lure than the full-timers do. One typical member of this cohort indicates that he has been "invited to social functions by other students, but have mostly declined. Any time I have outside of class and studying I want to spend with my wife, the law school widow." That said, "The social life among the part-timers is pretty good considering we all have a lot of things going on; we still find time to occasionally go out for some drinks or whatever." Like most part-timers at most law schools, those here think they are "less competitive than the full-timers, for a variety of reasons—most of us work, most have other life priorities, [and] most realize grades aren't everything."

Students happily note that "there are a ton of meetings with free food every week." As one explains, "You can manage a free lunch at least twice a week just by going to lectures and meetings." Students "love the location," though a few mention that the school sits "in a pretty gnarly part of town."

Getting In

Bowen's admissions standards are comparable to its sister school in Fayetteville, so if you get in there, you have a very good shot at getting in here, too (and vice versa). A B-plus/A-minus undergraduate grade point average and an LSAT score in the mid-150s makes you a competitive candidate here, if not a shoo-in. For those with marks below these, note that the Admissions Office considers the personal statement the most important factor in its admissions decision-making process, so a compelling argument can go a long way in getting you through the door.

ADMISSIONS

Selectivity Rating	**82**
# applications received	1,322
# applicants accepted	267
# acceptees attending	134
Average LSAT	154
LSAT Range	150–157
Average undergrad GPA	3.28
Regular application	4/15
Regular notification	Rolling
Rolling notification	Yes
Early application program	No
Transfer students accepted	Yes
Evening division offered	Yes
Part-time accepted	Yes
LSDAS accepted	Yes

Applicants Also Look At
University of Arkansas—Fayetteville,
University of Missouri—Columbia,
The University of Tulsa.

International Students

TOEFL required of international students	No
TOEFL recommended of international students	Yes

FINANCIAL FACTS

Annual tuition (resident)	$8,610
Annual tuition (nonresident)	$18,540
Books and supplies	$1,000
Tuition per credit (resident)	$287
Tuition per credit (nonresident)	$618
Room and board (off-campus)	$9,476
Financial aid application deadline	7/1
% first-year students receiving some sort of aid	69
% receiving some sort of aid	79
% of aid that is merit based	50
% receiving scholarships	30
Average grant	$5,090
Average loan	$19,500
Average total aid package	$19,500
Average debt	$26,000

EMPLOYMENT INFORMATION

		Grads Employed by Field (%)	
Career Rating	**61**		
Rate of placement (nine months out)	85	Academic	2
Average starting salary	$47,097	Business/Industry	12
State for bar exam	AR, TN, TX, GA, FL	Government	17
Pass rate for first-time bar	77	Judicial clerkships	10
Employers Who Frequently Hire Grads		Private practice	55
Wright, Lindsey, and Jennings; Friday,		Public Interest	4
Eldredge and Clark; prosecuting attorney;			
Mitchell, Williams, Selig; Gates and			
Woodyard.			
Prominent Alumni			
Vic Snyder, member, U.S. Congress;			
Annabelle Clinton-Imber, State Supreme			
Court; Andrea Layton Roaf, State Court of			
Appeals.			

UNIVERSITY OF BALTIMORE
SCHOOL OF LAW

INSTITUTIONAL INFORMATION

Public/private	Public
Student-faculty ratio	18:1
% faculty part-time	58
% faculty female	32
% faculty minority	11
Total faculty	104

SURVEY SAYS...

Heavy use of Socratic method
Diverse opinions accepted
in classrooms
Great library staff
Abundant externship/internship/
clerkship opportunities

STUDENTS

Enrollment of law school	972
% male/female	49/51
% out-of-state	15
% full-time	69
% minority	19
% international	1
Average age of entering class	27

ACADEMICS

Academic Experience Rating	**74**
Profs interesting rating	70
Profs accessible rating	64
Hours of study per day	5.33

Academic Specialties

Commercial law, corporation securities law, criminal law, e-commerce, environmental law, government services, intellectual property law, international law, labor law, legal history, legal philosophy, property, taxation.

Advanced Degrees Offered

LLM (taxation), LLM (law of the United States).

Combined Degrees Offered

JD/MBA 4 years, JD/MS (criminal justice) 4 years, JD/MPA 4 years, JD/PhD (policy science in conjuction with the University of Maryland—Baltimore County) 4 years, JD/LLM (taxation) 4 years, JD/MS (negotiation and conflict management) 4 years.

Academics

"My professors are, for the most part, really great," beams a 1L at the University of Baltimore School of Law. "There are a few who are absolutely amazing educators, and have really inspired me. Overall, this is a great place to go to law school." Students tell us that, without question, "the greatest strength of UB is its caring and devoted faculty." These "easily approachable and highly accessible" professors often go out of their way to help students. A 3L relates: "During my first practical legal job, I had an evidence question. I called my professor, while at work, and she talked me through." "I have had the learning experience of a lifetime at UB." Students love their "responsive and very supportive" administration as well. "Students are treated as individuals" and the deans and the rest of the staff are "very involved in ensuring" that students are "prepared to become contributing members of the legal profession."

Course offerings and clinical programs are innovative and incredibly broad. Once students get all their meat-and-potatoes 1L courses out of the way, UB offers no fewer than 13 upperclass areas of concentration that allow students to gain in-depth knowledge about a particular area of law. Examples include business law, criminal practice, family law, international and comparative law, litigation and advocacy, and real estate practice. (However, UB students aren't required to complete an area of concentration.) You'll also find a wide variety of practical skills and simulation courses at UB and a very cool "lab to market" program allows law students to collaborate with business school students to develop and implement plans for the commercialization of technology developed in federal laboratories. There are also scores of opportunities to work with real, live clients—very often disadvantaged litigants—in BU's impressive array of "rigorous" clinical programs. Proximity to nearby Washington, DC, provides many opportunities for internships with government agencies and public-interest organizations. Joint-degree programs include a JD/MBA, a JD and a master's degree in public administration or criminal justice, and a unique program that allows law students to graduate with both a JD and an LLM in taxation.

Students who ponder life after graduation will find the Career Services Center "helpful." "Our alumni are very strong as well," promises a 3L. "I haven't met an alumnus of the school yet who hasn't offered to help me in big ways." "Wireless Internet access" is another plus. The library comes equipped "with a staff that can find anything for you at the drop of a hat." However, the library itself is "way too small, and there are few quiet study areas." Some students claim that the classrooms and building "need refurbishing," or that "the school could use a new building" altogether. "We are growing rather quickly and, before long, our building won't be able to hold everyone," says a 3L. "We could also use more parking."

MARK BELL, ASSISTANT DIRECTOR OF ADMISSIONS
1420 NORTH CHARLES STREET, BALTIMORE, MD 21201
TEL: 410-837-4459 FAX: 410-837-4450
E-MAIL: LWADMISS@UBMAIL.UBALT.EDU • INTERNET: LAW.UBALT.EDU

Life

About 20 percent of the law students at UB are members of an ethnic minority. There are a few more women than men in the full-time program, but the evening student population is a little more than 50 percent male. In general, the career-oriented students say that they get along well with one another. Competitiveness is not a problem: "UB does not have horror stories of pages in library books going missing. We help each other out when we can," explains a 3L.

Life outside of the classroom has its ups and downs. "Student-run activities occur regularly." "We have a variety of thought-provoking lectures and events," says one student. Many members of the faculty and staff attend these events, "adding to the sense of community." UB is also located in the midst of Baltimore's cultural corridor. The Lyric Opera House, Symphony Hall, and at least two prominent museums are all within a few blocks from the law school. The biggest problem at UB, according to students, is safety when they leave campus at night. There is a light rail station and commuter rail station located near campus. However, if you drive (as many students do), "The school is located pretty poorly, in an area of Baltimore that is not known as safe." Because of the inadequate parking situation, students who drive often have to hoof it through some sketchy neighborhoods to get to their cars. "There is very little security presence," frets a first-year student. "I often worry that simply walking to the parking lot is not safe."

Getting In

With nearly 1,000 students, the UB School of Law is pretty enormous. Median LSAT scores for entering students are around 152. The median GPA is approximately 3.13. Enrolled students at the 25th percentile have an LSAT score of 150 and a GPA of about 2.8. Enrolled students at the 75th percentile have an LSAT score of 157 and a GPA of about 3.5. Like many schools, UB takes more than quantitative factors into consideration, including the level of difficulty of the undergraduate major, graduate degrees, and work experience. Students must also submit a personal essay, a resume, and two letters of recommendation.

EMPLOYMENT INFORMATION

Career Rating	61	Grads Employed by Field (%)	
Average starting salary	$39,391	Academic	1
State for bar exam	MD	Business/Industry	6
Pass rate for first-time bar	72	Government	13
Employers Who Frequently Hire Grads		Judicial clerkships	31
Law firms; judges; government agencies;		Private practice	47
corporations; Whiteford, Taylor, and		Public Interest	2
Preston; Law Offices of Peter Angelos;			
DLA Piper.			
Prominent Alumni			
Kendel S. Ehrlich, First Lady of Maryland;			
Honorable Catherine Coran O'Malley,			
Baltimore City District Court, First Lady of			
Baltimore; C.A. Dutch Ruppersberger, U.S.			
Congress, House of Representatives.			

Clinical program required	No
Legal writing course requirement	Yes
Legal methods course requirement	Yes
Legal research course requirement	Yes
Moot court requirement	No
Public interest law requirement	No

ADMISSIONS

Selectivity Rating	78
# applications received	3,388
# applicants accepted	849
# acceptees attending	333
Average LSAT	154
LSAT Range	150–157
Average undergrad GPA	3.3
Application fee	$60
Regular application	4/1
Regular notification	Rolling
Rolling notification	Yes
Early application program	No
Transfer students accepted	Yes
Evening division offered	Yes
Part-time accepted	Yes
LSDAS accepted	Yes

Applicants Also Look At
American University, The Catholic University of America, University of Maryland, Widener University (PA).

International Students

TOEFL required of international students	No
TOEFL recommended of international students	Yes

FINANCIAL FACTS

Annual tuition (resident)	$17,469
Annual tuition (nonresident)	$29,981
Books and supplies	$850
Fees per credit (resident)	$81
Fees per credit (nonresident)	$81
Tuition per credit (resident)	$790
Tuition per credit (nonresident)	$1,158
Room and board (off-campus)	$10,000
Financial aid application deadline	4/1
% receiving some sort of aid	68
% receiving scholarships	10
Average grant	$4,000
Average loan	$12,500
Average debt	$38,300

UNIVERSITY OF CALIFORNIA—BERKELEY
BOALT HALL SCHOOL OF LAW

INSTITUTIONAL INFORMATION

Public/private	Public
Student-faculty ratio	14:1
% faculty part-time	49
% faculty female	32
% faculty minority	10
Total faculty	166

SURVEY SAYS...
Great library staff
Abundant externship/internship/
clerkship opportunities
Liberal students
Students love Berkeley, CA

STUDENTS

Enrollment of law school	879
% male/female	41/59
% out-of-state	33
% full-time	100
% minority	30
# of countries represented	22
Average age of entering class	25

ACADEMICS

Academic Experience Rating	**93**
Profs interesting rating	89
Profs accessible rating	86
Hours of study per day	3.9

Academic Specialties
Business law and economics, comparative legal studies, corporation securities law, environmental law, intellectual property law, international law, law and technology, social justice.

Advanced Degrees Offered
LLM 1 year, JSD, PhD (jurisprudence and social policy) 6 years.

Combined Degrees Offered
JD/MA (economics) 4 years, JD/PhD (economics), JD/MBA (school of business) 4 years, JD/MA (Asian studies) 4 years, JD/MA (international area studies) 4 years, JD/MCP (city and regional planning) 4 years, JD/MJ (journalism) 4 years, JD/MPP (public policy) 4 years, JD/MSW (social welfare) 4 years, JD/MA 4 years, JD/PhD (information management systems), JD/PhD (legal history), JD/MS (energy and resources) 4 years

Academics

California public institutions of higher education have in recent years suffered some substantial and well-publicized cuts in state funding. Despite the effects that these cuts have had on all of the schools in the University of California system, students at renowned Boalt Hall insist that their law school continues to uphold its well-earned, long-standing reputation for academic excellence. In particular, students praise the unwavering commitment and quality of the school's faculty and staff. A 2L tells us, "Coming from an economically flush private undergrad, I was not expecting that a public university in economically beleaguered California would have a staff that is as accessible, knowledgeable, helpful, and cheerful as the one here at Boalt." A 3L adds, "For a large public school in a state beset with serious financial issues, I believe that Boalt does an excellent job of focusing on providing the best teaching possible in a world of limited funds." While Boalt's academic excellence has not diminished in the face of such fiscal adversity, tuition and fees are on the rise. In fact, Boalt's price tag has nearly doubled in the past four years, making it roughly "comparable [with] other top schools," particularly if you are not a California resident. The good news for nonresident students is that they may establish residency (if they take certain steps) after their first year, meaning that they would be eligible for the much lower resident rates in their second and third years.

In addition to cost hikes, students also warn us that the aging facilities could use some improvements. "If only the school had more money to improve facilities!" is a common refrain, but one 3L notes that despite all this, "A number of real improvements have been made since I started—more classrooms have outlets for each student [laptop]. In addition, the computer labs are all great." Besides, "People don't come to Boalt because it's shiny, new, or pretty. They come because it is a great institution with tremendously helpful faculty and a very cool, friendly, and mellow student body."

As a part of the world-renowned University of California—Berkeley, Boalt benefits in many ways. In particular, Boalt offers a number of joint-degree programs in conjunction with other graduate schools within the university. "One of the greatest, and least known, strengths is that Boalt houses an interdisciplinary PhD program (jurisprudence and social policy). This program allows for a broad range of courses and faculty that are not necessarily found in other law schools." In general, students say the law school sustains an intellectual vibe. One 3L looks back and muses, "Academically, I understand why Berkeley is a top 10 school. When you can have a semester composed of four constitutional law classes with some of the country's paramount scholars, the experience of law school transcends the vocational and becomes more akin to the scholarship of a true graduate school experience."

While academically superior, Boalt distinguishes itself from some of its peer schools by promoting a casual, non-competitive atmosphere, even in the classroom. According to one 2L, "Boalt's faculty and administration make a concerted effort to keep students sane and happy. Relaxation is nearly a rule, and the general ethos is one in which hyperachievers are a curiosity." Students point to Boalt's unconventional grading system (which awards pass, fail, or honors, rather than letter grades) as particularly responsible for the lack of cutthroat grade-grubbing. A 3L says, "Although it's rough for 60 percent of the class to get merely a pass, it actually makes students focus less on grades. Also, because our grades can't be reduced to a GPA, employers have to look more closely at how we've done in other areas."

UC—Berkeley is well known for its liberal politics, and the law school is no exception. When considering Boalt Hall, keep this in mind: "If you consider yourself moderate

EDWARD TOM, DIRECTOR OF ADMISSIONS
FIVE BOALT HALL, BERKELEY, CA 94720-7200
TEL: 510-642-2274 FAX: 510-643-6222
E-MAIL: ADMISSIONS@LAW.BERKELEY.EDU • INTERNET: WWW.LAW.BERKELEY.EDU

anywhere else, be prepared to be labeled a crazy right-winger at Boalt. Some professors are not afraid to make it very clear where they stand politically (very liberal) and you might have to take that into consideration when writing exams." Most students seem to be in the right place for their politics, however, as they praise the school's lively, liberal atmosphere and commitment to philanthropy. "I applaud the social-justice activities and events that occur daily on campus," writes one 2L. Another adds, "The student body is very active in social and political causes, and there is a general sense that Boalt students don't just see their law degree as a ticket to a prestigious firm." Even so, students say it is close to a piece of cake to land a plumb job after graduation from Boalt. "I'm a third-year student, and by September most of my friends already had job offers from incredibly prestigious law firms," is how one student puts it. Another 2L puts it this way: "Almost every Boalt student [who] wants such a job will be earning $125,000-plus right after graduation."

Life

While Boalt students spend a lot of time praising their school's location, academic programs, prestige, and mellow atmosphere, they spend much more time praising one another. "My classmates are one of the greatest strengths of this school. I am constantly impressed that people so intellectually capable can also be as collegial and humble as they are," beams one 2L. Boalt values diversity and students say their classmates run the gamut. "The Berkeley community—students and faculty alike—remains true to type: quirky, eccentric, diverse, and incredibly intelligent," writes one student. After class, students enjoy "cocktail and snack parties in the school's courtyard, amazing speakers, and the rotating 'Bar Review' pub night." Students also say that making friends at Boalt should be easy. Why? Because, as one first-year student puts it, "There's a niche for every interest a person could have and the social and academic outlets to enhance those interests."

Getting In

Good luck. Boalt Hall receives between 5,000 and 8,000 applications annually for fewer than 300 first-year spots. The average GPA for enrolled students is 3.79, and the average LSAT score is 166, but the LSAT range is quite broad. Boalt Hall also prides itself on considering more than just an applicant's grades and test scores, reviewing extracurricular activities, achievements, and the overcoming of obstacles when making an admissions decision.

Clinical program required	No
Legal writing	
course requirement	Yes
Legal methods	
course requirement	Yes
Legal research	
course requirement	Yes
Moot court requirement	Yes
Public interest	
law requirement	No

ADMISSIONS

Selectivity Rating	**98**
# applications received	7,159
# applicants accepted	791
# acceptees attending	266
Average LSAT	166
LSAT Range	163–169
Average undergrad GPA	3.75
Application fee	$75
Regular application	2/1
Regular notification	4/1
Rolling notification	Yes
Early application program	No
Transfer students accepted	Yes
Evening division offered	No
Part-time accepted	No
LSDAS accepted	Yes

Applicants Also Look At
Columbia University, Georgetown University, New York University, Stanford University, University of California—Hastings, University of California—Los Angeles, University of Southern California.

International Students

TOEFL required	
of international students	Yes
Minimum paper TOEFL	570
Minimum computer TOEFL	230

FINANCIAL FACTS

Annual tuition	
(nonresident)	$12,245
Books and supplies	$1,495
Room and board	$14,608
Financial aid application	
deadline	3/2
% receiving some sort of aid	94
% of aid that is merit based	1
% receiving scholarships	74
Average grant	$10,102
Average loan	$24,210
Average total aid package	$31,958
Average debt	$68,831

EMPLOYMENT INFORMATION

Career Rating	**94**	
Rate of placement (nine months out)	99	
Average starting salary	$125,000	
State for bar exam	CA	
Pass rate for first-time bar	87	

Employers Who Frequently Hire Grads
Roughly 450 employers recruit at Boalt Hall each fall including national firms, multinational corporations, public interest groups, and governmental agencies.

Grads Employed by Field (%)	
Academic	1
Business/Industry	2
Government	1
Judicial clerkships	14
Private practice	69
Public Interest	13

UNIVERSITY OF CALIFORNIA—DAVIS

SCHOOL OF LAW

INSTITUTIONAL INFORMATION

Public/private	Public
Student-faculty ratio	14:1
% faculty part-time	38
% faculty female	36
% faculty minority	31
Total faculty	76

SURVEY SAYS...

Diverse opinions accepted
in classrooms
Great library staff
Liberal students

STUDENTS

Enrollment of law school	582
% male/female	45/55
% full-time	100
% minority	34
% international	1
# of countries represented	7
Average age of entering class	24

ACADEMICS

Academic Experience Rating	**83**
Profs interesting rating	84
Profs accessible rating	85
Hours of study per day	4.05

Academic Specialties

Business, criminal law, environmental law, human rights law, intellectual property law, international law, social justice, taxation.

Advanced Degrees Offered

LLM 1 year.

Combined Degrees Offered

JD/MBA 4 years, JD/MA, JD/MS 4 years.

Clinical program required	No
Legal writing	
course requirement	Yes
Legal methods	
course requirement	Yes
Legal research	
course requirement	Yes
Moot court requirement	No
Public interest	
law requirement	No

Academics

The "cozy" University of California—Davis, School of Law is "one of the smallest law schools in California." The "dynamic" professors here "know what they're talking about" and are "passionate about teaching." Sure, some are "mean and unhappy," but overall, "The faculty is the best part of King Hall." "Most use some form or other of the Socratic Method." "My professors have at least added humor to my life, ranging from role play (like arresting people in class) and poking fun at our being stumped over relatively simple questions just because it's sometimes terrifying to be called on," relates a 2L. These "incredibly approachable" professors are also "willing to help in anyway they can to enhance your education or career goals." Tutors in the highly praised teaching assistant program "hold office hours and review sessions to solidify big-picture concepts" for 1Ls. The UCD administration is good at "seeking student involvement in decision-making."

The whopping 11 clinics at UCD "are a great way to really understand how to practice law." The prison law clinic in particular "has enjoyed a great deal of success and acclaim." There are certificate programs in public service law and environmental law, and students say they are "truly are committed to public interest work." "We take the fact that we are named after Martin Luther King Jr. very seriously," asserts a 2L. "It's great to be in an environment where people truly care about cause lawyering." However, many students pine for more of a course selection. "About one-fourth of a class has the opportunity to take Pre-trial Skills, but there are so many classes like Latinos and the Law and Disability Rights with classrooms that sit half empty."

As for employment, alumni are "supportive," and with San Francisco and Sacramento nearby, "Davis is conveniently connected to two powerful cities that are full of federal, state, and local agencies as well as important judicial offices." Students complain that the "inept" Career Services staff "needs to get its act together." "'Big-law' possibilities are fairly good," and "approximately 25 percent of the student body will work in a large law firm after graduation." There is "an awesome loan forgiveness program" for graduates who pursue public interest careers.

The "depressing" King Law building is "run down and showing its age." "There's not a lot of windows," and "Space is a big issue." The "ancient" chairs are "very uncomfortable." The library is an "exceptional" research facility, but it's "grungy," "with a little bit of a 1960s industrial feel." "Fortunately the school is about to undergo a dramatic facelift." "Future classes should have newer and more spacious facilities."

Life

Student diversity is comparatively strong on campus, with a visible "Asian and Pacific Islander" presence and a "decent" Hispanic student population. "There are active Jewish, Muslim, and Catholic student groups in the law school, as well as a feminist forum, a pro-choice group, a GLBT group, and a Federalist society." Politically, "Students are often very liberal or very conservative" and "Moderates aren't very vocal."

"There is certainly competition" among students, but "the King Hall Spirit" "keeps it from getting dirty or uncomfortable." "A laid-back atmosphere" permeates. "People loan notes and books without a qualm." "Not that we all hold hands in the hallway and sing Kumbaya," elaborates a 3L, "but everybody is very respectful and has a good time together." Socially, "Most people find a niche," and events and parties occur "pretty much every weekend." "There are a large number of traditions at King Hall that students

SHARON L. PINKNEY, DIRECTOR OF ADMISSION
SCHOOL OF LAW–KING HALL, 400 MRAK HALL DRIVE, DAVIS, CA 95616-5201
TEL: 530-752-6477 FAX: 000-000-0000
E-MAIL: ADMISSIONS@LAW.UCDAVIS.EDU • INTERNET: WWW.LAW.UCDAVIS.EDU

really get into" as well, including "softball and bowling leagues, the law school talent show, and a law school prom." "While these may seem lame and tacky, they are actually really fun, and the large majority of students get involved," explains a 3L. There's also "a co-op nursery, so students with children can drop their kids off while in class."

"The city of Davis is a delightful college town." "You don't have to fight traffic, and people are just downright friendly." "Armies of students ride bicycles to classes, and the fun downtown area is a short walk from campus." There is a "dearth of interesting restaurants," but "The weather is nice." "You can focus," notes a 3L, because "It's quiet." "Davis is a fantastic place to spend three years of graduate school," adds another 3L.

"Sacramento is 15 minutes away and the Bay Area is only an hour [away]." "Great skiing" and "wine country" are not far. Davis is also "a town where hippies settle down after . . . making high salaries." As a result, apartments aren't cheap. "The housing crunch cannot be overstated enough," warns a 2L. "Students considering Davis should immediately check Craigslist and do everything in their power to get housing secured as soon as they accept."

Getting In

Admitted students at the 25th percentile have LSAT scores of about 161 and GPAs of nearly 3.5. Admitted students at the 75th percentile have LSAT scores of 166 and GPAs of 3.8. Most of the time, UC–Davis will consider all LSAT scores but it won't hurt (and it might even help) to add an addendum explaining why your highest score is the one the admissions staff ought to consider.

ADMISSIONS

Selectivity Rating	86
# applications received	3,493
# applicants accepted	981
# acceptees attending	188
Average LSAT	162
LSAT Range	160–164
Average undergrad GPA	3.53
Application fee	$75
Regular application	2/1
Regular notification	Rolling
Rolling notification	Yes
Early application program	No
Transfer students accepted	Yes
Evening division offered	No
Part-time accepted	No
LSDAS accepted	Yes

Applicants Also Look At
University of California—Berkeley, University of California—Hastings, University of California—Los Angeles.

International Students

TOEFL required of international students	Yes
TOEFL recommended of international students	Yes
Minimum paper TOEFL	600
Minimum computer TOEFL	250

FINANCIAL FACTS

Annual tuition (nonresident)	$12,245
Books and supplies	$987
Room and board (off-campus)	$10,251
Financial aid application deadline	3/2
% first-year students receiving some sort of aid	86
% receiving some sort of aid	87
% of aid that is merit based	1
% receiving scholarships	79
Average grant	$8,700
Average loan	$22,232
Average total aid package	$30,200
Average debt	$57,611

EMPLOYMENT INFORMATION

Career Rating	80	Grads Employed by Field (%)	
Rate of placement (nine months out)	95	Academic	1
Average starting salary	$91,864	Business/Industry	14
State for bar exam	CA	Government	5
Pass rate for first-time bar	76	Judicial clerkships	3
Employers Who Frequently Hire Grads		Military	1
State of California; private law firms; district attorneys, public defenders; public interest entities.		Other	1
		Private practice	64
		Public Interest	11

University of California
Hastings College of the Law

INSTITUTIONAL INFORMATION

Public/private	Public
Student-faculty ratio	18.9:1
% faculty part-time	59
% faculty female	39
% faculty minority	18
Total faculty	166

SURVEY SAYS...

Diverse opinions accepted
in classrooms
Abundant externship/internship/
clerkship opportunities
Students never sleep
Liberal students

STUDENTS

Enrollment of law school	1,242
% male/female	46/54
% full-time	100
% minority	33
# of countries represented	22
Average age of entering class	24

ACADEMICS

Academic Experience Rating	**79**
Profs interesting rating	82
Profs accessible rating	65
Hours of study per day	4.21

Academic Specialties
Civil litigation, criminal law, international law, public interest law, taxation.

Advanced Degrees Offered
JD 3 years.

Combined Degrees Offered
JD/MBA, other masters degrees (in conjunction with other institutions) 4 to 5 years.

Clinical program required	No
Legal writing course requirement	Yes
Legal methods course requirement	No
Legal research course requirement	Yes
Moot court requirement	Yes

Academics

The University of California's Hastings College of the Law "is like the redheaded stepchild among public law schools in California." While Hastings offers a "great commitment to legal education, an ambitious student body, and a wonderful alumni reputation," it's often underrated. Plus, there are "way too many students." (1L sections have "about 85 people.") Some students tell us that the grading curve is "ruthless"; others note that "most students get B's." Hastings has "a number of notable legal scholars," many whom have "written their own casebooks." "The problem is that there are not enough of them." Faculty accessibility can be sparse, too, though "Some of the professors genuinely care about students' learning and even their well-being." Administratively, "Hastings is a great school for making you feel wanted and treating you like an adult." "There's not a lot of hand-holding here, but the support is there (in ample supply) when you need it." The deans tend to be "invisible" though, and "The school is overly bureaucratic."

At Hastings, "If you walk away without practical experience, it's your own fault," admonishes a 2L. "The focus is on getting students to actually practice the law, rather than just study it." "Theories are taught when necessary." "Hastings is right next to practically every courtroom in Northern California," so "There are unparalleled opportunities to extern." Clinics are abundant. The "invaluable" moot court program is "one of the best in the country." Other highlights include the Legal Education Opportunity Program, an academic support program for students who have had to face a lot of educational obstacles.

Career Services "is very helpful," offering "tons of forums and panels pertaining to different types of law." Students appreciate that the "responsive" staff is "honestly interested in helping students find the right job for them." Others are highly critical. "They focus way too much on the top 25 percent of the class," leaving the rest to "just fend for [them]selves," charges a 3L. A happy contingent of students brags about the "huge" alumni network, particularly in the area. "Just about every big law firm comes to interview," enthuses a 2L. Hastings is also "very good at pointing out alternatives to a traditional law firm." "The school does a good job of encouraging public interest work." Hastings is also "a big feeder" for district attorney and public defender offices.

Hasting's "busy, urban campus" is in "the worst neighborhood in an otherwise beautiful city." "A seismic retrofit renovation" of the facilities is pretty much completed. However, student say it's still "an ugly school" (and "the lack of working copy machines and printers" can be annoying). On the upside, "Classrooms are spacious and modern," "with comfortable chairs." There is "wireless everywhere" and "The library is completely brand new."

Life

Students here are "intelligent and hardworking." Though Hastings students are a left-leaning, liberal bunch, "Everyone is welcome, even conservatives." "Contrary to popular myth," claims a 1L, "Hastings is not competitive." Other students tell us that "there are definitely some very competitive students." "You will have at least one time when you're slapped in the face with the fact that people are trying to outdo you." Still others describe a more nuanced situation. "Hastings gets a bad rap from young students who should have been out in the world for a while before coming here, and who have a chip on their shoulders because they didn't get into Boalt." Ultimately, "Hastings is designed for people

GREG CANADA, DIRECTOR OF ADMISSIONS
200 MCALLISTER STREET, SAN FRANCISCO, CA 94102
TEL: 415-565-4623 FAX: 415-581-8946
E-MAIL: ADMISS@UCHASTINGS.EDU • INTERNET: WWW.UCHASTINGS.EDU

with thick skin." "I am now thoroughly calloused," explains a 3L. "If you want to be known as a tough lawyer, go to Hastings."

"Hastings is basically a commuter school," and it can be "hard to feel connected" here. On the other hand, there are "lots of ways for students to get involved and pursue their own interests." "There are micro-communities if you join a student organization like the public interest group or a journal," and "If you want to participate in something that interests you, this is a place that will definitely support and encourage it." "Most of the social life is centered on the students living in the campus housing." "There's free beer every other Thursday on the concrete patio affectionately called 'The Beach.'"

Hastings is "right in the heart of San Francisco," "a world-class city" with "good public transportation" and teeming with cultural activity. On the downside, Hastings is located in a "homeless Mecca" called The Tenderloin, "the epicenter of drugged-out craziness on the West Coast." "This is humanity at its lowest, at its down-and-outest," warns a 2L. "For some, it's an opportunity to engage with a community in need." "For others, it's a source of annoyance, hassle, and fear." "I would be dumbfounded to hear that an alumnus ever came back to campus for nostalgic purposes," suggests one student. "I recommend everyone interested in attending Hastings at least come and check out the neighborhood so they know what it's like."

Getting In

Students admitted to Hastings at the 25th percentile have LSAT scores of 159 and GPAs of about 3.4. Admitted students at the 75th percentile have LSAT scores of 164 and GPAs of about 3.75. If you feel like you've faced a lot of cultural or economic obstacles in your academic career, check out the Legal Education Opportunity Program, which accepts students with lower numbers but requires a more complex application.

Public interest law requirement	No

ADMISSIONS

Selectivity Rating	88
# applications received	5,526
# applicants accepted	1,479
# acceptees attending	421
Average LSAT	162
LSAT Range	159–164
Average undergrad GPA	3.6
Application fee	$75
Regular application	3/1
Regular notification	5/30
Rolling notification	Yes
Early application program	No
Transfer students accepted	Yes
Evening division offered	No
Part-time accepted	No
LSDAS accepted	Yes

Applicants Also Look At

University of California—Berkeley, University of California—Davis, University of California—Los Angeles, University of San Francisco, University of Southern California.

International Students

TOEFL required of international students	No
TOEFL recommended of international students	No

FINANCIAL FACTS

Annual tuition (resident)	$22,190
Annual tuition (nonresident)	$33,415
Books and supplies	$1,100
Room and board	$14,031
% first-year students receiving some sort of aid	87
% receiving some sort of aid	89
% of aid that is merit based	1
% receiving scholarships	74
Average grant	$6,210
Average loan	$28,502
Average total aid package	$33,928
Average debt	$79,485

EMPLOYMENT INFORMATION

		Grads Employed by Field (%)	
Career Rating	90		
Rate of placement (nine months out)	97	Academic	2
Average starting salary	$95,891	Business/Industry	9
State for bar exam	CA, NY	Government	13
Pass rate for first-time bar	84	Judicial clerkships	3
Employers Who Frequently Hire Grads		Other	1
Major San Francisco and Los Angeles large and medium-sized law firms.		Private practice	67
Prominent Alumni		Public Interest	5
Associate Justice Marvin Baxter, CA Supreme Court; Willie Brown, former Mayor of San Francisco; Associate Justice Carol Corrigan, CA Supreme Court; Joseph Cotchett, founding partner, Cotchett, Pitre, and Simon.			

UNIVERSITY OF CALIFORNIA—LOS ANGELES
SCHOOL OF LAW

INSTITUTIONAL INFORMATION

Public/private	Public
Student-faculty ratio	12:1
% faculty part-time	37
% faculty female	35
% faculty minority	11
Total faculty	136

SURVEY SAYS...

Great research resources
Great library staff
Students love Los Angeles, CA

STUDENTS

Enrollment of law school	1,021
% male/female	53/47
% out-of-state	26
% full-time	100
% minority	13
% international	1
# of countries represented	8
Average age of entering class	25

ACADEMICS

Academic Experience Rating	**93**
Profs interesting rating	89
Profs accessible rating	78
Hours of study per day	3.58

Academic Specialties

Business law and policy, constitutional law, corporation securities law, criminal law, critical race studies, environmental law, human rights law, intellectual property law, international law, labor law, property, public interest law and policy, taxation.

Advanced Degrees Offered

LLM 1 year, SJD.

Combined Degrees Offered

JD/MA (African American studies) 4 years, JD/MA (American Indian studies) 4 years, JD/MBA 4 years, JD/MPH, 4 years JD/MA (public policy) 4 years, JD/MSW (social welfare) 4 years, JD/MA (urban planning) 4 years.

Academics

"If you are looking for professors who encourage you, want you to do well, and want to interact with you outside of school, UCLA School of Law is ideal," proclaims a satisfied 1L. Though class sizes "are probably larger than they are at most schools," "UCLA has a very positive academic atmosphere." "The resources are boundless," and students brag that they are receiving "a world-class legal education in a beautiful city." "Superstar professors" regularly teach 1L courses and the faculty as a whole is full of "amazing and dedicated teachers" who are "quite witty and entertaining." They "will cold-call students, but if you're not able to answer the question, saying 'I don't know' is fine, and they'll leave you alone." The administration is hit-or-miss. Some administrators are "amazingly accessible." "One particular time I went in to get an extension on an independent study paper and wound up playing Barrel of Monkeys for 20 minutes with the Dean of Students," relates a 3L. "I won and she wants a rematch." "The Financial Aid Office seems to get very little right," though, and the bureaucracy can be "horribly inefficient and a pain to wade through." "I don't know how much of that is the law school's fault as opposed to the UC system's," offers a 1L.

"The grading curve is not particularly brutal." "About 60 percent get B's," estimates one student. The curriculum stresses theory as well as practical skills (though one student calls the legal writing curriculum "completely impractical"). The "incredibly valuable" clinical program "is truly the institution's crown jewel." "Trial advocacy is the best class that I have taken at any level," attests a 3L, and the "incredible" public interest program "can turn out lawyers who want to make the world better." Still, many wish that there was less focus placed upon gearing students towards corporate law.

Graduates don't have much of a problem finding jobs. "It is completely standard to leave here and earn $130,000" in your first year as an attorney. UCLA has an "excellent reputation among the big firms in Los Angeles" and is "highly regarded nationally." "Many students also go to work in New York and Washington, DC." "Those who, for some absurd reason, want to leave behind the fantastically high quality of life offered here and instead earn the same money but for more hours in Manhattan seem to have no problem doing so," notes a 1L.

The UCLA campus as a whole is "stunning." "The school is located on the most beautiful part of the generally gorgeous UCLA campus, in one of the most upscale parts of Los Angeles." "The law school building looks great on the outside, but is outdated on the inside." "Classes, bathrooms, and the library are all overcrowded." The "cramped" classrooms "are equipped for laptops," but "need some aesthetic upgrading." On the upside, the "luxurious and modern law library" has "big windows," making it "a pleasing place to study."

Life

Students describe themselves as "very smart." A lot of students complain about the lack of ethnic diversity on campus; "It bears no resemblance to the demographics of the population of the United States, much less that of California." Whatever the case, students "interact well with each other." "Different backgrounds and opinions are not merely tolerated, they are encouraged and respected." "UCLA has a large and active GLBT community, with a think tank and an academic journal both housed at the law school dedicated to sexual orientation law and policy." Politically, "students seem predominantly liberal but there are definitely conservatives too."

KARMAN HSU, DIRECTOR OF ADMISSIONS
BOX 951445, LOS ANGELES, CA 90095-1445
TEL: 310-825-2080 FAX: 310-825-9450
E-MAIL: ADMISSIONS@LAW.UCLA.EDU • INTERNET: WWW.LAW.UCLA.EDU

"People get quite stressed and preoccupied with grades and jobs" and "There is a serious spirit of competition" at UCLA. It's "not personal," though. "Students generally root for each other, rooting for themselves just a bit more." Also, you can easily "find your own space away from the gunners." At the end of the day, it's hard to be stressed out "when you study so close to the beach" (in "shorts and flip-flops"), and "It's 80 degrees in January." "The sunny weather compromises students' ability to stay indoors and study," admits a 1L.

"Lunch in the courtyard is probably the best part of being at UCLA." "People are always outside, reading or eating lunch, with the sun beaming down and the giant redwoods providing shade." "People study hard" but social activities are very prevalent (particularly early in each semester). There is "no shortage of people going out on a random Thursday night." "Rent is fairly expensive" in the surrounding area, but "UCLA offers pretty good, convenient housing to many law students." "If you can deal with a commute, there are many cheaper areas to live that are not too far" as well. Overall, UCLA students are among the more satisfied groups of law students in the country. "After my brother asked me how law school was going, he listened patiently to my answer and then told me that it sounded like Club Med with some required reading," says a 3L. "I couldn't be happier with my experience."

Getting In

Recently admitted students at UCLA at the 25th percentile have LSAT scores of 162 and GPAs in the 3.5 range. Admitted students at the 75th percentile have LSAT scores of 169 and GPAs of roughly 3.8.

Clinical program required	No
Legal writing course requirement	Yes
Legal methods course requirement	Yes
Legal research course requirement	No
Moot court requirement	No
Public interest law requirement	No

ADMISSIONS

Selectivity Rating	**96**
# applications received	5,834
# applicants accepted	1,105
# acceptees attending	340
Average LSAT	165
LSAT Range	162–169
Average undergrad GPA	3.61
Application fee	$75
Regular application	2/1
Regular notification	Rolling
Rolling notification	Yes
Early application program	No
Transfer students accepted	Yes
Evening division offered	No
Part-time accepted	No
LSDAS accepted	Yes

Applicants Also Look At

Georgetown University, New York University, University of California—Berkeley, University of California—Hastings, University of Southern California.

International Students

TOEFL required of international students	No
TOEFL recommended of international students	No

FINANCIAL FACTS

Annual tuition (resident)	$25,463
Annual tuition (nonresident)	$36,387
Books and supplies	$1,881
Room and board (off-campus)	$12,927
Financial aid application deadline	3/2
% first-year students receiving some sort of aid	85
% receiving some sort of aid	87
% receiving scholarships	66
Average grant	$8,424
Average loan	$28,000
Average total aid package	$45,353
Average debt	$83,866

EMPLOYMENT INFORMATION

Career Rating	**91**	**Grads Employed by Field (%)**	
Rate of placement (nine months out)	99	Academic	1
Average starting salary	$102,190	Business/Industry	8
State for bar exam	CA	Government	6
Pass rate for first-time bar	86	Judicial clerkships	12
Employers Who Frequently Hire Grads		Military	1
Leading employers from law firms, corporations, government agencies, and public interest organizations.		Other	1
		Private practice	65
		Public Interest	6
Prominent Alumni			
Honorable Henry Waxman, U.S. House of Representatives (29th District); Nelson Rising, president/CEO, Catellus Development Corporation.			

THE UNIVERSITY OF CHICAGO
THE LAW SCHOOL

INSTITUTIONAL INFORMATION

Public/private	Private
Student-faculty ratio	9:1
% faculty part-time	46
% faculty female	19
% faculty minority	6
Total faculty	127

SURVEY SAYS...

Heavy use of Socratic method
Diverse opinions accepted
in classrooms
Great library staff
Abundant externship/internship/
clerkship opportunities

STUDENTS

Enrollment of law school	600
% male/female	55/45
% full-time	100
% minority	30
% international	2
Average age of entering class	24

ACADEMICS

Academic Experience Rating	**99**
Profs interesting rating	99
Profs accessible rating	90
Hours of study per day	4.42

Academic Specialties

Civil procedure, commercial law, constitutional law, corporation securities law, criminal law, environmental law, government services, human rights law, intellectual property law, international law, labor law, legal history, legal philosophy, property, taxation.

Advanced Degrees Offered

JD 3 years, LLM 1 year, JSD up to 5 years, MCompL, DCompL.

Combined Degrees Offered

JD/MBA 4 years, JD/PhD (in conjunction with Graduate School of Business), JD/AM (public policy) 4 years, JD/AM (international relations) 4 years.

Clinical program required	No

Academics

The rigorous and ultra-prestigious Law School at The University of Chicago offers "an incredibly dynamic educational environment full of quirky but brilliant professors and an eclectic mix of students." "Expectations are high" and a unique trimester system means "There is little rest for the weary." Even so, students report that "there is no other place like The University of Chicago when it comes to intellectual curiosity." Course work is cerebral and highly analytical. Classes "have a strong theoretical bent" and are "geared to those who like thinking about the law." Chicago is virtually synonymous with the interdisciplinary combination of law and economics. The humanities, the social sciences, and the natural sciences are all integrated into the curriculum as well.

Students swear that their school has, "without a doubt, the best faculty in the country." The professors are "unquestionably the greatest part of this school." Somehow "they manage to produce brilliant work" while maintaining "a real emphasis on teaching" and making students "feel like top priority." "It's incredible to take classes from Cass Sunstein, Richard Epstein, and numerous others as a 1L, and to find out how accessible they are," beams one satisfied student. These "rock stars of legal academia" "treat students with respect," "are often in the common areas, and readily have lunch with students." "I have been amazed by the accessibility of my professors, particularly considering who they are," says a 3L. "They are always available for office hours." "The professors can help you get amazing jobs, can impart unparalleled wisdom, and are the people who write the books you use," explains another student. "I don't know where they find the time."

The administration "makes the experience seamless" and is quite popular with most students. "I would call the administration extremely overqualified if it weren't for the negative implications of that label," says a 1L. "I can't imagine a more enthusiastic and at-your-service administration." "The law school tries harder than any other school I've heard of to make its students happy," declares another student. Career Services does a good job too. There are "no worries about jobs." "Over 600 employers compete for only 190 students in each class," so "everyone will get a great job (public or private) making top dollar." There are some complaints, though. "The grading system is a little bizarre. It's tough on the ego because nearly everyone gets the same grade." Students must "lottery" into many seminars and clinical programs. Consequently, while the nine clinics are "great" for real-world experience, "practically no one" gets into the clinics they want. "You are very lucky if you are able to obtain practical experience through credited work." Though the recent introduction of a summer public interest program has guaranteed funding for public interest jobs, a 3L warns, "This is a school for corporate lawyers."

"The facilities are state of the art" at the U of C, though the "boringly modern" architecture won't exactly elevate your soul—unless, of course, a floating-cube-of-glass design is your idea of beautiful. Inside the law school, "The 1L classrooms are gorgeous but cramped." The library has undergone extensive renovation recently and boasts "a great number of resources and a willing and helpful staff."

Life

Chicago is "small" and home to "an intense intellectual environment." "It's quite an experience to know that some of my friends will clerk for the Supreme Court and work at the highest level in the field," relates one student. Debates are "constant and vibrant." "Our faculty and student body has many liberals, libertarians, moderates, and conservatives," explains a 2L. "The political views . . . range from ultra-liberal to ultra-conservative, but all

ANN PERRY, ASSISTANT DEAN FOR ADMISSIONS
1111 EAST 60TH STREET, CHICAGO, IL 60637
TEL: 773-702-9484 FAX: 773-834-0942
E-MAIL: ADMISSIONS@LAW.UCHICAGO.EDU • INTERNET: WWW.LAW.UCHICAGO.EDU

viewpoints are respected. Great weight is placed on academic inquiry and discussion, as opposed to vacuous politicking." "People are very interested in learning and maturing as legal thinkers."

Many students tell us that the academic environment is "easygoing" and "mostly non-competitive." "It is an extremely friendly school with a low degree of competition," they say, where "2L and 3L students frequently offer their assistance to the 1L class." However, other students tell us "The competition is tough." "Students are definitely not laid-back about getting jobs," observes a 3L. "Even though everyone ends up with plenty of great job offers, students are intense and cutthroat."

Socially, there is "community atmosphere" and "a great attitude on campus." People are "interesting and cool" and "genuinely excited to be a part of the law school." "Lots of people . . . participate in social events." Because many people hail from outside the Midwest, everyone arrives looking for friends. "The 1L class bonds quickly." "The small class size is a phenomenal advantage because I feel as if I get to know everyone," comments a 1L. Also, "weekly events such as Wine Mess and Coffee Mess" are perennial social institutions where students mingle with classmates and professors. "Nearly every day there is free food for some political or legal guest speaker," which is great if you like "sandwiches, pizza, or Thai food." The biggest complaint about life here appears to be the law school's affordable but "inconvenient" Hyde Park location. When students need to get away for work or any other reason though, downtown Chicago is "easy enough to live in and get to school" by car, bike, or public transportation.

Getting In

If you can get admitted here, you can get admitted to virtually any law school in the country. Admitted students at 25th percentile have LSAT scores of about 169 and GPAs of about 3.5. Admitted students at 75th percentile have LSAT scores of 172 and GPAs of about 3.8. If you take the LSAT a second time, Chicago will consider your higher score.

Legal writing course requirement	Yes
Legal methods course requirement	Yes
Legal research course requirement	Yes
Moot court requirement	Yes
Public interest law requirement	No

ADMISSIONS

Selectivity Rating	98
# applications received	4,818
# applicants accepted	766
# acceptees attending	192
Average LSAT	171
LSAT Range	169–172
Average undergrad GPA	3.67
Application fee	$75
Regular application	2/1
Regular notification	Rolling
Rolling notification	Yes
Early application program	Yes
Early application deadline	12/1
Early application notification	12/31
Transfer students accepted	Yes
Evening division offered	No
Part-time accepted	No
LSDAS accepted	Yes

Applicants Also Look At
Columbia University, Harvard University, New York University, Stanford University, University of Pennsylvania, University of Virginia.

International Students

TOEFL required of international students	Yes
Minimum paper TOEFL	600

FINANCIAL FACTS

Annual tuition	$37,334
Books and supplies	$1,650
Room and board	$13,455
Financial aid application deadline	3/1
% first-year students receiving some sort of aid	90
% receiving some sort of aid	82
% of aid that is merit based	75
% receiving scholarships	52
Average grant	$11,600
Average loan	$42,171
Average total aid package	$43,700
Average debt	$113,000

EMPLOYMENT INFORMATION

Career Rating	98
Rate of placement (nine months out)	99
Average starting salary	$135,000
State for bar exam	IL, NY
Pass rate for first-time bar	98

Employers Who Frequently Hire Grads
Cravath, Swain, and Moore; Latham and Watkins; Gibson, Dunn, and Crutcher; Sidley and Austin, Kirkland and Ellis; Skadden, Arps, Slate, Meagher, and Flom.

Grads Employed by Field (%)	
Academic	1
Business/Industry	1
Government	5
Judicial clerkships	15
Private practice	76
Public Interest	1

UNIVERSITY OF CINCINNATI
COLLEGE OF LAW

INSTITUTIONAL INFORMATION

Public/private	Public
Student-faculty ratio	11:1
% faculty part-time	42
% faculty female	35
% faculty minority	9
Total faculty	55

SURVEY SAYS...

Diverse opinions accepted
in classrooms
Great library staff
Abundant externship/internship/
clerkship opportunities
Good social life

STUDENTS

Enrollment of law school	376
% male/female	51/49
% out-of-state	33
% full-time	100
% minority	18
% international	1
# of countries represented	3
Average age of entering class	24

ACADEMICS

Academic Experience Rating	**78**
Profs interesting rating	73
Profs accessible rating	81
Hours of study per day	4.36

Academic Specialties

Criminal law, environmental law,
human rights law, intellectual property law, international law, labor law,
taxation.

Advanced Degrees Offered

JD 3 years, JD/MBA, JD/MA
(women's studies), JD/MCP (community planning), JD/MSW,
JD/PhD-MA (political science).

Combined Degrees Offered

JD/MBA 4 years, JD/MCP 4.5 years,
JD/MA (women's studies) 4 years,
JD/MSW 4 years.

Clinical program required	No
Legal writing course requirement	Yes

Academics

Students at the University of Cincinnati get the "small class sizes" and "intimate environment" typical of a private college while paying the comfortable, low tuition you would expect from a public institution. With roughly 125 students in each entering class, the school strikes an "excellent" balance with "its affordability, reputation, small class size, and excellent faculty. Students agree that UC professors are an "amazing and diverse group of people who care just as much for teaching and students as they do about publishing their own work." UC is particularly noted for its focus on "public interest" and "international" law; however, "There is no shortage of brilliant legal minds in a broad range of subjects—that goes for students as well as the professors." In addition to the accomplished tenured faculty, students rave about the school's recent acquisition of "exceptional young faculty members that have great teaching skills to match their great scholarship." A 2L sums it up, "As one of the smallest public law schools in the country, I feel my educational experience has been fantastic, and yet, at very little cost. Because our class consists of only 128 people, all of my professors know my name."

University of Cincinnati runs several "amazing" legal institutes and research centers focused on unique topics such as domestic violence, law and psychiatry, and corporate law. Through these centers, students can earn credit hours while doing fulfilling and useful work in the community. Many students make particular note of the Ohio Innocence Project, an institute at the University of Cincinnati through which students research and write reports, and work on real criminal cases. The institute also brings notable speakers to campus. Students also have the opportunity to research and write for the school's renowned publications, including the Human Rights Quarterly and Tenant Information Project. While students at other schools might scramble for spots on the school's law review or clinic programs, "Since the school is small, each student can participate in get involved in a number of organizations."

Thanks to an "ambitious but not overly competitive student body," the learning environment is charged, but not cutthroat, at University of Cincinnati. A 3L attests, "While academic achievement is always a numbers game in law school, the atmosphere at UC is nonpretentious and noncontentious." When it comes to the job and internship placements, University of Cincinnati maintains a "deep and well-regarded history as a legal educational institution" both locally and nationally. As a result, most students say the school "is a great place for students with all different kinds of career aspirations, and especially has a public interest/human rights orientation that I think is unparalleled in the Midwest." In fact, "Public interest students can actually obtain funding for their summer jobs through the school's Public Interest Group." Most UC grads stay in the Cincinnati area and meet with good results while those looking outside the region must do a little extra legwork to find a good placement. "While plenty of our grads go on to excellent careers in major firms, federal clerkships, and other government positions, I don't feel like our school does enough PR work to get out-of-town employers interested in our students," says one student.

AL WATSON, ASSISTANT DEAN AND DIRECTOR OF ADMISSION AND FINANCIAL AID
PO BOX 210040, CINCINNATI, OH 45221
TEL: 513-556-6805 FAX: 513-556-2391
E-MAIL: ADMISSIONS@LAW.UC.EDU • INTERNET: WWW.LAW.UC.EDU

Life

For starving students/aspiring lawyers, Cincinnati is an excellent home base offering the unbeatable combination of "small town prices (housing, dining, entertainment) with big city amenities." For both professional and recreational pursuits, the UC campus is pleasantly located "close to downtown so it's easy to get to work, ballgames, and entertainment." While Cincinnati has its charms, students complain that the law school "building looks like a 1950s bomb shelter" and could use "more outlets and better lighting." "Windows would be nice," adds another. However, students are optimistic that the school will consider remodeling the law school along with other campus projects. The good news is that "the new parking garage has been built, and there are brand-new (and attractive) living units pretty much right across the street." Not to mention that a few "Ice cream shops have opened within a short walk from school."

Despite the rigors of the academic curriculum, "The students that are here create a suitable balance between academic and social life. There are plenty of opportunities to go out and have fun and not be completely overwhelmed with school." On and off campus, "There are frequently SBA social events for students, such as happy hours at local bars." In fact, the SBA is very active and "most of the students are friends and spend time together outside of the law school." On the other hand, students remind us that Cincinnati also attracts "a large contingent of commuter students who spend little if no time involved in the school outside of actual class."

Getting In

To apply to the University of Cincinnati College of Law, students must submit LSAT scores and register with the Law School Data Assembly Service Report. If the LSAT was taken more than once, the highest score will be considered by the Admissions Committee. For Fall 2006, over 1,000 hopefuls applied for 135 spots in the JD program. Students in the 25th percentile had LSAT scores of 157 and GPAs of 3.31, while those in the 75th percentile had LSAT scores of 161 and GPAs of 3.80.

Legal methods course requirement	No
Legal research course requirement	Yes
Moot court requirement	No
Public interest law requirement	No

ADMISSIONS

Selectivity Rating	82
# applications received	1,183
# applicants accepted	407
# acceptees attending	113
Average LSAT	159
LSAT Range	157–161
Average undergrad GPA	3.5
Application fee	$35
Regular application	3/1
Regular notification	Rolling
Rolling notification	Yes
Early application program	Yes
Early application deadline	12/1
Early application notification	1/15
Transfer students accepted	Yes
Evening division offered	No
Part-time accepted	No
LSDAS accepted	Yes

Applicants Also Look At

Case Western Reserve University, Indiana University—Bloomington, Northern Kentucky University, The Ohio State University, University of Dayton.

International Students

TOEFL required of international students	Yes

FINANCIAL FACTS

Annual tuition (resident)	$18,532
Annual tuition (nonresident)	$32,652
Books and supplies	$4,992
Room and board	$9,765
Financial aid application deadline	3/1
% first-year students receiving some sort of aid	80
% receiving some sort of aid	80
% receiving scholarships	64
Average grant	$8,000
Average loan	$20,122
Average total aid package	$28,122
Average debt	$50,084

EMPLOYMENT INFORMATION

		Grads Employed by Field (%)	
Career Rating	80		
Average starting salary	$72,105	Academic	4.2
State for bar exam	OH	Business/Industry	16
Pass rate for first-time bar	93	Government	9.2
Employers Who Frequently Hire Grads		Judicial clerkships	7.6
All major law firms in Cincinnati and other		Private practice	56.3
Ohio cities as well as other Midwestern		Public Interest	5
cities.			

Prominent Alumni

Stan Chesley, class action; Cris Collinworth, journalist; Charles Luken, Mayor of Cincinnati; Billy Martin, Washington, DC–based, high-profile case attorney; Andrew Savage, *Survivor*.

UNIVERSITY OF COLORADO
SCHOOL OF LAW

INSTITUTIONAL INFORMATION

Public/private	Public
Student-faculty ratio	14:1
% faculty part-time	32
% faculty female	38
% faculty minority	16
Total faculty	69

SURVEY SAYS...
Beautiful campus
Students love Boulder, CO

STUDENTS

Enrollment of law school	511
% male/female	49/51
% out-of-state	15
% full-time	100
% minority	23
# of countries represented	4
Average age of entering class	25

ACADEMICS

Academic Experience Rating	**86**
Profs interesting rating	84
Profs accessible rating	78
Hours of study per day	4.81

Academic Specialties
Civil procedure, commercial law, constitutional law, corporation securities law, criminal law, environmental law, government services, human rights law, intellectual property law, international law, labor law, legal history, legal philosophy, property, taxation.

Advanced Degrees Offered
JD 3 years.

Combined Degrees Offered
JD/MBA 4 years, JD/MPA 4 years, JD/Master of Science and Technology 4 years, JD/Master of Environmental Law 4 years, tax emphasis 3 years, environmental policy certificate 3 years.

Clinical program required	No
Legal writing	
course requirement	Yes
Legal methods	
course requirement	Yes

Academics

The University of Colorado School of Law has much coming by way of recommendations. The faculty and the small student population are "eclectic and diverse." CU Law's "solid and growing" clinical programs boast "fantastic" facilities that help in "spreading its practical wings." Students in the Indian Law Clinic, for example, represent low-income Native American clients with specific Indian law-related problems. There are three law journals and five joint-degree programs. Though the international law program is "seriously lacking," there is a "particularly strong" specialization in environmental law, and CU has strong connections "within the environmental law community." Students here can participate in "cutting-edge climate change and renewable energy work" through the law school's Energy and Environment Security Initiative. CU is also a "very affordable school" and, if you come from another state, it is reportedly "easy to get in-state tuition your second year."

The "whip-smart" and "amazingly accomplished" professors here "could teach anywhere but choose the lifestyle that Colorado affords." While "The curriculum is rigorous," professors "use the Socratic Method in a friendly way that makes students feel comfortable in the classroom." Somehow, "It isn't very intimidating." Outside of class, the faculty is "accessible," "frequently attending student events and very willing to talk with students." Bureaucracy does exist, but the "very chill" administration is generally "polite, service-oriented, and very responsive to student needs." "They treat you like one of their own from the first day," claims a 1L.

Student opinion on the Office of Career Development is mixed. Some students tell us that job prospects are "excellent" thanks to the "hard work" of the "great" staff "coupled with a good local and regional job market." "I feel confident that I will get a great job," declares a 1L. Other students complain that CU "provides virtually no assistance" to those "looking for a job outside of Colorado or the surrounding states," and feel that special attention is paid to the top 10 percent of the class.

CU Law's "brand-spanking-new" and otherwise "stunning" building "has the latest and greatest bells and whistles" (including "three plugs for every law student"). "The layout of the building is not very conducive to socializing," but "It's a great place to spend most of your time." "Breathtaking" views are everywhere. "The cafeteria has an entire wall of glass windows looking out onto the flatirons." Classrooms are "comfortable and designed for discussion" and have "the latest modern technology" as well as "good old-fashioned chalk boards." The "inviting" library is "huge and has everything."

Life

"There is a good mix" of "traditional" and "older students" here. CU law students describe themselves as "genuinely kind and cooperative" and "diligent but laid-back." They also hasten to add that "a lot of the stereotypes about Boulder (yuppies, hippies, liberals, potheads, etc.) do not apply to the law school." There are "ski bums and outdoorsy people who are in the mountains every weekend," but "very few students are actually Teva-wearing, beard-growing sorts of people," explains one student. "Most are completely ordinary, and dress professionally if not casually." Politically, "While this is a generally liberal town and school, there are a surprising number of conservatives at the law school, balancing the diehard liberals out and making the atmosphere very middle-of-the-road." If anything, "The student body overall seems slightly apathetic" when it comes to "political or philosophic issues."

KRISTINE H. MCCORD, ASSISTANT DEAN FOR ADMISSIONS AND FINANCIAL AID
403 UCB, BOULDER, CO 80309-0403
TEL: 303-492-7203 FAX: 303-492-2542
E-MAIL: LAWADMIN@COLORADO.EDU • INTERNET: WWW.COLORADO.EDU/LAW

Life outside the classroom here is reportedly awesome. "There have been dozens of occasions where someone has uncontrollably muttered, 'I'm so glad I'm here,'" observes a 1L. "It's just such a great place." "Everyone knows everyone," and CU Law "can be gossipy," but it's "a friendly place with a serious work ethic." "Sharing notes" is common. "Competition between students is barely noticeable." In fact, "Competitions such as mock trial are friendly and in fun." You may even "find legal writing answers underlined in reference books for research exercises." The "very active" student government "is fantastic at addressing student concerns" and "contributes a lot to a relatively low-stress atmosphere." "Free beer . . . almost every Friday" is another great perk and, while the party scene isn't raging, "There is something going on almost every weekend."

The surrounding college town of Boulder is "outrageously expensive." If you can find the means, though, "Boulder is a unique and interesting place" that "offers a broad variety of experiences ranging from the cultural to the bizarre." With "300 days of sunshine a year" and an "absolutely gorgeous physical environment," it's "an outdoor rec haven" as well. "Skiing is fantastic during the winter, and you can't beat a Boulder summer." The law school is "perfectly situated at the base of the Front Range to allow for ample ways to relieve stress by being physically active all year long," explains one student. "Ski trips happen regularly" and "You can leave class and go for a hike in the mountains without having to get in your car." In the odd event that students would want to leave the Boulder area, "Denver's less than an hour away."

Getting In

The 25th percentile of admitted students has LSAT scores of about 159 and GPAs of about 3.4. Admitted students at the 75th percentile have LSAT scores of roughly 165 and GPAs of about 3.75. CU Law will consider all of your scores if you take the LSAT multiple times.

Legal research course requirement	Yes
Moot court requirement	No
Public interest law requirement	No

ADMISSIONS

Selectivity Rating	**89**
# applications received	2,517
# applicants accepted	661
# acceptees attending	172
Average LSAT	163
LSAT Range	159–165
Average undergrad GPA	3.56
Application fee	$65
Regular application	3/15
Regular notification	5/31
Rolling notification	Yes
Early application program	No
Transfer students accepted	Yes
Evening division offered	No
Part-time accepted	No
LSDAS accepted	Yes

Applicants Also Look At
Boston College, The George Washington U., Georgetown U., U. of California—Berkeley, U. of California—Hastings, U. of Denver, The U. of Texas at Austin.

International Students

TOEFL required of international students	No
TOEFL recommended of international students	Yes

FINANCIAL FACTS

Annual tuition (resident)	$16,738
Annual tuition (nonresident)	$30,814
Books and supplies	$1,592
Room and board (on/off-campus)	$12,814/$12,069
Financial aid application deadline	3/1
% first-year students receiving some sort of aid	90
% receiving some sort of aid	86
% of aid that is merit based	43
% receiving scholarships	73
Average grant	$3,450
Average loan	$20,802
Average total aid package	$25,000
Average debt	$58,874

EMPLOYMENT INFORMATION

Career Rating	**78**	Ritter, Governor of Colorado; Karen Mathis, president, ABA.
Rate of placement (nine months out)	97	**Grads Employed by Field (%)**
Average starting salary	$63,778	
State for bar exam	CO	Academic — 1
Pass rate for first-time bar	91	Business/Industry — 14
Employers Who Frequently Hire Grads		Government — 18
Arnold and Porter; Davis, Graham, and		Judicial clerkships — 20
Stubbs; Faegre and Benson; Hogan and		Military — 1
Hartson; Holland and Hart; Holme, Roberts,		Private practice — 43
and Owen; Kutak Rock; Otten Johnson.		Public Interest — 3
Prominent Alumni		
Associate Justice Wiley B. Rutledge, U.S.		
Supreme Court; former Chief Justice Luis		
D. Rovira, Colorado Supreme Court; Roy		
Romer, former Governor of Colorado; Bill		

UNIVERSITY OF CONNECTICUT
SCHOOL OF LAW

INSTITUTIONAL INFORMATION

Public/private	Public
Student-faculty ratio	11:1
% faculty part-time	50
% faculty female	29
% faculty minority	11
Total faculty	126

SURVEY SAYS...

Great research resources
Great library staff
Beautiful campus

STUDENTS

Enrollment of law school	704
% male/female	54/46
% out-of-state	30
% full-time	68
% minority	17
% international	1
# of countries represented	5
Average age of entering class	25

ACADEMICS

Academic Experience Rating	**82**
Profs interesting rating	72
Profs accessible rating	69
Hours of study per day	3.9

Academic Specialties

Commercial law, constitutional law, corporation securities law, criminal law, environmental law, government services, human rights law, insurance law, intellectual property law, international law, labor law, legal history, legal philosophy, property, taxation.

Advanced Degrees Offered

JD 3 to 4 years, LLM (U.S. legal studies) 1 year, LLM (insurance) 1 year.

Combined Degrees Offered

JD/MBA 4 years, JD/MLS 4 years, JD/MPA 4 years, JD/MSW 4 years, JD/MPH 4years, JD/LLM (insurance law) 4 years.

Clinical program required	No
Legal writing course requirement	No

Academics

University of Connecticut's undergraduate campus is located in the town of Storrs, whereas the law school makes its home on a "small" and "pretty" campus in the state's capital of Hartford. Without suffering from the distractions of a larger university but retaining the strength of the UConn name and reputation, students benefit from a close-knit academic atmosphere in which "You really get to know everyone within the law school community." While many UConn professors are "big names in law," students reassure us that "the faculty feel more like allies than oppressors," taking an active interest in professional and academic development of their students. Academically, UConn emphasizes both practical and theoretical aspects of the law, drawing a faculty comprised of "practicing lawyers, superior and appellate court judges, the chief disciplinary counsel and many other practicing professionals with real life experience who have not learned what they teach from a book." Catering to students interested in many legal fields, UConn operates "20-plus clinics for practical skills, even though they only reference 3 or 4 on our website, and the course selection is quite varied for a school of our size."

Like 1Ls across the nation, you'll have your fill of late-night cram sessions at UConn. However, students assure us that the "academic experience is challenging but fun." A student relates, "As a 1L, you will stress out over the workloads, but you will also get everything done without killing yourself." While competition doesn't reach cutthroat levels, it's still a legal pressure cooker because "Professors grade on a B-median scale, meaning that . . . you end up competing against the other people in your classes for the best grades, since most of you will receive B's." However, students also reassure us that, "Traditional academic rigor and competition are very well balanced with a very friendly, collegial environment. Students are smart, hardworking, and friendly."

In addition to the teaching staff, "Administration really supports the student, both academically, personally, and professionally. They attend and participate in all student organized events, help students think about different jobs, and counsel students about problems at school or home." However, many students at this public school also feel that despite their good intentions, "The administration tends to be out of step with the needs and wishes of the student body." One student explains, "We always joke that any change around here needs a legislative act . . . sadly, that is true!" On the other hand, students don't overlook the quality of the Career Services Office that helps the school to maintain its "very strong connection to CT firms and lawmakers, which is good if you plan to practice here." A current student shares: "The Career Services Office helped me, as an evening student, find a full-time job working as a law clerk with some of the best lawyers in the country." However, like most schools that are deeply invested in their community, students at UConn feel that "more emphasis needs to be given to acquiring interviewing firms from outside New England."

Life

University of Connecticut's student population is largely comprised of students in their mid-20s but also includes a decent number of recent college grads. As a result, there's an active group of students who are ready to enjoy both work and play during law school. A current student tells us, "UConn's biggest strength is a quality social life. We have a lot of parties, and a lot of sports teams to play on, including soccer, hockey, basketball, and softball."

KAREN DEMEOLA, ASSISTANT DEAN FOR ADMISSIONS AND STUDENT FINANCE
45 ELIZABETH STREET, HARTFORD, CT 06105
TEL: 860-570-5100 FAX: 860-570-5153
E-MAIL: ADMIT@LAW.UCONN.EDU • INTERNET: WWW.LAW.UCONN.EDU

In addition to the traditional program, the school also supports a fairly large evening program, whose students tend to differ from day students in that they are "pretty focused on school and their lives with family and friends outside school, and may have graduated from college some time ago." However, there are some who would like the school to provide "greater access to programs for evening students, as most of the student groups meet during the day, when most of the evening class is working." While they praise the campus as having a "very nice community feel," many students mention a general lack of diversity on campus (both on the faculty and within the student body), admitting to us that "there is not a ton of interaction between students of different races/ethnicities."

While hometown Hartford "won't win any style or fun points," the school is located in "a charming residential neighborhood" on a "pretty, Gothic-style" campus. Plus, Hartford's dicey reputation doesn't match up with reality. One current student assures that "Hartford is . . . on the way up, offering some surprisingly good cultural opportunities." Another agrees, "I think Hartford is coming out of its shell as a city, and UConn Law students are leading the charge in some of the bars and restaurants downtown."

Getting In

Students are admitted to UConn School of Law once annually, for entry in the fall semester. No numeric index is used to rank applicants to UConn School of Law and each applicant is considered individually. Connecticut residents receive special consideration in an admissions decision, though no absolute preference is given. Of the 210 1Ls accepted in 2006, the median undergraduate GPA was 3.46 and the median LSAT score was 161.

Legal methods course requirement	Yes
Legal research course requirement	Yes
Moot court requirement	Yes
Public interest law requirement	No

ADMISSIONS

Selectivity Rating	**96**
# applications received	2,598
# applicants accepted	356
# acceptees attending	209
Average LSAT	161
LSAT Range	159–163
Average undergrad GPA	3.45
Application fee	$30
Regular application	3/1
Regular notification	Rolling
Rolling notification	Yes
Early application program	No
Transfer students accepted	Yes
Evening division offered	Yes
Part-time accepted	Yes
LSDAS accepted	Yes

Applicants Also Look At
American U., Boston College, Boston U., George Mason U., Tulane U., U. of California—Hastings, Yeshiva U.

International Students

TOEFL required of international students	Yes

FINANCIAL FACTS

Annual tuition (resident)	$17,520
Annual tuition (nonresident)	$36,960
Books and supplies	$1,100
Fees per credit (resident)	$710
Fees per credit (nonresident)	$710
Tuition per credit (resident)	$730
Tuition per credit (nonresident)	$1,289
Room and board (off-campus)	$10,900
Financial aid application deadline	3/1
% first-year students receiving some sort of aid	88
% receiving some sort of aid	87
% of aid that is merit based	1
% receiving scholarships	69
Average grant	$9,484
Average loan	$26,209
Average total aid package	$23,713
Average debt	$58,615

EMPLOYMENT INFORMATION

		Grads Employed by Field (%)	
Career Rating	**84**	**Grads Employed by Field (%)**	
Rate of placement (nine months out)	95	Academic	3
Average starting salary	$80,709	Business/Industry	15
State for bar exam	CT, NY, MA, IL, NJ	Government	8
Pass rate for first-time bar	90	Judicial clerkships	13
Employers Who Frequently Hire Grads		Military	3
Adler, Pollock, and Sheehan; Akin, Gump,		Private practice	48
Strauss, Hauer, and Feld LLP; Axinn,		Public Interest	6
Veltrop, and Harkrider; Bernstein, Shur,			
Sawyer, Nelson; Bingham McCutchen LLP;			
Bond, Schoeneck, and King, PLLC;			
Bowditch and Dewey.			
For a complete list please see			
www.law.uconn.edu/careers/employers/			
employer-list.htm.			

University of Dayton

School of Law

INSTITUTIONAL INFORMATION

Public/private	Private
Affiliation	Roman Catholic
Student-faculty ratio	9:1
% faculty part-time	45
% faculty female	41
% faculty minority	8
Total faculty	51

SURVEY SAYS...

Great research resources
Great library staff
Beautiful campus

STUDENTS

Enrollment of law school	458
% male/female	57/43
% out-of-state	38
% full-time	100
% minority	12
% international	2
# of countries represented	1
Average age of entering class	25

ACADEMICS

Academic Experience Rating	**64**
Profs interesting rating	66
Profs accessible rating	66
Hours of study per day	4.81

Academic Specialties

Advocacy and dispute resolution, civil procedure, computer/cyberspace law, criminal law, intellectual property law, personal and transactional law, property, taxation.

Advanced Degrees Offered

JD 2.5 to 3 years.

Combined Degrees Offered

JD/MBA 4 years, JD/MSEd 4 years.

Clinical program required	Yes
Legal writing course requirement	Yes
Legal methods course requirement	Yes
Legal research course requirement	Yes
Moot court requirement	No
Public interest law requirement	No

Academics

"There is no more state-of-the-art law school than the University of Dayton School of Law," say its students. UDSL is home to a notable program in intellectual property law, and its "smaller class sizes" provide students with lots of "one-on-one interaction" with "engaging, passionate" professors. With the exception of the occasional "highly intimidating, *Paper Chase*-esque" professor, most of the faculty is "down to earth and approachable". "In the weeks before finals," says one 1L, "I had an almost daily correspondence with my property professor." The legal writing program is nationally renowned. "I feel that the greatest strength of our school is our legal writing program," emphasizes a 3L. It's "the torture we all feared about law school but it's definitely worth the stress."

The administration gets more mixed reviews. Some students tell us that the top brass "will work tirelessly to help every student in any way possible." Others call the administration "not responsive and very difficult to work with." "Class scheduling has been a problem" as well; a glut of night classes "makes having a family difficult."

Recent and pretty massive "curriculum change" has kept students on their toes. The most radical change was shaving one semester from the traditional three years of law school. "We are the first school in the nation to attempt a five-semester option," explains an optimistic 2L. "This gives highly motivated individuals the opportunity to graduate" with less debt and "without sacrificing an excellent legal education." Other students aren't so upbeat: "The requirement to begin our law experience with 18 credit hours per semester is too much," complains one. Some students worry about burnout and the effect the five-semester option will have on the school's reputation; one 2L thinks the school will be come known as a watered-down "quickie degree" institution. Another contentious issue involves the actual course work. First-year students choose one of "three tracks (advocacy, general, or technology)." Many students praise this aspect of Dayton because they are "able to take career-specific courses very early in the curriculum" and the track they choose "carries over into other classes." "For instance, I am on the Intellectual Property track," says a 1L. "All of our writing assignments have been based around various IP legal questions." According to other students, though, the mandatory track choice "pigeonholes" them, making them choose before they have an idea of the field of law they would like, and leaving them "unprepared for even the basics of other fields." Other gripes about the program include an "idiotic schedule-your-own-exam policy that rewards students who cheat" and a Career Services Center that provides "almost no opportunities for students who want to leave the Dayton/Cincinnati area."

One feature that garners unanimous student praise is the facilities. UDSL's "new, large, and aesthetically pleasing" law school building is an "architectural jewel" that boasts "open areas, natural light, and large windows" as well as "a huge library and high-tech classrooms," making it a nice place to be "trapped 10 hours a day." Technology is readily accessible: "There is wireless Internet all over campus and the library maintains a great computer lab." Many students complain, however, that the Web is "always down."

JANET L. HEIN, ASSISTANT DEAN, DIRECTOR OF ADMISSIONS AND FINANCIAL AID
300 COLLEGE PARK, 112 KELLER HALL, DAYTON, OH 45469-2760
TEL: 937-229-3555 FAX: 937-229-4194
E-MAIL: LAWINFO@NOTES.UDAYTON.EDU • INTERNET: LAW.UDAYTON.EDU

Life

The "small, tight-knit" law school community at UDSL is "wonderful and encouraging." Students are "easy to work with" and "not overly competitive." Students help each other out and frequently share study aids. "Even though we are all busy with our own school work, family life, etc., we'll still take time to help out a fellow classmate," says a 2L. "We aren't cutthroat (except a few nutty people who think they are at a top-tier school)."

UDSL students describe themselves as "relaxed, open, and friendly." A reasonably "diverse student body adds to the cultural background." Students run the gamut politically and socially. "It's like all organizations," advises a 2L. "There are some liberals, some conservatives, some losers, some snobs, some overachievers, some slackers." "There are some very bright students here, but we have others who seem to just be doing enough to get a JD." "Dayton is a lot like high school because there are well-defined cliques," explains another student.

Social life at UDSL has its ups and downs. On the plus side, "Dayton is a good place to go to law school because there aren't many distractions." On the contrary, as one 2L complains, Dayton has "the crime of Detroit, the pollution of LA, the weather of the Dakotas, and the intellectual vigor of the most insular small town in America." When students go out, they "always hit up the same bars" ("and sometimes the professors meet students" there for drinks).

Getting In

The University of Dayton School of Law is relatively small; its entering class is only about 120 students. Enrolled students last year at the 25th percentile had an LSAT score of 152 and a GPA of roughly 2.8. Enrolled students at the 75th percentile had an LSAT score of 156 and a GPA of roughly 3.4. Applicants must submit a personal statement and two letters of recommendation. Aside from quantitative factors, according to the school, "Admissions decisions are influenced by diversity of experiences, leadership, motivation, the ability to overcome hardships, and a breadth and depth of skills and interests." Applicants whose first language is not English must earn a TOEFL score of at least 600 on the paper-based test or 250 on the computer-based test.

ADMISSIONS

Selectivity Rating	**74**
# applications received	2,400
# applicants accepted	926
# acceptees attending	181
Average LSAT	152
LSAT Range	150–155
Average undergrad GPA	3.22
Regular application	5/1
Regular notification	Rolling
Rolling notification	Yes
Early application program	No
Transfer students accepted	Yes
Evening division offered	No
Part-time accepted	No
LSDAS accepted	Yes

Applicants Also Look At
Capital University, Cleveland State University, Florida Coastal School of Law, Ohio Northern University, Thomas M. Cooley Law School, The University of Akron, Valparaiso University.

International Students
TOEFL required	
of international students	No
TOEFL recommended	
of international students	Yes
Minimum paper TOEFL	600
Minimum computer TOEFL	250

FINANCIAL FACTS

Annual tuition	$31,536
Books and supplies	$1,200
Room and board	$9,911
Financial aid application	
deadline	5/1
% first-year students	
receiving some sort of aid	90
% receiving some sort of aid	90
% of aid that is merit based	80
% receiving scholarships	54
Average grant	$10,000
Average loan	$26,288
Average total aid package	$31,296
Average debt	$79,654

EMPLOYMENT INFORMATION

		Grads Employed by Field (%)	
Career Rating	**72**	**Grads Employed by Field (%)**	
Rate of placement (nine months out)	91	Academic	2
Average starting salary	$55,892	Business/Industry	17
State for bar exam	OH, FL, GA, KY, IN	Government	2
Pass rate for first-time bar	78	Judicial clerkships	3
Employers Who Frequently Hire Grads		Military	9
Proctor and Gamble; Ohio Attorney		Private practice	61
General; Thompson Hine; Fronst Brown		Public Interest	6
Todd LexisNexis; Jackson Kelly PLLC;			
Dinsmore and Shohl LLP.			
Prominent Alumni			
Honorable Barbara Gorman, Common			
Pleas Court; Ron Brown, CEO, Milacron			
Inc.; Helen Jones-Kelley, Director, Ohio			
Department of Job and Family Services.			

UNIVERSITY OF DENVER
STURM COLLEGE OF LAW

INSTITUTIONAL INFORMATION

Public/private	Private
Student-faculty ratio	16:1
% faculty female	42
% faculty minority	8
Total faculty	60

SURVEY SAYS...

Great research resources
Beautiful campus
Students love Denver, CO

STUDENTS

Enrollment of law school	1,129
% male/female	54/46
% out-of-state	70
% full-time	73
% minority	24
% international	5
# of countries represented	15
Average age of entering class	26

ACADEMICS

Academic Experience Rating	**80**
Profs interesting rating	74
Profs accessible rating	73
Hours of study per day	4.25

Academic Specialties

Civil procedure, corporation securities law, elder law, environmental law, human rights law, international law, taxation.

Advanced Degrees Offered

LLM (American and comparative law) 1 year, LLM (taxation) 1 year, LLM (natural resources).

Combined Degrees Offered

Business, geography, history, international management, international studies, legal administration, mass communications, professional psychology, psychology, social work, sociology.

Clinical program required	No
Legal writing course requirement	Yes
Legal methods course requirement	Yes

Academics

The luxury liner of law schools, the University of Denver Sturm College of Law boasts "amazing" facilities, "several" journals and clinical experiences, an "increasing" endowment, and a "strong" alumni network in the Denver metropolitan area. This large private school is "great" for its public interest and environmental law programs, though a wider range of interests, such as a Lawyering in Spanish program and "numerous opportunities for those of us that want to work for a corporate law firm" also garner praise. Diverse as the courses they teach, DU's "kind, brilliant, tough, and challenging" faculty is comprised of a "mixture of tenure-track professors and practicing attorneys." Despite the variety, students find that "the scheduling and availability of classes could be a little more diverse," especially when it comes to "basics" and "bar classes." Some students report "concern" over "bar-passage rates," though note that the "new administration is iron-fisted with purpose of bringing [them] up."

A practical perspective is paramount to the academic experience at University of Denver. For those interested, Career Services hosts frequent—almost daily—sessions (including free lunch) on "topics in international law, human rights, politics, practical career advice, debates on current issues, etc." Students say that these daily extra talks allow them to gain a better grasp of "life out of law school and after law school, which is a huge help." Through the mentorship program, "All students have regular opportunities to get career advice and direction from lawyers in the Denver community." To top it off, the school operates a large number of clinic programs, five law journals, and, from day one, "1Ls are invited and encouraged to participate in almost every moot court competition, so students develop exceptional trial advocacy skills early on."

Students explain that "as with any large law school there are some administrative problems"; however, one student sums it up this way: "Right now DU is like a teenager whose metaphysical development is just a little behind his or her physical growth. Make no mistake, all indications are that DU's going to be a stunner; however, on occasion administrative clumsiness leads to collective student body headaches." That said, students dole out praise for the new and spacious facilities, housed in an environmentally friendly (aka "green") building. One student explains, "The building is beautiful and well designed. There are lots of commons areas, and it would be nearly impossible to make it through a day without interacting with other people."

Students get a jump start on their career through the school's "outstanding" internship program that offers "internships with sole practitioners, large firms, and judges in legal fields ranging from water law to criminal law to administrative law." Come graduation, satisfied students praise the school's "incredible alumni network in the community and its incredible reputation in Denver and Colorado." Job-seekers are given an additional edge due to the fact that "DU is the only law school in Denver, and one of only two law schools in the state of Colorado, which makes it easy for DU graduates to find jobs." Plus, the Career Development Center does an "excellent" job introducing students to the local legal community. A current student elaborates, "Between guest speakers, networking events, on-campus interviews, resume and writing sample coaching, and weekly e-mails announcing new job/internship opportunities, if you don't have a job or at least some leads when you graduate, it's because you didn't want it."

KAREN HIGGANBOTHAM, DIRECTOR OF ADMISSIONS
2255 EAST EVANS AVENUE, DENVER, CO 80208
TEL: 303-871-6135 FAX: 303-871-6992
E-MAIL: ADMISSIONS@LAW.DU.EDU • INTERNET: WWW.LAW.DU.EDU

Life

While DU is a large school, the program is structured in a way that creates a more intimate atmosphere. One student says, "Day students are divided into one of three sections comprised of 80 students. I see the same people day in and day out for every class." Many find this "very helpful for forming close friendships" since it allows students to get "to know and become comfortable" with each other while "forming study groups." No matter what your background, you're likely to find a friend or two amongst the large student body. "There's a wide range of social groups, from 'high school' gossiping, partying groups, to academic and career-centered groups," explains one student. In addition, "There's a club for every interest you could think of, which is great."

Not surprisingly, many law students admit that they are "too busy studying to go out and have a social life." However, if you are looking for a good time, "The straight-out-of-college crew is probably the most social, or at least the ones that seem to go out and hang out the most," and "There are lots of informally organized nights at the local restaurant or bar that are open to all." Students agree that "Denver is a great city" with "so much to do." And being only "an hour from the mountains," winter sport fans find that "you can be in court in the morning and on the slopes by afternoon."

Getting In

Applicants to the University of Denver Sturm College of Law must have a bachelor's degree from an accredited college and current LSAT scores. Competition is steep as for the 2006 entering class, the school received a little over 3,500 applications and enrolled 266 full-time and 77 part-time students. The median LSAT score for matriculated students was 158 with a median GPA of 3.4.

EMPLOYMENT INFORMATION			
Career Rating	72	**Grads Employed by Field (%)**	
Rate of placement (nine months out)	91	Academic	2
Average starting salary	$50,000	Business/Industry	15
State for bar exam	CO	Government	17
Pass rate for first-time bar	72	Judicial clerkships	8
Employers Who Frequently Hire Grads		Other	7
Small, medium and large law firms; government agencies (DA office, AG's office, etc.); corporations; nonprofit organizations.		Private practice	45
		Public Interest	5

Legal research course requirement	Yes
Moot court requirement	No
Public interest law requirement	Yes

ADMISSIONS

Selectivity Rating	**83**
# applications received	3,199
# applicants accepted	824
# acceptees attending	259
Average LSAT	158
LSAT Range	155–160
Average undergrad GPA	3.4
Application fee	$60
Regular application	5/30
Regular notification	Rolling
Rolling notification	Yes
Early application program	No
Transfer students accepted	Yes
Evening division offered	Yes
Part-time accepted	Yes
LSDAS accepted	Yes

International Students

TOEFL required of international students	Yes
Minimum paper TOEFL	580
Minimum computer TOEFL	213

FINANCIAL FACTS

Annual tuition	$30,360
Books and supplies	$1,698
Tuition per credit	$1,012
Room and board	$8,783
Financial aid application deadline	3/30
% first-year students receiving some sort of aid	83
% receiving some sort of aid	86
% of aid that is merit based	26
% receiving scholarships	26
Average grant	$13,500
Average loan	$26,793
Average total aid package	$32,254
Average debt	$88,556

UNIVERSITY OF THE DISTRICT OF COLUMBIA*
DAVID A. CLARKE SCHOOL OF LAW

INSTITUTIONAL INFORMATION

Public/private	Public
Student-faculty ratio	11:1
% faculty female	45
% faculty minority	45
Total faculty	18

SURVEY SAYS...

Liberal students
Students love Washington, DC

STUDENTS

Enrollment of law school	235
% male/female	39/61
% full-time	100
% minority	44
% international	5 Average age of
entering class	27

ACADEMICS

Academic Experience Rating	**77**
Profs interesting rating	88
Profs accessible rating	95
Hours of study per day	5.5

Academic Specialties

Public interest law.

Advanced Degrees Offered

JD 3 years.

Clinical program required	Yes
Legal writing course requirement	Yes
Legal methods course requirement	No
Legal research course requirement	No
Moot court requirement	Yes
Public interest law requirement	Yes

Academics

"An up-and-coming school with an emphasis on public interest and public service," the David A. Clarke School of Law was founded with the mission to train students from groups underrepresented at the bar to become skilled and ethical public advocates and private attorneys. This unique mission is carried out through the school's extensive clinical programs, which include, among others, an Immigrant Law Program, an HIV law clinic, and a housing and consumer law clinic. At these free legal centers, students advise on real, ongoing legal cases under the supervision of a practicing attorney, representing clients in the DC area who would otherwise be unable to afford legal counsel. While these clinics provide a meaningful service to the DC community, they also offer important, hands-on legal experience to the UDC student body. As a result, UDC "students and alumni enter the legal field extremely well prepared for practical application of their legal skills." A 3L boasts, "Due to the public interest and practice focus of the school, my classmates and I will graduate with a full resume of legal experience as we enter the workplace." Another adds, "The school trains you to be a 'street lawyer'—an advocate for the people, focusing on the disenfranchised."

While the extensive clinical training is a distinguishing characteristic of UDC, students tell us that the traditional academic program is excellent, describing their course work as "challenging and stimulating." Professors are "competent and very knowledgeable about their subject areas" and are likewise "exceptional pedagogues." In addition, UDC teachers bring important, practical experience to the classroom, as most "are experts in their field, having practiced (or are still practicing) in that area." As diversity is a cornerstone of the educational experience at UDC, students also note with pleasure that the variety of background within the teaching staff is particularly strong at their school.

When slogging through the first-year workload, UDC students appreciate the fact that their professors are "very accessible and truly want to see you succeed." On top of that, the school maintains relatively small class sizes, which foster bonds between faculty and students. "It's rigorous, but the best part about it is that you truly develop a one-on-one relationship with the faculty and staff," comments a 2L. In fact, professors treat students like colleagues and, after class, "They are not above going to the dive bar across the street to share a beer with you." Administrators, likewise, are reputed to be "always available and extremely helpful," so much so that students claim "It's a bit of a shock when, after the first month, the deans all know you by name."

While students praise the quality of their education, some worry that "as a provisionally accredited school, we underestimate ourselves and look at things from the position of underdog." However, they have great faith in the strength of the UDC program and feel that continued improvements will soon impact the school's reputation. A 3L explains, "I think this school is a diamond in the rough and will see national recognition and accolades when it gets final ABA accreditation." Students also feel the school's growing pains in its physical structure, saying that "the facilities are not always the best, having been inherited from the underfunded undergraduate school." However, they are quick to remind us that "things get better every year" at UDC. Furthermore, philanthropic UDC students say "It's not about the edifice; it's about the individuals who are trained to make a difference in the lives of people." While the classrooms may be antiquated, UDC has given students a "great new law library."

*Provisionally approved by the ABA.

VIVIAN CANTY, ASSISTANT DEAN OF ADMISSION
4200 CONNECTICUT AVENUE, NORTHWEST, WASHINGTON, DC 20008
TEL: 202-274-7336 FAX: 202-274-5583
E-MAIL: VCANTY@UDC.EDU • INTERNET: WWW.LAW.UDC.EDU

Life

Located in a residential neighborhood in Washington, DC, the UDC campus is just a short bus ride away from Capitol Hill, local and federal courts, and the many public and private agencies located downtown. Reflecting the multicultural population of the surrounding city, UDC "is a very diverse and accepting school for people of all races, religions, genders, and sexual orientations." Underrepresented minorities make up about half of the student body.

While they hail from varied backgrounds, "Students work cooperatively and respect each other's opinions." "Despite our diverse backgrounds, there is no one I'd feel uncomfortable walking up to and striking up a conversation with," writes a 1L. While seriously studious, students are only moderately competitive with each other. "The environment is like a family of brothers and sisters: competitive, but always supportive!" In fact, "If a classmate misses a class for whatever reason (even if they were out too late at the bar the night before), there are always other students willing to share their notes for the missed class."

Getting In

About half of UDC law students are underrepresented minorities, and the school seeks to admit students who represent a broad spectrum of society, culture, age, ethnicity, and gender. Because of the school's commitment to diversity and underrepresented communities, both academic and non-academic criteria are weighed heavily in an admissions decision. In particular, a demonstrated commitment to public service is a great asset to an application.

ADMISSIONS

Selectivity Rating	73
# applications received	1,344
# applicants accepted	276
# acceptees attending	95
Average LSAT	151
Average undergrad GPA	3.1
Application fee	$35
Regular application	3/15
Regular notification	Rolling
Rolling notification	Yes
Early application program	No
Transfer students accepted	Yes
Evening division offered	No
Part-time accepted	No
LSDAS accepted	Yes

Applicants Also Look At
American University, The Catholic University of America, City University of New York—Queens College, George Mason University, Howard University, University of Baltimore, University of Maryland.

International Students
TOEFL required of international students	Yes

FINANCIAL FACTS

Annual tuition (resident)	$7,350
Annual tuition (nonresident)	$14,700
Books and supplies	$4,500
Room and board (off-campus)	$25,150
Financial aid application deadline	3/31
% receiving some sort of aid	90
% of aid that is merit based	46
% receiving scholarships	78
Average grant	$4,000
Average debt	$66,000

EMPLOYMENT INFORMATION

Career Rating	63	Grads Employed by Field (%)	
Rate of placement (nine months out)	73	Academic	5
Average starting salary	$54,500	Business/Industry	20
State for bar exam	MD, DC, VA, CA, FL	Government	7
Pass rate for first-time bar	56	Judicial clerkships	5
Employers Who Frequently Hire Grads		Private practice	51
Local and federal government agencies; legal services providers; litigation-oriented law firms; public interest law firms and organizations; judicial clerkships; business and industry.		Public Interest	12

UNIVERSITY OF FLORIDA
LEVIN COLLEGE OF LAW

INSTITUTIONAL INFORMATION

Public/private	Public
Student-faculty ratio	17.6:1
% faculty female	49
% faculty minority	17
Total faculty	82

SURVEY SAYS...

Diverse opinions accepted
in classrooms
Abundant externship/internship/
clerkship opportunities
Good social life

STUDENTS

Enrollment of law school	1,364
% male/female	53/47
% out-of-state	9
% full-time	100
% minority	17
% international	4
# of countries represented	4
Average age of entering class	24

ACADEMICS

Academic Experience Rating	**66**
Profs interesting rating	69
Profs accessible rating	67
Hours of study per day	4.04

Academic Specialties

Environmental law, estates and trusts practice, family law, intellectual property law, international law, taxation.

Advanced Degrees Offered

LLM (taxation) 1 year, LLM (international taxation) 1 year, LLM (comparative law) 1 year, SJD (taxation) multiyear.

Combined Degrees Offered

More than 30 joint-degree programs (JD/masters and PhD); length of program varies.

Clinical program required	No
Legal writing course requirement	Yes
Legal methods course requirement	No

Academics

The University of Florida Levin College of Law is said to be "the best" law school in the state and "one of the best in the South." Also, the outrageously cheap in-state tuition "is hard to beat." Academic strengths include a nationally recognized tax law program and scores of joint-degree programs—from standards like accounting and business administration to more unique offerings like sport sciences and environmental engineering. Study abroad programs send UF students to Cape Town, South Africa, for international comparative law; Montpellier, France, for international business; and San Jose, Costa Rica, for environmental law.

Many students tell us that one of UF's greatest strengths is its "excellent professors who are seemingly at the top of their profession." One student professes that "the faculty are godly in their expertise, yet human in their compassionate approach in instruction." (The school's writing and legal skills instructors were singled out as "superb.") Professors in all departments "respect us and hold us to the highest standards" and are "extremely available out of class for questions concerning their class or any matter you may wish to discuss." Some appear to have "left-wing agendas" and most "are tough," but one UF student tells us, "I've laughed in almost every class this year. Professors are interested in developing you into an ethical lawyer who is a tribute to the profession." Going beyond the classroom, "There is a collegial atmosphere here that encourages communication between students, faculty, and administration. And all three groups participate in social events outside the law school."

Students approve of the classes offered too: "I cannot think of a law school which emphasizes practical lawyering more than UF. We have excellent tax, intellectual property, elder law, and environmental programs." Students only wish there were "greater variety in course offerings. I know there is more out there, but I see the same courses semester after semester."

Students and faculty alike speak highly of the $25-million-dollar expansion project that resulted in "brand-new classrooms with state-of-the-art technology." "They're gorgeous and definitely worth the hassle of construction," says one student. Another believes that now "The quality of the law school's physical appearance matches the quality of education a student receives here. They are spacious, bright, and ready to take us into the future." With a sparkling new library (double the size of the old one), the school has entered Phase III, the construction of a new trial advocacy center. As one student tells us, "For a school undergoing a complete face-lift, the faculty, students, and staff have done remarkably well in maintaining a high quality of education and an extremely professional environment. As these construction projects continue to resolve, the facilities are becoming among the best in the country."

J. MICHAEL PATRICK, ASSISTANT DEAN FOR ADMISSIONS
BOX 117622, GAINESVILLE, FL 32611
TEL: 352-273-0890 FAX: 352-392-4087
E-MAIL: ADMISSIONS@LAW.UFL.EDU • INTERNET: WWW.LAW.UFL.EDU

Life

There are more than 1,200 students at the UF College of Law. They are "for the most part in their early 20s" and from Florida. Although one in five is a student of color, some complain of a homogenous student body. "The school is not as diverse as it could be," one student says. "There should be more diversity [in] the faculty, too." The school has instituted a variety of new programs and initiatives to this end. Socially, UF is home to the usual suspects. "There are those who party every night and those who live in the library, afraid someone might get ahead of them." Students report a very "Greek" feel to the social environment. "People get along well and socialize a lot" but, with so many students, there are bound to be "lots of cliques." One student says, "If you find one you like, you're grand. But even if not, nearly everyone is friendly and nice." Students seem to experience competitiveness in varying degrees at UF, as some say there is zilch, while others call it "cutthroat." However, "Despite the obvious underlying competitiveness of law school, students are always willing to help each other out." This is what helps to form "a strong bond between UF law students that carries on well after graduation" and create "great opportunities to form a strong alumni network."

The University of Florida is located in Gainesville, "a big college town where there is not much" to do. (Except study, of course.) Beyond the standard undergraduate fare, "Gainesville has nothing to offer." For students seeking a more urban vibe, "The nearest city is Orlando, which is an hour and a half away." Gainesville does have its merits, though. The weather is mostly good, particularly if you can avoid the sweltering heat in the summer. Perhaps most importantly, "It is cheap to live here."

Getting In

Accepting fewer than one in every three candidates, admission to Levin is tough. About 90 percent of the student body are residents of the state of Florida, but there is no cap on the percentage of the student body who can come from out of state, so your nonresident status is not a strike against you in the admissions process.

Legal research course requirement	Yes
Moot court requirement	No
Public interest law requirement	No

ADMISSIONS

Selectivity Rating	**82**
# applications received	2,535
# applicants accepted	1,044
# acceptees attending	447
Average LSAT	158
LSAT Range	155–161
Average undergrad GPA	3.59
Application fee	$30
Regular application	1/15
Regular notification	4/1
Rolling notification	Yes
Early application program	No
Transfer students accepted	Yes
Evening division offered	No
Part-time accepted	No
LSDAS accepted	Yes

Applicants Also Look At

American University, Emory University, Florida Coastal School of Law, Florida State University, Georgetown University, Stetson University, University of Georgia, University of Miami, The University of North Carolina at Chapel Hill.

International Students

TOEFL required of international students	Yes
Minimum paper TOEFL	550
Minimum computer TOEFL	213

FINANCIAL FACTS

Annual tuition (resident)	$9,861
Annual tuition (nonresident)	$29,227
Books and supplies	$920
Room and board (on/off-campus)	$7,530/$7,640
Financial aid application deadline	4/1
% first-year students receiving some sort of aid	85
% receiving some sort of aid	82
% of aid that is merit based	1
% receiving scholarships	13
Average grant	$3,790
Average loan	$18,018
Average total aid package	$18,166
Average debt	$49,612

EMPLOYMENT INFORMATION

Career Rating	74	Grads Employed by Field (%)	
Rate of placement (nine months out)	93	Academic	1
Average starting salary	$58,921	Business/Industry	9
State for bar exam	FL, GA	Government	16
Pass rate for first-time bar	83	Judicial clerkships	6
Employers Who Frequently Hire Grads		Military	3
Foley and Lardner; King and Spalding;		Private practice	58
Holland and Knight; White and Case;		Public Interest	7
Greenberg Traurig; Hunton and Williams;			
Troutman Sanders.			

Prominent Alumni

Martha Barnett, Holland and Knight LLP, ABA president 2000; W. Reece Smith Jr., Carlton Fields, ABA president 1980.

UNIVERSITY OF HAWAII—MANOA
WILLIAM S. RICHARDSON SCHOOL OF LAW

Academics

Nestled at the "crossroads of the Pacific," the University of Hawaii—Manoa William S. Richardson School of Law offers local, national, and international students an equal opportunity to get a law degree while enjoying a little piece of heaven on earth. Don't be fooled by the laid-back nature of the students and faculty—academics here are plenty "rigorous," particularly in the school's strong Pacific Island law and environmental law programs. Fortunately, it's easy to wind down from a long day of hitting the books when you're surrounded by beaches and happy fellow students. As a second-year student eloquently observes: "Just the right mix of *aloha* and Socratic thrashing yields capable, happy lawyers."

Richardson's "first-rate" faculty has a reputation for being "very accessible and easy to work with," and it's obvious to students that "they take pride in teaching." Even the handful of students who aren't raving about their instructors can only offer up the mildest criticism, as one second-year demonstrates: "A few I've encountered are just okay." Abiding by an open-door policy and demonstrating an openness "to discussing topics at most anytime," Richardson professors take the time to make sure that everyone understands the concepts, while at the same time being "very supportive of independent research." "I generally feel that I am able to explore my intellectual pursuits as I deem fit, with guidance and support from the faculty," states a 2L.

The "very friendly" administration is certainly accessible; the Richardson School of Law is "the kind of school where the dean is seen in the halls everyday and says hello to you by name," and administrators are often spotted participating in school activities. In return, they ask for student input on many school matters, such as the hiring of professors, expansion of the school library, and improving student services. Richardson students speak very highly of the regard shown by the entire campus community for the well-being of first-year students, from the "truly concerned" deans to "supportive" upperclassmen. The island is a magnet for a great deal of "very impressive" adjunct faculty and visiting lecturers. "Professors from top law schools are always looking for an excuse to spend a semester or a year in paradise," surmises a 2L. "[During] my 1L year, I had two visiting professors from Georgetown and one from Duke, in addition to the excellent professors tenured at UH." Networking opportunities are "exceptional if you're staying in Hawaii," although some students seeking employment in the continental United States wish they had more assistance in their job search.

Both the facilities and the library are "useful" and sufficient for the typical student's needs, and include "access to up-to-date online sources, as well some print materials." Unsurprisingly, students prefer to congregate outside whenever possible, and a "courtyard where students can relax or talk" is usually where you'll find them. Even so, students clamor for more study and meeting rooms, and complain about the state of the library and the "very cold" air conditioning levels in classrooms. Luckily, the law school facilities are up for renovation within the next few years.

Life

A good mix of students fresh out of undergrad and those with more life experience bring diversity to Richardson' student population. Some students say that the school is "trying too hard to get diversity," which results in the enrollment of "lots of mainland people who will get their degree and bolt back." "Diversity of opinion and views is important, but not at the expense of the community at large," says a student. Still, there's

LAURIE TOCHIKI, ASSISTANT DEAN
2515 DOLE STREET, HONOLULU, HI 96822
TEL: 808-956-3000 FAX: 808-956-3813
E-MAIL: LAWADM@HAWAII.EDU • INTERNET: WWW.HAWAII.EDU/LAW

not many downsides to life at Richardson. As one can imagine, "It's a very tightly knit community." Most students agree that competition at this "small, intimate" school is present and "healthy," but it takes a back seat to "learning how to be both a zealous advocate for clients and a responsible officer of the court." Classmates definitely "don't claw each other to get to the top of the class." It's hard to imagine all that much back-stabbing going on when "The culture and values of Hawaii permeate the school and administration," and the general happiness of students contributes to a "communal atmosphere" in which students "build ties and form lifelong bonds." "You become *ohana* (family) when you attend the Richardson School of Law," says one student. Still, there's a bit of "Hawaiian/not Hawaiian, *haole*/not *haole* tension" present on the island, but "in general, it's civil." The options of things to do in your downtime are unrivaled. "How many schools have a Surf Club?" asks a first-year. There are a "wide variety" of student clubs and organizations on campus (it's also easy to start one), and these groups do "a nice job" of promoting events such as guest speakers and symposiums.

Getting In

As the only ABA-accredited law school in the Pacific Asia region, the University of Hawaii—Manoa Richardson School of Law can afford to be selective. They've got a lock on the local talent and anyone looking to practice within the area will be competing for a limited number of seats. The school is very strict about its deadlines, and all applications must be received by March 1. LSAT scores prior to 2004 will not be accepted.

ADMISSIONS

Selectivity Rating	87
# applications received	1,091
# applicants accepted	203
# acceptees attending	96
Average LSAT	158
LSAT Range	156–161
Average undergrad GPA	3.4
Application fee	$60
Regular application	3/1
Regular notification	4/15
Rolling notification	No
Early application program	No
Transfer students accepted	Yes
Evening division offered	No
Part-time accepted	No
LSDAS accepted	Yes

Applicants Also Look At

Santa Clara University, University of California—Berkeley, University of California—Hastings, University of California—Los Angeles, University of San Diego.

International Students

TOEFL required	
of international students	Yes
Minimum paper TOEFL	600
Minimum computer TOEFL	250

FINANCIAL FACTS

Annual tuition (resident)	$12,120
Annual tuition (nonresident)	$20,784
Books and supplies	$800
Room and board (on/off-campus)	$9,378/$12,563
Financial aid application deadline	3/1
Average grant	$5,724
Average loan	$11,885
Average total aid package	$5,724
Average debt	$46,512

EMPLOYMENT INFORMATION

Career Rating	70	Grads Employed by Field (%)	
Rate of placement (nine months out)		Academic	1
Average starting salary	$53,800	Business/Industry	12
State for bar exam	HI, CA, WA, OR, NY	Government	10
Pass rate for first-time bar	91	Judicial clerkships	25
Employers Who Frequently Hire Grads		Military	2
Hawaii State Judiciary; Office of the		Other	13
Prosecuting Attorney; Public Defenders		Private practice	35
Office; Ashford and Wriston; Bays Deaver		Public Interest	2
et al.			

Prominent Alumni

John Waihee, former Governor of Hawaii; Jack Fritz, Speaker, House of Congress of Fed. State of Micronesia; Mari Matsuda, professor, Georgetown University Law Center.

UNIVERSITY OF HOUSTON
LAW CENTER

Academics

As large and lively as the state of Texas, the University of Houston Law Center enrolls over 1,000 students in its diverse and challenging JD, LLM, and joint-degree programs. Drawing top names from the Houston legal community, professors are "either extremely accomplished attorneys or nationally renowned experts in a particular field of law." Though they represent the top of their field, "There are no 'bigger than Texas' egos with any of the faculty." In fact, "The entire faculty is very accessible and willing to help students learn in any way they can." Students agree that their professors are "not only available during office hours, many professors host lunches or parties in their homes to learn more about their students."

In the classroom, the professors are "very much focused on teaching us to think creatively" and throughout the JD program the "Practical aspects of lawyering are stressed." Things here begin with a bang as "All first-year students are required to take part in a moot court competition and it's a great experience for everyone." In addition, "There are six different law journals in which a student may participate, including the Houston Law Review, which consistently ranks in the top 50 of all Law Reviews in the country." What's more, the school operates a number of clinics and research institutes that augment classroom experiences with hands-on experience. "I have spent three semesters working at the Immigration and Civil Clinic and will always remember this time as the most exciting and rewarding aspect of my law school experience," explains one clinic participant. "We are given enormous responsibility for our clients and the experience has given me an invaluable opportunity to learn actual lawyering skills."

Those looking for great value relative to cost in their education will be extremely satisfied with U of H. Students love that they get a "high-value education for a low cost in a great legal market." If you can manage a "scholarship" or are "a Texas resident" it only sweetens the proverbial deal. Even so, students admit there are some sacrifices associated with a U of H education, particularly with regard to the school's facilities which most agree "need improvement." There are no ivy-lined walls at U of H; instead, think "East-German-bunker school of architecture." However, most students take the environs in stride. "Students who enter with high expectations of facilities will be disappointed," says one student. "But you learn at this school in an environment conducive to learning." On that note, U of H "fosters a community and not a rivalry among students. Fellow students are always willing to answer a question, share notes, and form study groups."

Outside the classroom, "There are lots of opportunities to work with major law firms and other community organizations during the summer and during the school year," and the "Office of Career Services is particularly helpful for summer job opportunities." After graduation, Houston is a well-suited environment for future attorneys, boasting its reputation as one of the "largest legal markets in the country." A current student insists, "If you want to succeed, you can, and you can get a great job when you graduate too— with all the top firms in Texas including all the elite New York satellite offices."

Life

Students say the school is a great place to work on your powers of persuasion as there's lots of debate on the U of H campus. A student explains, "Because the student body is fairly conservative, but, at the same time, lawyers generally exhibit liberal thinking (at least in the social realm), you get a nice balance of liberal and conservative, often

JAMIE HAMMERS, ASSISTANT DEAN FOR ADMISSIONS
100 LAW CENTER, HOUSTON, TX 77204-6060
TEL: 713-743-2280 FAX: 713-743-2194
E-MAIL: LAWADMISSIONS@UH.EDU • INTERNET: WWW.LAW.UH.EDU

leading to lively debate absent from more liberal institutions." Even so, don't expect "any cutthroat type of competitive environment" here since students agree that "even if they have polar opposite views in the classroom, afterwards they hang out."

On campus, the prevailing atmosphere is "friendly" with "an awesome SBA that is very active in helping make UHLC a better place." Students tend to form strong friendships in their first-year sections, and when the weekend arrives "Plenty of people . . . go out on a regular basis." Night students are generally less involved in the campus community, admitting that there is something of a "social divide between part-time and full-time students"; many complain that events and activities take place during the day (while they are working) and that "most of the social events are geared towards single people or those without children."

Unfortunately, the campus isn't much of a social hub because "It is in a part of Houston that nobody really cares to live in, so most people come in for class and then head home." However, the cosmopolitan city of Houston is a great place to live, offering "a standing symphony, opera, and ballet, NFL, NBA, MLB, and MLS sports teams (and minor league ice hockey) a great zoo and museums, and a multitude of golfing opportunities."

Getting In

There is no set minimum LSAT score or undergraduate GPA required for acceptance to the University of Houston Law Center; all applicants are reviewed individually. In 2006, the lowest LSAT score accepted was in the mid-140s, while the median score for accepted applicants was 161. The median GPA was 3.6. Non-Texans comprise approximately 33 percent of the student population and the acceptance rate is equally competitive for out-of-state and in-state residents.

Legal methods	
course requirement	Yes
Legal research	
course requirement	Yes
Moot court requirement	Yes
Public interest	
law requirement	No

ADMISSIONS

Selectivity Rating	**84**
# applications received	3,032
# applicants accepted	886
# acceptees attending	247
Average LSAT	159
LSAT Range	157–162
Average undergrad GPA	3.49
Application fee	$70
Regular application	2/15
Regular notification	5/15
Rolling notification	Yes
Early application program	Yes
Early application deadline	11/1
Early application notification	2/15
Transfer students accepted	Yes
Evening division offered	Yes
Part-time accepted	Yes
LSDAS accepted	Yes

Applicants Also Look At
Baylor U., Southern Methodist U., Texas Tech U., The U. of Texas at Austin.

International Students

TOEFL required	
of international students	Yes
Minimum paper TOEFL	600
Minimum computer TOEFL	250

FINANCIAL FACTS

Annual tuition (resident)	$11,656
Annual tuition	
(nonresident)	$18,106
Books and supplies	$1,050
Fees per credit	$1,612
Tuition per credit (resident)	$389
Tuition per credit	
(nonresident)	$604
Room and board	
(on/off-campus)	$6,888/$8,772
Financial aid application	
deadline	4/1
% first-year students	
receiving some sort of aid	85
% receiving some sort of aid	85
% of aid that is merit based	43
% receiving scholarships	59
Average grant	$3,323
Average loan	$20,828
Average total aid package	$21,869
Average debt	$58,010

EMPLOYMENT INFORMATION

Career Rating	**86**	**Grads Employed by Field (%)**	
Rate of placement (nine months out)	96	Business/Industry	25
Average starting salary	$85,215	Government	6
State for bar exam	TX	Judicial clerkships	5
Pass rate for first-time bar	90	Military	1
Employers Who Frequently Hire Grads		Private practice	60
Baker and Botts; Locke, Liddell, and Sapp;		Public Interest	3
Fulbright and Jaworski; Vinson and Elkins;			
Bracewell and Giuliani; Harris Co. D.A.;			
Weil, Gotshal, and Manges.			
Prominent Alumni			
Richard Haynes, litigation; John O'Quinn,			
litigation; Charles Matthews, vice president			
and general counsel, ExxonMobil.			

UNIVERSITY OF IDAHO
COLLEGE OF LAW

Academics

"Handwritten on my letter of acceptance were the words 'We would love to have you in the Idaho family,'" beams a 1L at the University of Idaho College of Law. "I didn't think anything of it at the time, but it really does have that kind of feel here." "The low tuition is a bargain," and "The administration is kind, fair, and involved." Plus, "The Dean rocks." "There are a few profs here and there who obviously just want to do their research, and teaching is a bit of a dead weight for them, but they are definitely in the minority." Most "dedicated" professors at this "small public law school" are "unbelievably friendly and accessible" and "genuinely care about the students." The faculty "knows students by name by the end of their first year, even if you do not have a class with them." "I've never seen anything like it, quite frankly," says an impressed 1L. "Sure, one moment they're using the Socratic Method to grill you in class," says a 2L, "but after class they take the time to discuss any topic with you."

Some students complain that "practical legal skills, other than writing, seem to get short shrift." Others contend that there are "ample opportunities for pro bono work" and "other ways to allow students to get some practical experience before they graduate." "Many of these programs are student run, which I think is great," notes a 1L. "The externship, internship, clinic, and semester-in-practice programs are wonderful."

U of I is the only law school in Idaho, "and its graduates are extremely well respected throughout the state and throughout the geographic region in general." "Because Idaho is a small state with a relatively small legal community, alumni are very actively involved at the law school." "During orientation, a group of us were eating lunch on the lawn outside the law school," explains a 1L. "A man approached us and asked to join us. Only after five minutes of casual conversation did he mention that he was the Attorney General for the state of Idaho." "There are quite a few job opportunities in the area surrounding Moscow," but "It is hard to get good placements" for jobs, internships, and externships because of the school's relatively remote location. "You pretty much have to live in Spokane or Boise for the summer to get a really well-paid job with valuable experience."

The "somewhat old" and "small" law school facilities are "functional," but "could be more aesthetically pleasing." The administration is "working to improve aesthetics" but "It's very dark inside; there are no windows in the halls or in the class rooms, and the lighting is extremely poor." The computer lab is "the worst." On the plus side, the study areas are "roomy and nice," and classrooms are "comfortable" and "very large," though not very modern. "There is a beautiful courtroom where the Idaho Supreme Court and Court of Appeals come twice a year and provide the students an opportunity to observe actual proceedings." The library is "pretty good for a small school."

Life

The administration "is striving to increase diversity," but it's not easy because U of I is "somewhat isolated by its location and lack of diversity in the general population." Students do run the gamut in terms of age. "I am enjoying my experience of returning to school as an older student," says a 2L. Also, "There is a sizeable Mormon population." Politically, the student population is "divided between extreme conservatives and extreme liberals," which "creates tension" occasionally.

STEPHEN M. PEREZ, DIRECTOR OF ADMISSIONS
SIXTH AND RAYBURN STREETS, MOSCOW, ID 83844-2321
TEL: 208-885-2300 FAX: 208-885-5709
E-MAIL: LAWADMIT@UIDAHO.EDU • INTERNET: WWW.LAW.UIDAHO.EDU

"This is a tremendously friendly law school." Students describe themselves as "cooperative and accepting." "The 1Ls, though competitive," demonstrate a "strong camaraderie." Cliques do tend to form, though, and gossip runs "rampant." Outside of class, there is "a lot of student involvement." "Because of the limited number of students [at the law school], there are countless opportunities for involvement in extracurricular activities, legal aid clinics, positions in student groups, and for membership on administration committees." "About half of the students socialize on a regular basis," and there are "some pretty hard partiers."

Moscow is "a fairly remote," "beautiful," rural hamlet "in northern Idaho," "closer to Seattle than Boise," and "two hours from a city of any size (Spokane, Washington)." Idaho boasts "many recreational opportunities." "If you love hiking, biking, skiing, and the outdoors, then it is heaven," counsels a 2L. "If you need constant activity and entertainment, U of I is not for you, but if you're serious about getting a good-quality, inexpensive education, you'll get both here." "The cost of living is affordable," and "There is a large food co-op" and "an impressive farmer's market." There are "great parks" and "many festivals" as well. It's "easy to walk anywhere." "There isn't an apartment in town that isn't five minutes from the school."

Getting In

Admitted students at the 25th percentile have LSAT scores of 151 and GPAs a little over 3.1. Admitted students at the 75th percentile have LSAT scores of 158 and GPAs of nearly 3.7. If you take the LSAT more than once, the U of I "may put more weight on the most recent score, especially when there is several years between scores."

Moot court requirement	Yes
Public interest law requirement	Yes

ADMISSIONS

Selectivity Rating	**75**
# applications received	782
# applicants accepted	302
# acceptees attending	105
Average LSAT	155
LSAT Range	151–157
Average undergrad GPA	3.44
Application fee	$50
Regular application	2/15
Regular notification	4/15
Rolling notification	Yes
Early application program	No
Transfer students accepted	Yes
Evening division offered	No
Part-time accepted	No
LSDAS accepted	Yes

Applicants Also Look At

Gonzaga University, Seattle University, University of Nevada—Las Vegas, Willamette University.

International Students

TOEFL required of international students	Yes
TOEFL recommended of international students	Yes
Minimum paper TOEFL	560
Minimum computer TOEFL	280

FINANCIAL FACTS

Annual tuition (resident)	$9,540
Annual tuition (nonresident)	$19,140
Books and supplies	$1,388
Room and board	$7,236
Financial aid application deadline	2/15
% first-year students receiving some sort of aid	99
% receiving some sort of aid	94
% of aid that is merit based	100
% receiving scholarships	43
Average grant	$4,683
Average loan	$18,278
Average total aid package	$19,278

EMPLOYMENT INFORMATION

Career Rating	72
Rate of placement (nine months out)	92
Average starting salary	$48,816
State for bar exam	ID, WA, UT, OR, NV
Pass rate for first-time bar	76

Employers Who Frequently Hire Grads

Employers with offices in Idaho, Washington, Oregon, Utah, Nevada.

Prominent Alumni

Justice Linda Copple Trout, Idaho Supreme Court; Frank A. Shrontz, former CEO, Boeing Co.; Dennis E. Wheeler, president, Coeur: The Precious Metals Co.; James A. McClure, former United States Senator.

Grads Employed by Field (%)	
Academic	2
Business/Industry	10
Government	9
Judicial clerkships	24
Private practice	48
Public Interest	7

UNIVERSITY OF ILLINOIS
COLLEGE OF LAW

INSTITUTIONAL INFORMATION

Public/private	Public
Student-faculty ratio	14:1
% faculty part-time	35
% faculty female	28
% faculty minority	11
Total faculty	71

SURVEY SAYS...

Diverse opinions accepted
in classrooms
Great research resources
Great library staff

STUDENTS

Enrollment of law school	626
% male/female	61/39
% out-of-state	35
% full-time	100
% minority	32
% international	1
# of countries represented	12
Average age of entering class	24

ACADEMICS

Academic Experience Rating	**90**
Profs interesting rating	87
Profs accessible rating	90
Hours of study per day	4.5

Academic Specialties

Civil procedure, commercial law, constitutional law, corporation securities law, criminal law, environmental law, government services, human rights law, intellectual property law, international law, labor law, legal history, legal philosophy, property, taxation.

Advanced Degrees Offered

JD 3 years, LLM 1 year.

Combined Degrees Offered

JD/MBA 4 years, JD/PhD 6 years, JD/DVM 6 years, JD/MD 6 years, JD/MUP 4 years, JD/MHRIR 3.5 years, JD/MED 3.5 years, JD/MSChem 3.5 years, JD/MSJourn 3.5 years, JD/MCS 3 years, JD/MSNRES 3.5 years.

Clinical program required	No
Legal writing course requirement	Yes

Academics

"You'll definitely get the bang for your buck" at the University of Illinois College of Law, "a jewel amid the cornfields [that boasts] the best mix of academic excellence, social interaction, and human decency for the best price available." Tuition is especially affordable for in-state students. The "tireless [administration] is also very accessible" and extraordinarily popular among students. "The new dean is extremely supportive of the students and does a wonderful job of building community."

Students at the U of I tell us emphatically that "the faculty is the school's greatest strength." The "tough but not unreasonable" professors are "prolific writers [who are] clearly brilliant and accomplished." Students say the professors "are, for the most part fantastic, both in and out of the classroom [and] always able to clarify concepts that are confusing. More significant, they are completely available [and] genuinely interested in teaching and working with students." The professors make an effort to be reached in that they "have open-door policies and are available for discussions with students about class, a job, or just life in general." Students also note that the school "employs a nice mix of tenured and adjunct faculty, which makes for a perfect balance of legal theory and real-world experience. The primary complaint that students have with regard to the faculty is "keeping the good professors around. "One student explains, "There's not much reason for them to stay in central Illinois. The school really needs to make an effort to not let the good ones get away."

Graduates enjoy "a great employment rate" thanks to an aggressive Career Services Office. As one transfer student attests, "I'm in a unique position in that I've seen how two different law schools operate. I was blown away by the quality of the Career Services Department at the University of Illinois. The administration goes to great lengths to make sure that not only do all University of Illinois College of Law graduates get jobs, but that they get the jobs they want." "If you do well here, nothing in Chicago will be off limits." However, students complain that the college "needs to broaden its resources [and] expand beyond the Midwestern market." Until that happens, "It is difficult to get much traction" on either coast "when searching for jobs in Champaign."

The facilities at the U of I "are good" in that large chunks "are wired," and the research resources of the library are as abundant as you'll find anywhere. Overall, though, the "rather Spartan [College of Law] could use some serious help." Suffice it to say, the "incredibly ugly and cheap-looking [building] does not give anyone goose bumps for the grand study of the law." One student writes, "There are no windows in any of the rooms." It's like going to school in a casino." Students note, "Sometimes seats are scarce [in the] crowded" classrooms, as well as in the "cramped" library, though now that the school has reduced the size of the incoming class, this should help to alleviate the problem. Also, wear layers because "There also seems to be a bit of a temperature control problem" no matter what the season.

Life

If they do say so themselves, the students at the U of I are "very amiable, noncompetitive, [and] very intellectually minded, yet not stuck on themselves." These are the "brightest [and] most fun" people—"all the cool, smart kids." Students at the U of I are also "a bit neurotic [and] love to hear their own voices." The student population "has a wonderful mix of student ethnicities, religions, sexual orientation, and gender." There is also a laid-back atmosphere on campus. "Everybody really cares about you. They want you to succeed, and it's almost difficult not to."

PAUL D. PLESS, ASSISTANT DEAN FOR ADMISSIONS AND FINANCIAL AID
504 EAST PENNSYLVANIA AVENUE, ROOM 201, MC-594, CHAMPAIGN, IL 61820
TEL: 217-244-6415 FAX: 217-244-1478
E-MAIL: ADMISSIONS@LAW.UIUC.EDU • INTERNET: WWW.LAW.UIUC.EDU

"The school truly is a community because of its manageable size. Lunches with the dean" are common, and there are "endless other ways to connect with the other students and, more important, the faculty." One content student writes, "The cafeteria has good food and, best of all, they carry Starbucks coffee." Students also say, "Although U of I is located in the corn fields of Illinois, it is impossible to feel isolated" because the administration "is constantly bringing in lecturers, symposiums, and guest speakers." In addition, the College of Law sponsors "a weekly happy hour, [at which] professors and administrators act as the celebrity bartenders."

Life outside the classroom has many positive aspects. Students are very "sports-oriented" and say "It is great to be on a Big Ten campus and be able to devote yourself to the study of law full-time," and surprising though it seems, "There is actually a lot to do in Urbana-Champaign." There are "great bars, coffee houses, [and] centers for the arts." There is also "a progressive music scene." Some students gripe that "social life can seem dominated by a frat/sorority type atmosphere," even at the law school level. "The town is basically designed for college students, so it gets a little dullsville at times." Many students would "prefer to be in a larger city," with Chicago being the example of choice. "Socially, we do the best we can with the town we're in," asserts one student. "That means we drink a lot [and] go en masse to football and basketball games."

Getting In

The average LSAT score for admitted students is 166. The median GPA is 3.5. Those numbers are serious but not forbidding. Note also that, while it's substantially cheaper for Illinois residents to attend the college, residency in the Land of Lincoln will not get you one iota of special treatment from the admissions office.

Legal methods course requirement	No
Legal research course requirement	Yes
Moot court requirement	No
Public interest law requirement	No

ADMISSIONS

Selectivity Rating	93
# applications received	3,221
# applicants accepted	742
# acceptees attending	186
Average LSAT	166
LSAT Range	160–167
Average undergrad GPA	3.5
Application fee	$50
Regular application	3/15
Regular notification	Rolling
Rolling notification	Yes
Early application program	Yes
Early application deadline	10/31
Early application notification	12/15
Transfer students accepted	Yes
Evening division offered	No
Part-time accepted	No
LSDAS accepted	Yes

Applicants Also Look At
Illinois Institute of Technology, Indiana University—Bloomington, Northwestern University, University of Iowa, University of Michigan, University of Wisconsin, Washington University.

International Students

TOEFL required of international students	Yes
Minimum paper TOEFL	600
Minimum computer TOEFL	250

FINANCIAL FACTS

Annual tuition (resident)	$18,102
Annual tuition (nonresident)	$29,100
Books and supplies	$3,020
Room & board	$8,532
Financial aid application deadline	3/15
% first-year students receiving some sort of aid	99
% receiving some sort of aid	99
% of aid that is merit based	90
% receiving scholarships	58
Average grant	$8,000
Average loan	$21,556
Average total aid package	$35,000
Average debt	$62,223

EMPLOYMENT INFORMATION

Career Rating	87
Rate of placement (nine months out)	99
Average starting salary	$75,072
State for bar exam	IL, CA, DC, NY, MO
Pass rate for first-time bar	93

Employers Who Frequently Hire Grads
Baker and McKenzie; Brinks, Hofer, Gilson, and Lione; Bell, Boyd, and Lloyd; Foley and Lardner; Sidley, Austin, Brown, and Wood; McGuire and Woods, McAndrews, Held, and Malloy; Deloitte Touche Tohmatsu; Gardner, Carton, and Douglas; Husch and Eppenberger; Jenner and Block; Jones Day; Kirkland and Ellis; KMZ Rosenman; Latham and Watkins; Littler and Mendelson.

Grads Employed by Field (%)	
Academic	3
Business/Industry	12
Government	9
Judicial clerkships	13
Military	2
Private practice	58
Public Interest	3

The University of Iowa
College of Law

Academics

Students at the affordable University of Iowa College of Law are unanimous on one point: Iowa is "the most underrated school in the country." "If you want to learn from the best without giving an arm and a leg for tuition," they say, "come to this school." The "sympathetic" faculty at Iowa is "very concerned with providing the best academic experience." "Professors are demanding in a way that I know will make me a better lawyer," relates 2L. "They are brilliant yet not egomaniacs." "Some scare the crap out of you, and some create a warm classroom environment." Outside of class, "The professors are, for the most part, interesting and cool people," and interaction between students and professors is exceedingly common. Sure, they are "awkward socially," but "Even the most distinguished professors welcome you into their offices, and it's not uncommon to go out to dinner with your professor and a few classmates."

Classes here "tend toward the theoretical." "Iowa presents kind of a contradiction," proffers a 2L. "It is a theory-driven program that produces mostly practicing attorneys." Iowa's 10 practice clinics are "very strong," "and there are plenty of slots available" (though you do have to lottery into them). "The Iowa City/Cedar Rapids area has opportunities to practice while in law school, but those opportunities are somewhat limited." The legal writing program garners mixed reviews. "We are learning to write legal briefs and memos from the best," contends a satisfied 1L. Others feel "cheated." "We could use a lot more hands-on training with writing and research," says one student. Pretty much everyone who mentions the moot court program is unhappy with it. "The faculty can't be bothered to provide meaningful coaching or instruction," laments one student.

The Career Services staff here "is a group of all-stars" that provides "all of the assistance you need." "The top 25 to 30 percent of students don't seem to have any trouble finding work in cities across the country, including New York, San Francisco, Los Angeles, and Boston." By and large, though, students end up practicing in one of "several large markets" throughout the Midwest. Some students complain that "Iowa could do better in attracting and encouraging employers outside of the Midwest." "If you want to work in the Midwest, this school is considered good, and employers are eager to interview you," advises a 2L. "If you want to work anywhere else, go to law school in that region."

The "really space-constrained" law school building is "functional, though it looks pretty awful." "It was built in the early 80s, and I think at that time people thought it was cool and futuristic," adds a 2L, "but now it just looks like something out of Star Trek IV." "Classrooms are pretty typical," though students "appreciate the plentiful outlets and wireless Internet." "There is no shortage of PCs available in the computer labs" and "The school also has very friendly tech gurus." The "extensive" law library is "a little bubble of greatness." It's "open late" and "always staffed by friendly librarians who know more about the law than anyone ever should."

Life

Students are "mostly White and from Iowa or Illinois," but there is also "a surprisingly large number of kids from the coasts." "I was actually surprised by how many non-Midwestern students are currently at the school," admits a 1L. Overall, it's "a good mix of people from all walks of life." There are "some very conservative points of view" but "young crazy liberals" predominate. There are "a lot of do-gooders who are very socially conscious and commit a tremendous amount of time to community and national issues."

JAN BARNES, ADMISSIONS COORDINATOR
320 MELROSE, IOWA CITY, IA 52242
TEL: 319-335-9095 FAX: 319-335-9646
E-MAIL: LAW-ADMISSIONS@UIOWA.EDU • INTERNET: WWW.LAW.UIOWA.EDU

"U of I law students and most of the professors have a definite liberal slant," says a 2L. "If you're conservative and not articulate and able to defend your opinions, you'll never survive classroom discussion."

"Students at Iowa are competitive, certainly." "I was surprised by how many gunners there actually are," relates a 3L. It's "friendly" gunning, though. Iowa students are "a group of people who have their priorities in order, who are willing to lend a hand, and who are remarkably grounded in reality." "There's an earnestness and commitment to integrity and excellence that Iowa students, faculty, and staff all share," enthuses a 3L. "It makes Iowa a unique place, and it makes me hopeful for the legal profession as a whole. As a jaded California native and East Coast private college graduate, I never cease to be surprised by the quality and professionalism I've found here in the heartland."

Socially, though "People tend to buckle down when it is demanded," "You can be sure to find friends out at a bar" on virtually any given weekend night. "Everyone is very good friends with each other," and Iowa City is "a fun town." Coffee shops, libraries, bookstores, and great restaurants abound. There are "weekly Law Nights held at a local drinking establishment." "There's no such thing as a grad student bar in Iowa City," and there is "a pretty big divide between people who took time off and people who came straight from undergrad."

Getting In

Admitted students at the 25th percentile have LSAT scores of 158 and GPAs in the range of 3.3. Admitted students at the 75th percentile have LSAT scores of 163 and GPAs of around 3.8.

Legal research course requirement	Yes
Moot court requirement	Yes
Public interest law requirement	No

ADMISSIONS

Selectivity Rating	**86**
# applications received	1,809
# applicants accepted	567
# acceptees attending	193
Average LSAT	160
LSAT Range	157–163
Average undergrad GPA	3.59
Application fee	$60
Regular application	3/1
Regular notification	Rolling
Rolling notification	Yes
Early application program	No
Transfer students accepted	Yes
Evening division offered	No
Part-time accepted	No
LSDAS accepted	Yes

Applicants Also Look At
Drake University, The George Washington University, University of Illinois, University of Minnesota, University of Notre Dame, University of Wisconsin, Washington University.

International Students

TOEFL required of international students	Yes
Minimum paper TOEFL	620
Minimum computer TOEFL	260

FINANCIAL FACTS

Annual tuition (resident)	$13,374
Annual tuition (nonresident)	$28,818
Books and supplies	$2,300
Room and board (off-campus)	$9,180
Financial aid application deadline	1/1
% first-year students receiving some sort of aid	94
% receiving some sort of aid	94
% of aid that is merit based	7
% receiving scholarships	53
Average grant	$13,374
Average loan	$23,234
Average total aid package	$30,210
Average debt	$63,798

EMPLOYMENT INFORMATION

		Grads Employed by Field (%)	
Career Rating	**79**		
Rate of placement (nine months out)	99	Academic	2
Average starting salary	$69,068	Business/Industry	13
State for bar exam	IA, IL, MN, MO, AZ	Government	9
Pass rate for first-time bar	93	Judicial clerkships	9
Employers Who Frequently Hire Grads		Military	1
Business/industry, national law firms, government agencies, state and federal judges.		Other	3
		Private practice	57
Prominent Alumni		Public Interest	6
Justice Rita Garman, Illinois Supreme Court; Victor Alvarez, partner, White and Case; John J. Bouma, chairman, Snell and Wilmer; Margaret Tobey, vice president of regional affairs, NBC Universal, Inc.			

UNIVERSITY OF KANSAS
SCHOOL OF LAW

INSTITUTIONAL INFORMATION

Public/private	Public
Student-faculty ratio	13:1
% faculty part-time	31
% faculty female	33
% faculty minority	10
Total faculty	60

SURVEY SAYS...

Diverse opinions accepted
in classrooms
Great research resources
Great library staff
Abundant externship/internship/
clerkship opportunities

STUDENTS

Enrollment of law school	500
% male/female	57/43
% out-of-state	25
% full-time	100
% minority	18
% international	2
# of countries represented	8
Average age of entering class	24

ACADEMICS

Academic Experience Rating	**80**
Profs interesting rating	79
Profs accessible rating	92
Hours of study per day	3.34

Academic Specialties

Commercial law, constitutional law, corporation securities law, criminal law, elder law certificate and LLM, environmental law, intellectual property law, international law, media law and policy, Native American law certificate, property, taxation.

Advanced Degrees Offered

An accelerated degree option so that students can complete the JD in 26 months, or in the traditional 3 years.

Combined Degrees Offered

JD/MBA 4 years, JD/MA 4 years, JD/MPA 4 years, JD/MA 4 years, JD/Master of Social Welfare 4 years, JD/Master of Health Policy and Management 4 years, JD/Master of Indigenous Nations Studies 4 years.

Academics

The "extremely affordable" University of Kansas School of Law "produces good attorneys and loyal alumni." "If you like the Midwest, you can't get better than KU," declares a 1L. "If you don't like the Midwest but ended up here anyway, you really can't get any better than KU." There are "a lot of different kinds of clinical opportunities available" for students looking to gain practical experience. Certificate programs at KU include elder law, environmental law, tax law, and tribal law. There is also a program in international trade and finance. Another nifty feature here is a Summer Start program which allows first-year students to enroll in 1L courses during the summer before the traditional first semester begins. It was "a big help in getting plugged in to the social aspect of law school," reports a student. Career Services "does an excellent job of bringing potential employers from all over the country for on-campus interviews." However, students do note that the legal research and writing program could use some "improvement."

KU's "sharp" and "funny" professors are "highly qualified, both academically and professionally." "The faculty seems genuinely interested in seeing the students happy and successful at the end of the day," explains a student. "We have a good balance between the more 'scholarly' professors—the ones who do lots of research and writing and are known in their field for these activities but maybe only practiced a few years—and professors who have lots of real-world experience," says a 2L. The Socratic Method, though "scary at first," "really helps students to learn." Outside of class, KU professors are notoriously "approachable" and "friendly." "I feel comfortable walking into any professor's office, whether I'm currently taking a class from them or not," claims a 3L.

Many students tell us that KU's "very student-oriented" administration maintains "an open-door policy" and is "available to help students in a variety of ways." "You can tell the administration is truly concerned about student satisfaction and preparation," gushes a 1L. Other students see room for improvement, citing the "outdated" law building.

KU Law is located on "one of the prettiest campuses in the country." Though "There have recently been renovations" to the law building, students complain that the facilities are "far too small" and could use "an interior designer." That said, the "state-of-the-art classrooms" are "laptop friendly," and Internet access is "anywhere and everywhere." However, the library "needs more printers and computers." "The long and ridiculous lines at the restrooms are a serious consideration" as well. On the bright side, common areas are "aesthetically pleasing" and offer "a comfortable place to spend the time between classes."

Life

KU is "generally a young school, so if you are coming just out of undergrad you will be pretty happy," says one student. The "dynamic student body" also includes students "who have worked for a few years" and "those who have lived and worked throughout their lives and are now returning in their 40s and 50s." Students here come primarily from Kansas and its neighboring states and exhibit plenty of "Midwestern charm." Though students would like to see KU "encouraging diversity," members of ethnic minorities feel quite at home. "Everyone knows me and treats me with respect," says one minority student. Politics are "rarely discussed in classes," though that isn't to say that people don't "have opinions and vote." Ultimately, "There are just as many conservative students as there are liberal." "I wouldn't say that students are obnoxious in their liberality, it is just part of the package at a university like KU," explains a 2L.

JACQLENE NANCE, DIRECTOR OF ADMISSIONS
1535 WEST FIFTEENTH STREET, LAWRENCE, KS 66045-7577
TEL: 785-864-4378 FAX: 785-864-5054
E-MAIL: ADMITLAW@KU.EDU • INTERNET: WWW.LAW.KU.EDU

Students report that "there is some competition," but this is mostly a "cooperative and friendly" group. By and large, KU Law has a "very collegial" and "laid-back" atmosphere. "Students tend to get along pretty well" and, "as a whole, do not tolerate rudeness." "There are some cliques," says one student, but, by and large, "Camaraderie and good will" are the rule. "We regularly trade outlines, discuss cases, and help each other out," says a happy 1L.

"The social life is pretty great at KU," and "Most students find a good balance between school and personal life." Student-organized activities are popular. "If you attend student organization meetings, you can enjoy several free pizza lunches each week and learn more about different areas of law," explains a student. "The student body has numerous pub crawls and other events" as well. The surrounding college town of Lawrence provides for off-campus fun, and when students want to escape to the plains, Kansas City is only a short drive away.

Getting In

Admitted students at the 25th percentile have LSAT scores of roughly 154 and GPAs of roughly 3.3. Admitted students at the 75th percentile have LSAT scores of about 160 and GPAs of just under 3.8. If you are coming to KU from another state, note that it is very tough to become recognized as a resident of Kansas for tuition purposes if you aren't one already.

Clinical program required	No
Legal writing course requirement	Yes
Legal methods course requirement	Yes
Legal research course requirement	Yes
Moot court requirement	No
Public interest law requirement	No

ADMISSIONS

Selectivity Rating	**81**
# applications received	1,121
# applicants accepted	347
# acceptees attending	157
Average LSAT	158
LSAT Range	154–160
Average undergrad GPA	3.57
Application fee	$50
Regular application	3/15
Regular notification	Rolling
Rolling notification	Yes
Early application program	No
Transfer students accepted	Yes
Evening division offered	No
Part-time accepted	No
LSDAS accepted	Yes

Applicants Also Look At
Empire College, U. of Denver, U. of Missouri—Kansas City, U. of Missouri—Columbia, U. of Nebraska—Lincoln, U. of Oklahoma, Washburn U.

International Students

TOEFL required of international students	Yes
Minimum paper TOEFL	600
Minimum computer TOEFL	250

FINANCIAL FACTS

Annual tuition (resident)	$10,216
Annual tuition (nonresident)	$19,738
Books and supplies	$700
Room and board	$8,270
Financial aid application deadline	3/15
% first-year students receiving some sort of aid	80
% receiving some sort of aid	80
% of aid that is merit based	85
% receiving scholarships	71
Average grant	$3,304
Average loan	$18,415
Average total aid package	$18,500
Average debt	$44,917

EMPLOYMENT INFORMATION

		Grads Employed by Field (%)	
Career Rating	**77**	**Grads Employed by Field (%)**	
Rate of placement (nine months out)	96	Academic	3
Average starting salary	$55,785	Business/Industry	12
State for bar exam	KS, MO, CA, CO, TX	Government	20
Pass rate for first-time bar	86	Judicial clerkships	9
Employers Who Frequently Hire Grads		Other	1
Baker, Sterchi, Cowden, and Rice;		Private practice	51
Blackwell, Sanders, Peper, Martin; Bryan		Public Interest	4
Cave; Hinkle Elkouri; Husch and			
Eppenberger; Lathrop and Gage; Lewis, Ric,			
and Fingersh; Shook, Hardy, and Bacon.			
Prominent Alumni			
Carla Stovall, Attorney General of Kansas;			
Sam Brownback, United States Senate;			
Honorable Mary Beck Briscoe, U.S Court			
of Appeals, 10th Circuit.			

UNIVERSITY OF KENTUCKY
COLLEGE OF LAW

INSTITUTIONAL INFORMATION

Public/private	Public
Student-faculty ratio	15:1
% faculty female	33
% faculty minority	13
Total faculty	32

SURVEY SAYS...

Heavy use of Socratic method
Diverse opinions accepted
in classrooms
Good social life

STUDENTS

Enrollment of law school	425
% male/female	56/44
% out-of-state	20
% full-time	100
% minority	8
% international	1
# of countries represented	5
Average age of entering class	23

ACADEMICS

Academic Experience Rating	**75**
Profs interesting rating	86
Profs accessible rating	83
Hours of study per day	4.07

Academic Specialties

Advocacy, civil procedure, commercial law, constitutional law, corporation securities law, criminal law, environmental law, government services, human rights law, intellectual property law, international law, labor law, legal philosophy, property, taxation.

Advanced Degrees Offered

JD.

Combined Degrees Offered

JD/MPA 4 years, JD/MBA 4 years, JD/Masters in Diplomacy and International Commerce, 4 years.

Clinical program required	No
Legal writing course requirement	Yes
Legal methods course requirement	No
Legal research course requirement	Yes

Academics

A personable public school with strong regional ties, University of Kentucky offers a challenging JD program in the context of a super-student-friendly environment. Professors here "maintain an appropriate level of publication and research, but focus primarily on teaching the students." In fact, when it comes to their personal pursuits, professors "are always eager to include students in their research outside the classroom." While students admit that there are a few professors "who are not up to typical UK standards," most agree that the school remains "a great place to get a classical legal education." The program is nonetheless difficult, requiring a major time commitment and willingness to put yourself on the line. But that doesn't mean you won't get a little help from the "engaging" faculty who are "concerned with helping you do the best can—if you're willing to do the work to do so."

Though students find their "academic training rigorous," they do note that "practical experience is seriously lacking." Most here would like to feel better prepared "upon graduation . . . to enter a courtroom." Others mention they'd like to see more "clinical opportunities" since there is only "one legal clinic and roughly 20 3Ls may participate" though "There are over 130 3Ls." On the other hand, "Steps are being taken to increase the diversity of classes being offered." In addition to its traditional strength in corporate law, UK is now "a great place to study equine law, and a number of health law courses have proven quite popular this year."

From professors and students to staff and administrators, a friendly and hospitable vibe permeates the UK campus. When it comes to the higher ups, students say "The Dean is one of the most personable deans one could have." On top of that, "The librarians are the best. They help on completely unrelated topics besides legal research." Unfortunately, the pleasantness of UK community is not reflected in its shabby facilities. Students warn us that "the building is outdated and desperately needs work." Fortunately, UK Law is "scheduled to break ground on the new building in the next two years," so future students will be sitting pretty. In the meantime, most UK students are willing to forgo the frills in exchange for a "personalized" and "very thorough" education. Plus, the school manages to uphold high standards in the most important arenas. For example, students rave that their "Research facilities couldn't be better" and classrooms (though in need of sprucing up) are "technologically updated and super wired."

The immitigable goal of any law student is to get a job after graduation, and UK grads say their school amply prepares them for a competitive position. A current 3L enthuses, "Overall, my experience has been excellent. I got a job at a top-five national firm, and felt like I was competitive with my peers during my summer clerking experience." On the other hand, "Many students are frustrated with the level of service provided by the Career Services Office"—in particular, complaints arise from those students who hail from out of state and would like to consider jobs in geographical regions other than Kentucky.

Life

Expect a dose of Southern hospitality in the amiable state of Kentucky, a place filled with "nothing but friendly people." In and out of the classroom, "Students get along well, helping one another out, and no one attempts to sabotage the success of another student." One 1L explains, "There is such a familial feeling here . . . [with] instant camaraderie and friendship." However, as the school tends to draw students of similar

DRUSILLA V. BAKERT, ASSOCIATE DEAN
209 LAW BUILDING, LEXINGTON, KY 40506-0048
TEL: 859-257-6770 FAX: 859-323-1061
E-MAIL: DBAKERT@E-MAIL.UKY.EDU • INTERNET: WWW.UKY.EDU/LAW

backgrounds from the surrounding community, students also admit that "there could stand to be more diversity among the student body." A student agrees, "It may be more diverse than many Kentuckians are accustomed to, but I think if it were compared to national law school demographics, UK would not fare very well."

Though there isn't a lot of extra time for socializing in law school, students are pleased to report that "the student government here is amazing in keeping social activities going so that there are always chances to meet more people." In particular, "The Student Bar Association is very active in providing frequent, enjoyable social events." However, those who do not enjoy a typical night of partying and carousing won't be alone. "There has recently been a movement among nontraditional, nonalcoholic students to create more low-key and family-friendly social activities," says one student. "I think they've succeeded. It seems everyone who wants to be socially active among their colleagues has a way to do that."

Getting In

The University of Kentucky relies heavily on a prospective student's LSAT scores and GPA when making an admissions decision. However, all applications are reviewed in full and other academic factors (such as writing ability, grade trends, and letters of recommendation) are also considered. Last year, the school extended just 385 offers of admission to over 1,200 candidates. The median LSAT score for the entering class was 159 and their median GPA was 3.64.

Moot court requirement	Yes
Public interest law requirement	No

ADMISSIONS

Selectivity Rating	**85**
# applications received	1,255
# applicants accepted	384
# acceptees attending	138
Average LSAT	159
LSAT Range	155–162
Average undergrad GPA	3.64
Application fee	$50
Regular application	3/1
Regular notification	Rolling
Rolling notification	Yes
Early application program	No
Transfer students accepted	Yes
Evening division offered	No
Part-time accepted	No
LSDAS accepted	Yes

Applicants Also Look At

Indiana University—Bloomington, Northern Kentucky University, University of Cincinnati, University of Georgia, University of Louisville, University of Tennessee, Vanderbilt University.

International Students

TOEFL required of international students	Yes
Minimum paper TOEFL	650
Minimum computer TOEFL	280

FINANCIAL FACTS

Annual tuition (resident)	$12,114
Annual tuition (nonresident)	$22,544
Books and supplies	$900
Room and board	$10,300
Financial aid application deadline	4/1
% first-year students receiving some sort of aid	85
% receiving some sort of aid	75
% receiving scholarships	60
Average grant	$5,000
Average loan	$18,500
Average total aid package	$23,500
Average debt	$48,460

EMPLOYMENT INFORMATION

		Grads Employed by Field (%)	
Career Rating	**75**	**Grads Employed by Field (%)**	
Rate of placement (nine months out)	96	Academic	2
Average starting salary	$61,500	Business/Industry	8
State for bar exam	KY	Government	6
Pass rate for first-time bar	89	Judicial clerkships	19
Employers Who Frequently Hire Grads		Private practice	59
All KY legal employers; major firms in Cincinnati, Nashville, West Virginia, DC, NYC and Atlanta.		Public Interest	6
Prominent Alumni			
Mitch McConnell, U.S. Senator; Hal Rodgers, U.S. Representative; Ben Chandler, U.S. Representative; Steve Bright, National Public Interest Attorney; Honorable Jennifer Coffman, federal judge.			

UNIVERSITY OF LA VERNE*
COLLEGE OF LAW

INSTITUTIONAL INFORMATION

Public/private	Private
Student-faculty ratio	12:1
% faculty part-time	14/32
% faculty female	9/32
% faculty minority	5/32
Total faculty	32

SURVEY SAYS...
Heavy use of Socratic method
Diverse opinions accepted
in classrooms
Great research resources
Great library staff

STUDENTS

Enrollment of law school	261
% male/female	148/113
% out-of-state	17
% full-time	148/261
% minority	85/261
# of countries represented	5
Average age of entering class	27

ACADEMICS

Academic Experience Rating	**68**
Profs interesting rating	70
Profs accessible rating	81
Hours of study per day	4.99

Academic Specialties
Civil procedure, commercial law, constitutional law, corporation securities law, criminal law, environmental law, government services, human rights law, intellectual property law, international law, labor law, legal philosophy, property, taxation. See catalogue.

Advanced Degrees Offered
JD 3 to 4 years.

Combined Degrees Offered
JD/MBA 4 years, JD/MPA 4 years.

Clinical program required	No
Legal writing course requirement	Yes
Legal methods course requirement	Yes

Academics

It's a satisfying time to be a student at University of La Verne College of Law. Having recently received provisional accreditation from the ABA, "there is a sense of excitement and a feeling that the school is on the rise." Offering a grounded and practical legal education, "La Verne seems to be a 'meat and potatoes' school interested in preparing future lawyers" rather than dallying over theory and concepts. In the classroom, professors draw heavily on real world examples, and "While the theoretical side of law is covered to some extent, the emphasis seems to be on the practical application of law." A student elaborates, "Professors usually incorporate their personal legal experiences into the lecture; this could range from having a federal judge give his legal perspective on civil rights to a cutting-edge professor speaking about gaming law and how the ever-changing laws have affected the legal games he has created." As the school grows its reputation, it has likewise expanded the diversity of coursework and extracurricular offerings. For example, "ULV was the first ABA school in the country to offer a course devoted to the computer game industry and its applicable laws. Other interesting/specialized electives include: terrorism and the law, white-collar crime, entertainment law, immigration law and patent law." In addition, the school operates "a great externship program with ties to many of the local governmental and nonprofit offices/organizations."

Getting a JD from ULV is no walk in the park. The school's uniformly small class sizes "force you to prepare for each class because you will be called on," and the "harsh grading curve" has students struggling to keep up with academic standards. Fortunately, "The school does a great job at supporting the 1Ls and helping prepare them for the rigors of the first-year law school exams." For example, "The school holds ungraded practice exam sessions in formal conditions," as well as the opportunity to enroll in "great optional workshops on briefing, outlining, and exam preparation." On top of that, stress is soothed by the school's supportive academic atmosphere. One student shares, "I love that when I have a question regarding material discussed in class I can go straight to my professor rather than having to go through a TA." Another student adds, "The school is very small, so you have an opportunity to get one-on-one instruction and help in almost every class."

Once they've got their JD in hand, prospects are good for La Verne grads. Thanks to strong bar preparation courses, "Students who earn GPAs higher than 2.6 have a 97 percent chance of passing on the first attempt!" On top of that, La Verne lawyers have a corner on a significant job market. One student explains, "Since ULV is the only law school in the Inland Empire region of California, which is growing rapidly, there are ample opportunities for not only great externships, but employment." Even so, students fret over the school's tough grading policies, saying it puts them at a professional disadvantage. A student elaborates, "Grading system is not on par with schools in the local area, which makes it harder for graduates from La Verne to match up without having to explain why GPAs are traditionally lower."

* Provisionally approved by the ABA.

ALEXIS THOMPSON, ASSISTANT DEAN OF ADMISSIONS
320 EAST D STREET, ONTARIO, CA 91764
TEL: (909) 460-2001 FAX: (909) 460-2082
E-MAIL: LAWADM@ULV.EDU • INTERNET: LAW.ULV.EDU

Life

La Verne is law school on a first-name basis. On this personable campus, "Class sizes are small, so we have the opportunity to get to know each other," and the program structure fosters personal relationships among the students. A student elaborates, "Since the one 1Ls are split into two groups, it is as if the 30 or so students grouped together learn how to read each other and understand how others think and relate to the law." Despite the school's tough grading policies, students insist that competition is minimal, and "A majority of the students are very willing to help one another in comparing class notes or answering questions." However, students also warn us, "Since this is such a small school, it has a junior high atmosphere where everyone knows and gossips about your personal life like it's a sitcom on MTV."

Socially, there is a noticeable rift between day and evening students, who don't have much overlap in their schedules or interests. Evening students also say it's harder for them to participate in campus clubs and activities, since most are held during the day. For full-timers, there are plenty of ways to get involved in campus life through "activities like softball, membership in the SBA, Delta Theta Phi, and Sports and Entertainment Law Society that bring together the three years of students."

About 10 miles away from the main university campus, "The school is located in the city center close to the main library, city hall, [and] restaurants." However, students say Ontario "isn't exactly paradise," and the school itself is situated in a dicey part of town. On the upside, "It's only 45 minutes from LA and 30 minutes from OC [Orange County]."

Getting In

University of La Verne College of Law is committed to admitting students from diverse educational and professional backgrounds. The school admits students with a strong academic background and competitive LSAT scores. The school also considers qualitative factors, such as an applicant's verbal skills, letters of recommendation, community service work, leadership, and maturity.

Legal research course requirement	Yes
Moot court requirement	No
Public interest law requirement	No

ADMISSIONS

Selectivity Rating	**64**
# applications received	641
# applicants accepted	271
# acceptees attending	89
Average LSAT	149
LSAT Range	148–151
Average undergrad GPA	3.08
Application fee	$60
Regular application	Rolling
Regular notification	Rolling
Rolling notification	Yes
Early application program	No
Transfer students accepted	Yes
Evening division offered	Yes
Part-time accepted	Yes
LSDAS accepted	Yes

Applicants Also Look At

Chapman University, Southwestern University School of Law, Western State University College of Law, Whittier College.

International Students

TOEFL required of international students	No
TOEFL recommended of international students	Yes
Minimum paper TOEFL	550
Minimum computer TOEFL	213

FINANCIAL FACTS

Annual tuition	$29,800
Books and supplies	$1,314
Tuition per credit	$1,000
Room and board (off-campus)	$11,484
Financial aid application deadline	3/2
% first-year students receiving some sort of aid	98
% receiving some sort of aid	97
% receiving scholarships	70
Average grant	$13,965
Average loan	$23,000
Average total aid package	$31,400

EMPLOYMENT INFORMATION

		Grads Employed by Field (%)	
Career Rating	**65**	Business/Industry	14
Rate of placement (nine months out)	96	Government	10
Average starting salary	$61,277	Private practice	76
Pass rate for first-time bar	57		

Employers Who Frequently Hire Grads
Private law firms; business/industry; government.

Prominent Alumni
Thomas M. Finn, HSC regional director (s. region), Dublin, Ireland; Honorable Dennis Aichroth, Los Angeles Superior Court; Honorable Jean Pfeiffer Leonard, Riverside Juvenile Court; Eileen M. Teichert, City Attorney for Sacramento.

UNIVERSITY OF MAINE
SCHOOL OF LAW

Academics

1Ls may spend most of their first year at the University of Maine School of Law in a single classroom "incredibly restricted by physical space," but they say that "what Maine lacks in state-of-the-art facilities it more than makes up for in faculty strength and availability." A mere 22 professors make up the Maine law faculty, meaning "It's easy to become close with your peers, faculty, and the administration." A 3L tells us, "I have close working and personal relationships with several faculty members, which is exactly why I chose a small law school. That kind of access has vastly enhanced my academic experience." Students repeatedly give props to professors for "the way they treat us, always ready and willing to answer questions, offer advice, and talk with us about more than just the classes they teach." Instructors generate an environment where "The amount of humor and laughter during each class is amazing, and the mutual respect for everyone's ideas is clearly evident." Socratic tactics are "supported by a combination of articles, book reviews, cases, trial transcripts, and other materials. They work to create a functional use of the law, rather than a memorization of rules and procedural elements."

Some of the school's unique course offerings center on the Ocean and Coastal Law Program and its affiliated Marine Law Institute, the one of only two marine policy think-tank associated with a law school in the Northeast. "Other course offerings focus on intellectual property and commerce—including an intellectual property critic—at the school's Center for Law and Innovation, which provides patent advice to inventors, researchers, and businesses." Some students combine their JD with a master's in public policy and management, community planning and development, business development, or health policy and management. The academic vibe combines a desire to serve people in a practical way with an intellectual commitment to the best of the profession's principles. "Pursuit of knowledge and truth is stressed," reflects a 1L, "a refreshing recentering of values in an educational society where we sometimes lose track of what really is important: justice."

Arguably, the one person with the biggest impact on the University of Maine School of Law is the architect. The building looks like a "postmodern fortress of justice" to some. "Third-world, dismal, silly—take your pick; there's no escaping the backdrop." A 2L assures us that "most people have a good sense of humor about it," like the student who marvels that walking amid the 1970s decor "kind of feels like going back in time." Somewhat anachronistically, wireless coverage does function, though outlets can be hard to come by.

Students take pride in their work beyond grades or career prospects: "Even though our tiny school doesn't have a well-known reputation outside the state, the professors do not hold back on expectations for excellence," comments one student. The legal writing program and clinic experiences are singled out as highlight of academic life. For example, the Cumberland Legal Aid Clinic allows 3Ls to put their learning into practice under faculty supervision in "a uniquely great program" that provides legal services to the poor.

Students make a point of hinting at the offbeat nature of academic life at Maine Law. "Don't come for fancy facilities or super-specialized course offerings. Do come if you want to be a part of a very small, truly interesting student body," is how one student articulates a common sentiment. Students are eager to cultivate this original environment. An ambitious 2L writes, "We need more money for a physically larger school, a sophisticated computer lab, more scholarships, and a larger career counseling staff to

DAVID PALLOZZI, ASSISTANT DEAN FOR ADMISSIONS
246 DEERING AVENUE, PORTLAND, ME 04102
TEL: 207-780-4341 FAX: 207-780-4239
E-MAIL: MAINELAW@USM.MAINE.EDU • INTERNET: MAINELAW.MAINE.EDU/

expand our knowledge and contacts beyond northern New England." Already, students see the school's reputation on the rise and assure prospective applicants: "Attending Maine doesn't mean you have to stay in Maine. You will graduate prepared to enter any legal environment." Currently, students get the sense that "there aren't a whole lot of potential employers with open arms for us." However, students emphasize, "The legal community in the area is so involved in the law school." If you come to this school, start collecting business cards early.

Life

Maine Law runs like one long outdoor leadership and team-building retreat that just happens to be a law school. With just more than 90 students per class, the school is "large enough to have a unique student body, but small enough to get to know almost everyone personally." The overall vibe resembles that of "a small liberal arts college, given the number of students from New England's many liberal arts schools." Most people have taken a nice long academic vacation between undergrad and law school, however. "Your average 1L has seen something of the world and the workplace." People demonstrate "a healthy attitude about competition and genuinely support each other in job searches and tryouts for moot court." Many students agree that "you will not find snobbishness or cut-throat, uncomfortable competition in this extremely friendly and collaborative" setting. They have achieved a "friendly rivalry of intelligent peers that inspires rather than intimidates." The semester wraps up with a party with entertainment provided by the 1Ls. (An upperclassman swears, "It's not hazing!") Barhopping ranks high among popular diversions, and no Maine student would allow anything to interfere with their "outdoor-loving lifestyle." The school integrates well with the community in Portland, a city that "gives us everything we need to succeed." On a small supportive campus in a small supportive city, "You realize how special the intimacy and closeness of a school can be."

Getting In

Though the deadline doesn't come until March 1, decisions are already being made in January: Get in early. Students applying from Massachusetts, New Hampshire, Rhode Island, Vermont, or Canada pay slightly less tuition than normal out-of-state rates.

ADMISSIONS

Selectivity Rating	**75**
# applications received	760
# applicants accepted	325
# acceptees attending	101
Average LSAT	155
LSAT Range	153–159
Average undergrad GPA	3.34
Application fee	$50
Regular application	3/1
Regular notification	Rolling
Rolling notification	Yes
Early application program	Yes
Early application deadline	11/15
Early application notification	12/31
Transfer students accepted	Yes
Evening division offered	No
Part-time accepted	No
LSDAS accepted	Yes

International Students

TOEFL required of international students	Yes

FINANCIAL FACTS

Annual tuition (resident)	$16,590
Annual tuition (nonresident)	$26,280
Books and supplies	$944
Fees per credit (resident)	$625
Fees per credit (nonresident)	$625
Tuition per credit (resident)	$553
Tuition per credit (nonresident)	$876
Room and board	$10,727
Financial aid application deadline	2/15
% receiving some sort of aid	87
% of aid that is merit based	20
% receiving scholarships	49
Average grant	$3,300
Average loan	$19,636
Average debt	$61,170

EMPLOYMENT INFORMATION

		Grads Employed by Field (%)	
Career Rating	**73**	**Grads Employed by Field (%)**	
Rate of placement (nine months out)	91	Academic	0
Average starting salary	$49,062	Business/Industry	19
State for bar exam	ME	Government	10
Pass rate for first-time bar	84	Judicial clerkships	12
Employers Who Frequently Hire Grads		Other	0
Maine/New England law firms and corporations; federal/state government; federal/state courts.		Private practice	48
		Public Interest	11

UNIVERSITY OF MARYLAND
SCHOOL OF LAW

INSTITUTIONAL INFORMATION

Public/private	Public
Student-faculty ratio	11:1
% faculty part-time	54
% faculty female	39
% faculty minority	15
Total faculty	119

SURVEY SAYS...

Great research resources
Great library staff
Beautiful campus

STUDENTS

Enrollment of law school	826
% male/female	40/60
% out-of-state	43
% full-time	82
% minority	31
% international	2
# of countries represented	10
Average age of entering class	24

ACADEMICS

Academic Experience Rating	88
Profs interesting rating	80
Profs accessible rating	79
Hours of study per day	4.39

Academic Specialties

Clinical law, constitutional law, corporation securities law, criminal law, environmental law, health care law, human rights law, intellectual property law, international law, litigation/advocacy, public interest/policy.

Advanced Degrees Offered

JD 3 to 4 years.

Combined Degrees Offered

JD/PhD 7 years, JD/MA 4 years, JD/MBA 4 years, JD/MA 4 years, JD/MA 3.5 to 4 years, JD/MSW 3.5 to 4 years, JD/MA 4 years, JD/MA 4 years, JD/PharmD 7 years, JD/MPH 4 years, JD/MS 4 years, JD/MS 4 years.

Clinical program required	Yes
Legal writing course requirement	Yes
Legal methods course requirement	Yes

Academics

"Considering the price and the quality of education," you can't beat the "fun, interesting, and hard" University of Maryland School of Law. Boasting a notable "commitment to public service," Maryland Law "has one of the best environmental and health law programs in the country" further abetted by a "terrific alumni network." The "mandatory clinical program" offers two-dozen courses and is "excellent," though some "think that the clinical subjects should be expanded to include the interests of a broader array of students." The legal writing program "is a strength, though very demanding," say some students to which it was taught "by full professors and not adjuncts."

Maryland Law's "mix of professors" ranges from "lively and Socratic" to "quiet lecturers." "Eighty percent of the professors are good," says one 2L, "though some don't have a clue how to teach." "Some professors stand out as excellent and some are the worst teachers I have ever had in my academic career." "All but one of four of my professors were extremely intelligent, enthusiastic, and passionate about the material they were teaching," adds a 1L. The "not-too-bad" administration is "always available," though too much "hand-holding" can be a bit of a problem. "They think that a long informational session needs to be had on everything" when an e-mail would "be a better use of everyone's time." Administrators are "extremely dedicated to racial and economic diversity" both in the student body and faculty. Sometimes, "They overstress diversity," suggests a 2L.

"The Career Development Office, which has continued to improve both years I've attended, needs to continue getting better," says a 2L. Maryland Law has a "solid reputation in the Mid-Atlantic region," and many students "have landed jobs at some of the best firms in DC." There is "little competition for 'big law' positions" locally, while students compete nationally in the school's regional interview programs in other cities. "The opportunities for practical experience with law firms, political organizations, and judges in Baltimore and DC are really impressive," adds a 3L. "Even if you don't achieve the traditional law school honors (top 10 percent, Law Review, moot court, etc.) you can get a lot out of your law school experience and establish an impressive resume record that will help you find a job after school."

The "absolutely beautiful" facilities at Maryland Law are "new, with all the amenities you expect of a top-flight law school." An enclosed, private patio area next to the library allows students "to study or eat outside." There are "comfortable chairs all over." Wireless Internet appeared on campus recently, and now Maryland Law is "well equipped technologically." The library needs "longer hours," and the cafeteria "tries to be trendy" with sometimes "overpriced food and often not-too-accessible hours." The school's location isn't ideal according to many students. "It is in the inner city," cautions a 1L, "but I think that is important for the clinical program to work."

Life

Maryland Law's "very capable and motivated" student population "is composed of a diverse group of students with different interests and academic backgrounds." "The small sections in the first year give you a real chance to get to know classmates and at least one professor well." "It helps you to not feel lost in the shuffle." "The competition at the school is invigorating and healthy, and almost everyone gets along well," says a 2L. Maryland Law's day students and evening students often have wildly different law school experiences. The "vibrant evening program" has "no social life but is less competitive." "There is a strong sense among the students that we are in this together," relates one happy evening student. Day students are "moderate-to-cutthroat competitive with a more active social life." Politically, students (and faculty) are "pretty heavily weighted to the left." Some students at Maryland Law "have a chip on their shoulder because they feel they should have gotten into Georgetown or George Washington." "We have a bit of an inferiority complex, but we seem to be getting over it," notes a 3L.

"One thing that can be improved is the neighborhood" surrounding Maryland Law. The law school is located downtown, "which is not quite the safest area." "Going out alone at night around the law school is scary." There are a lot of security guards and "a free door-to-door shuttle service after 5:00 P.M." "A lot of money has been pumped into redeveloping the entire area. Each year, newly converted loft apartments and restaurants open up, and many plans are continually coming to life." UMD is also "next to other graduate schools and in great proximity to" Baltimore's iconic Inner Harbor and many "stylish bars." Oriole Park at Camden Yards is "within easy walking distance." The absence of undergraduates "in the near vicinity" creates "a unique vibe." "Socializing with other students consists of the traditional Thursday- or Friday-night Bar Reviews." "There is a decent amount of social activities, but students will only participate the first half of the semester; after that they are in crazy-study mode." "Housing near campus is cramped and overpriced," but "local neighborhoods, such as Fells Point, Federal Hill, and Canton offer the charm that makes Baltimore so terrific."

Getting In

Admitted students at the 25th percentile have LSAT scores of approximately 157 and GPAs around 3.3. Admitted students at the 75th percentile have LSAT scores of 161 and GPAs in the 3.7 range.

Legal research course requirement	Yes
Moot court requirement	Yes
Public interest law requirement	Yes

ADMISSIONS

Selectivity Rating	94
# applications received	3,790
# applicants accepted	627
# acceptees attending	207
Average LSAT	162
LSAT Range	160–165
Average undergrad GPA	3.61
Application fee	$65
Regular application	3/1
Regular notification	Rolling
Rolling notification	Yes
Early application program	No
Transfer students accepted	Yes
Evening division offered	Yes
Part-time accepted	Yes
LSDAS accepted	Yes

Applicants Also Look At
American U., George Mason U., The George Washington U., Georgetown U., U. of Baltimore.

International Students

TOEFL required of international students	No
TOEFL recommended of international students	Yes
Minimum paper TOEFL	600
Minimum computer TOEFL	250

FINANCIAL FACTS

Annual tuition (resident)	$18,371
Annual tuition (nonresident)	$28,650
Books and supplies	$8,357
Fees per credit (resident)	$496
Fees per credit (nonresident)	$496
Tuition per credit (resident)	$582
Tuition per credit (nonresident)	$1,036
Room and board (on/off-campus)	$11,817/$15,480
Financial aid application deadline	3/1
% first-year students receiving some sort of aid	87
% receiving some sort of aid	87
% of aid that is merit based	25
% receiving scholarships	69
Average grant	$7,068
Average loan	$26,963
Average total aid package	$48,628
Average debt	$59,960

EMPLOYMENT INFORMATION

		Grads Employed by Field (%)	
Career Rating	**79**		
Rate of placement (nine months out)	98	Academic	5
Average starting salary	$61,498	Business/Industry	10
State for bar exam	MD	Government	12
Pass rate for first-time bar	88	Judicial clerkships	26
Employers Who Frequently Hire Grads		Military	2
Skadden, Arps, et al; DLA Piper; Arnold		Other	1
and Porter; Venable; Covington and		Private practice	39
Burling; Dickstein, Shapiro, and Morin,		Public Interest	5
LLP; U. S. Department of Justice.			

Prominent Alumni
Frank Burch, chairman, DLA Piper; Martin O'Malley, Governor of Maryland; Benjamin Cardin, U.S. Senator; Henry H. Hopkins, general counsel, T. Rowe Price; Miriam Fisher, partner, Morgan Lewis; Patricia Gatling, New York Commissioner of Human Rights; Joanne Pollak, general counsel, Hopkins Hospital System; Mark Treanor, general counsel, Wachovia Corp.

UNIVERSITY OF MEMPHIS
CECIL C. HUMPHREYS SCHOOL OF LAW

Academics

An affordable, practical-minded, and utterly personable law school program, the University of Memphis is the ideal training ground for future attorneys in the mid-South. Through course work and extracurricular activities, this friendly public school distinguishes itself through its "emphasis on training you to be a lawyer and not just a student of the law." Throughout the curriculum, professors place a "strong emphasis on oral argument abilities," and required course work includes instruction in many of the practical skills you'll need in the real world. For example, "Course work required for the legal methods class is incredibly helpful in learning good writing, oral communication, and other lawyering skills." Students further appreciate the inclusion of Tennessee law into the curriculum—a facet that is particularly useful to those planning to practice in the state.

Offering an intimate academic atmosphere at a friendly price, "U of M Law is one of the best values available." Unlike programs at larger public schools, Memphis students don't have to clamor for attention from their brilliant professors; with an enrollment of about 150 students per class, "The school is small enough that personal attention is readily available, and professors are always willing to talk." With little exception, students say the school's accomplished faculty is its greatest strength. A 1L agrees: "I have never before been taught by so many excellent professors at one time." Outside the classroom, students can augment course work through participation in one of three legal clinics, the General Litigation Clinic, Elder Law Clinic, and the Child and Family Litigation Clinic, through which they can represent elderly and indigent clients in the Memphis area. For those who want practice in the courtroom, the school operates a competitive moot court program. In a very lawyerly fashion, a current student attests: "Our moot court people kick ass."

If there is one thing University of Memphis students unanimously criticize, it's the school's ramshackle facilities. From the shabby library to the hot and under-equipped computer lab, students say the facilities certainly don't reflect the quality of the U of M law experience. At times, the building even has adverse effects on academics. A case in point: "In some of the classrooms, the professors have to use microphones because you cannot hear anything but the air conditioner." The good news for prospective students is that the school recently bought a historic building in downtown Memphis, which will serve as the law school's new home in 2009. Optimistic students are sure that their educational experience will "dramatically improve once we move to the new building." In fact, they reassure us, "Once the school moves downtown into the Customs House, this school is likely to become one of the premier public law schools in the South."

The school's excellent bar-passage rate is among its major selling points. At 95 percent for first-time test-takers, it's "unusually high for a small state school." Another appealing facet of a U of M degree is the school's "very high job-placement rate" and its strong "ties with the Memphis community." Deeply entwined in the local legal market, "For a person looking to practice in Memphis, or anywhere else in Tennessee, the school's reputation is outstanding." Of course, there are always a handful of students who are looking for jobs in other regions; given the school's regional strength, its not surprising that these students complain Career Services isn't "much help outside of the Memphis area."

Life

This urban law school attracts all types of students, the range of which includes "college athletes, war veterans, people in their second careers, mothers re-entering the workforce." While they are all scrambling to score the best grades, there is surprisingly little

Dr. Sue Ann McClellan, Assistant Dean for Law Admissions
207 Humphreys Law School, Memphis, TN 38152-3140
Tel: 901-678-5403 Fax: 901-678-5210
E-mail: lawadmissions@mail.law.memphis.edu • Internet: www.law.memphis.edu

friction between students at U of M. One student explains, "The environment, despite the building, is very positive and upbeat. You don't get the feeling that the guy or girl next to you is looking to stab you in the back." Because the school comprises "a much smaller community than most of us are used to after undergraduate at large schools" and the curriculum requires an incredible time commitment, Memphis students get to know each other well. A student elaborates: "We spend an unbelievable amount of time around each other, so it is to be expected that people will date, people will bicker, people will complain, and people will make up."

University of Memphis is a commuter school, so most "Students attend class and then go their separate ways." However, for those who'd like to participate in campus culture, there are plenty of opportunities and a "fairly small group who consistently attend the law school's social functions." A current student shares, "All in all, we have a lot of fun when we aren't studying, and we are able to find a common bond with pretty much everyone with which we go to school."

Getting In

Of more than 1,000 students who applied to the University of Memphis JD and joint-degree programs, only 26 percent were successful. The entering class of 2009 had a median undergraduate GPA of 3.36 and median LSAT scores of 155. Students range in age from 21 to 43, but the median age is 25.

ADMISSIONS

Selectivity Rating	81
# applications received	1,113
# applicants accepted	290
# acceptees attending	144
Average LSAT	155
LSAT Range	153–158
Average undergrad GPA	3.36
Application fee	$25
Regular application	3/1
Regular notification	4/15
Rolling notification	Yes
Early application program	No
Transfer students accepted	Yes
Evening division offered	No
Part-time accepted	Yes
LSDAS accepted	Yes

Applicants Also Look At

Florida Coastal School of Law, Georgia State University, Mississippi College, Samford University, University of Arkansas at Little Rock, University of Mississippi, University of Tennessee.

International Students

TOEFL required	
of international students	Yes
Minimum paper TOEFL	600
Minimum computer TOEFL	283

FINANCIAL FACTS

Annual tuition (resident)	$10,028
Annual tuition (nonresident)	$28,466
Books and supplies	$1,500
Fees per credit (resident)	$6
Fees per credit (nonresident)	$6
Tuition per credit (resident)	$487
Tuition per credit (nonresident)	$1,331
Room and board	$7,509
Financial aid application deadline	4/1
% first-year students receiving some sort of aid	100
% receiving some sort of aid	80
% of aid that is merit based	9
% receiving scholarships	34
Average grant	$4,500
Average loan	$18,509
Average total aid package	$19,091
Average debt	$54,029

EMPLOYMENT INFORMATION

Career Rating	**77**	
Rate of placement (nine months out)	97	
Average starting salary	$55,676	
State for bar exam	TN, GA, FL, MS, AR	
Pass rate for first-time bar	92.4	

Employers Who Frequently Hire Grads

Major area and regional law firms; Tennessee Attorney General; public defenders office; TN Supreme Court and Court of Appeals; major area corporate legal departments; city and county government.

Prominent Alumni

John Wilder, Speaker of the Tennessee House; Honorable Bernice Donald, U.S. District Court.

Grads Employed by Field (%)

Academic	1
Business/Industry	3
Government	18
Judicial clerkships	8
Military	1
Other	1
Private practice	59
Public Interest	1

UNIVERSITY OF MIAMI
SCHOOL OF LAW

INSTITUTIONAL INFORMATION

Public/private	Private
Student-faculty ratio	18:1
% faculty part-time	41
% faculty female	35
% faculty minority	21
Total faculty	114

SURVEY SAYS...

Great library staff
Students love Coral Gables, FL
Good social life

STUDENTS

Enrollment of law school	1,208
% male/female	55/45
% out-of-state	65
% full-time	96
% minority	23
% international	4
# of countries represented	24
Average age of entering class	24

ACADEMICS

Academic Experience Rating	**67**
Profs interesting rating	65
Profs accessible rating	62
Hours of study per day	3.9

Academic Specialties

Civil procedure, commercial law, constitutional law, corporation securities law, criminal law, environmental law, government services, human rights law, intellectual property law, international law, labor law, property, taxation.

Advanced Degrees Offered

LLM (comparative law—for graduates of foreign law schools), estate planning, inter-American law, international law, ocean and coastal law, real property development (taxation) 1 year.

Combined Degrees Offered

JD/MBA 3.5 years, JD/MPH 3.5 years, JD/MS (marine affairs) 3.5 years, JD/LLM (taxation) 3.5 years.

Clinical program required	No

Academics

Getting a degree at the University of Miami may sound like fun in the sun, but students at this large program say you'd better come prepared for a serious legal education. With 400-plus students per entering class, the school's ample size makes a big impact on the academic experience. Many see the size as an advantage, explaining: "There are many different people with diverse viewpoints contributing, rather than a small class where you hear the same people again and again." But don't expect to hide among the masses: "The professors have seating charts with each student's photo and, thus, still love the Socratic Method." While class is engaging, Miami professors "do not have the typical Draconian preparation requirements one comes to expect from a law school"; nonetheless, course work is substancial. A 1L tells us, "I went to an Ivy League school for my undergraduate degree, and I find the work load to be significantly more intense than undergrad and the people to be more competitive." On top of that, the grading system is based on a curve, inspiring a fairly high level of competitiveness within the classes.

Attracting a stellar fleet of faculty, "Professors are very impressive, and several have made names for themselves in obscure, yet interesting, legal niches. Many are prolific writers, and they really seem to enjoy learning and teaching about the law." However, because "The faculty is generally chosen based on their superior credentials and research ability," there is a mix of teaching styles, some better than others. One student laments, "Unfortunately, a national, (or in many cases, international) reputation for excellence in a field does not always translate to excellence in teaching." Within the school's broad academic offerings, the "Latin American focus of the school is unique," and "Students hoping to specialize in litigation, tax, or international law find truly excellent opportunities to develop their skills in school and to network in an effort to secure jobs upon graduation." However, students uniformly complain about the required course called Elements, which they describe as "a course experiment from the 70s that didn't catch on, and this school won't let it die."

Miami places an "emphasis on academic study of law, rather than simply focusing on how to be a lawyer." However, if you are itching to get your feet wet, the school offers a small selection of clinical and pro bono activities, including "the opportunity for lawyers interested in public work to get great hands-on experience by taking part in the school's Center for Ethics and Public Service." Ambitious students may take advantage of "the opportunity for judicial internships at the federal level" through a program coordinated by the Career Center. While some feel Career Services could be more proactive in national recruiting, Miami is home to "tons of law firms, courthouses, and public interest organizations" in the region. Plus, "The diverse population of Miami and range of opportunities available make this the perfect location to learn about the law and to begin a career."

Life

Miami may be known for its crashing waves, nightclubs, and bikinis, but sun-lovers take heed: "Students work so hard here, you sometimes completely forget the beach is only a few miles away." On the other hand, the sunny atmosphere is nothing to complain about. "You walk out of the library, after spending eight hours readings casebooks, and there's sunshine and palm trees," gloats a 2L. The school's pleasant campus is a great place to spend time, and many students take a break at The Bricks, "a large courtyard and fountain with lots of tables, in the middle of the law school, where any time of day people will be sitting out there having lunch, socializing, studying, or just passing through." After class, many stay on campus to participate in one of the many student clubs and associations; plus, "Law Students play a variety of intramural sports against the medical students at UM, from darts and billiards, to track, soccer, flag football, and soccer." Lest we forget: "Beer is a very important element of law school. Thus, the Student Bar Association sponsors a bimonthly "Beer at the Rat" event where they provide free beer to all law students."

The school's location has its benefits and drawbacks, as "Coral Gables is beautiful, but the nearest activities still require a drive down the constantly packed US-1." In addition, "Because students live in all of the various sub-areas in Miami, they are spread apart, and the sense of community here isn't extremely strong." On the other hand, the school is so large that you'll certainly find a few like minds amongst the student body. For those who like the nightlife, Miami is as good as it gets. A current student enthuses, "There are tons of places to go out partying, and we take advantage of them all!" However, on the whole, "Certain students enjoy the social life of Miami more than they probably should, but most students strike an appropriate balance."

Getting In

The University of Miami admits students once annually for entry in the fall semester. Admissions decisions are made on a rolling basis beginning in December. For the 2006 entering class, the 75th percentile LSAT score and GPA were 160 and 3.65, respectively. Multiple LSAT scores are averaged in the admissions process. The Admissions Committee reviews an applicant's academic performance, evaluating courses that demonstrate writing and logic skills.

Legal writing course requirement	Yes
Legal methods course requirement	Yes
Legal research course requirement	Yes
Moot court requirement	No
Public interest law requirement	No

ADMISSIONS

Selectivity Rating	**76**
# applications received	4,923
# applicants accepted	2,340
# acceptees attending	420
Average LSAT	158
LSAT Range	156–160
Average undergrad GPA	3.43
Application fee	$60
Regular application	7/31
Regular notification	Rolling
Rolling notification	Yes
Early application program	No
Transfer students accepted	Yes
Evening division offered	No
Part-time accepted	No
LSDAS accepted	Yes

Applicants Also Look At
American University, Florida State University, The George Washington University, Nova Southeastern University, Stetson University, Tulane University, University of Florida.

International Students

TOEFL required of international students	Yes
Minimum paper TOEFL	600
Minimum computer TOEFL	250

FINANCIAL FACTS

Annual tuition	$32,820
Books and supplies	$1,067
Tuition per credit	$1,420
Room and board (off-campus)	$10,464
Financial aid application deadline	3/1
% first-year students receiving some sort of aid	82
% receiving some sort of aid	82
% of aid that is merit based	17
% receiving scholarships	33
Average grant	$15,232
Average loan	$20,058
Average total aid package	$39,279
Average debt	$89,674

EMPLOYMENT INFORMATION

Career Rating	**80**	**Grads Employed by Field (%)**	
Rate of placement (nine months out)	91	Academic	1
Average starting salary	$81,000	Business/Industry	7
State for bar exam	FL, NY, IL, GA, CA	Government	12
Pass rate for first-time bar	85	Judicial clerkships	4
Employers Who Frequently Hire Grads		Military	1
Holland and Knight; Greenberg Traurig;		Private practice	70
Hunton and Williams; Steel Hector and		Public Interest	5
Davis; White and Case.			

Prominent Alumni
Chief Justice Fred Lewis, Florida Supreme Court; Sue M. Cobb, Florida Secretary of State; Roy Black, prominent criminal defense attorney, legal expert.

UNIVERSITY OF MICHIGAN
LAW SCHOOL

INSTITUTIONAL INFORMATION

Public/private	Public
Student-faculty ratio	14:1
% faculty part-time	34
% faculty female	35
% faculty minority	10
Total faculty	140

SURVEY SAYS...
Great research resources
Beautiful campus

STUDENTS

Enrollment of law school	1,130
% male/female	55/45
% out-of-state	73
% full-time	100
% minority	29
% international	3
# of countries represented	29
Average age of entering class	24

ACADEMICS

Academic Experience Rating	**98**
Profs interesting rating	94
Profs accessible rating	82
Hours of study per day	4.46

Academic Specialties
Asylum and refugee law, civil procedure, commercial law, constitutional law, corporation securities law, criminal law, environmental law, government services, human rights law, intellectual property law, international law, labor law, legal history, legal philosophy, property, taxation.

Advanced Degrees Offered
LLM, LLM (international tax), MCL, SJD.

Combined Degrees Offered
JD/MBA 4 years, JD/PhD 5 year, JD/MPP 4 years, JD/MHSA 4 years, JD/MPH 4 years, JD/MSI 4 years, JD/MSW 4 years, JD/MUP 4 years, JD/MS 4 years, JD/MA 3.5 to 4 years, JD/MA 3.5 to 4 years, JD/MA 3.5 to 4 years, JD/MA 3.5 to 4 years, JD/MA 3.5 to 4 years.

Academics

The University of Michigan Law School "is definitely a special place." "Just entering the Law Quad puts into perspective the good fortune students have in attending this great institution," says a 3L. A faculty features "a good mix of 'institutions' and up-and-comers," making for "an interesting and unique educational experience." The "engaging" and "hilarious" professors here are "academic rock stars" who "challenge you and help you think about the law in novel ways." "Our professors are definitely brain ninjas," declares a 2L. Professors "have open-door policies" and are "truly available to meet with you and help you in any way they can." The administration is "very approachable." "Michigan students adore their school, and the school adores them right back," says one student. "I've e-mailed various deans and had my e-mails returned within minutes." Such first-class treatment comes at a hefty price, though. Students wish that tuition were more "affordable."

The "massive course selection" provides "an interdisciplinary perspective to the law and promotes interdisciplinary learning." "Cutting-edge legal theory" is the norm, and course work tends to focus more on "policy implications of the law," meaning that the campus doesn't function as "a factory of corporate lawyers." Several clinics including the Environmental Law Clinic and the Urban Communities Clinic provide "options that allow you to get real experience in the courtroom." Nevertheless, many students insist that there should be more of an emphasis on "practical skills for lawyering."

"Career Services is incredibly well organized" and "the Michigan reputation" is an "asset" since "Employers fall all over themselves for you." "About 700 employers" come to campus to interview, and they "can't screen by GPA," which many students find allows them to "interview with top firms even if [they] are at the bottom of the class." "My successful job hunts on the West Coast and in the South showed me that a Michigan degree opens doors all over the country," boasts a 3L. "I have friends who will be practicing everywhere from New York to Phoenix." For graduates wishing to pursue careers in public interest, there is "a generous loan repayment program."

Michigan's "Gothic" and "beautiful" Law Quad is "definitely what you imagine when you think about what 'law school' should look like." "The stone buildings are covered in climbing ivy" and the "somewhat dauntingly quiet and eerie" Reading Room ("open until 2:00 A.M.") is "like a cathedral to learning." While "No one . . . wants to lose the feel" of such impressive sights, many lament that "modern amenities sometimes take a back seat" on campus. Some buildings "lack plug space." Wireless access is adequate though "blocked during class" to the chagrin of many students. The most pressing problem at Michigan Law appears to be a severe bathroom shortage. "More toilets! Working toilets!" demands a 3L.

Life

Students state that "Michigan is more diverse than any other law school out there." "A range of geographic, ideological, religious, and ethnic backgrounds" is represented. Michigan is also a "very tolerant" place for gay students. "The Admissions Office does an amazing job of selecting individuals who are talented, diverse, friendly, and normal," says one student. "The student body is a hotbed of intellectual discussion, but then we all play flip-cup on the weekends." "Michigan draws not only incredible smart individuals but also individuals with personality."

SARAH C. ZEARFOSS, ASSISTANT DEAN AND DIRECTOR OF ADMISSIONS
726 OAKLAND AVENUE, ANN ARBOR, MI 48104
TEL: 734-764-0537 FAX: 734-647-3218
E-MAIL: LAW.JD.ADMISSIONS@UMICH.EDU • INTERNET: WWW.LAW.UMICH.EDU

"The atmosphere is highly conducive to learning the law with an absolute minimum of stress." Generally, "Everyone wants everyone to do well." "The theory is, 'We're all smart; we all deserve to be here; if we all help out each other then we can get the most out of law school.'" However, some students disagree with this view. Students are "always sizing others up," they say. "People are secretly competitive."

"Michigan's social scene is one of its greatest strengths." The law school's dorm ("Lawyers Club") is very popular, and many students eat "lunch and dinner" together on campus. ("The food is not too bad either.") "Finals are stressful," of course, but "The rest of the year is very laid-back, and there are plenty of opportunities to engage in social activities." "In some respects," Michigan Law "still has a college feel to it." "Many law students attend the home football games" and "Going out to the local watering holes happens almost every night (even first year)." "If your social life doesn't involve drinking, there aren't many organized activities for you," gripe some students. Others say that "there is a great deal to do in Ann Arbor besides [going] to the bar." "There is a downtown area that is geared more towards adults." There is "a show, symphony, or concert somewhere in Ann Arbor at any point in time." Most here "love" Ann Arbor, though several students long for "a more hip area."

Getting In

Michigan Law is a tough nut to crack. Admitted students at 25th percentile have LSAT scores of 166 and GPAs of about 3.5. Admitted students at 75th percentile have LSAT scores of 170 and GPAs of about 3.8. If you take the LSAT multiple times, Michigan will give the most weight to the highest scores but will consider the average score as well.

Clinical program required	No
Legal writing course requirement	Yes
Legal methods course requirement	Yes
Legal research course requirement	Yes
Moot court requirement	No
Public interest law requirement	No

ADMISSIONS

Selectivity Rating	97
# applications received	5,664
# applicants accepted	1,165
# acceptees attending	369
Average LSAT	168
LSAT Range	166–170
Average undergrad GPA	3.67
Application fee	$60
Regular application	2/15
Regular notification	Rolling
Rolling notification	Yes
Early application program	Yes
Early application deadline	11/15
Early application notification	12/15
Transfer students accepted	Yes
Evening division offered	No
Part-time accepted	No
LSDAS accepted	Yes

Applicants Also Look At

Columbia U., Cornell U., Duke U., Georgetown U., Harvard U., New York U., Pennsylvania State U., Northwestern U., The U. of Chicago, U. of Virginia.

International Students

TOEFL required of international students	No
TOEFL recommended of international students	No

FINANCIAL FACTS

Annual tuition (resident)	$35,312
Annual tuition (nonresident)	$38,312
Books and supplies	$4,800
Room and board	$9,680
% first-year students receiving some sort of aid	91
% receiving some sort of aid	90
% of aid that is merit based	52
% receiving scholarships	50
Average grant	$11,774
Average loan	$35,441
Average total aid package	$40,196
Average debt	$90,700

EMPLOYMENT INFORMATION

Career Rating	99	Grads Employed by Field (%)	
Rate of placement (nine months out)	99	Academic	2
Average starting salary	$135,000	Business/Industry	4
State for bar exam	NY, IL	Government	3
Pass rate for first-time bar	97	Judicial clerkships	12
		Military	1
		Private practice	73
		Public Interest	5

UNIVERSITY OF MISSISSIPPI
SCHOOL OF LAW

INSTITUTIONAL INFORMATION

Public/private	public
Student-faculty ratio	16:1
% faculty part-time	34
% faculty female	28
% faculty minority	9
Total faculty	49

SURVEY SAYS...
Diverse opinions accepted
in classrooms
Good social life

STUDENTS

Enrollment of law school	568
% male/female	55/45
% out-of-state	12
% full-time	100
% minority	11
# of countries represented	3
Average age of entering class	23

ACADEMICS

Academic Experience Rating	**77**
Profs interesting rating	76
Profs accessible rating	85
Hours of study per day	3.5

Academic Specialties
Commercial law, corporation securities law, criminal law, environmental law, international law, remote sensing and space law, taxation.

Combined Degrees Offered
JD/MBA 4 years, JD/MA (tax) 4 years, JD/MA (accounting) 4 years.

Clinical program required	No
Legal writing	
course requirement	Yes
Legal methods	
course requirement	Yes
Legal research	
course requirement	Yes
Moot court requirement	No
Public interest	
law requirement	No

Academics

Students at Ole Miss love the combination of "a down-home, small-town atmosphere where everyone knows your name" and a law degree that is "given much credit within the state." Though "academically strenuous," the school's "laid-back atmosphere" prevails, and students praise the "easily accessible" staff, the "large student mall with plenty of couches and chairs for discussions between classes," and the "professors with awesome senses of humor." By all accounts, Ole Miss is not a school that "makes you feel like they are trying to weed you out." As one student explains, "I love the dynamics of the classes and the size of the student body. It is nice to be friends with 2Ls and 3Ls and not feel like a freshman again." "Everyone in the administration is incredibly friendly and helpful," a classmate adds. "If you have any question, even if it has nothing to do with their particular job, they will do everything they can to get you the right answer." Professors here hail from "a broad diversity of backgrounds" and "are all extremely knowledgeable and very experienced." Not only do they "present the material in an entertaining way," they "take a special interest" in students, "which can help build up [students'] confidence and help them to excel."

The professors at Ole Miss are a major reason why its students say the school is a "great value." "It is not nearly as expensive to go to school here as the other schools to which I applied or was accepted," says one student. "I can still get pretty much any job I want coming out of Ole Miss, yet I have zero debt." Other students, however, temper such expectations, noting that while Ole Miss' "Career Services Office is always there to help with a resume or to provide Tylenol during exams," securing a job outside of Mississippi can be an uphill battle. That said, this situation seems to be on the upswing thanks to the school's "great relationship with alumni" and also in that "Ole Miss changed their grading curve for 2Ls 2 years ago and that has significantly helped those who are looking to get a job out of state."

Students consistently report that the faculty is one of the school's "greatest strengths." "They take away the mundane, stereotypical experience of law school and present the material in an entertaining way without compromising the integrity of the institution," says one student. Many feel that "there is a lot of potential in the legal writing and research classes"; however, they are damaged by "the lack of communication between . . . departments." Others would like "more classes to choose from," particularly in the area of entertainment law. Students are divided on the school's aesthetics, finding that the "great library" is "extremely up to date with the latest technology" while the building itself is "not very pretty" and "somewhat outdated." A 1L provides some perspective, explaining that "the law school building would be aesthetically pleasing at most major schools, but when compared to the columned architecture and tree-lined walkways of the rest of the campus, you can immediately tell it is a relic of the early 70s. . . . Instead of being 'postmodern,' it simply looks out of place." However, "a new state-of-the-art building" "will soon be under construction."

Life

Ole Miss students emphasize that theirs is a "relaxed learning environment," one that "promotes collaboration between students instead of the cutthroat competition that you hear about at other law schools." The school divides 1Ls into sections of "about 60 students." While this can be "good for making friends" and forming "study groups and TV nights," it can at times seem "like high school all over again with the distinct social circles." "In true Southern form," law students at Ole Miss "like to work hard and play

BARBARA VINSON, DIRECTOR OF ADMISSIONS
OFFICE OF ADMISSIONS, PO BOX 1848, LAMAR LAW CENTER, UNIVERSITY, MS 38677
TEL: 662-915-6910 FAX: 662-915-1289
E-MAIL: LAWMISS@OLEMISS.EDU • INTERNET: WWW.LAW.OLEMISS.EDU

hard," and "There is a huge effort to make sure that students do more than study." "There is a great Law School Social Board (LSSB) that throws parties, organizes intramural teams, and puts together community-service projects so that students have a way to get to know each other and put the books down for a few hours," a 1L reports. When they do take a break, Ole Miss students find themselves in a pleasant location. The university's campus is "beautiful," and hometown Oxford is "a unique place" with "a healthy social scene." Though most will tell you that "drinking is a big part of social life" here, popular opinion states that "you can absolutely have a good time without drinking." "There are two great new movie theaters, and there are plans to open a 'New Square,'" says one student. "Oxford is constantly growing, and hopefully there will be a lot more for students to do soon." One thing that students agree could be improved a more "diverse student body."

Getting In

The early bird gets the worm at Ole Miss since admitted first-year students can begin their studies during the summer. Certain factors, such as "residency, undergraduate institution, difficulty of major, job experience, social, personal or economic circumstances, non-academic achievement, letters of recommendation and grade patterns and progression," can impact your application favorably, according to the school. Admitted students at the 25th percentile have an LSAT score of 152 and a GPA of 3.25. Admitted students at the 75th percentile have an LSAT score of 158 and a GPA of 3.76.

ADMISSIONS

Selectivity Rating	78
# applications received	1,550
# applicants accepted	489
# acceptees attending	175
Average LSAT	155
LSAT Range	152–158
Average undergrad GPA	3.47
Application fee	$40
Regular application	3/1
Regular notification	4/15
Rolling notification	Yes
Early application program	No
Transfer students accepted	Yes
Evening division offered	No
Part-time accepted	No
LSDAS accepted	Yes

Applicants Also Look At
Mississippi College, University of Alabama—Tuscaloosa, University of Tennessee.

International Students

TOEFL required of international students	Yes
Minimum paper TOEFL	625
Minimum computer TOEFL	263

FINANCIAL FACTS

Annual tuition (resident)	$8,300
Annual tuition (nonresident)	$16,180
Books and supplies	$1,300
Room & board	$14,858
% of aid that is merit based	90
Average grant	$5,788
Average loan	$15,334
Average debt	$41,632

EMPLOYMENT INFORMATION

		Grads Employed by Field (%):	
Career Rating	76		
Rate of placement (nine months out)	93	Academic	2
Average starting salary	$64,025	Business/Industry	6
State for bar exam	MS, TN, GA, FL, TX	Government	10
Pass rate for first-time bar	92	Judicial clerkships	18
Employers Who Frequently Hire Grads		Military	2
Top regional employers from across the South and Southeast.		Private practice	58
Prominent Alumni		Public Interest	4
C. Trent Lott, U.S. Senator; Thad Cochran, U.S. Senator; John Grisham, author; Richard Scruggs, attorney for first tobacco case; Robert C. Khayat, Chancellor, The University of Mississippi.			

UNIVERSITY OF MISSOURI—COLUMBIA
SCHOOL OF LAW

Academics

The University of Missouri—Columbia School of Law, "provides a high-quality legal education at an affordable price." Its small size, collegial atmosphere and "absolutely outstanding" faculty make Mizzou a "place where you can find all the challenge you want in a law school, without unnecessary stress on top of it." In the words of one student, "If you want to practice in the state of Missouri, there's no better place. Our law school consistently produces the future leaders of Missouri."

Students offer nothing but the utmost praise for their faculty. "The professors are intelligent yet not intimidating; they really care about the students." They "are leading scholars in their field yet available outside the classroom." "Although the Socratic Method is used throughout the first year, and often in other classes, it is used effectively, to help teach students to think like lawyers, but not to embarrass them." Of particular note, one student expresses pleasure in discovering that "classes integrate well with each other, in that professors seem aware of the other classes students are taking, and they draw connections between various fields of the law, thus helping students see how the law comes together." In the words of one particularly enthusiastic student, "The university is the reason I chose MU School of Law, but the faculty is why I would recommend it to any future students. Go Tigers!"

Similar feelings resonate over the administration. One student shares, "The dean of the law school teaches one of my classes. That's probably one of the coolest things about the law school—everyone is so attainable. The administration knows me, and probably every other student in the school, and they genuinely do have our best interests in sight." An older student returning to school after having a family, remarks, "The administration and professors are willing to work with students when those pesky issues of life come along and interfere with the school schedule." Another fan declares, "Law school is hard, MU made it easier."

Academically, students are challenged "within the comfort of a community." Students appreciate "the rigor and intensity of the curriculum" and especially call attention to Mizzou's noteworthy program in alternative dispute resolution. However, of greatest frustration to students are course offerings that conflict with scheduling. One student explains, "Although the course catalog offers a nice variety, students sometimes will have only one opportunity to take a particular class during their student careers, since some 2L/3L classes are offered only every other year." Unfortunately, the wait for in-demand classes can range from a semester to a year, depending on availability.

Career services receive mixed reviews. One student feels that "Career Services does an excellent job with the top 25 percent of the class, but the other three-fourths could use more attention, in my opinion." Another agrees, remarking that "the career development services are probably the most deserving of attention." Specifically, some feel that "the Career Office could do a better job attracting employers from more geographical areas." Fortunately, it appears that Career Services is addressing some of these issues; as one student reports, due to recent changes, "Career Services has done a much better job at providing job and internship opportunities for the students."

Mizzou's facilities—specifically the lack of technology in classrooms—seem to be one of its few weaknesses. "The classrooms do not have electrical outlets, which makes it difficult to take notes on a computer when you have class for four hours straight." As a result, "students are commonly seen lugging around extension cords" with them on campus.

DONNA L. PAVLICK, ASSISTANT DEAN
103 HULSTON HALL, COLUMBIA, MO 65211
TEL: 573-882-6042 FAX: 573-882-9625
E-MAIL: UMCLAWADMISSIONS@MISSOURI.EDU • INTERNET: WWW.LAW.MISSOURI.EDU

Additionally, students feel that "physical facilities are starting to show their age and need to be remodeled."

Life

"Mizzou is a great place for law school, the vast majority of people get along well with everyone else, and we all socialize together as well." "As [for] social life—you can get exactly what you want out of it. If you want to be involved, you got it. If you want to be a hermit and just come in for class," go ahead. "It is an environment that allows people to be flexible with their time, but it is also demanding in a sense that it has the proper time constraints to get people motivated." "Furthermore, Columbia is a great city, and the law school is right in the heart of campus with easy access to the recreation center as well as all of the amenities of downtown."

The degree of competition varies depending on who you ask. One student notes, "The thing I like best about this school is that very few individuals are worried about hiding books from each other in the library in order to get that cutthroat best grade." Another explains, "Students are friendly, but not shy about competition. We are here to learn how to be good lawyers, not to tear each other up." "MU is not a love fest though; people are here because they want to succeed."

Getting In

While application decisions are made on a rolling basis as long as the entering class has openings (class size is 150), the school recommends early application, preferably in the fall of the year prior to enrollment. Admitted students at the 25th percentile have an LSAT score of 156 and a GPA of 3.2. Admitted students at the 75th percentile have an LSAT score of 160 and a GPA of 3.7.

Legal methods	
course requirement	Yes
Legal research	
course requirement	Yes
Moot court requirement	Yes
Public interest	
law requirement	No

ADMISSIONS

Selectivity Rating	**80**
# applications received	875
# applicants accepted	381
# acceptees attending	152
Average LSAT	158
LSAT Range	156–160
Average undergrad GPA	3.49
Application fee	$50
Regular application	3/1
Regular notification	Rolling
Rolling notification	Yes
Early application program	Yes
Early application deadline	11/15
Early application notification	12/31
Transfer students accepted	Yes
Evening division offered	No
Part-time accepted	Yes
LSDAS accepted	Yes

Applicants Also Look At
Saint Louis U., U. of Missouri—
Kansas City, Washington U.

International Students

TOEFL required	
of international students	Yes
Minimum paper TOEFL	600
Minimum computer TOEFL	250

FINANCIAL FACTS

Annual tuition (resident)	$14,752
Annual tuition	
(nonresident)	$28,176
Books and supplies	$1,372
Fees per credit (resident)	$476
Fees per credit (nonresident)	$476
Tuition per credit	
(nonresident)	$433
Room and board	$7,590
Financial aid application	
deadline	3/1
% first-year students	
receiving some sort of aid	90
% receiving some sort of aid	90
% of aid that is merit based	22
% receiving scholarships	52
Average grant	$4,000
Average loan	$16,500
Average total aid package	$18,500
Average debt	$57,889

EMPLOYMENT INFORMATION

Career Rating	**75**	**Grads Employed by Field (%)**	
Rate of placement (nine months out)	93	Business/Industry	4
Average starting salary	$52,022	Government	15
State for bar exam	MO, IL, TX, KS, CA	Judicial clerkships	12
Pass rate for first-time bar	89	Military	4
Employers Who Frequently Hire Grads		Other	4
Missouri law firms of all sizes; Missouri,		Private practice	49
federal and governmental agencies; busi-		Public Interest	5
ness, accounting and insurance industries;			
federal and state judges, both inside and			
outside the state of Missouri.			
Prominent Alumni			
Claire McCaskill, U.S. Senator; Ted			
Kulongowski, Governor of Oregon; John R.			
Gibson, U.S. Court of Appeals, 8th Circuit.			

UNIVERSITY OF MISSOURI—KANSAS CITY
SCHOOL OF LAW

INSTITUTIONAL INFORMATION

Public/private	Public
Student-faculty ratio	14:1
% faculty part-time	36
% faculty female	30
% faculty minority	9
Total faculty	47

SURVEY SAYS...

Diverse opinions accepted
in classrooms
Great research resources
Great library staff
Students love Kansas City, MO

STUDENTS

Enrollment of law school	489
% male/female	58/42
% out-of-state	39
% full-time	97
% minority	9
# of countries represented	2
Average age of entering class	23

ACADEMICS

Academic Experience Rating	**84**
Profs interesting rating	80
Profs accessible rating	82
Hours of study per day	4.87

Academic Specialties

Business and entrepreneurial law,
child and family law, urban, land
use and environmental law, litigation, taxation.

Advanced Degrees Offered

LLM 1 to 3 years.

Combined Degrees Offered

JD/MBA 3 to 4 years, JD/MPA 3 to
4 years, JD/LLM 3.5 to 4 years.

Clinical program required	No
Legal writing	
course requirement	Yes
Legal methods	
course requirement	No
Legal research	
course requirement	Yes
Moot court requirement	Yes

Academics

The University of Missouri—Kansas City School of Law already offers good value, and with the bar-passage rate climbing each year, the investment just looks better and better. Students enjoy being part of a school "new in its success" and support the administration's aspiration to climb the rankings.

UMKC professors provide the thrust behind the upward momentum. "Some particularly big names have arrived recently, and the law school appears to be leapfrogging up the rankings as a result." The adjunct faculty, made up of practitioners, judges, and congressional representatives, add their perspectives to the mix. Many instructors draw on a background in "prominent public interest work, making the social-service aspects of the law clearly appreciable." That compassion carries over to their students. A 1L writes, "The entire faculty is aware of stressful times and makes general comments of encouragement along the way." Many students express pleasant surprise at having "such student-oriented professors." If anyone misses class, "they will sit with you one-on-one to explain what we went over." After their first year, students have offices in close proximity to faculty offices, creating an integrated community. However, come grade time, the generosity of spirit seems to dry up; professors are serious about "weeding people out after the first semester."

The predominant teaching style features somewhat leftist politics (by Missouri standards) and "old-fashioned" Socratic questioning by way of the Inquisition. Apparently, "someone forgot to tell the faculty here that law school isn't supposed to be like the book *One L* anymore." But professors aren't completely without a sense of humor when lecturing and most will "throw in a joke or two just to make sure the students are still awake." The majority appreciates courses' practical focus but beg for more problem-based teaching methods. Many new students would be at a loss were it not for the structured study groups and tutors in place to ease the transition. A 1L writes, "The mentor program is very positive. We are placed with a 2L or 3L that is studying our area of interest. The 1Ls can pick the upper-level student's brains about classes, professors, exams, and outlines."

About half of the lecture halls have been turned into "the classroom of the future," but the rest "still have a 1970s vibe going on." Climate-control issues force people "to wear coats during class on cold days." The library lacks "in terms of atmosphere, seating, and number of volumes," according to a 2L, but the "extremely gifted researchers" on staff "strive to help all who ask." Summer programs in China and Ireland provide additional resources for students.

Students prepare for the real world at the child and family services clinic by helping to establish permanency for children. In the words of a 3L, "Working at the clinic really makes you think about the power a law degree can give you and the responsibility to use that power wisely." Some people will parlay these skills into a public sector job, but most of the career emphasis lies on big-firm litigation. Everyone with a class ranking in the double digits feels abandoned by their friends at career services, but networking can pick up the slack. Faculty members help out by "organizing meet-and-greets with local attorneys to help you begin networking," to the relief of a 1L. "If you are willing to work in the Kansas City area, opportunities abound for graduates of UMKC Law."

DEBBIE BROOKS, ASSISTANT DEAN
UMKC SCHOOL OF LAW, 5100 ROCKHILL ROAD, KANSAS CITY, MO 64110
TEL: 816-235-1644 FAX: 816-235-5276
E-MAIL: LAW@UMKC.EDU • INTERNET: WWW.LAW.UMKC.EDU

Life

Incoming classes are divided into three sections, which either gel into supportive groups or devolve to petty infighting. "Gunners" keep the curve respectable and the laid-back environment from losing its edge. Orientation emphasizes that "the competitive aspects of school should not overshadow professionalism and collegiality." The pervasive "Midwestern values" also help to keep things friendly, and since "Most everyone understands that we will all be practicing together," there is good reason to keep the backstabbing to a minimum. Law students tend to "have other things going on in their lives"; one nontraditional student appreciates the school's efforts to "help me find a schedule that is conducive to my lifestyle and family obligations." Students see plenty of opportunities "to combine social life and networking while in law school." For example, the Inn program, run by a small group of students, professors, and UMKC alumni practicing in the Kansas City area, coordinates social events as well as field trips to the courthouse or a law firm, fostering continuity and camaraderie in the bar. Faculty and students look forward to the annual Halloween party, Barrister Ball, and school-wide softball tournament. First-years haunt the on-campus lounge, "a 1L's second home," and happy hour always draws a crowd. People inevitably start butting heads over politics, given the split population, but "For the most part, we are accepting of other views and happy to talk with people of differing beliefs." A 2L explains, "While most people come from similar backgrounds, there is enough of a mix to spice things up."

Getting In

Students who don't quite have the numbers to get into Mizzou's Columbia campus still have a shot at Kansas City. Applicants who can't commit to the full-time program may want to consider the part-time "flex" program, which allows students up to five years to complete the JD degree. Applications are accepted any time after September 1, but procrastinators beware—most seats are filled by the end of February.

Public interest	
law requirement	No

ADMISSIONS

Selectivity Rating	**89**
# applications received	1,141
# applicants accepted	423
# acceptees attending	161
Average LSAT	154
LSAT Range	152–156
Average undergrad GPA	3.47
Application fee	$50
Regular application	Rolling
Regular notification	Rolling
Rolling notification	Yes
Early application program	No
Transfer students accepted	Yes
Evening division offered	No
Part-time accepted	Yes
LSDAS accepted	Yes

Applicants Also Look At
University of Kansas, University of Missouri—Columbia,

International Students

TOEFL required	
of international students	Yes
Minimum paper TOEFL	650
Minimum computer TOEFL	280

FINANCIAL FACTS

Annual tuition (resident)	$12,365
Annual tuition	
(nonresident)	$24,416
Books and supplies	$3,900
Room and board	
(on/off-campus)	$23,458/$25,778
Financial aid application	
deadline	3/1
% receiving some sort of aid	100
% of aid that is merit based	99
% receiving scholarships	39
Average grant	$8,600
Average loan	$23,923
Average total aid package	$26,115
Average debt	$64,606

EMPLOYMENT INFORMATION

Career Rating	**76**	**Grads Employed by Field (%)**	
Rate of placement (nine months out)	96	Academic	3
Average starting salary	$54,056	Business/Industry	7
State for bar exam	MO, KS	Government	4
Pass rate for first-time bar	86	Judicial clerkships	14
Employers Who Frequently Hire Grads		Other	1
Blackwell, Sanders, Peper, Martin LLP;		Private practice	66
Bryan Cave LLP; Husch and Eppenberger,		Public Interest	5
LLC; Jackson County Circuit Court;			
Lathrop and Gage LC.			
Prominent Alumni			
Harry S. Truman, President of the United			
States; Justice Charles E. Whittaker, U.S.			
Supreme Court; Clarence Kelley, Director			
of the FBI.			

UNIVERSITY OF NEBRASKA—LINCOLN
COLLEGE OF LAW

INSTITUTIONAL INFORMATION

Public/private	Public
Student-faculty ratio	12:1
% faculty part-time	46
% faculty female	21
% faculty minority	4
Total faculty	48

SURVEY SAYS...

Diverse opinions accepted
in classrooms
Great research resources
Great library staff

STUDENTS

Enrollment of law school	399
% male/female	53/47
% out-of-state	28
% full-time	99
% minority	13
% international	1
# of countries represented	2
Average age of entering class	26

ACADEMICS

Academic Experience Rating	**89**
Profs interesting rating	98
Profs accessible rating	83
Hours of study per day	3.6

Academic Specialties

Commercial law, corporation securities law, environmental law, intellectual property law, international law, labor law, taxation, litigation.

Advanced Degrees Offered

JD 3 years, MLS 1 year.

Combined Degrees Offered

JD/PhD (psychology) 6 years, JD/MA (economics), JD/MBA 4 years, JD/MPA 4 years, JD/political science 4 years, JD/community of regional planning 4 years, JD/PhD (ed. adm.) 5 years, JD/MA (international affairs) 4 years.

Clinical program required	No
Legal writing	
course requirement	Yes
Legal methods	
course requirement	No

Academics

The University of Nebraska—Lincoln College of Law offers a high-quality education at an unbeatable price. One student incredulously declares, "I pay about $9,000 a semester for books and tuition. Where else can you get a top-rate legal education for that cheap?" Students say that UNL offers a first-rate education with a "brilliant and very approachable" staff. "Not only are the professors walking through the library, talking to the students and answering questions, but the staff throughout the college is amazing."

The administration, faculty and research staff undoubtedly serve as UNL's greatest assets. One student remarks, "Honestly, I don't think that one could find a better school administration or research librarians. They always meet you with a helpful smile," and are willing to do all that they can to assist students. Another notes, "The faculty and staff at Nebraska law care about the success of each student," and help "student[s] find their place within the law." According to many, professors are "extremely engaging" and "are able to connect the subject matter to practical experience and real-life cases, which makes class more interesting."

Students warn that "the first year is extremely demanding, especially spring semester [since] our classes are a year long and most of the tests in the spring are cumulative." While April and May in the first year might be "almost unbearable," one seasoned 3L reassures us that "during my three years at UNL, most of my classes have been very interesting. Some of them have changed my life and outlook on the world." Students rave about UNL's prosecutorial clinic, as it is one of the few of its kind amongst an array of defense clinics. One student emphatically declares it "the best class that I took at UNL. Another student is of the opinion that though "there are a lot of classes in varying subjects, [UNL] is lacking in public interest/pro bono–type classes or topics for students wanting a different type of experience."

Students are divided when it comes to the subject of employment after graduation. One student expresses an appreciation for "how UNL is trying to branch out and help students land jobs outside of Nebraska." Another argues that while "The school is great for finding jobs for students with higher grades that want to stay in Nebraska," "There is not enough emphasis on employment after law school if a student wants to work in public interest." One 3L would like "employers more involved in recruiting for clerkships," but in the same breath concedes that "most [students] were able to get clerkships if they wanted them as a 2L."

"The renovation of the school is almost complete," students gladly report. "It's great having brand new classrooms and facilities, as well as complete access to technology anywhere in the building." The almost fully renovated classrooms are "extremely comfortable" and "all have wireless access and plugs for laptops." Additionally, the "auditorium is set for renovation, and [the school is] adding on to accommodate larger class sizes." Overall, students seem content with the refurbished facilities and as one satisfied 1L affirms, "After six years on the East Cost, the beautiful library and outstanding professors made returning to the Midwest an easy decision."

Environment

"UNL recruits some very intelligent and exceptionally talented students," and students agree that "the law school does a really good job of creating community among the students." Specifically, the small class size creates a "close-knit group mentality" and particularly helpful is the practice of scheduling first years "so they have at least one

SARAH GLODEN, ASSISTANT DEAN OF ADMISSIONS
PO BOX 830902, LINCOLN, NE 68583-0902
TEL: 402-472-2161 FAX: 402-472-5185
E-MAIL: LAWADM@UNL.EDU • INTERNET: LAW.UNL.EDU

class with most of the students" in their cohort. One reassured student remarks from experience, "I know that if I need any help, albeit from a librarian, administrator, faculty member, or fellow law student, that I will receive it."

There is no shortage of social opportunities at UNL. "People take the initiative to organize mixers and activities to help people get to know one another and to keep law school stress at bay as much as possible." One student observes, "The social life at Nebraska is great if you like to drink. Many of the students like to go to the bars on the weekends (or on Mondays or Tuesdays), and there's almost always alcohol at Student Bar Association events. Heck, even our Civil Procedure professor took our class out to the bar after a particularly tough week." The bottom line remains clear as expressed in one student's words, "students aren't just classmates—we're friends."

Getting In

LSAT scores and undergraduate GPA are the main factors that UNL's Admissions Committee consider when evaluating applications. Admitted students at the 25th percentile have an LSAT score of 154 and a GPA of 3.2. Admitted students at the 75th percentile have an LSAT score of 160 and a GPA of 3.8. UNL pays particular attention in reviewing applications from members of minority groups that historically have been under-represented in the legal profession.

Legal research course requirement	Yes
Moot court requirement	No
Public interest law requirement	No

ADMISSIONS

Selectivity Rating	**78**
# applications received	877
# applicants accepted	366
# acceptees attending	144
Average LSAT	156
LSAT Range	154–160
Average undergrad GPA	3.64
Application fee	$25
Regular application	3/1
Regular notification	Rolling
Rolling notification	Yes
Early application program	No
Transfer students accepted	Yes
Evening division offered	No
Part-time accepted	No
LSDAS accepted	Yes

Applicants Also Look At

Arizona State University, Creighton University, Drake University, University of Denver, University of Iowa, University of Kansas, Washburn University.

International Students

TOEFL required of international students	Yes
Minimum paper TOEFL	600
Minimum computer TOEFL	250

FINANCIAL FACTS

Annual tuition (resident)	$6,856
Annual tuition (nonresident)	$19,223
Books and supplies	$1,230
Tuition per credit (resident)	$208
Tuition per credit (nonresident)	$583
Room and board (on/off-campus)	$7,106/$6,846
Financial aid application deadline	5/1
% first-year students receiving some sort of aid	46
% receiving some sort of aid	44
% of aid that is merit based	38
% receiving scholarships	44
Average grant	$7,000
Average loan	$15,880
Average total aid package	$20,428
Average debt	$44,910

EMPLOYMENT INFORMATION

Career Rating	**77**	**Grads Employed by Field (%)**	
Rate of placement (nine months out)	95	Academic	5
Average starting salary	$52,589	Business/Industry	13
State for bar exam	NE, IA, MO, SD, WA	Government	11
Pass rate for first-time bar	90	Judicial clerkships	6
Employers Who Frequently Hire Grads		Military	2
Very small firms (2 to 10 attorneys); small		Other	1
firms (11 to 25 attorneys); state government.		Private practice	55
Prominent Alumni		Public Interest	7
Ted Sorensen, special counsel to president John F. Kennedy; Harvey Perlman, chancellor, University of Nebraska—Lincoln; Ben Nelson, U.S. Senator and former Governor of Nebraska; Lee Rankin, former Solicitor General of the United States.			

UNIVERSITY OF NEVADA—LAS VEGAS
WILLIAM S. BOYD SCHOOL OF LAW

INSTITUTIONAL INFORMATION

Public/private	Public
Student-faculty ratio	14:1
% faculty part-time	21
% faculty female	40
% faculty minority	15
Total faculty	53

SURVEY SAYS...

Diverse opinions accepted
in classrooms
Great research resources
Abundant externship/internship/
clerkship opportunities
Beautiful campus

STUDENTS

Enrollment of law school	471
% male/female	50/50
% out-of-state	
% full-time	72
% minority	26

ACADEMICS

Academic Experience Rating	86
Profs interesting rating	84
Profs accessible rating	80
Hours of study per day	4.31

Combined Degrees Offered
JD/MBA 4 years, JD/MSW 4 years.

Clinical program required	No
Legal writing course requirement	Yes
Legal methods course requirement	Yes
Legal research course requirement	Yes
Moot court requirement	No
Public interest law requirement	Yes

Academics

A young and recently ABA-accredited law school, many students feel "The greatest strength of Boyd is its newness," which lends a sense of optimism, excitement, and challenge to the campus. Because it's not "steeped in tradition, there's an entrepreneurial spirit here. Everyone senses we're building something special." With a quality teaching staff, top-notch facilities, a talented student body, and reasonable tuition costs, students are confident that their school will continue to climb in the ranks. In fact, this sense of excitement extends throughout the city and state. Boyd is the only law school in Nevada; students report that "the legal community and the community in general are excited to have us here and the whole city is invested in all of us succeeding."

Professors boast impressive educational and professional backgrounds and are known to be both "intelligent and well respected in their fields." More important, they are "stimulating individuals who are skilled teachers." Students are "consistently amazed by the ease with which the faculty so effectively employs the Socratic Method, such that the student body . . . is able to break down even the most complex legal scenarios and digest them as fully understandable rules and concepts." Outside the classroom, "Professors are extremely approachable, even for a shy student."

The administration is generally regarded as "accessible and very pro-student." A 2L affirms, "The administrators I deal with on any sort of regular basis are fantastic. Not only do they know their stuff; they are anxious to help and are just all-around fabulous people." Students particularly applaud the efforts the administration has made to help new students make the transition into law school, citing the "optional 30-minute classes once a week where we are taught exam skills, note-taking, and outlining tips."

Built just a few years ago, classrooms at Boyd are "new and clean" and very high-tech. The "top quality facilities" include "wireless Internet and cable Internet hook-ups throughout the building," as well as "a state-of-the-art library." Off campus, students say that "being the only law school in Nevada, in the middle of one of the fastest-growing economies in the United States, opportunities abound." For example, UNLV students "have opportunities for something close to 30 judicial externships each year (out of a class of 150)" and additionally "have extraordinary access to the local, regional, and state governments." When it comes to landing a job after graduation, UNLV is extremely well located. In the city of Las Vegas "The local law firms are eager to hire graduates, and the private sector opportunities in gaming, hospitality, real estate, corporate, entertainment and litigation are abundant and highly lucrative."

KATIE LYON, ADMISSIONS COUNSELOR AND RECRUITER
4505 MARYLAND PARKWAY, BOX 451003, LAS VEGAS, NV 89154-1003
TEL: (702) 895-2440 FAX: (702) 895-2414
E-MAIL: REQUEST@LAW.UNLV.EDU • INTERNET: WWW.LAW.UNLV.EDU

Life

While located in the heart of Las Vegas, "Most of the students commute into campus . . . and that can put a strain on the nearby social scene." In lieu of a hopping campus life, "Student organizations are great and have become central to social events at the school." Students have no trouble making friends among their interesting and talented classmates since "The people make the school." One student writes, "I love coming to school because I've made really great friends and don't mind seeing them everyday."

Commuter student or not, "Being in the center of Las Vegas, there is always something to do and somewhere new to go." You may be surprised to learn, however, that law school in Sin City is actually quite serious. At Boyd, "Students are very competitive, and you can feel that in the air." Some students feel the competitiveness is a product of the high caliber of the student body. A 1L explains that many "of the students in the entering class are in their 40s, and several of them are doctors and dentists, so the bar is set quite high." In addition to their diligence, UNLV students are a fairly homogenous and quite conservative group. One student points out that some of "The faculty is comprised of very liberal individuals from a diverse background, whereas a majority of the students are very conservative and tend to have similar life experiences."

Getting In

When selecting applicants, the Admissions Committee looks for students with demonstrated academic capability, including depth and breadth of undergraduate course work, grades, concurrent work experience, and extracurricular activities. The school also considers non-academic factors, such as community service and work experience. Older students should feel particularly welcomed at Boyd.

ADMISSIONS

Selectivity Rating	**88**
# applications received	2,205
# applicants accepted	358
# acceptees attending	156
Average LSAT	158
LSAT Range	155–160
Average undergrad GPA	3.5
Application fee	$50
Regular application	3/15
Regular notification	4/30
Rolling notification	Yes
Early application program	No
Transfer students accepted	Yes
Evening division offered	Yes
Part-time accepted	Yes
LSDAS accepted	Yes

Applicants Also Look At

Arizona State University, California Western, Southwestern University School of Law, Thomas Jefferson School of Law, University of Arizona, University of the Pacific, University of San Diego.

International Students

TOEFL required	
of international students	No
TOEFL recommended	
of international students	No

FINANCIAL FACTS

Annual tuition (resident)	$8,900
Annual tuition (nonresident)	$17,800
Books and supplies	$1,080
Tuition per credit (resident)	$317
Tuition per credit (nonresident)	$635
Room and board (off-campus)	$8,370
Financial aid application deadline	2/1
% of aid that is merit based	90
% receiving scholarships	41
Average grant	$4,400
Average loan	$17,400

EMPLOYMENT INFORMATION

		Grads Employed by Field (%)	
Career Rating	**73**	**Grads Employed by Field (%)**	
Rate of placement (nine months out)	87	Business/Industry	16
Average starting salary	$64,000	Government	12
State for bar exam	NV, AZ, UT, CA	Judicial clerkships	17
Pass rate for first-time bar	78	Private practice	47
Employers Who Frequently Hire Grads		Public Interest	8
Local and state private firms; local and state governmental agencies; local and state judiciary.			

UNIVERSITY OF NEW MEXICO

SCHOOL OF LAW

INSTITUTIONAL INFORMATION

Public/private	Public
Student-faculty ratio	10:1
% faculty female	51
% faculty minority	40
Total faculty	35

SURVEY SAYS...

Great research resources
Great library staff
Abundant externship/internship/
clerkship opportunities
Liberal students

STUDENTS

Enrollment of law school	343
% male/female	50/50
% full-time	100
% minority	45
% international	1
# of countries represented	3
Average age of entering class	28

ACADEMICS

Academic Experience Rating	**84**
Profs interesting rating	84
Profs accessible rating	94
Hours of study per day	3.74

Academic Specialties
Environmental law, Indian law.

Advanced Degrees Offered
JD 3 years.

Combined Degrees Offered
JD/MBA, JD/MA (water resources)
JD/MA (Latin American studies)
JD/MA (public administration) 4
years.

Clinical program required	Yes
Legal writing	
course requirement	Yes
Legal methods	
course requirement	Yes
Legal research	
course requirement	Yes
Moot court requirement	No
Public interest	
law requirement	No

Academics

The University of New Mexico School of Law "offers [students] an absolutely amazing experience." By all accounts, it's "a very affordable, friendly, ideal place to study law." Highlights include "a small community"—there are only about 350 law students—"and a really encouraging faculty." "The small size limits the number of classes that are offered," but they also "give a greater opportunity to connect with professors and students alike, not just academically but on a personal level as well." The Family Law curriculum is popular, and certificates are available in Natural Resources Law and in the "superb" Native American Law program. Dual-degree programs include a JD/MA in Latin American Studies. There's also study abroad opportunities in Mexico, Canada, and Tasmania. "The other great thing about UNMSOL is the clinical program." "Participating in clinic has been one of the most rewarding and useful experiences of my law school career," gushes one student. "I've had the opportunity to personally represent actual clients in actual cases with help from an experienced attorney." Also, "The trial practice classes give you real trial experience in front of current judges and real jurors."

The administration is "very accessible and open to student input." "Law students in general always have complaints about everything, but this administration seems to be fairly responsive to student concerns," notes a 2L. Students tell us that teaching is "the focus of the law school." "While some teachers are better than others, the overall experience has been great so far," says a 2L. The faculty "includes some brilliant legal minds" and "could not be more knowledgeable." "Our professors are the best lawyers in the state in their given fields," asserts a 2L. Many "have literally written the book on a given area of New Mexico law." Professors are "accessible" and "student friendly" as well. "Most of my professors know who I am, and I can easily get in contact with most—if not all—of them," declares a 3L.

UNM does a pretty good job of helping students fulfill "a broad array of career goals." There is "great access to externships and clerkships both during and after law school." "Any student can set up an externship with any lawyer in the state." Career Services "is sometimes disorganized and so students often have to go on their own to find jobs." "That's not very difficult to do," though, because "There's no other law school in the state." UNM graduates often have their pick of jobs in The Land of Enchantment.

The facility here is something like "a concrete bungalow surrounded by parking lots." (By the way, "Parking is, and always will be, a hassle.") "The newer wing of the school is beautiful and bright, but the older building could use some aesthetic improvements." "Classroom walls are thin, and you can often hear the professor next door." "The chairs are dismal in some of the classrooms" too. The best feature is probably the library, which is "open and bright with plenty of private spots for intense study."

Life

The diversity of the student population is a tremendous strength at this school. UNM "works hard to ensure that the student population is diverse and reflects the actual demographics" of the state. There is a "strong Mexican American and Native American presence." Students here are "cool, interesting, admirable, energetic, fun people of different ages." They are often "prone to open, heated debate" and "very open to discussion whenever a point of contention might arise." Politically, it's an "overwhelmingly leftist student body," which makes some students uncomfortable. "As a Hispanic who is a moderate Democrat, I cannot believe how . . . intolerant this institution is," gripes a 3L.

SUSAN MITCHELL, ASSISTANT DEAN FOR ADMISSIONS AND FINANCIAL AID
MSC 11-6070, ONE UNIVERSITY OF NEW MEXICO, ALBUQUERQUE, NM 87131-0001
TEL: 505-277-0958 FAX: 505-277-9958
E-MAIL: ADMISSIONS@LAW.UNM.EDU • INTERNET: LAWSCHOOL.UNM.EDU

Other students disagree. "I (as a conservative student) still feel that I have a voice that is heard and considered whenever there is a debate, whether it's in class or in the parking lot." There isn't a ton of academic competition. "Most everyone is very friendly; the only serious, cutthroat competition takes place at the Ping-Pong table in the Student Forum."

"Students all know each other, and there is an active social scene" on campus. "It is a tight community." "I have made a lot of really great friends," proclaims a 2L. There are a very high number of student organizations on campus, but "Some of those organizations tend to have a low level of activity due to the small number of students at the school." The surrounding city of Albuquerque (population: about 700,000) is "an extremely affordable place to live with low crime and moderate traffic which makes it great for students." "Albuquerque is just a great place to live, especially for people who like the outdoors." Summers are relatively hot, and it does snow during the mild winters, making it possible to ski in the nearby mountains in the morning and play a comfortable round of golf in the afternoon. "Lots of students are athletic and run or bike; there are extensive trail systems around campus."

Getting In

Admitted students at the 25th percentile have LSAT scores in the range of 152 and GPAs of a little over 3.0. Admitted students at the 75th percentile have LSAT scores of 158 and GPAs just over 3.7.

ADMISSIONS

Selectivity Rating	83
# applications received	1,405
# applicants accepted	248
# acceptees attending	115
Average LSAT	155
LSAT Range	152–158
Average undergrad GPA	3.34
Application fee	$50
Regular application	2/15
Regular notification	Rolling
Rolling notification	Yes
Early application program	No
Transfer students accepted	Yes
Evening division offered	No
Part-time accepted	No
LSDAS accepted	Yes

International Students

TOEFL required of international students	Yes
Minimum paper TOEFL	600
Minimum computer TOEFL	250

FINANCIAL FACTS

Annual tuition (resident)	$9,565
Annual tuition (nonresident)	$23,212
Books and supplies	$1,308
Room and board (on/off-campus)	$6,590/$7,614
Financial aid application deadline	3/1

EMPLOYMENT INFORMATION

Career Rating	79	
Rate of placement (nine months out)	96	
Average starting salary	$48,818	
State for bar exam	NM	
Pass rate for first-time bar	95	

Employers Who Frequently Hire Grads
Private firms; government; federal and state judges; public interest organizations.

Prominent Alumni
Chief Justice Edward L. Chavez, New Mexico Supreme Court; Honorable Tom Udall, United States House of Representatives; Gary King, New Mexico Attorney General.

Grads Employed by Field (%)

Academic	4
Business/Industry	5
Government	18
Judicial clerkships	10
Private practice	50
Public Interest	13

THE UNIVERSITY OF NORTH CAROLINA AT CHAPEL HILL
SCHOOL OF LAW

Academics

The School of Law at The University of North Carolina at Chapel Hill is, according to students, "one of the best public law schools in the country." Many claim that "the faculty here couldn't be more down to earth and accessible." They have "a literal 'my-door-is-open-all-the-time policy' and never hesitate to "[take] the time to talk to every single student before class." Still, some students feel that "there is a strong liberal bias at the school" and that professors sometimes "bring their political views with them into the classroom." To correct this, they are calling for the law school to "improve on fostering a more diverse political atmosphere." UNC Law's "excellent" and "accessible" administration is "unparalleled" in its efforts to promote a "positive and supportive environment for the study of law." Everyone here seems to practice "the 'We're all family at UNC' motto to a fault."

Most UNC survey respondents are pretty pleased about their employment prospects. One student credits the Career Services Office as being "the greatest strength of UNC. Even when they are too busy for a brief meeting about resumes or cover letters, you can just leave your stuff under the door, and someone will get it back to you by the next day with recommendations about what you should fix." However, some feel that it could "stand to improve, particularly with communicating jobs to 1Ls." Others note a weakness in the "timeliness" with their grades. "We still don't have one grade in late February. How are we supposed to get a summer job?" asks one student. However, jobs in North Carolina and neighboring states are fairly abundant, though, in large part because the law school maintains "strong connections" with in-state employers.

Student organizations and learning opportunities are aplenty. According to one student, "There are lots of organizations to get involved in, and the pro bono program is one of the best." About one-third of all students do some kind of pro bono work—many during the summer or during winter or spring breaks. Students who have performed more than 75 hours of pro bono service receive certificates of acknowledgment from the state bar association, and those who perform more than 100 hours of pro bono service get special shout-outs at graduation. Other notables include UNC's clinical programs, in which students handle more than 350 civil and criminal cases every year and "really get a lot of hands-on experience" along with "solid academic[s]" in the process. Joint-degree programs include the standard JD/MBA as well as master's of public policy science and a handful of others. UNC also offers a summer program down under in Sydney, Australia, that concentrates on Pacific Rim issues and semester-long programs in Europe and Mexico.

The general consensus is that facilities at UNC are middling, but in terms of the availability of information, "The resources are outstanding." Also, "The school is improving the technology of each classroom every year." It's a pretty slow process, though. As of now, "Half the facilities are brand-new. Once they get around to renovating the other half, they'll be golden." In the meantime, a cry of "More parking!" can be heard throughout campus.

MICHAEL J. STATES, ASSISTANT DEAN FOR ADMISSIONS
CB #3380, VAN HECKE-WETTACH HALL, UNC SCHOOL OF LAW—ADMISSIONS,
CHAPEL HILL, NC 27599-3380
TEL: 919-962-5109 FAX: 919-843-7939
E-MAIL: LAW_ADMISSION@UNC.EDU • INTERNET: WWW.LAW.UNC.EDU

Life

"Carolina offers a healthy balance between academic and student life." UNC is home to "diverse, interesting, charming, and intelligent people." One student exclaims, "I am constantly amazed by how interesting my classmates are." Most agree that "everyone gets along" in this "very friendly" and "very cooperative" academic atmosphere. "It is competitive but not necessarily with each other. It seems we all want to see everyone do well," explains one student.

Students insist that "there is no better college town in the United States than Chapel Hill," a Southern hamlet of about 44,000 souls that offers a good supply of part-time jobs, affordable housing, and a mild climate. These fine qualities have not gone unnoticed: *Money* magazine named the Raleigh-Durham-Chapel Hill area the "Best Place to Live in the South" in 2000, and *Sports Illustrated* named Chapel Hill "the Best College Town in America" a few years earlier. "It's a great place to live," says one student. "The people are amazing" and the "campus and city are breathtaking." As one student puts it, "While you don't go to law school for the social life, it makes a big difference to have something to do when you actually do find free time."

"Social life is good" at Chapel Hill because "On the whole, students are very social outside of class." There are always a multitude of "school-sponsored social events in town" and "parties being thrown by law students to celebrate a wide array of milestones" (for instance, there is a "we just took our second practice exam" party). However, some students lament that there is little to do "for someone who does not drink."

Getting In

While perhaps easier than you might think, admissions here is no cakewalk. Admitted students at the 25th percentile have an LSAT score of 158 and a GPA of 3.4. Admitted students at the 75th percentile have an LSAT score of 164 and a GPA of 3.8. If applying as a nonresident, keep in mind that you'll want to be ready to dazzle with your academic prowess as around 75 percent of each admitted year at Chapel Hill are residents of North Carolina, and competition for the remaining quarter of the class is stiff.

Legal research	
course requirement	Yes
Moot court requirement	Yes
Public interest	
law requirement	No

ADMISSIONS

Selectivity Rating	95
# applications received	3,581
# applicants accepted	543
# acceptees attending	229
Average LSAT	162
LSAT Range	158–164
Average undergrad GPA	3.6
Application fee	$70
Regular application	2/1
Regular notification	Rolling
Rolling notification	Yes
Early application program	No
Transfer students accepted	Yes
Evening division offered	No
Part-time accepted	No
LSDAS accepted	Yes

Applicants Also Look At
American University, College of William & Mary, Duke University, The George Washington University, Georgetown University, University of Virginia, Wake Forest University (full-time MBA Program,

International Students

TOEFL required	
of international students	Yes
Minimum paper TOEFL	600
Minimum computer TOEFL	250

FINANCIAL FACTS

Annual tuition (resident)	$10,202
Annual tuition	
(nonresident)	$22,620
Books and supplies	$4,904
Room & board	$11,128
Financial aid application	
deadline	12/31
% first-year students	
receiving some sort of aid	86
% receiving some sort of aid	78
% of aid that is merit based	66
% receiving scholarships	53
Average grant	$4,665
Average loan	$18,748
Average total aid package	$22,803
Average debt	$59,329

EMPLOYMENT INFORMATION

Career Rating	92	Grads Employed by Field (%):	
Rate of placement (nine months out)	99	Academic	2
Average starting salary	$100,000	Business/Industry	7
State for bar exam	NC, NY, FL, GA, VA	Government	13
Pass rate for first-time bar	93	Judicial clerkships	13
Prominent Alumni		Private practice	59
John Edwards, U.S. Senator; Terry		Public Interest	6
Sanford, U.S. Senator; James Hunt, former			
Governor of North Carolina; Chief Justice			
Sarah Parker, NC Supreme Court; Chief			
Justice Henry Frye, NC Supreme Court.			

UNIVERSITY OF NORTH DAKOTA
SCHOOL OF LAW

INSTITUTIONAL INFORMATION

Public/private	Public
Student-faculty ratio	8:1
% faculty part-time	53
% faculty female	41
% faculty minority	13
Total faculty	32

SURVEY SAYS...

Diverse opinions accepted
in classrooms
Great library staff
Abundant externship/internship/
clerkship opportunities
Good social life

STUDENTS

Enrollment of law school	236
% male/female	54/46
% out-of-state	58
% full-time	100
% minority	10
% international	6
# of countries represented	6
Average age of entering class	26

ACADEMICS

Academic Experience Rating	**70**
Profs interesting rating	79
Profs accessible rating	84
Hours of study per day	4.58

Advanced Degrees Offered

JD 3 years.

Combined Degrees Offered

JD/MPA 4 years.

Clinical program required	No
Legal writing	
course requirement	Yes
Legal methods	
course requirement	Yes
Legal research	
course requirement	Yes
Moot court requirement	No
Public interest	
law requirement	No

Academics

If you are looking for a legal education at bargain basement prices, look no further than the University of North Dakota School of Law, where a "valuable and enriching education" can be had for an "extremely low price." Despite its affordability, quality teaching is a cornerstone of the academic experience at UND. One student says "[I am] more entertained while sitting in my first-year classes than I am watching prime-time TV." On top of their abilities to keep their students' attention, "The faculty really want students to succeed" and strive to make the material accessible. In doing so, "They use the Socratic Method, but not as a scare tactic." Professors are nothing if not personable; a 2L recalls that "on my first day, I wandered into the faculty lounge and was greeted by name by a professor who had taught my mother at the same law school 15 years earlier! He remembered when I was five years old and Mom had brought me to class when the babysitter was sick."

In addition to professors, the "administration clearly demonstrates an intention to help each student succeed in law school and beyond." Yet students feel that despite the intimate atmosphere, they give up little in terms of diversity and quality of courses and clinical experiences. Even so, students point out some weaknesses in the school's curriculum and course offerings. For example, some would like better programs in criminal and international law, as well as more emphasis on legal writing and research skills. A 3L adds, "This law school is in the middle of one of the greatest agricultural areas of the United States. However, it is not a center for agricultural law."

In addition to foundational course work, "Several legal research courses are offered as part of the curriculum, as well as voluntary training sessions that focus on developing your individual research skills." On top of that, "Practical experience is encouraged through things like moot court, trial advocacy competitions, and trial advocacy classes." Students also tell us that "the North Dakota Law Review is also a great opportunity to test and develop your legal research and writing skills" and that the school offers "a summer program abroad in Norway." The school is also proactive in seeking externships and clerkship opportunities within the state, and "Career Services, including internship placements, summer, and full-time employment opportunities, is very helpful." In addition, "The North Dakota Supreme Court selects graduating UND students as clerks each year."

In terms of enrollment, UND Law is tiny compared with other law schools, but students feel it is just the right size, "small enough to cater to individual students' interests and needs and large enough to have a good reputation nationally and internationally."

On campus, "facilities, particularly classrooms and the library, need more space and modernization," but students are satisfied with the level of bandwidth available, pointing out that "there is wireless Internet throughout the building, and even outside" and that professors make good use of technology in the classroom. Students report that the research facilities are excellent and "Research representatives from LexisNexis or Westlaw are available at all times to help out."

BEN HOFFMAN, DIRECTOR OF ADMISSIONS AND RECORDS
CENTENNIAL DRIVE, PO BOX 9003, GRAND FORKS, ND 58202
TEL: 701-777-2260 FAX: 701-777-2217
E-MAIL: HOFFMAN@LAW.UND.EDU • INTERNET: WWW.LAW.UND.NODAK.EDU

Life

On this low-key campus, "Classmates regularly coordinate group outings to local spots and really seem to get along with everyone." A number of clubs and student groups draw active members, and many make mention of the school's annual social events, like the "fabulous Halloween party" and the annual "Malpractice Bowl, in which the law school students play a football game against the medical students." Hometown Grand Forks gets the thumbs-up, and students tell us that "there are plenty of places to go for students who need to unwind."

In terms of demographics, "More diversity among the student body and faculty would be beneficial." While a few students claim the politics of the school leans to the left, most feel that UND "is a very conservative law school in a very conservative university in a very conservative town." Whatever their politics, "debates and discussions are always brewing between students." "Whether we are in class, studying, or out at the bar, there is always something to disagree on and challenge each other [about]." However, students insist that they are respectful of all viewpoints and opinions, and, "Aside from election time, there have been almost no squabbles."

Getting In

While there is no specific pre-law course work required for admission, demonstrated oral and written communication skills are paramount to an admissions decision at University of North Dakota. The applicant's undergraduate record, LSAT scores, and letters of recommendation are the most heavily weighted factors in an admissions decision; however, the school will consider all factors that may suggest a student is capable of completing a rigorous legal curriculum.

ADMISSIONS

Selectivity Rating	73
# applications received	632
# applicants accepted	191
# acceptees attending	77
Average LSAT	152
LSAT Range	149–155
Average undergrad GPA	3.34
Application fee	$35
Regular application	4/1
Regular notification	Rolling
Rolling notification	Yes
Early application program	No
Transfer students accepted	Yes
Evening division offered	No
Part-time accepted	No
LSDAS accepted	Yes

International Students

TOEFL required of international students	No
TOEFL recommended of international students	No

FINANCIAL FACTS

Annual tuition (resident)	$5,780
Annual tuition (nonresident)	$15,432
Books and supplies	$900
Room and board	$8,100
Financial aid application deadline	4/15
% first-year students receiving some sort of aid	92
% receiving some sort of aid	91
% of aid that is merit based	1
% receiving scholarships	25
Average grant	$500
Average loan	$19,627
Average total aid package	$18,500
Average debt	$53,684

EMPLOYMENT INFORMATION

Career Rating	67	Supreme Court.	
Rate of placement (nine months out)	96	**Grads Employed by Field (%)**	
Average starting salary	$44,800	Academic	2
State for bar exam	ND, MN, NC, SD, NM	Business/Industry	4
Pass rate for first-time bar	91	Government	11
Employers Who Frequently Hire Grads		Judicial clerkships	30
Judicial systems of ND and MN; private firms in ND and MN.		Military	2
Prominent Alumni		Private practice	44
Earl Pomeroy, ND Congressman; Chief Justice H.F. Gierke, U.S. Armed Forces Court of Appeals; Honorable Kermit Bye, U.S. Court of Appeals, 8th Circuit; Honorable Rodney Webb, U.S. District Court; Honorable Mary Maring, ND		Public Interest	7

UNIVERSITY OF NOTRE DAME
LAW SCHOOL

INSTITUTIONAL INFORMATION

Public/private	Private
Affiliation	Roman Catholic
Student-faculty ratio	15:1
% faculty part-time	47
% faculty female	36
% faculty minority	9
Total faculty	88

SURVEY SAYS...

Diverse opinions accepted
in classrooms
Great library staff
Conservative students

STUDENTS

Enrollment of law school	571
% male/female	63/37
% out-of-state	89
% full-time	100
% minority	22
% international	1
# of countries represented	4
Average age of entering class	24

ACADEMICS

Academic Experience Rating	**87**
Profs interesting rating	90
Profs accessible rating	85
Hours of study per day	4.64

Academic Specialties

Human rights law, international law, trial advocacy.

Advanced Degrees Offered

LLM (international human rights) 1 year, JSD (international human rights) 3 to 5 years, LLM (international and comparative law—London campus only) 1 year.

Combined Degrees Offered

JD/MBA 4 years, JD/ME 4 years, JD/MA (English) 3 to 4 years, JD/MS 3 to 4 years, JD/PhD.

Clinical program required	No
Legal writing course requirement	Yes
Legal methods course requirement	Yes

Academics

Notre Dame Law School provides "a sense of community that doesn't exist elsewhere," "strong traditions," and a "large network throughout the United States." Arguably its greatest asset, the alumni connection allows students to "go anywhere in the country and find someone who has a link to the school and, more importantly, who is willing to go out of his or her way to help out a fellow Domer." "The school takes its Catholic faith and heritage seriously, and a majority of the student body does as well. Don't come here expecting a watered-down Catholicism."

"Uniformly personable and approachable," "The professors are one of the best things about Notre Dame." "They've ranged from rising stars who have clerked in the Supreme Court, to veteran public officials who came to teaching after years in the Justice Department or White House." "Some of the professors here have a reputation of using the Socratic Method so efficiently [that] they often leave students arguing the opposite of their original point within seconds." However, one 2L observes, "'Conservative' jurisprudential views are more common among the faculty here than at other law schools, and they actually predominate in the student body, but this hasn't kept me from being exposed to a broad range of legal perspectives."

There is general consensus that the administration is disconnected from its students. Categorized by students as "infamously inflexible and unresponsive," "The higher up the administration chain, the less interested they seem to be in the welfare of the students," though in the past year, this has led the administration to make a commitment to improving responsiveness. One particular example of the "administration's ambivalence towards the students," is that they "react poorly to unforeseen contingencies," such as a recent professor shortage that required them to bring an emeritus professor out of retirement to teach a property law class.

Students say that their overall academic experience has been first rate but warn prospective students of the "very conservative nature of the student body." Others note that "there is a surprisingly large percentage of students who hold moderate to liberal views on socially divisive issues which is very refreshing and leads to great discussion in classes such as Con Law."

"Although the school boasts one the most beautiful neo-Gothic facades in the country, the interior leaves much to be desired as much the classrooms and study areas are in need of updating." One student explains, "Notre Dame has history around every corner; unfortunately for many of the students those corners don't come with the amenities of other law schools." The source of particular frustration is the cramped classrooms, as one student illustrates: "There's slightly more room in your seat than there is in coach on a plane." Fortunately, these problems should be alleviated with the construction of the new building, which broke ground in Fall 2007. On a positive note, the building's "two jewels" are its library and courtroom. Students tell us that "the library's main reading room is a wonderful place to study, and its resources are well-proportioned. The courtroom is starting to show its age, but it is still a good place to watch and practice oral arguments."

MARIE BENSMAN, DIRECTOR OF ADMISSIONS AND FINANCIAL AID
NOTRE DAME LAW SCHOOL, 112 LAW SCHOOL, NOTRE DAME, IN 46556
TEL: 574-631-6626 FAX: 574-631-5474
E-MAIL: LAWADMIT@ND.EDU • INTERNET: WWW.LAW.ND.EDU

Life

Students agree that "there isn't any of the unsavory competitiveness you might find in other places." In fact, "Most schools only say their students are non-cutthroat; here, the administration practically makes it mandatory. NDLS doesn't rank students, there is no forced curve, and OCI interviews are based off of a lottery system rather than class rank." "Plus the relatively small class size ensures that you know almost everyone in your class (if not the whole law school!) and that makes the whole experience very enjoyable."

"Thanks to Fightin' Irish football, Notre Dame may be the one law school where even a 1L can forget the pain of first year, if only for a few hours on Saturdays in the fall." "Most students participate in intramural sports like flag football and softball. Nearly all students participate in the springtime bowling league, which promises kegs of beer and tons of laughs." One student describes the makeup of the study body very simply: "There are two predominate social groups at NDLS: (1) single and fun loving, who frequent the handful of bars in South Bend and have fun doing so, and (2) married with children who have a great community of fellowship, babysitting arrangements, Bible studies, and general fun neighborhood-type activities." All in all, students are very close. One 3L concludes, "South Bend is not a particularly nice city, so Notre Dame students have to make their own fun [and] we do a pretty good job."

Getting In

Applicants are encouraged to take the LSAT in June, September/October or December in the year preceding enrollment, as doing so provides the advantage of receiving full consideration for fellowship assistance. Admitted students at the 25th percentile have an LSAT score of 164 and a GPA of 3.3. Admitted students at the 75th percentile have an LSAT score of 167 and a GPA of 3.7. It is NDLS policy to review the highest LSAT score when an applicant has taken the LSAT more than once within a five-year period.

Legal research course requirement	Yes
Moot court requirement	Yes
Public interest law requirement	No

ADMISSIONS

Selectivity Rating	**91**
# applications received	3,502
# applicants accepted	853
# acceptees attending	198
Average LSAT	166
LSAT Range	164–167
Average undergrad GPA	3.5
Application fee	$55
Regular application	3/1
Regular notification	Rolling
Rolling notification	Yes
Early application program	Yes
Early application deadline	11/1
Early application notification	12/15
Transfer students accepted	Yes
Evening division offered	No
Part-time accepted	No
LSDAS accepted	Yes

Applicants Also Look At
Boston College, Boston University, Duke University, The George Washington University, Georgetown University, University of Michigan, Vanderbilt University.

International Students
TOEFL required of international students	Yes

FINANCIAL FACTS

Annual tuition	$33,670
Books and supplies	$6,850
Room and board	$7,250
Financial aid application deadline	2/15
% of aid that is merit based	95
% receiving scholarships	66
Average grant	$13,455
Average debt	$82,409

EMPLOYMENT INFORMATION

		Grads Employed by Field (%)	
Career Rating	**95**		
Rate of placement (nine months out)	99	Academic	2
Average starting salary	$105,000	Business/Industry	5
State for bar exam	IL	Government	12
Pass rate for first-time bar	93	Judicial clerkships	10
Employers Who Frequently Hire Grads		Military	1
Major law firms in locations throughout the country and abroad, judges at all levels, government agencies, corporations and public interest organizations.		Private practice	65
		Public Interest	5

UNIVERSITY OF OKLAHOMA
COLLEGE OF LAW

INSTITUTIONAL INFORMATION

Public/private	Public
Student-faculty ratio	12:1
% faculty part-time	30
% faculty female	31
% faculty minority	11
Total faculty	62

SURVEY SAYS...

Great research resources
Great library staff
Beautiful campus

STUDENTS

Enrollment of law school	501
% male/female	55/45
% out-of-state	16
% full-time	100
% minority	24
Average age of entering class	24

ACADEMICS

Academic Experience Rating	**81**
Profs interesting rating	74
Profs accessible rating	80
Hours of study per day	4.21

Academic Specialties

Civil procedure, commercial law, constitutional law, corporation securities law, criminal law, environmental law, intellectual property law, international law, labor law, property, taxation, Native American law.

Combined Degrees Offered

JD/MBA 4 years, JD/MPH 4 years, JD/generic dual degree 4 years.

Clinical program required	No
Legal writing course requirement	Yes
Legal methods course requirement	No
Legal research course requirement	Yes
Moot court requirement	Yes
Public interest law requirement	No

Academics

"An incredible, first-class facility" is one of the most appealing aspects of the University of Oklahoma College of Law. Chief new features of the remodeled law school building include: "A new library and a new state-of-the-art courtroom, which has brought several appellate courts, including the *en banc* Tenth Circuit, to hold hearings at OU, video conferencing capabilities in the classrooms [that] make distance learning from specialized lawyers possible, in-house clinical facilities, and a designated lab for writing and research." The recent expansion and renovation is just the tip of the iceberg. According to one student, "The administration is committed to shaking down the alumni to continue to build up OU's facilities as well as its scholarship fund."

Posh surroundings might make the school a comfortable place to study, but its professors are what garner the most unequivocal student praise. These dedicated professionals are both knowledgeable and accessible: they're "always wandering the halls talking to students outside of class." It's worth noting that OU students describe their law professors in terms seldom (if ever) uttered about any law professor anywhere: Namely, "Our professors are so cool." One first-year student reports that his professors for constitutional law and torts "both play in bands"—one "actually invited our section to come and hear his jazz band play, and they were good." Savvy recruitment has something to do with the presence of such uncommon law professors. "As far as the professors go we have some hidden gems at our law school, which in large part is due to our Dean, Andrew Coats. We have brought in some incredible professors, especially bright and engaging women," a contingent one student sees missing at other schools. The addition of these "new, young professors in the past few years has been an invaluable addition to the school, providing instruction from varied backgrounds from throughout the country." Students can easily get to know these brilliant young minds because "Small sections provide very good access to faculty." The administration earns equally high marks: administrators are "open to suggestions by students who wish to begin new programs or expand the curriculum in a new direction. Innovation, enthusiasm, and activism by the student body is both encouraged and appreciated."

As far as career planning goes, student opinion is divided. While some think that "our Career Services Office could be better funded in order to assist the students in finding the best career, not just a job," others contend that the "College of Law offers outstanding career opportunities within the Midwest and Southwest, but . . . is only slowly gaining the national prominence needed to place well outside of these regions."

KATHIE G. MADDEN, ADMISSIONS COORDINATOR
ANDREW M. COATS HALL, 300 TIMBERDELL ROAD, NORMAN, OK 73019
TEL: 405-325-4728 FAX: 405-325-0502
E-MAIL: KMADDEN@OU.EDU • INTERNET: WWW.LAW.OU.EDU

Life

While small size might be a boon to students in the classroom, it can be a bit of a problem outside of it. At OU "The student body is so small and spends so much time around each other that we often morph into high school students, including the rumor mill." This cliquishness "can be disappointing to see in aspiring professionals, but also teaches you to watch your step and remember that your colleagues are going to be observing your actions [when] forming their opinions of you." Unlike many law school student bodies, "OU's student community encourages us to work hard and excel, but doesn't have the issues with 'gunner' students who will do anything to succeed." Most students agree that "the student body on the whole possesses the proper balance between commitment to academic excellence and being a normal well-rounded person with a life outside of law school." Politically, "The student population is somewhat conservative," but "The classrooms are full of debate, and everyone is treated fairly."

There are "lots of clubs" at OU and "student organization participation is excellent." "There is never a shortage of social events hosted by someone affiliated with the law school," and the "Halloween party" and "Law School Prom" are popular events. Off-campus entertainment options are also plentiful, as the school is within easy reach of Oklahoma City.

Getting In

Admission to OU is "highly competitive," with just over a quarter of applicants accepted. The average GPA of accepted students last year was 3.51, and the average LSAT score was 157. Both GPA and LSAT score are large factors in admissions, but so are personal statements and letters of recommendation. The school's website states that "in addition to giving considerable weight to the LSAT and undergraduate grade point average, the Admissions Committee also examines the other more personal variables of motivation, character, and capability. Insight into these variables can be derived from a careful examination of your resume, personal statement, and other contents in the file."

ADMISSIONS

Selectivity Rating	83
# applications received	1,055
# applicants accepted	341
# acceptees attending	164
Average LSAT	157
LSAT Range	154–160
Average undergrad GPA	3.57
Application fee	$50
Regular application	3/15
Regular notification	Rolling
Rolling notification	Yes
Early application program	No
Transfer students accepted	Yes
Evening division offered	No
Part-time accepted	No
LSDAS accepted	Yes

Applicants Also Look At
Baylor University, Oklahoma City University, Southern Methodist University, Texas Tech University, Texas Wesleyan University, The University of Texas at Austin, The University of Tulsa.

International Students
TOEFL required of international students	No
TOEFL recommended of international students	No

FINANCIAL FACTS
Annual tuition (resident)	$10,198
Annual tuition (nonresident)	$20,127
Books and supplies	$950
Room and board (on/off-campus)	$13,751/$15,185
Financial aid application deadline	3/1
% first-year students receiving some sort of aid	89
% receiving some sort of aid	89
% of aid that is merit based	63
% receiving scholarships	76
Average grant	$2,500
Average loan	$18,277
Average total aid package	$18,500
Average debt	$63,868

EMPLOYMENT INFORMATION

Career Rating	77	Grads Employed by Field (%)	
Rate of placement (nine months out)	94	Academic	2
Average starting salary	$62,163	Business/Industry	18
State for bar exam	OK, TX, GA, MO, KS	Government	13
Pass rate for first-time bar	98	Judicial clerkships	3
Employers Who Frequently Hire Grads		Military	2
McAfee and Taft; Crowe and Dunlevy;		Private practice	57
Conner and Winters; Gable and Gotwals;		Public Interest	5
Hall, Estill, Hardwick, Gable, and Nelson.			

Prominent Alumni
Frank Keating, former Governor of Oklahoma; David L. Boren, president of OU, former U.S. Senator; William T. Comfort, president, CitiCorp Venture Capital.

UNIVERSITY OF OREGON
SCHOOL OF LAW

INSTITUTIONAL INFORMATION

Public/private	Public
Student-faculty ratio	7:1
% faculty part-time	54
% faculty female	42
% faculty minority	13
Total faculty	72

SURVEY SAYS...

Great research resources
Liberal students
Beautiful campus

STUDENTS

Enrollment of law school	536
% male/female	58/42
% out-of-state	61
% full-time	100
% minority	20
% international	2
Average age of entering class	25

ACADEMICS

Academic Experience Rating	**82**
Profs interesting rating	82
Profs accessible rating	89
Hours of study per day	4.81

Academic Specialties

Appropriate dispute resolution, business law, civil procedure, commercial law, constitutional law, corporation securities law, criminal law, environmental law, government services, human rights law, intellectual property law, international law, property, taxation.

Advanced Degrees Offered

The University of Oregon School of Law offers a 2-year master's degree program in conflict and dispute resolution. We will also be offering an LLM degree in environmental and natural resources law in 2007–2008.

Combined Degrees Offered

JD/MBA 4 years, JD/MA (environmental studies) or JD/MS (environmental studies) 4 years, JD/MA (international studies) 4 years, JD/MA (conflict resolution) or JD/MS (conflict resolution), 4 years.

Academics

The University of Oregon School of Law offers a "diverse" and "amazing" array of opportunities "to see what practice is like before getting out into the field." The school has "a strong pro bono and public interest program." It's also a "great school" for ocean and coastal or environmental law. Students in the "fantastic" clinics get a chance to help to advance cutting-edge and previously untested legal theories. Every year, the Public Interest Environmental Law Conference is "an unbelievable mash-up of activists and public interest attorneys." The Center for Law and Entrepreneurship works to "integrate the Portland campus into business law study." A litany of other clinics is available as well. Despite the breadth of hands-on opportunities, students gripe that UO Law could "offer a few more practical courses" and "use a bit more diversity in the classes offered."

"The course work is challenging" but the "intelligent and often quirky" professors are "supportive and enthusiastic." "They have high expectations while demonstrating genuine interest in students," reports one student. "The business law professors are fantastic," although "A couple of professors are extremely confusing and hard to follow." Nearly all professors here are "excellent teachers." "Overall, I'd say B-plus," assesses a 3L. "Stimulating class discussions about a wide variety of topics" are the norm. Also, "the entire faculty" is "very approachable outside of class" and "willing to help." "Oregon is probably one of the most liberal schools" anywhere and some note that "the liberal bias in the faculty is rather extreme"—a good or bad thing depending on your perspective. The "friendly" and "helpful" administration is also "very approachable" and "singularly focused on making law school the smoothest experience possible for the students." However, registration "is a work in progress." "The course scheduling" is "routinely disappointing," and "popular classes" are "too small."

UO grads face a highly competitive local job market. Some students find that "it is harder to find a job in Oregon than elsewhere" since Portland is "a desirable place to live," and the big Portland firms can "easily" import new attorneys from other states. Also, "A lot of students come here thinking they will return to their home state, but end up wanting to stay." "Opportunities for jobs and externships are particularly limited" in the surrounding college town of Eugene. "Our removed location makes it more difficult to network in other areas of Oregon," advises a 3L. "Many students need to relocate during the summers or commute during the school year for the better jobs."

The "new" building here is "gorgeous" and "very well designed," "allow[ing] for lots of light." "Students enjoy spending time at the school and the common area acts as a social meeting place," says one student. The facility is "super wired" and generally "a great place to have classes." "State-of-the-art" classrooms provide "the ability to do multimedia presentations." A student explains, "Many faculty members have added multimedia aspects to class to enhance lessons, aid understanding, and even entertain. (One professor shows clips of *The Simpsons* and *Saturday Night Live* to illustrate the rules of evidence)."

Life

UO Law is "small," and students appreciate the "congenial atmosphere." "The school has the feel of a small community within the larger UO campus," notes one student. The student body is "fun but serious, and many are committed to making positive social change through the law." There are "lots of very active minority student groups," and "Lots of students are California transplants." "There certainly is a competitive environment but in a good way" due to the "strong feeling of getting through this together rather

LAWRENCE SENO JR., ASSISTANT DEAN OF ADMISSIONS
1221 UNIVERSITY OF OREGON, EUGENE, OR 97403-1221
TEL: 541-346-3846 FAX: 541-346-3984
E-MAIL: ADMISSIONS@LAW.UOREGON.EDU • INTERNET: WWW.LAW.UOREGON.EDU

than competing against one another." What's more is that "even the most alpha and turbo students can't help but be calmed by the surrounding community's hippie culture." "The cooperative spirit among the students is pretty amazing," says an awed 2L. "When you need to miss class, students are very happy to provide notes or to pass along outlines or answer questions."

"Student groups are very active on campus," but life "behind the Granola Curtain" in "very small" Eugene, Oregon is "laid-back." There are "cultural activities" and "big-name music performances throughout the year," but "Eugene is not a glamorous town." "Don't come here if you are looking for a cosmopolitan experience," warns one student. However, "The great thing about Oregon is there are several ways to disconnect yourself from the inherent stress." While "It would be fair to classify UO as a 'party law school,'" students here "are very outgoing, and there's always something you could do on any night of the week." "Most social events include alcohol, and UO students are serious about fitting in time for social gatherings." Also, the "geographically breathtaking location" affords "biking trails, hills to climb, [and] outdoor activities galore."

Getting In

When applying to a strong law program located in a gorgeous setting, expect some competition. Oregon's admitted students at the 25th percentile have LSAT scores of 157 and GPAs of 3.08. Admitted students at the 75th percentile have LSAT scores of 161 and GPAs of 3.63.

Clinical program required	No
Legal writing	
course requirement	Yes
Legal methods	
course requirement	No
Legal research	
course requirement	Yes
Moot court requirement	No
Public interest	
law requirement	No

ADMISSIONS

Selectivity Rating	**80**
# applications received	2,015
# applicants accepted	807
# acceptees attending	178
Average LSAT	159
LSAT Range	157–161
Average undergrad GPA	3.41
Application fee	$50
Regular application	3/1
Regular notification	Rolling
Rolling notification	Yes
Early application program	No
Transfer students accepted	Yes
Evening division offered	No
Part-time accepted	No
LSDAS accepted	Yes

Applicants Also Look At
Lewis & Clark College, Seattle University, University of California—Hastings, University of Colorado, University of Denver, University of Washington, Willamette University.

International Students

TOEFL required	
of international students	Yes
Minimum paper TOEFL	600
Minimum computer TOEFL	250

FINANCIAL FACTS

Annual tuition (resident)	$18,690
Annual tuition	
(nonresident)	$23,262
Books and supplies	$1,600
Room and board	
(off-campus)	$7,524
Financial aid application	
deadline	3/1
% first-year students	
receiving some sort of aid	89
% receiving some sort of aid	95
% receiving scholarships	50
Average grant	$3,872
Average loan	$23,763
Average total aid package	$25,355
Average debt	$62,177

EMPLOYMENT INFORMATION

Career Rating	**75**
Rate of placement (nine months out)	93
Average starting salary	$58,738
State for bar exam	OR, CA, WA, NY, DC
Pass rate for first-time bar	80

Employers Who Frequently Hire Grads
Lane County and Portland-area state and trial courts; Oregon Department of Justice; Washington Attorney General's Office, Western Prosecutor and Public Defender Offices.

Prominent Alumni
Ron Wyden, U.S. Senator; former Chief Judge Alfred T. Goodwin, U.S. Court of Appeals, 9th Circuit; Jim Carter, VP and general counsel, Nike; Matthew McKeown, Acting Assistant Attorney General, Environmental Resources, U.S. Dept. of Justice; Katherine Gurun, former VP and general counsel, Bechtel Corporation.

Grads Employed by Field (%)

Academic	1
Business/Industry	10
Government	14
Judicial clerkships	13
Military	1
Private practice	48
Public Interest	13

UNIVERSITY OF THE PACIFIC
McGEORGE SCHOOL OF LAW

INSTITUTIONAL INFORMATION

Public/private	private
Student-faculty ratio	13:1
% faculty part-time	37
% faculty female	39
% faculty minority	16
Total faculty	76

SURVEY SAYS...

Diverse opinions accepted in classrooms
Great library staff
Beautiful campus

STUDENTS

Enrollment of law school	1,043
% male/female	52/48
% out-of-state	21
% full-time	62
% minority	10
% international	1
# of countries represented	13
Average age of entering class	24

ACADEMICS

Academic Experience Rating	**79**
Profs interesting rating	76
Profs accessible rating	78
Hours of study per day	4.33

Academic Specialties

Advocacy and dispute resolution, criminal law, environmental law, government services, intellectual property law, international law, property, taxation.

Advanced Degrees Offered

JD 3 to 4 years, JSD (international water law), LLM (transnational business practice) 1 year, LLM (international law) 1 year, LLM (government and public policy) 1 year, LLM (teaching of advocacy).

Combined Degrees Offered

JD/MBA 4 years, JD/MPPA 4 years, JD/MA or MS 4 years.

Clinical program required	No
Legal writing course requirement	Yes

Academics

Located in the capital of the Golden State, the University of the Pacific McGeorge School of Law offers a modern, pragmatic, and rigorous legal education to over 1,000 future lawyers. Practical experience is fundamental to instruction at McGeorge. One 2L writes, "Every single one of my professors has actually practiced law at some point in his or her career, and so I know that the advice and insight is actually meaningful and not just theoretical." On top of that, every student is required to successfully complete a rigorous program in legal writing and research. Also, "The appellate and international advocacy programs are very good. Both courses are challenging for second-year students but prepare students well for the everyday practice of law with their emphasis on brief writing and oral argument." Real-world experiences are also emphasized outside the classroom. Crediting the school's favorable location, law students report that "the availability and ease with which students are able to obtain externships is fantastic!" In addition, almost every student singles out for praise the school's "excellent study abroad programs, and excellent moot court and mock trial competition teams."

With a sizable student body, McGeorge is able to offer "one of the broadest curricula in the nation," boasting more than "140 courses and 6 specializations." Even so, McGeorge students must complete a high number of required classes to receive the JD, the majority of which, we are told, are both rigorous and challenging. A 3L insists, "McGeorge is one of the harder, more disciplined law programs." In fact, students inform us that in the first year you can expect "an average of six to eight hours a day of reading." But there's a light at the end of the tunnel. On that note, students claim that despite the challenges, classes are extremely stimulating and well worth the effort you put in. A 2L writes, "This has been the most difficult, yet rewarding academic experience of my life." On top of that, the faculty is readily available to help students who are struggling with the material.

"The administration is working to improve the quality of education and the image of the school," and many tell us that the "school has been steadily beautified and upgraded." In general, students are pleased to report that the administration "is aggressively reshaping itself academically and physically to be a more recognized (and higher-rated) law school." At the same time, a number of students express concerns that "the administration at McGeorge has become overly focused on improving the school's reputation and has lost sight of its most important commodity: its students." Students do feel that the dean listens and responds to their concerns, however. "With the arrival of Dean Parker, whose first year was my first year," writes one 3L, "every needed improvement was put on a 'to do' list, and she is getting things done. She has been relentless; no detail [is] too small, and the school continues to improve in all aspects."

Students assure us that, "within the Northern California legal community, McGeorge is known for producing top-rate practicing attorneys," and students are able to find excellent jobs, especially in-state. A 3L explains, "Many of the local employers know that even though other schools may have a better GPA, a McGeorge graduate has the good foundation and is ready to hit the ground running, rather than needing extensive training." While the school's connections run deepest within hometown Sacramento, McGeorge alumni currently practice in every state in the nation.

ADAM W. BARRETT, DEAN OF ADMISSIONS
3200 FIFTH AVENUE, SACRAMENTO, CA 95817
TEL: 916-739-7105 FAX: 916-739-7134
E-MAIL: ADMISSIONSMCGEORGE@PACIFIC.EDU • INTERNET: WWW.MCGEORGE.EDU

Life

With such demanding course work, it is no surprise that some McGeorge students can be rather competitive in the classroom. Students insist, however, that friendliness overrides any of the negative implications of their academic rivalries. "McGeorge students are competitive, but there manages to be a collegial attitude despite the competitiveness." A 3L likewise reasons, "Obviously you can't take the competitive nature out of law school entirely, but there is a general feeling of goodwill and friendship toward your fellow students." For example, "The Bar Review every Thursday night is a well-attended drink fest" held at a different Sacramento location each week. If you are looking for a very close-knit campus community, however, McGeorge will disappoint you. While "people form close relationships with those in their class, the school is too large to feel a real sense of community."

Most students describe their classmates as being slightly more politically conservative, but there's also a healthy balance of liberals to even things out; the school is large enough to promote some difference of opinion and background on campus. A 1L shares, "There are a wide range of student clubs, from the Federalist Society to the Lambda GLBT side." In addition, the school's evening program encourages students of different ages and backgrounds to join the community. When it comes to lifestyle, students approve of affordable Sacramento, telling us that the city "is becoming a great place to live with all new restaurants, lots of culture, and a fun nightlife." However, the school itself is located in a dodgy part of town, described by many as "sort of scary." A small number of students feel safety is an issue, so the school attempts to keep the campus safe, and "The campus police are visible, especially after dark when students are going home."

Getting In

At McGeorge, the most important factors in an admissions decision are a student's previous academic record, LSAT scores, graduate school or post-college career experience, and community service or extracurricular activities. McGeorge also looks for students who might add a diversity of background or perspective to the campus community.

Legal methods	
course requirement	No
Legal research	
course requirement	Yes
Moot court requirement	Yes
Public interest	
law requirement	No

ADMISSIONS

Selectivity Rating	82
# applications received	3,401
# applicants accepted	1,086
# acceptees attending	354
Average LSAT	158
LSAT Range	155–160
Average undergrad GPA	3.42
Application fee	$50
Regular application	5/1
Regular notification	Rolling
Rolling notification	Yes
Early application program	No
Transfer students accepted	Yes
Evening division offered	Yes
Part-time accepted	Yes
LSDAS accepted	Yes

Applicants Also Look At
Loyola Marymount University, Santa Clara University, University of California—Davis, University of California—Hastings, University of San Francisco.

International Students

TOEFL required	
of international students	Yes
Minimum paper TOEFL	550
Minimum computer TOEFL	213

FINANCIAL FACTS

Annual tuition	$32,832
Books and supplies	$950
Tuition per credit	$1,094
Room & board	$16,062
% first-year students	
receiving some sort of aid	95
% receiving some sort of aid	93
% of aid that is merit based	94
% receiving scholarships	35
Average grant	$8,160
Average loan	$27,290
Average total aid package	$34,032
Average debt	$89,982

EMPLOYMENT INFORMATION

Career Rating	**74**	**Grads Employed by Field (%):**	
Rate of placement (nine months out)	98	Academic	8
Average starting salary	$67,935	Business/Industry	14
State for bar exam	CA, NV, HI, OR, DC	Government	24
Pass rate for first-time bar	73	Judicial clerkships	3
Employers Who Frequently Hire Grads		Other	2
National and California law firms; federal and California state agencies; Sacramento County DA and PD.		Private practice	47
		Public Interest	2
Prominent Alumni			
Scott Boras, sports agent, baseball; Bill Lockyer, California Attorney General; Steve Martini, novelist; Johnnie Rawlinson, U.S. Court of Appeals, 9th Circuit; Consuelo M. Callahan, U.S.Court of Appeals, 9th Circuit.			

UNIVERSITY OF PENNSYLVANIA
LAW SCHOOL

INSTITUTIONAL INFORMATION

Public/private	Private
Student-faculty ratio	11:1
% faculty part-time	51
% faculty female	28
% faculty minority	12
Total faculty	125

SURVEY SAYS...

Diverse opinions accepted
in classrooms
Great research resources
Great library staff
Abundant externship/internship/
clerkship opportunities

STUDENTS

Enrollment of law school	777
% male/female	55/45
% out-of-state	85
% full-time	100
% minority	34
% international	4
# of countries represented	23
Average age of entering class	24

ACADEMICS

Academic Experience Rating	**94**
Profs interesting rating	88
Profs accessible rating	88
Hours of study per day	4.19

Academic Specialties

Civil procedure, commercial law, constitutional law, corporation securities law, criminal law, environmental law, government services, human rights law, intellectual property law, international law, labor law, legal history, legal philosophy, property, taxation.

Advanced Degrees Offered

JD 3 years, LLM 1 year, SJD 1 year, LLCM 1 year.

Combined Degrees Offered

JD/MBA 4 years, JD/MA or PhD 4+ years, JD/MA or PhD 6 years, JD/PhD 6 years, JD/MA 3+ years, JD/MCP 4 years, JD/MSW 4 years, JD/MBioethics 3 years, JD/MD, JD/MA 3 years, JD/MS 4 years, JD/MA/MS 4 years, JD/PhD 6 years.

Academics

The University of Pennsylvania attracts the big legal names you would expect to find at an Ivy League school; however, it is also a true teaching college, where classroom excellence is taken seriously. You won't sleep through any dry lectures at Penn. The Socratic Method will keep you on your toes, and "Most of the professors are great teachers and make class fun." How fun can law school be? A current student insists, "It feels more like I'm going to see a stand-up comedian than a law professor at some points." Penn's teaching staff excels at being both "ridiculously accomplished and truly happy to have a lot of student interaction." Outside the classroom, "Professors are available to meet with students, and it is tradition for all 1Ls to have lunch with their professors at some point during the semester." Guiding their students professionally, personally, and academically, professors "teach us more than legal scholarship; they elevate us from disorganized, arrogant, first-year students into fine, sophisticated, and yet tough advocates."

In addition to the prestige carried by Penn's well-established name, law students benefit from their association with the university in other ways. Adding uniqueness and depth to their JD, "Most students take law-related classes at some of Penn's other graduate schools." For those with a specific academic interest, the school offers "a series of 'certificate' programs offered in conjunction with other schools, including a certificate from the Wharton School of Business and a certificate in Politics from the Fels Institute of Government." Students further augment traditional legal course work by participating in the school's legal journals and clinics, including the Interdisciplinary Child Advocacy Clinic, the Entrepreneurship Legal Clinic, and the Legislative Clinic. The only gripe that many Penn students express is with the first-year legal writing program. While some report positive experiences, many complain that the program is of poor quality and "instructed by third-year law students that often don't have a lot of real-world experience outside of the summer clerking opportunities."

Penn's administration receives gold stars for friendliness, effectiveness, and accessibility. Highly responsive to student concerns, "If you ever have a problem with anything, relate it to an administrator and expect to have it either fixed or about to be fixed." In particular, "The Associate Dean of Student Affairs is a much-loved character around the law school and is the highly accessible 'point man' for anyone and everyone's problems." This friendly attitude permeates campus, and students likewise promote a supportive and noncompetitive atmosphere. "A common phrase around the law school is 'feel the love,' because you do. The students here are a very cooperative, social bunch," insists a 1L. Students surmise that the non-competitive attitude is partially due to the fact that "there is no ranking and no formal GPA at Penn," so students aren't pitted against each other to win choice jobs. On the contrary, "Students freely share notes and study together for finals." When it's time to consider life after graduation, "The school has an incredible Career Services Program," and "Everyone gets a top-tier job. Everyone." On the other hand, those looking for public interest or judicial internships find their desires slightly suffocated in this "pre-professional wonderland."

Life

Penn promotes a well-balanced lifestyle, attracting students who "want to enjoy their time at law school as well as get an excellent education." Campus is a hub of activity, and "The central courtyard really pulls the school together, especially when there are kegs out there." After class, "People spend hours hanging out at school, chatting and doing crossword puzzles." As they spend many hours confined to such close quarters, students admit, "Sometimes it's tiring to hang out with only law students, and a small community of law students at that. Penn Law doesn't do much to encourage mingling with other grad schools at Penn." However, the vast majority of Penn students feel that "law school is a social paradise—there is always plenty to drink and plenty people willing to drink with you!" Indeed, "There is almost always a law school group holding an event or happy hour on any given weekend (except for maybe finals)—the school encourages students to get away from studying and have a real life."

Penn students enjoy the school environment, telling us "Philadelphia can be 'gritty,' but there is a lot to do in the city, and the campus itself is clean and safe." Students also mention, "Philadelphia is now attracting more and more grad students and young professionals. If hanging out with other law students isn't your thing, there are plenty of people around; you just have to find them yourself."

Getting In

Last year, the University of Pennsylvania received more than 5,500 applications for an entering class of 249 students. The entering class had a median LSAT score of 170 and a median GPA of 3.7. Fifteen percent already held graduate degrees before entering law school, whereas 33 percent enrolled directly from college. Penn evaluates an applicant's entire academic history, including grade trends and rigor of course work. The Admissions Committee also evaluates a candidate's writing ability, as well as leadership experience, personal background, and achievements.

Clinical program required	No
Legal writing course requirement	Yes
Legal methods course requirement	Yes
Legal research course requirement	Yes
Moot court requirement	No
Public interest law requirement	Yes

ADMISSIONS

Selectivity Rating	99
# applications received	6,396
# applicants accepted	801
# acceptees attending	243
Average LSAT	169
LSAT Range	166–171
Average undergrad GPA	3.7
Application fee	$70
Regular application	2/15
Regular notification	Rolling
Rolling notification	Yes
Early application program	Yes
Early application deadline	11/1
Early application notification	12/31
Transfer students accepted	Yes
Evening division offered	No
Part-time accepted	No
LSDAS accepted	Yes

Applicants Also Look At
Columbia University, Georgetown University, Harvard University, New York University.

International Students
TOEFL required of international students	No
TOEFL recommended of international students	No

FINANCIAL FACTS

Annual tuition	$37,020
Books and supplies	$975
Room and board (on/off-campus)	$11,346/$10,346
Financial aid application deadline	3/1
% first-year students receiving some sort of aid	73
% receiving some sort of aid	78
% of aid that is merit based	16
% receiving scholarships	35
Average grant	$13,914
Average loan	$31,500
Average total aid package	$34,800
Average debt	$88,500

EMPLOYMENT INFORMATION

Career Rating	96	Grads Employed by Field (%)	
Rate of placement (nine months out)	99	Business/Industry	2
Average starting salary	$125,000	Government	3
State for bar exam	NY	Judicial clerkships	12
Pass rate for first-time bar	93	Other	1
Employers Who Frequently Hire Grads		Private practice	79
Variety of major corporate law firms nationwide; prestigious national fellowship organizations and public interest organizations; federal and state judges.		Public Interest	2

UNIVERSITY OF PITTSBURGH
SCHOOL OF LAW

INSTITUTIONAL INFORMATION

Public/private	Public
Student-faculty ratio	14:1
% faculty part-time	59
% faculty female	34
% faculty minority	8
Total faculty	143

SURVEY SAYS...
Diverse opinions accepted in classrooms
Great research resources
Great library staff

STUDENTS

Enrollment of law school	731
% male/female	58/42
% out-of-state	40
% full-time	100
% minority	15
% international	2
# of countries represented	5
Average age of entering class	24

ACADEMICS

Academic Experience Rating	**79**
Profs interesting rating	75
Profs accessible rating	80
Hours of study per day	4.14

Academic Specialties
Civil procedure, corporation securities law, environmental law, health law, intellectual property law, international law, taxation.

Advanced Degrees Offered
LLM (for foreign-trained attorneys) 1 year.

Combined Degrees Offered
JD/MPA (law and urban and public administration) 4 years, JD/MPIA (law and international affairs) 4 years; JD/MBA (law and business administration) 3.5 years, JD/MPH (law and public health) 3.5 years, JD/MA (law and medical ethics) 3.5 years, JD/MS (law and public management in conjunction with Carnegie Mellon University) 4 years, JD/MBA (in conjunction with Tepper School Carnegie Mellon University).

Academics

The "underrated" University of Pittsburgh School of Law has "a very good position in the Pittsburgh community" and features a "very strong" faculty. "Legal theory" is here, of course, and so is "real-world application." But there is also "a great deal of emphasis on practical skills such as legal writing, oral arguments, and externships." "Many strong clinical programs" include a tax clinic and a civil practice clinic that focuses on both health law and elder law. A host of "fantastic" certificate programs includes civil litigation and intellectual property. Students interested in international law will find "a strong and effective emphasis" on this area through study abroad opportunities, internships, and classes." There's also Jurist, a very comprehensive legal news and research online service run pretty exclusively by faculty and staff.

Pitt has "a number of highly energetic, brilliant, [and] helpful" professors. "Some members of the faculty are absolutely astounding" and several adjunct professors "are really impressive." "Many of our professors are active practitioners in the fields that they teach, giving students opportunities to participate in ongoing cases and to hear about the issues that are most pressing in the field at that moment," adds a 2L. However, "There are some truly awful professors here too." One student notes that the "younger ones tend to be better." Ultimately though, "almost all" of the professors are "very friendly" and "exceedingly accessible" outside of class. They "will go out of their way to make their vast connections applicable to whatever field you pursue."

Many students say that "aesthetically, Pitt could use an upgrade." The Law School building "sits right in the middle" of Pitt's "urban" campus. While the building "certainly isn't beautiful," one student says, "it isn't as bad as everyone likes to pretend." A 1L offers, "The building as a whole reminds me of a 1970s fort." Classrooms are "laptop friendly" but "can be quite uncomfortable and acoustically flawed," though wireless Internet has just been added to encompass the law school. The "gorgeous" library is the "showcase of the law school" that features a coffee lounge which serves Starbucks and where students can "relax" on "artsy couches."

Students would love to see course registration go "online." Many students tell us that "the administration is incredibly frustrating" and "often seems adrift." They say there is too much "needless bureaucracy." Other students have had a very different experience. They contend that the administration is "open and responsive to student concerns." "The school is small enough that you can get to know someone in the Registrar's Office, Career Services, and the Dean's Office," claims a satisfied 3L. Speaking of Career Services, it "still gets mixed reviews," but students report that "they are working hard at reaching out." Students also say that Pitt is "strong" regionally. If you want to practice law in Pennsylvania or in Washington, DC, "good job opportunities" are abundant, and the alumni network is solid.

Life

Students confide that Western Pennsylvania is "not the most diverse school in the world"; however, the campus has a "clear liberal bent" politically. Many here say that Pitt is "a warm, friendly place to learn." "Even during the first year," one student says, "Students at the school are generally pretty laid-back, friendly, and non-competitive." On the other hand, some find that "people are normal on the outside and freaking out on the inside." "I was really, really surprised at how friendly other students are," gushes a 1L. "If I miss a class I never have a problem getting notes from someone, and students tend to help each other out with research questions."

CHARMAINE C. McCALL, ASSISTANT DEAN FOR ADMISSIONS AND FINANCIAL AID
3900 FORBES AVENUE, PITTSBURGH, PA 15260
TEL: 412-648-1413 FAX: 412-648-1318
E-MAIL: ADMISSIONS@LAW.PITT.EDU • INTERNET: WWW.LAW.PITT.EDU

Outside of class, "There is a great social scene," and "Making friends is fairly easy." The Student Bar Association sponsors "a lot of social events." The 'Burgh is "a cheap city with lots of cultural activities" and it is perennially rated among the best cities in the United States in which to live and work. "Pittsburgh is far more beautiful than people who have never been here would imagine," promises a 1L. There are good bars "right across the street from the law school." "There is tons of cheap . . . housing within walking distance," and "nicer housing" is only "a bus ride away." (If you drive, though, students warn that "parking is a nightmare.") "You absolutely need a car," because many places you'll have to go "are all 15 miles away from each other." But for those that are still unsure, one student suggests: "Drive up Mt. Washington and look down on the Pittsburgh skyline and the rivers, and you'll be convinced."

Getting In

Admitted students at the 25th percentile have LSAT scores of roughly 158 and GPAs of 3.1. Admitted students at the 75th percentile have LSAT scores of about 161 and GPAs of just over 3.6. Pitt's administration says that it will consider your highest score if you take the LSAT multiple times.

Clinical program required	No
Legal writing course requirement	Yes
Legal methods course requirement	No
Legal research course requirement	Yes
Moot court requirement	No
Public interest law requirement	No

ADMISSIONS

Selectivity Rating	83
# applications received	2,369
# applicants accepted	736
# acceptees attending	243
Average LSAT	159
LSAT Range	158–161
Average undergrad GPA	3.4
Application fee	$55
Regular application	3/1
Regular notification	Rolling
Rolling notification	Yes
Early application program	No
Transfer students accepted	Yes
Evening division offered	No
Part-time accepted	No
LSDAS accepted	Yes

Applicants Also Look At
American University, Case Western Reserve University, The George Washington University, Pennsylvania State University, Temple University, University of Maryland, Villanova University.

International Students

TOEFL required of international students	Yes
Minimum paper TOEFL	600
Minimum computer TOEFL	250

FINANCIAL FACTS

Annual tuition (resident)	$20,758
Annual tuition (nonresident)	$29,056
Books and supplies	$1,500
Room and board	$13,780
Financial aid application deadline	3/1
% first-year students receiving some sort of aid	85
% receiving some sort of aid	85
% of aid that is merit based	27
% receiving scholarships	46
Average grant	$10,000
Average loan	$22,680
Average debt	$68,919

EMPLOYMENT INFORMATION

Career Rating	**77**	**Grads Employed by Field (%)**	
Rate of placement (nine months out)	97	Academic	2
Average starting salary	$68,000	Business/Industry	20
State for bar exam	PA, VA, MD, NY, CA	Government	5
Pass rate for first-time bar	90	Judicial clerkships	12
Employers Who Frequently Hire Grads		Military	2
Buchanan, Ingersoll, and Rooney;		Private practice	56
Kirkpatrick and Lockhart, Nicholson		Public Interest	3
Graham; Reed Smith; Morgan, Lewis and			
Bockius; Jones Day; Pepper Hamilton.			
Prominent Alumni			
Richard Thornburg, former U.S. Attorney			
General; Orrin Hatch, U.S. Senator, Utah;			
Honorable Joseph Weis, U.S. Court of			
Appeals, 3rd Circuit.			

UNIVERSITY OF RICHMOND
SCHOOL OF LAW

INSTITUTIONAL INFORMATION

Public/private	Private
Student-faculty ratio	15:1
% faculty part-time	65
% faculty female	40
% faculty minority	7
Total faculty	107

SURVEY SAYS...
Beautiful campus
Students love Richmond, VA

STUDENTS

Enrollment of law school	500
% male/female	53/47
% out-of-state	53
% full-time	100
% minority	10
% international	1
# of countries represented	5
Average age of entering class	24

ACADEMICS

Academic Experience Rating	**86**
Profs interesting rating	83
Profs accessible rating	86
Hours of study per day	4.43

Academic Specialties
Civil procedure, commercial law, constitutional law, corporation securities law, criminal law, environmental law, intellectual property law, international law, labor law, legal history, property, taxation, trial advocacy.

Advanced Degrees Offered
JD 3 years, certification in intellectual property law.

Combined Degrees Offered
JD/MBA 4 years, JD/MURP (urban planning) 4 years, JD/MHA (health administration) 4 years, JD/MSW (social work) 4 years, JD/MPA (public administration) 4 years.

Clinical program required	No
Legal writing course requirement	Yes

Academics

Those looking to receive a first-rate law education while enjoying "Southern hospitality at its finest" would be wise to look into University of Richmond School of Law, where students say "The open dialogue among students and between students and professors is truly special." By all accounts, a "very friendly," "almost family-like" atmosphere prevails at this small school. "It amazes me that I'm able to walk down the hallway and have even professors whose classes I have not taken greet me by name," a satisfied 3L writes. The "well-educated, well-published" faculty members here are "dedicated to bettering their students and compassionate to their needs as individuals." The majority of professors "offer their home numbers and cell phone numbers so that we can call whenever we need help, or even just a little advice."

Professorial love is of the tough variety in the classroom, where students say "the use of the Socratic Method" "can be a bit intimidating," particularly for first-year students, though "It makes class entertaining and ensures that you are prepared," a 1L offers. All students here go through "an outstanding lawyering skills program. During these courses, our legal writing and actual courtroom skills are emphasized in very precise, methodical ways," a 2L writes. If students run into academic difficulties, they can take advantage of Richmond's Academic Success Program, which provides a full-time faculty member to assist students with their course work. The downside to the school's small size is "limited course selection," and "only one section" of most upper-level classes each semester. To expand its offerings, the School of Law partners with other schools within the University of Richmond—for example, the Robins School of Business and the Jepson School of Leadership Studies—to offer students a "diversity of dual degrees" which allows students "to really focus on particular fields of interest."

Richmond enjoys "a tremendous reputation in the Commonwealth of Virginia" and students believe that "the fact that there are so many opportunities for legal experience in Richmond," the state capital, "is a great strength" of the school. "We have access to county, state, and district courts and often have lectures and course[s] taught by Virginia Supreme Court Justices," a sanguine student writes. Many clerkships and externships are made possible through a "highly involved alumni community" in the area and help students to figure out what type of practice they'd like to enter when they graduate. Because many students "fall in love with the city," the school's Career Services Office (CSO) has historically taken a somewhat provincial approach. However, it "recently hired a new dean and two new staff members," and students are beginning to feel that the CSO "has the resources to help any student find a job anywhere in the world."

Administrators are described as "doting," and most maintain an "open-door policy." While there are a few reports of disorganization—"It did take them four tries within a 5-hour period to get our second semester schedule correct," a 1L reports—the vast majority here believe the "personal approach" and lack of red tape transcend the minor difficulties. The "entire campus has wireless Internet access," which allows students to "study anywhere." In addition, "You are provided your own personal study carrel in the library, which functions as a locker and, most importantly, a nice quiet place to study." If students require more incentive to head to the library, "ample" staffing ensures that all customers "find what they are looking for." The student body's biggest complaint is that Richmond is "very underappreciated." "I have friends at Georgetown, UNC, Wake Forest, Duke, NYU, and UVA law schools, and none of them are as happy as I am at Richmond," a 2L boasts.

MICHELLE RAHMAN, ASSOCIATE DEAN FOR ADMISSIONS
LAW SCHOOL ADMISSIONS OFFICE, 28 WESTHAMPTON WAY, UNIVERSITY OF RICHMOND, VA 23173
TEL: 804-289-8189 FAX: 804-287-6516
E-MAIL: LAWADMISSIONS@RICHMOND.EDU • INTERNET: LAW.RICHMOND.EDU

Life

Not only is the University of Richmond campus "one of the most beautiful in the country," it is "surrounded by a safe and pristine neighborhood that is also easily affordable." Adding to the pleasant environment, "Competition among students is healthy and not overwhelming." "I almost enjoy the daily grind of law school when I can so easily relate to my fellow students," a 2L reports. "Little things, like taking lunch breaks at the dining hall or going through flashcards together during exams, [have] helped me find a comfortable niche here." Richmond is "a very social school," and "numerous events and groups meetings" are held "every week." In addition, "The school sponsors monthly happy hours in order to encourage students and faculty/staff to interact," and "There is always the opportunity for free food." The student body can be cliquey, however, "especially if you don't fit in with the pretty and party-oriented mid-20s crowd." Fortunately, "There's plenty to do in Richmond. I went to the opera with one of my friends and his wife," a 2L writes. Bars in the Fan district, "in the heart of Richmond," are very popular with students of all ages.

Diversity is "a big issue" at Richmond. While the school "is making great strides to diversify its student body and faculty," there currently "aren't very many minorities." "It is a little awkward for us (minorities) to adjust at first," a 1L reports. "The professors and students don't really know how to address or interact with us, oftentimes, without trying to seem as if they're treating us differently." A former bastion of conservatism, Richmond is "middle of the road these days, and there is a definite liberal presence on campus."

Getting In

Students frequently mention "the Admissions Office ladies" as a major resource of Richmond. "Literally, if you need a hug, they are there," a 2L reports. Their "personal acceptance phone call" initiates students to an environment in which "Every student is given plenty of attention." The advice the Associate Dean provides at http://law.richmond.edu/admissions/applyingadvice.php is another way in which the staff here goes above and beyond the call of duty.

EMPLOYMENT INFORMATION

Career Rating	79
Rate of placement (nine months out)	98
Average starting salary	$60,719
State for bar exam	NC, NY, FL, VA, DC
Pass rate for first-time bar	87

Employers Who Frequently Hire Grads

Baker Botts; Christian and Barton; Hirschler Fleischer; Hogan and Hartson; Hunton and Williams; Jackson and Kelly; Kaufman and Canoles; Kennedy Covington.

Prominent Alumni

Justice Lawrence L. Koontz, VA Supreme Court; Honorable Harvey E. Schlesinger, U.S. District Court, middle district of FL.

Grads Employed by Field (%)

Academic	1
Business/Industry	8
Government	20
Judicial clerkships	23
Military	2
Private practice	43
Public Interest	3

Legal methods course requirement	Yes
Legal research course requirement	Yes
Moot court requirement	No
Public interest law requirement	No

ADMISSIONS

Selectivity Rating	84
# applications received	1,873
# applicants accepted	626
# acceptees attending	158
Average LSAT	161
LSAT Range	159–162
Average undergrad GPA	3.36
Application fee	$35
Priority application	2/15
Regular notification	4/15
Rolling notification	Yes
Early application program	No
Transfer students accepted	Yes
Evening division offered	No
Part-time accepted	No
LSDAS accepted	Yes

Applicants Also Look At

American University, College of William and Mary, George Mason University, The George Washington University, University of Virginia, Wake Forest University, Washington and Lee University.

International Students

TOEFL required of international students	Yes
Minimum paper TOEFL	650
Minimum computer TOEFL	280

FINANCIAL FACTS

Annual tuition	$28,390
Books and supplies	$1,200
Tuition per credit	$1,420
Room and board (on/off-campus)	$6,376/$9,045
Financial aid application deadline	2/25
% first-year students receiving some sort of aid	78
% receiving some sort of aid	95
% of aid that is merit based	29
% receiving scholarships	75
Average grant	$6,985
Average loan	$30,700
Average total aid package	$32,920
Average debt	$84,690

UNIVERSITY OF SAN DIEGO
SCHOOL OF LAW

INSTITUTIONAL INFORMATION

Public/private	Private
Affiliation	Roman Catholic
Student-faculty ratio	14:1
% faculty part-time	32
% faculty female	38
% faculty minority	11
Total faculty	104

SURVEY SAYS...

Diverse opinions accepted
in classrooms
Beautiful campus
Students love San Diego, CA

STUDENTS

Enrollment of law school	1,035
% male/female	55/45
% out-of-state	31
% full-time	71
% minority	28
Average age of entering class	24

ACADEMICS

Academic Experience Rating	82
Profs interesting rating	85
Profs accessible rating	75
Hours of study per day	4

Academic Specialties

Administrative law, children's advocacy, civil procedure, commercial law, constitutional law, criminal law, environmental law, human rights law, intellectual property law, international law, public interest law, taxation.

Advanced Degrees Offered

JD 3 to 4 years (day), LLM (general, taxation, business and corporate, international, comparative law for foreign attorneys) 1 year.

Combined Degrees Offered

JD/MBA 4 to 4.5 years, JD/MA (international relations) 4 to 4.5 years, JD/IMBA (international master in business administration) 4 to 4.5 years.

Academics

A stalwart Southern California institution, the University of San Diego draws rave reviews for its fine faculty, practical programs, and, of course, weather. A large and diverse program, "USD attracts some of the finest professors from across the country, specializing in criminal law, corporate, international law, and IP." A current student enthuses, "Each professor is unique in their approach to teaching, and because most of them are the brightest minds in their field, they are able to give you the tools you will need to succeed as a practicing attorney." Academically, the "Socratic Method isn't so big at USD" and, on the whole, the curriculum is "conscious of the practical aspects of lawyering, and doesn't obsess over theory." Even so, course work is challenging, and faculty is "helpful and welcoming, yet not afraid to be blunt and mean business." When considering USD, students remind us of the school's Catholic affiliation, telling us that the professors are "rather conservative in their approach to teaching and the law in general." A current student shares, "It's no secret that the legal profession is a liberal one, so USD Law is a refreshing haven for more moderate and right-thinking students."

Despite the practical emphasis, many feel that USD could offer more courses that directly prepare you for the legal profession. For example, "USD offers no classes whatsoever in drafting or licensing, and what courses are offered in interviewing and negotiations are typically oversubscribed 2:1 [or] 3:1." However, those looking for practical experience will find "a multitude of opportunities outside of the classroom that simultaneously offer course credit." For example, the school operates a "competitive mock trial team, which provides very rigorous and thorough training and preparation for future trial practice." Students may also participate in one of "13 clinics in diverse areas that offer hands-on legal experience with a classroom component." A 3L shares, "I never got law school burnout because I was able to work for credit for a nonprofit, a government agency, and a court, which all kept me focused on my future career as a lawyer instead of the daily grind of a law student."

Techies beware: "If you want to go to law school in the twenty-first century, USD may not be for you." The wireless is spotty, many classrooms have no electrical outlets, and all administrative paperwork is actually done on paper (no online registration here). Plus, students point out that the "USD campus is beautiful, but the law school is outdated and needs a massive facelift." A student laments, "USD seems to spend all of their resources on manicuring the lawns and not the actual facilities." On the upside, "The library resources are also unparalleled. There are literally floors of books, journals, microfiches, and other legal resources."

Maybe it's the school's hefty tuition that has USD students dreaming of dollar signs; whatever the reason, "Most students that come to USD seem to be far more focused on fields that make money more than anything else, and the culture is very conservative." Lucky for them, "USD Law is considered the preeminent local law school, so networking and job opportunities abound." In fact, students insist, "This is a very 'hometown' area, and is not welcoming to outsiders. To employers here, USD really is a better school than Harvard."

Life

Beachside living and law school aren't necessarily a natural pair. A student bemoans, "There's nothing like spending three years living next to the beach yet never having time to actually go to the beach." However, students unanimously agree that the mellow San

CARL EGING, ASSISTANT DEAN OF ADMISSIONS AND FINANCIAL AID
5998 ALCALA PARK, SAN DIEGO, CA 92110
TEL: 619-260-4528 FAX: 619-260-2218
E-MAIL: JDINFO@SANDIEGO.EDU • INTERNET: WWW.LAW.SANDIEGO.EDU

Diego atmosphere really reduces the stresses of law school. "Being able to spend a Saturday at the beach or riding your bike or doing something outdoors on a regular basis makes a huge difference in how positive you feel about your life during law school," confesses a current student.

You'll bump into quite a few beamers in the USD parking lot, and students admit the school "has the SoCal rich-kid culture one would expect from a conservative, wealthy, private school with a student body drawn primarily from upper-class kids in and around the LA, OC, and San Diego regions." On the whole, however, "Most people are pleasant and friendly, help each other, and have interests beyond studying." If you want to connect with your classmates, "There are more than enough social opportunities including the famed Bar Review every week. There are also more alumni/networking events than anyone could every find time to attend." Around town, "San Diego is full of young people around my age, and there is always something to do whether it is hanging at the beach, going to the bars, or taking in a Chargers or Padres game." When its time to blow off steam, "San Diego has a great bar scene, and finals aside you'll never be lacking an excuse to go grab a beer."

Getting In

While there are no pre-legal courses required for entry to the USD law program, all applicants must have a bachelor's degree from an accredited college. LSAT scores and GPA are important to an admissions decision, as are the personal qualities and skills demonstrated by your personal statement and letters of recommendation. The 2006–2007 entering class had a median LSAT score of 161 and a median GPA of 3.33.

Clinical program required	No
Legal writing course requirement	Yes
Legal methods course requirement	No
Legal research course requirement	Yes
Moot court requirement	Yes
Public interest law requirement	No

ADMISSIONS

Selectivity Rating	**84**
# applications received	4,820
# applicants accepted	1,518
# acceptees attending	342
Average LSAT	161
LSAT Range	159–164
Average undergrad GPA	3.33
Application fee	$50
Regular application	Rolling
Regular notification	Rolling
Rolling notification	Yes
Early application program	No
Transfer students accepted	Yes
Evening division offered	Yes
Part-time accepted	Yes
LSDAS accepted	Yes

Applicants Also Look At
Loyola Marymount University, Pepperdine University, Santa Clara University, University of California—Davis, University of California—Hastings, University of California—Los Angeles, University of Southern California.

International Students
TOEFL required of international students	Yes
Minimum paper TOEFL	600
Minimum computer TOEFL	250

FINANCIAL FACTS
Annual tuition	$35,700
Books and supplies	$925
Tuition per credit	$1,235
Room and board	$17,884
Financial aid application deadline	3/1
% first-year students receiving some sort of aid	87
% receiving some sort of aid	84
% receiving scholarships	37
Average grant	$17,000
Average loan	$33,942
Average total aid package	$49,500
Average debt	$92,000

EMPLOYMENT INFORMATION

Career Rating	**80**	**Grads Employed by Field (%)**	
Rate of placement (nine months out)	86	Academic	2
Average starting salary	$74,600	Business/Industry	17
State for bar exam	CA, NV, AZ	Government	12
Pass rate for first-time bar	77	Judicial clerkships	2
Employers Who Frequently Hire Grads		Military	1
Gibson Dunn and Crutcher; Latham and		Private practice	61
Watkins; Fish and Richardson; Cooley		Public Interest	5
Godward; DLA Piper; Pillsbury Winthrop;			
Department of Justice.			

Prominent Alumni
Congresswoman Shelley Berkley, Nevada; Frances Townsend, Homeland Security Advisor; Honorable Thomas Whelan, U.S. District Court.

UNIVERSITY OF SAN FRANCISCO
SCHOOL OF LAW

Academics

A pretty, private school with a relaxed California attitude, University of San Francisco is a remarkably accommodating and comfortable place to study law. While course work is rigorous, students appreciate the small class sizes as well as the personal relationships they develop with the teaching and administrative staff. So while you may expect all the typical challenges of law school at USF, you never have to worry about being singled out or sabotaged. A 1L shares, "All my professors are amazing in their respective ways and foster a comfortable learning atmosphere, which was quite a departure from the horror stories I heard about the first year." Another adds, "Professors are all experienced both in the classroom and in practice. This faculty is more impressive than I had expected, but there's no pretension."

Outside of the lecture hall, students feel at ease with their accomplished teachers, turning to them as mentors and friends. Students maintain that "more than anything, the faculty and staff want to see you succeed" and that professors "make themselves available at all times and always take extra time in answering your questions." Such close interactions aren't restricted to the classroom or office hours, either: "I have shared numerous meals, drinks, and laughs with professors who treat me like a colleague," recalls one seasoned 3L.

With this kind of precedent set by the faculty, the whole campus follows suit, creating a learning atmosphere that is decidedly intimate and cooperative. At USF, "Students are supportive and down to earth . . . the librarians offer great advice, and the facilities are pleasant and comfortable to be in." On that note, "all the facilities are brand spanking new, and the views from the library and the lounge are spectacular."

Many students feel that the best part of a USF education is the school's "high emphasis on integrity and public interest law, a commitment to training socially responsible attorneys." In support of its progressive vision, "USF has numerous clinical opportunities through which students are able to gain practical legal experience under faculty and practitioner supervision." Students are active in many political and community issues, such as "closing down the School of the Americas, water resource allocation in the Western United States, and custodial care within the Family Courts." In addition, "Every summer students travel to the Hague to take part in the Human Rights Commission of the United Nations and others travel to the Deep South to take part in defending Death Row inmates." While the school's mission and philosophy may encourage students to seek public interest positions after graduation, many point out that it's difficult to make ends meet in a public service career after graduating from a private law school in pricey San Francisco. Many feel that "considering the crushing debt burden that a USF graduate emerges with, [the school] needs to place more resources toward loan repayment and forgiveness programs in order to ensure that competent young attorneys can feel comfortable going into public interest positions."

Financial worries aside, students have nothing but praise for the USF administration. "Things get done quickly and efficiently." "You don't have to wait in long lines or deal with mean and bitter staff like at so many public institutions." In addition, students applaud the administration for taking "consistent and deliberate steps in increasing the caliber of both the faculty and the facilities." Over the past decade, "The quality of the incoming students [has been] increasing and the profile of the faculty rising."

ALAN GUERRERO, DIRECTOR OF ADMISSIONS
2130 FULTON STREET, SAN FRANCISCO, CA 94117
TEL: 415-422-6586 FAX: 415-422-6433
E-MAIL: LAWADMISSIONS@USFCA.EDU • INTERNET: WWW.LAW.USFCA.EDU

Life

Perched on a hilltop in one of the world's most famous cities, "USF's location in San Francisco gives it a unique vibe as well as exposure to all that the city offers." USF students take advantage of their ideal surroundings through the "weekly bar nights" and report that there are "always a multitude of things to do a heartbeat away: museums, opera, hiking, nightclubs. You name it, San Francisco's got it!" On campus, "The general academic atmosphere is welcoming, not fierce and competitive." A 2L elaborates, "Students are driven, but not out to get each other, and I really appreciate that about the school." In addition, the school boasts a number of campus clubs and activities. A 3L writes that "our politically active student body has started over 15 new student organizations in the last two years, and student-sponsored activities are actively supported by the administration."

USF values a diverse and progressive educational experience, and this attitude is reflected in the student body. "Every class is diverse, not just in terms of race or gender but also in terms of experience and knowledge. I am always learning something new from a fellow classmate," writes one 2L. Students from USF, however, also have some things in common. For example, "The average student has taken time off after college," and the student population tends to be very liberal in their politics, which is not surprising given the school's location and commitment to public service. A 3L warns, "I would not recommend USFSL if you are a militant Rush Limbaugh/Ann Coulter Republican. You will find yourself in a very small minority."

Getting In

University of San Francisco carefully evaluates each applicant's pre-law transcripts and curriculum, admitting students whose undergraduate course work demonstrates success in a broad set of liberal arts courses, as well as an emphasis on oral and written skills. Last year, the school received more than 4,100 applications for just 250 first-year spots. The biggest five feeder undergraduate schools are all members of the University of California system.

EMPLOYMENT INFORMATION

Career Rating	81	
Rate of placement (nine months out)	97	
Average starting salary	$83,000	
State for bar exam	CA	
Pass rate for first-time bar	74	

Employers Who Frequently Hire Grads
Bingham and McCutcheon; Morgan, Lewis and Brockius; Reed Smith; Wilson, Sonsini, Goodrich, and Rosati.

Prominent Alumni
Justice Ming Chin, CA Supreme Court; Honorable Martin Jenkins, U.S. District Court Northern California; Honorable Saundra B. Armstrong, U.S. District Court Northern California.

Grads Employed by Field (%)

Field	%
Academic	1
Business/Industry	11
Government	7
Judicial clerkships	2
Other	6
Private practice	65
Public Interest	8

Public interest law requirement	No

ADMISSIONS

Selectivity Rating	**81**
# applications received	3,090
# applicants accepted	1,031
# acceptees attending	178
Average LSAT	159
LSAT Range	157–161
Average undergrad GPA	3.32
Application fee	$60
Regular application	2/1
Regular notification	Rolling
Rolling notification	Yes
Early application program	No
Transfer students accepted	Yes
Evening division offered	Yes
Part-time accepted	Yes
LSDAS accepted	Yes

Applicants Also Look At
Golden Gate University, Loyola Marymount University, Santa Clara University, University of California—Davis, University of California—Hastings, University of the Pacific, University of San Diego.

International Students

TOEFL required of international students	Yes
Minimum paper TOEFL	600
Minimum computer TOEFL	250

FINANCIAL FACTS

Annual tuition	$32,110
Books and supplies	$900
Fees per credit	$12
Tuition per credit	$1,150
Room and board (on/off-campus)	$10,580/$13,500
Financial aid application deadline	2/15
% first-year students receiving some sort of aid	92
% receiving some sort of aid	90
% of aid that is merit based	15
% receiving scholarships	30
Average grant	$10,950
Average loan	$30,216
Average total aid package	$24,000
Average debt	$92,500

UNIVERSITY OF SOUTH CAROLINA
SCHOOL OF LAW

INSTITUTIONAL INFORMATION

Public/private	Public
Student-faculty ratio	21:1
% faculty female	24
% faculty minority	9
Total faculty	45

SURVEY SAYS...
Diverse opinions accepted
in classrooms
Great library staff

STUDENTS

Enrollment of law school	706
% male/female	58/42
% out-of-state	23
% full-time	100
% minority	10
% international	1
# of countries represented	6
Average age of entering class	24

ACADEMICS

Academic Experience Rating	**79**
Profs interesting rating	77
Profs accessible rating	76
Hours of study per day	4.04

Advanced Degrees Offered
JD 3 years.

Combined Degrees Offered
IMBA (International Master of Business Admininistration) 4 years, MACC (accountancy) 4 years, MCJ (criminal justice) 4 years, MEERM, (earth and environmental resource management) 4 years, MHA (health administration) 4 years, MHR (human resources) 4 years, MPA (public administration) 4 years, MSB (business) 4 years, MSW (social work) 4 years, MSEL (environmental law with Vermont Law School) 4 years.

Clinical program required	No
Legal writing course requirement	Yes
Legal methods course requirement	No

Academics

Deeply enmeshed and dearly loved in the local legal community, the University of South Carolina boasts a prestigious faculty, a well-connected alumni network, and an ultra-friendly staff and student body. At USC, the classroom experience is top of the line, spearheaded by talented professors who are "very accessible and willing to interact with students formally and informally." A student raves, "The faculty really care about teaching and are always available to help explain or give you further enrichment. They are very encouraging, which is very important when you've had a hard day under the Socratic Method!" In addition to the impressive roster of tenured faculty, "The administration has done a great job of recruiting new, more dynamic professors in recent years." The resulting atmosphere is a "welcome mixture of the stuffy old law professors with the young, cutting-edge, recent academics." Even so, the program takes a fairly traditional approach to legal education, and some students say the school should "work on addressing more diverse needs than just the typical needs of the corporate lawyer-to-be."

Students adore the "the collegial, friendly, and open attitude" at USC, assuring us that "the faculty and administration will move mountains to help you make it through to graduation." Fellow students also form an important support network at USC. A 1L elaborates: "We are placed with a group of 12 students that comprise our legal writing class; you are with these students in almost every class your first year. They become like your law school family; everyone watches out for each other." Another adds, "My favorite part about the law school is the collegiality of the students; although there is healthy competition, we truly look out for one another's best interest."

There's no doubt about it: "If you want to be an attorney in South Carolina, this is the best place to be." Smack dab in the middle of the capital, USC is "just blocks away from the state legislature and the state supreme court, as well as to administrative agencies and local government," which offers students "a great opportunity to see the law in action while still in school." When looking for a job or internship, USC students enjoy "a wonderful reputation in the Southeast"; not to mention a corner on the regional market. "Because over 70 percent of the South Carolina Bar attended this law school," the alumni network is beyond compare. If that weren't enough, Career Services does "an excellent job informing us with local and regional opportunities and equipping us with skills to 'land the job' (i.e., interview workshops, resume workshops, and individual evaluations)."

Amidst glowing reviews, students give the school's aging facilities a decisive thumbs-down. Thinking like a future prosecutor, a 2L informs us, "The walls are filled with asbestos. The pipes are filled with lead. Not the smartest place to house a bunch of aspiring lawyers." Another student comments, "Apparently [they] have been planning on building a new one for decades but instead have used duct tape to keep it together. Literally, the window next to me is held up with duct tape." Fortunately, administrators are aware of the duct tape problem, and "The Law School is in the process of fund-raising for its new, top of the line building."

PAUL B. ROLLINS, ASSISTANT DEAN
701 SOUTH MAIN STREET, COLUMBIA, SC 29208
TEL: 803-777-6605 FAX: 803-777-7751
E-MAIL: USCLAW@LAW.SC.EDU • INTERNET: WWW.LAW.SC.EDU

Life

At USC, students enjoy the incomparable combination of an excellent academic program and a stellar social life. Attracting a fun-loving and outgoing student body, "There are very few law students you wouldn't invite to have a beer with after a rough week of classes." When they aren't hitting the books, "There is no shortage of social events at USC." For example, "Students put together tailgates during football season, and SBA puts on great theme parties and a formal [get-together] in the spring." Students also hang out casually, and "It's easy to find law students out every night of the week."

Besides drinking and studying, many students spend their free time participating in clubs, intramural sports, and extracurricular activities. Demonstrating a community-oriented and philanthropic spirit, students organize "massive food-drive competitions with each class donating tens of thousands of pounds of canned goods, and most students donate their study guides and commercial outlines to the Public Interest Law Society's outline bank, which then sells them back to other students at highly discounted rates." Since they end up spending so much time together, students admit that law school is something like "High School II, complete with lockers and gossip, but at least we are old enough to legally drink."

A great mix of cosmopolitan and cozy, hometown Columbia is "small enough to be comfortable but large enough to have opportunities in private and corporate law." Thanks to USC's sizable undergrad and graduate programs, "The area has a 'happenin'" bar scene." More liberal thinkers beware: this Southern school has "a feeling of staunch South Carolina Republicans."

Getting In

At University of South Carolina, the Admissions Committee takes a holistic approach to reviewing applicants. LSAT scores and GPA are important factors among many considered. The Admissions Committee also considers a student's employment and life experiences, residency, letters of recommendation, personal statement, and ability to contribute to a diverse community. In 2006, USC received 1,600 applications for a class of 225 students (500 applicants were successful). The median LSAT score for the class was 159, and the median GPA was 3.4.

EMPLOYMENT INFORMATION		
Career Rating	**65**	
Average starting salary	$63,000	**Grads Employed by Field (%)**
State for bar exam	SC, NC, GA, FL, TX	Business/Industry — 4
Pass rate for first-time bar	89	Government — 12
Employers Who Frequently Hire Grads		Judicial clerkships — 22
Nelson, Mullins, Riley, and Scarborough;		Private practice — 53
Alston and Bird; Haynsworth Sinkler Boyd;		Public Interest — 4
Nexsen Pruet; Womble, Carlyle, Sandridge,		
and Rice.		
Prominent Alumni		
Richard W. Riley, former U.S. Secretary of Education; Lindsay Graham, U.S. Senate; Karren J. Williams, U.S. Court of Appeals, 4th Circuit; Joe Wilson, U.S. Congress.		

Legal research course requirement	Yes
Moot court requirement	No
Public interest law requirement	No

ADMISSIONS

Selectivity Rating	**84**
# applications received	1,609
# applicants accepted	535
# acceptees attending	222
Average LSAT	159
LSAT Range	156–161
Average undergrad GPA	3.43
Application fee	$60
Regular application	4/1
Regular notification	Rolling
Rolling notification	Yes
Early application program	No
Transfer students accepted	Yes
Evening division offered	No
Part-time accepted	No
LSDAS accepted	Yes

International Students

TOEFL required of international students	Yes

FINANCIAL FACTS

Annual tuition (resident)	$15,584
Annual tuition (nonresident)	$31,476
Books and supplies	$838
Room and board (off-campus)	$15,092
Financial aid application deadline	4/15
% receiving some sort of aid	78
% of aid that is merit based	72
% receiving scholarships	24
Average grant	$7,600
Average loan	$8,300
Average total aid package	$23,200
Average debt	$64,203

THE UNIVERSITY OF SOUTH DAKOTA

SCHOOL OF LAW

INSTITUTIONAL INFORMATION

Public/private	Public
Student-faculty ratio	18:1
% faculty part-time	1
% faculty female	26
% faculty minority	1
Total faculty	15

SURVEY SAYS...

Diverse opinions accepted
in classrooms
Great research resources
Great library staff

STUDENTS

Enrollment of law school	235
% male/female	58/42
% out-of-state	32
% full-time	98
% minority	4
Average age of entering class	25

ACADEMICS

Academic Experience Rating	**72**
Profs interesting rating	73
Profs accessible rating	87
Hours of study per day	4.45

Academic Specialties

Environmental law, Indian law.

Combined Degrees Offered

JD/MBA, JD/MPA (professional accountancy), JD/M (education administration), JD/M (English), JD/M (history), JD/M (political science), JD/M (public administration), JD/M (psychology), JD/M (administrative studies).

Clinical program required	No
Legal writing course requirement	Yes
Legal methods course requirement	Yes
Legal research course requirement	Yes
Moot court requirement	No
Public interest law requirement	No

Academics

If you plan to practice law in the Mount Rushmore state, the University of South Dakota is the best place to lay the foundation for your career. If you want to study the law in South Dakota at an ABA-accredited law school, USD is the only place to do it. As such, attending USD has many advantages. Simply put, "USD students have unparalleled access to members of the South Dakota bar." The school's ongoing "relationship with practicing attorneys and judges in the state provides an opportunity for quality hands-on education and guidance." The result of all this is South Dakotan legal interconnectivity. "It is commonplace to find members of the SD Supreme Court, the attorney general, the governor of SD, local politicians, leaders of the various [Native American] nations, SD state bar leaders, and numerous accomplished USD Law alumni walking the halls here." As if that weren't enough, USD offers a unique opportunity: Each spring semester, "The SD Supreme Court holds [its March] session at the USD Law School, taking great care to pick interesting and difficult cases to hear before the student body."

In addition to enhancing their educational experience, the school's legal connections create many opportunities for practice after graduation. A student explains, "South Dakota is a small bar, and the majority of lawyers in SD went to USD, and they look within the state to recruit first." Some feel, however, that the school is too singularly focused on South Dakota and that "students aren't encouraged to look for positions outside of the fall interview days or out of state." Some also feel their career opportunities could be enhanced with the addition of more practical, hands-on opportunities, such as moot court activities and internships.

Reflecting the small population of its home state, USD boasts a tiny student body and a good student/teacher ratio. Students say the small enrollment benefits them because they "get to know teachers and administrators on a much more personal basis." The result is a supportive academic atmosphere in which students look upon faculty and staff as mentors, not just instructors. Here you can expect to be a part of "a small and extremely close-knit community where the faculty and administration have a genuine concern for their students." "Professors take the time to work with us in the academic setting," writes one student, "but are interested in getting to know us personally outside of the classroom as well." Indeed, USD students agree that their professors and classmates have relationships that extend beyond the law. For example, one proud student boasts, "I've played golf with the dean, I've shared single malt scotches with a few professors, and I've spent countless hours discussing my personal life with members of the administration."

The school's affordable price tag is the icing on the cake. Without exception, students describe USD as a great bargain. Some go so far as to say it is "surely one of America's best-kept secrets and a flat-out steal of a legal education." "You cannot beat the price, and the legal instruction is on par, and may even exceed, some of the top schools." With so much to offer for so little cash, it's also not surprising that USD boasts "an extremely low attrition rate."

Jean Henriques, Admission Officer/Registrar
414 East Clark Street, Vermillion, SD 57069-2390
Tel: 605-677-5443 Fax: 605-677-5417
E-mail: Law.School@usd.edu • Internet: www.usd.edu/law

Life

Students describe their classmates as friendly and studious and tell us that the school maintains "a good blend of traditional and nontraditional students." But while "The correct harmony between the 'real' world and the 'academic' world are represented in every class," South Dakota isn't a very ethnically or culturally diverse state. As one student succinctly puts it, "Though USD tries, our student body diversity is sorely lacking." Located in a small town, USD is a tight-knit community where students socialize, study together, and build lasting friendships. In fact, "Law students have been going to the same bar for what seems to be forever, so there is rarely a question of where to find your friends." While most students love the friendly and intimate atmosphere, some would prefer a more cosmopolitan environment. One disgruntled student goes so far as to describe the law school as offering an "overpriced high school atmosphere, under the best of circumstances."

Getting In

The University of South Dakota School of Law seeks students who demonstrate intelligence, a strong desire to practice law (especially in the state of South Dakota), and commitment to helping others through legal advocacy. You are a competitive applicant with a solid B undergraduate GPA and an LSAT score above 153.

ADMISSIONS

Selectivity Rating	**74**
# applications received	445
# applicants accepted	164
# acceptees attending	71
Average LSAT	153
LSAT Range	151–155
Average undergrad GPA	3.37
Application fee	$35
Regular application	Rolling
Regular notification	Rolling
Rolling notification	Yes
Early application program	No
Transfer students accepted	Yes
Evening division offered	No
Part-time accepted	Yes
LSDAS accepted	Yes

Applicants Also Look At
Creighton University, Drake University, Hamline University, Thomas M. Cooley Law School, University of North Dakota, The University of Tulsa, University of Wyoming.

International Students

TOEFL required	
of international students	Yes
Minimum paper TOEFL	600
Minimum computer TOEFL	250

FINANCIAL FACTS

Annual tuition (resident)	$4,364
Annual tuition (nonresident)	$12,647
Books and supplies	$1,300
Fees per credit (resident)	$132
Fees per credit (nonresident)	$132
Tuition per credit (resident)	$145
Tuition per credit (nonresident)	$422
Room and board (on/off-campus)	$4,373/$6,323
% first-year students receiving some sort of aid	89
% receiving some sort of aid	90
% of aid that is merit based	90
% receiving scholarships	20
Average grant	$2,631
Average loan	$19,278
Average total aid package	$19,291
Average debt	$51,636

EMPLOYMENT INFORMATION

Career Rating	**66**
Rate of placement (nine months out)	89
Average starting salary	$38,251
State for bar exam	SD, IA, MN, CO, NV

Employers Who Frequently Hire Grads
U.S. Court of Appeals, 8th Circuit; U.S. District Court; South Dakota Supreme Court; South Dakota Circuit Court; Minnehaha Public Defender, firms.

Prominent Alumni
Tim Johnson, U.S. Senator; Chief Justice David Gilbertson, SD Supreme Court; Justice Judith Meierhenry, SD Supreme Court.

Grads Employed by Field (%)

Academic	2
Business/Industry	11
Government	13
Judicial clerkships	24
Military	2
Private practice	40
Public Interest	8

UNIVERSITY OF SOUTHERN CALIFORNIA
GOULD SCHOOL OF LAW

Academics

The University of Southern California's Gould School of Law offers students "an excellent legal education on a beautiful campus in the middle of one of the most vibrant, diverse, and exciting cities in the world." "USC seems to cover it all," proclaims a 3L: "a near-perfect climate, affable students, engaging professors, a legal education that readies you for the top ranks of any practice, and a commitment to pro bono legal services that is inspiring." "If you want to be pushed and if you want be rewarded for your hard work, this place is perfect," adds a 2L. "The Public Interest Law Foundation is very large and active." The school's "very wide range" of clinical programs includes a cutting-edge Intellectual Property Clinic. Students say the "intensive" legal writing program at Gould is "amazing." "They are beating us over the head with writing and the importance of writing skills for our future until we are numb," says an exhausted 1L. However, "You really learn to appreciate it when you take your first summer job and realize how impressive a legal writer you are compared with law students from other schools."

Some professors "are very theoretical." "More emphasis on the practical side of things" would be nice, students say. On the whole, though, "Classes are quite good and a few professors are spectacular." They are always "available to have lunch, talk, and give advice." "The professors who go out of their way to make minority students feel welcome are the highlight of the law school," beams a 3L. Most students also seem pleased with the "very available and helpful" administration. "No matter how big or ridiculously small the problem, someone is there to help you," though "We have our share of lackluster profs who couldn't teach a dog to eat," confesses a 2L.

Career prospects are outstanding. "USC Law opens doors nationally" and is "absolutely worth every penny even though it is not cheap." "The USC Law community has amazing clout within Los Angeles," and "The alumni connections are unbelievable." "People may think the Trojan Family is a cheesy notion," but alumni are "crazy about USC, and they are incredibly loyal to the school and its graduates." The administration "formally sets you up with a mentor in the legal path of your interest during your first year," explains a 2L. "Mine is the general counsel to the Los Angeles Lakers." "More than half of the student body has no problem landing top corporate jobs paying $135,000 or more." However, many students are "still jobless in year three because they choose not to settle for a position with compensation less than California's highest market price." Some students worry that USC is "brainwashing students into being corporate peons." Others argue that "the Law School actually puts a huge effort into making it possible for students to pursue public interest work when they graduate."

The law school's "concrete," "late-60s-ugly" building "isn't that bad" but students agree that it "could be more aesthetic." The interior is "relatively pleasant" and "functional," despite a "terrible layout." "Some of the classrooms are dark, grim, and uberinstitutional." "I haven't seen a window in three years," laments a 3L. "The wireless network could suck less" too. On the plus side, "The library is new and hi-tech," and "The research librarians are amazing."

Life

"If you're 22 and gorgeous, you'll have a rollicking social life" at USC. "If you're already (gasp!) in your mid-20s, or older, it's tough to find mature, like-minded friends who aren't only interested in hooking up and partying." While "The immediate location of the campus is less than ideal, Southern California itself is a wonderful place to live."

CHLOE REID, ASSOCIATE DEAN
USC LAW SCHOOL, LOS ANGELES, CA 90089-0074
TEL: 213-740-2523 FAX: 213-740-4570
E-MAIL: ADMISSIONS@LAW.USC.EDU • INTERNET: WWW.LAW.USC.EDU

"Many students do not live near the USC area," though, because it "can be somewhat unsafe late at night."

Academically, USC is "tolerant and more laid-back than other law schools." Students are "generally very down-to-earth, helpful, and considerate." "Virtually everyone here is extremely motivated and wants to succeed but not at someone else's expense." As one 2L notes, "Overall, I believe that the University of Southern California really is the family atmosphere that it proclaims itself to be. Although we all operate in a competitive environment, students are in this thing together." It's "an incredibly communal place."

"The Law School is not the trust-fund stomping ground that the undergraduate college is" but "If you're a White person coming from an upper-middle-class or affluent background, you'll fit in perfectly here." Nevertheless, the law school boasts a "richly diverse student body" full of "top students with very interesting backgrounds." This "amazing blend of really different people with different backgrounds and interests mixes together and has a good time while they do it, both in class and out." Students say that "there's a creative energy [on campus] that's infused in everything." "You can see it in the students, on the students (their aesthetic mix), and in the work they do." As one student sums up: "If you want to work or study on the West Coast, you would be crazy to pass on the opportunity to join this community of entrepreneurial, bright, and personable individuals."

Getting In

The range of admitted applicants is pretty narrow. Admitted students at the 25th percentile have LSAT scores of 165 and GPAs of about 3.47. Admitted students at the 75th percentile have LSAT scores of 167 and GPAs of 3.75.

Clinical program required	No
Legal writing course requirement	Yes
Legal methods course requirement	No
Legal research course requirement	Yes
Moot court requirement	Yes
Public interest law requirement	No

ADMISSIONS

Selectivity Rating	95
# applications received	5,670
# applicants accepted	1,084
# acceptees attending	217
Average LSAT	166
LSAT Range	165–167
Average undergrad GPA	3.63
Application fee	$70
Regular application	2/1
Regular notification	Rolling
Rolling notification	Yes
Early application program	No
Transfer students accepted	Yes
Evening division offered	No
Part-time accepted	No
LSDAS accepted	Yes

Applicants Also Look At

Georgetown University, Loyola Marymount University, New York University, Stanford University, University of California—Berkeley, University of California—Los Angeles.

International Students

TOEFL required of international students	No
TOEFL recommended of international students	Yes

FINANCIAL FACTS

Annual tuition	$38,900
Books and supplies	$1,584
Room and board	$12,214
Financial aid application deadline	3/2
% first-year students receiving some sort of aid	89
% receiving some sort of aid	89
% of aid that is merit based	17
% receiving scholarships	52
Average grant	$12,000
Average loan	$36,800
Average total aid package	$56,766
Average debt	$97,416

EMPLOYMENT INFORMATION

Career Rating	92	Grads Employed by Field (%)	
Rate of placement (nine months out)	98	Academic	3
Average starting salary	$125,000	Business/Industry	7
State for bar exam	CA, NY, DC, WA, TX	Government	6
Pass rate for first-time bar	90	Judicial clerkships	8
Employers Who Frequently Hire Grads		Other	1
Private firms, corporations, federal judges, government and public interest nonprofits.		Private practice	72
		Public Interest	3

Prominent Alumni

Justice Joyce Kennard, California Supreme Court; Amy Trask, general manager, Oakland Raiders; Honorable Dorothy Nelson, U.S. Court of Appeals, 9th Circuit; Walter Zifkin, CEO of William Morris Agency; Carlos Moorehead, U.S. Congressman.

UNIVERSITY OF ST. THOMAS
SCHOOL OF LAW

Academics

If you are passionate, opinionated, and love a great debate, you will fit right in at the University of St. Thomas School of Law. On this spirited (and spiritual) campus, "The administration and faculty encourage rigorous debate in the community, and ideas are challenged from the left and the right." However, don't worry about entering a war zone. While "Students are not shy about expressing differing opinions," the whole community maintains an attitude that is respectful and collegial. All viewpoints, no matter how radical, are accepted at UST, a place where "Even the most conservative students have established life-long friendships with the most liberal students." A student jokes, "I wish Congress could learn to cooperate the way the students have here at UST. The freedom to express one's religious, social, and political views here is liberating!"

A Catholic institution, UST "strongly encourages students to evaluate their behavior as a lawyer with their values, morals, and beliefs" and "promotes integration of spiritual values into professional practice." The school also places an "emphasis on social justice." While students praise the open-minded attitude that pervades the campus, prospective students should be aware of the Catholic influence on the community. "Make no mistake that it is a Catholic law school," advises one first-year student. "We pray before class begins, and every event is related to Catholic issues." Even so, UST students say that the stress on moral thinking is valuable, even for non-Catholics. A 1L explains, "I am not Catholic, and I appreciate the emphasis on thinking about how my values will impact my career as an attorney."

University of St. Thomas School of Law is about as young as they come, having graduated its first JD class in May 2004. One decided benefit to attending such a new institution is getting to study in clean, modern, freshly built facilities. Students rave about UST's "absolutely beautiful" building in downtown Minneapolis, which boasts "an amazing library, state-of-the-art technology, and ample space for students to gather." There's also a palpable excitement within the campus environment, as the students and faculty work to build a name for the school. "It is very easy to access the faculty and administration with concerns regarding the direction in which the law school is going," reports one student. There are drawbacks, too, to the newness of the school, like the fact that "many of the bureaucratic processes have not solidified yet." This lack of formalized procedures "can produce unnecessary obstacles" or lead to an absence of communication between students and the administrative brass.

Despite how young the school is, St. Thomas has already assembled an outstanding team of accomplished, accessible, and talented faculty. "The faculty members with whom I have had contact are not only brilliant scholars and exceptional teachers, but they also care deeply about the students they teach," writes one student. "UST Law has extremely bright and energetic faculty who are accessible and really care about the students," adds another. Some would like to see the administration work harder to recruit minority faculty, but "There is a broad range of diversity among the faculty" in terms of politics, opinion, and teaching style.

CARI HAALAND, DIRECTOR OF ADMISSIONS
1000 LASALLE AVENUE, MSL 124, MINNEAPOLIS, MN 55403
TEL: (651) 962-4895 FAX: (651) 962-4876
E-MAIL: LAWSCHOOL@STTHOMAS.EDU • INTERNET: WWW.STTHOMAS.EDU/LAW

Graduates are in good shape if they want to practice in the Twin Cities. University of St. Thomas is located "close to a great number of businesses and law firms—many of whom have become involved in the school." The school makes the most of its location through an "excellent mentoring program" in which "each student is assigned a personal mentor for each of their three years." The school also offers a variety of other extracurricular programs to help students succeed, such as "a free academic success program to prepare students for the rigors of law school and frequent symposiums about various topics of interest," which are described as "a favorite with students." With a focus on social justice, the school also promotes other community-based projects, including the fall and spring "day of service" program.

Life

Students at St. Thomas love a debate, but they also know when to lay down their arguments and have some fun together. "Regardless of what is said in class, be it a conversation about abortion, gay rights, or living wages, we can always find time to walk across the street and have a beer," writes one student. Indeed, competition is kept at bay, and students say they "help each other learn" and that "most students participate in a study group or two." When they aren't hitting the books, students take advantage of downtown Minneapolis, where "There are many places to go grab lunch or a beer after a tough week of class." On campus, there is a "strong social life" and students enjoy events reminiscent of college, such as "a Halloween party, a talent show, a spring fling, Bar Review parties every Thursday night, [and] the annual chili cook-off."

Getting In

University of St. Thomas evaluates students on the following six criteria: LSAT score, undergraduate grades, writing skills, leadership potential, motivation, and demonstrated ability to contribute to UST's mission of integrating faith and reason and promoting social justice. In Fall 2006, the median LSAT score for entering students was 156.

ADMISSIONS

Selectivity Rating	74
# applications received	1,135
# applicants accepted	518
# acceptees attending	155
Average LSAT	156
LSAT Range	153–159
Average undergrad GPA	3.42
Application fee	$50
Regular application	7/1
Regular notification	Rolling
Rolling notification	Yes
Early application program	No
Transfer students accepted	Yes
Evening division offered	No
Part-time accepted	No
LSDAS accepted	Yes

Applicants Also Look At
Creighton University, DePaul University, Hamline University, Marquette University, University of Minnesota, University of Wisconsin, William Mitchell College of Law.

International Students

TOEFL required of international students	Yes
Minimum paper TOEFL	600
Minimum computer TOEFL	254

FINANCIAL FACTS

Annual tuition	$26,941
Books and supplies	$1,300
Financial aid application deadline	7/1
% first-year students receiving some sort of aid	89
% receiving some sort of aid	87
% of aid that is merit based	100
% receiving scholarships	70
Average grant	$14,595
Average loan	$18,284
Average total aid package	$27,485
Average debt	$66,640

EMPLOYMENT INFORMATION

Career Rating	90	Grads Employed by Field (%)	
Rate of placement (nine months out)	94	Business/Industry	22
Average starting salary		Government	8
State for bar exam	MN	Judicial clerkships	16
Pass rate for first-time bar	91	Military	1
		Private practice	33
		Public Interest	13

THE UNIVERSITY OF TENNESSEE
COLLEGE OF LAW

Academics

Affordable, practical, and blessed with a touch of Southern charm, the University of Tennessee is a friendly place to study the law and to learn to be a lawyer. Across the board, UT students praise their school's unequivocal "emphasis on practical and 'real' lawyering instead of just philosophical theory." The school's fleet of faculty is equipped with impressive real-world credentials, and "Several classrooms are laid out exactly like courtrooms" to help students hone their litigation skills. In addition to the tenured staff, the "Adjunct professors for skills-based classes are a wonderful resource." UT students can further augment course work through the school's ample and long-standing clinical programs, which teach lawyering skills through real-world experience, including a pro bono clinic for indigent clients. They can also pursue a specialization in advocacy through the Center for Advocacy and Dispute Resolution. While the practical offerings are outstanding, many students mention that they would like to see more diverse academic specializations. A student clarifies, "Classes in a wide number of specialties are available, but it wouldn't hurt to hire a few more professors to have more options available in a given semester. It would seem the school has taken a "quality-over-quantity" approach in this regard."

Although University of Tennessee is a stalwart Southern institution, "There are numerous professors that cater to a wide range of philosophical beliefs and legal theories . . . from the far-left stereotypical 'academics' all the way to the right side with Instapundit.com creator Glenn Reynolds." A stimulating academic atmosphere, "The class discussions that ensue between such a faculty and the geographically and academically diverse student body are most rewarding." The notorious Socratic Method remains a classroom favorite; however, it's never used to torture or embarrass. Rather, it "is a tool to encourage learning, and professors and students are seen as partners in that endeavor, as opposed to adversaries." Outside the classroom, "Teachers are willing to meet you after class and help you in anyway possible," and students reassure us that "there isn't a faculty member I would feel intimidated approaching." A satisfied student sums it up: "The laid-back attitude juxtaposed with expert instruction and the feeling that the UT College of Law, while already well ranked, is one of the most underrated schools and is by all means a rising star among law schools nationwide."

When transitioning to the real world, UT grads are prepared to hit the ground running. A 3L shares: "I worked at a big New York firm last summer with several Ivy Leaguers. Everyone was very smart, but many of them were just as lost when it came to advocacy skills (namely trial practice and negotiation). What I learned at Tennessee gave me an opportunity to shine in these areas." Another 3L chimes in, "I have a great job in Atlanta after graduation. When I was clerking down there this summer, I really enjoyed surprising people with how well prepared I am to practice." On that note, career placement is no problem for UT grads—especially those looking to work in the South; however, generally speaking, "The Career Services Center is geared towards students who want to practice in Tennessee or in big law firms elsewhere. Other career options are usually up to the students to pursue."

Life

The UT campus is a pleasant place for work and play, and students admit, "The beautiful classrooms and library make coming to school a lot easier." In and out of the classroom, "The majority of students are very friendly and cooperative," and most strike a good balance between recreation and study. To burn some calories and blow off steam,

Dr. Karen R. Britton, Director of Admissions and Career Services
1505 West Cumberland Avenue, Suite 161, Knoxville, TN 37996-1810
Tel: 865-974-4131 Fax: 865-974-1572
E-Mail: lawadmit@utk.edu • Internet: www.law.utk.edu

there are "law school teams in several of the intramural sports leagues on campus." When its time for a study break, there is a social event for almost every night of the week in Knoxville, a first-rate college town, boasting "a good music scene, an independent film theater, and lots of local festivals." Law students get together for "mixers every Thursday, bowling every Monday in the spring semester, and tailgates every Saturday in the fall." In addition to the weekly gatherings at local watering holes, the school sponsors many special events including "the yearly Halloween party called Chilla" and the enticing (or so students assure us) Learned Hand Bowling League. Within this tight-knit community, "Even if you don't go out every night you still develop good friendships with your peers."

Despite the social vibe, a student admits, "We have had some racial tension especially surrounding the hotly contested Tennessee Senate Race. We are trying to work on it and have less social segregation." Another student adds this perspective: "There are different social circles, but it is natural that people with common interests will be drawn to one another. On the whole, I feel that we have active and amiable community here."

Getting In

In 2006, UT received almost 1,400 applications for an entering class of 151 students. Undergraduate GPA and LSAT scores are important to an admissions decision; however, the school also considers qualitative factors including strength of undergraduate institution, extracurricular activities, and professional experience. The school has no minimum LSAT requirement; however, 75 percent of the 2006 entering class had an LSAT score 161 or lower, and 25 percent had an LSAT score of 155 or lower. Tennessee residents made up over 70 percent of entering students.

EMPLOYMENT INFORMATION

Career Rating	79
Rate of placement (nine months out)	99
Average starting salary	$64,260
State for bar exam	TN
Pass rate for first-time bar	88

Employers Who Frequently Hire Grads
Law firms; judges; government agencies; corporations; public interest organizations; academic institutions.

Prominent Alumni
Howard H. Baker Jr., government/public service; Joel A. Katz, entertainment lawyer; Jim Hall, former chair, NTSB; Art Stolnitz, former VP, Warner Bros.; former Justice Penny White, TN Supreme Court.

Grads Employed by Field (%)	
Business/Industry	7
Government	11
Judicial clerkships	11
Military	1
Private practice	65
Public Interest	4

ADMISSIONS

Selectivity Rating	84
# applications received	1,390
# applicants accepted	384
# acceptees attending	151
Average LSAT	158
LSAT Range	155–161
Average undergrad GPA	3.52
Application fee	$15
Regular application	3/1
Regular notification	3/15
Rolling notification	Yes
Early application program	No
Transfer students accepted	Yes
Evening division offered	No
Part-time accepted	No
LSDAS accepted	Yes

Applicants Also Look At
George Mason University, Samford University, University of Alabama, University of Georgia, University of Kentucky, The University of North Carolina at Chapel Hill, University of Memphis, Vanderbilt University.

International Students

TOEFL required of international students	Yes
TOEFL recommended of international students	Yes
Minimum paper TOEFL	213

FINANCIAL FACTS

Annual tuition (resident)	$9,142
Annual tuition (nonresident)	$24,198
Books and supplies	$1,470
Fees per credit (resident)	$35
Fees per credit (nonresident)	$51
Tuition per credit (resident)	$508
Tuition per credit (nonresident)	$1,345
Room and board	$8,464
Financial aid application deadline	3/1
% first-year students receiving some sort of aid	85
% receiving some sort of aid	89
% receiving scholarships	45
Average grant	$6,785
Average loan	$18,327
Average total aid package	$19,725
Average debt	$52,853

THE UNIVERSITY OF TEXAS AT AUSTIN
SCHOOL OF LAW

INSTITUTIONAL INFORMATION

Public/private	Public
Student-faculty ratio	14:1
% faculty part-time	45
% faculty female	34
% faculty minority	9
Total faculty	130

SURVEY SAYS...

Diverse opinions accepted
in classrooms
Great research resources
Great library staff
Students love Austin, TX

STUDENTS

Enrollment of law school	1,484
% male/female	60/40
% out-of-state	28
% full-time	100
% minority	31
% international	1
# of countries represented	18
Average age of entering class	24

ACADEMICS

Academic Experience Rating	**91**
Profs interesting rating	85
Profs accessible rating	71
Hours of study per day	3.23

Academic Specialties

Commercial law, constitutional law,
corporation securities law, criminal
law, environmental law, intellectual
property law, international law, labor
law, legal philosophy, property, taxation.

Advanced Degrees Offered

LLM, 1 year.

Combined Degrees Offered

JD/MBA, JD/MPA (public affairs),
JD/MA (Latin American studies),
JD/MS (community and regional planning), JD/MA (Russian, east European
and European studies), JD/MA
(Middle Eastern studies), JD/PhD
(government, history, or philosophy).

Clinical program required	No
Legal writing course requirement	Yes

Academics

Students at the University of Texas at Austin School of Law receive "the most bang for the buck in Texas" and a "great overall education." UT boasts a "huge network of alumni," a "focus on high-level analytical thinking," and a "diverse student body and faculty." Tuition is "relatively low," and graduates rack up very little debt. "I couldn't imagine a better law school as far as the quality of the professors," says one student. Another writes, "What I particularly appreciate is how they encourage us to try new areas of law. They show such enthusiasm and knowledge in the courses they teach that even the most boring or difficult course can be interesting and not so difficult after all." Another student brags, "In my first semester, I had the leading expert in admiralty law teach torts by singing songs on guitar, a contracts professor who could have been the stunt-double-professor in *The Paper Chase*, and a criminal law professor who clerked for Thurgood Marshall." Students praise the "writing program," "Constitutional law instruction," and "great clinics" that include a mental health clinic, a capital punishment clinic, and an actual innocence clinic, in which students screen and investigate claims of innocence from prison inmates. "The legal research and writing program is undervalued and under-funded," reports one student. Others would like to see "bar preparation improved" along with the addition of a "Loan Repayment Assistance Program." "Public interest law" could use more "interest" too. Students note smaller classes "would be nice." On the plus side, though, "going to such a large law school [guarantees a] wide range of courses."

When the time comes to get a real job, "The academic reputation enjoyed by Texas is unsurpassed in this part of the country." Thanks to this, students have "many great opportunities for jobs, internships, and clerkships." Being "right in the middle of one of the nation's biggest legal markets," UT maintains a "strong presence in the business and law communit[es]," effectively providing "ample employment opportunities." If you want to get out of the Lone Star State, no problem: More than 60 percent of the employers who interview on campus are from other states. Also, since 1995, eight UT grads have clerked for the United States Supreme Court. There are differing views on Career Services, with some students seeing them as focusing "too much on students that want to go into a big-firm environment," while others find them "open, helpful, [and] a valuable resource."

"The facilities are generally nice" at UT, though they "could use some updating." "The law school occupies an oddly cobbled together set of interconnected buildings representing a number of architectural styles," says one student. Unfortunately, "the older buildings were not built to accommodate the number of students that attend this law school—it can get quite crowded at times," and students complain of a shortage of outlets in which to plug in laptops. The "pretty" and "wonderfully comprehensive" law library is one of the "largest in the country," thanks to the "generous donations of alumni." Students are pleased that "the school is complete with wireless Internet throughout."

Life

Is UT competitive? It depends on whom you ask. According to one school of thought, "A lot of kids are really tough, [and] competition among 1Ls can be fierce." Others tell us that UT doesn't have "competitive tension running throughout the student body" and that the school "does a good job of making it seem more like a family and a support network."

MONICA INGRAM, ASSISTANT DEAN FOR ADMISSIONS AND FINANCIAL AID
727 EAST DEAN KEETON STREET, AUSTIN, TX 78705-3299
TEL: 512-232-1200 FAX: 512-471-2765
E-MAIL: ADMISSIONS@LAW.UTEXAS.EDU • INTERNET: WWW.UTEXAS.EDU/LAW

"Many political [and] social viewpoints are represented here," but lots of those viewpoints come from Texas. Most agree that the majority of students here were "born and raised in Texas." A student explains, "The saying that Texas is its own country and culture seems to be pretty accurate . . . . [Yet despite] these negative impressions, I am falling in love with the charm of the area and may even stay here upon graduation." Students do add that the school "could improve by having more students with life and work experience."

Because the school's law student population "is so large, there's not a real feeling of camaraderie." Nevertheless, "The campus is very social" and "There's always something fun to do." "There are a wide variety of student organizations, from political or ethnic groups, to journals or practice-oriented organizations, to a hugely successful variety show written, produced, and performed by law students," a student explains. Students can take advantage of "tons of opportunities to do extracurricular things off campus" as well.

If there's one thing people agree on, it's that "Austin is a truly fascinating city with a bundle of outdoor activities, social life, and dining experiences."

Getting In

Admitted students at the 25th percentile have an LSAT score of 162 and a GPA of 3.3. Admitted students at the 75th percentile have an LSAT score of 168 and a GPA of 3.8. If you take the LSAT more than once, the school will consider all scores—not just the average of them. Note also that nonresident matriculation can only constitute 35 percent of the student body.

Legal methods course requirement	No
Legal research course requirement	Yes
Moot court requirement	Yes
Public interest law requirement	No

ADMISSIONS

Selectivity Rating	97
# applications received	4,999
# applicants accepted	1,085
# acceptees attending	433
Average LSAT	166
LSAT Range	162–168
Average undergrad GPA	3.6
Application fee	$70
Regular application	2/1
Regular notification	4/1
Rolling notification	No
Early application program	Yes
Early application deadline	11/1
Early application notification	1/31
Transfer students accepted	Yes
Evening division offered	No
Part-time accepted	No
LSDAS accepted	Yes

Applicants Also Look At

Boston University, Cornell University, Duke University, The George Washington University, Southern Methodist University, University of California—Los Angeles, University of Houston, Vanderbilt University.

International Students

TOEFL required of international students	Yes
Minimum computer TOEFL	213

FINANCIAL FACTS

Annual tuition (resident)	$14,948
Annual tuition (nonresident)	$27,238
Books and supplies	$1,000
Room and board (on/off-campus)	$8,176/$8,472
Financial aid application deadline	3/31
% first-year students receiving some sort of aid	76
% receiving some sort of aid	71
% of aid that is merit based	46
% receiving scholarships	70
Average grant	$6,378
Average loan	$24,021
Average total aid package	$29,295
Average debt	$70,419

EMPLOYMENT INFORMATION

Career Rating	90	Grads Employed by Field (%)	
Rate of placement (nine months out)	96	Academic	2
Average starting salary	$101,111	Business/Industry	8
State for bar exam	TX, NY, CA, IL	Government	7
Pass rate for first-time bar	89	Judicial clerkships	10
Employers Who Frequently Hire Grads		Military	1
Akin, Gump, Strauss, Hauer, and Feld LLP;		Other	2
Baker Botts LLP; Bracewell and Giuliani		Private practice	64
LLP; Fulbright and Jaworski LLP; Haynes		Public Interest	1
and Boone LLP; Jones Day LLP.			
Prominent Alumni			
Joseph D. Jamail Jr., owner, Jamail and			
Kolius Law Firm; Kay Bailey Hutchison,			
U.S. Senator; Frederico Pena, former			
Secretary of Transportation.			

UNIVERSITY OF TOLEDO
COLLEGE OF LAW

INSTITUTIONAL INFORMATION

Public/private	Public
Student-faculty ratio	14:1
% faculty part-time	31
% faculty female	40
% faculty minority	4
Total faculty	45

SURVEY SAYS...

Diverse opinions accepted in classrooms
Abundant externship/internship/clerkship opportunities

STUDENTS

Enrollment of law school	524
% male/female	59/41
% out-of-state	41
% full-time	66
% minority	7
% international	1
# of countries represented	4
Average age of entering class	27

ACADEMICS

Academic Experience Rating	**86**
Profs interesting rating	89
Profs accessible rating	90
Hours of study per day	4.31

Academic Specialties

Civil procedure, commercial law, constitutional law, corporation securities law, criminal law, environmental law, government services, human rights law, homeland security law, intellectual property law, international law, labor law, legal history, legal philosophy, property, taxation.

Advanced Degrees Offered

JD 3 to 4 years, LLM 1 to 2 years.

Combined Degrees Offered

JD/MBA 3 to 3.5 years, JD/MSE 3 to 3.5 years, JD/Masters in Public Administration 3 to 3.5 years, JD/Masters in Criminal Justice 3 to 3.5 years, JD/MPH (public health) 3 to 3.5 years.

Clinical program required	No

Academics

With faculty who are "both intellectually stimulating and approachable and infinite resources," students at the University of Toledo can't stop singing the praises of their friendly, Midwestern school. Take it from an enthusiastic 1L, who exclaims, "The only way to comprehensively encapsulate my educational experience at UT is: Awesome, baby!" In particular, students tells us that the school's most laudable characteristic is the kindness and accessibility of their teachers, who "bend over backward to help students succeed, in academics, job searches, and life in general." Need an illustration? Take this one from a 2L: "Our property professor, who was about to nail us with our final exam, sought us out in the law library to see if we had questions rather than waiting for us to show up at his office hours." No wonder that most students agree that "it's the human component that makes this school shine."

In addition to their friendliness, students praise the quality and diversity of the teaching staff as "a superb mixture of old-fashioned ethical and young, modern, enthusiastic teachers." A 2L writes, "I feel like I can learn every aspect of any type of law just by picking the brains of the professors." Students at Toledo also appreciate the college's strong focus on the practical applications of their education. "The professors have a lot of experience in legal practice," explains one student. "It is always helpful to hear someone talk about actual cases and issues they have dealt with." Another adds, "One of our greatest strengths is the faculty and their real-world experiences. They use these experiences to demonstrate how the law is practiced in the real world."

The practical wisdom imparted by professors is augmented by the college's extensive and active extracurricular programs. At Toledo "there are an enormous number of avenues for students to get a chance to shine: moot court (appellate and trial advocacy), Law Review, clinics, externships, clerkships, independent research, Student Bar Association, and many more student organizations. A student only has to put forth an effort to get a world of experience."

Students admit that the college "could update the decor, especially in the library," but they are impressed with the level of technology available in the classrooms, which "are designed for the online experience—with SmartBoards and wireless Internet access." Some point out, however, that the human component may not be as modern as the hardware. Students confide that "the SmartBoards occasionally outfox the professors" and that "the wireless networking throughout the building seems to encourage more Web surfing than listening."

While most students are enrolled in the traditional, full-time day program, the college also operates a part-time day and evening program geared toward students with careers or families. According to participants in the evening program, the administration does a good job of catering to the diverse needs of the student body, including student parents. A participant in the evening program explains, "It would be nice to see more events tailored to nontraditional evening students. Other than that I think they do an admirable job." The college also offers several joint-degree programs (JD-MPH, JD-ME [engineering], JD-MBA, and JD-MCJ), as well as several certificates of concentration in environmental law, intellectual property law, international law, and labor and employment law.

CAROL E. FRENDT, ASSISTANT DEAN FOR ADMISSIONS
2801 WEST BANCROFT, TOLEDO, OH 43606
TEL: 419-530-4131 FAX: 419-530-4345
E-MAIL: LAW.ADMISSIONS@UTOLEDO.EDU • INTERNET: WWW.UTLAW.EDU

Life

Students at Toledo say their pretty, suburban campus is a laid-back and friendly place to study law. As part of the University of Toledo, law students can make use of the whole UT campus, which means they have "access to the undergraduate fitness facilities" or "can take part in undergraduate club sports like flag football, softball, and water polo, and attend some sporting events as well." The 500 students enrolled in the law school hail from "a wide range of backgrounds and places" and enjoy a generally non-competitive and collegial atmosphere. Students also enjoy socializing together and many attend the weekly Bar Reviews sponsored by the SBA. Students also like the school's location in the small, Midwestern city of Toledo. In Toledo, "The cost of living is low." However, "If you want a major city, Chicago, Detroit, Cleveland, Cincinnati, and Columbus . . . are only one to four hours away." If you want an international experience, the Canadian border is about that far away, too.

Getting In

To be accepted by the University of Toledo College of Law for the full-time day program, you should aim for an LSAT score in the high 150s and a B-plus undergraduate GPA. The college enrolls around 90 full-time students in each entering class, for which the college receives approximately 1,000 applications annually. Part-time programs are slightly less competitive in their admissions requirements.

Legal writing	
course requirement	Yes
Legal methods	
course requirement	No
Legal research	
course requirement	Yes
Moot court requirement	No
Public interest	
law requirement	No

ADMISSIONS

Selectivity Rating	**86**
# applications received	1,216
# applicants accepted	340
# acceptees attending	190
Average LSAT	158
LSAT Range	155–160
Average undergrad GPA	3.68
Application fee	$40
Regular application	Rolling
Regular notification	Rolling
Rolling notification	Yes
Early application program	No
Transfer students accepted	Yes
Evening division offered	Yes
Part-time accepted	Yes
LSDAS accepted	Yes

International Students

TOEFL required	
of international students	No
TOEFL recommended	
of international students	No

FINANCIAL FACTS

Annual tuition (resident)	$13,426
Annual tuition	
(nonresident)	$23,670
Books and supplies	$1,850
Fees per credit (resident)	$65
Fees per credit (nonresident)	$65
Tuition per credit (resident)	$559
Tuition per credit	
(nonresident)	$986
Room and board	
(off-campus)	$8,123
Financial aid application	
deadline	8/1
% first-year students	
receiving some sort of aid	100
% receiving some sort of aid	100
% of aid that is merit based	21
% receiving scholarships	47
Average grant	$14,370
Average loan	$20,059
Average total aid package	$23,557
Average debt	$45,251

EMPLOYMENT INFORMATION

		Grads Employed by Field (%)	
Career Rating	**74**	**Grads Employed by Field (%)**	
Rate of placement (nine months out)	93	Academic	4
Average starting salary	$63,074	Business/Industry	10
State for bar exam	OH, MI	Government	14
Pass rate for first-time bar	79	Judicial clerkships	3
Employers Who Frequently Hire Grads		Military	2
Shumaker, Loop, and Kendrick; Eastman		Other	6
and Smith; Kilpatrick Stockton; Jones Day;		Private practice	54
McDermott, Will and Emery; Baker and		Public Interest	7
Daniels; Squire, Sanders, and Dempsey.			
Prominent Alumni			
Honorable Judith Lanzinger, OH Supreme			
Court; Honorable Joseph Farnan, U.S.			
District Court, Wilmington, DE; Gerald			
Griffin, partner, Jones Day, Chicago.			

THE UNIVERSITY OF TULSA
COLLEGE OF LAW

INSTITUTIONAL INFORMATION

Public/private	Private
Affiliation	Presbyterian
Student-faculty ratio	14:1
% faculty part-time	32
% faculty female	35
% faculty minority	10
Total faculty	72

SURVEY SAYS...
Great research resources
Great library staff

STUDENTS

Enrollment of law school	540
% male/female	67/33
% out-of-state	60
% full-time	85
% minority	10
% international	1
# of countries represented	7
Average age of entering class	25

ACADEMICS

Academic Experience Rating	**71**
Profs interesting rating	74
Profs accessible rating	77
Hours of study per day	4.65

Academic Specialties
Alternative dispute resolution, environmental law, international law, Native American law, health law, practical skills, public policy.

Advanced Degrees Offered
LLM (American Indian and indigenous law) 1 to 2 years, LLM (American law for foreign lawyers) 1 year.

Combined Degrees Offered
History, industrial/organizational psychology, geosciences, biological sciences, anthropology, computer science, accounting, taxation, business administration, clinical psychology, English. Each joint-degree program takes approximately 4 years to complete.

Clinical program required	No

Academics

While the academic program at this midsize Southwestern law school is undeniably tough, Tulsa law students say they are soothed by their college's friendly environment. With a low student-faculty ratio, students are on a first-name basis with their accomplished instructors. Additionally, "Class sizes, for the most part, are small, which encourages class participation." By almost all accounts, professors are "interested, accessible, and knowledgeable in their fields," and outside the lecture hall "the faculty open-door policy is real rather than pro forma." What's more, they consider and support each student as individuals. As one 1L attests, "As a mother of two young children, the staff and faculty here have bent over backward to help me create a schedule that will work for me and my family." "I love the personal feeling at TU Law," echoes a 2L.

Students laud the "outstanding Native American law program and LLM for international students," as well as the new certificate program in entrepreneurial law. Beyond course work, many mention the quality of the school's two legal clinics in immigration law and Muscogee Creek Nation Indian Law, saying that these programs "do amazing work" within the greater community. Indeed, TU students praise the fact that "the student body cares about making a difference." While students get an excellent blend of practical and theoretical education through course work and clinics, many feel the school could improve by "requiring students to take more bar-oriented courses." A 2L explains, "We have a lot of flexibility in scheduling, which is wonderful, but when I graduate, I want to make sure I have adequately covered the bar material."

Like the faculty, "The administration is always there to help you." A new dean was just named to lead the college. With regards to that, many feel that "it is important that the new dean continue with the progress that has been made" in the recent past. However, given "the willingness of the student body to be involved, stay involved, and develop and improve the school," students are optimistic that the college will continue its climb in quality and prestige. Students also tell us that "the research facilities and the library are outstanding, and the library staff is helpful and knowledgeable and the library has been ranked very well."

As graduation approaches, "Career Services goes out of their way to help you find a job that is right for you." The staff "suggests all types of opportunities that you may not have ever thought of and give you the means to find that perfect job." Moreover, 35 percent of TU students receive scholarship awards and tell us that "the scholarship program is wonderful," ensuring a less stressful postgraduation job search. A 2L writes, "I received a scholarship, and I expect to have no academic debt when I graduate with a joint JD/Master of Taxation."

MARTHA CORDELL, ASSISTANT DEAN OF ADMISSIONS AND FINANCIAL AID
3120 EAST FOURTH PLACE, TULSA, OK 74104-3189
TEL: 918-631-2406 FAX: 918-631-3630
E-MAIL: MARTHA-CORDELL@UTULSA.EDU • INTERNET: WWW.LAW.UTULSA.EDU

Life

University of Tulsa attracts students from across the nation and a majority of current students hail from outside Oklahoma. However, "While we have students from a variety of states, the student body is not very diverse in ethnicity." For the size of the student population, however, "The number of student organizations is very broad, and this allows students many leadership opportunities." Off campus, many claim that surrounding Tulsa is a great place to get a JD, and students appreciate the fact that "the cost of living is reasonable enough to live well as a poor student on loans." In addition, "Tulsa is a beautiful town" with all the friendliness of a small community. A 2L writes, "Tulsa is small, but it is nice to see the people you know from school when you go out at night."

On the whole, TU is a friendly and cooperative environment. A 2L warns, however, that "while the students are friendly, there is definitely a competitive edge." Nonetheless, students enjoy being in the trenches with one another, saying their classmates are "unrivaled in their intellect, integrity, and amiability." A 3L writes, "We stress together, eat together, study together, and talk about our wives/husbands together." Another adds, "I have made some of my best friends at the University of Tulsa."

Getting In

Tulsa Law, like all law schools, admits students whose test scores and academic background suggest they will be successful in the study of law. It is also a little more welcoming of older students than many of its peers. Tulsa Law admits students from across the nation, and more than half of the student body hails from outside Oklahoma.

Legal writing course requirement	Yes
Legal methods course requirement	Yes
Legal research course requirement	Yes
Moot court requirement	No
Public interest law requirement	No

ADMISSIONS

Selectivity Rating	**70**
# applications received	1,436
# applicants accepted	588
# acceptees attending	183
Average LSAT	153
LSAT Range	150–155
Average undergrad GPA	3.23
Application fee	$30
Regular application	Rolling
Regular notification	Rolling
Rolling notification	Yes
Early application program	No
Transfer students accepted	Yes
Evening division offered	No
Part-time accepted	Yes
LSDAS accepted	Yes

Applicants Also Look At

Oklahoma City University, St. Mary's University, Texas Wesleyan University, University of Arkansas—Fayetteville, University of Missouri—Kansas City, University of Oklahoma, Washburn University.

International Students

TOEFL required of international students	Yes

FINANCIAL FACTS

Annual tuition	$25,264
Books and supplies	$1,500
Tuition per credit	$1,026
Room and board (on/off-campus)	$5,700/$7,800
% first-year students receiving some sort of aid	72
% receiving some sort of aid	87
% of aid that is merit based	25
% receiving scholarships	32
Average grant	$11,448
Average loan	$23,842
Average total aid package	$35,870
Average debt	$87,758

EMPLOYMENT INFORMATION

Career Rating	**74**	**Grads Employed by Field (%)**	
Rate of placement (nine months out)	90	Academic	2
Average starting salary	$48,953	Business/Industry	18
State for bar exam	OK, TX, MO, FL, CO	Government	11
Pass rate for first-time bar	90	Judicial clerkships	1
Employers Who Frequently Hire Grads		Military	1
Tulsa law firms.		Private practice	64
Prominent Alumni		Public Interest	3

Prominent Alumni

Paul J. Cleary, U.S. Magistrate Judge; Drew Edmondson, Oklahoma Attorney General; David Barclay Waller, deputy director general, International Atomic Energy Agency; Elizabeth Crewson Paris, Tax Counsel, U.S. Senate Finance Committee

UNIVERSITY OF UTAH
S. J. QUINNEY COLLEGE OF LAW

Academics

Students at the S.J. Quinney College of Law at the University of Utah are quite confident that they are receiving the "best law education available in the country for the price." The "extremely approachable" and "very student-oriented" professors "make every effort to meet with students and make sure they understand the material." "I went to an expensive liberal arts school for undergrad that advertised itself as offering available and motivated professors," relates a 3L. "My undergrad experience pales in comparison to the individual attention and encouragement I have received at this state school." "Professors here actually try to minimize stress rather than build it up," agrees a 1L. The standard Socratic Method is not en vogue. Some students tell us that professors' more easygoing approach allows "for a more comfortable environment in which to learn." Other students say it's "just too easy to doze off." "I know this sounds crazy," admits a 1L, "but I wish more of the professors would use the Socratic Method or, at least, engage the students in class more."

The administration at Utah "is always looking for new, creative ways to improve the school." "The new dean has brought a new vision of Dream Big," and administrators "demonstrate a great interest in not only hearing the students' voices, but in improving student experience, academic quality, and transition to real-world practice." "All the deans keep themselves highly available." "Nobody's got an attitude" and "No one is too busy to answer a question."

Students here are "right in the middle of Salt Lake City, surrounded by large and prestigious law firms." The College of Law has "a great relationship with practitioners and judges in the community" and "There are plenty of opportunities to gain practical experience." "It is fairly easy to do judicial clinics and other legal internships." "Terrific outreach programs afford students opportunities to work pro bono with public interest organizations." The "excellent first-year legal writing program" is "rigorous and well thought out." "You'll walk out of here writing better than most lawyers who have been practicing for years," claims a 2L. If you want to specialize, "There are plenty of courses, especially in natural resources law." Career Services is "friendly and helpful," but "A lot of students get jobs from other sources."

"A new [law school] building is in the works," but in the meantime, the current "aging" and "undersized" building is "from the late 60s and reflects that boring architecture." "Our building sucks, in a word," laments a 2L. "The campus seems designed to drive students off campus as soon as classes are over." "The bathrooms, though clean, have an odd smell." The computer network is "spotty in some places," and the library gets average reviews.

Life

"People at this school actually seem happy," and "There is a sense of community and connectedness" on campus. "We're small," explains one student. "You'll know most of the school and faculty by the time you're a 2L." "The U fosters a great environment, where everyone helps everyone else." "Individual personalities flourish and the interaction of personalities is like that among family members who have known each other their entire lives." "People here see the whole person. It's a very collaborative environment."

Students report that their peers are "equal parts brilliant, collegial, encouraging, competitive, and just flat-out a joy." It's "probably an older and more mature crowd than at the average law school." Many students "are married with children." "I don't regret for

Susan Baca, Operations Coordinator for Admissions and Financial
Admissions, 332 South 1400 East, Room 101, Salt Lake City, UT 84112-0730
Tel: 801-581-7479 Fax: 801-581-6897
E-mail: admissions@law.utah.edu • Internet: www.law.utah.edu

a moment choosing to come here as a 30-something, second-career mom," says a 2L. "I fit in." "The nontraditional demographic allows for an interesting mix and a few extra designated drivers." The Church of Latter-Day Saints is, of course, prevalent everywhere in Utah. "Don't think that because this isn't BYU there won't be plenty of Mormons." Politically, "The school is fairly evenly split between liberals and conservatives." "The divide can be fierce at times," but "Overall there is great acceptance of different viewpoints and lifestyles."

"The social life is not great" here. "Salt Lake culture is fairly conservative," and "The Mormon influence is felt both in the city and in the law school." Though wild parties are few, Utah sponsors "many social events which are geared toward building relationships between the school and the local bar." "Throughout the week there are plenty of opportunities to hang out with students in many different social settings and activities." Off campus, "Salt Lake City is a gorgeous place to live" "The city is clean; the crime rate is low." And It's surrounded by "one of the most scenic and beautiful areas in the country." "Outdoor life is great." "We are six hours away from red-rock desert and half an hour's drive from the greatest snow on earth," declares a 1L. "You can spend all that tuition money you're saving on ski passes and road trips."

Getting In

Recently admitted students at the 25th percentile have LSAT scores of 157 and GPAs of nearly 3.4. Admitted students at the 75th percentile have LSAT scores of 162 and GPAs of about 3.8. If you take the LSAT more than once, Utah will usually average your scores.

ADMISSIONS

Selectivity Rating	85
# applications received	1,130
# applicants accepted	360
# acceptees attending	122
Average LSAT	160
LSAT Range	157–162
Average undergrad GPA	3.58
Application fee	$60
Regular application	2/1
Regular notification	Rolling
Rolling notification	Yes
Early application program	No
Transfer students accepted	Yes
Evening division offered	No
Part-time accepted	No
LSDAS accepted	Yes

Applicants Also Look At

Arizona State University, Brigham Young University, University of Arizona, University of Colorado, University of Denver, University of Oregon, University of Washington.

International Students

TOEFL required of international students	Yes
TOEFL recommended of international students	Yes
Minimum paper TOEFL	600
Minimum computer TOEFL	250

FINANCIAL FACTS

Annual tuition (resident)	$11,423
Annual tuition (nonresident)	$25,595
Books and supplies	$1,812
Room and board	$8,964
Financial aid application deadline	3/15
% first-year students receiving some sort of aid	87
% receiving some sort of aid	83
% of aid that is merit based	27
% receiving scholarships	47
Average grant	$3,713
Average loan	$18,625
Average total aid package	$22,338
Average debt	$55,876

EMPLOYMENT INFORMATION

Career Rating	70	Grads Employed by Field (%)	
Rate of placement (nine months out)		Academic	2
Average starting salary	$62,889	Business/Industry	18
State for bar exam	UT, CA, NV, AZ, ID	Government	10
Pass rate for first-time bar	90	Judicial clerkships	11
Employers Who Frequently Hire Grads		Military	1
Utah Attorney General's Office; Parsons,		Private practice	55
Behle, and Latimer; Ray, Quinney, and		Public Interest	3
Nebeker.			

Prominent Alumni

Deborah Dugan, president, Disney Worldwide Publishing; Honorable Stephen Anderson, Court of Appeals, 10th Circuit; Gary Kennedy, general counsel and VP for American Airlines.

UNIVERSITY OF VIRGINIA
SCHOOL OF LAW

INSTITUTIONAL INFORMATION

Public/private	Public
Student-faculty ratio	14:1
% faculty part-time	49
% faculty female	21
% faculty minority	5
Total faculty	150

SURVEY SAYS...
Great research resources
Great library staff
Beautiful campus

STUDENTS

Enrollment of law school	1,146
% male/female	61/39
% out-of-state	57
% full-time	100
% minority	17
% international	1
# of countries represented	8
Average age of entering class	24

ACADEMICS

Academic Experience Rating	**96**
Profs interesting rating	93
Profs accessible rating	86
Hours of study per day	3.77

Academic Specialties
Civil procedure, commercial law, communication and media, constitutional law, corporation securities law, criminal law, environmental law, health law, human rights law, intellectual property law, international law, labor law, legal history, legal philosophy, public policy and regulation, race and law, taxation.

Advanced Degrees Offered
LLM 1 year, SJD 2 to 5 years.

Combined Degrees Offered
JD/MA 3 to 4 years, JD/MS 3.5 years, JD/MPH 3.5 years, JD/MBA 4 years, JD/Masters in Urban and Environmental Planning 4 years, JD/MPA 4 years, JD/MA 4 years, JD/MA 4 years.

Clinical program required	No
Legal writing course requirement	Yes

Academics

"You couldn't pay me to go anywhere else," says one of the many thrilled students attending the University of Virginia School of Law. "I don't think there is another law school that strikes such a perfect balance between rigorous academics and genuine fun. People are actually happy to be here and sad to leave." UVA offers a vast array of different concentrations; students can participate in no fewer than nine Law Review journals; and several interdisciplinary programs utilize the strengths of the medical and business schools. "There are many opportunities for independent research" as well.

By all accounts, Virginia Law's "enthusiastic, expert" professors are "tremendous." "Witty and entertaining," they are "teachers in the fullest sense of the word," and take an "extraordinary interest in their students." "They genuinely respect all opinions" and "People from both sides of the political spectrum are welcomed and encouraged to speak," proclaims a 2L. Outside of class, "friendly interactions" are the norm. "I have had lunch with every single professor this semester and so have most of my classmates," declares a 1L. The "totally responsive" administration is also "excellent." The deans and the staff "try their best to help" whenever students identify problems. "I hardly notice the administration, which says wonders," observes a 1L.

Not shy about singing UVA's praises, students rave: The facilities are "gorgeous, fantastic, [and] state of the art," and "The grounds are breathtakingly beautiful." "UVA has more windows than any law school in America," alleges one student. Classrooms with "wood paneling and super-comfy seats" "make it bearable to sit through an hour and 15 minutes of class." The honor code here is a big deal, and "It is not uncommon for students to leave laptops, purses, wallets, cell phones, and textbooks unattended in the library and study areas."

"Employment opportunities abound" for UVA Law graduates. "Professors are not afraid to pull strings to get students jobs, particularly in the public interest sectors." Many students "with middling to low GPAs still get positions with large law firms." The school "tends to channel students into traditional career paths," explains a 2L. "This law school aims to produce law firm lawyers," and most students "expect to graduate and make a salary upwards of $130,000." UVA's "clerkship reputation is phenomenal," and the "dedicated and comprehensive" public service program "offers generous loan repayment" options.

Life

"UVA School of Law is the summer camp of all law schools" and has arguably the "greatest quality of life of any law school." "There is beer on the quad every Thursday afternoon and a law-school-wide party at a local bar every Thursday evening." For many students, "Social life revolves largely around softball and beer," "with some reading on the side." Others say that "the whole 'beer-and-softball thing' is always exaggerated." Pretty much everyone agrees, though, that "UVA Law strikes an ideal balance between work and fun, study and softball, theoretical and practical." "People will go out three to four nights a week, but will still be sitting in torts class the next morning no less brilliant for being hung over," claims an impressed 1L. "The most overwhelming thing about UVA in the first few weeks is not its academics," admits another 1L. "It's the sheer number of social events." Be warned, however: "This is not a slacker school." "There is a lot of pressure" when exams get close.

SUSAN PALMER, ASSOCIATE DEAN OF ADMISSIONS
580 MASSIE ROAD, CHARLOTTESVILLE, VA 22903-1738
TEL: 434-924-7351 FAX: 434-982-2128
E-MAIL: LAWADMIT@VIRGINIA.EDU • INTERNET: WWW.LAW.VIRGINIA.EDU

UVA's "easygoing" students describe themselves as "intelligent and insightful," not to mention "industrious and well-rounded." "Students are competitive without being negatively so," says a 3L. "Any competition here is healthy, and the students who choose to perform exceptionally well have an opportunity [to do so]," while "Those who want to just work hard enough to get good (but not great) grades can do so with no pressure or fear that they won't get a desirable job." Some students say that "the school could stand to be a bit more diverse" ethnically, but students definitely display "varying opinions" and "varied interests." "One class of mine has a former Navy fighter pilot, a neurosurgeon, and a top Division I basketball player," says a first-year student. Politically, UVA is home to "a mix of both conservatives and liberals," which "provides for more interesting conversation." "Tolerance for diverse opinions and a general laid-back attitude make this place a real joy to be at day in and day out," says a 2L.

Off campus, the surrounding town of Charlottesville has a "very cool downtown," a thriving "bohemian art scene," and "a surprisingly sophisticated host of restaurants" and "small clubs." The local music scene is fabulous too. "The only people who will be unhappy at UVA Law are those who worship city life," says one student. "Charlottesville can be a very small place for anyone who has ever lived in even a moderately sized city."

Getting In

Admitted students at the 25th percentile have LSAT scores of roughly 167 and GPAs of about 3.5. Admitted students at the 75th percentile have LSAT scores of about 171 and GPAs of just over 3.8. UVA has a policy of not having a policy when it comes to evaluating multiple LSAT scores. It's purely case by case.

Legal methods	
course requirement	Yes
Legal research	
course requirement	Yes
Moot court requirement	No
Public interest	
law requirement	No

ADMISSIONS

Selectivity Rating	**96**
# applications received	4,869
# applicants accepted	1,225
# acceptees attending	375
Average LSAT	169
LSAT Range	167–171
Average undergrad GPA	3.68
Application fee	$75
Regular application	3/1
Regular notification	4/16
Rolling notification	Yes
Early application program	Yes
Early application deadline	11/15
Early application notification	12/15
Transfer students accepted	Yes
Evening division offered	No
Part-time accepted	No
LSDAS accepted	Yes

Applicants Also Look At
Columbia University, The George Washington University, Georgetown University, Harvard University, New York University, University of Michigan, University of Pennsylvania.

International Students

TOEFL required	
of international students	Yes
Minimum paper TOEFL	600
Minimum computer TOEFL	250

FINANCIAL FACTS

Annual tuition (resident)	$28,944
Annual tuition	
(nonresident)	$33,768
Books and supplies	$1,500
Room and board	$14,100
Financial aid application	
deadline	3/1
% first-year students	
receiving some sort of aid	93
% receiving some sort of aid	92
% of aid that is merit based	19
% receiving scholarships	62
Average grant	$13,745
Average loan	$36,146
Average total aid package	$40,400
Average debt	$86,260

EMPLOYMENT INFORMATION

Career Rating	95	Grads Employed by Field (%)	
Rate of placement (nine months out)	99	Business/Industry	5
Average starting salary	$125,000	Government	3
State for bar exam	NY, VA	Judicial clerkships	17
Pass rate for first-time bar	94	Military	2
Employers Who Frequently Hire Grads		Private practice	71
Graduates are employed in every top 100 firm in the country.		Public Interest	2

UNIVERSITY OF WASHINGTON
SCHOOL OF LAW

INSTITUTIONAL INFORMATION

Public/private	Public
Student-faculty ratio	11:1
% faculty part-time	49
% faculty female	37
% faculty minority	14
Total faculty	105

SURVEY SAYS...

Great research resources
Great library staff
Students love Seattle, WA

STUDENTS

Enrollment of law school	544
% male/female	43/57
% out-of-state	30
% full-time	100
% minority	20
% international	4
# of countries represented	6
Average age of entering class	25

ACADEMICS

Academic Experience Rating	**84**
Profs interesting rating	74
Profs accessible rating	76
Hours of study per day	4.75

Academic Specialties

Asian law, civil procedure, commercial law, constitutional law, corporation securities law, criminal law, dispute resolution, environmental law, government services, health law, human rights law, intellectual property law, international and comparative law, international law, labor law, legal history, legal philosophy, property, taxation.

Advanced Degrees Offered

LLM (Asian law) 1 year, LLM (law of sustainable international development) 1 year, LLM (taxation) 1 year, LLM (intellectual property) 1 year.

Combined Degrees Offered

Can set up with 90 graduate programs at UW.

Clinical program required	No
Legal writing course requirement	Yes

Academics

According to students, the goal of the University of Washington School of Law is to "do all the weeding in the admissions process so that everyone who makes it in can and should graduate. This means that there is no pressure to compete or flunk out." Academically, the administration and teaching staff "tries to deemphasize the 'cutthroat competition' aspects of law school and allow students to focus on learning." Here you will find "relaxed and open faculty who place a serious emphasis on teaching quality." "The professors are all easy-going and only practice a Socratic-light method. That is, you either know well in advance when you'll be called on in class or, if you're called on randomly, they won't grill you until you start crying," writes a 1L. While they go easy in the classroom, UW professors are nonetheless top-notch. "The professorial staff that I have encountered has been exceptional. Each one has a unique style of instruction and educational background," writes a 2L.

With a student faculty ratio of 11:1, "Each 1L has at least one or two classes of 30 students," so there is plenty of opportunity to work one-on-one with professors. Moreover, "Professors are eager to discuss almost anything" and make an effort to be available to students outside of the classroom. A 2L recounts, "The professors are not only brilliant, but [also] actually care about the students. I've had professors take me out to coffee or lunch just because I needed someone to talk to." Students single out the school's taxation and intellectual property programs for praise and applaud the fact that "professional responsibility and pro bono work is stressed" throughout the curriculum. Despite the progressive focus in the curriculum, students admit that the UW population is fairly homogeneous and that the "school desperately needs more professors of color."

Like the teaching staff, the UW administration is "organized, accessible, highly competent, and, most important, kind." In particular, many students tell us that "Dean Joe Knight is an inspiring and motivating force of nature and all-around great guy." In addition to its positive attitude, the administration at UW works hard to support students in their personal lives, not just academically. Among the most striking examples is that "the school offers unlimited, free psychotherapy with the country's leading lawyer psychologist." "Given that law school drives us crazy," comments one 2L, "he is an invaluable resource." The school is also "incredibly family- and child-friendly." In fact, on every level, UW expects students to have a life outside law school. A satisfied 2L adds, "While UW has provided me with all the necessary tools and connections to pursue a stellar career, I can still take time on the weekends to ski, kayak, and even run marathons. This place has allowed me to maintain and nurture all the facets of my life. It's quite rare." In fact, the environment is so non-competitive and encouraging that a 2L goes so far as to suggest that "if you want a school where you can find out how you rank and how you are doing, don't go here."

The school recently built "new, state-of-the-art facilities" funded by Seattle's most famous resident, Bill Gates. The law library, "with its towering skylights and ample use of windows, is affectionately known on campus as the 'shark tank' [and] swarms with undergrads because it's the best place on campus to study." While the quality and technological capabilities of the facility are indisputable, many lament the fact that "the physical space of the law school is not the most student-user friendly, as there are few spaces for students to congregate, and none, other than classrooms, where more than 50 to 75 people could meet at once."

KATHY SWINEHART, ADMISSIONS SUPERVISOR
WILLIAM H. GATES HALL, BOX 353020, SEATTLE, WA 98195-3020
TEL: 206-543-4078 FAX: 206-543-5671
E-MAIL: LAWADM@U.WASHINGTON.EDU • INTERNET: WWW.LAW.WASHINGTON.EDU

Life

Think of law school. Now, think of its opposite. "I've been shocked that being around a bunch of lawyers can feel so little like being around a bunch of lawyers," writes one 1L. But the UW student body is more than just friendly faces; it is a group of extremely talented and accomplished individuals. "The single greatest strength of the law school is the range of experience of the student body. We have students [who] hold science PhDs, we have Olympic-caliber athletes, we have professional writers, and any profession in between," comments one student. The community is active in a wide range of social and philanthropic activities, which means that "it's easy to get involved with student groups and do something relevant."

While UW has a famously "mellow, welcoming environment," students are diligent and studious, which leads to some "healthy competition" in an overall atmosphere of teamwork and support. When they aren't studying, students maintain active personal lives, and many are eager to socialize with their classmates in the evenings or on the weekends. "No one is obsessed with school, and someone throws a party just about every weekend (except during finals)," reports a 2L. You will not, however, encounter the "work hard, play hard" attitude prevalent at many other law schools. "There is also the famous 'Seattle reserve' to contend with: People aren't unfriendly, but they don't necessarily bounce around the halls in ecstasy, either."

Getting In

It's tough getting admitted to the University of Washington, but the school follows your basic law school admissions policy: It puts heavy weight on applicants' undergraduate records and LSAT scores, also considering letters of recommendation, work and volunteer experience, and personal statements. The vast majority of enrollees (about 70 percent) are residents of Washington State; however, residency is not a major factor in an admissions decision.

Legal methods course requirement	Yes
Legal research course requirement	No
Moot court requirement	No
Public interest law requirement	Yes

ADMISSIONS

Selectivity Rating	**91**
# applications received	2,545
# applicants accepted	537
# acceptees attending	179
Average LSAT	162
LSAT Range	159–166
Average undergrad GPA	3.67
Application fee	$50
Regular application	1/15
Regular notification	4/1
Rolling notification	No
Early application program	No
Transfer students accepted	Yes
Evening division offered	No
Part-time accepted	No
LSDAS accepted	Yes

Applicants Also Look At

The George Washington University, Georgetown University, Seattle University, University of California—Berkeley, University of California—Hastings, University of California—Los Angeles, University of Southern California.

International Students

TOEFL required of international students	No
TOEFL recommended of international students	No

FINANCIAL FACTS

Annual tuition (resident)	$16,255
Annual tuition (nonresident)	$23,878
Books and supplies	$1,500
Room and board	$15,000
Financial aid application deadline	2/28
% first-year students receiving some sort of aid	85
% receiving some sort of aid	85
% of aid that is merit based	10
% receiving scholarships	43
Average grant	$7,000
Average loan	$22,000
Average total aid package	$28,000
Average debt	$59,411

EMPLOYMENT INFORMATION

Career Rating	84	Grads Employed by Field (%)	
Rate of placement (nine months out)	99	Academic	5
Average starting salary	$85,000	Business/Industry	11
State for bar exam	WA	Government	16
Pass rate for first-time bar	84	Judicial clerkships	16
Employers Who Frequently Hire Grads		Other	1
Preston, Gates, and Ellis; Davis Wright		Private practice	40
Tremaine; Perkins Coie; Stoel Rives; King		Public Interest	11
County Prosecuting Attorney; Garvey,			
Schubert, and Barer.			
Prominent Alumni			
Tom Foley, former Speaker, U.S. House of			
Representatives; Chief Justice Gerry			
Alexander, Washington Supreme Court.			

UNIVERSITY OF WISCONSIN—MADISON
LAW SCHOOL

INSTITUTIONAL INFORMATION

Public/private	Public
Student-faculty ratio	13:1
% faculty part-time	50
% faculty female	52
% faculty minority	15
Total faculty	114

SURVEY SAYS...
Liberal students

STUDENTS

Enrollment of law school	865
% male/female	52/48
% out-of-state	37
% full-time	100
% minority	26
% international	2
# of countries represented	8
Average age of entering class	25

ACADEMICS

Academic Experience Rating	**83**
Profs interesting rating	83
Profs accessible rating	77
Hours of study per day	4.38

Academic Specialties

Biotechnology law, civil procedure, commercial law, constitutional law, corporation securities law, criminal law, environmental law, estate planning, family law, government services, health law, human rights law, intellectual property law, international law, Islamic law, labor law, law practice skills, legal history, legal philosophy, property, taxation.

Advanced Degrees Offered
JD, LLM, SJD.

Combined Degrees Offered
Joint-degree with environmental studies, business, public affairs, sociology, political science, library information science, Latin American studies, philosophy.

Clinical program required	No
Legal writing	
course requirement	Yes

Academics

The University of Wisconsin Law School takes its motto "law in action" very seriously. The law in action philosophy is "the notion that the law on the books must be understood in the context of the way the law really works on the ground." To that end, the "school places a big emphasis on clinical programs," with "numerous and varied" opportunities to gain "practical experience with clients—even during 1L year." "The Innocence Project and Consumer Law Clinics," for example, "are busy around the clock" and the latter routinely "wins class actions that help fund itself." What's more, the practical impact of the law is not divorced from the approach to teaching law in the classroom: "Many if not most professors adopt a pragmatic approach to teaching the law, focusing as much on the public policy as the doctrine."

Students say professors here "are very knowledgeable in their fields. Many of them are well-known figures across the state, have a tremendous influence on the state government, and are excellent 'people to know' if you plan to remain in the state of Wisconsin." "Professors employ a modified Socratic Method to make students more comfortable," which "is refreshing at first but can lead to classes that drag if they depend on student participation." Exhibiting a particular "strength in contracts," Wisconsin's "public interest and criminal law classes are world class." However, students say the business law courses "[are] not taught by a strong business law faculty."

"Wisconsin does not have the most attractive law building"—"dark, depressing, stale" is how one student describes it. However, it does have certain features that recommend it. There is, for example, "excellent wireless Internet throughout the building." In addition, "The library is magnificent!" It has "one end composed entirely of glass, overlooking Bascom Hill (the heart of the university)." Inside, you will find "library staff [who] are extremely friendly and willing to go the extra mile to help you find what you are looking for." If they can't do it for you, the "Lexis and Westlaw reps are knowledgeable and accessible."

Cost-conscious and risk-averse students should note that "in-state tuition and automatic bar admission are two of the best deals around." Automatic bar admission? Yes, you read correctly. The University of Wisconsin Law School is only one of two law schools in the Badger State (the other being Marquette) that enjoys a certain "diploma privilege which allows you to be licensed in Wisconsin without taking the bar exam."

Life

One of the signature traits of the Wisconsin law experience is the school's "laid-back atmosphere." "Considering [that] law school is supposed to be some sort of nightmare where everything is like the *The Paper Chase*" students are constantly "surprised [by] how uncompetitive UW is." For example, "If you miss a lecture, it is commonplace for a classmate to e-mail you notes without being asked."

Students across the board say "This is a very left-wing law school, on par with Berkeley and Boulder." A lot of students love the liberal atmosphere on campus, but others complain that the "overall learning environment is hindered by an absence of diversity in thought." "Conservative ideas are not seriously considered in classes while liberal ideas are," observes one student. Despite their pervasive liberal ethos, students note that "there is definitely a degree of de facto segregation within the student body." Students point to "the large number of student orgs designed around different minority groups," which they feel sometimes "creates an 'us against them' mentality."

Michael A. Hall, Assistant Dean for Admissions and Financial Aid
975 Bascom Mall, Madison, WI 53706
Tel: 608-262-5914 Fax: 608-263-3190
E-mail: admissions@law.wisc.edu • Internet: www.law.wisc.edu

Socially, "The attitude among students is to work hard and play hard." Lucky for them "The law school is a very active environment. Students who want to be involved have a number of different organizations they can join and the student government offers a number of social events to facilitate interaction not only within classes but from year to year." A little-known fact is that UW was the first university to open a campus pub after passage of the twenty-first amendment, and a proud drinking culture still perseveres in the law school. Some students go so far as to say that there is "too much drinking." Bar Reviews, Dean Mixers, and similar social events "always have a keg."

Hometown "Madison is a fantastic place to be in school—it's a beautiful city with lots to do, but the cost of living is very affordable and the city isn't so distracting that you end up neglecting your studies." Students also "love their proximity to Chicago" for those times when they do crave the distractions that can help them to neglect their studies.

Getting In

Incoming students at the 25th percentile have an LSAT score of 156 and a GPA of 3.2. Incoming students at the 75th percentile have an LSAT score of 163 and a GPA of 3.7. UW Law School excels in minority student recruitment, and minority applicants who meet all the traditional criteria for admission often have a better shot at getting in. If you are in any way a unique or nontraditional student, it could work in your favor here.

Legal methods course requirement	Yes
Legal research course requirement	Yes
Moot court requirement	No
Public interest law requirement	No

ADMISSIONS

Selectivity Rating	**86**
# applications received	3,037
# applicants accepted	774
# acceptees attending	283
Average LSAT	159
LSAT Range	156–163
Average undergrad GPA	3.47
Application fee	$45
Regular application	2/1
Regular notification	Rolling
Rolling notification	Yes
Early application program	No
Transfer students accepted	Yes
Evening division offered	No
Part-time accepted	No
LSDAS accepted	Yes

International Students

TOEFL required of international students	Yes

FINANCIAL FACTS

Annual tuition (resident)	$12,654
Annual tuition (nonresident)	$30,817
Books and supplies	$2,100
Room and board	$7,202
Financial aid application deadline	3/1
% first-year students receiving some sort of aid	90
% receiving some sort of aid	90
% of aid that is merit based	22
% receiving scholarships	22
Average grant	$11,700
Average total aid package	$18,500

EMPLOYMENT INFORMATION

Career Rating	**89**	
Rate of placement (nine months out)	97	
Average starting salary	$81,371	
State for bar exam	WI	
Pass rate for first-time bar	100	

Employers Who Frequently Hire Grads
Foley and Lardner; Sidley and Austin; Mayer Brown Rowe and Maw; Jenner and Block; Quarles and Brady; Godfrey and Kahn.

Prominent Alumni
Tommy Thompson, former secretary of Health and Human Services, former govenor of WI; Tammy Baldwin, U.S. House of Representatives.

Grads Employed by Field (%)

Academic	1
Business/Industry	10
Government	17
Judicial clerkships	5
Private practice	60
Public Interest	7

UNIVERSITY OF WYOMING
COLLEGE OF LAW

INSTITUTIONAL INFORMATION

Public/private	Public
Student-faculty ratio	13:1
% faculty part-time	25
% faculty female	41
% faculty minority	11
Total faculty	27

SURVEY SAYS...

Diverse opinions accepted
in classrooms
Great research resources
Great library staff
Students never sleep

STUDENTS

Enrollment of law school	231
% male/female	55/45
% out-of-state	41
% full-time	100
% minority	11
% international	2
# of countries represented	3
Average age of entering class	26

ACADEMICS

Academic Experience Rating	**71**
Profs interesting rating	68
Profs accessible rating	90
Hours of study per day	4.63

Academic Specialties
Environmental law, natural
resources law.

Advanced Degrees Offered
JD 3 years.

Combined Degrees Offered
JD/MPA 3.5 years, JD/MBA 3.5 to
4 years.

Clinical program required	No
Legal writing	
course requirement	Yes
Legal methods	
course requirement	No
Legal research	
course requirement	Yes
Moot court requirement	Yes
Public interest	
law requirement	No

Academics

The University of Wyoming College of Law is one of the smallest law schools in the country and, according to students here, "completely underrated." They tell us that "small class sizes" (roughly 80 in each first-year class), "low cost," "a friendly and unintimidating atmosphere," and a "wonderfully approachable" faculty make UW "a great school." "At the University of Wyoming you can be on a first-name basis with the deans and all the professors," boasts a 1L. "The deans have an open-door policy" and the "extremely supportive" administration "has to be one of the best around."

Legal writing is solid and "Opportunities for practical experience are top-notch." Five real-world legal clinics and a wealth of externships provide "a lot of great practical opportunities" for students. A "huge environmental law contingent" takes advantage of internships and externships associated with the "excellent" environment and natural resources program. There is "great networking within the state" and "plenty of opportunity for employment" reportedly awaits students upon graduation. "Wyoming—including the law school—tends to take care of its own," explains one student. "I am confident, if I want to work outside of Wyoming, I will be able to find a job," adds a fearless 1L.

The "highly qualified" professors at UW "teach a wide variety of course subjects" and "most" are "pretty good at teaching the material." "Some of the professors are the best you could hope for." Others "are less inspiring" and "Some courses they teach might not truly be their expertise." However, "The professors are extremely helpful and will give you all the individual attention that you need and want," explains a 2L. "Of course, this leaves little chance of 'blending' to escape notice." "I have never felt intimidated to approach any of them in order to ask a question or advice," adds a 2L. "I have professors who have offered to look over sample exam answers and who have given their home telephone numbers out."

Students say that the facilities "could use some work," but they are "by no means hideous." Some aspects of the College of Law building are "a relic of the 1970s," including the "limited space" and "dated décor." At least "There are a few nice classrooms that are really updated for the new technology requirements of school. There are a few other classrooms that still need updating." Wireless capabilities and the number of electrical outlets facilities have been "vastly improved" in recent years. "In every carrel in the library, there is a power outlet for a laptop" and "There is no lack of computer stations." Tech support is "very helpful" as well.

Life

Many students say the University of Wyoming "clearly lacks diversity in terms of ethnic minorities" but they also note that geography is a limitation in this regard. "I don't think that the lack of diversity is caused by lack of effort in recruiting," observes a 2L. "I just don't think that many people want to move to Wyoming." There are quite a few non-traditional students here but "Most students are traditional students" just a few years out of undergrad.

Academically, a "competitive yet cooperative spirit" prevails. "Students are very friendly and helpful to each other." They actually "leave their laptops unlocked overnight." The "very small" size of UW "is a great strength of the school" because it fosters "a very strong sense of community" and "a real camaraderie" "regardless of class rank." Students here become lifelong friends and colleagues. "We are able to have a much more intimate relationship with the faculty and staff, administration, and

CAROL PERSSON, COORDINATOR OF ADMISSIONS
DEPARMENT 3035, 1000 EAST UNIVERSITY AVENUE, LARAMIE, WY 82071
TEL: 307-766-6416 FAX: 307-766-6417
E-MAIL: LAWADMIS@UWYO.EDU • INTERNET: WWW.UWYO.EDU/LAW

classmates," explains a 2L. "We don't let the competition of getting a high ranking get in the way of establishing meaningful relationships." "I transferred in from another law school that was just [an] overly competitive environment," elaborates another 2L. "Students here are much more friendly and helpful toward one another."

"The people of Wyoming are the nicest people in the world," and "no one's complaining about the 'lower cost' of living in Wyoming." However, Laramie—the surrounding town of about 30,000 souls—isn't much in the way of culture and nightlife. At 7,200 feet, Laramie is also home to "the highest elevation law school in the country." "It's bloody cold up here," cautions a 1L. It's also "safe" and "very Western." "You will typically run into other law students no matter where you go." "Everyone congregates at certain bars in town on weekends" like "one big, happy family." "The social life is limited," though. "That is, if you're not particularly fond of the Cowboy Bar." "The rumor mill runs rampant" in the tiny College of Law universe as well. "Everyone is well aware of who is dating who, who broke up with who." When students need a break, outstanding skiing, hiking, hunting, and fishing are easily accessible and "larger towns like Denver and Fort Collins" are a short drive south.

Getting In

The 25th percentile of admitted students has LSAT scores of 150 and GPAs of a little over 3.1. Admitted students at the 75th percentile have LSAT scores of 154 and GPAs of about 3.6. A whopping 70 percent of all the law students at UW receive scholarships of some kind.

ADMISSIONS

Selectivity Rating	74
# applications received	809
# applicants accepted	212
# acceptees attending	85
Average LSAT	152
LSAT Range	150–154
Average undergrad GPA	3.32
Application fee	$50
Regular application	3/1
Regular notification	4/1
Rolling notification	Yes
Early application program	Yes
Early application deadline	2/1
Early application notification	3/15
Transfer students accepted	Yes
Evening division offered	No
Part-time accepted	No
LSDAS accepted	Yes

Applicants Also Look At

University of Colorado, University of Denver, University of Idaho, University of Montana, University of Nebraska—Lincoln, University of Nevada, Las Vegas, University of Utah.

International Students

TOEFL required	
of international students	Yes
Minimum paper TOEFL	525
Minimum computer TOEFL	195

FINANCIAL FACTS

Annual tuition (resident)	$6,840
Annual tuition (nonresident)	$15,360
Books and supplies	$1,200
Room and board	$8,932
Financial aid application deadline	3/1
% first-year students receiving some sort of aid	89
% receiving some sort of aid	86
% of aid that is merit based	18
% receiving scholarships	79
Average grant	$1,610
Average loan	$16,579
Average total aid package	$18,181
Average debt	$37,340

EMPLOYMENT INFORMATION

Career Rating	71	Grads Employed by Field (%)	
Rate of placement (nine months out)	86	Academic	3
Average starting salary	$50,524	Business/Industry	5
State for bar exam	WY, CO, AK, CA, MT	Government	13
Pass rate for first-time bar	80	Judicial clerkships	18
Employers Who Frequently Hire Grads		Military	5
Government (attorney general, federal and district courts, supreme court, public defender, county attorney); general practice firms.		Private practice	53
		Public Interest	3
Prominent Alumni			
Gerry Spence, trial lawyer, author, television commentator; Mike Sullivan, former U.S. Ambassador to Ireland, Governor of Wyoming.			

VALPARAISO UNIVERSITY
SCHOOL OF LAW

INSTITUTIONAL INFORMATION

Public/private	Private
Affiliation	Lutheran
Student-faculty ratio	16.6:1
% faculty part-time	50
% faculty female	42
% faculty minority	6
Total faculty	50

SURVEY SAYS...
Diverse opinions accepted
in classrooms
Great research resources
Abundant externship/internship/
clerkship opportunities

STUDENTS

Enrollment of law school	523
% male/female	55/45
% out-of-state	65
% full-time	92
% minority	11.5
% international	2
# of countries represented	4
Average age of entering class	24

ACADEMICS

Academic Experience Rating	**77**
Profs interesting rating	81
Profs accessible rating	84
Hours of study per day	4.87

Academic Specialties
Civil procedure, commercial law, constitutional law, corporation securities law, criminal law, environmental law, government services, human rights law, intellectual property law, international law, labor law, legal history, legal philosophy, property.

Advanced Degrees Offered
JD 3 to 5 years, LLM 1 year.

Combined Degrees Offered
JD/MBA 4 years, JD/CMHC 4 years, JD/PSY 4 years, JD/MA (international commerce and policy) 4 years, JD/MA (sports administration) 4 years, JD/MALS (create your own program) 4 years, JD/MA CS (Chinese studies).

Academics

For students seeking a small and community-oriented law school, they should know that a "truly personal manner of teaching" is what distinguishes a Valparaiso education. At Valpo, small class sizes are the rule and classes are generally taught through the Socratic Method and group discussion. Students call their professors "true scholars" as well as great teachers and describe classes as "thorough, difficult, rewarding, and fair." They're also enjoyable; take it from this 1L, who tells us, "There is never a day when you don't laugh. The professors here combine a fun and open learning atmosphere while maintaining professionalism and responsibility for the material."

In addition to their flair for teaching, Valpo professors are some of the most congenial in the business. They "go out of their way to make sure you are at ease with them and the school" and help to engender in a students a feeling of community. In addition to the campus wide "open-door policy," Valpo professors are generous with their time, willing to support students academically, personally, and socially. For example, they are "ready, willing, and able to step up and act as judges for moot court competitions and to help with practice rounds." They're also not above showing up for student events, dinners, and various extracurriculars. A great "example of this is Cardozo Cup, our fall softball tournament. The faculty and staff come out in force for this event and form their own team to play the various classes of students."

Valparaiso augments its traditional legal course work with an extensive legal writing and research program. Whereas many law schools limit their legal writing courses to the first year, at Valpo "legal writing skills are not only stressed in the first year, but throughout your time" as well, since the program includes "a full year dedicated to legal research and three years dedicated to legal writing." These skills are extremely valuable in the real world: "Several of us who worked at large firms were the only summer associates who did not have significant problems transferring our skills to a practical environment, and the employers noticed," writes one 3L. On top of the legal writing program, "there are a lot of practical, hands-on experiences available," including the school's "great clinical program, which is really respected in the community." In addition, "externship opportunities abound" with a list of possible placements including "local prosecutors, in-house work for hospitals and steel corporations, the United States Attorney's Office, federal judicial externships, state judicial exterships, and nonprofits." A 2L exclaims, "My first summer I had the opportunity to work with the Federal Community Defender's office on a death penalty case. Talk about an education!"

In most cases, Valpo students go on to take jobs in regional firms, and "if you are from the Midwest and want to stay, Valparaiso has great contacts, and the alumni are very faithful." By most accounts, "The Career Center is very motivated to help the students and truly care about the results," though some would like to see more support for career searches on a national level. Many students confide that, until recently, Career Services at Valparaiso struggled to place students in big firm jobs in metropolitan areas; however, students say that the administration "has really listened to our needs and helped improve job placement." A 3L attests, "I found a great job, as did my fiancée and a lot of my friends here. The 2L class below us has amazing job placement all over the Chicago area and Indianapolis, as well as other cities in Indiana and Michigan."

TONY CREDIT, JD, EXECUTIVE DIRECTOR OF ADMISSIONS
WESEMANN HALL, VALPARAISO, IN 46383
TEL: 888-825-7652 FAX: 219-465-7808
E-MAIL: VALPOLAW@VALPO.EDU • INTERNET: WWW.VALPO.EDU/LAW

Life

Life on this small town campus is lively, active, and extremely social. Students keep busy through a wide variety of extracurricular clubs, and "There is always a social event, guest lecturer, charity drive, or similar happening taking place." What's more, it's easy to make friends in this open, community-oriented environment; "I'm friends with everyone in my class and have a very personal relationship with my professors," writes one 3L. An enthusiastic 1L brags, "All the social events, which are nearly weekly, revolve around my two favorite things: free food and free beer." If that weren't enough, there is a long list of annual events for students and faculty, which include "a softball competition, a Halloween costume party, the boat cruise, the spring play that students and faculty put on together as a fund-raiser, a big Spring Ball, Law Week, which consists of tons of competitions, and end-of-the-year dinners and banquets."

While the environment is decidedly collegial, not all Valpo students hail from the same background or viewpoint and, especially when it comes to politics, they are surprisingly diverse. At Valparaiso, you can expect lively classroom debates, as "Some students are very strong liberals and some are extremely conservative." On this friendly campus, however, "There is always a place for someone, no matter what their political beliefs," and students welcome the liveliness and interest that diversity brings to the campus. Debates aside, you won't find competitiveness at Valparaiso, where "There is a strong sense of community among students" and everyone looks out for everyone else. According to newbies, "2Ls and 3Ls are always there to answer questions and lend a helping hand."

Getting In

To apply to Valparaiso, you must submit a completed application, a personal statement, two letters of recommendation, an undergraduate transcript, and LSAT scores. While LSAT score and GPA are important factors in an admissions decision, Valparaiso also considers a candidate's background, work experience, contribution to the community, and commitment to the study of law.

Clinical program required	No
Legal writing course requirement	Yes
Legal methods course requirement	Yes
Legal research course requirement	Yes
Moot court requirement	No
Public interest law requirement	Yes

ADMISSIONS

Selectivity Rating	**75**
# applications received	2,589
# applicants accepted	775
# acceptees attending	174
Average LSAT	151
LSAT Range	144–162
Average undergrad GPA	3.31
Application fee	$60
Regular application	6/1
Regular notification	Rolling
Rolling notification	Yes
Early application program	No
Transfer students accepted	Yes
Evening division offered	No
Part-time accepted	Yes
LSDAS accepted	Yes

International Students

TOEFL required of international students	Yes
Minimum paper TOEFL	575
Minimum computer TOEFL	230

FINANCIAL FACTS

Annual tuition	$28,250
Books and supplies	$2,000
Fees per credit	$22
Tuition per credit	$1,107
Room and board	$7,300
Financial aid application deadline	4/1
% first-year students receiving some sort of aid	90
% receiving some sort of aid	95
% of aid that is merit based	35
% receiving scholarships	34
Average grant	$15,214
Average loan	$18,500
Average total aid package	$39,850
Average debt	$56,000

EMPLOYMENT INFORMATION

Career Rating	66	Grads Employed by Field (%)	
Average starting salary	$56,000	Academic	1
State for bar exam	IN, IL, MI, WI, GA	Business/Industry	16
Pass rate for first-time bar	84	Government	12
Prominent Alumni		Judicial clerkships	4
Stephan Todd, VP Law and Environment,		Military	1
U.S. Steel Corporation; Cornell Boggs, VP		Private practice	63
and general counsel, Tyco Plastics and		Public Interest	2
Adhesives; Honorable Nancy Vaidik,			
Indiana Court of Appeals; Koreen Ryan,			
senior council, South Asia McDonald's			
Corporation; Honorable Robert Rucker,			
Supreme Court of Indiana.			

VANDERBILT UNIVERSITY
LAW SCHOOL

INSTITUTIONAL INFORMATION

Public/private	Private
Student-faculty ratio	15:1
% faculty part-time	58
% faculty female	34
% faculty minority	12
Total faculty	120

SURVEY SAYS...

Diverse opinions accepted
in classrooms
Great research resources
Beautiful campus

STUDENTS

Enrollment of law school	631
% male/female	54/46
% out-of-state	86
% full-time	100
% minority	18
% international	3
# of countries represented	17
Average age of entering class	23

ACADEMICS

Academic Experience Rating	**96**
Profs interesting rating	97
Profs accessible rating	89
Hours of study per day	4.5

Academic Specialties

Civil procedure, commercial law, constitutional law, corporation securities law, criminal law, environmental law, government services, human rights law, intellectual property law, international law, labor law, legal history, legal philosophy, property, taxation. Students can also craft their own specializations.

Advanced Degrees Offered

LLM 1 year.

Combined Degrees Offered

JD/MBA 4 years, JD/MA 5 years, JD/PhD 7 years, JD/MDiv 5 years, JD/MTS 4 years, JD/MD 6 years, JD/MPP 4 years, LLM/MA (Latin American studies) 2 years, PhD (law and economics) 5 to 6 years.

Academics

More than a law school, Vanderbilt is "a home away from home," students here tell us. The school is remarkably "student friendly." One 1L elaborates, "Not only does [the Dean of Students] know your name, she knows about you and actually cares about your progress." Impressive facilities are a matter of course. "Our law building is gorgeous," a 3L reports. "It underwent massive renovations a few years ago, so our classrooms are spacious, comfortable, and equipped with all of the latest technology. The building also has a ton of windows to let in natural light, a great asset when you spend every daylight hour inside." Professors, "despite being legal scholars of national fame . . . are approachable people [who] can explain the law in a way that is easy to understand." They are also remarkably helpful. "A week before my torts exam, my professor gave the 100-person class his private cell phone number and told us we could call him with questions between 8:00 A.M. and 11:00 P.M. as long as there was no heavy breathing. That's commitment."

The course selection at Vanderbilt leans to a "general legal education." In recent years, however, many students have called for "more formal specialization programs," and the "responsive" administration is taking action. Already in possession of a "very strong business law program," the school is "currently working on creating . . . a program in technology and entertainment law." In addition, "new concentrations [are] being developed by the faculty" in areas such as "regulatory concerns and litigation." Students here have also called upon the school "to better prepare us for legal practice, rather than engage us in theoretical discussions about how the law should be." The administration, as expected, has heeded their calls. Vanderbilt's "new dean" is "making positive moves towards incorporating more practical experience in the curriculum," and some here believe the school is "on the cusp of a fairly radical curriculum change" that will "make Vandy on the cutting edge of approaching legal education in a more practical way." Recently, the school has also provided "more encouragement for students to pursue careers outside private law firms," such as "public interest work and government work." In particular, "The school is putting a great effort into expanding its public interest profile with the addition of a Public Interest Institute in the coming years." To that end, students say "more clerkships and government opportunities" would also be appreciated as well as "better loan-forgiveness programs for students" who plan to enter those fields.

Students believe "Vandy's Career Cervices Department is top-notch, with motivated and dedicated people running the department." A top-third class rank seems to be key and "can get you a big-firm job in a major city." A 3L writes, "Like many of my classmates, I had a job early on in my third year. I am not at the top of my class (probably top third), but I've had plenty of offers and opportunities. I will be working in the (Midwestern) city of my choice next year and making a little over $100,000." While some students question the reach of Vanderbilt's Career Services Office, it is now "bringing more employers" "from the Northeast and West Coast" to campus. In nearly all areas, "The school's willingness to change to reflect what students need makes it stand out." One notable exception is the legal writing program, which students have long felt "could use some improvement," namely "less emphasis on grades and more opportunities for constructive criticism." In addition, "Registration is needlessly complicated."

Life

"The best thing about Vanderbilt is, by far, the students," a 2L asserts. Students say "Vandy has the types of diversity that count: ideological, experiential, and geographical. Students hail from all over the country; some are Marines, some are hippies; some are Bible thumpers, some are atheistic intellectuals; some are conservative, some are liberal; most are somewhere in between." Perhaps most importantly, "Vandy is a law school filled with non-lawyers." A 2L quips: "Unlike every other law school I have encountered, where 75 percent of the people are unfit for human society, only about a quarter of the people [here] are." On the whole, students "provide a lot of support for one another, and keep things in perspective. People are friendly, generally upbeat, and willing to help out." "You'll never have a hard time finding someone to study or eat with you during the day or to go out with you at night," a sanguine 1L adds. Competition here "is low; most people are self-motivated but go out of their way to seem under-motivated. Actually, it can be annoying sometimes how anti-competitive people are; they will profess not to be working, but you know they are spending some extra hours here and there to do their best."

Vanderbilt's "Campus is beautiful and serene, which compensates for the stress of finals." Hometown Nashville "is a fantastic and up-and-coming city," an enthusiastic 1L writes. "I have been extremely impressed by the culture and environment. The town is much more cosmopolitan than [a] New York City girl would expect." In case you haven't heard, "People party" at Vanderbilt. A lot. In fact, "The social demands of the school might consume more time than the classwork, depending on who your professors are and what you take." Social options include "Bar Review every Thursday night for students who want to do the bar scene" and "lots of gatherings among friends." In addition, "Every Friday the school buys kegs, and both students and professors come together for a drink." The prevalence of alcohol here—"all after-class student activities at the law school include a generous amount of beer and wine"—leads one incredulous student to exclaim, "We all still drink like undergrads!"

Getting In

A plethora of qualified candidates apply to Vanderbilt each year, and the school's rolling selection policy allows it to take the time it needs to carefully consider each application. Applicants who take the LSAT in December or February are at no disadvantage here.

Clinical program required	No
Legal writing course requirement	Yes
Legal methods course requirement	No
Legal research course requirement	Yes
Moot court requirement	No
Public interest law requirement	No

ADMISSIONS

Selectivity Rating	**92**
# applications received	3,640
# applicants accepted	921
# acceptees attending	190
Average LSAT	166
LSAT Range	164–167
Average undergrad GPA	3.7
Application fee	$50
Regular application	3/15
Regular notification	5/1
Rolling notification	Yes
Early application program	No
Transfer students accepted	Yes
Evening division offered	No
Part-time accepted	No
LSDAS accepted	Yes

Applicants Also Look At
Cornell University, Duke University, Georgetown University, University of Michigan, University of Virginia.

International Students

TOEFL required of international students	Yes

FINANCIAL FACTS

Annual tuition	$36,000
Books and supplies	$1,528
Room and board (off-campus)	$11,944
Financial aid application deadline	2/15
% first-year students receiving some sort of aid	90
% receiving some sort of aid	87
% of aid that is merit based	86
% receiving scholarships	65
Average grant	$15,000
Average loan	$36,860
Average total aid package	$56,672
Average debt	$101,408

EMPLOYMENT INFORMATION

Career Rating	**96**	**Grads Employed by Field (%)**	
Rate of placement (nine months out)	98	Academic	2
Average starting salary	$115,000	Business/Industry	5
State for bar exam	TN, GA, NY, DC, TX	Government	4
Pass rate for first-time bar	95	Judicial clerkships	10
Employers Who Frequently Hire Grads		Military	1
King and Spalding; Alston and Bird;		Private practice	76
Shearman and Sterling; Kirkland and Ellis		Public Interest	2
Bass, Berry, and Sims; Waller, Lansden,			
Dortch, and Davis; Locke, Liddell, and Sapp			
Prominent Alumni			
Greg Abbott, Texas Attorney General; Fred Thompson, U.S. Senator, counsel Watergate Committee, actor; Honorable Martha Daughtrey, U.S. Circuit Court judge.			

VERMONT LAW SCHOOL

INSTITUTIONAL INFORMATION

Public/private	Private
Student-faculty ratio	13:1
% faculty female	47
% faculty minority	10
Total faculty	48

SURVEY SAYS...

Liberal students
Beautiful campus

STUDENTS

Enrollment of law school	552
% male/female	48/52
% out-of-state	90
% full-time	100
% minority	15
% international	2
# of countries represented	5
Average age of entering class	26

ACADEMICS

Academic Experience Rating	**72**
Profs interesting rating	77
Profs accessible rating	87
Hours of study per day	5

Academic Specialties

Civil procedure, commercial law, constitutional law, corporation securities law, criminal law, environmental law, government services, human rights law, international law, labor law, legal history, legal philosophy, property, taxation.

Advanced Degrees Offered

JD, 3 years; MSEL, environmental law, 1 year; LLM, environmental law, 1 year.

Combined Degrees Offered

JD/Master of Studies in Environmental Law 3 years.

Clinical program required	No
Legal writing course requirement	Yes
Legal methods course requirement	Yes
Legal research	

Academics

"If you are into environmental law, this is the place to be," declares a 3L at Vermont Law School, a "stand-alone law school" in the "picturesque, tranquil, [and] rural" Green Mountains. "Classes are small" and "Environmental law permeates even the traditional core curriculum." There is also "a lot of emphasis on public policy and ethics." Unique summer sessions allow students to analyze dozens of highly specialized aspects of environmental law. In the Semester-in-Practice program, students gain experience working for government agencies, NGOs, and law firms in—among other places—Washington, DC and Montreal. The Environmental and Natural Resources Law Clinic affords students the opportunity to work with leading public-interest attorneys. Other great ways to gain practical experience include the "wonderful" judicial externship program and internships in the Vermont General Assembly.

The "incredibly approachable" faculty members "genuinely care about your success" and are "always available for help." "Some of the top" environmental law professors "in the country" call this school home. "Most professors have a passion for teaching" and "share their enthusiasm." "We have so many top-notch scholars who could be at much higher-ranked law schools but who teach here because they want to live in Vermont, or because they believe in the ethos of the school," brags a 2L. "The Socratic Method isn't used a lot," though, "which sometimes lead to a quiet classroom." Unfortunately, "each first-year section is stuck with exactly one professor who is almost universally dreaded and subject to poor reviews," discloses a 2L. Also, "Some professors are so overly liberal that it impairs their ability to be evenhanded." The administration is "generally fine" but "can sometimes seem unorganized." It also "has its quirks." Students note, for example, that the dean leads "weekly hikes."

Some students call Career Services "decent" while others say that "finding a job after graduating from VLS can be very hard, even in Vermont." Students also gripe about the school's relatively low bar-passage rate. Frustration about school finances is another hardy perennial. "Frankly, VLS alums need to give back to the school," asserts a 2L. While environmental law "will always be" the "bread and butter," a few students feel that "all other areas of the law are ignored."

The "environmentally progressive" facilities here are "very conducive to learning." "Large parts of the school have been either recently built or are newly renovated" providing "plenty of power outlets." The library's environmental collection is "unparalleled" but it's "very limited when it comes to more general topics." Wireless access is not always speedy. The "rudimentary gym on campus" is "pretty pathetic." Many elements of the buildings are "green" and "reflect the school's strong environmental and public policy focus." As such, the heating, cooling, and lighting systems are designed to minimize energy consumption. At mealtime, the "organic cafeteria food" is "unexpectedly tasty." Few other schools can boast that the "freaking awesome" composting toilets—which, somehow, don't involve any water—"are a real treat."

Life

"There is a real mix of students" here—including everyone "from 22-year-olds right out of college who still like to party" to "50-year-olds whose kids are grown." These "smart, fun" students describe themselves as "generally athletic" and "voraciously outdoorsy." Some are "very open and accepting." Others are "judgmental and opinionated." A common bond grows from the fact that students are "passionate" about the environment, social

KATHY HARTMAN, ASSOCIATE DEAN FOR ENROLLMENT MANAGEMENT
CHELSEA STREET, SOUTH ROYALTON, VT 05068-0096
TEL: 888-277-5985 FAX: 802-763-7071
E-MAIL: ADMISS@VERMONTLAW.EDU • INTERNET: WWW.VERMONTLAW.EDU

course requirement	Yes
Moot court requirement	Yes
Public interest	
law requirement	No

ADMISSIONS

Selectivity Rating	**69**
# applications received	1,119
# applicants accepted	632
# acceptees attending	202
Average LSAT	154
LSAT Range	151–157
Average undergrad GPA	3.27
Application fee	$60
Regular application	3/15
Regular notification	4/1
Rolling notification	Yes
Early application program	No
Transfer students accepted	Yes
Evening division offered	No
Part-time accepted	No
LSDAS accepted	Yes

Applicants Also Look At
Franklin Pierce Law Center, Lewis and Clark College, Pace University, State University of New York at Albany, Suffolk University, University of Colorado, University of Denver.

International Students

TOEFL required	
of international students	Yes
Minimum paper TOEFL	600

FINANCIAL FACTS

Annual tuition	$29,730
Books and supplies	$950
Room and board	
(off-campus)	$9,530
Financial aid application	
deadline	3/1
% first-year students	
receiving some sort of aid	94
% receiving some sort of aid	95
% of aid that is merit based	39
% receiving scholarships	52
Average grant	$7,000
Average loan	$18,500
Average total aid package	$31,000
Average debt	$111,567

justice, and human rights. One student finds it all "very refreshing." Another calls it "the personification of the hippy, tree-hugger establishment."

VLS boasts "an unrivaled community." "There really aren't any cutthroat students here," so a "great feeling of camaraderie" prevails. "You can leave your laptop in the library and no one will touch it." "Anyone can send an e-mail to everyone," reports a 2L, "so you are informed about all kinds of things ranging from a lost pair of mittens to the date when the Vermont Supreme Court will next hear oral arguments at the school." There is "absolutely no anonymity," though, and "lots of gossip." "The grapevine is pervasive, but not super vindictive."

"Rural Vermont" has "New England charm" but it's "definitely not for diehard city slickers." The surrounding "natural beauty" "takes your breath away every single day." "It's truly amazing to wake up to," lauds a 1L. "For the nature enthusiast," hiking, rafting, "and all other sorts of outdoor activities" are plentiful. Skiing and snowboarding abound as well. Just "Get used to skiing on ice." ("Builds character," notes a 3L.) Ultimately, though, "You are a long way from anywhere" here. "Vermont Law School is in a 'town' populated by approximately 2,000 permanent residents" called South Royalton where "Rent is extremely high." "SoRo has a bank, a post office, a pizza place, a laundromat, a great co-op," and a "local dive bar." The nearest grocery store is in New Hampshire," which is "25 minutes away." "Students without a car should not come here," advises a 3L. Socially, "the SBA is a little overzealous" and there is "incredible participation in student groups." "There are many student-run conferences and activities—and parties—throughout the school year, which complement those sponsored by the school." Students can join "organized soccer, hockey, softball, and rugby teams" as well. "Though it's a small town, I had a great house to live in, a great housemate to share it with, and have met people here with whom I know I'll be in touch 10 years from now," predicts a 3L. "I actually enjoyed law school."

Getting In

The 25th percentile of admitted students has LSAT scores of 149 and GPAs of just a tad under 3.0. Admitted students at the 75th percentile have LSAT scores of 157 and GPAs of about 3.5.

EMPLOYMENT INFORMATION

Career Rating	**71**	**Grads Employed by Field (%)**	
Rate of placement (nine months out)	91	Academic	3
Average starting salary	$48,804	Business/Industry	17
State for bar exam	VT, MA, NY, CO, NJ	Government	13
Pass rate for first-time bar	61	Judicial clerkships	16
Employers Who Frequently Hire Grads		Private practice	33
Federal and state judges in the northeast;		Public Interest	18
law firms throughout New England;			
Beveridge and Diamond; federal and state			
agencies.			
Prominent Alumni			
Glenn Berger, partner, Skadden Arps;			
Charles diLeva, lead, Environmental			
Counsel World Bank; Linda Smiddy,			
professor of law, Vermont Law School.			

VILLANOVA UNIVERSITY
SCHOOL OF LAW

INSTITUTIONAL INFORMATION

Public/private	Private
Affiliation	Roman Catholic
Student-faculty ratio	17:1
% faculty part-time	49
% faculty female	35
% faculty minority	10
Total faculty	109

SURVEY SAYS...

Diverse opinions accepted
in classrooms
Great library staff
Abundant externship/internship/
clerkship opportunities
Students love Villanova, PA

STUDENTS

Enrollment of law school	729
% male/female	52/48
% out-of-state	40
% full-time	100
% minority	17
% international	1
# of countries represented	5
Average age of entering class	23

ACADEMICS

Academic Experience Rating	**83**
Profs interesting rating	89
Profs accessible rating	81
Hours of study per day	5.5

Advanced Degrees Offered

JD 3 years, LLM (taxation) 24 credits.

Combined Degrees Offered

JD/MBA 3 to 4 years, JD/PhD (psychology) 7 years, JD/LLM (taxation) 3.5 years.

Clinical program required	No
Legal writing	
course requirement	Yes
Legal methods	
course requirement	No
Legal research	
course requirement	Yes
Moot court requirement	Yes
Public interest	
law requirement	No

Academics

At Villanova University School of Law, students find "a good balance in an interactive and educational atmosphere" through a blend of lecture, discussion, and serious hands-on experience. Students say the "absolutely wonderful" professors are the heart and soul of the program. "Instructors are all extremely intelligent and have a wealth of real-world experience, yet remain in touch with students," says a 1L. In fact, he tells us, "My law school professors are much more helpful and approachable than my undergrad professors were." Another student agrees that the "Professors' knowledge and experience is fundamental to the Villanova experience." Many here happily report a lack of the "heavy competitive atmosphere that you hear about at other schools," noting that "we all encourage each other to do well."

Villanova takes a fairly traditional approach to introductory course work, and students say "There is still a heavy reliance on the Socratic Method and many classes use a lecture format (especially in the first year)." In the next two years, students continue studying the basic principals of law, while adding elective courses to their schedule. Experiential learning is emphasized throughout the curriculum, and students dole out praise for the school's strong legal writing and research courses, simulation programs, clinics, and externships. The school has a "clear emphasis" on "solidifying students' legal writing skills." In addition, students take on real legal work thanks to the school's "strong commitment to community service and pro bono work."

For a Catholic institution, it should come as no surprise that a "Catholic identity" reigns supreme. However, some students wish opportunities for service were not restricted by the administration's commitment to Catholic values. ("No 'regular hours' in the 40-hour workweek can be spent helping efforts to litigate for women's reproductive freedom, and the participating organization must be aware of the policy.") Ultimately, many wonder "how the administration will balance the school's Catholic mission with its mission as a legal institution."

After bemoaning that the school had "really outgrown its building and parking areas," (many students cite the "severe lack of classrooms, computers, parking spots, hallways, lockers, and space in general") students happily report "a new building is in the works." This new development's plans call for a brand new state-of-the-art law school on a site adjacent to the university's suburban Philadelphia campus. While they may complain that the campus has a "high school atmosphere," students also say they leave Villanova well-prepared for their professional career in the adult world. Students insist that "opportunities for practical experience are abundant," and the "Career Services Department works really hard to help students find jobs in the private and public sectors." They note that the school has "strong professional contacts in Pennsylvania, New Jersey. and Delaware" and that "major firms routinely interview on campus and hire many Villanova graduates."

Life

When they are not hitting the books, Villanova students live the high life at the many bars, clubs, and restaurants in Philadelphia, as well as at campus events. A student assures us, "The Student Bar Association spends a lot of time planning activities to students. There are many active students groups as well." According to another, "Students get along well and the ones that choose to socialize together have a great time."

NOE BERNAL, ASSISTANT DEAN FOR ADMISSIONS
299 NORTH SPRING MILL ROAD, VILLANOVA, PA 19085
TEL: 610-519-7010 FAX: 610-519-6291
E-MAIL: ADMISSIONS@LAW.VILLANOVA.EDU • INTERNET: WWW.LAW.VILLANOVA.EDU

Still, many students choose to maintain a life outside of school, living off-campus with their friends or spouses. Getting to campus is easy since "The train runs literally out the front door of the law school." One student advises, "There is a bar that students usually hang out at which can be fun, but sometimes after seeing these people all day and every day, it's good to do something away from the law school crowd." Luckily, that is easy to accomplish at Villanova thanks to the school's "amazing" location. One student enthuses, "It is 25 minutes from Philadelphia, as well as a short drive to New York City, Washington DC, Baltimore, the beaches, and skiing!"

Most students say that they get along with their classmates, though some say the student body is pretty "homogenous" and "not exactly diverse." However, "Villanova has openly stated that they feel that diversity is a compelling interest at the institution" and many believe that "in time, Villanova will be one of the more diverse legal institutions."

Getting In

For the admitted class of 2006, admitted students in the 25th percentile had an average LSAT score of 160 and a 3.27 GPA. Admitted students in the 75th percentile had an average LSAT score of 163 and a 3.62 GPA. However, Villanova may consider students with a lower GPA if they offer other important qualities, such as commitment to service, volunteer work, or unique professional experience. The majority of students who enter do so within a year or two of college, and the average age of a Villanova student in their first year is 23.

ADMISSIONS

Selectivity Rating	84
# applications received	2,834
# applicants accepted	1,022
# acceptees attending	248
Average LSAT	162
LSAT Range	160–163
Average undergrad GPA	3.44
Application fee	$75
Regular application	3/1
Regular notification	Rolling
Rolling notification	Yes
Early application program	No
Transfer students accepted	Yes
Evening division offered	No
Part-time accepted	No
LSDAS accepted	Yes

Applicants Also Look At

American University; Boston College; The George Washington University; Rutgers, The State University of New Jersey; Temple University; University of Pennsylvania.

International Students

TOEFL required of international students	No
TOEFL recommended of international students	No

FINANCIAL FACTS

Annual tuition	$29,150
Books and supplies	$4,738
Room and board (off-campus)	$13,950
Financial aid application deadline	3/1
% first-year students receiving some sort of aid	85
% receiving some sort of aid	82
% of aid that is merit based	3
% receiving scholarships	19
Average grant	$10,671
Average loan	$38,538
Average total aid package	$45,635
Average debt	$98,326

EMPLOYMENT INFORMATION

		Grads Employed by Field (%)	
Career Rating	82		
Rate of placement (nine months out)	94	Academic	2
Average starting salary	$80,786	Business/Industry	12
State for bar exam	PA, NJ, NY, DE	Government	8
Pass rate for first-time bar	85	Judicial clerkships	14
Employers Who Frequently Hire Grads		Private practice	60
Law firms in the Mid-Atlantic region; state		Public Interest	4
and federal judges; government agencies			
at all levels.			

Prominent Alumni
Honorable Edward G. Rendell, Governor of Pennsylvania; Honorable Marjorie O. Rendell, U.S. Court of Appeals, 3rd Circuit; Jeffrey S. Moorad, general partner, Arizona Diamondbacks.

WAKE FOREST UNIVERSITY
SCHOOL OF LAW

Academics

"Litigation-oriented" Wake Forest University School of Law "is an unbelievable experience." "The size of the school is perfect." At Wake Forest, you will not "get swallowed up and just become a number." "There are no more than 40 people in any first-year class," and this "allows you to get to know your professors and your professors to get to know you," exalts one student. An "emphasis on practical applications of the law and on-trial advocacy are two of the greatest strengths" of the curriculum. "Hands-on experience" is available through several clinics. "Structured study groups, practice exams, and one-on-one tutoring" mitigate some of the first-year stress. "I find that there is almost an overwhelming amount of support here," observes an appreciative 1L. The "practical and thorough" three-semester-long legal research and writing curriculum "helps to teach real-world skills." To top it off, "Wake Forest offers a large number of full-tuition scholarships which make it possible to attend law school and take the job you want rather than the job you need in order to pay off debt."

Wake's "approachable, knowledgeable, generous" professors are "invaluable resources." "Learning trial practice from a federal prosecutor and human rights law from someone who negotiated treaties at the U.N. made me feel like I was really getting something useful out of my classroom time," comments one student. Professors are "truly dedicated to excellent teaching," and they "genuinely care about their students." They "also have a great deal of brilliant individual personality, which makes class a lot more fun and makes them kind of like rock stars." Some have "intimidating nicknames" (e.g., "Mad Dog") but they "seem to remember what it was like to be on the other end of the stick and are compassionate." In class, "Discourse is encouraged." "It's not just the loud mouths who chime in." Outside of class, professors "welcome students dropping by their offices at almost any time of the day." The administration here is "available for questions, general help, and crisis situations. "Nothing is ever done in a timely fashion," though.

Some students rave that Career Services "will do just about anything to help you" "if you take the time to actually go in there." They note that Wake "is successfully working to improve its reputation outside the Southeast." A disgruntled faction contends that Career Services is "out of touch with the needs of students." "For on-campus interviews, there aren't as many big New York or DC firms," observes one student.

Wake's facilities are "drab and basically awful." The elevators are "slow [and] small." The bathrooms are "outdated" and "There aren't enough" of them. "Classrooms are always very cold." "The hallways are too narrow. When the bell rings between classes (yes, there's a bell), they fill up with dense mobs of the only thing more obnoxious than middle schoolers: law students." "Wake Forest is at the top of the class when it comes to technological advancement," though. "The wireless Internet and on-call staff make access to all sorts of information easy." The library has "very little study space" and "needs some updating" to accommodate laptops but it contains "a broad range of research materials."

MELANIE E. NUTT, DIRECTOR OF ADMISSIONS AND FINANCIAL AID
PO BOX 7206 REYNOLDA STATION, WINSTON-SALEM, NC 27109
TEL: 336-758-5437 FAX: 336-758-3930
E-MAIL: ADMISSIONS@LAW.WFU.EDU • INTERNET: WWW.LAW.WFU.EDU

Life

"Wake does a good job recruiting students from across the country." In terms of ethnic diversity, though, "The law school could use some work." "They have made steps in the last couple years, but there is still room for improvement." Politically, "Students tend toward the conservative." ("The professors are generally much more liberal.") "Some students are more competitive than others" but "It's not an 'I'm-only-here-to-look-out-for-myself' kind of atmosphere." "People are willing to share their outlines, notes, etc."

A "genuinely friendly atmosphere" makes "going to law school a much more comfortable experience than it might otherwise be." "The welcoming atmosphere at Wake Forest has made the last three years a wonderful experience," reminisces a 3L. "It is really easy to make friends" because "Everyone knows everyone else." Occasionally, "You can get a little too much togetherness": "The gossip mill runs amok. It often feels like high school." However, the student population is "diverse enough socially" that "Everyone can find a niche to fit into." On campus, there is "a fairly strong divide between the 'cool kids'" (who have more of a "throw-down-and-drink mentality") "and the others (who don't)." A large number of older students "tends to have moved past the beer-hazed weekend revelry and, as such, they can do other activities together."

While some students concede that Winston-Salem "isn't the greatest social scene in the world," they "make the best of it." If you are seeking "a good place to buy a home some time this century and raise a family," Winston-Salem is "ideal." "If you want nightclubs open until 4:00 A.M., you should probably consider another city." When students here "need to escape, there is always Charlotte, Greensboro, or Raleigh-Durham."

Getting In

Wake Forest is a little bit of a diamond in the rough in the sense that it is nationally recognized as a top law school but not quite as hard to get into as some of its peers. Admitted students at the 25th percentile have LSAT scores of 162 and GPAs of about 3.2. Admitted students at the 75th percentile have LSAT scores of 166 and GPAs of about 3.6.

Moot court requirement	No
Public interest law requirement	No

ADMISSIONS

Selectivity Rating	**88**
# applications received	2,422
# applicants accepted	571
# acceptees attending	154
Average LSAT	162
LSAT Range	162–166
Average undergrad GPA	3.4
Application fee	$60
Regular application	4/1
Regular notification	4/15
Rolling notification	Yes
Early application program	No
Transfer students accepted	Yes
Evening division offered	No
Part-time accepted	No
LSDAS accepted	Yes

Applicants Also Look At

American University, College of William and Mary, Emory University, The George Washington University, The University of North Carolina at Chapel Hill, Tulane University, Vanderbilt University.

International Students

TOEFL required of international students	No
TOEFL recommended of international students	Yes
Minimum paper TOEFL	650

FINANCIAL FACTS

Annual tuition	$27,900
Books and supplies	$800
Room and board (off-campus)	$14,000
Financial aid application deadline	5/15
% first-year students receiving some sort of aid	78
% receiving some sort of aid	78
% of aid that is merit based	74
% receiving scholarships	36
Average grant	$19,800
Average loan	$30,562
Average total aid package	
Average debt	$75,418

EMPLOYMENT INFORMATION

Career Rating	71	Grads Employed by Field (%)	
Average starting salary	$63,831	Business/Industry	5
State for bar exam	NC, VA, GA, NY, FL	Government	15
Pass rate for first-time bar	92	Judicial clerkships	13
Employers Who Frequently Hire Grads		Military	2
For a representative list see Career Services website at www.law.wfu.edu.		Other	2
		Private practice	62
		Public Interest	1

WASHBURN UNIVERSITY
SCHOOL OF LAW

Academics

Its "small size" and "close-knit" atmosphere make Washburn University School of Law a popular choice for students. Washburn's "reputation for graduating outstanding trial lawyers" is matched by its "proud historical commitment to public service," not to mention an "exceptional" and "dedicated" faculty. The "family-style setting" makes acclimating to law school an easy process. One student conveys, "I felt very comfortable at Washburn Law the second I entered the school, and that comfort and acceptance has not wavered."

The law school's cozy size allows students to receive one-on-one attention from faculty. Students say the friendly and supportive professors "make law school such a pleasure," and they "are more than willing to help out in any way that they can, as long as you ask." Students rave about the accessibility of the professors and the quality of instruction, saying that "they are tough but compassionate" but most importantly, "really care about your success." According to one student, "They truly want me to be successful and always equal or exceed the effort I put into my education. Here, I feel like I am on a team that wants to win."

Students have mixed feelings about the administration. Some students feel "The administration is fantastic in some respects and completely inept in others. The ones who know what they are doing are wonderful, and the ones who don't unfortunately can make spectacles of themselves at school functions." Others say that the administration is "second to none" and "seems to jump [into action] when a law student asks for something." Overall, there is a feeling that "problems or concerns students have are addressed by the administration promptly."

Students rate their overall academic experience as positive, but many wish that Washburn would offer a wider variety of courses or at least more time slots for required classes. One student observes, "We have great certificate opportunities, but it is very difficult to schedule the necessary classes because class availability is sparse with non-bar classes." On the other hand, students are quick to note that Washburn's legal writing program (one of only eight in the country taught by tenure-track faculty) is excellent, as is its clinic program. One student remarks, "In addition to a functioning law clinic where third-years can actually practice law under supervision (almost like medical school) there are tons of course offerings that address exactly what lawyers actually do, applying the 'book law' and research and writing skills as you go." "Hitting the real world of law is, of course, scary, but I feel quite confident in both my abilities and familiarity with what to expect thanks to my school."

Students report that "the school itself is well equipped with an amazing legal library, knowledgeable library staff, and great resources at every turn." As a Federal Depository library, Washburn's library has "great access to current government materials," and "The classroom and research facilities at the school are adequate for what every law student would ever need or conceive of needing." On the downside, "Parking is a genuine problem and, though it seems petty, it's a legitimate gripe. Law students should not have to be

KARLA BEAM, DIRECTOR OF ADMISSIONS
1700 COLLEGE, TOPEKA, KS 66621-1140
TEL: 785-670-1185 FAX: 785-670-1120
E-MAIL: ADMISSIONS@WASHBURNLAW.EDU • INTERNET: WASHBURNLAW.EDU

treated like royalty, but they deserve [better] than to have to park three blocks from the school and walk through snow to class."

Life

The congenial atmosphere at Washburn has students appreciating its "laid-back, non-competitive tone." Student organizations on campus also work hard to foster student activities and collaboration. Some feel that an air of competition exists, but that this is not necessarily a negative. As one student remarks, Washburn is "competitive, intimate, and tough, but we have all gotten to know each other very well. I have made some wonderful friends. It's weird, like being on a team where we all play the same position." Another satisfied customer reports, "I can honestly say that my choice in going to Washburn was the best I could have made, and I don't think that I would have been happier at another school."

"Truly the only downfall to Washburn is the fact that it is located in Topeka, Kansas, but that downfall may be exactly what provides an ideal location to foster more studying and less partying." One student feels that "Topeka gets a little bit of a bad rap. I think it's fair when students laugh about how *not* hopping Topeka is, but the fact that it is the state capital (with all the jobs and internship opportunities that it provides) far outweighs the fact that it's a dull city." Additionally, students report that Lawrence, a nice college town, is only 25 minutes away, and Kansas City is an hour drive. As one student observes, "If there's not satisfactory action at those two places, law school should probably be postponed."

Getting In

Washburn's Admissions Committee does not base its admissions decisions solely on numerical scores but considers a variety of factors including a sincere interest in the legal profession, a record of excellence, and improvement in grade history. Admitted students at the 25th percentile have an LSAT score of 152 and a GPA of 3.0. Admitted students at the 75th percentile have an LSAT score of 157 and a GPA of 3.7.

ADMISSIONS

Selectivity Rating	73
# applications received	963
# applicants accepted	411
# acceptees attending	137
Average LSAT	154
LSAT Range	152–157
Average undergrad GPA	3.37
Application fee	$40
Regular application	4/1
Regular notification	6/1
Rolling notification	Yes
Early application program	No
Transfer students accepted	Yes
Evening division offered	No
Part-time accepted	No
LSDAS accepted	Yes

Applicants Also Look At
University of Kansas, University of Missouri—-Kansas City.

International Students

TOEFL required	
of international students	Yes
Minimum paper TOEFL	550
Minimum computer TOEFL	213

FINANCIAL FACTS

Annual tuition (resident)	$13,530
Annual tuition (nonresident)	$22,260
Books and supplies	$1,698
Tuition per credit (resident)	$451
Tuition per credit (nonresident)	$742
Room and board	$7,654
Financial aid application deadline	7/1
% first-year students receiving some sort of aid	92
% receiving some sort of aid	92
% of aid that is merit based	12
% receiving scholarships	39
Average grant	$7,186
Average loan	$22,453
Average total aid package	$24,351
Average debt	$65,821

EMPLOYMENT INFORMATION

Career Rating	76	Grads Employed by Field (%)	
Rate of placement (nine months out)	92	Academic	2
Average starting salary	$50,347	Business/Industry	18
State for bar exam	KS, MO	Government	14
Pass rate for first-time bar	90	Judicial clerkships	6
Prominent Alumni		Military	1
Lillian A. Apodaca, past president,		Private practice	49
Hispanic Bar Association; Robert J. Dole,		Public Interest	10
former U.S. Senator; Bill H. Kurtis,			
journalist/American justice; Delano E.			
Lewis, former U.S. Ambassador to South			
Africa; Ron Richey, chair of Executive			
Committee, Torchmark Corp.			

WASHINGTON AND LEE UNIVERSITY
SCHOOL OF LAW

INSTITUTIONAL INFORMATION

Public/private	Private
Student-faculty ratio	10:1
% faculty part-time	15
% faculty female	28
% faculty minority	10
Total faculty	39

SURVEY SAYS...

Diverse opinions accepted
in classrooms
Great research resources
Great library staff
Abundant externship/internship/
clerkship opportunities

STUDENTS

Enrollment of law school	403
% male/female	59/41
% out-of-state	86
% full-time	100
% minority	19
% international	3
# of countries represented	14
Average age of entering class	24

ACADEMICS

Academic Experience Rating	**90**
Profs interesting rating	95
Profs accessible rating	98
Hours of study per day	4.74

Advanced Degrees Offered

LLM (United States law).

Combined Degrees Offered

JD/MHA 6 years.

Clinical program required	No
Legal writing	
course requirement	Yes
Legal methods	
course requirement	No
Legal research	
course requirement	No
Moot court requirement	No
Public interest	
law requirement	No

Academics

A small student body, a rural location, and a lack of a part-time program combine to create a distinctive academic experience at Washington and Lee University School of Law. "This is not a school where you will go to classes and have a job," a 2L writes. "School is your life; the administration makes that very clear to you when you step on campus." This contributes to a "nurturing and family environment" where students and staff are "on a first-name basis," and "It is not unusual for the deans to stop you in the hall [to] check up on all aspects of your life or for your classmates to send you their notes when you miss a class." Full-time faculty members are "here because they care deeply about teaching." They're also "remarkably good" lawyers—"Several argue before the Supreme Court on a regular basis," a 1L informs—and they "work really hard to get to know you and help you succeed outside the classroom. I interviewed for a federal judicial clerkship, and the judge said that the recommendation that my professor wrote was the best she had ever read. This particular professor was determined that I would get a federal clerkship and went above and beyond the call of duty to ensure that I did," a 3L reports. The school's small size also "allow[s] for significant involvement in a variety of activities, such as moot court and journals." The intimate setting does have its drawbacks, however, as "course selection is limited and the schedule is structured in such a way that you're often prevented from taking a lot of the courses you want to. Many classes are only offered once a year, or once every two years, and it seems that a large portion of classes tend to be offered at the same time." While the school "has a policy of providing any course requested by a minimum number of students, such courses are typically taught by visiting professors" of "varying quality."

Many here believe that Washington and Lee needs "more diversity in its faculty and student body." A 1L explains: "Because there are certain ethnic groups that are still underrepresented, there is a tendency by both the faculty and student body to make assumptions and close their eyes to other important points of view in the world." Compounding the issue, hometown Lexington, Virginia is "in the sticks," so "Students are isolated, with no place to turn but [the school]. This cannot help but narrow their perspective of the world." To broaden perspectives, the school "successfully expends energy and resources" to bring "many notable speakers, including District and Circuit Court judges, political appointees, top international and national lawyers, and policy experts," to campus. Still, a 3L writes: "For me, the hardest part of law school has not been the 'school' aspect, but rather the challenge of doing law school in a very small, very isolated, rural area with a very small group of peers." The upside of this unique experience is that it engenders "a strong alumni base. W&L graduates are always willing to help out fellow alums."

While the active alumni base ensures that Washington and Lee's "reputation among those professionals who are 'in the know'" is strong, students here find it "difficult" to "pursue a legal career outside of the Southeast (especially DC, Virginia, South Carolina, and Alabama)." The school's Office of Career Planning and Professional Development "has made progress helping students break into the New York market," but students say that "if you want to get to the Northeast, the Midwest, or the West, be prepared for a lot of individual legwork." The school's library is "wonderful." "Every student . . . has their own personal study carrel that has a little closet. It is great to have my own space in the law school," a 1L tells us. Classrooms are "state of the art," "well lit, spacious, and comfortable." The new Moot Court Room is "beautiful."

ANDREA HILTON HOWE, DIRECTOR OF ADMISSIONS
SYDNEY LEWIS HALL, LEXINGTON, VA 24450
TEL: 540-458-8503 FAX: 540-458-8586
E-MAIL: LAWADM@WLU.EDU • INTERNET: WWW.LAW.WLU.EDU

Life

Washington and Lee is located in "an extremely isolated, rural area," and law students report "little contact with undergrads, VMI students, and townies." In this potentially "claustrophobic" environment, the school's honor code, now more than 100 years old, is a calming presence. "We can leave our laptops around the school without fear of theft or vandalism," a 1L reports. "There are never any stolen or missing books, and if I have a question I can count on my friends [to give] me an honest answer. There are enough opportunities for everybody, and class rank is not disclosed, so people don't feel a need to compete against anybody but themselves." By all accounts, "Students form very close relationships" with each other. "Law school sports are of paramount importance" here, and students report "a full docket" of them, including "kickball, football, dodgeball, basketball, hockey, and softball." Among these, football is king, and "Every Friday during the fall we play football on the law school lawn and drink kegs of beer." Throw in "cocktail parties" "every other weekend," and some will grouse that "activities held at the school always center [on] alcohol. This focus is less appealing for those who have progressed beyond the drunken days of fraternity and sorority life in undergraduate school." Even if sports and keg beer define fun for you, know that "Almost everyone gets stir crazy to some degree here."

Getting In

Admitted students at the 25th percentile have an LSAT score of 162 and a GPA of 3.2. Admitted students at the 75th percentile have an LSAT score of 167 and a GPA of 3.7.

ADMISSIONS

Selectivity Rating	88
# applications received	2,764
# applicants accepted	867
# acceptees attending	126
Average LSAT	166
LSAT Range	162–167
Average undergrad GPA	3.61
Application fee	$50
Regular application	2/1
Regular notification	4/1
Rolling notification	Yes
Early application program	No
Transfer students accepted	Yes
Evening division offered	No
Part-time accepted	No
LSDAS accepted	Yes

Applicants Also Look At
College of William and Mary, University of Virginia, Vanderbilt University.

International Students
TOEFL required
of international students   Yes

FINANCIAL FACTS

Annual tuition	$30,500
Books and supplies	$1,600
Room and board (off-campus)	$14,095
Financial aid application deadline	2/15
% first-year students receiving some sort of aid	94
% receiving some sort of aid	94
% of aid that is merit based	100
% receiving scholarships	65
Average grant	$12,377
Average loan	$33,377
Average total aid package	$38,471
Average debt	$75,549

EMPLOYMENT INFORMATION

		Grads Employed by Field (%)	
Career Rating	85	Academic	2
Rate of placement (nine months out)	98	Business/Industry	11
Average starting salary	$76,431	Government	6
Employers Who Frequently Hire Grads		Judicial clerkships	19
Visit http://law.wlu.edu/career/ and click on		Military	2
"Prospective Students" for information		Other	2
about recruiting employers.		Private practice	54
		Public Interest	4

WASHINGTON UNIVERSITY
SCHOOL OF LAW

INSTITUTIONAL INFORMATION

Public/private	Private
Student-faculty ratio	14:1
% faculty part-time	66
% faculty female	31
% faculty minority	2
Total faculty	177

SURVEY SAYS...

Diverse opinions accepted
in classrooms
Great research resources
Beautiful campus

STUDENTS

Enrollment of law school	788
% male/female	58/42
% full-time	99
% minority	18
% international	4
# of countries represented	9
Average age of entering class	23

ACADEMICS

Academic Experience Rating	**92**
Profs interesting rating	88
Profs accessible rating	86
Hours of study per day	4.26

Academic Specialties

Civil procedure, commercial law, constitutional law, corporation securities law, criminal law, environmental law, government services, human rights law, intellectual property law, international law, labor law, legal history, legal philosophy, property, taxation.

Advanced Degrees Offered

JD 3 years, JSD, LLM (foreign lawyers), LLM (taxation), LLM (intellectual property and technology law).

Combined Degrees Offered

JD/MBA, JD/MS (economics,) JD/MSW (social work), JD/MA (Jewish, Islamic and Near Eastern studies), JD/MA (East Asian studies), JD/PHD (political science), JD/MA (health administration).

Clinical program required	No
Legal writing course requirement	Yes

Academics

Washington University School of Law in St. Louis is a "student-centered institution" with "outstanding" clinical programs. One of the biggest draws here is that "all students are guaranteed the opportunity to participate in at least one clinic during law school." Those clinics are stellar. In the Congressional and Administrative Law Clinic, as one example, 3Ls get to spend their spring semester interning in Congress and federal agencies. Notable joint-degree programs include the traditional JD/MBA as well as a unique JD/MA in East Asian studies. "Excellent specializations" include international law, intellectual property, and business law.

WashU's "diverse" and "accomplished" faculty is "available virtually all the time to answer student questions." Many professors here are "great teachers and terrific human beings" who "have a passion for imparting their knowledge upon the students." "Several rank among the best instructors I've had in my educational career," gloats a 2L. However, there are "some mediocre" professors in the mix. Another 2L elaborates: While "a handful of my professors have exceeded my highest expectations as instructors, in a few other classes, I am certain I could teach more effectively than my professors given a month's notice." Administratively, "There is really almost no red tape." The "wonderful," "student-focused" administration "will do anything to help a student survive and flourish." "They do their best to make law school as touchy-feely an experience as possible," describes one student. "From Admissions to the Registrar's Office to various professors' assistants, everyone at WULaw is just great." "Financial aid is lightning fast too."

Students are irreconcilably split when it comes to Career Services. One faction maintains that the staff has a "willingness to get you where you want to go." In addition to St. Louis and other Midwestern metropolises, "Many grads go to DC and New York City." "I think that Career Services does a good job of getting people national exposure," agrees a 2L. "I had callbacks in DC, Orlando, Chicago, Philadelphia, Minneapolis, and New York, and I didn't finish in the top 25 percent." Another faction contends that Career Services is "not very helpful" and "could do more to bring in employers." "The vast majority of students will tell you that CSO is worthless unless you are in the top 15 percent or want to work in the public interest sector in St. Louis," asserts a 2L. "We have some of the best law students in the country, and some employers seem to not recognize this."

The "beautiful" facilities at WashU "seem brand new." Anheuser-Busch Hall "is an amazing place to go to school every day" and "what an undergraduate student dreams of when they think about law school." The law school building is "only a few years old and it has its own cafeteria," an indoor courtyard, and "impressive architectural details." Students do complain a lot about "wireless dead spots," though. Otherwise, the research facilities and technological resources are "nothing short of absolutely satisfactory" and "really enhance the law school experience." "The library is outstanding" and "has lots of study rooms," though it "can be a little congested at times." "The reading room is amazing."

Janet Bolin, Associate Dean of Admissions and Student Services
One Brookings Drive, Campus Box 1120, St. Louis, MO 63130-4899
Tel: 314-935-4525 Fax: 314-935-8778
E-mail: admiss@wulaw.wustl.edu • Internet: law.wustl.edu

Life

WashU is pretty small, so "You will definitely not be lost in the shuffle." There is a "unique group of talented, intelligent," and "well-rounded" students here and, if these students do say so themselves, they are "the friendliest and funniest people you will ever meet." It tends to be a younger crowd and, while "the paradigmatic law student wearing social blinders" is easily recognizable at WashU, the social scene is very much "a priority." "The students at the law school take its name"—Anheuser-Busch Hall—"very seriously." "We have fun, smart, competitive students who are generally as interested in having a social life as they are in ranking toward the top of our class," explains a 2L. "Every Friday," the school hosts a "well-attended" happy hour in the courtyard. "Students, professors, kegs, and, yes, beer pong," is how one student characterizes the event. "Plenty of organized school activities" also include an annual student-produced comedy called the "Barely Legal Law Revue."

Academically, a few students claim that WashU is "becoming more competitive," but most tell us that "competition is unspoken and left to dark corners of the library." "I have yet to sense any competitiveness among students, even when exams came around," observes a discerning transfer student. "The student population is very laid-back" and students "are always willing to help one another understand the material." Self-scheduled exams for 2Ls and 3Ls help ease some of the tension.

"The WashU campus is located in an upscale suburb of St. Louis with an air of subdued sophistication." The campus is "right by Forest Park, home to the largest free zoo in the country, as well as many other attractions" and not far from bars, restaurants, and things to do. It's a fine place to spend a few years as a student. "St. Louis is not as chic as a lot of cities in the country," admits a 1L, "but it is cheap."

Getting In

The 25th percentile of admitted students has LSAT scores of about 161 and GPAs of about 3.2. Admitted students at the 75th percentile have LSAT scores of roughly 167 and GPAs of about 3.7.

Legal methods	
course requirement	No
Legal research	
course requirement	Yes
Moot court requirement	No
Public interest	
law requirement	No

ADMISSIONS

Selectivity Rating	**91**
# applications received	3,325
# applicants accepted	933
# acceptees attending	241
Average LSAT	165
LSAT Range	162–167
Average undergrad GPA	3.6
Application fee	$70
Regular application	3/1
Regular notification	4/15
Rolling notification	No
Early application program	Yes
Early application deadline	12/1
Early application notification	12/15
Transfer students accepted	Yes
Evening division offered	No
Part-time accepted	No
LSDAS accepted	Yes

Applicants Also Look At
Boston College, Boston University, The George Washington University, Georgetown University, Northwestern University, University of Southern California, Vanderbilt University.

International Students

TOEFL required	
of international students	No
TOEFL recommended	
of international students	Yes
Minimum paper TOEFL	600

FINANCIAL FACTS

Annual tuition	$35,670
Books and supplies	$2,000
Room and board	
(off-campus)	$12,000
Financial aid application	
deadline	3/1
% first-year students	
receiving some sort of aid	86
% receiving some sort of aid	87
% of aid that is merit based	100
% receiving scholarships	57
Average grant	$10,000
Average loan	$36,435
Average total aid package	$54,000
Average debt	$97,000

EMPLOYMENT INFORMATION

Career Rating	87	Grads Employed by Field (%)	
Rate of placement (nine months out)	98	Academic	1
Average starting salary	$89,505	Business/Industry	5
State for bar exam	MO, IL, CA, NY	Government	15
Employers Who Frequently Hire Grads		Judicial clerkships	11
Bryan Cave; Winston and Strawn; Paul		Military	1
Weiss; Arnold and Porter; public defender,		Private practice	61
U.S. Department of Justice.		Public Interest	6

WAYNE STATE UNIVERSITY
LAW SCHOOL

Academics

The Law School at Wayne State University is efficient, low in cost, rich in diversity, and favorably located for future lawyers looking to practice in southeastern Michigan. The school's excellent teaching staff draws praises all around, and students assure us that "the academics are stellar." This is at least partly attributable to the fact that, as one 2L puts it, "The faculty are amazing, and all boast the highest credentials. We are all confident that we are receiving a premier education." In addition, "Most professors are good teachers and dedicated to imparting knowledge."

While the classrooms could use a touch-up, the school's research and technological facilities are top-notch. A 1L reports, "The law library is extremely well-equipped, and Wayne State is continually improving the technological resources." Yet all this quality comes with a very low price tag. Wayne State students insist that "with [in-state] costs of only $13,000 or so a year, Wayne State deserves even greater recognition as an 'excellent value' in education."

Many students at Wayne State say that one of the school's greatest assets is "the wonderful support given by the administrative staff." Honestly attentive to the student body, administrators are "approachable and always give you advice that you can use" and, furthermore, are extremely efficient at their jobs. A 2L claims that "getting things done at the law school is effortless." In particular, many students have kind words for the charismatic new dean, claiming that "in one year, he has turned the administration around and revitalized the faculty and students." A 2L raves, "One of our greatest strengths? Dean Wu! The man's awesome. I mean, come on, how many other law schools have a dean that rides a motorcycle?"

While the Wayne curriculum will provide you with ample doses of legal theory, there is a strong focus on practical aspects of law. Many of the professors are practicing attorneys and incorporate their expertise into classroom instruction. A 2L explains, "The professors at Wayne are the perfect balance between scholars and practicing lawyers. They help you develop the analytical/theoretical tools you need for a long legal career while also breaking it down to what you really need to know in the real world." In addition, there is "an incredible internship program at Wayne that gives students such great real-world exposure to the legal profession." A 2L shares, "I had a judicial internship at the Federal District Court this semester and am participating in the Urban Housing and Community Development Clinic next semester!" While students appreciate the quality and content of their courses and extracurriculars, some feel that "though the faculty is wonderful, it is too small," and that the school needs to "offer a wider range of classes each semester and improve class scheduling." Students are hopeful that the variety of course offerings will widen shortly as the school "will be adding at least four new tenure-track professors in 2005."

One of the greatest attributes of Wayne State is its location. A 2L boasts, "It is a fabulous location for a law school in general because it is so close to the courts and major MI law firms, as well as very close to Canada. That location alone opens up many opportunities that other MI law schools just cannot compete with." However, students are adamant that the location really pays off after graduation and that "if you want to be a lawyer or a judge in Michigan, Wayne is a great place to be." In fact, more than "half of the judges and 75 percent of the lawyers practicing in southeast Michigan are Wayne graduates." Additionally, "The alumni are very active and willing to help other graduates."

LINDA FOWLER SIMS, ASSISTANT DEAN FOR RECRUITMENT AND ADMISSIONS
471 WEST PALMER, DETROIT, MI 48202
TEL: 313-577-3937 FAX: 313-993-8129
E-MAIL: LAW.INQUIRE@WAYNE.EDU • INTERNET: WWW.LAW.WAYNE.EDU

Life

If you are looking to relive your undergraduate years, you may be disappointed with Wayne State. Students warn that "Detroit is not a college town" and that "most students commute to Wayne State, which obviously leads to a different environment than if students lived on campus." This cosmopolitan city is nonetheless "an interesting place to go to school—we have big industry, great suburbs, and lots of diversity." Additionally, "a strong portion of the student body gets together and socializes a great deal," and students say it is easy to make friends among their interesting and talented classmates. A 1L remarks, "The student body is awesome. My section is extremely friendly and we spend a great deal of time together. I see my classmates more than I do my family." While "Everyone works well together," be aware that "there is a great deal of competition" academically.

Interacting with their classmates is an important part of the educational experience at Wayne, and within the student body, "There is diversity between races, religions, socio-economic, and prior educational backgrounds." Students say Wayne is the type of place where "You can learn first-hand about people whom you may never have had the opportunity to learn about before," as the environment is "very open and rarely uncomfortable." The "wealth of experience in the student body . . . is an extremely important attribute because, as prospective students will come to find out, you tend to learn as much from your fellow students as you do from you professors."

Getting In

Wayne State admits students on a rolling basis, accepting applications after October 1 for an August start date. Wayne State admits students with competitive LSAT scores and a strong academic record; however, the school also considers relevant personal qualities and characteristics demonstrated through previous leadership positions, community service, or communication ability.

ADMISSIONS

Selectivity Rating	77
# applications received	1,256
# applicants accepted	507
# acceptees attending	214
Average LSAT	156
LSAT Range	144–170
Average undergrad GPA	3.48
Application fee	$50
Regular application	Rolling
Regular notification	Rolling
Rolling notification	Yes
Early application program	No
Transfer students accepted	Yes
Evening division offered	Yes
Part-time accepted	Yes
LSDAS accepted	Yes

Applicants Also Look At

DePaul University, Michigan State University College of Law, Thomas M. Cooley Law School, University of Detroit Mercy, University of Michigan.

International Students

TOEFL required of international students	No
TOEFL recommended of international students	No

FINANCIAL FACTS

Annual tuition (resident)	$16,355
Annual tuition (nonresident)	$31,228
Books and supplies	$1,030
Fees per credit (resident)	$25
Fees per credit (nonresident)	$25
Tuition per credit (resident)	$584
Tuition per credit (nonresident)	$1,115
Room and board	$12,326
Financial aid application deadline	3/15
Average grant	$5,490
Average loan	$18,500
Average total aid package	$21,500
Average debt	$58,232

EMPLOYMENT INFORMATION

Career Rating	77	Grads Employed by Field (%)	
Average starting salary	$70,808	Business/Industry	17
State for bar exam	MI, NY, IL, CA, GA	Government	9
Pass rate for first-time bar	80	Judicial clerkships	2
Employers Who Frequently Hire Grads		Private practice	62

Employers Who Frequently Hire Grads
Leading law firms in Michigan, in-house legal departments of *Fortune* 500 and other corporations and governmental agencies.

Prominent Alumni
Robert Sedler, con. law; David Moran, criminal law; Ralph Slovenko, behavioral science; Joan Mahoney, children's rights.

WEST VIRGINIA UNIVERSITY
COLLEGE OF LAW

INSTITUTIONAL INFORMATION

Public/private	Public
Student-faculty ratio	15:1
% faculty part-time	11
% faculty female	31
% faculty minority	14
Total faculty	30

SURVEY SAYS...

Diverse opinions accepted
in classrooms
Great research resources
Great library staff

STUDENTS

Enrollment of law school	477
% male/female	55/45
% out-of-state	23
% full-time	99
% minority	10
# of countries represented	2
Average age of entering class	26

ACADEMICS

Academic Experience Rating	**73**
Profs interesting rating	77
Profs accessible rating	78
Hours of study per day	5.05

Academic Specialties

Civil procedure, commercial law, constitutional law, corporation securities law, criminal law, environmental law, government services, human rights law, international law, labor law, legal history, legal philosophy, property, taxation.

Advanced Degrees Offered

JD 3 years.

Combined Degrees Offered

JD/MPA 4 years, JD/MBA 4 years.

Clinical program required	No
Legal writing course requirement	Yes
Legal methods course requirement	Yes
Legal research course requirement	Yes
Moot court requirement	No

Academics

The West Virginia University College of Law offers a unique community experience that "fosters intellectual growth and collegiality at the same time." Students say that "WVU can provide a great legal education if you are willing to put in the work." "For the price you can't beat the experiences and the opportunity that WVU Law offers." "If you want to work in West Virginia, or simply get a great 'bang for your buck,' WVU College of Law is a wonderful choice."

Students across the board rave about WVU's personable faculty and note that, while "The school isn't perfect," "Most of the professors are constantly striving to improve." Professors are described as "the type of people you'd like to bump into at a bar and talk [with] for hours." The "phenomenal teaching staff" is "willing to meet with a student anytime, anywhere to discuss topics beyond those addressed in the classroom." "The faculty's greatest strength is their passion," reports one 2L. "Our professors are much more than just our teachers . . . they are our mentors, our confidantes, and our friends."

Students report that "the business law classes are superb and provide an excellent business focus." WVU places a large emphasis on research and writing skills, though the legal research and writing program garners mixed reviews. One self-proclaimed "worst writer in the world" says that WVU's "legal research and writing [curriculum], along with the writing seminars, has improved my writing ability." Other students think the legal writing curriculum "is ridiculously tedious and time consuming." "A lot of time is wasted teaching a legal writing format and citation format not currently utilized in most practices." Some students wish for programs that allow for specialization in various areas of law.

Students find little fault with Career Services, which has reportedly improved significantly over the past three years. Described as "extremely proactive and effective [and] a jewel in the law school's crown," students say that the Career Service Center "offers a great deal of assistance and advice in searching for summer jobs and permanent jobs." While some students complain that "little help is provided outside of [help] obtaining a private law firm job," for those students planning to stay in the area, "The relationship with the state bar is phenomenal and opens up the door to many opportunities in the state." One student confidently tells us, "I can always rest assured that getting my law degree from WVU will [assist] me in finding employment opportunities in West Virginia."

Students bemoan the law school facilities, saying that they are in desperate need of a "makeover," particularly when it comes to expanding technology and classroom infrastructure. "Classes are forced into rooms that are much too small to accommodate." While the majority of students wish for a new, more modern building, one 2L is not overly concerned: "The building may be a box, but it does have everything a student needs to prepare for the practice of law." Fortunately, the law school facility is scheduled to be remodeled in the summer of 2007 "to meet the needs and technological requirements of today's law student." As one student sums up, "We may not be the highest-ranked school in the nation, but we can go head to head with any other school out there."

JANET ARMISTEAD, ASSISTANT DEAN FOR ADMISSIONS
PO BOX 6130, MORGANTOWN, WV 26506-6103
TEL: 304-293-5304 FAX: 304-293-6891
E-MAIL: WVULAW.ADMISSIONS@MAIL.WVU.EDU • INTERNET: WWW.WVU.EDU/~LAW

Life

Students appreciate that WVU Law offers them a well-rounded experience. "Although it is not a social paradise, the students organize both intellectual and social events on a monthly basis" that are well attended by both students and faculty. Students in general are very supportive of one another. "Most people are willing to share outlines or help you find a certain case. There are always a couple [of] exceptions, but most people laugh at the ultra-competitive people." As one student explains, "We are more than a small school; we're a family . . . sharing shoulders to lean on, sibling rivalry, and a few 'eccentric' relatives included."

"The social scene in Morgantown is one in a million," claims one student. "There are a ton of things to do for fun in our town." "Arts and entertainment, concerts, skiing, hiking, athletics, [and] nights out on the town" are just a few of the options available to WVU students outside of the classroom. Students say it's easy to achieve a balance between life and work: "I make time to exercise, attend church, volunteer in the community, and engage in extracurricular activities at the law school, such as Law Review and mock trial competitions, as well as [find] time to socialize with friends at dinner or athletic events. This type of well-roundedness is evident throughout the student body and contributes to a happy and healthy environment at the school."

Getting In

Admitted students at the 25th percentile have an LSAT score of 148 and a GPA of 3.2. Admitted students at the 75th percentile have an LSAT score of 155 and a GPA of 3.7.

Applicants are required to submit three letters of recommendation from people who have personal knowledge of their character, skills, and aptitude for law study and practice. At least one recommendation must be from a former professor.

Public interest law requirement	No

ADMISSIONS

Selectivity Rating	**72**
# applications received	903
# applicants accepted	354
# acceptees attending	166
Average LSAT	152
LSAT Range	148–155
Average undergrad GPA	3.42
Application fee	$50
Regular application	2/1
Regular notification	Rolling
Rolling notification	Yes
Early application program	No
Transfer students accepted	Yes
Evening division offered	No
Part-time accepted	Yes
LSDAS accepted	Yes

Applicants Also Look At
College of William and Mary, University of Pennsylvania, University of Pittsburgh.

International Students

TOEFL required of international students	Yes
Minimum paper TOEFL	600
Minimum computer TOEFL	250

FINANCIAL FACTS

Annual tuition (resident)	$4,926
Annual tuition (nonresident)	$14,278
Books and supplies	$1,125
Fees per credit (resident)	$492
Fees per credit (nonresident)	$826
Tuition per credit (resident)	$552
Tuition per credit (nonresident)	$1,592
Room and board	$11,356
Financial aid application deadline	3/1
% first-year students receiving some sort of aid	36
% receiving some sort of aid	91
% of aid that is merit based	1
% receiving scholarships	32
Average grant	$1,822
Average loan	$15,800
Average total aid package	$19,150
Average debt	$54,881

EMPLOYMENT INFORMATION

Career Rating	72	Grads Employed by Field (%)	
Rate of placement (nine months out)	92	Business/Industry	8
Average starting salary	$52,610	Government	4
State for bar exam	WV	Judicial clerkships	21
Pass rate for first-time bar	75	Private practice	60
Employers Who Frequently Hire Grads		Public Interest	1
Law firms, state and federal judges/courts, business/corporate, government agencies.			

WESTERN NEW ENGLAND COLLEGE
SCHOOL OF LAW

INSTITUTIONAL INFORMATION

Public/private	Private
Student-faculty ratio	16:1
% faculty part-time	38
% faculty female	38
% faculty minority	2
Total faculty	56

SURVEY SAYS...

Diverse opinions accepted
in classrooms
Great research resources
Great library staff

STUDENTS

Enrollment of law school	553
% male/female	56/44
% out-of-state	56
% full-time	69
% minority	10
% international	5
# of countries represented	11
Average age of entering class	26

ACADEMICS

Academic Experience Rating	**66**
Profs interesting rating	71
Profs accessible rating	76
Hours of study per day	4.64

Advanced Degrees Offered
LLM (estate planning and elder law)
2 to 3 years.

Combined Degrees Offered
JD/MRP (Masters in Regional
Planning with the University of
Masssachusetts) 4 years, JD MSW
(with Springfield College) 4 years,
JD/MBA (with Western New
England College) 4 years.

Clinical program required	No
Legal writing	
course requirement	Yes
Legal methods	
course requirement	Yes
Legal research	
course requirement	Yes
Moot court requirement	No
Public interest	
law requirement	No

Academics

Western New England College School of Law is a small, private institution with an accomplished teaching staff, diverse student body, and growing national reputation. Students report that their classes are "engaging" and that professors are "simply phenomenal," capable of bringing not just expertise, but also passion to the study of law. "The professors are very knowledgeable and interesting. Their enthusiasm about and devotion to the law, especially their areas of specialization, is apparent in every classroom discussion," reports one 1L. Indeed, the "open and inviting" classroom atmosphere inspires student participation, and "Debate is encouraged both in and out of the classroom." At WNEC "Teaching occurs through the Socratic Method (99 percent of the time) and by means of answering students' questions (1 percent)." Therefore, students must come prepared to participate in class and be ready to think on their feet. The effort pays off. WNEC students report that they "easily master Black Letter law" and feel well prepared for the bar exam, as well as future practice.

While courses are tough, the academic environment at WNEC is decidedly supportive and student friendly. From their first day on campus, "Each student is appointed a faculty advisor," and the school offers an optional Legal Education Achievement Program (LEAP) for first- and second-year students, designed to help them improve their study and organizational skills. On top of that, Western New England College "places a heavy emphasis on accessibility of the faculty," and students feel comfortable asking their professors for extra guidance. For example, one 2L reports, "During a writing assignment, I called a professor on a Saturday at home, and she called me back! That is a professor who cares!" Beyond academic concerns, WNEC teachers "encourage students to access them outside of the classroom in order to establish a more personal relationship" and some "even go to bars with the students after class." As a result, professors become more like mentors or friends, willing to lend an ear in any manner of discussion. Similarly, the administration at WNEC works to develop a personal connection with students. A 2L elaborates, "The administration is great. You can always get in to see them, and the dean interacts with the students quite often when he hosts the Dean's Tea."

Outside traditional course work, students at WNEC build their resumes and experience through the school's numerous extracurricular programs, including "many volunteer opportunities for 1Ls," clinics, simulations, and externship placements in the Boston area. In addition, the administration works to maintain a lively academic atmosphere and "Many outstanding lecturers have already spoken on campus by mid-semester." However, while the day students are highly satisfied with the extracurricular activities and programs available to them, participants in the evening program feel their needs are often overlooked; one such student writes, "Most programs and opportunities seem to be geared toward day students," adding that evening and working students are "limited in opportunities because activities, office hours, and training are scheduled during the middle of the day or afternoons."

Students insist that they receive "a quality education that is comparable [with] (although perhaps less theoretical than) the top-tier law schools," but many do worry that the school's reputation is still lagging behind where it should be. A 2L laments, "If I could change one thing about WNEC Law, I would match the school's reputation with the outstanding education it provides." Students say administrators "do not do enough to promote the school" or its alumni. However, things may change as the school "becomes more of a national draw." In addition to more widespread recruiting, the

MICHAEL A. JOHNSON, ASSISTANT DEAN AND DIRECTOR OF ADMISSIONS
1215 WILBRAHAM ROAD, SPRINGFIELD, MA 01119
TEL: 413-782-1406 FAX: 413-796-2067
E-MAIL: ADMISSIONS@LAW.WNEC.EDU • INTERNET: WWW.LAW.WNEC.EDU

administration is committed to constant improvement in the curriculum, campus, and facilities. Students tell prospective students to look for updates in a number of other areas. For example, "The classrooms are being updated as we speak," and "The school is expanding its wireless Internet network." Moreover, the school is constantly offering new programs and classes, such as a recently instituted bar review course.

Life

While the WNEC student body is small, the school boasts "a wide age range, race range, and socioeconomic range." As a result, it's not surprising that "not everyone agrees socially or politically." Students insist, however, that the diversity of opinion and background "makes WNEC rich and interesting" and that "disagreements only spark discussion, not argument." Out of class, WNEC students are far from competitive. By almost all accounts "The school environment is relaxed," and students are generally described as "cooperative and helpful with each other." While studious WNEC students have a strong work ethic and desire to succeed, they are always willing to lend a hand to a colleague. A 1L explains, "There is a strong sense that everyone wants to do well, but not at the expense of another."

WNEC is home to a fairly active student body, and there are a number of campus-based social activities and academic clubs that attract the younger day students. Full-timers say that "everyone is friendly and social" and that it is easy to make friends on this small campus. Some would like to see the extracurricular offerings expanded to include more intellectual or professional activities, rather than primarily social events. In addition, some students in the part-time program feel they aren't well-integrated into the campus community, as the majority of activities take place in the afternoons. "I can say that as an evening student, I do feel that we miss out on a lot of things," complains one 2L.

Getting In

WNEC accepts students on a rolling basis for fall admission until March 15 of each year. Among law schools, the admissions process is fairly forgiving, with about two of every five applicants accepted. More than a quarter of students are in the part-time program.

ADMISSIONS

Selectivity Rating	**67**
# applications received	1,860
# applicants accepted	919
# acceptees attending	201
Average LSAT	153
LSAT Range	151–157
Average undergrad GPA	3.03
Application fee	$50
Regular application	Rolling
Regular notification	Rolling
Rolling notification	Yes
Early application program	No
Transfer students accepted	Yes
Evening division offered	Yes
Part-time accepted	Yes
LSDAS accepted	Yes

Applicants Also Look At
New England School of Law, New York Law School, Quinnipiac University, Roger Williams University, State University of New York at Albany, Suffolk University.

International Students
TOEFL required	
of international students	Yes

FINANCIAL FACTS

Annual tuition	$29,456
Books and supplies	$1,386
Room and board	
(on/off-campus)	$7,000/$11,578
% first-year students	
receiving some sort of aid	97
% receiving some sort of aid	95
% receiving scholarships	54
Average grant	$14,651
Average loan	$30,273
Average total aid package	$37,679
Average debt	$76,719

EMPLOYMENT INFORMATION

Career Rating	**70**	**Grads Employed by Field (%)**	
Rate of placement (nine months out)	85	Academic	2
Average starting salary	$51,664	Business/Industry	25
State for bar exam	CT, MA, NY, NJ, PA	Government	18
Pass rate for first-time bar	76	Judicial clerkships	7
Employers Who Frequently Hire Grads		Military	1
Law firms (e.g. Bingham Dana; Day, Berry		Private practice	43
and Howard; Shipman and Goodwin);		Public Interest	4
accounting firms; insurance companies			
and government agencies.			

WHITTIER COLLEGE*
WHITTIER LAW SCHOOL

INSTITUTIONAL INFORMATION

Public/private	Private
Student-faculty ratio	17:1
% faculty part-time	47
% faculty female	48
% faculty minority	14
Total faculty	88

SURVEY SAYS...
Diverse opinions accepted
in classrooms
Students never sleep
Students love Costa Mesa, CA

STUDENTS

Enrollment of law school	244
% male/female	67/33
% out-of-state	18
% full-time	55
% minority	20
% international	1
# of countries represented	10
Average age of entering class	24

ACADEMICS

Academic Experience Rating	**62**
Profs interesting rating	63
Profs accessible rating	61
Hours of study per day	5.1

Academic Specialties
Commercial law, criminal law, intellectual property law, international law, children's rights, health law.

Advanced Degrees Offered
JD 3 to 4 years, LLM (foreign legal studies) 1 year.

Clinical program required	No
Legal writing	
course requirement	Yes
Legal methods	
course requirement	Yes
Legal research	
course requirement	Yes
Moot court requirement	Yes
Public interest	
law requirement	No

Academics

Full disclosure: The ABA recently placed Whittier Law School on probation for a lower-than-desired first-time bar-passage rate. Being placed on ABA probation is a big issue for any law school. Many students responding to our survey mentioned this fact, as well as what the school is doing to remedy the problem. For starters, the administration is focused on "rearranging the curriculum" by adding more "required courses in preparation for the bar" (some students think the administration has added "too many" new requirements in a "knee-jerk" reaction). Another move to improve the school is "bringing in a higher caliber of student than in the past. Continuing that trend should be a priority" in order "to ensure higher bar passage rates and the school's ABA status."

Students believe that "the classroom experience at Whittier is positive." "Professors are all top-notch, with a deep knowledge of the subject matter they're teaching." Faculty members "work on their own outside of the classroom, so they know what it's like in the 'real world' as well." They are also focused on students, as they "show consistent concern from the beginning [in] preparing you for the bar." Occasionally, of course, "We will get an adjunct who is basically learning the subject matter right out of the book at the same time as the students." Regardless of the regular/adjunct split in quality, students appreciate the fact that "professors are accessible and receptive to student questions, feedback, and input." Students also praise the school for "encouraging hands-on experience and emphasizing practical applications of the material we learn, rather than purely theoretical topics."

Whittier has a reputation for being a "liberal safe haven in the middle of Orange County," and this characterization is particularly true with "regards to the faculty. Most faculty express very liberal leanings." Given the political sensibilities, it seems logical that there is a "focus on public interest" law. But "Whittier also has the strongest intellectual property program in the area." And when not learning how to save the world or patent the next big thing, students take advantage of "lots of opportunities to study abroad."

The exceptional and cost-minded student should note that Whittier "offer[s] a lot of scholarships, so chances are good that you will not have to take as many loans. It is also sometimes rewarding that it is a 'little pond,' so if you are a good student, it is easy to be the 'big fish.'" The one student complaint about the school is that "there is no wireless Internet." "But with all of the wired locations around campus," the lack of wireless access is "not that big of a deal."

* Currently on ABA probation for a period of two years, effective August 9, 2005.

BETTY VU, DIRECTOR OF ADMISSIONS
3333 HARBOR BOULEVARD, COSTA MESA, CA 92626
TEL: 714-444-4141 FAX: 714-444-0250
E-MAIL: INFO@LAW.WHITTIER.EDU • INTERNET: WWW.LAW.WHITTIER.EDU

Life

Whittier is a small school, with fewer than 300 students in each entering class. Its size is a big factor in determining student life: "The campus is small and intimate, everyone is quite friendly," and the limited number of students roaming the halls gives the school a "family feeling." Another contributor to the family atmosphere is the relative lack of competition: According to one 2L, "The forced curve gives the perception of competition, but most students are helpful to others."

The most significant demographic breakdown of the Whittier student body is between the full-time and part-time students. About 40 percent of students here are part-time, and of those, "The majority work during the day and have class at night. When we are not working or attending class, we are studying. For us, there is no time for socializing." However, "Small groups do work cooperatively together on studying." Among the full-time students, there is a perception of "cliquishness." One 1L tells us that "most students seem to be rich kids that just don't want to grow up." Despite this stereotype, however, "They are great people that I am proud to know."

Of course, student life at Whittier is enhanced by its gorgeous location. For those who seek an endless summer in which to study, Whittier Law School is a good choice. You just "can't beat being 10 minutes away from the beaches" of SoCal.

Getting In

In weighing applicants to its program, Whittier considers undergraduate transcripts, LSAT scores, a resume, two letters of recommendation, and a personal statement. In the past, Whittier was a solid choice those students who may not have been in the top quarter of their undergraduate classes, but who were nonetheless hard workers. In other words, a C-plus undergraduate average did not necessarily rule you out. However, as you have probably guessed if you read the "Academics" section above, all that may start to change with the school's urgent need to get more students to pass the bar exam on their first try. So this is one school where it may be substantially more difficult to gain admission in the year you are reading this than it had been in the recent past. The school's 2005 student profile lists an average LSAT score of 154 and an average GPA of 3.1 and Whittier seeks candidates who will deliver a solid academic performance with enduring stamina during their tenure at the law school.

ADMISSIONS

Selectivity Rating	70
# applications received	2,362
# applicants accepted	961
# acceptees attending	189
Average LSAT	153
LSAT Range	151–155
Average undergrad GPA	3.12
Application fee	$50
Regular application	Rolling
Regular notification	Rolling
Rolling notification	Yes
Early application program	No
Transfer students accepted	Yes
Evening division offered	Yes
Part-time accepted	Yes
LSDAS accepted	Yes

Applicants Also Look At

California Western, Chapman University, Pepperdine University, Southwestern University School of Law, University of the Pacific, University of San Diego, University of San Francisco.

International Students

TOEFL required of international students	Yes
Minimum paper TOEFL	600
Minimum computer TOEFL	250

FINANCIAL FACTS

Annual tuition	$30,750
Books and supplies	$6,406
Tuition per credit	$1,025
Room and board (off-campus)	$10,084
Financial aid application deadline	5/1
% first-year students receiving some sort of aid	83
% receiving some sort of aid	86
% of aid that is merit based	25
% receiving scholarships	57
Average grant	$8,904
Average loan	$34,990
Average total aid package	$34,500
Average debt	$86,000

EMPLOYMENT INFORMATION

		Grads Employed by Field (%)	
Career Rating	67		
Rate of placement (nine months out)	93	Academic	3
Average starting salary	$65,000	Business/Industry	36
State for bar exam	CA	Government	6
Pass rate for first-time bar	59	Judicial clerkships	1
Employers Who Frequently Hire Grads		Private practice	48
Small law firm practices (2 to 10 attorneys).		Public Interest	5
Prominent Alumni			
Honorable Florence Marie Cooper, U.S. District Court; Garo Mardirossian, Mardirossian and Associates, personal injury; Judith Ashmann-Gerst, California Court of Appeal; Honorable Mablean Ephraim, *Divorce Court*.			

WIDENER UNIVERSITY
SCHOOL OF LAW—DELAWARE CAMPUS

Academics

Many students at Widener's Delaware campus believe the school's "greatest strength" is "flexibility of scheduling; whether you are a full-time student or working professional, Widener offers the opportunity to study law," and nearly half here are enrolled in the school's four-year evening program. Students tell us the school's Admissions Office is also rather accommodating. "Most of our students, including myself, are students who may not have gotten a chance to pursue a legal career otherwise due to low LSAT scores or [a] low undergrad GPA," a 3L writes. With many at Widener happy just to have a chance to study law, the school could provide students with the bare minimum they need to get a JD. Instead, Widener impresses students at almost every turn. Students say, "The campus and its facilities are improving almost daily," and "The school has upgraded [its] principal classrooms to include SmartBoards and other modern capabilities." While "facilities outside of the main law building" could still use improvement—the "spotty" wireless network is a common complaint—the library—(i.e., "the only law library in Delaware)" is "beautiful and well equipped." In addition, "students get free access to both Westlaw and LexisNexis and receive plenty opportunities to be trained in both sources." With a campus that is "solely comprised of the law school," students report that "the focus is totally on law and the students. This allows for law students to feel like a major priority here."

Professors at Widener hail from "well-respected schools" and "bring a great real-world perspective to the classes." They're also accessible: "Any professor in this law school will take time out of their day to help a student out with a difficult concept, write a recommendation for employment, or . . . chat with students who want to hear a war story." There are a few duds, however, "so you have to ask around to find out who people like." Classes "are fast paced and engaging in a way that makes even the driest of subjects comprehensible and interesting." The curriculum here leans more to the practical than the theoretical and includes a "strong" writing program. The school's location in the state of Delaware—where, because of tax laws, "many major banks, credit card companies, etc. are located"—"is a real asset for those students who are focusing on corporate law." Programs in health law and trial advocacy are also top notch. As Widener is "the only law school in Delaware," its students "have almost exclusive access to externships with the Delaware Chancery Court and Delaware Supreme Court. Some of the Justices are our teachers, and many well-recognized judges are also our teachers," a 2L writes. An aspiring trial attorney reports that he has been "trained and taught by successful practicing prosecutors, plaintiff's attorneys, and defense attorneys, both civil and criminal. Now in my last semester of law school here at Widener, I feel like I . . . have the skills and abilities to win a case. My clinical externship program at the Attorney General's Office in New Castle County, Delaware has placed me in court trying cases against real defense attorneys and their juvenile clients . . . and the last trial I had resulted in a victory over a respected defense attorney."

Students tell us Widener's Career Development Office "is always creating seminars for [those] seeking job[s]" and regularly organizes "mock interviews with attorneys and judges." However, "most" here currently find work through "sources other than the university." As such, students call for more job leads and on-campus interviews. Many gripe that Widener "does not get much respect from potential employers," and several suggest that the administration "offer tours to prospective employers in the area to show them what a commodity that Widener Law students are." Students believe Widener's "C curve," "meaning that the majority of the class gets a C," also complicates their job search. "Other law schools in the area are all on the 'B curve,' so our average GPA is much lower than [theirs]," a 3L writes. "We constantly have to clarify this at job interviews where we compete against those students because to employers it just seems like

BARBARA AYARS, ASSISTANT DEAN FOR ADMISSIONS
PO BOX 7474, 4601 CONCORD PIKE, WILMINGTON, DE 19803-0474
TEL: 302-477-2162 FAX: 302-477-2224
E-MAIL: LAWADMISSIONS@MAIL.WIDENER.EDU • INTERNET: WWW.LAW.WIDENER.EDU

we just have lower grades." Those attending Widener part-time in the school's Extended Division report a trade-off: "I'm an Evening Division student, and, as such, I miss out on certain activities and resources made available for day students," a 3L writes. "However, I believe it is more than compensated for by the wonderfully diverse, real-world experiences the evening division student body brings to the table."

Life

Perception on campus is that "evening and day students are two completely different animals," and they "run in different packs." And while evening students tend to be more mature and don't interact much with their fellow evening students outside of class—day students at least "congregate every Wednesday night at a local bar"—there are more similarities than differences between them. "We are all very intellectual people in the same boat, so we watch out for each other while still being competitive," a 1L writes. "Students are willing to share notes, form study groups, etc."

The school "is located on a major four-lane artery that leads right into Wilmington and is surrounded by a mall, strip malls, fast-food restaurants, and motels." Students say the campus is "more or less aesthetically pleasing—with the exception of Polishook Hall, which should be torn down." The campus has earned the nickname "Camp Widener" for its summer-camp-like amenities: "There are three tennis courts, one basketball court, and a huge gym where yoga [and] other aerobic lessons are available," a 2L writes. There could, however, "be more on-campus apartments. The dorms are adequate but begin to feel cell-like to people who have been out of college for a certain amount of time and are accustomed to a certain amount of living space." Dorms also "lack kitchen facilities," which is an issue as the food on campus is reportedly "terrible," and students often have "long days and no time to leave campus to get food."

Getting In

While the admissions standards for Widener's part-time (aka evening) program are less stringent than the standards for its full-time program, the program itself can involve some difficult choices. A 2L elaborates: "In order to complete a judicial externship/internship, they suggest 'saving your vacation time at work' and taking it all at once. . . . How many full-time employees get so much vacation time that they could use it for an internship?"

EMPLOYMENT INFORMATION

Career Rating	71
Rate of placement (nine months out)	89
Average starting salary	$52,518
State for bar exam	PA, NJ, DE, MD, NY
Pass rate for first-time bar	71

Employers Who Frequently Hire Grads
Law firms, judges, corporations and other government employers.

Prominent Alumni
William G. Bush, IV, legal counsel to Delaw; Cynthia Rhoades Ryan, chief counsel, National Geospatial Intelligence Agency; Brian P. Tierey, CEO, Philadelphia Media Holdings LLC; Honorable Lee A. Solomon, Superior Court of New Jersey.

Grads Employed by Field (%)	
Academic	1
Business/Industry	22
Government	15
Judicial clerkships	20
Military	1
Private practice	38
Public Interest	3

Legal research course requirement	Yes
Moot court requirement	No
Public interest law requirement	No

ADMISSIONS

Selectivity Rating	67
# applications received	1,940
# applicants accepted	863
# acceptees attending	216
Average LSAT	152
LSAT Range	150–155
Average undergrad GPA	3.08
Application fee	$60
Regular application	5/15
Regular notification	Rolling
Rolling notification	Yes
Early application program	No
Transfer students accepted	Yes
Evening division offered	Yes
Part-time accepted	Yes
LSDAS accepted	Yes

Applicants Also Look At
Penn State University; Rutgers, The State University of New Jersey; Temple University; Thomas M. Cooley Law School; University of Baltimore, Villanova University.

International Students

TOEFL required of international students	No
TOEFL recommended of international students	Yes
Minimum paper TOEFL	550
Minimum computer TOEFL	220

FINANCIAL FACTS

Annual tuition	$29,330
Books and supplies	$1,000
Tuition per credit	$975
Room and board	$8,300
Financial aid application deadline	4/15
% first-year students receiving some sort of aid	89
% receiving some sort of aid	89
% of aid that is merit based	11
% receiving scholarships	19
Average grant	$7,270
Average loan	$26,325
Average total aid package	$28,255
Average debt	$78,977

WIDENER UNIVERSITY
SCHOOL OF LAW—HARRISBURG CAMPUS

INSTITUTIONAL INFORMATION

Public/private	Private
Student-faculty ratio	16:1
% faculty part-time	30
% faculty female	48
% faculty minority	4
Total faculty	47

SURVEY SAYS...

Diverse opinions accepted
in classrooms
Great research resources
Great library staff

STUDENTS

Enrollment of law school	449
% male/female	56/44
% full-time	66
% minority	7
Average age of entering class	23

ACADEMICS

Academic Experience Rating	**74**
Profs interesting rating	81
Profs accessible rating	80
Hours of study per day	4.18

Academic Specialties

Constitutional law, corporation
securities law, environmental law,
government services, health law,
international law.

Combined Degrees Offered

JD/MSLS (library sciences in conjunction with Clarion University of
PA) 4 years.

Clinical program required	No
Legal writing	
course requirement	Yes
Legal methods	
course requirement	Yes
Legal research	
course requirement	Yes
Moot court requirement	No
Public interest	
law requirement	No

Academics

At Widener's Harrisburg campus, "small class sizes" and a location "tuck[ed] away from the hustle of a large university setting" ensure that "the focus of the school is completely and totally on the law student." As "the only [law] school in the state capital" of Pennsylvania, Widener is "an excellent place for any student who is interested in a career in politics—from being a politician to researching and drafting legislation," a 3L reports. "Students at Widener have a very easy time getting internships and clinics with local lawyers, Pennsylvania Supreme Court judges, senators, and representatives." Despite Widener's environmental advantages, many students maintain that the school's "biggest asset is its faculty." Professors here are reportedly "very accessible"—"most have an open-door policy"—and are, just as importantly, "approachable." They also possess "unique eccentricities" that "keep the class interested in the material." "You are never quite sure how it is going to be presented to you," a 1L tells us. While a few "can be a bit condescending," "Most try to associate with the students outside of the class" and "sponsor a collegial atmosphere that is emulated by the students." Many professors bring considerable "real-life experience" to the classroom: "Last semester I took Sports Law which was taught by the author of the book, which is used around the country; I often see professors on television or local news giving opinions on cases that affect the local community," a 2L writes. With the school's part-time program attracting "many students with maturity, life experience, and practical insights," a pragmatic approach is ubiquitous here. Most see Widener's "focus on legal writing and lawyering skills" as a major strength. The school offers 3Ls "a bar review class for credit" and provides "numerous electives that focus on the practice of litigation and trial methods. This is invaluable." In some areas, however, the school's practical approach leaves students unsatisfied. Many here would like the school to "open up the first-year curriculum. Taking the same five classes all year long is boring and unnecessary." And with Widener's "nationally ranked concentrations, corporate law and health care law," only available at the school's Delaware campus, students would also like to see more opportunities for specialization: "[Widener's] emphasis is on [a] general educational background in the law, but there are obviously adjuncts with impressive credentials," a 3L writes. "Concentrations . . . may attract a greater pool of top recruits to the student body." With existing programs, the school could utilize area resources better: "We have access to a lot of state government resources, but our law and government program is not what it should be."

By all accounts, Widener is a school "constantly seeking to improve," and students here report a "great environment" in which they can "speak to the deans just as candidly" as they do to professors. Both conditions are fortunate, as students have numerous complaints. An evenhanded student puts it this way: "Widener is slowly advancing into the twenty-first century." While many of the classrooms have outlets for laptop computers, a small percentage of them do not. The on-campus "wireless network signal is extremely low"—depending on who you talk to, it either works in "some classrooms" or only "a handful of rooms in the library building"—and, while the school has "two computer labs," "the computers [in each] need to be updated." Widener's "reference librarians are excellent" students say, but maintain that the library could use "bigger study areas" and more comfortable classroom facilities. Policy-wise, the school "allows teachers 25 days from the last final to submit their grades for each semester," which means Widener students receive their grades significantly later than most law school students. In addition, students describe the bookstore as problematic because it doesn't release information about required course texts—not to mention that it's only open for seven

BARBARA AYARS, ASSISTANT DEAN OF ADMISSIONS
3800 VARTAN WAY, PO BOX 69381, HARRISBURG, PA 17106-9381
TEL: 717-541-3903 FAX: 717-541-3999
E-MAIL: LAWADMISSIONS@MAIL.WIDENER.EDU • INTERNET: WWW.LAW.WIDENER.EDU

hours a day, four days a week. Part-time, predominantly evening students gripe that they "do not get the same breadth of academic offerings nor the same level of administrative support services as do the day students." A big-picture student puts it all in perspective: "While I'm sure Widener does not have the most lavish research facilities and class-rooms, [the school] nonetheless provides its students with everything they need to be successful in law school."

Life

"The bottom 10 percent get kicked out after the first year, and the bottom one-third get put into an academic support class after the first semester," so it makes sense that "students are high strung and competitive the first year. Students become more social at the end of the second year and during the third, after the weak links have been academically dismissed and class ranks have settled." Evening students seem to exist outside these peaks and valleys: "We're much more likely to help each other out and share outlines and notes," a 1L writes. "I've found all the horror stories of people backstabbing you in law school and trying to make you look like a fool in class to be generally untrue. Everyone pretty much respects each other." Overall, the atmosphere at Widener is "competitive but friendly, with many of the 2Ls and 3Ls willing to help the incoming students." However, students warn that it can be "hard to get social groups going," and the ones already in place "are pretty tight." Regarding the facilities, "Most classes are in one building, which makes everything very convenient." Unfortunately, "the nearest ATM is one mile away," and "The school's cafeteria operates on a cash-only basis." Its hours are also limited: "One cannot even purchase a cup of coffee on campus in the evening, let alone a sand-wich or anything other than crackers or a candy bar from a vending machine," a 3L writes.

Getting In

Students who apply to both Widener campuses are charged only one application fee by the school. Such students, however, waive their right to choose between locations—the school only grants accepted applicants admission to one campus. It tends to populate each campus with students of roughly equal caliber.

ADMISSIONS

Selectivity Rating	**68**
# applications received	827
# applicants accepted	363
# acceptees attending	126
Average LSAT	151
LSAT Range	149–153
Average undergrad GPA	3.18
Application fee	$60
Regular application	5/15
Regular notification	Rolling
Rolling notification	Yes
Early application program	No
Transfer students accepted	Yes
Evening division offered	Yes
Part-time accepted	Yes
LSDAS accepted	Yes

Applicants Also Look At
New England School of Law; Penn State University; Rutgers, The State University of New Jersey; Temple University; Thomas M. Cooley Law School; University of Baltimore; Villanova University.

International Students

TOEFL required	
of international students	No
TOEFL recommended	
of international students	Yes
Minimum paper TOEFL	550
Minimum computer TOEFL	220

FINANCIAL FACTS

Annual tuition	$29,330
Books and supplies	$1,000
Tuition per credit	$975
Room and board	$8,300
Financial aid application deadline	4/1
% first-year students receiving some sort of aid	90
% receiving some sort of aid	90
% of aid that is merit based	11
% receiving scholarships	18
Average grant	$7,505
Average loan	$28,401
Average total aid package	$30,769
Average debt	$85,207

EMPLOYMENT INFORMATION

Career Rating	**74**	**Grads Employed by Field (%)**	
Rate of placement (nine months out)	95	Business/Industry	24
Average starting salary	$49,537	Government	20
State for bar exam	PA, NJ	Judicial clerkships	16
Pass rate for first-time bar	78	Private practice	37
Employers Who Frequently Hire Grads		Public Interest	3

Law firms; judges; corporations; government employers.

Prominent Alumni
Honorable Mark Cohen, member, Pennsylvania House of Representatives; Honorable Peter J. Daley, member, Pennsylvania House of Representatives; P. Kevin Brobson, partner, Buchanan Ingersoll P.C.

WILLAMETTE UNIVERSITY
COLLEGE OF LAW

INSTITUTIONAL INFORMATION

Public/private	Private
Affiliation	Methodist
Student-faculty ratio	15:1
% faculty part-time	21
% faculty female	29
% faculty minority	10
Total faculty	56

SURVEY SAYS...
Diverse opinions accepted
in classrooms
Great research resources
Great library staff
Beautiful campus

STUDENTS

Enrollment of law school	424
% male/female	57/43
% out-of-state	66
% full-time	99
% minority	12
Average age of entering class	27

ACADEMICS

Academic Experience Rating	**70**
Profs interesting rating	68
Profs accessible rating	65
Hours of study per day	4.7

Academic Specialties
Government services, dispute resolution, law and business, international and comparative law.

Advanced Degrees Offered
LLM (transnational law) 1 year.

Combined Degrees Offered
JD/MBA (with Atkinson Graduate
School of Management) 4 years.

Clinical program required	No
Legal writing course requirement	Yes
Legal methods course requirement	No
Legal research course requirement	Yes
Moot court requirement	Yes
Public interest law requirement	No

Academics

Willamette University College of Law is a "small, intimate" school located in Oregon's capital city, Salem. One benefit to its small size is the administration, which is "committed to the success of the students here." "From finding open office doors to running into the dean in the hallway," guarantees one student, students will have no problem making contact with administrators: "There is always someone available to answer your questions." Other students are less enthusiastic. "The administration is probably typical of most law schools," maintains a 1L, "friendly and accessible, but not exactly pro-student." As for the professors, students tell us of an "incredibly devoted teaching faculty." Don't expect someone to hold your hand, though. Professors are often "pretty tough and really jab you with the Socratic Method." Many adjunct professors work in important positions in the state government, contributing substantial "expertise and vitality" to the academic atmosphere. "For the most part," the faculty is "accessible" outside the classroom. However, certain professors can be "unhappy and aloof, hard to locate," let alone "engage in meaningful input and guidance." In terms of particular academic subjects, students give kudos to the legal research and writing program. Willamette also offers certificate programs in dispute resolution, business law, international and comparative law, and law and government and offers study-abroad programs in Hamburg, Germany; Quito, Ecuador; and Shanghai, China.

"Overall, I am happy with my school," declares a 1L. Nevertheless, students at Willamette do have some complaints. Many students think that "course selection is insufficient." The fairly strict grading curve is also a source of serious frustration. "Willamette practices 'grade deflation,'" explains one student. "Our median GPA is lower than other schools, which makes our grades look worse than those of graduates of other schools." "Also, the school kicks out a number of students each semester for low grades, so the atmosphere is tense to say the least," adds a 1L. "This is not a kinder, gentler law school." There's also the "hardly aggressive" Office of Career Services. Other students, perhaps more thoughtfully, suggest that employment problems are more structural. "Career Services is on the rise," says a 3L, "but since Oregon is a professionally appealing state, competition is fierce in a small legal market with substantial out-of-state competition."

On a positive note, Willamette's "facilities are the best I have seen in Oregon or Washington," brags a 2L. "You have access to the library 24/7" as well as "wireless networking and great computer labs." The location is also fabulous, "right next to the state capitol," providing students lots of opportunities for internships and externships. Classrooms "are quite up-to-date and provide comfortable environments for lecture." "The library is small but the printing is free" (a real perk when you need to print some appellate judge's 200-page tome).

Life

Willamette's cozy size "creates a wonderful, cohesive atmosphere, which is conducive to learning and to feeling comfortable in general." The "friendly" students definitely "aren't at each other's throats all the time." "There have been no horror stories of ultra-competitiveness or selfishness," reports a 2L. "Students help out when asked and often will volunteer help. This is the best aspect of Willamette in my opinion." "Here everything is so personal," agrees a 1L. "The reference librarian knew my name within the first two days."

One aspect of student life that is a bit less ideal is the fact that you won't find a ton of ethnic diversity. "I can count the minority students on my hands," claims a 1L. While the situation isn't actually that extreme, the student population here is definitely "not very diverse." Then again, of course, "neither is Oregon in general." A bit more diversity exists on Willamette's campus in terms of the age and experience of its student body— there are "a lot of older students who are looking to transition into another, more lucrative career;" many students are "married with children and planning to settle in the area or return to their home or college town." The general student body is comprised of "independent" sorts, so there is no "overall theme or political bent."

Some students consider the "small" surrounding burg of Salem "an inexpensive and livable town in a pleasant state." "The greatest strength is Willamette's location," they contend. Other students call Salem "the backwaters of Oregon." "There is a lack of cultural activity," they complain. "There is very little college town atmosphere and most attractions are over 45 minutes away." However, let's focus on the positives. The attached undergraduate campus is "pretty" and offers "the benefits of sports" and a gym. Temperatures are mild all year long and the surrounding area is an outdoor sports paradise. Lakes, mountains, trails, and rivers are all nearby.

Getting In

The Admissions Committee considers the GPAs and LSAT scores of its applicants, as well as relevant work experience and a personal statement. Enrolled students at the 25th percentile have an LSAT score of 153 and a GPA of 3.1. Enrolled students at the 75th percentile have an LSAT score of 157 and a GPA of 3.6. Almost 60 percent of the students at Willamette come from outside the Beaver State.

ADMISSIONS

Selectivity Rating	77
# applications received	1,329
# applicants accepted	511
# acceptees attending	159
Average LSAT	157
LSAT Range	155–160
Average undergrad GPA	3.23
Application fee	$50
Regular application	4/1
Regular notification	Rolling
Rolling notification	Yes
Early application program	No
Transfer students accepted	Yes
Evening division offered	No
Part-time accepted	No
LSDAS accepted	Yes

International Students

TOEFL required of international students	Yes
TOEFL recommended of international students	Yes
Minimum paper TOEFL	600
Minimum computer TOEFL	250

FINANCIAL FACTS

Annual tuition	$25,400
Books and supplies	$1,350
Room and board	$13,500
Financial aid application deadline	3/1
% first-year students receiving some sort of aid	87
% receiving some sort of aid	92
% of aid that is merit based	7
% receiving scholarships	53
Average grant	$12,697
Average loan	$30,513
Average total aid package	$36,896
Average debt	$88,720

EMPLOYMENT INFORMATION

		Grads Employed by Field (%)	
Career Rating	72		
Rate of placement (nine months out)	87	Business/Industry	11
Average starting salary	$50,500	Government	12
State for bar exam	OR, WA, CA, UT, NV	Judicial clerkships	11
Pass rate for first-time bar	87	Military	1
Employers Who Frequently Hire Grads		Other	2
Stoel Rives; Schwabe Williamson Wyatt;		Private practice	57
Washington State Attorney General; Lane		Public Interest	6
County Circuit Court; Bullivant House			
Bailey; Oregon Department of Justice.			

Prominent Alumni

Lisa Murkowski, U.S. Senator from Alaska; Chief Justice Paul De Muniz, Oregon Supreme Court; Lindsay D. Stewart, vice president, law and corporate affairs, Nike.

WILLIAM MITCHELL COLLEGE OF LAW

INSTITUTIONAL INFORMATION

Public/private	Private
Student-faculty ratio	24:1
% faculty part-time	84
% faculty female	41
% faculty minority	24
Total faculty	252

SURVEY SAYS...
Great research resources
Great library staff
Students love St. Paul, MN

STUDENTS

Enrollment of law school	1,103
% male/female	45/55
% out-of-state	32
% full-time	67
% minority	10
# of countries represented	7
Average age of entering class	28

ACADEMICS

Academic Experience Rating	**77**
Profs interesting rating	73
Profs accessible rating	77
Hours of study per day	4.31

Academic Specialties
ADR, commercial law, corporate, criminal law, estates, family, government services, intellectual property law, international law, labor law, litigation, property, taxation, torts and insurance.

Advanced Degrees Offered
JD 3 to 4 years.

Combined Degrees Offered
JD/MA (public administration in conjunction with Minnesota State University—Mankato) 4 to 6 years, JD/MS (community health in conjunction with Minnesota State University—Mankato) 4 to 6 years.

Clinical program required	No
Legal writing	
course requirement	Yes
Legal methods	
course requirement	Yes

Academics

William Mitchell College of Law is unique among law schools for its strong evening program. The curriculum for both day and evening programs stresses a practical approach to the law. While first-year students get a dose of "hard-core Socratic teachers," in the second and third years "The professors at Mitchell stress the 'real-world' concept of teaching and actual, practical use of law in the real world." "Many of the specialized upper-division courses are taught by practicing attorneys from large and small firms, industry, and government, all of whom have a commitment to teaching. This provides an unparalleled blend of theory and practical knowledge, along with a little bit of networking!" exclaims one 3L. The school further promotes practical applications of law by augmenting traditional classroom instruction with intensive legal writing and research courses and a dynamic clinical program.

William Mitchell professors are demanding yet "exceptional in their commitment to the students." In fact, every member of the campus community treats individuals with respect and personal attention: "The administration and faculty are easily accessible, the librarians are always there and eager to help with any task, even the security guards always greet people with they enter the building," notes a 3L. Many point out the superb quality of the research facilities and staff. A 2L recounts, "The research librarians are super-helpful. You can e-mail them anytime and typically hear back from them within the hour. They are even happy to help when you call them in a panic from your law clerk job."

William Mitchell was founded as a part-time law school and has since developed a more traditional, full-time program. Still, "one third of the students are part-time," and the program preserves much of its original structure and attitude, always keeping the diverse needs of nontraditional or working students in mind. In fact, "You can even switch back and forth between being full-time and part-time." A 2L notes that "the professors understand the rigors of full-time employment while attending law school; they won't coddle you, but they will work with you." While designed to support part-time students, the school's flexible scheduling system benefits those in the full-time programs as well. A 2L explains, "Classes are offered all throughout the day, including evenings, so it is easy to accommodate any type of work or volunteer schedule." However, many students complain that the school's attempt to offer classes at irregular hours results in conflicts for traditional students, as too many mandatory courses overlap during the evening hours: "Class offerings and times could be spread out a bit more. Too often classes I want to take are offered at the same time, so I can only take one," writes one 3L.

"William Mitchell is growing and changing quickly at the moment," and students say it's a propitious time to be a part of the college community. In particular, a new set of administrators has joined the staff, taking positive steps to promote the college and develop its regional and national reputation: "The administration of the college has changed. It is too early to know, but all evidence appears to suggest a forward-thinking, progressive administration interested in enhancing the national public image of the college," writes one student. In addition, the college is physically expanding, and "a new building, student center, and lounge were opened this fall, all of which redefine 'state of the art.'" In fact, the William Mitchell campus draws praises all around for its "beautiful student area for studying and socializing, lots of lockers, beautiful grounds, state-of-the-art classrooms, and many small courtrooms for trial exercises."

KENDRA DANE, ASSISTANT DEAN AND DIRECTOR OF ADMISSIONS
875 SUMMIT AVENUE, ST. PAUL, MN 55105
TEL: 651-290-6476 FAX: 651-290-6414
E-MAIL: ADMISSIONS@WMITCHELL.EDU • INTERNET: WWW.WMITCHELL.EDU

Life

Given the strength of its evening program, it's not surprising that William Mitchell College of Law attracts many older, nontraditional students who have experience in other career fields. Many say the diversity of the student body is the school's greatest strength, as it "allows people to see how the law would affect different people in different ways." For example, "In my 90-student section we have a doctor, a dentist, two PhDs, a dozen engineers, and almost that many MBAs," writes a 3L. No matter who you are or what your background is, you will feel comfortable at William Mitchell. Whether among kindred spirits or polar opposites, the college promotes tolerance and respect. For example, a 2L tells us, "The law school is extremely supportive of diversity! I specifically chose this law school because of its good standing with the gay community. The school is very GLBT-friendly and supportive."

A friendly college within a friendly city, competition is kept at a minimum at William Mitchell, and "The college provides a collegial atmosphere; most students prefer to work together to learn concepts, rather than compete with each other." For example, "If someone forgets a book for class, another is likely to either forward notes or offer to allow the student to copy his/her book." In particular, many of the evening students claim that they function as a surrogate family, helping each other through the challenges of full-time employment and the legal education. While "students are very, very friendly," you won't find a very social atmosphere on the William Mitchell campus. With many older classmates, "Students work hard, but have well-rounded lives outside of school." Even so, there are a few opportunities to get down with your classmates: "The social event held every semester is widely attended and looked forward to by the entire student population."

Getting In

The Admissions Committee at William Mitchell College of Law evaluates students based on both academic and non-academic factors. Therefore, a student's resume of extracurricular and professional experience is heavily weighted, in addition to grades and LSAT scores.

Legal research	
course requirement	Yes
Moot court requirement	No
Public interest	
law requirement	No

ADMISSIONS

Selectivity Rating	**73**
# applications received	1,323
# applicants accepted	631
# acceptees attending	237
Average LSAT	155
LSAT Range	150–158
Average undergrad GPA	3.43
Application fee	$50
Regular application	5/1
Regular notification	Rolling
Rolling notification	Yes
Early application program	No
Transfer students accepted	Yes
Evening division offered	Yes
Part-time accepted	Yes
LSDAS accepted	Yes

Applicants Also Look At
Hamline University, St. Thomas University, University of Minnesota.

International Students

TOEFL required	
of international students	Yes
Minimum paper TOEFL	600
Minimum computer TOEFL	250

FINANCIAL FACTS

Annual tuition	$27,480
Books and supplies	$1,550
Room and board	
(off-campus)	$13,920
Financial aid application	
deadline	3/15
% first-year students	
receiving some sort of aid	94
% receiving some sort of aid	96
% of aid that is merit based	17
% receiving scholarships	66
Average grant	$8,856
Average loan	$26,864
Average total aid package	$35,068
Average debt	$70,315

EMPLOYMENT INFORMATION

Career Rating	**77**	
Rate of placement (nine months out)	91	
Average starting salary	$63,634	
State for bar exam	MN, WI, IL, NY, CA	
Pass rate for first-time bar	92	

Employers Who Frequently Hire Grads
Briggs and Morgan; Faegre and Benson; Gray Plant Mooty; Robins, Kaplan, Miller, and Ciresi; Leonard, Street, and Deinard.

Prominent Alumni
Chief Justice Warren E. Burger, U.S. Supreme Court; former Justice Rosalie Wahl, Minnesota Supreme Court; former Chief Justice Douglas Amdahl, Minnesota Supreme Court.

Grads Employed by Field (%)	
Academic	1
Business/Industry	25
Government	10
Judicial clerkships	11
Military	1
Other	1
Private practice	46
Public Interest	5

YALE UNIVERSITY
LAW SCHOOL

INSTITUTIONAL INFORMATION

Public/private	Private
Student-faculty ratio	7:1
% faculty female	20
% faculty minority	8
Total faculty	71

SURVEY SAYS...

Great research resources
Great library staff
Abundant externship/internship/
clerkship opportunities
Beautiful campus

STUDENTS

Enrollment of law school	576
% male/female	52/48
% full-time	100
% minority	30
# of countries represented	22
Average age of entering class	24

ACADEMICS

Academic Experience Rating	**87**
Profs interesting rating	69
Profs accessible rating	67
Hours of study per day	3.5

Advanced Degrees Offered
JD 3 years, LLM 1 year, MSL 1 year,
JSD up to 5 years.

Combined Degrees Offered
JD/PhD (history), JD/PhD (political
science), JD/MS (forestry), JD/MS
(sociology), JD/MS (statistics),
JD/MBA and JD/PhD (with Yale
School of Management) and others.

Clinical program required	No
Legal writing course requirement	No
Legal methods course requirement	No
Legal research course requirement	No
Moot court requirement	No
Public interest law requirement	No

Academics

It's hard to beat Yale Law School, where the atmosphere is "highly intellectual" and classes are mostly "small" (first-year classes vary in size from 15 to 90 students). One of the many uniquely cool things about Yale is that "there aren't very many required courses." All 1Ls must complete course work in constitutional law, contracts, procedure, and torts. There's also a small, seminar-style legal research and writing course, and that's pretty much it. Best of all, there are "no grades." First semester classes are graded pass/fail and everybody passes. After first semester, there is some semblance of grades but, since Yale doesn't keep track of class rank, it's not a big deal.

Academically, "This is the best place in the world." "It's easy to learn about whatever you're interested in, from medieval European law to helping immigrants in the modern-day United States," says one student. Yale is home to cutting-edge centers and programs galore. Clinical opportunities are vast and available "in your first year," which is a rarity. You can represent family members in juvenile neglect cases, provide legal services for nonprofit organizations, or participate in complicated federal civil rights cases. It's also "easy" to obtain joint-degrees or simply "cross-register for other classes" at Yale. A particularly unique program allows students to get a joint-degree at the Woodrow Wilson School of Public and International Affairs at Princeton.

Student report that the administration is "generally friendly." Word on the faculty is mixed. "I love all my professors," beams a 2L. "They will help me with anything." Nearly all agree that "most professors are delighted to help you." When jobs and clerkships are on the line, it's not uncommon for professors to personally make calls on behalf of students "to high-profile firms or government officials." Other students, however, tell us the faculty isn't all it's cracked up to be. "Quality teaching is not valued enough," gripes a critic. "Professors are hired based on their scholarship rather than their ability to teach or their interest in interacting with students."

Employment prospects are simply awesome. A degree from Yale virtually guarantees "an easy time finding a good job" and a lifetime of financial security. There is "very solid career support" (including "lots of free wine" at recruiting events). But did you know that Yale prolifically produces public interest attorneys? It's true. Every one of Yale's graduates could immediately take the big firm route but, each year, hordes of them don't. Yale "encourages diverse career paths" and "nontraditional routes" ("especially in academia and public interest") and annually awards dozens of public interest fellowships to current students and newly minted grads. There's a "great" loan forgiveness program too.

Facilities are phenomenal. Yale boasts Internet access at every classroom seat, wireless common areas, and perhaps the greatest law library in the history of humanity. "The research facilities are spectacular." Aesthetically, "Everything is beautiful," especially if you are into "wood paneling, stained glass windows, and hand-carved moldings." "If you care about architecture and Ivy League ambiance, come to Yale."

Life

Though the student population "is a bit Ivy heavy," it doesn't necessarily follow that everyone is wealthy. Approximately 80 percent of the lucky souls here receive financial assistance of some kind. It does follow, however, that students are pretty conceited about their intelligence and their privileged educational status. "If egos were light, an astronaut on the moon would have to shade his eyes from the glare of New Haven," analogizes one

ASHA RANGAPPA, ASSISTANT DEAN
PO BOX 208329, NEW HAVEN, CT 06520-8329
TEL: 203-432-4995 FAX: 000-000-0000
E-MAIL: ADMISSIONS.LAW@YALE.EDU • INTERNET: WWW.LAW.YALE.EDU

student. "I'm not sure there's a cure for that, but it might not be wise to tell us in the first week of torts that many of us will wind up on the federal bench."

"There are parties," swears a 1L. However, for many students, the social scene at Yale is simply an extension of academic life. Lectures and cultural events of all kinds are, of course, never-ending. The surrounding city of New Haven is lively in its own way and New York City and Boston are both easily accessible by train. On campus, Yale offers an "encouraging environment" and a "wonderful community." "Because of the small size of each class and the enormous number of activities, it is incredibly easy to get involved with journals (even the *Journal*) and any other student group you might want to try." "Students are very engaged and motivated, but not generally in a way that stresses everyone else out," explains one student. "The no-grades policy for first semester completely eliminates the competition I expect exists at other schools." "People ask me what law school is like, and I can honestly say, 'I work pretty hard, but it's fun,'" says a satisfied student. "Then those people stare at me oddly, and maybe they're right that 'fun' isn't exactly the right word. But I've found it enriching and enjoyable and the people I've met here have been great."

Getting In

Let's not sugarcoat the situation: It's ridiculously hard to get into Yale Law School. Consider: with a stellar grade-point average of 3.75 and a near-perfect LSAT score of, say, 176, you have about a 40 percent chance of getting accepted. With a perfectly good GPA of 3.4 and a perfectly good LSAT score of 168, your shot at getting into Yale is a little more than 1 percent. The folks in admissions at Yale say that they don't use any kind of formula or index. They consider many factors including grades; LSAT scores (including multiple LSAT scores), extracurricular activities, ethnic and socioeconomic diversity, and letters of recommendation.

ADMISSIONS

Selectivity Rating	99
# applications received	3,677
# applicants accepted	249
# acceptees attending	189
Average LSAT	173
LSAT Range	170–176
Average undergrad GPA	3.89
Application fee	$75
Regular application	2/15
Regular notification	Rolling
Rolling notification	Yes
Early application program	No
Transfer students accepted	Yes
Evening division offered	No
Part-time accepted	No
LSDAS accepted	Yes

International Students

TOEFL required of international students	No
TOEFL recommended of international students	No

FINANCIAL FACTS

Annual tuition	$39,500
Books and supplies	$1,000
Room and board (on-campus)	$14,700
Financial aid application deadline	3/15
% first-year students receiving some sort of aid	75
% receiving some sort of aid	75
% receiving scholarships	49
Average grant	$18,412
Average loan	$32,719
Average debt	$81,733

EMPLOYMENT INFORMATION

Career Rating	90	Grads Employed by Field (%)	
Rate of placement (nine months out)	99	Academic	2
State for bar exam	NY	Business/Industry	2
Pass rate for first-time bar	94	Government	2
		Judicial clerkships	51
		Private practice	37
		Public Interest	6

YESHIVA UNIVERSITY
BENJAMIN N. CARDOZO SCHOOL OF LAW

Academics

Despite having only been around about 30 years, Benjamin N. Cardozo School of Law "has accomplished much" in that time and offers "a top-notch legal education" to its students. Academic life at the "underrated, under-known" law school in New York City is pretty exciting. There are "weekly debates featuring legal experts from around the country on topics that run the gamut from post-9/11 national security policy to the impact of labor unions on Major League Baseball." Plus, there are lunches or roundtables "every single day with public officials like the New York City Police Commissioner."

Offering "a strong balance of theory and practice," Cardozo provides "superb" opportunities for practical experience. Students also love the "envied" clinical opportunities available. "I've spent a full semester in the New York DA's office, tried a civil case from pleadings to judgment, and this week will argue an appeal at the NY's Appellate Division First Department," says one student. Likewise, a participant in Cardozo's Innocence Project tells us, "Spending eight straight hours in the library doesn't seem so bad after you meet a guy who spent 18 years in jail for a crime he didn't commit." Cardozo also boasts a strong intellectual property program, a unique Public Service Scholars program, several "great journals," and study abroad programs.

Student are "continually impressed" by the "high caliber" of Cardozo's professors. "The faculty is composed of nationally recognized scholars who care deeply about their specialized fields of law and their students' progress within it," says one student. They "really care about how you are progressing." Not only are they "smart," but they also make "fantastic teachers, which don't always go hand in hand." However, "Some teachers are clearly experts in their field, but are unable to convey their knowledge as effective instructors," claims one student. Another remarks, "Cardozo's faculty is a mix of brilliant young stars who have clerked in high places and old-school Socratic Method actors straight out of *The Paper Chase*. My experiences vary so widely from those of 1Ls in other sections that it's as though we go to different schools."

Students find that "some areas of the administration are very strong and certain administrators are particularly sensitive to the needs of the students." However, some students would like to see "more emphasis . . . placed on weeding out the weakest of the administrators and shoring up the more poorly performing departments." Most students are satisfied with their career prospects. "The school's reputation is growing by leaps and bounds," however, Cardozo graduates "unfortunately have to compete with intense competition from Columbia, NYU, and Fordham grads for jobs."

Students applaud the "great facility face-lift in the last few years" and "amazing" location. One student reports that "it's a pretty aesthetically pleasing place to be these days." Many find the moot court room "impressive" but say that "technology across the board" (especially the "website, online course reviews, e-mail system, [and] online research resources") could be improved. Also, technology is not cutting-edge. Cardozo's library has "great reading rooms," but many students complain because it is "closed every Friday night and Saturday." (Cardozo is a Jewish-affiliated law school.)

Life

Besides the fact that the library is closed on Saturdays, "Cardozo does not feel like a religious law school." There are "exceptionally hardworking and dedicated" students of every "religion, ethnicity, and background." Another student adds, "Law school is not about religion, unless one wishes to specialize in religious law." One student explains, "We feel that

DAVID G. MARTINIDEZ, DEAN OF ADMISSIONS
55 FIFTH AVENUE, NEW YORK, NY 10003
TEL: 212-790-0274 FAX: 212-790-0482
E-MAIL: LAWINFO@YU.EDU • INTERNET: WWW.CARDOZO.YU.EDU

the school is consistently underrated." This feeling gives students "a strong bond and sense of community," however the school is "shedding its underdog character every year" as its profile rises and successful alumni base expands. Students are divided when it comes to the level of competition at Cardozo. Some perceive a "very competitive" atmosphere. Others "would like nothing better then to give you their notes." "The students are more competitive with themselves than with other students," writes a student in the latter camp. "There is generally a very supportive and friendly environment among students."

Cardozo's location in "the heart of New York City is its best asset." Certainly, getting a legal education in the world's capital of business and finance has its perks. If urban life is what you are after, you would be hard-pressed to do better. However, it can be somewhat of a "commuter school," and the location "drives students into the city, not into school to socialize." Also, housing comes at a hefty premium in New York City. Some students find housing in Greenwich Village, Tribeca, SoHo, and other nearby neighborhoods. Others aren't so lucky. The law school also has a residence hall, (but space is limited and priority is given to out-of-towners), although it has been possible to accommodate all students in recent years.

Getting In

Admitted students at the 25th percentile have an LSAT score of 161 and a GPA of 3.23. Admitted students at the 75th percentile have an LSAT score of 166 and a GPA of 3.72. If you take the LSAT more than once, Cardozo will review all scores and may give consideration to the highest LSAT score. If you score significantly better on one LSAT, write an explanatory letter to the Admissions Committee—it can do wonders. Finally, note that you can enter Cardozo in January and May as well as in September.

Legal methods	
course requirement	Yes
Legal research	
course requirement	Yes
Moot court requirement	Yes
Public interest	
law requirement	No

ADMISSIONS

Selectivity Rating	**88**
# applications received	4,411
# applicants accepted	1,226
# acceptees attending	268
Average LSAT	163
LSAT Range	161–166
Average undergrad GPA	3.55
Application fee	$65
Regular application	4/1
Regular notification	Rolling
Rolling notification	Yes
Early application program	Yes
Early application deadline	11/15
Early application notification	12/15
Transfer students accepted	Yes
Evening division offered	No
Part-time accepted	Yes
LSDAS accepted	Yes

Applicants Also Look At
Boston University, Brooklyn Law School, Columbia University, Fordham University, The George Washington University, New York University.

International Students
TOEFL required	
of international students	No
TOEFL recommended	
of international students	No

FINANCIAL FACTS

Annual tuition	$36,900
Books and supplies	$1,000
Tuition per credit	$1,650
Room and board	
(on/off-campus)	$18,000/$18,050
Financial aid application	
deadline	4/15
% first-year students	
receiving some sort of aid	85
% receiving some sort of aid	84
% of aid that is merit based	42
% receiving scholarships	60
Average grant	$13,996
Average loan	$36,579
Average total aid package	$34,704
Average debt	$100,292

EMPLOYMENT INFORMATION

Career Rating	**88**	
Rate of placement (nine months out)	98	
Average starting salary	$86,971	
State for bar exam	NY, NJ	
Pass rate for first-time bar	91	

Employers Who Frequently Hire Grads
International and national law firms of all sizes; corporations; federal and state judges nationwide; government entities and public interest organizations.

Prominent Alumni
Randi Weingarten, president, United Federation of Teachers; Honorable Sandra J. Feuerstein, judge, U.S. District Court; David Samson, president, Florida Marlins, Keff Marx, co-writer, "Avenue Q."

Grads Employed by Field (%)
Academic	1
Business/Industry	17
Government	14
Judicial clerkships	3
Private practice	60
Public Interest	5

LAW SCHOOL DATA LISTINGS

In this section you will find data listings of the ABA-approved schools not appearing in the "Law School Descriptive Profiles" section of the book. Here you will also find listings of the California Bar Accredited, but not ABA-approved law schools, as well as listings of Canadian law schools. Explanations of what each field of data signifies in the listings may be found in the "How to Use This Book" section.

BARRY UNIVERSITY

School of Law

6441 East Colonial Drive, Orlando, FL 32807 United States
Admissions Phone: *321-206-5600 • **Admissions Fax:** 321-206-5620*
Admissions E-mail: *lawinfo@mail.barry.edu • **Website:** www.barry.edu/law*

INSTITUTIONAL INFORMATION

Public/private: Private
Affiliation: Roman Catholic
Student/faculty ratio: 19:1
Total faculty: 29
% part time: 16
% female: 34
% minority: 17

STUDENTS

Enrollment of law school: 511
% Out of state: 40
% Male/female: 50/50
% Full time: 56
% International: 1
% minority: 23
Average age of entering class: 27

ACADEMICS

Clinical program required: No
Legal writing course requirements: Yes
Legal methods course requirements: Yes
Legal research course requirements: Yes
Moot court requirement: No
Public interest law requirement: Yes

ADMISSIONS INFORMATION

Admissions Selectivity Rating: 62
Application fee: $50
Regular application deadline: 4/1
Early application program: No
LSDAS accepted: Yes
Average GPA: 2.9
Range of GPA: 2.6–3.4
Average LSAT: 148
Range of LSAT: 145–153
Transfer students accepted: Yes
Evening division offered: Yes
Part-time accepted: Yes
Applicants also look at: Nova Southeastern University, St. Thomas University, Stetson University, University of Miami.
Number of applications received: 1,500
Number of applicants accepted: 739
Number of acceptees attending: 241

INTERNATIONAL STUDENTS

TOEFL required for international students: Yes
Minimum Paper TOEFL: 600
Minimum Computer-based TOEFL: 250

FINANCIAL FACTS

Annual tuition: $26,000
Room & board (off-campus): $10,400
Books and supplies: $1,400
Financial aid application deadline: 6/30
% receiving scholarships: 67
Average grant: $6,779
Average loan: $28,400
% of aid that is merit-based: 16
% receiving some sort of aid: 94
% first year students receiving some sort of aid: 90
Average total aid package: $32,598
Average debt: $70,780
Tuition per credit: $925
Average starting salary: $57,275
State for bar exam: FL
Pass rate for first-time bar: 58

Grads employed by field:	%
Academic	6
Business/Industry	26
Government	23
Military	2
Private practice	41
Public Interest	2

CALIFORNIA WESTERN SCHOOL OF LAW

225 Cedar Street, San Diego, CA 92101 United States
Admissions Phone: *619-525-1401 • **Admissions Fax:** 619-615-1401*
Admissions E-mail: *admissions@cwsl.edu • **Website:** www.californiawestern.edu*

INSTITUTIONAL INFORMATION

Public/private: Private
Student/faculty ratio: 18:1
Total faculty: 103
% part time: 53
% female: 44
% minority: 12

STUDENTS

Enrollment of law school: 835
% Out of state: 46
% Male/female: 51/49
% Full time: 88
% International: 1

% Minority: 27
Average age of entering class: 25

ACADEMICS

Academic Specializations: Biotech law, constitutional law, creative problem solving, criminal law, environmental law, family law, health law, human rights law, intellectual property law, international law, labor law, taxation, telecomm law.
Advanced Degrees Offered: JD 2 to 3 years, MCL/LLM (comparative law, laws on comparative law) 9 months, LLM (trial advocacy) 1 year.
Combined Degrees Offered: JD/MSW (social work) 4 years, JD/MBA 4 years, JD/PhD (political science or history) 5 years.
Clinical program required: No
Legal writing course requirements: Yes
Legal methods course requirements: Yes
Legal research course requirements: Yes
Moot court requirement: No
Public interest law requirement: No

ADMISSIONS INFORMATION

Admissions Selectivity Rating: 70
Application fee: $45
Regular application deadline: 4/1
Regular notification: Rolling
Early application program: No
LSDAS accepted: Yes
Average GPA: 3.29
Range of GPA: 3.0–3.5
Average LSAT: 153
Range of LSAT: 151–156
Transfer students accepted: Yes
Evening division offered: No
Part-time accepted: Yes
Applicants also look at: University of San Diego
Number of applications received: 2,777
Number of applicants accepted: 1,299
Number of acceptees attending: 318

INTERNATIONAL STUDENTS

TOEFL required for international students: Yes
Minimum Paper TOEFL: 600
Minimum Computer-based TOEFL: 250

FINANCIAL FACTS

Annual tuition: $32,280
Room & board (off-campus): $15,816
Books and supplies $1,088
Financial aid application deadline: 3/31
% receiving scholarships: 30
Average grant: $15,778
Average loan: $35,193
% of aid that is merit-based: 11
% receiving some sort of aid: 86
% first year students receiving some sort of aid: 91
Average total aid package: $39,314
Average debt: $89,192
Tuition per credit: $1,130

EMPLOYMENT INFORMATION

Rate of placement (nine months out): 93
Average starting salary: $64,047
State for bar exam: CA, NV, AZ, NY
Pass rate for first-time bar: 86

Employers who frequently hire grads: Multiple private, public, and nonprofit employers of all sizes from many regions nationally.
Prominent Alumni: Lisa Haile, partner, DLA Piper, Rudnick, Gray, Cary; Hon. Garland Burrell, U.S. District Court; Duane Layton, partner, Mayer, Brown, Rowe and Maw; David Roger, DA, Clark County, Nevada; Hon. James Lorenz, U.S. District Court.

Grads employed by field:	%
Academic	2
Business/Industry	15
Government	10
Judicial clerkships	5
Private practice	63
Public Interest	5

DUQUESNE UNIVERSITY
School of Law

900 Locust Street Pittsburgh, PA 15282 United States
Admissions Phone: *412-396-6296* • **Admissions Fax:** *412-396-1073*
Admissions E-mail: *campion@duq.edu* • **Website:** *www.law.duq.edu*

INSTITUTIONAL INFORMATION

Public/private: Private
Student/faculty ratio: 23:1
Total faculty: 26
% female: 21
% Minority: 16

STUDENTS

Enrollment of law school: 630
% Out of state: 38
% Male/female: 50/50
% Full time: 65
% minority: 7
Average age of entering class: 23

ACADEMICS

Academic Specializations:
Combined Degrees Offered: JD/MBA 4 years, JD/MDiv 5 years, JD/M (environmental science and management) 4 years, JD/MS (taxation) 4 years.
Clinical program required: No
Legal writing course requirements: Yes
Legal methods course requirements: Yes
Legal research course requirements: Yes
Moot court requirement: No
Public interest law requirement: No

ADMISSIONS INFORMATION

Admissions Selectivity Rating: 60*
Application fee: $50
Regular application deadline: 4/1
Regular notification: Rolling
Early application program: No
LSDAS accepted: Yes
Average GPA: 3.4
Average LSAT: 154

Transfer students accepted: Yes
Evening division offered: Yes
Part-time accepted: Yes

INTERNATIONAL STUDENTS
TOEFL required for international students: Yes
Minimum Paper TOEFL: 600

FINANCIAL FACTS
Annual tuition: $19,394
Room & board (off-campus): $8,000
Books and supplies: $1,000
Average grant: $4,500
Average loan: $12,000
% of aid that is merit-based: 50
% receiving some sort of aid: 35
% first year students receiving some sort of aid: 40
Average total aid package: $11,000
Average debt: $35,000

EMPLOYMENT INFORMATION
Average starting salary: $59,693
State for bar exam: PA
Pass rate for first-time bar: 71
Employers who frequently hire grads: Reed Smith; Kirkpatrick and Lockhart; Buchanon Ingersoll; Eckert; Seamans.

Grads employed by field:	%
Academic	1
Business/Industry	25
Government	4
Judicial clerkships	6
Private practice	61
Public Interest	3

FLORIDA A&M UNIVERSITY*

College of Law

PO Box 3113 Orlando, FL 32802 United States
Admissions Phone: 407-254-3268 • Admissions Fax: 407-254-3213
Admissions E-mail: famulaw.admissions@famu.edu • Website: www.famu.edu/law

INSTITUTIONAL INFORMATION
Public/private: Public
Student/faculty ratio: 13:1
Total faculty: 40

STUDENTS
Enrollment of law school: 293
% Male/female: 40/60
% Full time: 69
% Minority: 53
Average age of entering class: 33

ACADEMICS
Advanced Degrees Offered: JD 3 to 4 years.
Clinical program required: Yes
Legal writing course requirements: No
Legal methods course requirements: Yes
Legal research course requirements: No
Moot court requirement: No
Public interest law requirement: Yes

ADMISSIONS INFORMATION
Admissions Selectivity Rating: 67
Application fee: $20
Regular application deadline: 5/1
Regular notification: Rolling
Early application program: No
LSDAS accepted: Yes
Average GPA: 3.1
Range of GPA: 2.6–3.4
Average LSAT: 148
Range of LSAT: 143–150
Transfer students accepted: No
Evening division offered: Yes
Part-time accepted: Yes
Number of applications received: 540
Number of applicants accepted: 194
Number of acceptees attending: 120

INTERNATIONAL STUDENTS
TOEFL required for international students: No

FINANCIAL FACTS
Annual tuition (resident): $7,140
Annual tuition (nonresident): $26,580
Books and supplies: $13,591
Financial aid application deadline: 4/1
% receiving scholarships: 16
Average grant: $1,800
Average loan: $18,500
% receiving some sort of aid: 92
% first year students receiving some sort of aid: 88
Tuition per credit (resident): $239
Tuition per credit (nonresident): $88,600

*Provisionally approved by the ABA.

FLORIDA COASTAL SCHOOL OF LAW

8787 Baypine Road, Jacksonville, FL 32256 United States
Admissions Phone: *904-680-7710* • **Admissions Fax:** *904-680-7692*
Admissions E-mail: *admissions@fcsl.edu* • **Website:** *www.fcsl.edu*

INSTITUTIONAL INFORMATION
Public/private: Private
Student/faculty ratio: 20:1
Total faculty: 93
% part-time: 39
% female: 47
% Minority: 16

STUDENTS
Enrollment of law school: 1,278
% Out of state: 60
% Male/female: 54/46
% Full time: 19
% International: 1
% minority: 17
Average age of entering class: 26

ACADEMICS
Academic Specializations: Civil procedure, commercial law, constitutional law, corporation securities law, criminal law, environmental law, government services, human rights law, intellectual property law, international law, labor law, legal history, legal philosophy, property, taxation.
Advanced Degrees Offered: JD 2.5 to 4 years.
Clinical program required: Yes
Legal writing course requirements: Yes
Legal methods course requirements: Yes
Legal research course requirements: Yes
Moot court requirement: Yes
Public interest law requirement: No

ADMISSIONS INFORMATION
Admissions Selectivity Rating: 65
Regular application deadline: Rolling
Regular notification: Rolling
Early application program: No
LSDAS accepted: Yes
Average GPA: 3.24
Range of GPA: 2.9–3.5
Average LSAT: 151
Range of LSAT: 149–154
Transfer students accepted: Yes
Evening division offered: No
Part-time accepted: Yes
Applicants also look at: Florida State University, Mercer University, Nova Southeastern University, St. Thomas University, Stetson University, University of Florida, University of Miami.
Number of applications received: 4,940
Number of applicants accepted: 2,365
Number of acceptees attending: 622

INTERNATIONAL STUDENTS
TOEFL required for international students: No
Minimum Paper TOEFL: 600
Minimum Computer-based TOEFL: 250

FINANCIAL FACTS
Annual tuition: $25,888
Room & board (off-campus): $16,470
Books and supplies: $1,200
Financial aid application deadline: 8/1
% receiving scholarships: 25
Average grant: $6,200
Average loan: $18,500
% of aid that is merit-based: 11
% receiving some sort of aid: 85
% first year students receiving some sort of aid: 85
Average total aid package: $23,000
Average debt: $60,000

EMPLOYMENT INFORMATION
Rate of placement (nine months out): 87
Average starting salary: $48,525
State for bar exam: FL
Pass rate for first-time bar: 76
Employers who frequently hire grads: Small to midsized Florida firms; Florida prosecutors' and public defenders' offices.

Grads employed by field:	%
Academic	1
Business/Industry	15
Government	16
Judicial clerkships	5
Military	1
Other	2
Private practice	48
Public Interest	12

GOLDEN GATE UNIVERSITY*
School of Law

536 Mission Street, Law Admissions Office, San Francisco, CA 94105 United States
Admissions Phone: *415-442-6630* • **Admissions Fax:** *415-442-6631*
Admissions E-mail: *lawadmit@ggu.edu* • **Website:** *www.ggu.edu/law*

INSTITUTIONAL INFORMATION
Public/private: Private
Student/faculty ratio: 22:1
Total faculty: 156
% part time: 66
% female: 40
% minority: 22

STUDENTS
Enrollment of law school: 851
% Out of state: 40
% Male/female: 43/57
% Full time: 79
% International: 1
% minority: 25
Average age of entering class: 26

ACADEMICS

Academic Specializations: Business law, criminal law, environmental law, intellectual property law, international law, labor law, litigation, property, public interest law, taxation.

Advanced Degrees Offered: JD 3 to 4 years; LLM 1 year; SJD 1 year.

Combined Degrees Offered: JD/MBA 4 years, JD/PhD 7 years.

Clinical program required: No

Legal writing course requirements: Yes

Legal methods course requirements: No

Legal research course requirements: Yes

Moot court requirement: Yes

Public interest law requirement: No

ADMISSIONS INFORMATION

Admissions Selectivity Rating: 70

Application fee: $60

Regular application deadline: 4/1

Regular notification: Rolling

Early application program: No

LSDAS accepted: Yes

Average GPA: 3.21

Range of GPA: 2.9–3.4

Average LSAT: 153

Range of LSAT: 150–156

Transfer students accepted: Yes

Evening division offered: Yes

Part-time accepted: Yes

Applicants also look at: California Pacific School of Law, California Western, Santa Clara University, Thomas Jefferson School of Law, University of California, Hastings, University of San Francisco, Whittier College.

Number of applications received: 2,475

Number of applicants accepted: 943

Number of acceptees attending: 220

INTERNATIONAL STUDENTS

TOEFL required for international students: Yes

Minimum Paper TOEFL: 600

Minimum Computer-based TOEFL: 250

FINANCIAL FACTS

Annual tuition: $30,900

Room & board (off-campus): $13,500

Books and supplies: $1,200

% receiving scholarships: 80

Average grant: $13,175

Average loan: $28,747

% of aid that is merit-based: 90

% receiving some sort of aid: 95

% first year students receiving some sort of aid: 92

Average total aid package: $48,200

Average debt: $89,337

Tuition per credit: $1,030

EMPLOYMENT INFORMATION

Rate of placement (nine months out): 70

Average starting salary: $54,364

State for bar exam: CA

Pass rate for first-time bar: 44

Employers who frequently hire grads: Small, medium, and large firms; government agencies; public interest organizations, businesses and corporations.

Prominent Alumni: Justice Jesse Carter (deceased), California Supreme Court; Philip Burton (deceased), former U.S. Congressman; Peter M. Carroon, Mayor of Salt Lake City; Mark S. Anderson, vice president and general counsel, Dolby Labs; Marjorie Randolph, senior vice president for HR and admin., Walt Disney Studios.

Grads employed by field:	%
Academic	5
Business/Industry	18
Government	7
Judicial clerkships	3
Other	12
Private practice	47
Public Interest	8

* Currently on ABA probation for a period of two years, effective December 9, 2005.

HOFSTRA UNIVERSITY

School of Law

121 Hofstra University, Hempstead, NY 11549 United States

Admissions Phone: 516-463-5916 • **Admissions Fax:** 516-463-6264

Admissions E-mail: lawadmissions@Hofstra.edu • **Website:** law.hofstra.edu

INSTITUTIONAL INFORMATION

Public/private: Private

Student/faculty ratio: 18:1

Total faculty: 86

% part-time: 52

% female: 22

% minority: 5

STUDENTS

% International: 2

% minority: 22

Average age of entering class: 25

ACADEMICS

Academic Specializations: Civil procedure, commercial law, constitutional law, corporation securities law, criminal law, environmental law, family law, government services, health law, human rights law, intellectual property law, international law, labor law, property, taxation, trial advocacy.

Advanced Degrees Offered: JD 3 to 4 years, LLM (family law, international law, real estate and development law, American legal studies—for foreign lawyers) 1 to 2 years.

Combined Degrees Offered: JD/MBA 4 years, JD/MS (taxation) 4 years.

Clinical program required: No

Legal writing course requirements: Yes

Legal methods course requirements: Yes

Legal research course requirements: Yes

Moot court requirement: Yes

Public interest law requirement: No

ADMISSIONS INFORMATION

Admissions Selectivity Rating: 76

Application fee: $60

Regular application deadline: 4/15

Regular notification: Rolling

Early application program: Yes

LSDAS accepted: Yes

Average GPA: 3.5

Range of GPA: 3.2–3.6

Average LSAT: 157

Range of LSAT: 153–159
Transfer students accepted: Yes
Evening division offered: Yes
Part-time accepted: Yes
Applicants also look at: Brooklyn Law School, Fordham University, New York Law School, New York University, Pace University, St. John's University, Yeshiva University.
Number of applications received: 4,811
Number of applicants accepted: 2,088
Number of acceptees attending: 413

INTERNATIONAL STUDENTS

TOEFL required for international students: Yes
Minimum Paper TOEFL: 580
Minimum Computer-based TOEFL: 237

FINANCIAL FACTS

Annual tuition: $30,824
Room & board (on/off-campus): $9,616/$12,960
Books and supplies: $900
Financial aid application deadline: 4/15
Average grant: $8,553
Average loan: $3,161
% of aid that is merit-based: 50
Tuition per credit: $1,100

EMPLOYMENT INFORMATION

Average starting salary: $68,799
State for bar exam: NY, NJ, CT, FL, CA
Employers who frequently hire grads: The most prestigious law firms in New York City and Long Island regularly recruit at the law school; government agencies; public interest organizations.

Grads employed by field:	%
Business/Industry	16
Government	12
Judicial clerkships	4
Other	2
Private practice	64
Public Interest	1

JOHN MARSHALL LAW SCHOOL—ATLANTA

1422 West Peachtree Street Northwest, Atlanta, GA 30309 United States
Admissions Phone: *404-872-3593* • **Admissions Fax:** *404-873-3802*
Admissions E-mail: *admissions@johnmarshall.edu* • **Website:** *www.johnmarshall.edu*

INSTITUTIONAL INFORMATION

Public/private: Private
Student/faculty ratio: 12:1
Total faculty: 44
% part time: 47
% female: 56
% minority: 15

STUDENTS

Enrollment of law school: 358
% Male/female: 53/47
% Full time: 56
% minority: 27
Average age of entering class: 25

ACADEMICS

Academic Specializations:
Advanced Degrees Offered: JD 3 to 4 years.
Clinical program required: No
Legal writing course requirements: Yes
Legal methods course requirements: No
Legal research course requirements: Yes
Moot court requirement: No
Public interest law requirement: No

ADMISSIONS INFORMATION

Admissions Selectivity Rating: 68
Application fee: $50
Regular application deadline: Rolling
Regular notification: Rolling
Early application program: No
LSDAS accepted: Yes
Average GPA: 3.02
Range of GPA: 2.6–3.3
Average LSAT: 151
Range of LSAT: 149–153
Transfer students accepted: Yes
Evening division offered: Yes
Part-time accepted: Yes
Applicants also look at: Barry University, Florida Coastal School of Law, Georgia State University, Mercer University, University of Georgia.
Number of applications received: 1,244
Number of applicants accepted: 473
Number of acceptees attending: 158

INTERNATIONAL STUDENTS

TOEFL required for international students: Yes

FINANCIAL FACTS

Annual tuition: $26,430
Room & board (off-campus): $13,400
Books and supplies: $1,730
Financial aid application deadline: 6/6
% receiving scholarships: 1
Average loan: $45,067
% receiving some sort of aid: 82
% first year students receiving some sort of aid: 87
Average total aid package: $33,248
Average debt: $59,204
Tuition per credit: $881

EMPLOYMENT INFORMATION

Rate of placement (nine months out): 97
Average starting salary: $57,700
State for bar exam: GA, FL, TN, SC
Pass rate for first-time bar: 72
Employers who frequently hire grads: Georgia public interest organizations; Georgia district attorneys; Georgia public defenders; Georgia solicitor generals. Additionally, many John Marshall grads start their own law firm.
Prominent Alumni: Honorable Alan Blackburn, presiding judge, Court of Ap-

peals; Honorable Brooks Blitch, chief judge, Alapaha Circuit; Honorable James Bodiford, chief judge, Cobb Superior Court; Joan Boilen Sasine, partner, Powell Goldstein; Adam Malone, attorney, Malone Law Office.

Grads employed by field:	%
Academic	1
Business/Industry	5
Government	4
Private practice	26
Public Interest	1

LIBERTY UNIVERSITY*

School of Law

1971 University Boulevard, Lynchburg, VA 24502 United States
Admissions Phone: *434-592-5300* • **Admissions Fax:** *434-592-5400*
Admissions E-mail: *law@liberty.edu* • **Website:** *law.liberty.edu*

INSTITUTIONAL INFORMATION
Public/private: Private
Student/faculty ratio: 12:1
Total faculty: 16
% female: 25
% minority: 6

STUDENTS
Enrollment of law school: 157
% Out of state: 78
% Male/female: 62/38
% Full time: 100
% International: 4
% minority: 22
Average age of entering class: 28

ACADEMICS
Academic Specializations: Constitutional law.
Advanced Degrees Offered: JD 3 years.
Clinical program required: No
Legal writing course requirements: Yes
Legal methods course requirements: Yes
Legal research course requirements: Yes
Moot court requirement: Yes
Public interest law requirement: No

ADMISSIONS INFORMATION
Admissions Selectivity Rating: 69
Application fee: $50
Early application program: No
LSDAS accepted: Yes
Average GPA: 3.21
Range of GPA: 2.7–3.6
Average LSAT: 151
Range of LSAT: 148–153
Transfer students accepted: Yes
Evening division offered: No
Part-time accepted: No
Number of applications received: 203

Number of applicants accepted: 102
Number of acceptees attending: 70

INTERNATIONAL STUDENTS
TOEFL required for international students: Yes
Minimum Paper TOEFL: 650
Minimum Computer-based TOEFL: 280

FINANCIAL FACTS
Annual tuition: $23,000
Room & board (on-campus): $6,900
Books and supplies: $1,500
Financial aid application deadline: 6/1
% receiving scholarships: 100
Average grant: $17,474
Average loan: $18,071
% of aid that is merit-based: 57
% receiving some sort of aid: 100
% first year students receiving some sort of aid: 100
Average total aid package: $31,687

* Provisionally approved by the ABA.

PENNSYLVANIA STATE UNIVERSITY

The Dickinson School of Law

150 South College Street, Carlisle, PA 17013 United States
Admissions Phone: *717-240-5207* • **Admissions Fax:** *717-241-3503*
Admissions E-mail: *dsladmit@psu.edu* • **Website:** *www.dsl.psu.edu*

INSTITUTIONAL INFORMATION
Public/private: Public
Student/faculty ratio: 12:1
Total faculty: 95
% part time: 41
% female: 34
% minority: 12

STUDENTS
Enrollment of law school: 609
% Out of state: 36
% Male/female: 54/46
% Full time: 89
% International: 2
% minority: 22
Average age of entering class: 25

ACADEMICS
Academic Specializations: Civil procedure, commercial law, constitutional law, corporation securities law, criminal law, dispute resolution, environmental law, government services, human rights law, intellectual property law, international law, labor law, legal history, legal philosophy, property, taxation.

Advanced Degrees Offered: JD 3 years LLM (comparative law), 1 year.

Combined Degrees Offered: JD/MBA (with Penn State's Smeal College of Business Administration), JD/MBA (with Penn State Harrisburg), JD/MPA (with Penn State Harrisburg School of Public Affairs), JD/3 Environmental Pollution Control degrees (with Penn State Harrisburg), JD/MSIS (information systems with Penn State Harrisburg), JD/5 counseling degree programs (with Shippensburg University).

Clinical program required: No

Legal writing course requirements: Yes

Legal methods course requirements: No

Legal research course requirements: Yes

Moot court requirement: Yes

Public interest law requirement: No

ADMISSIONS INFORMATION

Admissions Selectivity Rating: 81

Application fee: $60

Regular application deadline: 3/1

Regular notification: Rolling

Early application program: No

LSDAS accepted: Yes

Average GPA: 3.31

Range of GPA: 2.9–3.7

Average LSAT: 157

Range of LSAT: 154–159

Transfer students accepted: Yes

Evening division offered: No

Part-time accepted: Yes

Applicants also look at: American University, Syracuse University, Temple University, University of Pittsburgh, Villanova University, Widener University (PA).

Number of applications received: 3,350

Number of applicants accepted: 959

Number of acceptees attending: 181

INTERNATIONAL STUDENTS

TOEFL required for international students: No

FINANCIAL FACTS

Annual tuition (resident): $27,600

Annual tuition (nonresident): $27,600

Room & board: $8,460

Books and supplies: $1,200

Financial aid application deadline: 3/1

% receiving scholarships: 29

Average grant: $7,769

Average loan: $30,530

% of aid that is merit-based: 80

% receiving some sort of aid: 94

% first year students receiving some sort of aid: 91

Average total aid package: $35,843

Average debt: $78,967

Tuition per credit (resident): $1,150

Tuition per credit (nonresident): $1,150

EMPLOYMENT INFORMATION

Average starting salary: $62,930

State for bar exam: PA

Pass rate for first-time bar: 80

Employers who frequently hire grads: Dickinson graduates are hired by a variety of employers each year including national law firms, small firms, federal and state judges, government agencies, public interest organizations, and other entities.

Prominent Alumni: Hon. Thomas Ridge, Secretary of Homeland Security and PA Governor; Hon. Pedro Cortes, PA Secretary of the Commonwealth; Hon. D. Brooks Smith, Third Circuit Court of Appeals; Lisa A. Hook, president and CEO, SunRocket; Hon. J. Michael Eakin, PA Supreme Court.

Grads employed by field:	%
Academic	3
Business/Industry	15
Government	12
Judicial clerkships	15
Other	1
Private practice	51
Public Interest	3

SAINT LOUIS UNIVERSITY
School of Law

3700 Lindell Boulevard, Morrissey Hall, Suite #120, St. Louis, MO 63108 United States
Admissions Phone: 314-977-2800 • **Admissions Fax:** 314-977-1464
Admissions E-mail: admissions@law.slu.edu • **Website:** law.slu.edu

INSTITUTIONAL INFORMATION

Public/private: Private

Affiliation: Roman Catholic

Student/faculty ratio: 16:1

Total faculty: 51

% female: 43

% minority: 8

STUDENTS

Enrollment of law school: 945

% Out of state: 58

% Male/female: 50/50

% Full time: 75

% minority: 11

Average age of entering class: 23

ACADEMICS

Academic Specializations: Civil procedure, commercial law, constitutional law, corporation securities law, criminal law, environmental law, government services, health law, human rights law, intellectual property law, international law, labor law, legal history, legal philosophy, property, public law, taxation, urban planning and development.

Advanced Degrees Offered: LLM (health law) 1 to 2 years, LLM (foreign lawyers) 1 year.

Combined Degrees Offered: JD/MBA 3.5 years, JD/MA (public administration) 4 years; JD/M.P.H., 4 years, JD/MA in urban affairs, 4 years; JD/PhD in health care ethics, 4 to 6 years

Grading system: Letter and numerical system, 4.0 scale.

Clinical program required: No

Clinical program description: In-House Clinic (including various areas of General Practice), The Externship Program, The Judicial Process Clinic, The Criminal Public Defender Clinic, The Corporate Counsel Externship Clinic, Immigration Law Project, Health Law Clinic, Litigation Clinic, Housing and Finance Clinic, Civil Clinic, Real Estate Development, Special Education, Disability Benefits, Estate Planning, Family Law, Criminal Law, Mediation

---

Legal writing course requirements: Yes
Legal writing description: Legal Research and Writing I (3 credits); Legal Research and Writing II (3 credits); Legal Research and Writing, a course required for all students, is taught in a small section of 25 to 30 students.
Legal methods course requirements: No
Legal research course requirements: Yes
Legal research description: Legal Research and Writing I (3 credits); Legal Research and Writing II (3 credits); Legal Research and Writing, a course required for all students, is taught in a small section of 25 to 30 students.
Moot court requirement: No
Moot court description: Moot Court, Jessup Moot Court (International), Giles Sutherland Rich Moot Court (Intellectual Property/Patent Law), Saul Lefkowitz Moot Court (Intellectual Property/Patent Law), National Health Law Moot Court
Public interest law requirement: No
Public interest law description: Public Interest Careers, Public Interest Law Fellowships, Make a Difference Day-Homeward Bound, Habitat for Humanity, CASA, Stand Down for Homeless Veterans, Tax Assistance Project, PILG (Public Interest Law Group), Public Service Awards (The David Grant Clinic Award, The Legal Service Award and The Community Service Award)
Academic journals: *The Saint Louis University Law Journal*, *Saint Louis University Public Law Review* and *Journal of Health Law*

RESEARCH FACILITIES
Research resources available: ITS has made arrangements for a Symantec Anti-Virus copy to all law students.
% of JD classrooms wired: 100
School-supported research centers: Saint Louis University campus (including the School of Law) maintains a wireless network.

ADMISSIONS INFORMATION
Admissions Selectivity Rating: 76
Application fee: $50
Regular application deadline: 3/1
Regular notification: Rolling
Early application program: No
LSDAS accepted: Yes
Average GPA: 3.5
Range of GPA: 3.3–3.7
Average LSAT: 157
Range of LSAT: 155–159
Transfer students accepted: Yes
Evening division offered: Yes
Part-time accepted: Yes
Applicants also look at: DePaul University, University of Illinois, University of Missouri—Columbia, University of Missouri—Kansas City, Valparaiso University, Washington University.
Number of applications received: 2,005
Number of applicants accepted: 910
Number of acceptees attending: 244

INTERNATIONAL STUDENTS
TOEFL required for international students: No
Minimum Computer-based TOEFL: 232

FINANCIAL FACTS
Annual tuition: $30,040
Room & board (off-campus): $11,988
Books and supplies: $1,040
Financial aid application deadline: 6/1
% receiving scholarships: 44
Average grant: $14,000
Average loan: $32,500
% of aid that is merit-based: 44

% receiving some sort of aid: 92
% first year students receiving some sort of aid: 92
Average debt: $83,500
Tuition per credit: $1,420

EMPLOYMENT INFORMATION
Rate of placement (nine months out): 94
Average starting salary: $56,000
State for bar exam: MO, IL
Pass rate for first-time bar: 89
Employers who frequently hire grads: Bryan Cave, LLP; Husch and Eppenberger; Lewis, Rice, and Fingersh; Armstrong Teasdale, LLP; Sonnenschein, Nath and Rosenthal; Greensfelder, Hemker, and Gale; Blackwell, Sanders, Peper, Martin; Missouri state public defender; Evans and Dixon; Brown and James; King and Spalding; Proskruer Rose; Thompson Coburn; Shook, Hardy, and Bacon; United States Postal Service; Missouri Attorney General.

Grads employed by field:	%
Academic	1
Business/Industry	16
Government	11
Judicial clerkships	6
Military	1
Other	1
Private practice	59
Public Interest	5

STETSON UNIVERSITY
College of Law

1401 Sixty-first Street South, Gulfport, FL 33707 United States
Admissions Phone: *727-562-7802 •* **Admissions Fax:** *727-343-0136*
Admissions E-mail: *lawadmit@law.stetson.edu •* **Website:** *www.law.stetson.edu*

INSTITUTIONAL INFORMATION
Public/private: Private
Student/faculty ratio: 18:1
Total faculty: 125
% part time: 54
% female: 23
% minority: 6

STUDENTS
Enrollment of law school: 1,031
% Out of state:
% Male/female: 47/53
% Full time: 78
% International:
% minority: 23

ACADEMICS
Academic Specializations: International law, advocacy, elder law, higher education law and policy.
Advanced Degrees Offered: JD 3 to 4 years, JD/MBA 3 to 4 years, LLM 1 year.
Combined Degrees Offered: JD/MBA 3 to 4 years.
Clinical program required: No

Legal writing course requirements: Yes
Legal methods course requirements: No
Legal research course requirements: Yes
Moot court requirement: Yes
Public interest law requirement: Yes

ADMISSIONS INFORMATION

Admissions Selectivity Rating: 79
Application fee: $55
Early application program: No
LSDAS accepted: Yes
Average GPA: 3.44
Range of GPA: 3.2–3.6
Average LSAT: 155
Range of LSAT: 152–157
Transfer students accepted: Yes
Evening division offered: Yes
Part-time accepted: Yes
Applicants also look at: Barry University, Florida Coastal School of Law, Florida State University, Nova Southeastern University, St. Thomas University, University of Florida, University of Miami.
Number of applications received: 2,707
Number of applicants accepted: 768
Number of acceptees attending: 274

INTERNATIONAL STUDENTS

TOEFL required for international students: Yes
Minimum Paper TOEFL: 600
Minimum Computer-based TOEFL: 250

FINANCIAL FACTS

Annual tuition: $27,660
Room & board (on/off-campus): $8,520/$11,704
Books and supplies: $1,200
% receiving scholarships: 13
Average grant: $17,000
Average loan: $40,000
% of aid that is merit-based: 59
% receiving some sort of aid: 82
% first year students receiving some sort of aid: 83
Average total aid package: $40,000
Average debt: $103,000

EMPLOYMENT INFORMATION

Rate of placement (nine months out): 98
Average starting salary: $67,750
State for bar exam: FL, GA, DC, VA, MD
Pass rate for first-time bar: 80
Employers who frequently hire grads: Small, medium, and large firms in the greater Tampa Bay area; state attorneys' offices; public defenders' office.
Prominent Alumni: Justice Carol Hunstein, Supreme Court of Georgia; Hon. Elizabeth Kovachevich, U.S. District Court; Rich McKay, president and general manager, Atlanta Falcons; Bruce Jacob, Dean Emeritus and professor of law, argued Gideon v. Wainwright, 372 U.S. 335 (1963); Rhea F. Law, president and CEO, Fowler White.

Grads employed by field:	%
Academic	1
Business/Industry	12
Government	20
Judicial clerkships	5
Military	1
Private practice	53
Public Interest	8

TEXAS SOUTHERN UNIVERSITY

Thurgood Marshall School of Law

3100 Cleburne Avenue, Houston, TX 77004 United States
Admissions Phone: 713-313-7114 • Admissions Fax: 713-313-1049
Admissions E-mail: lawadmit@tsulaw.edu • Website: www.tsulaw.edu

INSTITUTIONAL INFORMATION

Public/private: Public
Student/faculty ratio: 17:1
Total faculty: 35
% female: 20
% minority: 83

STUDENTS

Enrollment of law school: 541
% Male/female: 57/43
% Full time: 100
% minority: 77

ACADEMICS

Academic Specializations: Commercial law, corporation securities law.
Clinical program required: No
Legal methods course requirements: No

ADMISSIONS INFORMATION

Admissions Selectivity Rating: 62
Application fee: $50
Regular application deadline: 4/1
Regular notification: Rolling
Early application program: No
LSDAS accepted: No
Average GPA: 2.8
Range of GPA: 2.5–3.2
Average LSAT: 141
Range of LSAT: 138–144
Transfer students accepted: Yes
Evening division offered: No
Part-time accepted: No
Number of applications received: 1,460
Number of applicants accepted: 540
Number of acceptees attending: 265

INTERNATIONAL STUDENTS

TOEFL required for international students: No

FINANCIAL FACTS

Annual tuition (resident): $4,466
Annual tuition (nonresident): $7,562
Room & board (off-campus): $6,000
Books and supplies: $700

EMPLOYMENT INFORMATION

State for bar exam: TX
Pass rate for first-time bar: 68

Grads employed by field:	%
Government	2
Judicial clerkships	4
Private practice	87
Public Interest	5

THOMAS JEFFERSON SCHOOL OF LAW

2121 San Diego Avenue San Diego, CA 92110 United States
Admissions Phone: *619-297-9700* • **Admissions Fax:** *619-294-4713*
Admissions E-mail: *admissions@tjsl.edu* • **Website:** *www.tjsl.edu*

INSTITUTIONAL INFORMATION

Public/private: Private
Student/faculty ratio: 21:1
Total faculty: 61
% part time: 40
% female: 50
% minority: 6

STUDENTS

Enrollment of law school: 838
% Out of state: 65
% Male/female: 58/42
% Full time: 73
% International: 1
% minority: 17
Average age of entering class: 24

ACADEMICS

Academic Specializations: Civil procedure, commercial law, constitutional law, corporation securities law, criminal law, environmental law, family law, government services, health law, human rights law, intellectual property law, international law, labor law, litigation and dispute resolution, property, sports and entertainment law, taxation.
Advanced Degrees Offered: JD 3 to 4 years.
Clinical program required: No
Legal writing course requirements: Yes
Legal methods course requirements: No
Legal research course requirements: No
Moot court requirement: No
Public interest law requirement: No

ADMISSIONS INFORMATION

Admissions Selectivity Rating: 70
Application fee: $35
Regular application deadline: Rolling
Regular notification: Rolling
Early application program: No
LSDAS accepted: Yes
Average GPA: 3
Range of GPA: 2.7–3.3
Average LSAT: 153
Range of LSAT: 147–157
Transfer students accepted: Yes
Evening division offered: Yes

Part-time accepted: Yes
Applicants also look at: California Western, Chapman University, Southwestern University School of Law, Whittier College.
Number of applications received: 3,300
Number of applicants accepted: 1,206
Number of acceptees attending: 288

INTERNATIONAL STUDENTS

TOEFL required for international students: Yes

FINANCIAL FACTS

Annual tuition: $30,100
Room & board: $11,500
Books and supplies: $3,228
Financial aid application deadline: 4/25
% receiving scholarships: 40
Average grant: $10,394
Average loan: $27,607
% of aid that is merit-based: 15
% receiving some sort of aid: 92
% first year students receiving some sort of aid: 94
Average total aid package: $30,078
Average debt: $99,000
Tuition per credit: $18,900

EMPLOYMENT INFORMATION

Rate of placement (nine months out): 84
Average starting salary: $59,251
State for bar exam: CA, NV, AZ, CO, FL
Pass rate for first-time bar: 67
Employers who frequently hire grads: Various private law firms throughout California, Nevada, Arizona, Florida and Illinois; government agencies, such as attorney general, district attorney, city attorney and public defender; national and international corporations.
Prominent Alumni: Bonnie Dumanis, San Diego District Attorney; Duncan Hunter, member, U.S. Congress; Hon. Roger Benitez, U.S. District Court; Mattias Luukkonen, Baker and McKenzie; Dan Vrechek, Qualcomm.

Grads employed by field:	%
Business/Industry	25
Government	13
Judicial clerkships	4
Military	1
Private practice	47
Public Interest	10

University of Detroit Mercy

School of Law

651 East Jefferson Avenue, Detroit, MI 48226 United States
Admissions Phone: 313-596-0264 • **Admissions Fax:** 313-596-0280
Admissions E-mail: udmlawao@udmercy.edu
Website: www.law.udmercy.edu

INSTITUTIONAL INFORMATION

Public/private: Private
Affiliation: Roman Catholic
Student/faculty ratio: 19:1

STUDENTS

Enrollment of law school: 408
% Male/female: 53/47
% Full time: 64
% International: 11
% minority: 8
Average age of entering class: 28

ACADEMICS

Academic Specializations: Comprehensive legal education with courses in all areas.
Advanced Degrees Offered: JD 3 years, JD/MBA 4 years, JD/LLB 3 years.
Combined Degrees Offered: JD/MBA 4 years, JD/LLB 3 years.
Clinical program required: No
Legal writing course requirements: Yes
Legal methods course requirements: Yes
Legal research course requirements: Yes
Moot court requirement: Yes
Public interest law requirement: No

ADMISSIONS INFORMATION

Admissions Selectivity Rating: 65
Application fee: $50
Regular application deadline: 4/15
Regular notification: Rolling
Early application program: No
LSDAS accepted: Yes
Average GPA: 3.2
Range of GPA: 3.0–3.4
Average LSAT: 150
Range of LSAT: 146–153
Transfer students accepted: Yes
Evening division offered: Yes
Part-time accepted: Yes
Applicants also look at: Michigan State University—College of Law, Wayne State University.
Number of applications received: 543
Number of applicants accepted: 255
Number of acceptees attending: 91

INTERNATIONAL STUDENTS

TOEFL required for international students: Yes

FINANCIAL FACTS

Room & board (off-campus): $14,327
Books and supplies: $1,020
Financial aid application deadline: 4/1
% receiving scholarships: 15
Average grant: $10,000
Average loan: $19,300
Average debt: $69,678
Tuition per credit: $798

EMPLOYMENT INFORMATION

Average starting salary: $55,500
State for bar exam: MI
Pass rate for first-time bar: 81
Employers who frequently hire grads: County prosecutors; Dickinson Wright PLLC; Dykema Gossett PLLC; Michigan Court of Appeals; Butzel Long; Bodman Longley; Howard & Howard; Michigan Supreme Court.

Grads employed by field:	%
Business/Industry	15
Government	8
Judicial clerkships	8
Other	1
Private practice	68

University of Georgia

School of Law

225 Herty Drive, Athens, GA 30602-6012 United States
Admissions Phone: 706-542-7060 • **Admissions Fax:** 706-542-5556
Admissions E-mail: ugajd@uga.edu • **Website:** www.law.uga.edu

INSTITUTIONAL INFORMATION

Public/private: Public
Student/faculty ratio: 15:1
Total faculty: 88
% part time: 24
% female: 19
% minority: 6

STUDENTS

Average age of entering class: 25

ACADEMICS

Academic Specializations: Commercial law, constitutional law, criminal law, environmental law, government services, intellectual property law, international law, labor law, property, taxation.
Advanced Degrees Offered: LLM 1 year.
Combined Degrees Offered: JD/MBA 4 years, JD/Master of Historic Preservation 4 years, JD/Master of Public Administration 4 years, JD/Master of Social Work 4 years, JD/MA (various fields), JD/PhD (various fields).
Clinical program required: Yes
Legal writing course requirements: Yes
Legal methods course requirements: Yes
Legal research course requirements: Yes
Moot court requirement: No
Public interest law requirement: No

ADMISSIONS INFORMATION

Admissions Selectivity Rating: 89
Application fee: $30
Regular application deadline: 2/1
Regular notification: Rolling
Early application program: No
LSDAS accepted: Yes
Average GPA: 3.62
Range of GPA: 3.3–3.8
Average LSAT: 163
Range of LSAT: 158–164
Transfer students accepted: Yes
Evening division offered: No
Part-time accepted: No
Applicants also look at: Emory University, Georgia State University, Mercer University, University of Florida, University of Tennessee, University of Virginia, Vanderbilt University.
Number of applications received: 2,449
Number of acceptees attending: 232

INTERNATIONAL STUDENTS

TOEFL required for international students: No

FINANCIAL FACTS

Annual tuition (resident): $8,136
Annual tuition (nonresident): $26,112
Room & board (on/off-campus): $7,926/$8,950
Books and supplies: $1,000
Financial aid application deadline: 3/1
% receiving scholarships: 33
Average grant: $2,000
Average loan: $12,500
% of aid that is merit-based: 20
% receiving some sort of aid: 89
% first year students receiving some sort of aid: 91
Average debt: $34,000

EMPLOYMENT INFORMATION

Rate of placement (nine months out): 99
Average starting salary: $80,000
State for bar exam: GA
Pass rate for first-time bar: 92
Employers who frequently hire grads: Alston and Bird; King and Spalding; Jones Day; Greenberg Traurig; U.S. Department of Justice; public defenders and prosecutors; federal district and circuit court judges.

Grads employed by field:	%
Academic	2
Business/Industry	5
Government	9
Judicial clerkships	13
Military	2
Private practice	65
Public Interest	4

UNIVERSITY OF LOUISVILLE
Louis D. Brandeis School of Law

University of Louisville, Wyatt Hall, Room 107, Louisville, KY 40292 United States
Admissions Phone: *502-852-6364* • **Admissions Fax:** *502-852-8971*
Admissions E-mail: *lawadmissions@louisville.edu*
Website: *www.louisville.edu/brandeislaw*

INSTITUTIONAL INFORMATION

Public/private: Public
Student/faculty ratio: 14:1
Total faculty: 35
% part time: 17
% female: 34
% minority: 10

STUDENTS

Enrollment of law school: 417
% Out of state: 23
% Male/female: 58/42
% Full time: 76
% minority: 5
Average age of entering class: 24

ACADEMICS

Advanced Degrees Offered: JD 3 to 4 years.
Combined Degrees Offered: JD/MBA, JD/MSSW, JD/MDiv, JD/MA (humanities), JD/MA (political science), JD/MA (urban planning).
Clinical program required: Yes
Legal writing course requirements: Yes
Legal methods course requirements: Yes
Legal research course requirements: Yes
Moot court requirement: Yes
Public interest law requirement: Yes

ADMISSIONS INFORMATION

Admissions Selectivity Rating: 81
Application fee: $50
Regular application deadline: 5/15
Regular notification: Rolling
Early application program: No
LSDAS accepted: Yes
Average GPA: 3.48
Range of GPA: 3.1–3.7
Average LSAT: 157
Range of LSAT: 155–159
Transfer students accepted: Yes
Evening division offered: Yes
Part-time accepted: Yes
Applicants also look at: Northern Kentucky University, University of Cincinnati, University of Dayton, University of Kentucky, University of Memphis, University of Tennessee, Vanderbilt University.
Number of applications received: 1,065
Number of applicants accepted: 348
Number of acceptees attending: 102

INTERNATIONAL STUDENTS

TOEFL required for international students: No

FINANCIAL FACTS

Annual tuition (resident): $11,410
Annual tuition (nonresident): $23,554
Room & board: $6,618
Books and supplies: $1,000
Financial aid application deadline: 4/15
% receiving scholarships: 65
Average grant: $5,000
Average loan: $18,500
% of aid that is merit-based: 100
% receiving some sort of aid: 85
% first year students receiving some sort of aid: 85
Average total aid package: $23,500
Tuition per credit (resident): $475
Tuition per credit (nonresident): $981

EMPLOYMENT INFORMATION

Rate of placement (nine months out): 95
Average starting salary: $45,000
State for bar exam: KY, IN, TN, OH
Pass rate for first-time bar: 89
Employers who frequently hire grads: Frost, Brown, and Todd; Dinsmore and Shohl; Greenebaum, Doll, and McDonald; Wyatt, Tarrant, and Combs; Stites and Harbison.
Prominent Alumni: Chris Dodd, U.S. Senator; Ron Mazzoli, former U.S. Congressman; Hon. Joseph Lambert, Chief Justice of Kentucky; Stanley Chauvin, former ABA president; Ernie Allen, Director, National Center for Missing and Exploited Children.

Grads employed by field:	%
Academic	2
Business/Industry	10
Government	15
Judicial clerkships	7
Military	2
Private practice	60
Public Interest	4

UNIVERSITY OF MINNESOTA

Law School

290 Mondale Hall, 229 Nineteenth Avenue South, Minneapolis, MN 55455 U.S.
Admissions Phone: *612-625-3487* • **Admissions Fax:** *612-626-1874*
Admissions E-mail: *umnlsadm@umn.edu* • **Website:** *www.law.umn.edu*

INSTITUTIONAL INFORMATION

Public/private: Public
Student/faculty ratio: 13:1
Total faculty: 61
% female: 38
% minority: 18

STUDENTS

Enrollment of law school: 801
% Out of state: 56
% Male/female: 57/43
% Full time: 100
% International: 2
% minority: 16
Average age of entering class: 25

ACADEMICS

Academic Specializations: Labor law.
Advanced Degrees Offered: JD LLM (for foreign lawyers) 1 year.
Combined Degrees Offered: JD/MBA 4 years, JD/MPA 4 years, JD/MA, JD/MD, JD/MPP 4 years, JD/MURP 4 years, JD/MS 4 years, JD/PhD, JD/MP, JD/MBT, JD/MBS, JD/MPH.
Clinical program required: No
Legal writing course requirements: Yes
Legal methods course requirements: No
Legal research course requirements: Yes
Moot court requirement: No

ADMISSIONS INFORMATION

Admissions Selectivity Rating: 93
Application fee: $70
Regular application deadline: 3/1
Regular notification: 4/1
Early application program: Yes
LSDAS accepted: Yes
Average GPA: 3.53
Range of GPA: 3.3–3.8
Average LSAT: 165
Range of LSAT: 163–167
Transfer students accepted: Yes
Evening division offered: No
Part-time accepted: No
Number of applications received: 3,147
Number of applicants accepted: 757
Number of acceptees attending: 257

INTERNATIONAL STUDENTS

TOEFL required for international students: Yes
Minimum Paper TOEFL: 630
Minimum Computer-based TOEFL: 267

FINANCIAL FACTS

Annual tuition (resident): $19,000
Annual tuition (nonresident): $28,500
Room & board (on/off-campus): $10,972/$13,392
Financial aid application deadline: 2/1
% receiving scholarships: 52
Average grant: $7,581
Average loan: $24,643
% receiving some sort of aid: 98
% first year students receiving some sort of aid: 95
Average total aid package: $28,632
Average debt: $73,930

EMPLOYMENT INFORMATION

Rate of placement (nine months out): 99
Average starting salary: $83,309
Employers who frequently hire grads: Gibson Dunn; Fried Frank; Dorsey and Whitney; Dewey Ballantine; Sidley and Austin; Mayer Brown; Bryan Cave; Arnold and Porter; Faegre and Benson; Minnesota Supreme Court; Minnesota Court of Appeals; U.S. Department of Justice.

Prominent Alumni: Walter Mondale, former Vice President of the U.S.; Keith Ellison, U.S. Representative; Jean E. Hanson, partner, Fried, Frank, Harris, Shriver, and Jacobson; Catharine F. Haukedahl, Deputy Director, Mid-Minnesota Legal Assistance; Joyce A. Hughes, professor Northwestern School of Law.

State for bar exam: MN, WI, CA, NY, IL
Pass rate for first-time bar: 99

Grads employed by field:	%
Academic	3
Business/Industry	12
Government	9
Judicial clerkships	19
Private practice	52
Public Interest	5

UNIVERSITY OF MONTANA
School of Law

Admissions Office, Missoula, MT 59812 United States
Admissions Phone: *406-243-2698* • **Admissions Fax:** *406-243-2576*
Admissions E-mail: *heidi.fanslow@umontana.edu* • **Website:** *www.umt.edu/law*

INSTITUTIONAL INFORMATION
Public/private: Public
Student/faculty ratio: 19:1
Total faculty: 22
% part time: 18
% female: 32
% minority: 5

STUDENTS
Enrollment of law school: 241
% Out of state: 29
% Male/female: 56/44
% Full time: 100
% minority: 3
Average age of entering class: 28

ACADEMICS
Academic Specializations: Environmental law, taxation, Indian law, trial advocacy.
Advanced Degrees Offered: JD 3 years.
Combined Degrees Offered: JD/MPA 3 years, JD/MBA 3 years, JD/MS-EVST 4 years.
Clinical program required: Yes
Legal writing course requirements: Yes
Legal methods course requirements: Yes
Legal research course requirements: Yes
Moot court requirement: No
Public interest law requirement: Yes

ADMISSIONS INFORMATION
Admissions Selectivity Rating: 79
Application fee: $60

Regular application deadline: 3/1
Regular notification: Rolling
Early application program: No
LSDAS accepted: Yes
Average GPA: 3.4
Range of GPA: 3.2–3.6
Average LSAT: 155
Range of LSAT: 152–157
Transfer students accepted: Yes
Evening division offered: No
Part-time accepted: No
Applicants also look at: Gonzaga University, Lewis & Clark College, University of Denver, University of Idaho, University of Oregon, University of Wyoming.
Number of applications received: 550
Number of applicants accepted: 178
Number of acceptees attending: 79

INTERNATIONAL STUDENTS
TOEFL required for international students: Yes
Minimum Paper TOEFL: 600

FINANCIAL FACTS
Annual tuition (resident): $8,710
Annual tuition (nonresident): $17,475
Room & board: $9,300
Books and supplies: $1,010
Financial aid application deadline: 3/1
% receiving scholarships: 40
Average grant: $1,457
Average loan: $14,350
% of aid that is merit-based: 3
% receiving some sort of aid: 88
% first year students receiving some sort of aid: 85
Average total aid package: $14,619
Average debt: $48,504

EMPLOYMENT INFORMATION
Rate of placement (nine months out):
Average starting salary: $41,063
State for bar exam: MT, WA
Pass rate for first-time bar: 80
Employers who frequently hire grads: Church, Harris, Johnson, and Williams; Moulton, Bellingham, Longo and Mather; Crowley, Haughy, Hanson, Toole and Dietrich; Towe, Ball Enright, Mackey and Summerfeld; Smith, Walsh, Clark, and Gregoire; Jardine, Stephenson, Blewett and Weaver; Montana Supreme Court; Montana district courts; Montana federal district courts.

Grads employed by field:	%
Academic	11
Business/Industry	6
Government	12
Judicial clerkships	23
Private practice	35

CAL NORTHERN SCHOOL OF LAW

1395 Ridgewood Drive, Chico, CA 95973 United States
Admissions Phone: *530-891-6900* • **Admissions Fax:** *530-891-3429*
Admissions E-mail: *info@calnorthern.edu* • **Website:** *www.calnorthern.edu*

INSTITUTIONAL INFORMATION
Public/private: Private
Student/faculty ratio: 4:1
Total faculty: 18
% part time: 100
% female: 28

STUDENTS
Enrollment of law school: 70
Average age of entering class: 35

ACADEMICS
Advanced Degrees Offered: JD 4 years.
Clinical program required: No
Legal writing course requirements: Yes
Legal research course requirements: Yes
Moot court requirement: Yes
Public interest law requirement: No

ADMISSIONS INFORMATION
Admissions Selectivity Rating: 61
Application fee: $50
Regular application deadline: 6/1
Regular notification: 7/3
Early application program: No
LSDAS accepted: No
Average GPA: 2.98
Range of GPA: 2.6–3.6
Average LSAT: 145
Transfer students accepted: Yes
Evening division offered: Yes
Part-time accepted: Yes
Number of applications received: 28
Number of applicants accepted: 22
Number of acceptees attending: 25

INTERNATIONAL STUDENTS
TOEFL required for international students: No

FINANCIAL FACTS
Annual tuition: $7,590
Books and supplies: $700
Average grant: $250
Average loan: $8,000
% receiving some sort of aid: 5
Tuition per credit: $330

EMPLOYMENT INFORMATION
State for bar exam: CA
Pass rate for first-time bar: 54
Prominent Alumni: Rick Keene, California assemblyman.

EMPIRE COLLEGE
School of Law

3035 Cleveland Avenue, Santa Rosa, CA 95403 United States
Admissions Phone: *707-546-4000* • **Admissions Fax:** *707-284-2814*
Admissions E-mail: *dstiles@empirecollege.com* • **Website:** *www.empcol.edu*

INSTITUTIONAL INFORMATION
Public/private: Private
Student/faculty ratio: 4:1
Total faculty: 47
% part time: 100
% female: 17
% minority: 2

STUDENTS
Enrollment of law school: 146
% Male/female: 100/0
Average age of entering class: 36

ACADEMICS
Clinical program required: No
Legal writing course requirements: Yes
Legal methods course requirements: No
Legal research course requirements: Yes
Moot court requirement: Yes
Public interest law requirement: No

ADMISSIONS INFORMATION
Admissions Selectivity Rating: 61
Application fee: $50
Regular application deadline: Rolling
Regular notification: Rolling
Early application program: No
LSDAS accepted: No
Average GPA: 3.1
Range of GPA: 2.5–3.9
Transfer students accepted: Yes
Evening division offered: Yes
Part-time accepted: Yes
Number of applications received: 106
Number of applicants accepted: 105
Number of acceptees attending: 96

INTERNATIONAL STUDENTS
TOEFL required for international students: No

FINANCIAL FACTS

Annual tuition: $7,119
Books and supplies: $300
Tuition per credit: $339

EMPLOYMENT INFORMATION

State for bar exam: CA
Employers who frequently hire grads: Office of the District Attorney; public defender's office; private business.
Prominent Alumni: Jeanne Buckley, Superior Court Commissioner (retired); Hon. Raima Ballinger, Sonoma County Superior Court; Hon. Francisca Tisher, Napa County Municipal Court; Thomas S. Burr, juvenile court referee, Merced County Superior Court; Hon. Ron Brown, Mendocino County Superior Court.

GLENDALE UNIVERSITY
College of Law

220 North Glendale Avenue, Glendale, CA 91206 United States
Admissions Phone: 818-247-0770 • Admissions Fax: 818-247-0872
Admissions E-mail: admissions@glendalelaw.edu • Website: www.glendalelaw.edu

INSTITUTIONAL INFORMATION

Public/private: Private
Student/faculty ratio: 25:1

STUDENTS

Enrollment of law school: 130
% Male/female: 100/0
Average age of entering class: 32

ACADEMICS

Advanced Degrees Offered: JD 4 years.
Clinical program required: No
Legal writing course requirements: Yes
Legal methods course requirements: No
Legal research course requirements: Yes
Moot court requirement: Yes
Public interest law requirement: No

ADMISSIONS INFORMATION

Admissions Selectivity Rating: 63
Application fee: $65
Regular application deadline: Rolling
Regular notification: Rolling
Early application program: No
LSDAS accepted: No
Average GPA: 3.00
Average LSAT: 145
Transfer students accepted: Yes
Evening division offered: Yes
Part-time accepted: Yes
Number of applications received: 160
Number of applicants accepted: 80
Number of acceptees attending: 60

INTERNATIONAL STUDENTS

TOEFL required for international students: No

FINANCIAL FACTS

Books and supplies: $800
Tuition per credit: $335

EMPLOYMENT INFORMATION

State for bar exam: CA
Pass rate for first-time bar: 50

HUMPHREYS COLLEGE
School of Law

6650 Inglewood Avenue, Stockton, CA 95207 United States
Admissions Phone: 209-478-0800 • Admissions Fax: 209-478-8721
Admissions E-mail: selopez@humphreys.edu • Website: www.humphreys.edu/law

INSTITUTIONAL INFORMATION

Public/private: Private
Student/faculty ratio: 6:1
Total faculty: 12
% part time: 83
% female: 17

STUDENTS

Enrollment of law school: 60
Average age of entering class: 33

ACADEMICS

Clinical program required: No
Legal methods course requirements: Yes

ADMISSIONS INFORMATION

Admissions Selectivity Rating: 62
Application fee: $20
Regular application deadline: 6/1
Regular notification: Rolling
Early application program: No
LSDAS accepted: No
Average GPA: 2.8
Average LSAT: 149
Transfer students accepted: Yes
Evening division offered: Yes
Part-time accepted: Yes
Number of applications received: 52
Number of applicants accepted: 32
Number of acceptees attending: 19

INTERNATIONAL STUDENTS

TOEFL required for international students: Yes
Minimum Paper TOEFL: 450

FINANCIAL FACTS

Annual tuition: $7,062
Books and supplies: $650
Average loan: $14,658

% receiving some sort of aid: 66
% first year students receiving some sort of aid: 21
Average total aid package: $14,658
Average debt: $48,000
Tuition per credit: $214

EMPLOYMENT INFORMATION
State for bar exam: CA
Pass rate for first-time bar: 54
Employers who frequently hire grads: DA offices; police departments.

Grads employed by field:	%
Academic	5
Business/Industry	5
Government	30
Private practice	60

JOHN F. KENNEDY UNIVERSITY

School of Law

100 Ellinwood Way, Pleasant Hill, CA 94523 United States
Admissions Phone: 925-969-3330 • Admissions Fax: 925-969-3331
Admissions E-mail: law@jfku.edu • Website: www.jfku.edu/law

INSTITUTIONAL INFORMATION
Public/private: Private
Student/faculty ratio: 30:1
Total faculty: 54
% part time: 94
% female: 54

STUDENTS
Enrollment of law school: 154
% Male/female: 43/57
% Full time: 94
Average age of entering class: 37

ACADEMICS
Clinical program required: No
Legal writing course requirements: Yes
Legal methods course requirements: Yes
Legal research course requirements: Yes
Moot court requirement: No
Public interest law requirement: No

ADMISSIONS INFORMATION
Admissions Selectivity Rating: 63
Application fee: $75
Regular application deadline: 7/1
Regular notification: Rolling
Early application program: No
LSDAS accepted: Yes
Average GPA: 3.03
Average LSAT: 148
Transfer students accepted: Yes

Evening division offered: Yes
Part-time accepted: Yes
Applicants also look at: Golden Gate University, New College of California.
Number of applications received: 122
Number of applicants accepted: 53
Number of acceptees attending: 23

INTERNATIONAL STUDENTS
TOEFL required for international students: Yes
Minimum Computer-based TOEFL: 213

FINANCIAL FACTS
Annual tuition: $9,920
Books and supplies: $1,540
Average loan: $18,500
% of aid that is merit-based: 1
% receiving some sort of aid: 70
% first year students receiving some sort of aid: 70
Average total aid package: $18,500
Average debt: $70,000
Tuition per credit: $620

EMPLOYMENT INFORMATION
State for bar exam: CA
Pass rate for first-time bar: 45

LINCOLN LAW SCHOOL OF SACRAMENTO

3140 J Street, Sacramento, CA 95816 United States
Admissions Phone: 916-446-1275 • Admissions Fax: 916-446-5641
Admissions E-mail: info@lincolnlaw.edu • Website: www.lincolnlaw.edu

INSTITUTIONAL INFORMATION
Public/private: Private
Student/faculty ratio: 40:1
Total faculty: 25
% part time: 100
% female: 20
% minority: 10

STUDENTS
Enrollment of law school: 275
Average age of entering class: 35

ACADEMICS
Academic Specializations: Applied legal reasoning, civil procedure, constitutional law, corporation securities law, criminal law, environmental law, family law, government services, intellectual property law, labor law, legal history, legal philosophy, property, taxation.
Advanced Degrees Offered: JD 4 years.
Clinical program required: No
Legal writing course requirements: Yes
Legal methods course requirements: Yes
Legal research course requirements: Yes
Moot court requirement: Yes

ADMISSIONS INFORMATION

Admissions Selectivity Rating: 61
Application fee: $30
Regular application deadline: Rolling
Regular notification: Rolling
Early application program: No
LSDAS accepted: Yes
Average GPA: 2.8
Range of GPA: 2.1–4.0
Average LSAT: 145
Transfer students accepted: Yes
Evening division offered: Yes
Part-time accepted: Yes
Applicants also look at: Golden Gate University, Humphreys College, John F. Kennedy University, University of California, Davis, University of the Pacific.
Number of applications received: 150
Number of applicants accepted: 105
Number of acceptees attending: 95

INTERNATIONAL STUDENTS

TOEFL required for international students: No

FINANCIAL FACTS

Annual tuition: $7,000
Room & board (off-campus): $6,000
Books and supplies: $500
Financial aid application deadline: 6/1
% receiving scholarships: 20
Average grant: $500
Average loan: $10,000
% of aid that is merit-based: 2
% receiving some sort of aid: 20
% first year students receiving some sort of aid: 10
Average total aid package: $7,000
Average debt: $10,500
Tuition per credit: $350

EMPLOYMENT INFORMATION

Average starting salary: $40,000
State for bar exam: CA, OR, NV, AZ, CO
Pass rate for first-time bar: 60
Employers who frequently hire grads: District attorney's office; attorney general's office; public defender's office; local private firms.
Prominent Alumni: Jan Scully, Sacramento County District Attorney; Brad Fenocchio, Placer County District Attorney; Robert Holzapfel, Glenn County District Attorney; Hon. Gerald Bakarich, Sacramento County Superior Court; Hon. Sue Harlan, Amador County Superior Court.

Grads employed by field:	%
Business/Industry	10
Government	30
Judicial clerkships	5
Private practice	50
Public Interest	5

LINCOLN LAW SCHOOL OF SAN JOSE

One North First Street, San Jose, CA 95113 United States
Admissions Phone: 408-977-7227 • **Admissions Fax:** 408-977-7228
Admissions E-mail: admissionlincoln@earthlink.net
Website: www.lincolnlawsj.edu

INSTITUTIONAL INFORMATION

Public/private: Private
Student/faculty ratio: 1:1

STUDENTS

Enrollment of law school: 153

ACADEMICS

Clinical program required? No
Legal methods course requirements? No

ADMISSIONS INFORMATION

Admissions Selectivity Rating: 60*
Application fee: $35
Regular application deadline: Rolling
Regular notification: Rolling
Early application program: No
LSDAS accepted? No
Transfer students accepted? Yes
Evening division offered: Yes
Part-time accepted: Yes

FINANCIAL FACTS

Tuition per credit: $499

INTERNATIONAL STUDENTS

TOEFL required for international students? No
Minimum Paper TOEFL: 600
Minimum Computer-based TOEFL: 60

MONTEREY COLLEGE OF LAW

100 Col. Durham Street, Seaside, CA 93955 United States
Admissions Phone: 831-582-4000 • **Admissions Fax:** 831-582-4095
Admissions E-mail: wlariviere@montereylaw.edu • **Website:** www.montereylaw.edu

INSTITUTIONAL INFORMATION

Public/private: Private
Student/faculty ratio: 25:1
Total faculty: 44
% part time: 100
% female: 23
% minority: 2

STUDENTS

Enrollment of law school: 100
Average age of entering class: 30

ACADEMICS

Academic Specializations: Civil procedure, commercial law, constitutional law, corporation securities law, criminal law, environmental law, government services, human rights law, intellectual property law, international law, labor law, property, taxation.
Advanced Degrees Offered: JD 4 years, Master of Legal Studies, 2 years.
Clinical program required: Yes
Legal writing course requirements: Yes
Legal methods course requirements: Yes
Legal research course requirements: Yes
Moot court requirement: Yes
Public interest law requirement: No

ADMISSIONS INFORMATION

Admissions Selectivity Rating: 72
Application fee: $75
Regular application deadline: 5/1
Regular notification: Rolling
Early application program: Yes
LSDAS accepted: No
Average GPA: 3.17
Range of GPA: 2.7–4.0
Average LSAT: 153
Range of LSAT: 141–169
Transfer students accepted: Yes
Evening division offered: Yes
Part-time accepted: Yes
Applicants also look at: Lincoln Law School of San Jose, Santa Clara University.
Number of applications received: 120
Number of applicants accepted: 53
Number of acceptees attending: 54

INTERNATIONAL STUDENTS

TOEFL required for international students: No

FINANCIAL FACTS

Books and supplies: $1,000
% receiving scholarships: 25
Average grant: $750
Average loan: $5,000
% of aid that is merit-based: 30
% receiving some sort of aid: 55
% first year students receiving some sort of aid: 26
Tuition per credit: $450

EMPLOYMENT INFORMATION

Rate of placement (nine months out): 90
Average starting salary: $35,000
Employers who frequently hire grads: Governmental offices; public agencies; private law firms; public defender's office; district attorney's office.
Prominent Alumni: Hon. John Salazar, judge; Hon. Kim Baskett, judicial commissioner; Hon. Denine Guy, judge; Hon. Russel Scott, judge; Hon. Sam Lavarato Jr., judge.
State for bar exam: CA
Pass rate for first-time bar: 40

Grads employed by field:	%
Business/Industry	35
Government	5
Private practice	40
Public Interest	20

NEW COLLEGE OF CALIFORNIA

School of Law

50 Fell Street, San Francisco, CA 94102 United States
Admissions Phone: *415-241-1374 •* **Admissions Fax:** *415-241-9525*
Admissions E-mail: *Lawadmissions@newcollege.edu*
Website: *www.newcollege.edu*

INSTITUTIONAL INFORMATION

Public/private: Private
Student/faculty ratio: 15:1
Total faculty: 36
% female: 50
% minority: 50

STUDENTS

Enrollment of law school: 200
% Out of state: 10
% Male/female: 35/65
% Full time: 75
% International: 10
% minority: 35
Average age of entering class: 35

ACADEMICS

Academic Specializations: Constitutional law, environmental law, government services, human rights law, labor law, property.
Advanced Degrees Offered: JD 3 to 4 years.
Clinical program required: No
Legal writing course requirements: Yes
Legal methods course requirements: Yes
Legal research course requirements: Yes
Moot court requirement: No
Public interest law requirement: Yes

ADMISSIONS INFORMATION

Admissions Selectivity Rating: 63
Application fee: $55
Regular application deadline: 5/7
Regular notification: Rolling
Early application program: Yes
LSDAS accepted: Yes
Average GPA: 3.00
Range of GPA: 2.0–4.0
Average LSAT: 147
Transfer students accepted: Yes
Evening division offered: No

Part-time accepted: Yes
Number of applications received: 250
Number of applicants accepted: 110
Number of acceptees attending: 65

INTERNATIONAL STUDENTS

TOEFL required for international students: No

FINANCIAL FACTS

Annual tuition: $15,214
Books and supplies: $400
Financial aid application deadline: 8/7
Average grant: $500
Average loan: $18,500
% first year students receiving some sort of aid: 90
Average total aid package: $22,000
Tuition per credit: $180

EMPLOYMENT INFORMATION

Rate of placement (nine months out): 65
State for bar exam: CA
Pass rate for first-time bar: 25
Employers who frequently hire grads: All nonprofit agencies and small/solo law firms.

Grads employed by field:	%
Government	10
Private practice	30
Public Interest	60

SAN FRANCISCO LAW SCHOOL

20 Haight Street, San Francisco, CA 94102 United States
Admissions Phone: *415-626-5550* • **Admissions Fax:** *415-626-5584*
Admissions E-mail: *admin@sfls.edu* • **Website:** *www.sfls.edu*

INSTITUTIONAL INFORMATION

Public/private: Private
Student/faculty ratio: 25:1
Total faculty: 32
% part time: 100
% female: 13
% minority: 1

STUDENTS

Enrollment of law school: 115

ACADEMICS

Academic Specializations:
Advanced Degrees Offered: JD 4 to 4.5 years.
Clinical program required: No
Legal writing course requirements: Yes
Legal methods course requirements: No
Legal research course requirements: Yes
Moot court requirement: Yes
Public interest law requirement: No

ADMISSIONS INFORMATION

Admissions Selectivity Rating: 62
Application fee: $50
Regular application deadline: 6/5
Regular notification: Rolling
Early application program: No
LSDAS accepted: No
Average GPA: 2.8
Range of GPA: 2.0–3.8
Average LSAT: 148
Transfer students accepted: Yes
Evening division offered: Yes
Part-time accepted: Yes
Number of applications received: 150
Number of applicants accepted: 87

INTERNATIONAL STUDENTS

TOEFL required for international students: No

FINANCIAL FACTS

Annual tuition: $6,700
Room & board (off-campus): $25,000
Books and supplies: $350
% of aid that is merit-based: 40
Tuition per credit: $335

EMPLOYMENT INFORMATION

State for bar exam: CA
Pass rate for first-time bar: 30
Employers who frequently hire grads: San Francisco public defender; San Francisco DA; private sector.
Prominent Alumni: Edmund G. Brown (deceased), Governor of California; Milton Marks Jr. (deceased), California State Senator; Leo T. McCarthy, Lieutenant Governor, California; Hon. Lynn O'Malley Taylor, Superior Court; Hon. Henry Needham, Superior Court.

Grads employed by field:	%
Academic	5
Business/Industry	5
Government	20
Judicial clerkships	5
Private practice	60
Public Interest	5

SAN JOAQUIN COLLEGE OF LAW

901 Fifth Street, Clovis, CA 93612-1312 United States
Admissions Phone: *559-323-2100* • **Admissions Fax:** *559-323-5566*
Admissions E-mail: *jcanalin@sjcl.org* • **Website:** *www.sjcl.edu*

INSTITUTIONAL INFORMATION

Public/private: Private
Student/faculty ratio: 16:1
Total faculty: 36
% part time: 83
% female: 45
% minority: 14

STUDENTS

Enrollment of law school: 185
% Male/female: 54/46
% Full time: 13
% minority: 26
Average age of entering class: 33

ACADEMICS

Academic Specializations: Commercial law, corporation securities law, criminal law, environmental law, international law, labor law, taxation.
Advanced Degrees Offered: JD 3 to 5 years, MS (taxation) 2 years.
Clinical program required: Yes
Legal methods course requirements: Yes

ADMISSIONS INFORMATION

Admissions Selectivity Rating: 61
Application fee: $40
Regular application deadline: 6/30
Regular notification: Rolling
Early application program: No
LSDAS accepted: No
Average GPA: 2.9
Range of GPA: 1.8–3.9
Average LSAT: 148
Range of LSAT: 139–174
Transfer students accepted: Yes
Evening division offered: Yes
Part-time accepted: Yes
Number of applications received: 135
Number of applicants accepted: 108
Number of acceptees attending: 91

INTERNATIONAL STUDENTS

TOEFL required for international students: No

FINANCIAL FACTS

Annual tuition: $10,212
Books and supplies: $550
% receiving scholarships: 14
Average grant: $1,600
Average loan: $14,500
% of aid that is merit-based: 12
% receiving some sort of aid: 75
% first year students receiving some sort of aid: 75
Average total aid package: $18,500
Average debt: $62,500

EMPLOYMENT INFORMATION

State for bar exam: CA
Pass rate for first-time bar: 56
Employers who frequently hire grads: Local DA and DD; various small firms.

Grads employed by field:	%
Government	23
Private practice	70
Public Interest	5

SANTA BARBARA AND VENTURA COLLEGES OF LAW

Santa Barbara College of Law

20 East Victoria Street, Santa Barbara, CA 93101 United States
Admissions Phone: 805-966-0010 • **Admissions Fax:** 805-966-7181
Admissions E-mail: admit@venturalaw.edu
Web Address: www.santabarbaralaw.edu

INSTITUTIONAL INFORMATION

Public/private: Private
Student/faculty ratio: 11:1
Total faculty: 19
% part time: 100
% female: 26
% minority: 5

STUDENTS

Enrollment of law school: 917
% Male/female: 51/49

ACADEMICS

Clinical program required: Yes
Legal writing course requirements: Yes
Legal methods course requirements: No
Legal research course requirements: Yes
Moot court requirement: No
Public interest law requirement: No

ADMISSIONS INFORMATION

Admissions Selectivity Rating: 71
Application fee: $40
Regular application deadline: Rolling
Regular notification: Rolling
Early application program: No
LSDAS accepted: No
Average GPA: 3.2
Range of GPA: 3.0 to 3.5
Average LSAT: 156
Range of LSAT: 153–158
Transfer students accepted: No
Evening division offered: Yes
Part-time accepted: Yes
Applicants also look at: Syracuse University.
Number of applications received: 2,528
Number of applicants accepted: 1,265
Number of acceptees attending: 291

INTERNATIONAL STUDENTS

TOEFL required for international students: No

FINANCIAL FACTS

Annual tuition: $22,000
Room & board: $9,787
Books and supplies: $903
% receiving scholarships: 31

Average grant: $8,071
Average loan: $1
% of aid that is merit-based: 7
% receiving some sort of aid: 85
% first year students receiving some sort of aid: 77
Average debt: $60,379

EMPLOYMENT INFORMATION
Average starting salary: $58,000
State for bar exam: CA
Pass rate for first-time bar: 71

Grads employed by field:	%
Academic	2
Business/Industry	24
Government	8
Judicial clerkships	4
Military	1
Private practice	58
Public Interest	3

LSDAS accepted: Yes
Average GPA: 3.01
Range of GPA: 2.4 to 3.9
Transfer students accepted: Yes
Evening division offered: Yes
Part-time accepted: Yes

INTERNATIONAL STUDENTS
TOEFL required for international students: No

FINANCIAL FACTS
Books and supplies: $750
Average grant: $1,000
Average loan: $8,000
Tuition per credit: $355

EMPLOYMENT INFORMATION
State for bar exam: CA
Pass rate for first-time bar: 44

THE SANTA BARBARA AND VENTURA COLLEGES OF LAW
Ventura College of Law

4475 Market Street, Ventura, CA 93003 United States
Admissions Phone: 805-658-0511 • Admissions Fax: 805-658-0529
Admissions E-mail: admits@venturalaw.edu • Website: www.venturalaw.edu

INSTITUTIONAL INFORMATION
Public/private: Private
Student/faculty ratio: 12:1
Total faculty: 18
% part time: 100
% female: 27
% minority: 5

STUDENTS
Enrollment of law school: 141

ACADEMICS
Advanced Degrees Offered: JD 4 years.
Clinical program required: Yes
Legal writing course requirements: Yes
Legal methods course requirements: Yes
Legal research course requirements: Yes
Moot court requirement: No
Public interest law requirement: Yes

ADMISSIONS INFORMATION
Admissions Selectivity Rating: 60*
Application fee: $45
Regular application deadline: 7/15
Regular notification: Rolling
Early application program: No

SOUTHERN CALIFORNIA INSTITUTE OF LAW
College of Law

877 South Victoria Avenue, Ventura, CA 93003 United States
Admissions Phone: 805-644-2327 • Admissions Fax: 805-644-2367
Admissions E-mail: registrar@lawdegree.com
Website: www.lawdegree.com

INSTITUTIONAL INFORMATION
Public/private: Private
Student/faculty ratio: 5:1
% part time: 75
% female: 50
% faculty minority: 10

STUDENTS
Enrollment of law school: 50
% Male/female: 60/40
% minority: 15
Average age of entering class: 32

ACADEMICS
Legal methods course requirements? Yes

ADMISSIONS INFORMATION
Admissions Selectivity Rating: 60*
Early application program: No
LSDAS accepted? No
Transfer students accepted? No
Evening division offered: No
Part-time accepted: No
Number of applications received: 50

RESEARCH FACILITIES

Research resources available: Local courthouse library.

FINANCIAL FACTS

Annual tuition: $6,480
Books and supplies: $500
% of aid that is merit-based: 100
Tuition per credit: $200

INTERNATIONAL STUDENTS

TOEFL required for international students? Yes

EMPLOYMENT INFORMATION

Average starting salary: $30,000
Employers who frequently hire grads: Local law firms, government and state agencies.
State for bar exam: CA
Pass rate for first-time bar: 50

TRINITY INTERNATIONAL UNIVERSITY

Trinity Law School

2200 North Grand Avenue, Santa Ana, CA 92705 United States
Admissions Phone: 714-796-7100 • **Admissions Fax:** 714-796-7190
Admissions E-mail: deaton@tiu.edu • **Website:** www.tls.edu

INSTITUTIONAL INFORMATION

Public/private: Private
Affiliation: Protestant

ADMISSIONS INFORMATION

Admissions Selectivity Rating: 60*
Application fee: $35
Early application program: No
LSDAS accepted? Yes
Transfer students accepted? Yes
Evening division offered: Yes
Part-time accepted: Yes

FINANCIAL FACTS

Annual tuition: $17,500
Tuition per credit: $625

INTERNATIONAL STUDENTS

TOEFL required for international students? No

UNIVERSITY OF WEST LOS ANGELES

School of Law

9920 South La Cienega Boulevard, #404, Inglewood, CA 90301 United States
Admissions Phone: 310-342-5210 • **Admissions Fax:** 310-342-5295
Admissions E-mail: tsmith@uwla.edu • **Website:** www.uwla.edu

INSTITUTIONAL INFORMATION

Public/private: Private
Student/faculty ratio: 30:1
Total faculty: 36
% part time: 81
% female: 19
% minority: 17

STUDENTS

Enrollment of law school: 262
% Male/female: 45/55
% Full time: 13
% minority: 24

ACADEMICS

Academic Specializations:
Advanced Degrees Offered: JD 3 to 4 years.
Clinical program required: No
Legal writing course requirements: Yes
Legal methods course requirements: Yes
Legal research course requirements: Yes
Moot court requirement: No
Public interest law requirement: No

ADMISSIONS INFORMATION

Admissions Selectivity Rating: 64
Application fee: $55
Regular application deadline: Rolling
Regular notification: Rolling
Early application program: No
LSDAS accepted: Yes
Average GPA: 3.1
Range of GPA: 2.0–3.9
Average LSAT: 148
Transfer students accepted: Yes
Evening division offered: Yes
Part-time accepted: Yes
Number of applications received: 59
Number of applicants accepted: 28
Number of acceptees attending: 17

INTERNATIONAL STUDENTS

TOEFL required for international students: No
Minimum Paper TOEFL: 550
Minimum Computer-based TOEFL: 213

FINANCIAL FACTS

Annual tuition: $19,488
Books and supplies: $900
% receiving scholarships: 5
Tuition per credit: $695

EMPLOYMENT INFORMATION

State for bar exam: CA
Pass rate for first-time bar: 35
Prominent Alumni: Paula Zinneman, California Real Estate Commissioner; Gail Margolis, Director, Mental Health Services, State of California; Hon. Ron Skyers, LA Superior Court; Lael Rubin, District Attorney's Office.

WESTERN STATE UNIVERSITY
College of Law

1111 North State College Boulevard, Fullerton, CA 92831 United States
Admissions Phone: 714-459-1101 • Admissions Fax: 714-441-1748
Admissions E-mail: adm@wsulaw.edu • Website: www.wsulaw.edu

INSTITUTIONAL INFORMATION

Public/private: Private
Student/faculty ratio: 20:1
Total faculty: 41
% part-time: 39
% female: 33
% minority: 15

STUDENTS

Enrollment of law school: 155
% Out of state: 34
% Male/female: 50/50
% Full time: 83
% minority: 33
Average age of entering class: 26

ACADEMICS

Academic Specializations: Criminal law, business law.
Advanced Degrees Offered: JD 3 to 4 years.
Clinical program required: No
Legal writing course requirements: Yes
Legal methods course requirements: No
Legal research course requirements: Yes
Moot court requirement: Yes
Public interest law requirement: No

ADMISSIONS INFORMATION

Admissions Selectivity Rating: 67
Application fee: $50
Regular application deadline: Rolling
Regular notification: Rolling
Early application program: No
LSDAS accepted: Yes
Average GPA: 3.13
Range of GPA: 2.8–3.4
Average LSAT: 151
Range of LSAT: 149–154
Transfer students accepted: Yes
Evening division offered: Yes
Part-time accepted: Yes

Applicants also look at: California Western School of Law, Chapman University, Golden Gate University, Loyola Marymount University, Southwestern University School of Law, Thomas Jefferson School of Law, Whittier College.
Number of applications received: 1,637
Number of applicants accepted: 649
Number of acceptees attending: 155

INTERNATIONAL STUDENTS

TOEFL required for international students: Yes
Minimum Paper TOEFL: 550
Minimum Computer-based TOEFL: 213

FINANCIAL FACTS

Annual tuition: $27,220
Room & board (off-campus): $11,749
Books and supplies: $1,260
Financial aid application deadline: 3/2
% receiving scholarships: 44
Average grant: $11,000
Average loan: $26,000
% of aid that is merit-based: 12
% receiving some sort of aid: 91
% first year students receiving some sort of aid: 90
Average total aid package: $29,000
Average debt: $83,000
Tuition per credit: $17,440

EMPLOYMENT INFORMATION

Rate of placement (nine months out): 91
Average starting salary: $63,457
State for bar exam: CA, AZ, TX, OR, FL
Pass rate for first-time bar: 30
Employers who frequently hire grads: Medium-sized law firms; district attorneys; public defenders; corporations; state governments; federal governments.
Prominent Alumni: Pearl Mann, president, California Women Lawyers; Gary Kermott, president, First American Title Company; Hon. Richard Fields, presiding judge, Riverside Superior Court; Danni Murphy, Board of Governors, State Bar of California; Hon. Larry Allen, presiding judge, San Bernardino Superior Court.

Grads employed by field:	%
Academic	4
Business/Industry	10
Government	13
Judicial clerkships	3
Private practice	66
Public Interest	4

* Provisionally approved by the ABA.

CARLETON UNIVERSITY

Department of Law

C473 Loeb, 1125 Colonel By Drive, Ottawa, On K1S 5B6 Canada
Admissions Phone: *613-520-3690* • **Admissions Fax:** *613-520-4467*
Admissions E-mail: *law@carleton.ca* • **Website:** *www.carleton.ca/law*

INSTITUTIONAL INFORMATION
Public/private: Private

ADMISSIONS INFORMATION
Admissions Selectivity Rating: 60*
Early application program: No
LSDAS accepted? No
Transfer students accepted? No
Evening division offered: No
Part-time accepted: No

INTERNATIONAL STUDENTS
TOEFL required for international students? No

DALHOUSIE UNIVERSITY

Dalhousie Law School

Dalhousie Law School, Halifax, NS B3P 1P8 Canada
Admissions Phone: *902-494-2068* • **Admissions Fax:** *902-494-1316*
Admissions E-mail: *Rose.Godfrey@dal.ca*
Website: *www.dal.ca/law/admission.html*

INSTITUTIONAL INFORMATION
Public/private: public
Student/faculty ratio: 13:1
Total faculty: 35
% female: 45
% faculty minority: 6

STUDENTS
Enrollment of law school: 464
% Out-of-state: 88
% Male/female: 45/55
% Full-time: 98
% minority: 12
Average age of entering class: 24

ACADEMICS
Academic specializations: Commercial law, corporation securities law, environmental law, international law.
Advanced degrees offered: LLM, JSD.

Combined degrees offered: LLB/MBA, LLB/MLIS, LLB/MPA, LLB/MHSA.
Clinical program required? No
Clinical program description: Legal Aid Clinic.
Legal writing course requirements? Yes
Legal writing description: Required course, first year.
Legal methods course requirements? No
Legal research course requirements? Yes
Legal research description: Required course, first year.
Moot court requirement? Yes
Moot court description: Mandatory moot, second year.
Public interest law requirement? No
Academic journals: *Dalhousie Law Journal, Dalhousie Journal of Legal Studies, Canadian Journal of Law and Technology.*

ADMISSIONS INFORMATION
Admissions Selectivity Rating: 95
Application fee: $65
Regular application deadline: 2/28
Regular notification: 4/1
Early application program: No
LSDAS accepted? No
Average GPA: 3.8
Average LSAT: 161
Transfer students accepted? Yes
Evening division offered: No
Part-time accepted: Yes
Applicants also look at: Arizona State University, McGill University, Queen's University, University of British Columbia, University of Toronto, York University.
Number of applications received: 1,285
Number of applicants accepted: 279
Number of acceptees attending: 162

RESEARCH FACILITIES
% of JD classrooms wired: 100
School-supported research centers: Dalhousie Legal Aid Clinic, Health Law Institute, Law and Technology Institute, Marine and Environmental Law Institute.

FINANCIAL FACTS
Annual tuition: $9,492
Room & board (on-campus): $3,500
Books and supplies: $1,200
Financial aid application deadline: 10/31
Average grant: $4,212
Average loan: $8,000
% of aid that is merit-based: 43
Average total aid package: $2,500

INTERNATIONAL STUDENTS
TOEFL required for international students? Yes
Minimum Paper TOEFL: 600

EMPLOYMENT INFORMATION
Employers who frequently hire grads: Law firms, government, courts.
Grads employed by field: Academic, 1%; business/industry, 5%; government, 5%; judicial clerkships, 5%; private practice, 80%.

LAURENTIAN UNIVERSITY

Department of Law and Justice

935 Ramsey Lake Road, Arts Building, Room A-308, Sudbury, ON P3E 2C6 Canada
Admissions Phone: *705-675-1151 •* **Admissions Fax:** *705-675-4823*
Admissions E-mail: *Cneff@laurentian.ca*
Website: *http://laurentian.ca/justice/english*

INSTITUTIONAL INFORMATION
Public/private: Private

ADMISSIONS INFORMATION
Admissions Selectivity Rating: 60*
Early application program: No
LSDAS accepted? No
Transfer students accepted? No
Evening division offered: No
Part-time accepted: No

INTERNATIONAL STUDENTS
TOEFL required for international students? No

McGILL UNIVERSITY

Faculty of Law

3644 Peel Street, Room #406, Montreal, QC H3A 1W9 Canada
Admissions Phone: *514-398-6646 •* **Admissions Fax:** *514-398-8453*
Admissions E-mail: *gradadmissions.law@mcgill.ca*
Website: *www.law.mcgill.ca/graduate*

INSTITUTIONAL INFORMATION
Public/private: Public

STUDENTS
Average age of entering class: 35

ADMISSIONS INFORMATION
Admissions Selectivity Rating: 71
Application fee: $80
Regular application deadline: 3/1
Early application program: No
LSDAS accepted: No
Average GPA: 3.00
Transfer students accepted: No
Evening division offered: No
Part-time accepted: No
Number of applications received: 248
Number of applicants accepted: 122
Number of acceptees attending: 69

INTERNATIONAL STUDENTS
TOEFL required for international students: Yes
Minimum Paper TOEFL: 600
Minimum Computer-based TOEFL: 250

FINANCIAL FACTS
Room & board (on-campus): $9,600
Books and supplies: $800

QUEEN'S UNIVERSITY

Faculty of Law

Macdonald Hall, Room 200, 128 Union Street, Queen's University Kingston, ON K7L 3N6 Canada
Admissions Phone: *613-533-2220 •* **Admissions Fax:** *613-533-6611*
Admissions E-mail: *llb@post.queensu.ca •* **Website:** *law.queensu.ca*

INSTITUTIONAL INFORMATION
Public/private: Public
Student/faculty ratio: 6:1
Total faculty: 78
% part-time: 69
% female: 36

STUDENTS
Enrollment of law school: 486
% Male/female: 53/47
% Full time: 98
Average age of entering class: 26

ACADEMICS
Academic Specializations: Civil procedure, commercial law, constitutional law, corporation securities law, criminal law, environmental law, government services, human rights law, intellectual property law, international law, labor law, legal history, legal philosophy, property, taxation.
Advanced Degrees Offered: LLM.
Combined Degrees Offered: MIR/LLB (industrial relations), MPA/LLB (policy studies), MBA/LLB.
Clinical program required: No
Legal writing course requirements: Yes
Legal research course requirements: Yes
Moot court requirement: Yes
Public interest law requirement: Yes

ADMISSIONS INFORMATION
Admissions Selectivity Rating: 89
Application fee: $175
Regular application deadline: 11/1
Regular notification: Rolling
Early application program: No
LSDAS accepted: No
Average GPA: 3.7
Range of GPA: 3.0 to 4.0
Average LSAT: 162
Range of LSAT: 156–178
Transfer students accepted: Yes

Evening division offered: No
Part-time accepted: Yes
Applicants also look at: Dalhousie School of Law, McGill University, University of British Columbia, University of Calgary, University of Ottawa, University of Toronto, York University.
Number of applications received: 2,346
Number of applicants accepted: 575
Number of acceptees attending: 165

INTERNATIONAL STUDENTS
TOEFL required for international students: Yes
Minimum Paper TOEFL: 600
Minimum Computer-based TOEFL: 250

FINANCIAL FACTS
Annual tuition (resident): $10,452
Annual tuition (nonresident): $20,142
Room & board (on/off-campus): $4,891/$5,190
Books and supplies: $1,875
Financial aid application deadline: 10/31
% receiving scholarships: 22
Average grant: $2,327
Average loan: $4,752
% of aid that is merit-based: 13
% receiving some sort of aid: 78
% first year students receiving some sort of aid: 71
Average total aid package: $4,927
Tuition per credit (resident): $1,936
Tuition per credit (nonresident): $3,805

EMPLOYMENT INFORMATION
Rate of placement (nine months out): 98
Average starting salary: $71,000

Grads employed by field:	%
Academic	2
Business/Industry	1
Government	1
Judicial clerkships	1
Other	1
Private practice	92
Public Interest	1

ADMISSIONS INFORMATION
Admissions Selectivity Rating: 60*
Application fee: $39
Regular application deadline: 3/31
Early application program: No
LSDAS accepted? No
Transfer students accepted? No
Evening division offered: No
Part-time accepted: No

INTERNATIONAL STUDENTS
TOEFL required for international students? No

UNIVERSITÉ LAVAL
Faculté de Droit

Bureau du Registraire, Pavillon Jean-Charles-Bonenfant Pavillon Charles-De Koninck, QC GIK 7P4 Canada
Admissions Phone: *418-656-3080* • **Admissions Fax:** *418-656-5216*
Admissions E-mail: *info@vrdri.ulaval.ca* • **Website:** *www.ulaval.ca/fd*

INSTITUTIONAL INFORMATION
Public/private: Public

ADMISSIONS INFORMATION
Admissions Selectivity Rating: 60*
Early application program: No
LSDAS accepted? No
Transfer students accepted? No
Evening division offered: No
Part-time accepted: No

INTERNATIONAL STUDENTS
TOEFL required for international students? No

UNIVERSITÉ DE MONCTON
Faculté de Droit

Faculté de Droit, Université de Moncton, Moncton, NB E1A 3E9 Canada
Admissions Phone: *506-858-4564* • **Admissions Fax:** *506-858-4534*
Admissions E-mail: *edr@umoncton.ca* • **Website:** *www.umoncton.ca/droit*

INSTITUTIONAL INFORMATION
Public/private: Public

STUDENTS
Enrollment of law school: 50

UNIVERSITÉ DU QUÉBEC À MONTRÉAL
Faculté de Science Politique et de Droit

870, Boulevard de Maisonneuve Est, Bureau T-3600, Case postale 6190, succursale Centre-Ville, Montréal, QC H3C 4N6 Canada
Admissions Phone: *514-987-3132* • **Admissions Fax:** *514-987-8932*
Admissions E-mail: *admission@uqam.ca* • **Website:** *www.uqam.ca*

INSTITUTIONAL INFORMATION
Public/private: Public

ADMISSIONS INFORMATION

Admissions Selectivity Rating: 60*
Early application program: No
LSDAS accepted? No
Transfer students accepted? No
Evening division offered: No
Part-time accepted: No

INTERNATIONAL STUDENTS

TOEFL required for international students? No

ADMISSIONS INFORMATION

Admissions Selectivity Rating: 60*
Early application program: No
LSDAS accepted? No
Transfer students accepted? No
Evening division offered: No
Part-time accepted: No

INTERNATIONAL STUDENTS

TOEFL required for international students? No

UNIVERSITÉ DE SHERBROOKE

Faculté de Droit

2500, Boulevard de l'Université Sherbrooke, QC J1K 2R1 Canada
Admissions Phone: *800-267-8337* • **Admissions Fax:** *819-821-7652*
Admissions E-mail: *information@usherbrooke.ca*
Website: *www.usherbrooke.ca*

INSTITUTIONAL INFORMATION

Public/private: private

ADMISSIONS INFORMATION

Admissions Selectivity Rating: 60*
Early application program: No
LSDAS accepted? No
Transfer students accepted? No
Evening division offered: No
Part-time accepted: No

INTERNATIONAL STUDENTS

TOEFL required for international students? No

UNIVERSITY OF ALBERTA

Faculty of Law

University of Alberta, Law Centre, Edmonton, AB T6G 2H5 Canada
Admissions Phone: *780-492-3115* • **Admissions Fax:** *780-492-4924*
Admissions E-mail: *dmirth@law.ualberta.ca*
Website: *www.law.ualberta.ca*

INSTITUTIONAL INFORMATION

Public/private: Public

UNIVERSITY OF BRITISH COLUMBIA

Faculty of Law

1822 East Mall, Vancouver, BC V6T 1Z1 Canada
Admissions Phone: *604-822-6303* • **Admissions Fax:** *604-822-8108*
Admissions E-mail: *admissions@law.ubc.ca* • **Website:** *www.law.ubc.ca*

INSTITUTIONAL INFORMATION

Public/private: Public
Student/faculty ratio: 14:1
Total faculty: 675
% part-time: 3
% female: 51
% minority: 7

STUDENTS

Enrollment of law school: 673
% Out of state: 35
% Male/female: 48/52
% Full time: 90
% International: 1
% minority: 10
Average age of entering class: 25

ACADEMICS

Academic Specializations: Corporation securities law, environmental law, intellectual property law, legal history.
Advanced Degrees Offered: LLB 3 years, LLM 1 year, PhD 2 to 4 years.
Combined Degrees Offered: LLB/MBA 4 years, LLB/MA (MAPPS, Asian Pacific Policy) 3 years.
Clinical program required: No
Legal writing course requirements: Yes
Legal methods course requirements: No
Legal research course requirements: Yes
Moot court requirement: Yes
Moot court description: All first-year students are required to participate in a moot court program as part of their first-year curriculum. They must write an appeal factum and participate as an advocate in the mock appeal in the mock appeal in front of a bench of legal practitioners acting as judges. Students will wear robes and receive feedback from the judges.
Public interest law requirement: No

ADMISSIONS INFORMATION

Admissions Selectivity Rating: 94
Application fee: $80
Regular application deadline: 2/1
Regular notification: Rolling
Early application program: Yes
LSDAS accepted: No
Average GPA: 3.81
Average LSAT: 163
Range of LSAT: 153–175
Transfer students accepted: Yes
Evening division offered: No
Part-time accepted: Yes
Applicants also look at: University of Alberta, University of Calgary, University of Toronto, University of Victoria, York University.
Number of applications received: 1,637
Number of applicants accepted: 432
Number of acceptees attending: 208

INTERNATIONAL STUDENTS

TOEFL required for international students: No

FINANCIAL FACTS

Annual tuition (resident): $9,364
Annual tuition (nonresident): $18,749
Room & board (on/off-campus): $9,200/$10,400
Books and supplies: $1,600
Financial aid application deadline: 9/15
% receiving scholarships: 48
Average grant: $5,225
Average loan: $10,689
% of aid that is merit-based: 5
% receiving some sort of aid: 58
% first year students receiving some sort of aid: 60
Average total aid package: $13,097
Average debt: $16,226
Tuition per credit (resident): $312
Tuition per credit (nonresident): $586

EMPLOYMENT INFORMATION

Rate of placement (nine months out): 89
Average starting salary: $40,000
Employers who frequently hire grads: British Columbia law firms and government agencies (including Vancouver Island and interior); Ontario law firms and government agencies; Alberta law firms and government agencies; New York law firms; Canadian public interest groups; Canadian courts (both federal and provincial); corporate legal departments; Canadian crown corporations; Yukon/Northwest territories law firms.
Prominent alumni: Hon. Frank Iacobucci, former justice, Supreme Court of Canada; Hon. Lance Finch, chief justice, British Columbia; Kim Campbell, former Prime Minister of Canada; Hon. Don Brenner, chief justice, British Columbia Supreme Court; Ujjal Dosanjh, former Premier of British Columbia and Attorney General.
State for bar exam: BC, AB, NY, MA, ON
Pass rate for first-time bar: 99

Grads employed by field:	%
Business/Industry	1
Government	4
Judicial clerkships	9
Other	2
Private practice	83
Public Interest	1

UNIVERSITY OF CALGARY
Faculty of Law

Room 3390, Murray Fraser Hall, 2500 University Drive NW, Calgary, AB T2N 1N4 Canada
Admissions Phone: 403-220-8154 • **Admissions Fax:** 403-210-9662
Admissions E-mail: law@ucalgary.ca • **Website:** www.law.ucalgary.ca

INSTITUTIONAL INFORMATION

Public/private: Public
Student/faculty ratio: 12:1
Total faculty: 21
% female: 50

STUDENTS

Enrollment of law school: 238
% Male/female: 43/57
% Full time: 97
% International: 3
Average age of entering class: 26

ACADEMICS

Academic Specializations: Environmental law, natural resource, law legal skills program.
Advanced Degrees Offered: LLB 3 years, LLM 15 to 18 months.
Combined Degrees Offered: LLB/MBA 4 years, LLB/MEDes (environmental design).
Clinical program required: No
Legal writing course requirements: Yes
Legal methods course requirements: Yes
Legal research course requirements: Yes
Moot court requirement: Yes

ADMISSIONS INFORMATION

Admissions Selectivity Rating: 93
Application fee: $100
Regular application deadline: 2/1
Regular notification: rolling
Early application program: No
LSDAS accepted: No
Average GPA: 3.5
Range of GPA: 2.8 to 4.0
Transfer students accepted: Yes
Evening division offered: No
Part-time accepted: Yes
Applicants also look at: University of Alberta, University of British Columbia, University of Saskatchewan.
Number of applications received: 875
Number of applicants accepted: 136
Number of acceptees attending: 75

INTERNATIONAL STUDENTS

TOEFL required for international students: Yes
Minimum Paper TOEFL: 600
Minimum Computer-based TOEFL: 250

FINANCIAL FACTS

Annual tuition (resident): $11,080
Annual tuition (nonresident): $11,080

Room & board (on/off-campus): $8,000/$12,000
Books and supplies: $1,800

EMPLOYMENT INFORMATION

State for bar exam: AB

UNIVERSITY OF MANITOBA
Faculty of Law

424 University Centre, Enrollment Services/Admissions, University of Manitoba, Winnipeg, MB R3T 2N2 Canada
Admissions Phone: *204-474-8825* • **Admissions Fax:** *204-474-7554*
Admissions E-mail: *lawadmissions@umanitoba.ca*
Website: *www.umanitoba.ca/law*

INSTITUTIONAL INFORMATION

Public/private: Public
Student/faculty ratio: 15:1
Total faculty: 23
% part time: 43
% female: 30

STUDENTS

Enrollment of law school: 262
% Full-time: 97
Average age of entering class: 26

ACADEMICS

Advanced degrees offered: LLM
Clinical program required? No
Clinical program description: In clinical administrative law, the primary purpose is to train students in lawyering skills. Students are required to engage in classroom work and participate in simulated exercises. Emphasis is given to the difference between board and court advocacy. In clinical family law, instruction is given on an intensive basis in small groups. Students may be required to engage in classroom work, to participate in various forms of simulation exercises, and to conduct actual client based cases under the supervision of the instructor. Particular emphasis will be given to questions of professional responsibilities and ethics. In Clinical Criminal Law, instruction is given on an intensive basis in various forms of simulation exercises and to conduct actual client based cases under the supervision of the instructor. Particular emphasis will be given to questions of professional responsibility and ethics. Solicitors transactions is a study, involving practical exercises, of certain aspects of solicitors' work, including drafting. Advanced advocacy addresses advanced topics in trial presentation, procedure, and evidence with concentration on jury trials.
Legal writing course requirements? Yes
Legal writing description: An introduction to legal research and writing skills and oral advocacy.
Legal methods course requirements? Yes
Legal methods description: An introduction to legal research and writing skills and oral advocacy.
Legal research course requirements? Yes
Legal research description: An introduction to legal research and writing skills and oral advocacy.
Moot court requirement? Yes

Moot court description: In second and third years, students participate in moot courts, fictitious trials and appeals, which provide practice in research, examination of witnesses, and courtroom argument.
Public interest law requirement? No
Academic journals: *Manitoba Law Journal.*

ADMISSIONS INFORMATION

Admissions Selectivity Rating: 97
Regular application deadline: 11/1
Early application program: No
LSDAS accepted? No
Average LSAT: 158
Range of LSAT: 148-173
Transfer students accepted? Yes
Evening division offered: No
Part-time accepted: Yes
Number of applications received: 844
Number of applicants accepted: 102
Number of acceptees attending: 102

FINANCIAL FACTS

Annual tuition (resident): $5,000
Books and supplies: $1,600

INTERNATIONAL STUDENTS

TOEFL required for international students? Yes

UNIVERSITY OF NEW BRUNSWICK
Faculty of Law

Law Admissions Office, Faculty of Law, PO Box 44271, University of New Brunswick, Fredericton, NB E3B 6C2 Canada
Admissions Phone: *506-453-4693* • **Admissions Fax:** *506-458-7722*
Admissions E-mail: *lawadmit@unb.ca* • **Website:** *www.law.unb.ca*

INSTITUTIONAL INFORMATION

Public/private: Public
Student/faculty ratio: 11:1
Total faculty: 25
% part-time: 12
% female: 33

STUDENTS

Enrollment of law school: 239
% Male/female: 49/51
% Full time: 100
% International: 3
Average age of entering class: 25

ACADEMICS

Academic Specializations: Civil procedure, commercial law, constitutional law, criminal law, environmental law, human rights law, intellectual property law, international law, labor law, legal history, legal philosophy, taxation.

Advanced Degrees Offered: LLB 3 years.
Combined Degrees Offered: LLB/MBA 4 years.
Clinical program required: No
Legal writing course requirements: Yes
Legal methods course requirements: Yes
Legal research course requirements: No
Moot court requirement: Yes
Public interest law requirement: No

ADMISSIONS INFORMATION
Admissions Selectivity Rating: 87
Application fee: $50
Regular application deadline: 3/1
Regular notification: 3/2
Early application program: No
LSDAS accepted: No
Average GPA: 3.7
Range of GPA: 3.1–4.0
Average LSAT: 158
Range of LSAT: 151–173
Transfer students accepted: Yes
Evening division offered: No
Part-time accepted: No
Applicants also look at: Dalhousie School of Law.
Number of applications received: 828
Number of applicants accepted: 200
Number of acceptees attending: 89

INTERNATIONAL STUDENTS
TOEFL required for international students: No

FINANCIAL FACTS
Annual tuition (resident): $8,646
Annual tuition (nonresident): $8,646
Room & board (on-campus): $6,000
Books and supplies: $1,500
Financial aid application deadline: 11/15
% receiving scholarships: 21
Average grant: $5,000
% of aid that is merit-based: 82
% receiving some sort of aid: 45
% first year students receiving some sort of aid: 27
Average total aid package: $1,000

EMPLOYMENT INFORMATION
Rate of placement (nine months out): 80
State for bar exam: NB, NS, NL, PE, ON

Grads employed by field:	%
Government	6
Other	22
Private practice	72

UNIVERSITY OF OTTAWA
Faculty of Law

PO Box 450, Stn. A, 57 Louis Pasteur Street, Ottawa, ON K1N 6N5 Canada
Admissions Phone: 613-562-5800 • Admissions Fax: 613-562-5124
Admissions E-mail: comlaw@uottawa.ca • Website: www.commonlaw.uottawa.ca

INSTITUTIONAL INFORMATION
Public/private: Public
Student/faculty ratio: 17:1
Total faculty: 53
% part-time: 100
% female: 51
% minority: 15

STUDENTS
Enrollment of law school: 219
% Male/female: 42/58
% Full time: 94
Average age of entering class: 26

ACADEMICS
Academic Specializations: Environmental law, human rights law, intellectual property law, international law.
Combined Degrees Offered: LLB/JD 4 years, LLB/MBA 4 years, LLB/MA 4 years, LLB/LLL 4 years.
Clinical program required: No
Legal writing course requirements: No
Legal methods course requirements: No
Legal research course requirements: No
Moot court requirement: Yes
Public interest law requirement: Yes

ADMISSIONS INFORMATION
Admissions Selectivity Rating: 87
Application fee: $75
Regular application deadline: 11/1
Early application program: No
LSDAS accepted: No
Average GPA: 3.53
Transfer students accepted: Yes
Evening division offered: No
Part-time accepted: No
Number of applications received: 3,391
Number of applicants accepted: 620
Number of acceptees attending: 219

INTERNATIONAL STUDENTS
TOEFL required for international students: No

FINANCIAL FACTS
Annual tuition (resident): $9,180
Room & board (on-campus): $10,000
Books and supplies: $1,100
Financial aid application deadline: 3/15
% receiving scholarships: 16
Average grant: $1,815
Average loan: $1,159
% of aid that is merit-based: 67
% receiving some sort of aid: 65

% first year students receiving some sort of aid: 65
Average total aid package: $10,440
Tuition per credit (resident): $356

EMPLOYMENT INFORMATION

Rate of placement (nine months out): 60
State for bar exam: NY, MA
Pass rate for first-time bar: 95

Grads employed by field:	%
Government	1
Judicial clerkships	1
Other	40
Private practice	57
Public Interest	1

UNIVERSITY OF SASKATCHEWAN

College of Law

College of Law University of Saskatchewan, 15 Campus Drive, Saskatoon, SK S7N 5A6 Canada
Admissions Phone: 306-966-5045 • **Admissions Fax:** 306-966-5900
Admissions E-mail: law_admissions@usask.ca • **Website:** www.usask.ca/law

INSTITUTIONAL INFORMATION

Public/private: public
Total faculty: 38
% part-time: 18
% female: 20

STUDENTS

Average age of entering class: 25

ADMISSIONS INFORMATION

Admissions Selectivity Rating: 94
Application fee: $75
Regular application deadline: 2/1
Early application program: No
LSDAS accepted: No
Average GPA: 3.56
Average LSAT: 156
Range of LSAT: 150–167
Transfer students accepted: Yes
Evening division offered: No
Part-time accepted: Yes
Number of applications received: 901
Number of applicants accepted: 120
Number of acceptees attending: 120

INTERNATIONAL STUDENTS

TOEFL required for international students: No

FINANCIAL FACTS

Annual tuition (resident): $6,840
Annual tuition (nonresident): $6,840
Books and supplies: $1,000
Tuition per credit (resident): $228
Tuition per credit (nonresident): $228

UNIVERSITY OF TORONTO

Faculty of Law

78 Queens Park, Toronto, ON M5S 2C5 Canada
Admissions Phone: 416-978-3716 • **Admissions Fax:** 416-978-7899
Admissions E-mail: law.admissions@utoronto.ca • **Website:** www.law.utoronto.ca

INSTITUTIONAL INFORMATION

Public/private: Public
Student/faculty ratio: 10:1
Total faculty: 57
% female: 33

STUDENTS

Enrollment of law school: 585
% Male/female: 51/49
% Full time: 99
% minority: 30
Average age of entering class: 25

ACADEMICS

Academic Specializations:
Advanced Degrees Offered: LLM 1 year, SJD 1 year (plus thesis), MSL 1 year.
Combined Degrees Offered: JD/MBA 4 years, JD/MSW 4 years, JD/MA (criminology) 3 years, JD/MA (economics) 3 years, JD/MA (English) 3 years, JD/MA (political science, collaborative program in international relations) 3 years, JD/MA (European, Russian and Eurasian Studies) 4 years, JD/MISt (Masters of Information Studies) 4 years, JD/certificate in environmental studies 3 years, JD/PhD (economics) 4 years (plus dissertation), JD/PhD (philosophy) 4 years (plus dissertation), JD/PhD (political science) 4 years (plus dissertation).
Clinical program required: No
Legal writing course requirements: Yes
Legal methods course requirements: Yes
Legal research course requirements: Yes
Moot court requirement: Yes
Public interest law requirement: No

ADMISSIONS INFORMATION

Admissions Selectivity Rating: 97
Application fee: $75
Regular application deadline: 11/1
Regular notification: 1/4
Early application program: No
LSDAS accepted: No
Average GPA: 3.9
Range of GPA: 3.6 to 4.0
Average LSAT: 167
Range of LSAT: 158–179

Transfer students accepted: Yes
Evening division offered: No
Part-time accepted: Yes
Applicants also look at: Columbia University, Harvard University, McGill University, New York University, University of British Columbia, University of California, Berkeley, York University.
Number of applications received: 1,808
Number of applicants accepted: 273
Number of acceptees attending: 187

INTERNATIONAL STUDENTS

TOEFL required for international students: No

FINANCIAL FACTS

Annual tuition (resident): $17,280
Annual tuition (nonresident): $26,849
Room & board (on/off-campus): $10,250/$8,900
Books and supplies: $1,100
Financial aid application deadline: 7/15
Average grant: $7,587
Average loan: $6,274
% of aid that is merit-based: 4
% receiving some sort of aid: 45
% first year students receiving some sort of aid: 56

EMPLOYMENT INFORMATION

Rate of placement (nine months out):
Average starting salary: $60,000
Employers who frequently hire grads: All major Toronto law firms; provincial and federal government departments; many large New York and Boston law firms; large and midsize Vancouver, Halifax and Calgary law firms.
Prominent alumni: Justice Frank Iacobucci, former justice, Supreme Court of Canada; Justice Rosalie Abella, Supreme Court of Canada; Bob Rae & David Peterson, former Premiers of Ontario; Honorable Paul Martin, former Prime Minister of Canada; Justice Ian Binnie, Supreme Court of Canada.
State for bar exam: NY, MA, CA

Grads employed by field:	%
Business/Industry	1
Government	6
Judicial clerkships	8
Other	9
Private practice	74
Public Interest	2

UNIVERSITY OF VICTORIA
Faculty of Law

PO Box 2400, STN CSC, Victoria, BC V8W 3H7 Canada
Admissions Phone: *250-721-8151* • **Admissions Fax:** *250-721-6390*
Admissions E-mail: *lawadmss@uvic.ca* • **Website:** *www.law.uvic.ca*

INSTITUTIONAL INFORMATION

Public/private: Public
Affiliation: Baptist
Student/faculty ratio: 7:1
Total faculty: 60
% part-time: 43
% female: 30
% minority: 9

STUDENTS

Enrollment of law school: 360
% Out of state: 50
% Male/female: 40/60
% Full time: 98
% minority: 25
Average age of entering class: 26

ACADEMICS

Academic Specializations: Environmental law, intellectual property law, international law, alternative dispute resolution, Aboriginal law.
Advanced Degrees Offered: LLM 1 year, PhD 3 years.
Combined Degrees Offered: LLB/MPA 4 years, LLB/MBA 4 years, LLB/BCL 4.5 years, LLB/MAIG 4 years.
Clinical program required: No
Legal writing course requirements: Yes
Legal methods course requirements: Yes
Legal research course requirements: Yes
Moot court requirement: Yes
Public interest law requirement: No

ADMISSIONS INFORMATION

Admissions Selectivity Rating: 94
Application fee: $50
Regular application deadline: 2/1
Regular notification: 5/31
Early application program: No
LSDAS accepted: No
Average GPA: 3.82
Range of GPA: 3.4 to 4.0
Average LSAT: 164
Range of LSAT: 155–175
Transfer students accepted: Yes
Evening division offered: No
Part-time accepted: Yes
Applicants also look at: University of British Columbia, University of Toronto.
Number of applications received: 1,038
Number of applicants accepted: 277
Number of acceptees attending: 108

INTERNATIONAL STUDENTS

TOEFL required for international students: Yes
Minimum Paper TOEFL: 600
Minimum Computer-based TOEFL: 250

FINANCIAL FACTS

Annual tuition (resident): $7,721
Annual tuition (nonresident): $20,533
Room & board (on/off-campus): $7,000/$10,000
Books and supplies: $2,000
Financial aid application deadline: 6/1
Average grant: $2,500
Average loan: $10,880
% of aid that is merit-based: 35
Average total aid package: $4,000
Average debt: $30,000
Tuition per credit (resident): $576
Tuition per credit (nonresident): $1,929

EMPLOYMENT INFORMATION

Rate of placement (nine months out): 95
Employers who frequently hire grads: Local, provincial and national law firms; federal and provincial government; judicial clerkships; nonprofit organizations.
Prominent alumni: Sheridan Scott, Commissioner, Competition Bureau of Canada; Freya Kristjanson, partner, Borden, Ladner, Gervais, LLP; Gary Lunn, Federal Government Minister; Andrew Petter, Dean of Law.

Grads employed by field:	%
Academic	3
Government	10
Judicial clerkships	11
Other	8
Private practice	55
Public Interest	2

UNIVERSITY OF VICTORIA FACULTY OF LAW

Akitsiraq Law School

PO Box 2292, Iqaluit, NU X0A 0H0 Canada
Admissions Phone: 250-721-8151 • **Admissions Fax:** 250-721-6390
Admissions E-mail: lawadmss@uvic.ca • **Website:** www.law.uvic.ca

INSTITUTIONAL INFORMATION

Public/private: Public

ADMISSIONS INFORMATION

Admissions Selectivity Rating: 60*
Early application program: No
LSDAS accepted? No
Transfer students accepted? No
Evening division offered: No
Part-time accepted: No

INTERNATIONAL STUDENTS

TOEFL required for international students? No

THE UNIVERSITY OF WESTERN ONTARIO

Faculty of Law

Administrative Wing, Faculty of Law London, ON N5X 3T5 Canada
Admissions Phone: 519-661-3347 • **Admissions Fax:** 519-661-2063
Admissions E-mail: lawapp@uwo.ca • **Website:** www.law.uwo.ca

INSTITUTIONAL INFORMATION

Public/private: public
Student/faculty ratio: 7:1
Total faculty: 33
% part-time: 33
% female: 27

STUDENTS

Enrollment of law school: 161
% Out of state: 15
% Male/female: 52/48
% Full time: 98
Average age of entering class: 25

ACADEMICS

Academic Specializations: Business law, criminal law, intellectual property law, taxation.
Advanced Degrees Offered: LLB 3 years, LLM 1 year.
Combined Degrees Offered: LLB/HBA, LLB/BESc (engineering), LLB/BSc (computer science), honors BA (history)/LLB, BA (kin)/LLB, honors BA (MIT)/LLB, honors BA (political science)/LLB, LLB/MBA.
Clinical program required: No
Legal writing course requirements: Yes
Legal methods course requirements: Yes
Legal research course requirements: Yes
Moot court requirement: Yes
Public interest law requirement: No

ADMISSIONS INFORMATION

Admissions Selectivity Rating: 89
Application fee: $75
Regular application deadline: 11/1
Regular notification: Rolling
Early application program: No
LSDAS accepted: No
Average GPA: 3.72
Range of GPA: 3.3–4.0
Average LSAT: 160
Range of LSAT: 155–173
Transfer students accepted: Yes
Evening division offered: No
Part-time accepted: Yes
Applicants also look at: Queen's University, University of Ottawa, University of Toronto, University of Windsor, York University.
Number of applications received: 2,374
Number of applicants accepted: 504
Number of acceptees attending: 161

INTERNATIONAL STUDENTS

TOEFL required for international students: Yes
Minimum Paper TOEFL: 600
Minimum Computer-based TOEFL: 250

FINANCIAL FACTS

Annual tuition (resident): $11,372
Room & board (off-campus): $8,000
Books and supplies: $1,400
Financial aid application deadline: 10/7
% receiving scholarships: 50
Average grant: $5,000
% of aid that is merit-based: 80
% receiving some sort of aid: 50
% first year students receiving some sort of aid: 60
Average total aid package: $3,000

EMPLOYMENT INFORMATION

Rate of placement (nine months out): 99
Average starting salary: $50,000
State for bar exam: NY
Pass rate for first-time bar: 100

Grads employed by field:	%
Business/Industry	2
Government	3
Judicial clerkships	3
Private practice	91

UNIVERSITY OF WINDSOR

Faculty of Law

Faculty of Law, 401 Sunset Windsor, ON N9B 3P4 Canada
Admissions Phone: 519-253-3000 • **Admissions Fax:** 519-973-7064
Admissions E-mail: lawadmit@uwindsor.ca • **Website:** www.uwindsor.ca/law

INSTITUTIONAL INFORMATION

Public/private: Public
Student/faculty ratio: 15:1

STUDENTS

Enrollment of law school: 558
Average age of entering class: 24

ACADEMICS

Academic Specializations: Civil procedure, commercial law, constitutional law, corporation securities law, criminal law, environmental law, human rights law, intellectual property law, international law, labor law, legal history, legal philosophy, property, taxation.
Combined Degrees Offered: MBA/LLB 3 to 4 years, JD/LLB 3 years.
Clinical program required: No
Legal writing course requirements: Yes
Legal methods course requirements: Yes
Legal research course requirements: Yes
Moot court requirement: Yes
Public interest law requirement: No

ADMISSIONS INFORMATION

Admissions Selectivity Rating: 60*
Application fee: $175
Regular application deadline: 1/11
Regular notification: Rolling
Early application program: No
LSDAS accepted: No
Transfer students accepted: Yes
Evening division offered: No
Part-time accepted: Yes
Number of applications received: 1,763
Number of applicants accepted: 332
Number of acceptees attending: 151

INTERNATIONAL STUDENTS

TOEFL required for international students: No

FINANCIAL FACTS

Annual tuition (resident): $9,990
Annual tuition (nonresident): $15,387
Room & board (on-campus): $8,950
Books and supplies: $1,315
Average grant: $4,744
Average loan: $12,900
% of aid that is merit-based: 24

EMPLOYMENT INFORMATION

State for bar exam: ON, AB, BC, NS, NF
Pass rate for first-time bar: 99

Grads employed by field:	%
Government	5
Judicial clerkships	2
Other	2
Private practice	89

YORK UNIVERSITY

Osgoode Hall Law School

4700 Keele Street, Toronto, ON M3J 1P3 Canada
Admissions Phone: 416-736-5712 • **Admissions Fax:** 416-736-5618
Admissions E-mail: admissions@osgoode.yorku.ca
Website: www.osgoode.yorku.ca

INSTITUTIONAL INFORMATION

Public/private: Public
Student/faculty ratio: 8:1
Total faculty: 134
% part-time: 40
% female: 40

STUDENTS

Enrollment of law school: 954
% Male/female: 48/52
% Full time: 100
% minority: 30
Average age of entering class: 24

ACADEMICS

Academic Specializations: International law, litigation, taxation.
Advanced Degrees Offered: LLM; DJUR.
Combined Degrees Offered: JD (NYU)/LLB 4 years, LLB/LLM (NYU) 3.5 years, LLB/MBA 4 years, LLB/MES 4 years.
Clinical program required: Yes
Legal writing course requirements: Yes
Legal methods course requirements: No
Legal research course requirements: Yes
Moot court requirement: Yes
Public interest law requirement: Yes

ADMISSIONS INFORMATION

Admissions Selectivity Rating: 89
Application fee: $75
Regular application deadline: 11/1
Regular notification: Rolling
Early application program: No
LSDAS accepted: No
Average GPA: 3.7
Average LSAT: 84
Transfer students accepted: Yes
Evening division offered: No
Part-time accepted: No
Number of applications received: 2,397
Number of applicants accepted: 608
Number of acceptees attending: 302

INTERNATIONAL STUDENTS

TOEFL required for international students: Yes
Minimum Computer-based TOEFL: 250

FINANCIAL FACTS

Annual tuition (resident): $13,996
Annual tuition (nonresident): $13,996
Room & board: $10,000
Books and supplies: $1,300
Financial aid application deadline: 9/7
% receiving scholarships: 20
Average grant: $7,500
Average loan: $10,000
% of aid that is merit-based: 25
% receiving some sort of aid: 55
Average total aid package: $7,500

EMPLOYMENT INFORMATION

Average starting salary: $55,000
Employers who frequently hire grads: Aird and Berlis LLP; Baker and McKenzie; Bennet Jones LLP; Bereskin and Parr; Blake, Cassels, and Graydon LLP; Borden Ladner Gervais LLP; Cassels, Brock, and Blackwell LLP; Davies, Ward, Phillips and Vineberg LLP; Davis and Company; Department of Justice, Ontario regional office; Dimock Stratton Clarizio LLP; Fasken Martineau Dumoulin LLP; Fogler Rubinoff LLP; Fraser Milner Casgrain LLP; Gilbert's LLP; Goodman and Carr LLP; Goodmans LLP; Gowling, Lafleur, Henderson LLP; Heenan Blaikie LLP; Hicks, Morley, Hamilton, Stewart, Storie LLP; Hodgson, Tough, Shields, Desbrisay, O'Donnell LLP; Keyser, Mason, Ball LLP; Lang, Michener; Lenczner, Slaght, Royce, Smith, Griffin; Lerners LLP; Matthews, Dinsdale, and Clark LLP; McCarthy, Tétrault LLP; McMillan, Binch LLP; Miller, Thomson LLP; Ogilvy, Renault; Osler, Hoskin, and Harcourt LLP; Paliare, Roland, Rosenberg, Rothstein LLP; Ridout, Maybee LLP; Shearman and Sterling LLP; Skadden, Arps, Slate, Meagher and Flom LLP; Smart and Biggar; Stikeman, Elliott LLP; Torkin, Manes, Cohen, and Arbus LLP; Torys LLP; various provincial government ministries; Farris, Vaughan, Wills and Murphy; Lawson Lundell; Sangra Moller; Cadwalader, Wichersham and Taft; Clifford Chance; Davis, Polk, and Wardwell; Milbank, Tweed, Hadley and McCloy; Paul, Weiss, Rifkind, Wharton, and Garrison; Sidley Austin; Sullivan and Cromwell; Weil, Gotshal, and Manges; White and Case.
State for bar exam: ON
Pass rate for first-time bar: 98

Grads employed by field:	%
Business/Industry	1
Government	9
Judicial clerkships	6
Other	3
Private practice	77
Public Interest	4

SCHOOL SAYS

In this section you'll find schools with extended listings describing admissions, curriculum, internships, and much more. This is your chance to get in-depth information on programs that interest you. The Princeton Review charges each school a small fee to be listed, and the editorial responsibility is solely that of the university.

BAYLOR UNIVERSITY
School of Law

AT A GLANCE
Baylor Law School stands at the forefront of practice-oriented law schools nationally. Baylor is singularly clear about its mission—to equip students upon graduation to practice law effectively and ethically. That is the key difference. Students are trained and mentored in all facets of law, including theoretical analysis, practical application, legal writing, advocacy, professional responsibility, and negotiation and counseling skills.

Baylor graduates excel in top law firms, the judiciary, government service, business, and in all areas of the practice of law. They do so because they know how to practice law.

Baylor Law School is committed to enrolling classes that are highly credentialed and rich in diversity.

CAMPUS AND LOCATION
An excellent quality of life in a friendly environment awaits you in Waco. Baylor Law School is located on the campus of Baylor University in Waco, Texas. Waco is located in central Texas, has a population of more than 220,000, and offers a diverse and rich array of cultural activities. Baylor also is a member of the powerful Big 12 conference and offers students the excitement of Big 12 athletic events, ranging from football, basketball, baseball and softball to tennis, golf, track and field, volleyball, soccer, cross country, and equestrian.

PROGRAMS AND CURRICULUM
Baylor's required curriculum is structured to provide a logical progression for legal study from fundamental legal doctrine in first-year courses to increasingly more sophisticated and complex second- and third-year courses. The challenging curriculum, along with the opportunity to perform specialized lawyering tasks under the direct supervision of accomplished lawyers, prepares students for the rigors of any type of modern legal practice. Additionally, students have the opportunity to complete a more concentrated course of study and training in six areas of interest: general civil litigation, estate planning, business litigation, business transactions, criminal practice, and administrative practice.

The bedrock of Baylor's nationally ranked advocacy program is the third-year Practice Court program. Procedure, evidence, and advocacy are the tools of the trial lawyer, and the Practice Court program is an ultra-intensive study of these essentials. Students try multiple lawsuits from beginning to end. Whether or not students want to be a trial attorney, this course prepares all Baylor students to be confident, responsible, competent and ethical lawyers as they embark upon their chosen career path.

FACILITIES
The home of Baylor Law School is the award-winning Sheila & Walter Umphrey Law Center. The building houses every facility a modern law school requires: spacious and comfortable classrooms, practice courtrooms, an extensive law library, a student lounge and dining area, many interview, study, and conference rooms, and hard-wired and wireless connectivity throughout the building.

FACULTY
Baylor Law School has a dedicated faculty. Baylor is first a teaching school and one of the only law schools in the nation in which the granting of tenure is primarily based on a professor's teaching effectiveness. Faculty members hold degrees from law schools and universities throughout the nation. They are experts in their particular areas of the law and have significant practical experience as practicing lawyers —experience they bring to the classroom.

One of the distinctive features of the faculty is that professors maintain unrestricted hours for student consultation. Every professor is available for lending advice and guidance in all academic, professional, and other matters of concern to students.

ADMISSIONS
Baylor Law School's mission is to enroll classes that are highly credentialed and rich in diversity. It also seeks to enroll exceptionally motivated students who have strong work ethics, who will enrich the student body, and who will make a distinctive contribution to the legal profession. In addition to an applicant's undergraduate grade point average and LSAT score, the Admissions Committee takes into consideration such factors as letters of recommendation, academic achievements, extracurricular activities, work experience, other evidence of maturity, and a strong work ethic as well as the ability to contribute to the diversity of the Baylor community. The applicant's ability to communicate clearly and concisely, as evidenced through the personal statement, is also a key factor.

Baylor Law School operates on a quarter system, and one advantage of the quarter system is the flexibility it affords applicants in determining when to matriculate. The law school has classes in three of its four quarters—spring, summer, and fall. Each matriculating class has a separate application pool, and applicants are required to apply to the quarter in which they would like to begin.

CAREER SERVICES AND PLACEMENT
Employers value Baylor lawyers for three reasons: Our graduates are more prepared . . . they're more polished and professional . . . and they graduate knowing how to practice law. The Career Service Office is committed year-round to providing students with the support and resources they need in pursuing their chosen career paths. Shortly after graduation, 98 percent of our 2006 graduates were employed or enrolled in graduate degree programs. Our graduates have launched careers in practice, state, and federal judicial clerkships, government agencies, public interest organizations, as well as academic and business entities. Our graduates practice in 48 states and several foreign countries.

Baylor's record of success on the Texas bar exam is unsurpassed by any other Texas law school. In February 2007, 100 percent of Baylor graduates passed the Texas bar exam. This is compared to the average bar passage rate for the February bar exam in Texas of 79 percent. Baylor graduates taking other state bar exams have been exceptionally successful as well.

CHAPMAN UNIVERSITY
School of Law

AT A GLANCE

Chapman University was founded in 1861. The School of Law was established in 1995. The School of Law received ABA accreditation in 2002. In 2006, the School of Law received AALS accreditation.

Programs of study include Juris Doctor

Certificate Programs: Tax Law; Environmental, Land Use, and Real Estate Law; Advocacy and Dispute Resolution; Joint JD/MBA with Chapman's George L. Argyros School of Business; LLM Program in Taxation

Clinical programs in Tax Law, Elder Law, Constitutional Litigation, and Appellate Practice.

DEGREES

Chapman University School of Law offers the traditional Juris Doctor, the LLM degree in Taxation Law, and a dual JD/MBA degree.

GENERAL ACADEMIC PROGRAMS

The Law School requires 88 academic credits for graduation. First-year courses are required and cover traditional subjects: Contracts, Torts, Civil Procedure, Property, Criminal Law, and Legal Research and Writing. Several upper-level courses are also required in the following areas: constitutional law, corporations, evidence, federal income taxation, and professional responsibility.

Students may choose to focus their electives in one of three certificate areas: taxation, environmental/real estate/land use, or advocacy and dispute resolution.

Clinic offerings include courses in Appellate Practice, Elder Law, Constitutional Litigation, and Tax Law. These clinical opportunities allow students to represent actual clients in an array of legal settings.

The law school also offers an externship program in which students receive placements in the offices of appellate justices, trial judges, district attorneys, or public defenders, among others. In this program, students receive academic credit for hands-on legal experience.

EXPENSES AND FINANCIAL AID

Tuition: $32,780

Fees: $255

Estimated room and board per academic year:

On and off campus $13, 320

FACULTY

There are 36 full-time faculty members; 39 percent of our faculty are women and 11 percent of our faculty are minorities. The part-time faculty represents 40 percent of the total faculty. The 2006 student to faculty ratio was 16 to 1.

STUDENT BODY

Chapman University School of Law is an ideal environment for learning. The total student body of the law school numbers about 550.

The first-year students will be divided into three tracks of 60-65 students each. They will be further divided into considerably smaller sections of 12 to 15 students for the Legal Research and Writing component.

The minority representation of the entering class has been 26 percent. The average age is between 20 and 55. With respect to geographic representation, 18 percent of the 2006 entering class was from states other than California. The gender breakdown for the fall 2006 entering class was 58 percent men and 42 percent women.

ADMISSIONS

Chapman University School of Law has a rolling admissions policy. The application deadline for the Fall 2007 class was June 1. The February LSAT is the last test you can take to be considered for the Fall 2007 class.

The admissions process is highly competitive with over 2,300 applications for only 200 seats in the entering class.

Applicants are required to submit a formal application, personal statement, resume, two letters of recommendation, $60 nonrefundable application fee, and the LSDAS report from the Law School Admission Council (LSAC). The LSDAS report generally includes your LSAT score(s), official transcript(s), and letters of recommendation. A resume and addendums or optional essays are also acceptable.

Applicants should be advised that the law school reviews all LSAT scores and does not accept LSAT scores that are more than five years old.

Applicants who have graduated from college within the past five years are strongly encouraged to seek letters of recommendation from professors who have taught them in one or more courses.

Applicants may download a PDF version of the application from our website at www.chapman.edu/law, or elect to use the electronic application on the web from www.lsac.org. The electronic application is preferred.

When all of the aforementioned documents have been received by the Office of Admissions the file is considered complete and it advances to the Admissions Committee for careful review and decision. It generally takes a few weeks from the date an application is complete for a formal decision to be rendered and communicated to the applicant.

SPECIAL PROGRAMS

In addition to its three certificate programs and its clinical and externship programs, Chapman Law School offers a special JD/MBA joint-degree opportunity. This program affords students the ability to obtain two separate, accredited professional degrees in a shorter period than would normally be required to obtain the degrees independently. The adequately prepared student may obtain both degrees in four years rather than the typical five years. Chapman's George L. Argyros School of Business and Economics is AACSB accredited.

Chapman Law School also offers a Master of Laws in Taxation (LLM), and students in the JD program who are well-prepared in the taxation area may take courses otherwise open only to LLM students.

CAREER SERVICES AND PLACEMENT

Chapman law students successfully find satisfying employment with the assistance of the professionals in the Career Services Office. The office strives to provide Chapman students with the necessary skills to navigate the legal job market and to market the law school and its students to legal employers.

In recent years, approximately 85–90 percent of each graduating class has been able to secure employment within nine months of graduation.

Employment statistics for the Class of 2006 are as follows:

Employment nine months after graduation: 86%

Percentage of graduates enrolled in a full-time degree program: 7%

Percentage of graduates status unknown: 7%

Average starting salary of all 2006 graduates: $72,564

FAULKER UNIVERSITY
Thomas Goode Jones School of Law

AT A GLANCE

Faulkner University's Thomas Goode Jones School of Law is committed to the education of outstanding lawyers. In keeping with its distinctive Christian mission, the school embraces academic excellence and emphasizes a strong commitment to integrity within a caring Christian environment that sustains and nurtures faith. Students are encouraged to dedicate their lives to the service of others.

CAMPUS AND LOCATION

The School of Law is located in the capital of Alabama. Montgomery is widely known as the birthplace of the Confederacy and the Civil Rights movement.

The campus is located just a few miles from the Alabama State Capitol Building; the Alabama Judicial Building which houses the Alabama Supreme Court, the State Law Library, the Court of Civil Appeals and the Court of Criminal Appeals; and the Frank M. Johnson United States Courthouse Complex.

DEGREES

The school of law offers the Juris Doctor degree through a full-time program or part-time program.

ACADEMIC PROGRAMS GENERAL

The school of law's curriculum is comprised of fundamental courses such as Civil Procedure, Constitutional Law, Contracts Law, Criminal Law, Evidence, Professional Responsibility, Property Law and Torts Law. The school also offers an extensive Legal Research and Writing program and a broad elective curriculum with courses in every area of law. Each student is appointed a faculty advisor who assists with course selection, particularly if a student wishes to pursue a certain area in depth.

The school offers three clinical programs: the Mediation Clinic, the Family Violence Clinic, and the Elder Law Clinic. The Mediation Clinic allows students to mediate cases set for trial at Montgomery County District Court. The Family Violence Clinic provides pro bono services for clients unable to pay for representation, and works in conjunction with the Legal Services Corporation of Alabama and the Family Sunshine Center. The Elder Law Clinic allows students to represent low-income, elderly citizens in area counties. It works in cooperation with Legal Services Corporation of Alabama and the Alabama Department of Senior Services.

The School of Law's Advocacy Program is a vibrant program that provides students with the opportunity to hone their courtroom skills. Students can participate in national competitions in appellate advocacy and trial advocacy. Also, the school hosts the Greg Allen Intra-School Mock Trial Competition and 1L Moot Court Competition each year.

FACILITIES

The school of law is housed in a beautiful, neofederal-style building that accommodates the George H. Jones Jr. Law Library, the Judge Walter B. Jones Moot Court Room, and the Institute for Dispute Resolution. It includes state-of-the-art research and lecture Facilities with seven classrooms and two large conference rooms. All classrooms are outfitted for laptop computers and wireless Internet is available throughout the building and library.

EXPENSES AND FINANCIAL AID

Tuition for the academic year of 2007–08 is $22,000 for a full-time student and $16,500 for a part-time student. Cost of attendance for a full-time student is $40,900 (this includes tuition) and for a part-time student it is $27,440.

Students can seek educational loans through the Federal Stafford Loan program and through private lenders. The school of law offers merit-based scholarships to qualified entering students. Admitted applicants are automatically under scholarship consideration. Scholarships are limited in number therefore prospective students are encouraged to apply early in the admissions cycle.

FACULTY

The School of Law's curriculum is taught by a dynamic group of faculty. Professors challenge students, welcome ideas, and encourage debate. With a low student-to-faculty ratio and an emphasis on small class sizes and personalized instruction, the school provides a more intimate atmosphere that enhances a student's educational experience. The student-to-faculty to ratio is 11 to 1.

STUDENT BODY

The school of law hosts eleven student organizations. Those are: American Constitution Society, American Association for Justice, Black Law Students Association, Christian Legal Society, Delta Theta Phi, Federalist Society, Honor Court, Jones Law Review, Phi Alpha Delta, Student Bar Association, and Women Students Association.

ADMISSIONS

The school of law seeks to enroll a highly qualified and diverse student body. The two primary criteria used to make Admissions decisions are an applicant's LSAT score and cumulative undergraduate grade point average. Other factors considered are the applicant's personal statement, undergraduate school, undergraduate and/or graduate courses of study, grade trends, community service/involvement and professional employment history. Letters of recommendation are welcome but not required.

SPECIAL PROGRAMS

The Alternative Dispute Resolution (ADR) program enables law students to integrate their knowledge of conflict management principles and dispute resolution processes with professional skills. This program allows students to receive training normally available only through on-the-job experience after graduation.

Students can earn a certificate in ADR, which is not a supplemental degree but an opportunity for Juris Doctor candidates to enrich his or her skills training while still in law school. The certificate in ADR requires completion of the following courses: Arbitration, Dispute Resolution Processes, Interviewing/Counseling and Negotiation, Mediation Clinic, and an elective skills course. All of the certificate courses contain both an academic component and a skills component.

As part of a Christian university, the school of law seeks not only to provide legal knowledge and practical skills necessary to produce competent and ethical members of the legal community, but also to instill in students an attitude of service. This commitment to serve those who otherwise could not afford such assistance complements the legal profession's rich tradition of service.

The Public Interest program provides opportunities for students to begin their career of service while utilizing the practical skills obtained in their legal education. This program is voluntary and provides students with opportunities to work for nonprofit organizations, government agencies, and private attorneys or firms conducting pro bono legal work. Students are challenged to perform at least 35 hours of voluntary service during the academic year. This goal can be met in less than 4.5 hours per month.

CAREER SERVICES AND PLACEMENT

The School of Law's Career Services Office provides a full range of services to support students and alumni in their job search process. It actively develops relationships with employers, alumni, and professional organizations to assist students in developing a network of professional contacts. The school boasts a 96 percent placement rate for its graduates.

FLORIDA INTERNATIONAL UNIVERSITY
College of Law

AT A GLANCE

The College of Law at Florida International University offers a curriculum that prepares students for ethical and effective practice of law in an increasingly global and multicultural world. In addition to the traditional law course work, the curriculum incorporates important developments in the globalization of both public and private law. The academic program takes a pervasive approach to international and comparative law, incorporating these perspectives into all domestic law classes. The College of Law curriculum further provides students with extensive, rigorous legal research and writing experiences, introduces skills such as counseling and negotiation, and stresses the important professional values of civility and ethical practice.

CAMPUS AND LOCATION

FIU is location in beautiful Miami, part of South Florida. Surrounded by the natural beauty of the Everglades, Biscayne National Park, and the Florida Keys, Miami is a metropolitan destination known for its cultural diversity, bustling nightlife, and gorgeous beaches.

ACADEMIC PROGRAMS

In addition to the JD degree, FIU also offers a number of joint-degree programs: JD/MBA (Master of Business Administration); JD/MIB (Master of International Business); JD/MALACS (Master of Latin American and Caribbean Studies); JD/MPA (Masters of Public Administration); JD/MHSA (Masters of Health Services Administration); JD/MSW (Masters of Social Work).

Part-time and full-time programs are offered in the JD program.

PROGRAMS AND CURRICULUM

The College of Law curriculum seeks produce students that will practice law in an ethical, effective manner. Combining core classes found at most law schools, the College of Law's courses also feature a short comparison of other countries' handling of legal issues.

A student's first year curriculum consists of 31 hours of course work to provide the foundation for practicing law in Florida or anywhere else. The upper-level curriculum will vary for each student, depending on his or her interests. Only two courses are required: Legal Skills and Values III and Professional Responsibility, but courses must be taken in a broad range of subject matters.

FACILITIES

FIU's law library is available to all students, faculty, and the general public. With more than 200,000 volumes, the library is still growing. The library houses group study rooms, computer labs, carrels, and connections for laptops. Students have access to the library's electronic resources, including the web-based library catalog, subscription databases, and selected Internet resources.

EXPENSES & FINANCIAL AID

Tuition and Fees (full-time, resident): $8,848

Tuition and Fees (full-time, nonresident): $23,634

Room/Board: $10,060

Financial aid is available to students through loans and merit-based scholarships. To begin the process, students should fill out the Free Application for Federal Student Aid (FAFSA).

STUDENTS

Students will find plenty to do at FIU, on-campus and off. Student organizations include the Asian Pacific American Law Student Association, Black Law Student Association, Cuban-American Law Society, Criminal Law Society, Federalists Society, Hispanic Law Student Association, Human Rights and Environmental Law Society, International Human Rights and Environmental Law Society, Republican National Lawyers Association, Sports Entertainment Law Society, Student Bar Association, Women in Law.

ADMISSIONS

The College of Law seeks to enroll students that have succeeded academically and personally. In addition to the LSAT and academic record, the college also weighs the candidate's leadership experience, community service, command of global issues, work history, military service, any history of criminality or academic misconduct and evidence of obstacles that an applicant may have overcome (for example, English is not the applicant's native language, discrimination, economic or family hardship, severe medical condition, etc.).

To apply, please submit:

1. application for admission with $20 nonrefundable application fee
2. LSAT Test scores
3. official transcripts
4. academic honors, extracurricular activities, and work experience
5. three letters of recommendation

Please visit law.fiu.edu for information regarding International students and transfer students.

SPECIAL PROGRAMS

The FIU College of Law Review is a student-run scholarly law journal. Members are accepted after the first year (full-time students) or second year (part-time students) based on a writing competition.

The FIU Board of Advocates is a student-run moot court that enables students to use their knowledge in a variety of competitions. Competitions are held regionally and nationally in areas such as international appellate advocacy, trial advocacy, client counseling, mediation and negotiation.

FIU also sponsors international student exchanges with universities around the world. Students may spend a semester abroad at a foreign university and transfer the units toward their JD degree.

There are three clinics that enable students to apply their classroom learning to actual cases. The Carlos A. Costa Immigration and Human Rights Clinic, Community Development Clinic, and Criminal Law Clinic, which serves low-income clients, enabling students to represent real people in a supervised setting.

CAREER SERVICES AND PLACEMENT

The Career Planning & Placement Office provides resources and information for the College of Law. The office provides a career resource library, job search programs, job postings, individual counseling, and mock interviews.

Your success is the CPPO's goal. They can provide you with resume help—or help you land a judicial clerkship right after graduation.

FORDHAM UNIVERSITY
School of Law

AT A GLANCE

Fordham Law School prides itself on offering the complete legal education. Fordham educates lawyers' lawyers. Our students present some of the strongest credentials in the country with grades, scores, and experiences putting them in the top 15 student bodies in the country. They are supported by a full time faculty of 74 and countless adjuncts drawn from the best of the bar and bench in New York. Our graduates are represented in the top New York and national law firms. In fact, Fordham is the fifth most represented school among the 25 most profitable firms. Fordham alumni, supported by a generous LRAP, are also well represented in the public sector. As to government work, not only are our alumni federal and state judicial clerks, but Fordham has been the largest provider of Assistant District Attorneys to New York and Kings counties.

CAMPUS AND LOCATION

Located in New York City on the Upper West Side, across from Lincoln Center and a block from Central Park, Fordham is also a few blocks from midtown Manhattan, and a subway ride from Wall Street. It is in perhaps the best location in the greatest city in the world. Although admissions standards are quite competitive, Fordham has a reputation as a friendly law school where faculty-student collaboration is the norm and students work with, rather than against each other. Whether this is because of the opportunities available to our graduates, our clinical and dispute resolution programs or the innate qualities of the students themselves can be the subject of friendly debate.

DEGREES OFFERED

Fordham offers the JD degree through a full or part time program. In addition, three LLM degrees are offered in international trade, banking and intellectual property. Joint JD/MBA, JD/MA in International Political Economy, and JD/MSW are offered.

PROGRAMS AND CURRICULUM

Fordham offers 13 different clinics ranging from traditional criminal defense through family law, securities arbitration and community economic development. Through the clinics, more than 300 students annually are involved in live client and simulation courses.

There are six student edited journals at Fordham as well as two intramural moot court competitions. *Fordham Law Review* is among the top ten cited student law reviews nationally and the Fordham International Law Journal and *Fordham Urban Law Journal* are among the top ten cited specialty journals.

Fordham's programs in business law, alternative dispute resolution, law and philosophy, legal history and international law are ranked among the top 20 nationally.

Fordham offers summer programs in Ireland/Northern Irish Republic and in South Korea.

EXPENSES AND FINANCIAL AID

Tuition and fees in 2005–2006 full time was $35,141, part-time, $26,398

A private room (in a 3-bedroom apartment) in McMahon Hall – Lincoln Center Campus is $11,320 for the academic year.

About 80 percent of our students receive some sort of financial assistance. Fordham awards the majority of its aid on a need basis. There is limited merit aid that is guaranteed for all three (or 4 part-time) years.

FACULTY

Fordham has one of the largest law faculties nationally with 74 full-time faculty. Our faculty are drawn to our current faculty of teachers and researchers, superb students and the classroom. We are also fortunate to draw on the practical experience of the New York bench and bar to supplement this faculty. Our adjunct faculty are as drawn to our students and the teaching opportunities as our full-time faculty. There is much faculty-student and faculty/faculty collaboration. Our full-time faculty published over 100 articles, 14 books, and 13 book chapters/parts last year

STUDENTS

Learning and service continue outside of the classroom as well. There are 42 student groups and activities on campus. These range from the 14 groups affiliated with our Public Interest Law Center, to social, political, and co-curricular groups. Last year, our students provided in excess of 64,000 hours of pro bono public service while in law school. This service is an important part of the Fordham community. Of course, New York City can be its own diversion!

ADMISSIONS

In addition to top undergraduate grades and LSAT scores, Fordham is looking for students willing to engage with each other and work to bring out the best in each other. Whether in the classroom, study groups, informal groups gathering in the hall, student activities or service projects, Fordham students are part of an incredible learning community. We look for students to have been involved in their college campus life, their communities, and their work environment. We have historically been a "gateway" school, opening professional opportunities to generations of lawyers.

CAREER SERVICES AND PLACEMENT

Many of our students are attracted to Fordham for the placement opportunities after graduation. Most of our graduates choose to work in New York City after graduation, although many more are returning to their hometowns or working in other major markets. We also are a very strong feeder to government jobs, including judicial clerkships, district/state/federal attorneys and the public service. Our graduates win prestigious New York and national fellowships. The Office of Career Services provides programming throughout the year ranging from resume review and interview skills to regional programs to financial planning to on-campus interviews with over 5,000 employers, to individual counseling. Our alumni network, 15,000 members strong, and are great supporters of our students.

THE GEORGE WASHINGTON UNIVERSITY
Law School

CAMPUS AND LOCATION

The Law School is located on the main campus of The George Washington University in the downtown Washington, DC, area known as Foggy Bottom. GW's urban campus is spread over 18 city blocks, and its architectural details, brick courtyards, and green spaces help it fit seamlessly into the surrounding community. Across the street from the Law School are the World Bank and IMF, and the White House is just four blocks away. The State Department, Kennedy Center for the Performing Arts, and numerous other governmental and arts organizations are all in the immediate vicinity.

DEGREES OFFERED

In addition to the JD; GW offers several joint and advanced degrees. Joint degrees include: JD/MBA; JD/MPA; and JD/MP; J/MA; and JD/MPH. The Master of Laws (LLM) is an advanced degree program for law school graduates who wish to pursue an academic career or to enhance their knowledge for practice in a specialized area. The law school admits a very limited number of candidates for the Doctor of Juridical Science (SJD) degree.

ACADEMIC PROGRAMS

Students have the opportunity to sample a broad array of areas of the law with more than 250 elective courses and seminars. In addition to traditionally taught classes, the Law School offers a number of simulation, drafting, and writing skills courses that require students to translate the study of the law into action, and help to prepare graduates to work effectively in a broad range of practice areas. Many of these courses are taught or co-taught by judges and practicing attorneys.

The Law School's extensive clinical program gives students the opportunity to work with clients—many of whom might otherwise be without representation—while at the same time honing their counseling, advocacy, research, and negotiating skills. Drawing on surrounding institutions, the law school also provides unparalleled opportunities for students to pursue externships in government agencies, nonprofit organizations, and courts.

FACILITIES

The Law School's attractive and comfortable classrooms and moot court rooms incorporate technology to support a broad range of teaching methods. In addition, power outlets for notebook computers are provided at each student station in most classrooms, and there are more than 70 wireless access points throughout the facility.

The core of the Jacob Burns Law Library's research collection comprises more than 500,000 volumes. The library offers a variety of legal and law-related databases and automated indexes to enhance research capabilities. The staff administers and maintains the library during its liberal hours of operation and offers information, instruction, and other research support services. Students also have full access to the many amenities of the GW campus, including a state-of-the-art fitness complex.

EXPENSES AND FINANCIAL AID

The Law Financial Aid Office counsels and assists applicants and current students in applying for various sources of financial aid: federal and commercial loans at negotiated, competitive terms, need-based tuition grants, and outside scholarships. All applicants are considered for merit based aid. An estimated 85 percent of GW law students receive some sort of financial aid. The law school's Loan Reimbursement Assistance Program (LRAP) is designed to alleviate the financial burdens of graduates who pursue public interest employment.

FACULTY

One of the law school's greatest assets is an exceptionally talented and accessible faculty whose contributions are not limited to the classroom, but instead reach deeply into the students' academic and professional development. While dedicated to excellence in teaching, the faculty also remains at the forefront of legal scholarship both at the national and international level. Their practical experience adds an important perspective to their presentation of theoretical principles of the law.

STUDENT BODY

GW is one of the largest law schools in the U.S. In fall 2006, 1,919 degree candidates from the U.S. and more than 30 foreign countries were enrolled at the law school. The student body is one of the most diverse in the country, and this diversity greatly enhances the learning environment. For both full-time and part-time students, participation in the academic and social life of the school beyond the classroom greatly enhances and broadens their educational experience.

ADMISSIONS

In 2006, GW Law's entering JD class was selected from a pool of more than 9,800 applicants. All materials submitted by the applicant (including the personal statement and letters of recommendation, if submitted) are considered before a decision is made. There are no inflexible standards, nor are there minimum grade-point averages or LSAT scores that are required. However, students whose undergraduate records and LSAT scores indicate a high probability of success in law study are more likely to be admitted.

SPECIAL PROGRAMS

GW Law offers two summer programs: the Oxford–GW Summer Program in International Human Rights Law and the Munich Intellectual Property Summer Program; and two exchange programs: North American Consortium on Legal Education (NACLE), a consortium of nine law schools and research institutes from the NAFTA countries, and the GW University of Augsburg (Germany) Student Exchange Program.

CAREER SERVICES AND PLACEMENT

The CDO's mission is to provide effective career advising services to students enabling them to engage in a meaningful job search, to compete as professionals in the employment market, and to make well-informed choices leading to long-term career satisfaction. The CDO fulfills its mission through a broad range of services including individual counseling, group seminars, substantive legal practice area programs, interviewing programs, job and internship fairs, online job postings, a resource library, the *Alumni Career Advisor Network*, a biweekly newsletter, and a comprehensive website.

HAMLINE UNIVERSITY
School of Law

AT A GLANCE

Hamline University School of Law, founded in 1972, is accredited by the American Bar Association (ABA) and a member of the Association of American Law Schools (AALS). Hamline is located in the heart of the Twin Cities of Saint Paul and Minneapolis, noted as "one of the top ten cities in the US" by Cityrating.com.

CAMPUS AND LOCATION

Hamline Law School is located among 55 acres of wooded campus in the vibrant, urban centers of Minneapolis/St. Paul. The Twin Cities are home to many corporate headquarters, including 3M, Cargill, Medtronic, Target Corporation, and General Mills. Additionally, the Twin Cities are a center for diverse cultural, social, political and educational opportunities.

DEGREES OFFERED

Hamline Law School offers a full-time three year JD degree and a part-time, four year weekend program. An LLM degree for International lawyers is also offered.

Dual degrees are available in Public Administration, Management, Non-profit Management, Organizational Leadership, and Library and Information Science.

PROGRAMS AND CURRICULUM

Hamline's nationally-ranked Alternative Dispute Resolution (ADR) program provides a full range of ADR-related programming including a summer institute, January term courses, certificate programs, and a biannual symposium. A new Health Law Center will focus on the growth of health law, federal regulation, tort reform, medical device development and regulation, and ethics. The curriculum also supports twelve organized tracks of study or focus areas. These include: business representation, children and the law, civil dispute resolution, commercial law, criminal law, government and regulatory affairs, intellectual property, international law, labor and employment law, and social justice.

FACILITIES

Hamline Law School's architectural design encourages easy access to faculty and administrative offices. Wireless internet access is available throughout the building. The newly renovated moot courtroom is a technological showplace. Hamline's law library provides modern collections of print, electronic and microform resources. The library contains more than 266,000 volumes and numerous electronic databases. In addition, students have access to the libraries of seven other colleges and universities through a consortium arrangement. The library has a computer lab with 30 personal computers, wireless access, and numerous network ports.

EXPENSES AND FINANCIAL AID

Hamline University School of Law is a private school. Full-time tuition for the 2006-2007 academic year is $26,786. Hamline offers merit-based scholarships, diversity scholarships and endowed scholarships for first-year students.

FACULTY

Hamline Law School has 39 full-time faculty members: 18 women and 21 men. Adjunct faculty complements the faculty by teaching upper-division courses in specialty areas. Hamline has recently invested in growing its faculty, with nationally recognized experts in bio-ethics, intellectual property, international trade, corporate law, and critical race theory. These faculty members join a faculty nationally recognized for scholarship and academic leadership in dispute resolution, commercial law, state constitutional law, and many other fields. The Hamline faculty is committed to an "open door" policy to help students learn and enjoy the law.

STUDENT BODY

Hamline Law School's student body includes approximately 720 students from diverse backgrounds. As a student-centered community, Hamline student organizations play a key role in the vitality of the law school environment. More than 20 student organizations focus on students' cultural and professional interests.

ADMISSIONS

The admission selection process emphasizes a rigorous but fair examination of each person's application. In addition to the LSAT and undergraduate GPA, other factors are given significant weight including motivation, personal experiences, employment history, graduate education, maturity, letters of recommendation, and the ability to express one's interest in the study of law.

SPECIAL PROGRAMS

Hamline's ten clinics offer students the opportunity to develop litigation, transactional and alternative dispute resolution skills. The Practicum program combines 114 hours of field experience with a classroom component focused on enhancing a student's lawyering skills. Moot court and similar competitions involve legal research, brief writing, and oral argument. Hamline is home to three scholarly journals. Hamline law students staff the *Hamline Law Review* and the *Hamline Journal of Public Law and Policy*, and provide editorial assistance for *The Journal of Law and Religion*. Hamline law school offers unique study abroad opportunities in Norway, Italy, France, Hungary, England, Israel, and Puerto Rico.

CAREER SERVICES AND PLACEMENT

The Career Services Office (CSO) provides informational programs, mock interviews, one-on-one counseling, networking opportunities, and an online job bank. It also hosts on-campus interviews for interested employers and works extensively with employers to market Hamline law students.

NORTHERN ILLINOIS UNIVERSITY
College of Law

AT A GLANCE
NIU College of Law is a young and dynamic school celebrating its twenty-fifth anniversary. The college of law is accredited by the American Bar Association and is a member of the Association of American Law Schools. As the only public law school in the Greater Chicago area, the College of Law was founded on a core belief that a high-quality, challenging legal education should not be cost prohibitive.

CAMPUS & LOCATION
NIU College of Law is located in DeKalb, Illinois, 65 miles west of Chicago. The main campus spans 756 acres and offers students a tranquil but urban setting.

DEGREES OFFERED
JD; Part-time, full-time programs available

PROGRAMS AND CURRICULUM
The primary purpose of the college of law is to train effective lawyers through a program of quality legal education. The college has identified and continues to develop three special areas of emphasis: practice competence; public service/public interest; dispute resolution.

Students may choose to directly experience the practice of law in the hands-on settings afforded by the clinical experiences and externship programs.

Clinical courses allow students to experience the representation of clients, or the role of a neutral, in discreet areas of practice under the direct supervision of a well-qualified attorney. The clinical opportunities include: the Criminal Defense Clinic; the Domestic Abuse Clinic; the Elder Law Clinic; and the Mediation Clinic.

Externship programs permit qualified students to experience the daily practice of an attorney, mediator, or judicial clerk, under the direct supervision of a practicing attorney or sitting judge. Opportunities include: the Appellate Defender Externship; the Civil Externship; Criminal Externship; Judicial Externship; and Juvenile Mediation Externship.

FACILITIES
The David B. Shapiro Library houses more than 229,000 volumes including U.S. Government documents and audiovisual materials. The library also has a computer lab exclusively for law students with access to LexisNexis and WESTLAW. NIU law library is a member of the American Association of Law Libraries.

Zeke Giorgi Legal Clinic is a place for students to use their education in real-world cases. Advocacy and direct representation of clients allow students to build their understanding of the law and the professional responsibility necessary in the law profession.

EXPENSES
Educational & Living Expenses per Year

Tuition (in-state/out-of-state): $9,552/$19,104

Fees: $1,682

Insurance: $654

Books and supplies (approximately): $1,500

Housing: $7,850

Travel: $ 500

Miscellaneous personal expenses: $1,976

FACULTY
NIU College of Law's experienced faculty is committed to educating tomorrow's leaders. With the focus on the students, the faculty emphasizes public service. NIU's faculty members are recognized around the world as experts in their field and are recognized by serving on committees and being presenters at conferences around the country. The faculty is diverse, with 45 percent of the faculty being people of color.

STUDENTS
The students at NIU College of Law are a diverse group, enabling the study of law to be multicultural and multifaceted, as it is in the real-world. Last year's entering class of 133 students was 47 percent women, 14 percent minority, with an average age of 25.5 years.

Outside the classroom, students are part of a number of organizations such as the Asian Law Student Network, Black Law Students Association, and the Women's Law Caucus. The Student Bar Association enables students to become actively involved in their community, as the organization supports other law associations on campus and sponsors events such as picnics, parties, and special speakers.

NIU also has a student run moot court which allows students to participate in competitions within the school, as well as regional and national competitions.

ADMISSIONS
Students can apply to NIU College of Law by submitting the following documents:

- NIU College of Law application (either via the College of Law home page or the LSACD from Law Services.) A separate, additional application is required for the part-time option.

- A minimum of two letters to the Law Services' letter of recommendation that is part of the LSDAS registration subscription. The letter of recommendation forms are available online at www.lsac.org. All you need to do is identify your recommenders, print out your pre-filled letter of recommendation forms, and give the forms to the appropriate recommenders.

- A nonrefundable application fee of $50.

- A personal goal statement.

- An official transcript verifying your baccalaureate degree.

Applicants must also take the LSAT and complete the Law School Data Assembly Service (LSDAS) report.

The priority deadline for applications is March 1.

SPECIAL PROGRAMS
Externship programs permit qualified students to experience the daily practice of an attorney, mediator, or judicial clerk under the direct supervision of a practicing attorney or sitting judge. Opportunities include: the Appellate Defender Externship; the Civil Externship; Criminal Externship; Judicial Externship; and Juvenile Mediation Externship.

SUMMER PROGRAM IN FRANCE
NIU offers a summer program abroad in Agen, France. Courses are taught in international and comparative law by NIU law school faculty in cooperation with the law faculty of the University of Bordeaux-Montesquieu IV.

SAMFORD UNIVERSITY
Cumberland School of Law

AT A GLANCE
The Cumberland School of Law has been a member of the Association of American Law Schools (AALS) since 1952 and has been accredited by the American Bar Association (ABA) since 1949.

DEGREES OFFERED
To broaden their thinking or help them prepare for careers in special fields, Cumberland students may opt to pursue seven different joint degrees: JD/MAcc, JD/MBA, JD/MPH, JD/MPA, JD/MDiv, JD/MTS, and JD/MS in Environmental Management. The graduate degree of Master of Comparative Law (MCL) is offered to international law school graduates.

PROGRAMS AND CURRICULUM
Students select from a broad range of classes in areas such as corporate law, litigation, tax law, health law, intellectual property, environmental law, public interest law, family law, estate planning, international law, and others. (Please visit www.cumberland.samford.edu to view Cumberland School of Law's extensive course list.)

ADVOCACY AND SKILLS TRAINING
Cumberland's emphasis on teaching students the art and science of courtroom advocacy begins in the first-year curriculum, where a six-credit, two-semester course titled Lawyering and Legal Reasoning provides students hands-on practical instruction in prelitigation skills such as client interviewing, counseling, memorandum preparation, and negotitaion; pre-trial litigation skills, including summary judgment motions and making compelling oral arguments; and appellate litigation skills. This intensive course prepares students to work effectively in their first summer clerkships where they may be expected to research cases and write briefs in their first week.

The new Advanced Trial Advocacy Courtroom provides students with access to modern technology found in courtrooms across the country. In Cumberland's Advanced Trial Advocacy course, students can access databases and the internet at each counsel table and learn how to reproduce evidence with 3D digital presenters, video, and DVD re-enactments.

CENTER FOR BIOTECHNOLOGY, LAW, & ETHICS
Dedicated to furthering practical training in the legal disciplines critical to biotechnology, Cumberland's unique program builds on a base of intellectual property, health care, environmental, tort, and natural resources law.

INTERNATIONAL LAW
Cumberland conducts three ABA-approved international summer programs that are offered at Sidney Sussex College, Cambridge, England; The University of Victoria, British Columbia, Canada; and Federal University of Ceara, Fortaleza, Brazil. The graduate degree of Master of Comparative Law (MCL) is offered to international law school graduates.

ONLINE LEARNING AT CUMBERLAND SCHOOL OF LAW
Cumberland's iNetCourses represent special classes in which all or some portion of the substantive course materials are provided on the Internet.

EXPENSES AND FINANCIAL AID
Cumberland's tuition remains competitive with other private law schools in the region. Tuition for the 2006-2007 academic year is $26,190. Tuition for the flex program is $857 per hour. Other expenses associated with the cost of attendance are listed in the 2006-2007 Student Budget:

Tuition: $26,190°

Room/board: $13,000

Books/supplies: $1,500

Transportation: $1,410

Personal/Miscellaneous: $3,400

Total budget (COA): $45,500

°Tuition costs are subject to change for the 2007-2008 academic year.

The Samford University Financial Aid Office is committed to helping students make informed decisions as they review and discuss various financing options available for legal education.

Approximately 90 percent of Cumberland School of Law students receive some form of financial aid. Most students finance their education with federal and private loans. Over 30 percent of Cumberland students receive scholarships.

All admitted applicants are automatically considered for merit and recruiting scholarship awards. Various other scholarships are available to outstanding students who distinguish themselves academically, make outstanding contributions through leadership in the law school's program, or demonstrate financial need.

FACULTY
° 27 full-time professors and 3 full-time instructors with degrees from 19 law schools, including a federal judge and four members of the American Law Institute

° Faculty held 14 federal and state judicial clerkships have significant practice experience

° 43 adjunct faculty from the bar and bench

° Total 2005-2006 enrollment: 532 students from 151 different undergraduate colleges and universities

° Fall 2005 entering class profile: 175 students; average LSAT 156, GPA 3.23; 75th/25th percentiles: 158/154, 3.53/2.98

ADMISSIONS
Cumberland School of Law does not use a number index system or formula when choosing who will be admitted. Every applicant's file is thoroughly reviewed by the faculty admissions committee. In addition to the LSAT score and undergraduate GPA, other important factors considered are undergraduate school; grade trend and difficulty of major; extracurricular activities and/or employment while in undergraduate school; whether economic, physical, or other challenges have been overcome; graduate work; scholarly achievements; employment experience; personal statement; and letters of recommendation.

Admitted applicants are required to pay a nonrefundable $650 seat deposit that is credited toward tuition. The first installment of $150 is due April 1; the second installment of $500 is due June 15.

CAREER SERVICES AND PLACEMENT
Through the Career Services Office, the law school assists all law students in locating summer clerkships and part-time and permanent employment upon graduation. Students also receive individual counseling and take part in workshops. The office schedules on-campus interview programs during fall and spring semesters.

SEATTLE UNIVERSITY
School of Law

AT A GLANCE
Seattle University School of Law, founded in 1972, is fully accredited by the ABA and holds full membership in AALS. Students may pursue a Juris Doctor or an LLM in American Legal Studies (limited to students with law degrees from non-U.S. institutions).

CAMPUS AND LOCATION
The School of Law is located on the campus of Seattle University, an urban oasis distinguished by landscaped gardens atop First Hill, less than a mile from downtown Seattle, the Northwest's largest, most sophisticated city.

DEGREES OFFERED
In addition to the JD, the University offers five joint degrees that combine the Juris Doctor with either a Master of Business Administration (JD/MBA), a Master of International Business (JD/MIB), a Master of Science in Finance (JD/MSF), (J/MPAC), or Master of Professional Accounting and Master of Public Administration (JD/MA). Student participants of the joint-degree program must be admitted separately to both the School of Law and the Albers School of Business and Economics or the Institute of Public Service. The School of Law began the Master of Laws (LLM) in American Legal Studies for foreign lawyers in 2003.

ACADEMIC PROGRAMS GENERAL
In addition to nationally-recognized the legal writing and trial advocacy programs, and to an extensive externship programs, the Ronald A. Peterson Law Clinic gives students real-world experience as practicing attorneys under the supervision of six full-time and seven adjunct faculty members. Clinical courses cover the full range of legal issues, including administrative and bankruptcy law, general civil practice, trust and estates, immigration, and international human rights. An innovative entrepreneurship clinic provides hands-on transactional experience in addition to the more standard litigation focus of many clinics.

The Access to Justice Institute (ATJI) is a sophisticated center of legal activism that enables students to connect their classroom learning to real cases involving real clients. The Center on Corporations, Law & Society was established to foster interdisciplinary scholarship and dialogue about the roles and obligation of corporations in an increasingly privatized and interdependent global society.

FACILITIES
Sullivan Hall, home to the School of Law, lies on the eastern boundary of Seattle University's 46-acre campus.

COST OF ATTENDANCE
Financial aid is determined by need and cost of attendance. Your financial need is the difference between the cost of your education and your financial ability to pay for it. Your financial need is determined by an analysis of the information provided on your Free Application for Federal Student Aid (FAFSA). From this data, a federal calculation determines what you should be able to pay from your own resources. This amount is subtracted from your total cost of education. The difference is your financial need, and the amount we will try to help you meet with the various aid programs. Please note that there are aid programs available that are not need-based.

The cost of attendance includes tuition, books and supplies, room and board, transportation, and personal expenses while enrolled in law school. A standard student budget is comprised of these components, as specified by law, and financial aid cannot exceed the student budget amount. For 2004–2005, the cost of attendance, less tuition and books, averages approximately $15,4000 for the nine-month academic year.

For answers to any questions you have about financial aid, please contact the Office of Financial Aid at lawfa@seattleu.edu.

ADMISSIONS
In determining those applicants who will be admitted to the School of Law, the Admission Committee considers three primary factors:

Performance on the LSAT; undergraduate academic record; and personal accomplishments.

At least two evaluators review each application. In all cases, qualitative factors weigh heavily in the admission decision. These might include exceptional professional achievements, outstanding community service, and/or evidence of particular talent or background that will contribute specially and significantly to the law school community.

As a candidate for admission, you must have earned a bachelor's degree from an accredited college or university prior to your enrollment. In addition, you must have received a competitive score on the LSAT and have registered with the Law School Data Assembly Service. You should submit required application materials at the earliest possible date after they are available and complete your applicant file no later than April 1 of the year you wish to attend. As a rolling admissions school, we will begin receiving applications in the fall.

While the application deadline is April 1, you should submit your application materials at the earliest possible date after they are available. You need not wait until you have taken the LSAT and/or received your score.

Submit your application to our Admission Office, along with:

(a) an application fee of $50 (check or money order payable to the Seattle University School of Law);

(b) a two- or three-page personal statement that is typed, double-spaced, and signed;

(c) a resume detailing your academic endeavors, community service record, and employment history.

Take the LSAT. Application forms for the test and important information about it are available at your local college or university, Seattle University School of Law, or on the website of the Law School Admission Council.

Register with the Law School Data Assembly Service (LSDAS). Information on this service appears in the LSAT/LSDAS Registration and Information Book, available at Seattle University School of Law or from the Law School Admission Council website.

Send transcripts of all your undergraduate work directly to LSDAS. If admitted, you must submit an official transcript showing the award of a bachelor's degree prior to enrollment in the law school.

Arrange to have two (2) letters of recommendation submitted on your behalf. Of particular influence are evaluations from professors or professional colleagues who can comment on your ability to analyze complex material and to speak and write with fluency, economy, and precision. Your references may complete the applicant evaluation forms enclosed in our bulletin or they may send a separate letter in lieu of — or in addition to — these forms. References may be mailed directly to the law school, returned to you for forwarding to our Admission Office if sealed in an envelope with the writer's signature affixed across the sealed flap, or sent through the Law School Admission Council letter of recommendation service.

For answers to financial aid or admission questions, please contact lawadmis@seattleu.edu.

SETON HALL UNIVERSITY
School of Law

AT A GLANCE

Surveys, rankings, and other evidence convincingly demonstrate Seton Hall University School of Law's quality legal education. Seton Hall Law stands apart through the success of our graduates, the strength of our faculty and the range of professional opportunities provided to our students. Our alumni serve on federal and state benches, in major law firms, in public service, and as entrepreneurs, legal scholars, and civil and human rights advocates.

Our students are diverse, passionate, and success driven. Last year, Seton Hall law students achieved an 89 percent first-time pass rate on both the New York and New Jersey bar exams. And a total of 95 percent of our students were employed within nine months of graduation.

CAMPUS AND LOCATION

Our Newark location means Seton Hall Law is located in the midst of federal, appellate, state, and county courts; the state's major legal center; and hundreds of law firms and legal agencies. Also within easy access of New York City – by train, bus, or car – students at SHU Law are able to take advantage of all the region has to offer. The performing and visual arts, sports, great food, and architecture – an impressive range of professional opportunities – are all within easy reach. In addition, our convenient location along the Northeast corridor attracts world-renowned speakers, visiting faculty, and top employers.

DEGREES OFFERED

Seton Hall Law has full- and part-time divisions for students seeking a JD. The JD program requires 85 credits of study and can be completed on a full-time basis in three years or part-time in four years. SHU Law also offers a joint-degree program with the University of Medicine and Dentistry of New Jersey/ Robert Wood Johnson Medical School, where students can obtain a JD/MD in six years. There is a four-year JD/MBA program with the SHU Stillman School of Business, and a four-year JD/ MADIR program with the SHU School of Diplomacy and International Relations.

ACADEMIC PROGRAMS GENERAL

Seton Hall Law offers specialized programs in Intellectual Property, and Health and Pharmaceutical Law. We also have study abroad programs in Egypt, Ireland, Italy, and Zanzibar. In addition, our Center for Social Justice's for-credit clinical programs, extensive externship programs and summer public interest fellowships allow students to engage in a legal apprenticeship as they gain hands-on experience in the practice of law. In recent years, students have received funding to work with organizations such as the Urban Justice Center, International Human Rights Institute, Legal Aid Society of New York, and the NAACP Legal Defense and Educational Fund.

FACILITIES

Seton Hall Law is located in a striking five-story building with an open design that brings students and faculty together in an ongoing stream of activity. Open doors are both the metaphor and the reality at Seton Hall Law. The school provides wireless access, state-of-the-art classrooms, two moot court rooms, student organization and journal suites, reading areas, meeting rooms, a chapel, and student lounge.

The Peter W. Rodino Jr. Law Library contains more than 425,000 volumes and volume equivalents. Its areas of specialization include health and environmental law collections. The library also is a depository for U.S. and New Jersey State documents.

FACULTY

Seton Hall Law has a diverse and nationally respected faculty, consisting of 64 full-time members and approximately 145 adjuncts, providing a student-faculty ratio of 15 to 1. Faculty members are widely published and actively involved in research in innovative areas of the law. Recent research subjects that have commanded national and international attention include our reports on the status of detainees at Guantanamo Bay, and research on religious liberty, international human rights, property and the public interest, food and drug law, cyberspace law, bioethics, affirmative action, immigration justice, antitrust, science and the law, environmental policy, and employment discrimination.

STUDENT BODY

Our student body consists of approximately 1,140 students from diverse cultural, ethnic, and religious backgrounds, work experiences, and age groups. We have more than 30 student organizations that focus on a wide range of cultural and professional organizations, and publish four student journals. In addition, organizations at SHU Law sponsor career seminars on different areas of the law, host symposia and panel discussions focusing on current legal and societal issues, and plan annual banquets and networking receptions, adding to the value of the student experience.

ADMISSIONS

Seton Hall Law carefully considers each application's overall application in the admissions process. While undergraduate GPA and LSAT scores are important, all admissions files are holistically reviewed.

CAREER SERVICES AND PLACEMENT

At Seton Hall Law, we provide our students with real-world experiences, open career paths, and a wide variety of professional opportunities. Our close proximity to hundreds of large and small law firms in Newark and the surrounding area allows our students to gain critical legal experience as clerks, interns, and summer associates. In addition, we maintain close relationships with major law firms in New York City and Washington, DC, along with prominent employers, governmental, and legal agencies along the Northeast corridor.

ST. THOMAS UNIVERSITY
School of Law

AT A GLANCE

St. Thomas University School of Law is a highly-regarded student-centered law school where diversity is cherished, where a commitment to human rights and international law flourishes, and where the Catholic heritage of ethical behavior and public service is paramount.

One of the greatest strengths of our law school is the profound sense of community shared by students, St. Thomas is a leader in diversity, boasting one of the most culturally diverse student bodies in the country; and this global diversity within such a close-knit community facilitates a cosmopolitan learning environment where intellectual discovery flourishes.

St. Thomas places an institutional emphasis on social justice and ethical behavior. Our unwavering commitment to public service is manifest in everything we do. Our students and alumni are encouraged to live a deeply-felt sense of justice and charity, and to fully utilize their education and experience to lead the way in making our legal system one that truly champions the rights of the powerless.

CAMPUS AND LOCATION

St. Thomas University School of Law's location in Miami, Florida, provides an ideal setting for the study of law. Miami is a vibrant, thriving international community. A hub of domestic and international trade, an innovative center for fine arts, and one of the world's most popular vacation spots, Miami is a dynamic place to live and study. Miami enjoys a rapidly expanding multinational legal community and is home to federal and state trial and appellate courts.

DEGREES OFFERED

St. Thomas University School of Law offers the traditional JD degree as well as joint degrees, and an LLM and JSD degree. Joint degrees include:

JD/MBA or MS in Sports Administration

JD/MBA in International Business

JD/MBA in Accounting

JD/MS in Marriage and Family Counseling

St. Thomas University School of Law also offers advanced degrees: the LLM and the JSD in Intercultural Human Rights.

JD students are able to enroll in the classes offered through the LLM in Intercultural Human Rights as electives; and can earn a Certificate in Human Rights.

FACILITIES

The law school is designed to provide our students with an outstanding environment for learning the law.

Computers and printers are in abundant supply throughout the library. The law library offers Internet access to online databases and has been a leader in applying technology to legal education. Our wireless network allows students to conduct Internet-based research from anywhere on the law school's campus. Our classrooms and moot courtroom have all been recently renovated.

EXPENSES AND FINANCIAL AID

Tuition and fees for the JD degree for 2007-2008 are $26,580 per year. St. Thomas University School of Law offers merit-based scholarships to qualified students. St. Thomas also offers financial assistance apart from scholarships to eligible students in the form of loans, part-time employment, and grants. Many St. Thomas Law students receive some form of financial assistance.

FACULTY

The faculty at St. Thomas is committed to teaching, scholarship, and service. Our exceptional faculty have earned law degrees, and advanced law degrees from some of the nation's most prestigious institutions, including Harvard, Yale, Columbia, Michigan, Pennsylvania, Georgetown, and New York University. They are leaders in their field with impressive records of publication in the top law reviews and extensive practical experience.

A hallmark of the St. Thomas experience is the genuinely close relationship between Faculty and students. Professors maintain a congenial open door policy, meeting regularly with students.

STUDENT LIFE

St. Thomas University School of Law offers a rich student life. With more than 20 student organizations to choose from, students easily find activities that appeal to their interests. The Student Bar Association serves as the student government, planning activities and events, as well as working with the administration to communicate the student body's interests. Students also enjoy the wealth of activities, cultural and sporting events, and nightlife offered in Miami.

ADMISSIONS

Admissions decisions are made by the Law School Admissions Committee which evaluates each applicant's potential for excellence in the study of law. The LSAT score is a factor; however, consideration will also be given to factors such as the undergraduate record and grade point average, undergraduate institution, course of study, graduate degrees, work experience, community service, and so forth.

St. Thomas also offers an alternative process for admission for a select group of candidates called the Summer Conditional Admit Program. The program targets candidates who demonstrate excellent qualitative credentials but lack certain quantitative measurements. Successful candidates in the program are automatically offered admission to the law school for that year's fall entering class.

SPECIAL PROGRAMS

St. Thomas University School of Law is committed to student success both in law school and beyond. Using an interactive and cooperative approach to learning, the Academic Support Programs and the Legal Research and Writing Program assist students in developing the skills required for the successful study and practice of law.

Additionally, a series of classes is offered for students preparing for the Florida bar exam, focusing on both substance and techniques for success on the bar exam.

CAREER SERVICES AND PLACEMENT

St. Thomas provides first-rate career services that result in successful and rewarding employment for our graduates, whether their goals are to enter into private law practice, government, business and industry, or public interest. St. Thomas graduates are partners in major law firms from Florida to California, and the law school is represented in many of the most prestigious firms in the country.

THE UNIVERSITY OF THE DISTRICT OF COLUMBIA

David A. Clarke School of Law

AT A GLANCE

The University of the District of Columbia David A. Clarke School of Law (UDC-DCSL) is the only public law school of the nation's capital. The School of Law is unique among law schools, with a mission of recruiting and enrolling students from underrepresented communities, a nationally-recognized clinical program, and one of the most diverse student bodies in the country.

CAMPUS AND LOCATION

UDC-DCSL is located on the campus of the University of the District of Columbia, an urban land-grant public university. The university and School of Law are located in the upper northwest section of the district on one of the city's major thoroughfares. The UDC-Van Ness Metro subway stop on the Red Line is located directly in front of the university, making the campus easily accessible. The campus is very accessible by the Metro subway (UDC-Van Ness Red Line station), and surrounded by a quiet residential community, Rock Creek Park, the National Zoo, embassies, and small businesses.

DEGREES OFFERED

The School of Law offers the Juris Doctor (JD) degree and a full-time day program.

PROGRAMS AND CURRICULUM

The School of Law offers the best of both worlds for the study of law – a traditional legal education supplemented by hands-on clinical training. Students are required to complete 90 credits to graduate—14 from two semesters of clinical work. Clinics include Legislation, Juvenile and Special Education, Small Business and Community Development, the new Low-Income Tax and AIDS/HIV. Students are also required to complete 40 hours of community service.

FACILITIES

The School of Law is located in the upper northwest section of the nation's capital. The law school and university urban campus sits on several acres of land on Connecticut Avenue, Northwest.

The law school is located in Buildings 38 and 39 on Level Two. The $1.6 million newly-rennovated Mason Law Library is located in Building 39, Level B. Every seat in the library is wired and WIFI access is available everywhere in the library. The larger classrooms are wired and the large lecture classroom is wired.

EXPENSES AND FINANCIAL AID

The School of Law offers its students an affordable legal education and a comprehensive financial aid program. Tuition for District of Columbia resident students is about $7,000 a year. Tuition for non-DC resident students is about $14,00 a year. Non-DC resident students may be eligible for resident tuition after residing in the District for one year. Students may be eligible as well for the following financial assistance: federal loans; merit scholarships; need-based grants; work-study; dean's fellowships; continuing student scholarships; and summer public interest fellowships. For more information on the law school's financial aid program, you may visit www.law.udc.edu.

ADMISSIONS

The School of Law considers the entire applicant profile when rendering an admission decision. While the candidate's LSAT and grades play an important role in the admission process, other factors are also considered, e.g., the applicant's range of life experiences, the content and mechanics of the applicant's writing, community involvement, family background, and recommendations.

The average LSAT for the 2005 entering class was 152. The median LSAT was 151.

The Committee on Admission requests TOEFL on a case-by-case basis.

SPECIAL PROGRAMS

Other programs for students include the Equal Justice Works Summer Public Interest Fellowship Program and the Center for Immigration Law and Practice.

ADDITIONAL INFORMATION

Students enjoy an 11 to 1 student-faculty ratio and individualized attention from and access to faculty and administration. The small school also affords students a spirited, committed, and collegial setting and community in which to study law.

CAREER SERVICES AND PLACEMENT

Career Services includes general career exploration and planning, strategizing, resume and cover letter preparation, development of networking and interviewing skills, as well as how to consider and negotiate offers of employment. Programs include guest speakers from a wide variety of practice areas in the public and private sectors. Resources include extensive web site materials, online job databases and an email jobs bulletin, as well as a small library. The small size of the law school permits individualized counseling by the career services staff. For more information on Career Services and Placement, you may visit the school website at www.law.udc.edu or contact dbauman@udc.edu.

WESTERN NEW ENGLAND COLLEGE
School of Law

AT A GLANCE
2006 Full-time Entering Class

LSAT median: 154 (25th percentile: 151; 75th percentile: 157)

GPA median: 3.1

Average age: 26

Age range: 21–54

Minorities: 14%

States represented: 27

Total student enrollment: 553

CAMPUS AND LOCATION
Founded in 1919, the School of Law was originally part of Northeastern University and merged with Western New England College which itself was founded in 1951. Western New England College School of Law is located in Springfield, Massachusetts. Springfield is the third largest city in the Commonwealth, and home to a lively cultural scene. In the heart of the Pioneer Valley, Springfield is conveniently located near Boston, New York City, and Hartford, Connecticut.

DEGREES OFFERED
Western New England College School of Law offers many ways to earn a law degree. In addition to our three-year, full-time program, the School of Law also offers four-year, part-time evening and part-time day programs. Students may earn an advanced law degree in Estate Planning and Elder Law.

ACADEMIC PROGRAMS
Western New England College School of Law offers students the opportunity to combine our law degree with three other programs. These programs include the JD/MBA (Master of Business Administration) with Western New England College, the JD/MRP (Master of Regional Planning) with the University of Massachusetts, and the JD/MSW (Master of Social Work) with Springfield College.

WNEC School of Law affords students the opportunity to merge theory with practice. Students take advantage of clinical course work, a wide variety of simulation courses, and participate in a number of moot court teams in order to hone their lawyering skills. For more information on clinical opportunities, externships, and simulation courses visit our website at www.law.wnec.edu.

At WNEC School of Law, we keep our class size small to promote a collegial learning environment in which students are challenged to actively participate in their legal education. First-year students are grouped in sections of 50 to help promote this environment.

EXPENSES AND FINANCIAL AID
In 2006, tuition for full time students was $29,456; part-time students: $22,092, which include both the academic year and five credit hours of summer study. Institutional scholarships, including full-tuition scholarships, are typically awarded to 45 percent of each incoming class. Partial scholarships may range from $3,000 to 24,000 a year and may be renewed provided requirements are met. Many students receive our Oliver Wendell Holmes Jr. Scholarship which is a full-tuition scholarship. Holmes scholars typically have scored in the top 20 percent of the LSAT percentile and have graduated at the top of their class. Scholarships are also given based on background and life experiences.

Western New England College School of Law's support for public interest lawyering includes the establishment of its Public Interest Scholars Program. Public Interest Scholars receive three-year tuition scholarships in values ranging from $16,000 up to the cost of full tuition. In addition to the tuition scholarships, Public Interest Scholars are awarded a one-time public interest stipend of $3,500 for approved public interest work in the summer months after the first or second year of law school. Public Interest Scholars have access to a Public Interest Advisory Board, public interest mentoring, and clinical and externship opportunities.

For more information on scholarship and loan opportunities, visit our website at www.law.wnec.edu.

FACULTY
Our 34 full-time faculty members have been educated at the nation's most prestigious law schools. All have practiced law before joining our faculty and several hold additional graduate degrees in other disciplines. The School of Law places a strong emphasis on collaborative learning and student-professor interaction. Faculty members foster an open and collegial interaction with students that provides a positive legal education in a comfortable atmosphere. The School of Law also has more than 30 adjunct faculty members, including practicing attorneys and judges, who bring their current legal practices into the classroom setting.

STUDENT BODY
The Student Bar Association (SBA) is the student government of the School of Law. The SBA plays a significant role in the administration of the School of Law with representation at the faculty meeting and on the faculty/student committees.

Total enrollment of the law school: 553

% female/male: 46/54

% full-time enrolled: 71

Student/Faculty ratio: 15.7: 1

ADMISSIONS
Each year, the Admissions Committee assembles a talented, interesting, and diverse class of students. We enroll a class whose members come from various races and ethnicities, ages, academic, and professional backgrounds, and geographic areas.

Each completed application is read in its entirety and carefully reviewed to determine whether the applicant possesses the academic preparation and motivation necessary to complete the demanding workload of law school. Committee members attempt to gauge each applicant's prior academic performance, expected academic performance, and writing skills. While LSAT scores and undergraduate GPA are important to the Admissions Committee, they form just one part of the picture. We recognize that the ability to succeed in law school and contribute to our law school community and the legal profession is also demonstrated through personal statement, letters of recommendation, and supplemental essays provided by the applicant. We therefore review these materials closely.

We encourage you to submit your application early since admissions decisions are made on a rolling basis. The Admissions Committee begins admitting applicants in January and completes the majority of its work by April. It is strongly recommended that applications for full time enrollment be completed by March 15. Applications for part-time enrollment should be submitted by June 1. An applicant's chances may decrease after the suggested deadlines based on seat availability, as does the chance for scholarship awards.

Please visit our website at www.law.wnec.edu to view more details on admissions.

YESHIVA UNIVERSITY

Benjamin N. Cardozo School of Law

AT A GLANCE

Established in 1976, Benjamin N. Cardozo School of Law offers students a stimulating and dynamic educational experience. Its curriculum combines practical training in basic skills and legal doctrine, sophisticated study of recent developments in legal theory, and interdisciplinary approaches to the study of law.

CAMPUS AND LOCATION

Cardozo is located in an elegant residential neighborhood in the heart of Greenwich Village.

DEGREES

Cardozo offers a JD program where students may enter in September, January, or May. Those entering in January and May complete six semesters of law school in 2.5 years. This can be particularly appealing to mid-year graduates, juniors in college who wish to jump-start their graduate education, and returning students.

Cardozo offers Master of Laws (LLM) degrees (1 year full-time; 3 years part-time) in Intellectual Property Law, Comparative Legal Thought, and General Studies. Students may receive the JD/LLM degree in Intellectual Property in seven semesters. A joint-degree program between Cardozo and the Wurzweiler School of Social Work allows students to earn the JD/MSW in four years.

PROGRAMS AND CURRICULUM

Cardozo offers a rich curriculum that has been especially recognized for its offerings in Intellectual Property Law, Alternative Dispute Resolution, Criminal Law, Corporate Law, and International Law. Courses provide depth and breadth in all the standard subjects of legal study, as well as many more specialized ones.

Cardozo has a commitment to a particular style of education that seeks to blend theory and practice and teach our students the concrete skills and values they need to be first-rate attorneys. Cardozo offers over 15 clinical programs and externship opportunities that combine professional work experience with academic supervision, yielding students uniquely qualified to apply what they have studied.

FACILITIES

Cardozo's entire building has recently completed a $50 million renovation, expansion and upgrade. The Dr. Lillian and Dr. Rebecca Chutick Law Library is the center of student and faculty research at Cardozo. The library holds more than 531,000 books, periodicals, microforms, and audio and video materials. The library offers access to many law and law-related electronic resources, and maintains an exceptionally comprehensive reference collection.

EXPENSES AND FINANCIAL AID

Tuition in 2007-2008 is $39,100 with annual fees of $370.

Rents in the residence hall range from $5,750 to $8,750 per semester depending on the type of apartment.

Almost 85 percent of Cardozo students receive some sort of financial assistance. All admitted applicants are considered for merit-based scholarships. Both need- and merit-based scholarships are available. Approximately 60 percent of students receive scholarship aid.

A Public Service Scholars program awards scholarships to students who demonstrate an interest in public service through their application for admission. The Loan Repayment Assistance Program (LRAP) benefits graduates who choose to pursue careers in public interest/public service law by assisting with some of the burden of large educational debts.

FACULTY

Professors at Cardozo are vibrant, intellectually curious, accessible to students, and committed to the twin goals of teaching and scholarship. They are an interdisciplinary faculty, curious and serious about how the law relates to other expressions of the human spirit.

STUDENTS

The student body at Cardozo is a diverse and impressive. A typical entering class includes graduates from well more than 130 colleges and from over 35 states and several foreign countries. Roughly 20 percent of students are members of minority groups and 15–20 percent are returning to school after spending at least five years.

ADMISSIONS

Cardozo's Admissions Committee bases acceptances on previous academic performance, aptitude for the study of law, and personal criteria such as leadership ability and nonacademic accomplishments. In reviewing applications, the law school also seeks a geographically, racially, and culturally mixed study body. Requirements include: a baccalaureate degree, LSAT scores, registration with the Law School Data Assembly Service, letters of recommendation, and a personal statement. Each application is carefully and individually considered, with every effort made to find students who will contribute intellectually, ethically, and socially to the fabric of the Law School.

SPECIAL PROGRAMS

The Intellectual Property Law Program at Cardozo School of Law is consistently ranked among the top five in the nation. The Faculty includes two former Supreme Court clerks, a former attorney with the US Patent and Trademark Office, and leading experts in the field.

The Howard M. Squadron Program in Law, Media and Society, which brings nationally and internationally known broadcast journalists, artists, musicians, and media moguls to Cardozo, facilitates the lively exchange of information on issues related to publishing and entertainment law.

The Kukin Program for Conflict Resolution, which has a national reputation for excellence and innovation in the field of alternative dispute resolution, offers students many opportunities to explore theory and build skills both in the classroom and in the field. The program fosters an understanding and vision of the role of a lawyer as a problem solver, counselor, and peacemaker in additional to the traditional role of client advocate. It is among the first programs in the country to train law students as mediators.

The program in Family Law, Policy, and Bioethics brings together scholars with varied expertise, and offers a set of basic and advanced courses, a powerful collection of institutional resources, and series of special events to focus attention on the laws that govern marriage, divorce, and the rights of children.

The Samuel and Ronnie Heyman Center on Corporate Governance seeks to raise public and academic awareness of current corporate and securities law issues and to produce and disseminate research on a broad range of topics in these fields. The Center sponsors academic research as well as symposia and public lectures by business and political leaders and prominent legal scholars.

CAREER SERVICES AND PLACEMENT

Cardozo students benefit from a career services office staffed by professional counselors, all of whom have JD degrees, that offers individual assistance with interviewing techniques, résumé writing, and job search strategies as well as panels and other opportunities for learning about a variety of legal careers. An impressive 98.4 percent of those reporting from the class of 2006 were employed within several months of graduation.

INDEX

ALPHABETICAL INDEX

T

U

V

W

INDEX BY LOCATION

UTAH

VERMONT

VIRGINIA

WASHINGTON

WEST VIRGINIA

WISCONSIN

WYOMING

CANADA

INDEX BY COST

MORE THAN $30,000

ABOUT THE AUTHORS

Eric Owens, Esq., attended Cornell College for his undergraduate degree and Loyola University Chicago for law school. He is now an American diplomat.

John Owens, Esq., earned his undergraduate degree in accountancy at the University of Illinois, Urbana-Champaign. He then matriculated at Loyola University Chicago School of Law, where he earned his JD. John works in the tax department of a Chicago law firm. He is currently working on a book, which he hopes to finish up this year. In his spare time, John likes to rock.

Julie Doherty graduated from Stanford University in 1998 with a degree in English. She currently lives in San Miguel de Allende, Mexico, where she works in an art gallery and printmaking studio. She is the co-author of several Princeton Review titles, including *The Best 361 Colleges* and *Planning a Life in Medicine*. She is working on her first novel.

NOTES

NOTES

NOTES

NOTES

NOTES

FINDING THE FUNDS
What you should know about paying for your graduate school education

Furthering your education is an investment in your future. Laying down $120,000 — probably more — in exchange for a top-notch graduate school education requires just as much research and planning as deciding which school you'll hand that money over to.

The good news is that you still have a little time before you have to really worry about signing on the dotted line for any type of financial assistance. That gives you some time to research options, to properly calculate the actual costs of going to graduate school beyond just the sticker price, and to create a plan so that your potential future earnings cover your costs of living when you're out of school and using that degree you will have worked so hard for.

You're going to be responsible for the choices you make. Cutting your ancillary expenses for the next few years and building up an out-of-pocket school fund before you ever register for that first class might save you thousands of dollars in interest payments down the road. But how will you know if you don't come up with a plan?

No doubt you've accumulated some sort of credit history, most likely through undergrad student loans and/or some high-interest credit card debt, so you might think you have it all figured out when it comes to paying for graduate school. While you might understand the basics about how federal loans work and how scholarships, grants, and fellowships can help to cut down the final bill, there are lesser-known and fairly new options out there that can make your postgraduate life a little easier to enjoy.

OTHER PEOPLE'S MONEY

Scholarships and Grants

These are the best form of financial aid because they don't have to be paid back. Remember, though, that most scholarships require a minimum GPA and that some grants are good for only one year. When evaluating your payment options, make sure there is a reasonable expectation that the financial aid package being offered will be available for the full term of the degree requirement or that you have a way of managing funds if they are not enough.

Fellowships and Stipends

Fellowships come in many different forms. Sometimes partial tuition scholarships are called fellowships. These university-sponsored fellowships consist of a cash award that is promptly subtracted from your tuition bill. You can earn the amount of the award by teaching for a department or by completing research for a faculty member. The percentage of students who receive this type of fellowship and the amount paid to each will vary depending on the intended degree and field, enrollment status (full- or part-time), and years of enrollment.

It is important to note that survival on a fellowship alone is unlikely. Fellowships are taxable income — federal, state, county, and city — and you may be expected to pay for school fees, supplies, and books out of your fellowship, as well as tuition. If the fellowship doesn't cover the full cost of your attendance, you'll have to explore other financing options.

Employer-financed Opportunities:

Some employers will offer a tuition reimbursement or a limited financial sum for employees to attend graduate school part time. Employers expect the advanced degree to enhance your performance on the job or to make you eligible for a different job within the company. Be sure you understand all aspects of your employer's tuition reimbursement program before you sign on and be prepared to meet any commitments expected of you.

LOANS

When scholarships, grants, and fellowships don't cover the full cost of attendance, many students take out loans to help out with the rest.

Avoid loans if you can. A loan can best be described as renting money. There's a cost and it may not be an easy cost to bear.

Here's an interesting anecdote. Many students graduate without knowing what types of loans they received, who the lender was and how much they owe. The first time many students become aware of the scope of their obligation is when they receive their first bill—six months after graduation.

This is often because students are passive participants in the financial aid process and do not educate themselves or ask questions. Most students receive a list of "preferred lenders" from their financial aid office and simply go with the lender recommended to them. Over the course of the previous year, relationships between financial aid offices and lenders have been called into question by State Attorneys General, the Department of Education, and regulators. Financial aid offices in certain cases received revenue from lenders in exchange for being placed on the "preferred lender list." Some schools have even rented out their name and logo for use on loan applications. These practices occur without disclosure to parents and students.

It is important to know that the "preferred lenders" may not offer the best deals on your loan options. While your financial aid office may be very helpful with scholarships and grants, and is legally required to perform certain duties with regard to federal loans, many do not have staff researching the lowest cost options at the time you are borrowing.

Remember that your tuition payment equals revenue for the school. When borrowing to pay tuition, you can choose to borrow from any lender. That means you can shop for the lowest rate. Keep reading. This will tell you how.

TYPES OF LOANS

The federal government and private commercial lenders offer educational loans to students. Federal loans are usually the "first resort" for borrowers because many are subsidized by the federal government and offer lower interest rates. Private loans have the advantage of fewer restrictions

on borrowing limits, but may have higher interest rates and more stringent qualification criteria.

Federal Loans:

There are three federal loan programs. The Federal Perkins Loan Program where your school lends you money made available by government funds, the Federal Direct Loan Program (FDLP) where the government lends its money directly to students, and the Federal Family Education Loan Program (FFELP) where financial institutions such as MyRichUncle lend their own money but the government guarantees them. While most schools participate in the Federal Perkins Program, institutions choose whether they will participate in either the FFELP or FDLP. You will borrow from FFELP or FDLP depending on which program your school has elected to participate in.

The Federal Perkins Loan is a low-interest (5%) loan for students with exceptional need. Many students who do not qualify or who may need more funds can borrow FFELP or FDLP student loans. Under both programs, the Stafford loan is the typical place to start. The Stafford loan program features a fixed interest rate and yearly caps on the maximum amount a student can borrow. Stafford loans can either be subsidized (the government pays the interest while the student is in school) or unsubsidized (the student is responsible for the interest that accrues while in school). Starting July 1, 2007, the maximum amount a student can borrow for graduate school is $20,500.

It is often assumed that the government sets the rate on student loans. The government does not set the rate of interest. It merely indicates the maximum rate lenders can charge. These lenders are free to charge less than the specified maximum rate of 6.8% for Stafford loans. There is also a maximum origination fee of up to 2% dropping to 1.5% on July 1, 2007. In some cases you may also be charged up to a 1% guarantee fee. Any fees will be taken out of your disbursement.

Historically lenders have hovered at the maximum rate because most loans were distributed via the financial aid office

> The government only lends money directly to you under the Federal Direct Loan Program. Lenders provide loans guaranteed by the federal government in the Federal Family Education Loan Program.

whereby a few lenders received most of the loans. The end result was limited competition. At 1,239 institutions, one lender received more than 90% of the number of Stafford loans in 2006.

The GradPLUS loan is a federal loan that is another option for graduate and professional students. GradPLUS loans can be used to cover the full cost of attendance and have a fixed interest rate. The maximum rate a lender can charge for a GradPLUS loan is 8.5%. GradPLUS loans also have an origination fee of up to 3%, and a guarantee fee of up to 1%. Any fees will be taken out of your disbursement. Getting approved for one might be easier than getting approved for a private loan, so long as you don't have an adverse credit history.

For either program, the borrower submits a federal application known as the Free Application for Federal Student Aid (FAFSA). The application is available online at www.fafsa.ed.gov.

Certain lenders offer rate reductions, also known as borrower benefits, conditioned on the borrower making a certain number of on-time payments. Unfortunately, it is estimated that 90% of borrowers never qualify for these reductions.

Last year, MyRichUncle challenged this process by launching a price war. The company cut interest rates on Stafford loans and Graduate PLUS loans and introduced widespread price competition. These interest rate cuts are effective when students enter repayment and do not have any further qualification requirements. In addition, students only lose the rate reduction if they default.

Your financial aid office is legally required to certify for lenders that you are enrolled and based on your financial aid package, the amount in Federal loans you are eligible to borrow. You are free to choose any lender even if the lender is not on your financial aid office's preferred lender list.

To shop for low cost Federal loans, call a number of lenders before applying to determine their rates and fees. This is an effective approach because your application will not impact the price. Once you are comfortable that you have the lowest

cost option, apply and submit the Master Promissory Note to your lender of choice.

Private Loans:

Private student loans can make it possible to cover the costs of higher education when other sources of funding have been exhausted. Additionally, when you apply for federal loans, you can borrow up to what your institution has pre-defined as the annual cost of attendance. If your anticipated expenses are above and beyond this predefined cost because of your unique needs, it will take a series of appeals before your institution will allow you to borrow more federal loans. Private loans help you meet your true expectation of what you will need financially. Private loans can pay expenses that federal loans can't, such as application and testing fees and the cost of transportation.

When you apply for a private loan, the lending institution will check your credit history including your credit score and determine your capacity to pay back the money you borrow. For individuals whose credit history is less than positive, lenders may require a co-borrower: a credit-worthy individual who also agrees to be accountable to the terms of the loan. While private loans do not have annual borrowing limits, they often have higher interest rates, and interest rate caps are higher than those set by Federal loans. Generally, the loans are variable rate loans, so the interest rate may go up or down, changing the cost.

To shop for a private loan, after you've researched several options, apply to as many of them as you feel comfortable. Once you are approved, compare rates. Pick the lowest cost option.

EXTRA LESSONS

Borrow the minimum:

Just because someone is offering to lend you thousands upon thousands of dollars doesn't mean you should necessarily take them up on that offer. At some point, you'll have to repay the debt and you'll have to do it responsibly. Wouldn't it be better to use your money for something more worthwhile to you?

Know your rights:

Currently, student lending is an industry that is under heavy scrutiny. It is important, now more than ever, for parents and students to have an active voice and to make educational and financial choices that are right for them.

Some schools work with "preferred lenders" when offering federal and private loans. You are not required to choose a loan from one of these lenders if you can find a better offer. With respect to Federal loans, the financial aid office has a legislated role which is to certify for the lending institution that you the borrower are indeed enrolled and the amount you are eligible for. They are not legally empowered to dictate your choice of lender and must certify your loan from the lender of your choice. You have the right to shop for and to secure the best rates possible for your loans. Don't get bullied into choosing a different lender simply because it is preferred by an institution. Instead, do your homework and make sure you understand all of your options.

Know what you want:

When it's all said and done, you will have to take a variety of factors into account in order to choose the best school for you and for your future. You shouldn't have to mortgage your future to follow a dream, but you also shouldn't downgrade this opportunity just to save a few bucks.

MYRICHUNCLE
STUDENT LOANS

Call us:
1-800-926-5320
or learn more online:
MYRICHUNCLE.COM/LAW

MYRICHUNCLE

Who we are:
MyRichUncle is a national student loan company offering federal (Stafford, PLUS and GradPLUS) and private loans to undergraduate, graduate, and professional students. MyRichUncle knows that getting a student loan can be a complicated and intimidating process, so we changed it. We believe students are credit-worthy borrowers, and that student loan debt should be taken seriously by borrowers and lenders alike. We propose changes in the student loan industry that will better serve parents, schools, and most importantly, students.

Why it matters:
Your student loan will be your responsibility. When you enter into a loan agreement, you're entering into a long-term relationship with your lender — 15 years, on average. The right student loan with the right lender can help you avoid years of unnecessary fees and payments.

What we do:
MyRichUncle pays close attention to the obstacles students face. Removing these obstacles drives everything we do. MyRichUncle discounts federal loan rates at repayment rather than requiring years of continuous payments to earn the discount, which saves you money right from the start. We help you plan ahead, so you can choose the best loans and save.

Our credentials:
MyRichUncle is a NASDAQ listed company. Our symbol is UNCL. In 2006, MyRichUncle was featured in FastCompany Magazine's Fast 50 and in Businessweek's Top Tech Entrepreneurs. MyRichUncle and its parent company, MRU Holdings, are financed by a number of leading investment banks and venture capitalists, including subsidiaries of Merrill Lynch, Lehman Brothers, Battery Ventures and Nomura Holdings.

THE STUDENT LOAN COMPANY WITH A SECRET WEAPON:

REALLY LOW RATES.

LOW RATE FEDERAL AND PRIVATE LOANS. NO STRINGS ATTACHED.
MyRichUncle offers federal Stafford loans at the <u>discounted fixed rate of 5.8%</u>, effective at repayment. No strings attached. Even if you miss or are late on a payment, *you will not lose your discounted rate*, except in the event of default. We also offer private loans at some of the lowest rates around.

BE CAREFUL OF "LOW RATE IMITATORS"
We were the first to go below the government's set maximum rate on federal loans. Others have tried to follow. *But read their fine print!* In most cases, you'll find that qualifying for their discounts is very difficult and you'll end up paying more than if you had gone with **MyRichUncle**.

GO DIRECT. IT MATTERS NOW.
We advertise our student loans directly to students and parents instead of through financial aid offices. Our approach is free of conflicts-of-interest. Our borrowers save as a result. Remember: It's your loan. You're the one who has to pay. So, accept only the lowest rates and the most favorable terms. We invite you to call us to discuss in person, or visit our website to learn more.

GET A BETTER RATE ON YOUR STUDENT LOAN.
Talk to us in person at 1-800-926-5320 or visit WWW.MYRICHUNCLE.COM/LAW

Remember to ask about updates or changes to loan offers and always maximize your lowest cost loans first.

- Federal Stafford Loans
- Federal PLUS Loans
- Federal GradPLUS Loans
- Private Loans
- Low Rates
- Deferred Repayment

MYRICHUNCLE
STUDENT LOANS